# The Social Self in Zen
## and
# American Pragmatism

SUNY SERIES IN
CONSTRUCTIVE POSTMODERN THOUGHT
DAVID RAY GRIFFIN, EDITOR

# The Social Self in Zen
## and
# American Pragmatism

Steve Odin

STATE UNIVERSITY OF NEW YORK PRESS

Production by Ruth Fisher
Marketing by Bernadette LaManna

Published by
State University of New York Press, Albany

For information, address the State University of New York Press,
State University Plaza, Albany, N.Y. 12246

**Library of Congress Cataloging-in-Publication Data**

Odin, Steve, 1953–
    The social self in Zen and American pragmatism   /   Steve Odin.
        p.    cm. — (SUNY series in constructive and postmodern thought)
    Includes bibliographical references and index.
    ISBN 0–7914–2491–X. — ISBN 0–7914–2492–8 (pbk.)
    1. Self (Philosophy).    2. Philosophy, Japanese—20th century.
3. Pragmatism.    4. Philosophy, Comparative.    5. Zen Buddhism-
-Doctrines.    I. Title.    II. Series.
BD450.O35    1996
126'.09—dc20                                                    94–33404
                                                                       CIP

10  9  8  7  6  5  4  3  2  1

Dedicated to Robert C. Neville

# Contents

# Introduction to Suny Series in Constructive Postmodern Thought

The rapid spread of the term *postmodern* in recent years witnesses to a grow-ing dissatisfaction with modernity and to an increasing sense that the modern age not only had a beginning but can have an end as well. Whereas the word *modern* was almost always used until quite recently as a word of praise and as a synonym for *contemporary*, a growing sense is now evidenced that we can and should leave modernity behind—in fact, that we *must* if we are to avoid destroying ourselves and most of the life on our planet.

*Modernity*, rather than being regarded as the norm for human society toward which all history has been aiming and into which all societies should be ushered—forcibly if necessary—is instead increasingly seen as an aberra-tion. A new respect for the wisdom of traditional societies is growing as we realize that they have endured for thousands of years and that, by contrast, the existence of modern society for even another century seems doubtful. Likewise, *modernism* as a worldview is less and less seen as The Final Truth, in comparison with which all divergent worldviews are automatically regarded as "superstitious." The modern worldview is increasingly relativized to the status of one among many, useful for some purposes, inadequate for others.

Although there have been antimodern movements before, beginning perhaps near the outset of the nineteenth century with the Romanticists and the Luddites, the rapidity with which the term *postmodern* has become wide-spread in our time suggests that the antimodern sentiment is more extensive and intense than before, and also that it includes the sense that modernity can be successfully overcome only by going beyond it, not by trying to return to a premodern form of existence. Insofar as a common element is found in the various ways in which the term is used, *postmodernism* refers to a diffuse sentiment rather than to any common set of doctrines—the sentiment that humanity can and must go beyond the modern.

Beyond connoting this sentiment, the term *postmodern* is used in a con-fusing variety of ways, some of them contradictory to others. In artistic and literary circles, for example, postmodernism shares in this general sentiment but also involves a specific reaction against "modernism" in the narrow sense of a movement in artistic-literary circles in the late nineteenth and early twen-tieth centuries. Postmodern architecture is very different from postmodern literary criticism. In some circles, the term *postmodern* is used in reference to that potpourri of ideas and systems sometimes called *new age metaphysics*, although many of these ideas and systems are more premodern than postmodern. Even in philosophical and theological circles, the term *postmodern* refers to two quite different positions, one of which is reflected in this series. Each position seeks to transcend both *modernism* in the sense of the worldview that has developed out of the seventeenth-century Galilean-Cartesian-Baconian-Newtonian science, and *modernity* in the sense of the world order that both conditioned and was conditioned by this worldview. But the two positions seek to transcend the modern in different ways.

Closely related to literary-artistic postmodernism is a philosophical postmodernism inspired variously by pragmatism, physicalism, Ludwig Wittgenstein, Martin Heidegger, and Jacques Derrida and other recent French thinkers. By the use of terms that arise out of particular segments of this movement, it can be called *deconstructive* or *eliminative postmodernism*. It overcomes the modern worldview through an anti-worldview: it deconstructs or eliminates the ingredients necessary for a worldview, such as God, self, purpose, meaning, a real world, and truth as correspondence. While motivated in some cases by the ethical concern to forestall totalitarian systems, this type of postmodern thought issues in relativism, even nihilism. It could also be called *ultramodernism*, in that its eliminations result from carrying modern premises to their logical conclusions.

The postmodernism of this series can, by contrast, be called *constructive* or *revisionary*. It seeks to overcome the modern worldview not by eliminating the possibility of worldviews as such, but by constructing a postmodern worldview through a revision of modern premises and traditional concepts. This constructive or revisionary postmodernism involves a new unity of scientific, ethical, aesthetic, and religious intuitions. It rejects not science as such but only that scientism in which the data of the modern natural sciences are alone allowed to contribute to the construction of our worldview.

The constructive activity of this type of postmodern thought is not limited to a revised worldview; it is equally concerned with a postmodern world that will support and be supported by the new worldview. A postmodern world will involve postmodern persons, with a postmodern spirituality, on the one hand, and a postmodern society, ultimately a postmodern global order, on the other. Going beyond the modern world will involve transcending its individualism, anthropocentrism, patriarchy, mechanization, economism, consumerism, nationalism, and militarism. Constructive postmodern thought provides support for the ecology, peace, feminist and other emancipatory movements of our time, while stressing that the inclusive emancipation must be from modernity itself. The term *postmodern*, however, by contrast with *premodern*, emphasizes that the modern world has produced unparalleled advances that must not be lost in a general revulsion against its negative features.

From the point of view of deconstructive postmodernists, this constructive postmodernism is still hopelessly wedded to outdated concepts, because it wishes to salvage a positive meaning not only for the notions of the human self, historical meaning, and truth as correspondence, which were central to modernity, but also for premodern notions of a divine reality, cosmic meaning, and an enchanted nature. From the point of view of its advocates, however, this revisionary postmodernism is not only more adequate to our experience but also more genuinely postmodern. It does not simply carry the premises of modernity through to their logical conclusions, but criticizes and revises those premises. Through its return to organicism and its acceptance of non-sensory perception, it opens itself to the recovery of truths and values from various forms of premodern thought and practice that had been dogmatically rejected by modernity. This constructive, revisionary postmodernism involves a creative synthesis of modern and premodern truths and values.

This series does not seek to create a movement so much as to help shape and support an already existing movement convinced that modernity can and must be transcended. But those antimodern movements which arose in the past failed to deflect or even retard the onslaught of modernity. What reasons can we have to expect the current movement to be more successful? First, the previous antimodern movements were primarily calls to return to a premodern form of life and thought rather than calls to advance, and the human spirit does not rally to calls to turn back. Second, the previous antimodern movements either rejected modern science, reduced it to a description of mere appearances, or assumed its adequacy in principle; therefore, they could base their calls only on the negative social and spiritual effects of modernity. The current movement draws on natural science itself as a witness against the adequacy of the modern worldview. In the third place, the present movement has even more evidence than did previous movements of the ways in which modernity and its worldview *are* socially and spiritually destructive. The fourth and probably most decisive difference is that the present movement is based on the awareness that *the continuation of modernity threatens the very survival of life on our planet*. This awareness, combined with the growing knowledge of the interdependence of the modern worldview and the militarism, nuclearism, and ecological devastation of the modern world, is providing an unprecedented impetus for people to see the evidence for a postmodern worldview and to envisage postmodern ways of relating to each other, the rest of nature, and the cosmos as a whole. For these reasons, the failure of the previous antimodern movements says little about the possible success of the current movement.

Advocates of this movement do not hold the naively utopian belief that the success of this movement would bring about a global society of universal and lasting peace, harmony, and happiness, in which all spiritual problems, social conflicts, ecological destruction, and hard choices would vanish. There is, after all, surely a deep truth in the testimony of the world's religions to the presence of a transcultural proclivity to evil deep within the human heart, which no new paradigm, combined with a new economic order, new child-rearing practices, or any other social arrangements, will suddenly eliminate. Furthermore, it has correctly been said that "life is robbery": a strong element of competition is inherent within finite existence, which no social-political-economic-ecological order can overcome. These two truths, especially when contemplated together, should caution us against unrealistic hopes.

However, no such appeal to "universal constants" should reconcile us to the present order, as if this order were thereby uniquely legitimated. The human proclivity to evil in general, and to conflictual competition and ecological destruction in particular, can be greatly exacerbated or greatly mitigated by a world order and its worldview. Modernity exacerbates it about as much as imaginable. We can therefore envision, without being naively utopian, a far better world order, with a far less dangerous trajectory, than the one we now have.

This series, making no pretense of neutrality, is dedicated to the success of this movement toward a postmodern world.

David Ray Griffin
Series Editor

# Cover Painting

The cover painting is the tenth station from a famous Japanese version of the *Ten Oxherding Pictures*, attributed to Shūbun (active first half of the fifteenth century), the renowned Zen Buddhist artist-monk at Shōkoku-ji in Kyoto. Ueda Shizuteru (1982) interprets the *Ten Oxherding Pictures* using the Zen logic of Nothingness formulated by Nishida Kitarō and other thinkers related to the "Kyoto school" of modern Japanese philosophy. According to Ueda the *Ten Oxherding Pictures* illustrate the Zen Buddhist process of self-realization wherein the ego-self at the level of Being as portrayed in the first seven stations undergoes death or self-negation in the void of relative Nothingness as shown by the empty circle at the eighth station, only to be resurrected as a true self in the boundless openness of absolute Nothingness wherein emptiness is fullness and fullness is emptiness as portrayed by the last two stations. While the ninth station portrays how the true self returns from the void to the suchness of phenomena in the undivided aesthetic continuum of nature at the level of immediate experience, the tenth and final station depicts the realization of a relational self in the *between* of I and Thou as revealed by the iconographic image of a compassionate Bodhisattva returning from the void to everyday life in the human community. In the present work this Zen Buddhist process of crafting oneself into an ideal person through a dialectic of I-Thou relationships is interpreted through the communicative interaction model of the social self as a dialectic of I-Me relationships formulated by George Herbert Mead in classical American pragmatism. The ninth station depicting the suchness of events in nature is to be understood in terms of Mead's framework as the realization of *aesthetic quality* at the consummatory level of immediate experience. Finally, the tenth station depicting a compassionate Bodhisattva in the between of I and Thou is analyzed from the standpoint of Mead as a realization of the bipolar social self in the between of I and Me.

# Acknowledgments

This book was written during the period when I was a Visiting Scholar at Kyushu University in Fukuoka, Japan, funded by a 1991–92 Professional Fellowship from the *Japan Foundation*. The project was brought to completion on a return trip to Kyushu during the summer of 1992 funded by a *University of Hawaii Japan Studies Endowment Award*. I would like to thank Professor Inagaki Ryosuke of Kyushu University and Professor Fujikawa Yoshimi, President of Kyushu Women's University as well as Professor Matsunobu Keiji, President of the Japan Society for Whitehead-Process Studies, who all helped to arrange for my stay in Kyushu.

The material presented in this work has evolved during graduate and undergraduate courses on Japanese philosophy, American philosophy, and East-West comparative philosophy which I have taught over the past ten years in the Department of Philosophy at the University of Hawaii. As a global center for East-West dialogue, the scholarly community at the University of Hawaii has functioned as a Generalized Other enabling me to enter into a multiplicity of diverse theoretical and cultural perspectives. Concerning some of those at UH whose work has directly entered into my own research on the social self in American pragmatism and Japanese philosophy, I should first single out the great Buddhist scholar and Jamesian pragmatist David Kalupahana, who has long been a special resource for my studies. In Chinese philosophy the co-authored work of Roger Ames and David Hall interpreting the Confucian idea of self in terms of American pragmatism has also been particularly relevant, and is often referred to in this volume. In the area of Japanese studies I would like to express my deepest gratitude to Valdo Viglielmo, my colleague and *sensei* at the University of Hawaii for ten years, whose great expertise in Nishida Kitarō and modern Japanese philosophy have been of enormous value to my research in the field. Also, much appreciation goes to Joe Singer for his photography.

The evolution of this project can further be traced back to my graduate work in the Department of Philosophy at the State University of New York at Stony Brook, during which time I was fortunate to have attended the last seminars on classical American philosophy taught by Justus Buchler, who must be remembered as one of the greatest original thinkers in the recent period of American speculative metaphysics. In his books and seminars

Buchler would often point out that the semiotic communication theory of self as a linguistic web of relational "signs" worked out by Peirce, Royce, Mead, and Dewey provides the basis for a modern restatement of the ancient Greek concept of man as a social animal.

Otherwise, my single greatest debt of gratitude is to Robert Cummings Neville, who initiated me into the study of classical American pragmatism, A. N. Whitehead's process cosmology, Asian philosophy, and East-West comparative philosophy, all within the first semester of my freshman year as an undergraduate student of philosophy at the State University of New York at Purchase. Although Neville taught courses on a variety of Asian traditions, he favored neo-Confucianism wherein sagehood is not represented by the contemplative ideal of the isolated hermit, but rather by the social ideal of a "scholar-official" who exists on a continuum between the two poles of a private individual and public institutions, thus to establish the continuity of thought and action. Not only does Neville possess one of the foremost speculative minds of his generation; he has himself become an archetypal embodiment of this neo-Confucian ideal of a scholar-official. I have thus dedicated the present volume to my great teacher Robert C. Neville.

# Introduction: The Social Self as an Intercultural Theme for Comparative Philosophy and Religion

In recent years there has been a great resurgence of interest in classical American pragmatism, in part due to the widespread influence of Richard Rorty and Jürgen Habermas. The neopragmatism of Rorty describes the "pragmatization" or pragmatic turn of twentieth-century Western philosophy by clarifying how the linguistic turn of Wittgenstein and the deconstructive turn of Heidegger have converged with the nonfoundationalist theory of truth expounded by Dewey in American pragmatism. Hence, Rorty's three main philosophical heroes are Wittgenstein, Heidegger, and the Jamesian Dewey, all of whom deconstruct the substantialist image of mind as a Mirror of Nature, which itself underlies the essentialist notion of truth as correspondence to facts and the representationalist theory of knowledge as accuracy of reflection. However, while Rorty's neopragmatism focuses on the nonfoundationalist and nonessentialist elements of American philosophy in order to emphasize its deconstructive aspects, the communicative-action theory of Habermas instead concentrates upon the intersubjective or social dimensions of pragmatism. If for Rorty the heroes of American pragmatism are James and Dewey, for Habermas they are instead Mead and Peirce. Habermas above all else points to the shift toward a social pragmatism in the writings of George Herbert Mead. In *The Theory of Communicative Action*, Habermas announces the "The Paradigm Shift in Mead" (1989, 1–112; also, see Aboulafia: 1991, 137–68). Following in the direction of Habermas, Hans Joas underscores what he calls the "social turn" (1987, 1993) in G. H. Mead and the Meadian tradition of symbolic interactionism. According to Joas the intersubjectivist framework of Mead represents the "social turn of pragmatism" (1993, 24). Elsewhere, Joas describes "the steps that Mead took toward a 'social' or 'intersubjective' turn of the fundamental pragmatist model of action" (1993, 250). It can therefore be said that while both Rorty and Habermas have recognized the pragmatic turn of twentieth-century Western philosophy, Rorty sees this as a deconstructive turn, while German scholars like Habermas and Joas instead view it in more positive and reconstructive terms as a *social turn*. In the present work I focus precisely upon this

1

social turn represented by the paradigm shift in Mead. But at the same time
I have enlarged the scope of twentieth-century philosophy to include major
currents of Asian thought, arguing that there has been a social turn both in
the Zen tradition of modern Japanese philosophy in the East and the Meadian
tradition of classical American pragmatism in the West.[1]

The social turn of twentieth-century philosophy is here to be considered especially in terms of its expression in those models of the *social self*
which have been formulated in both Zen and American pragmatism. It is my
position that in the twentieth century, both in the East and the West, there
has been a shift or turn to a new communication theory of the bipolar social
self arising through an individual-society interaction. In the present volume I
have therefore set forth the notion of the *social self* as a transcultural motif
for East-West comparative philosophy and interfaith dialogue. The social self
is to be considered mostly in terms of its explicit articulation in two major
twentieth-century philosophical traditions: modern Japanese philosophy in
the East and classical American philosophy in the West. On the Eastern side
I examine those Zen Buddhist models of the social self as reformulated by
thinkers connected to the Kyoto school (Japanese *Kyōto-ha*) of modern Japanese philosophy with a special focus on the work of Nishida Kitarō and Watsuji
Tetsurō. On the Western side I then focus upon the social concept of self
which has been formulated in the tradition of classical American philosophy
running through Charles S. Peirce, William James, Josiah Royce, Charles
Horton Cooley, John Dewey, Alfred North Whitehead, and George Herbert
Mead. Within the tradition of classical American philosophy the concept of a
*social self* has especially been thematized in the Chicago school pragmatism
of G. H. Mead. Those fundamental insights into human selfhood at the heart
of classical American philosophy such as the social, temporal, and multiple
character of the self as well as the centrality of linguistic communication and
the significance of community for the social construction of the self have all
been crystallized in Mead's communicative-interaction model of the social
self as a dialectic of "I" and "Me" or individuality and sociality. Mead's framework also integrates those insights of classical American thinkers into the
value-centric nature of the social self as an artistic, creative process funded
throughout with pervasive aesthetic quality, so that each moment in the ends-
means continuum is both instrumental and consummatory. As a central point
of focus I therefore develop models of the social self which have emerged
from out of the academic schools most representative of these two twentieth-century philosophical traditions: namely, the Kyoto school of modern
Japanese Buddhist philosophy and the Chicago school of classical American
pragmatism.

In addition I examine G. H. Mead's symbolic interactionist framework of social psychology in relation to the *amae* psychology of Doi Takeo, focussing on the parallel between Mead's bipolar model of the social self and Doi's twofold *amae* or "dependency" model of the Japanese self. While cultural anthropologists like Nakane Chie have explained the Japanese self as rooted in the group, Doi shows how the groupism of Japanese selfhood is itself a function of the intrapsychic drive of *amae*, the need to depend on others. In this context I demonstrate how Doi's *amae* or dependency model of Japanese selfhood has been deeply influenced by the modern Japanese philosopher Kuki Shūzō, whose aesthetic ideal of *iki* (chic) as a tension between *amami* (sweetness) and *shibumi* (astringency) functions as a social norm for intersexual relationships in Japanese groupist culture. As a philosopher, Mead was commited to pragmatism with its effort to apply the scientific experimental method to all fields of inquiry, and process cosmology which articulates the temporal, relational character of the self and all phenomena in the creative advance of nature. However, as a social scientist Mead was especially noted for his outstanding contributions to social psychology, which analyzes the social construction of the human self through communicative interaction with others in the group to which it belongs. Whereas I use Mead's pragmatism and process cosmology to elucidate models of the social self in modern Japanese philosophy, I employ his social psychology to interpret the group-centered model of Japanese selfhood in Doi's *amae* psychology. Mead's communicative-interaction theory of the social self thereby establishes a unifying model for both philosophy and the social sciences which at the same time provides an interdisciplinary East-West transcultural framework for interpreting the Japanese concept of self.

An initial formulation of the basic thesis in this work can thus now be articulated: in the twentieth century there has occurred a *social turn* in both Zen and American pragmatism, thereupon resulting in a new model of the person as a bipolar social self arising through communicative interaction between individuality and sociality. By taking the social turn both the Zen Buddhist tradition of modern Japanese philosophy in the East and the American pragmatism of G. H. Mead in the West have converged upon a contextualist model of selfhood as socially constructed through a dialectic of I-Other relationships, altogether representing an intersubjective concept of the social self as an individual-society interaction as well as an ecological concept of the self as a human-nature interaction and a psychosomatic concept of the embodied self as a body-mind interaction. Furthermore it is argued that for both traditions the relationally defined self is not only a social self but also a temporal and multiple self which is fluid, open, shifting, decentered,

variable, and ever-changing according to context. At the value level of discourse it is shown that both underscore the aesthetic, consummatory, and
qualitative dimensions of human existence as a social self. Both the Zen tradition of modern Japanese philosophy and the Meadian tradition of Chicago
school pragmatism are shown to articulate human selfhood in terms of a
developmental process of socialization so that the self is not just something
fixed or given, but something which blossoms through social relations. In
both traditions the self is therefore something which is *constructed* through a
dynamic social process of constantly reconciling the I and Other, thereby
integrating the individual and society, the subject and object, the body and
mind, the self and nature. Hence, both Zen and Mead focus on the aesthetic
process of *crafting* oneself into an ideal person as a bipolar "social self" through
the dialectical interplay of individuation and sociation.

However, at the same time I argue that a conflict emerges between the
models of self articulated in Zen and American pragmatism with respect to
such problematics as individualism versus collectivism, liberalism versus
communitarianism, relativism versus universalism, and freedom versus determinism. Both Zen and American pragmatism have converged upon a
contextualist theory of selfhood as ontologically constituted by its
intersubjective relationships to others in a social context or situation. Yet
while the Zen idea of self moves in the direction of social determinism
whereby the self is constituted by its context, American pragmatism clarifies
how the self arises through creative reaction to its social context. It is my
contention that G. H. Mead's concept of a social self as an I-Me dialectic
establishes a middle way between the extremes of possessive individualism
and totalitarian collectivism more effectively than does the Zen model of
personhood in modern Japanese philosophy through an *asymmetrical* theory
of time wherein the self is determined by its social context in the past as a Me
and then responds with creative novelty in the emerging present as an I.
According to Mead's asymmetrical theory of time, although the self is conditioned by its social relations inherited from the past at the Me pole, it must
still unify them all with a free creative act of emergent synthesis in the present
at the I pole. For Mead it is this bipolar nature of selfhood wherein the emergent I in the present always responds to the socialized Me from the past which
constitutes the asymmetrical, irreversible, and cumulative nature of time's
arrow as a creative advance into novelty. Also, I argue that while the Zen
model of selfhood falls into moral relativism, Mead's concept of the social
self instead points the way to what Habermas calls a "communicative discourse ethics" based on a dialogical reformulation of Kant's moral universalism as expressed by the categorical imperative. While for the Zen model

ethical norms are relative to a particular social group within the Japanese family system, for Mead all validity claims in ethics must be generalized through public discourse into universally binding principles which transcend the group.

## Zen Models of the Social Self in Modern Japanese Philosophy

The founder of modern Japanese philosophy is Nishida Kitarō (1870–1945), who rose to fame with his Jamesian concept of an egoless "pure experience" devoid of subject-object bifurcation, which was then continually transformed throughout his career in terms of such notions as self-consciousness, absolute will, action intuition, absolute present, spatial locus, absolute nothingness, and the social-historical world. In his later years Nishida works out a Zen Buddhist ontology of the *basho* or "locus" of absolute Nothingness, the spatial horizon of disclosure wherein the true self is revealed in its bottomless depths through action-intuition in the absolute present. Insofar as Nishida's purpose was to elaborate an original reconstructive system of philosophy it is not correct to simply equate his thought with Zen philosophy. But it is well established that Nishida was a serious practitioner of Zen meditation and that his thought was rooted in Zen Buddhist philosophy. In terms of his fundamental orientation and especially in terms of his commitment to an ontology of absolute Nothingness he is therefore usually characterized by his interpreters both in the East and the West as a modern Zen Buddhist philosopher. Generally speaking, Nishida's philosophy can be characterized as an effort to formulate an original East-West philosophy and Buddhist-Christian interfaith dialogue within an overall Zen Buddhist framework of *mu* or Nothingness as expressed in terms of a paradoxical Zen Buddhist logic of *śūnyatā* (J. *kū*), emptiness.

Nishida's writings inspired the formation of the Kyoto school of modern Japanese philosophy. While most of Nishida's followers in the Kyoto school like Nishitani Keiji, Hisamatsu Shin'ichi, Ueda Shizuteru, and Abe Masao develop a Zen Buddhist concept of Nothingness as directly realized in immediate experience by the self-power method of intuition, several others like Tanabe Hajime and Takeuchi Yoshinori instead develop a Pure Land Buddhist concept of Nothingness as the salvific grace of absolute Other-power. Among those who are considered to be peripherally related to the Kyoto school, Nishida's associate D. T. Suzuki was strongly committed to Zen Buddhism, while the Zen concept of of *kū* or "emptiness" was the basic principle underlying Watsuji Tetsurō's ethical system. Even the decadent aestheticism of Kuki Shūzō has an important Zen influence insofar as his concept of the Edo period aesthetic ideal of *iki* (chic) synthesizes the three Japanese cultural elements of *bitai* or amorousness of the Geisha, *ikuji* or pride of the Samurai warrior, and *akirame* or detached resignation of the Zen Buddhist priest.

Traditional Zen Buddhism in Japan has been understood as a process of *koji-kyūmei*, "investigation of self." At the outset of his essay "The Standpoint of Zen" (1984, 1), Nishitani Keiji makes reference to a saying of the famous Zen master and founder of Daitokuji in Kyoto, Daitō Kokushi (1281–1338), who asserted that Zen is primarily to be understood as *koji kyūmei*, "investigation of self." Commenting on this, Nishitani states: "I think it most aptly indicates the unique character of the standpoint of Zen. Zen is that standpoint which exhaustively investigates the self itself" (1984, 1). Similarly, Abe Masao writes: "[T]he basic question of Zen is What is the self? . . . This is why the primary concern of Zen traditionally has been *koji-kyūmei*, 'investigation of self', which is to inquire into and awaken to one's own true self or 'original face'" (see Ives: 1992, viii). A paradigmatic expression of Zen as *koji kyūmei* or "investigation of self" which has frequently been cited by Nishida, Nishitani, Abe, and others in the Kyoto school, is to be found in the *Genjōkōan* fascicle of the *Shōbōgenzō* by Dōgen (1200–1253), founder of the Sōtō sect of Zen Buddhism: "To study the way of the Buddha is to study the self, and to study the self is to forget the self; and to forget the self is to be enlightened by others." It is therefore from the appropriation of this Zen Buddhist perspective of *koji kyūmei* that modern Japanese philosophy derives its own primary orientation as an inquiry into the human self. Generally speaking, Nishida and his followers in the Kyoto school develop a Zen Buddhist vision of the true self as an act of complete self-negation in absolute Nothingness, articulated both in terms of the Buddhist notion of *śūnyatā* (J. *kū*) or emptiness of self and the Christian idea of *kenōsis*, self-emptying. Similarly, Watsuji Tetsurō develops a Zen/Confucian idea of the person as *ningen* wherein there is a mutual emptying of the individual and the community in *kū* or emptiness as interrelational existence. It can be said that both Nishida and Watsuji developed a profoundly Zen Buddhist concept of the true self based on the *dependent co-arising of self and society* in a spatial locus of emptiness or nothingness. Hence, in the present work I focus especially upon the Zen Buddhist model of self as reformulated in twentieth-century Japanese philosophy by those scholars either centrally or peripherally related to the Kyoto school.

The *satori* or enlightenment of Zen Buddhism is not to be conceived as the experience of a transcendent, supernatural beyond such as a union with God, a realization of absolute Spirit, or an ascent to the One, but as a self-

Nishida Kitarō

awakening to the true self. Japanese Zen Buddhist philosophy develops the
nature of the true self on the basis of a metaphysics of Nothingness (*mu*) with
its correlate principles of "emptiness" (*kū*), "no-self" (*muga*), "impermanence"
(*mujō*), and "interrelational existence" (*engi*). As opposed to the monistic
Vedanta philosophy of Hinduism which taught the realization of a substantial
*ātman* or absolute Self of eternal Being-Consciousness-Bliss through Yoga
(union), early Buddhism instead taught realization of *anātman* or no-self

through the practice of Vipassana (insight), whereby through *sati* or "mindfulness" of ever-changing bodymind sensations one experiences the self and all phenomena to be a flux of events which are empty, impermanent, nonsubstantial, and dependent on chains of causation. In accord with the teachings of Buddha, Zen rejects the Hindu notion of *ātman* and argues for *anātman* (J. *muga*), no-self. Consequently, Zen Buddhist literature typically describes this true self in negativistic terms like no-self, no-soul, non-ego, or otherwise as self-emptying, self-negation, self-forgetting, self-extinction, and so forth. Again, the insubstantiality and contingency of the true self is articulated through the notion of *mujō*, "impermanence," as expressed at the cultural level through the reflection on temporality and death in Bushidō or the way of the Samurai warrior, and the aesthetic of perishability in Geidō or the way of the artist. While this emphasis on the emptiness, nonsubstantiality, and impermanence of the true self functions to deconstruct the idea of self as a kind of permanent substance with own-being or self-identity, it also often gives the impression that Zen is a form of nihilism culminating in a void of self-extinction. Elsewhere the true self of Zen is characterized in such terms of Buddha-Mind, Buddha-Nature, One Mind, and so forth. But insofar as such terms appear to reify or ontologize the true self as an absolute entity with substantial existence they are also misleading in that they too easily fall into the other extreme which the Buddha referred to as "eternalism." However, the true self of Zen/Chan Buddhism, as for Buddha, Nāgārjuna, and the Wisdom Text tradition, must always represent the middle way between nihilism and eternalism. While in negative terms the key Zen Buddhist principle of "emptiness" (J. *kū*; Sanskrit *śūnyatā*) signifies "no-self" (J. *muga*; Skt. *anātman*), in positive terms it designates the idea of "interrelational existence" or "dependent coorigination" (J. *engi*; Skt. *pratītya-samutpāda*). In the Tendai Buddhist philosophy, which itself exerted a significant influence upon the Japanese tradition of Zen Buddhism, this middle way conception of selfhood is expressed through a logic of the "three truths" wherein the true self occupies a "middle truth" (*chūtai*) between the "empty truth" (*kūtai*) of nihilism and the "conventional truth" (*ketai*) of eternalism. Hence, for Zen Buddhism in Japan, the true self is neither an absolute Self with substantial Being as taught by eternalism, nor a mere nothing, no-self or act of self-extinction as taught by nihilism, but a *relational self* as expounded by the middle way teachings of Mahāyāna Buddhism based on the underlying principle of *kū*, or emptiness, as interrelational existence. Nishida Kitarō and the Kyoto school reformulate this Zen Buddhist vision of the true self through a threefold process of kenotic self-emptying whereby the ego-self at the eternalistic standpoint of Being is emptied into no-self at the nihilistic standpoint of relative Nothingness and then reconstituted as a relational self in the openness of absolute Nothingness at the standpoint of the middle way between eternalism and nihilism. In the tradition of East Asian Buddhism this Zen process of self-awakening to the true self has long been illustrated by means of the famous *Ten Oxherding Pictures*, which passes through the various stages of eternalism and nihilism, finally leading to the achievement of a relational self depicted by the iconographic image of a compassionate Bodhisattva in fellowship with others in society.

Although a social or relational concept of selfhood has been implicit in the Zen concept of a true self since the very beginning, it has received a more explicit articulation through its reformulation in modern Japanese philosophy. While traditional Zen Buddhist writings express the nature of the true self in mostly negativistic terms as a no-self, selfless self or non-ego, modern Japanese thinkers have attempted to futher define the true self in positive terms as a relational, contextual, or social self. It is only with the rise of the social sciences in the twentieth century that the category of the "social" (J. *shakaitcki*) came into general usage in Japanese Buddhist thought. Influenced by the social turn of twentieth-century thought, post-Meiji period Japanese intellectuals like Nishida, Watsuji, and their followers have attempted to articulate the true self of Zen Buddhism in terms of those explicit social categories borrowed from the newly emerging disciplines of sociology, social psychology, anthropology, political science, and the other social sciences. Moreover, influenced by Western concepts of "individualism" (*kojinshugi*) they have also endeavored to further clarify the role of the individual in relation to the social aspects of human existence. As paradigm cases of such theories I focus on Nishida Kitarō's Zen model of the social self arising through an I-Thou dialectic in the spatial locus of *mu* or Nothingness, and Watsuji Tetsurō's Zen/Confucian idea of self as *ningen* existing in the *aidagara* or *between* of the individual and society in *kū*, emptiness. Both Nishida and Watsuji clarify the twofold or double-sided nature of the true self as an individual-society interaction so as to make fully explicit the social nature of the self while also giving an increased recognition to the status of the individual. By contrast to the impersonalism characterizing traditional Zen Buddhism based on the doctrine of no-self (J. *muga*; Skt. *anātman*), Watsuji's ethics is directed toward becoming a "person" (*ningen*), just as Nishida argues that the highest good is the achievement of "personality" (*jinkaku*). Ueda Shizuteru of the Kyoto school combines the thought of Nishida and Watsuji by showing how the final picture in the *Ten Oxherding Pictures* results in the achievement of a relational self as the *between* of I and Thou in the locus of absolute Nothingness. While modern Japanese philosophers like Nishida, Watsuji, and

Ueda establish the metaphysical basis of the social self through the Zen Buddhist principle of *kū* or "emptiness" as interrelational existence, the Japanese psychiatrist Doi Takeo works out the underlying psychological basis of the social self by positing the notion of *amae* (indulgent dependency) as an intrapsychic "drive," "desire," or "need" to depend on others. From the standpoint of social psychology Doi Takeo argues that the Japanese notion of personhood, including both the traditional Zen Buddhist model of self and its reformulation in the modern Japanese philosophy of Nishida Kitarō, is to be understood through his notion of *amae* as a nexus of dependency relationships. Moreover, he specifies that the Japanese dependency model of selfhood has a double structure characterized by the private aspect of "personal reaction" (*honne*) and the public aspect of "social institutions" (*tatemae*). In this way modern Japanese thinkers have come to clarify how the Japanese self is a twofold social self wherein the individual and society are not opposing but interactive processes.

## G. H. Mead's Communicative Interaction Model of the Social Self

While George Herbert Mead (1863–1931) has always been regarded as an important figure in classical American philosophy he has not generally received the same widespread attention as others in the American philosophical tradition such as C. S. Peirce, William James, Josiah Royce, George Santayana, John Dewey, and A. N. Whitehead. However, in recent years there has been a renaissance of interest in the philosophy of Mead, triggered especially by its remarkable development into the communicative-interaction theory and communicative-discourse ethics of Jürgen Habermas. It is only now that Mead's communicative-interaction model of the social self is coming to be recognized as one of the crowning achievements of classical American philosophy.

Mead's framework is often identified with that of pragmatism in American philosophy and symbolic interactionism in the social sciences. Furthermore, Mead is generally regarded as a process philosopher in the tradition of American speculative thinkers including Peirce, James, Dewey, Whitehead, and Hartshorne. In *World Hypotheses* (1942) Stephen C. Pepper articulates a typological classification scheme of four "world hypotheses" and their underlying *root metaphors*, including (1) Formism (Plato, Aristotle), based on the root metaphor of Similarity; (2) Mechanism (Descartes, Locke, Hume), based on the root metaphor of Machine; (3) Organicism (Hegel, Bradley, Royce), based on the root metaphor of Organism; and (4) Contextualism (Bergson,

George Herbert Mead

Peirce, James, Dewey, Mead), based on the root metaphor of an Event or Context. As indicated above, in Pepper's meta-philosophical taxonomy G. H. Mead is classified together with representatives of pragmatism and process metaphysics under the world hypothesis of contextualism. Although in his

early work he regarded A. N. Whitehead as an eclectic who oscilates between different paradigms, in Pepper's (1961) later writings he suggests that
Whitehead's process metaphysics signifies an original world hypothesis based
on the new root metaphor of a Creative Act such as that of an artist, inventor, or imaginative scientist. Charles Hartshorne (1987, 369) argues that the
process models of Peirce, Bergson, and Whitehead have all converged in a
new paradigm of aesthetic creationism insofar as all three recognize the primacy of artistic creativeness or aesthetic self-creativity in immediate experience. However, I would argue that while the framework of G. H. Mead shares
much in common with the world hypothesis of contextualism, it should ultimately be classified together with those of Peirce, Bergson, Whitehead, and
Hartshorne under the paradigm of aesthetic creationism based on the root
metaphor of the creative act. As Pepper himself asserts, the two root metaphors
of context and creative act share much in common, for instance, the relational and qualitative character of events. But in contrast to the contextualist
paradigm wherein the self is understood in Darwinian evolutionary terms as
an arising through a mechanistic adjustment or adaptation of organism to
environment, in the aesthetic creationist paradigm the self is now understood in terms of the creative evolutionism of Bergson as arising through the
*creative response* of an individual organism to its social environment in the
production of novel aesthetic events with intrinsic value. Hans Joas (1993,
248) has underscored the significance of Mead's concept of selfhood as a creative actor. Joas points out that the highly original concept of selfhood worked
out by Mead in American pragmatism at once combines the intersubjective
constitution of the social self with the creative subjectivity of the acting self.
Mead's pragmatist idea of self as an actor specifically involves an understanding
of human intersubjective praxis as *creative* action (1993, 4). This is a new idea
of interpreting creativity of action in that the guiding root metaphor is neither poetic expression nor material production but creative problem-solving
by an experimenting intelligence (1993, 128; also 248). For Joas the Meadian
concept of a social self thereby functions to clarify the interconnection of
creativity and situation (1993, 4). Thus, while Mead's social pragmatism in
some respects designates a contextualist model, it ultimately represents an
aesthetic creationist model of the human self as a creative problem-solver in
an experimental situation. Or in terms of the communicative action theory
of Jürgen Habermas (1989, 59), it can be said that Mead has elaborated a
communication model of the human self as a communicative actor which
emerges from the creative, spontaneous, and unpredictable response of an
individual I to the socialized Me during the symbolic process of communicative interaction.

The Life and Works of Mead

George Herbert Mead was born in 1863 in South Hadley, Massachusetts, where his father was a Congregational minister. His mother became President of Mount Holyoke College (1890–1900). Mead did his undergraduate studies at Oberlin College (1879–83), and his graduate work at Harvard University (1887–89), Leipzig, and Berlin (1889–91). At Harvard University he studied under William James and Josiah Royce, and in Germany he studied under Wilhelm Dilthey. After teaching at Michigan (1891–94) where he came under the influence of John Dewey and C. H. Cooley, he moved to the philosophy department at the University of Chicago where he taught until his death in 1931.

While Mead stands as one of the preeminent figures in the classical tradition of American philosophy, his writings have long been neglected by scholars in the field. At least one reason for this neglect of Mead's thought is that he did not publish any books within his own lifetime, although over thirty of his articles were published in scholarly journals. And even those of Mead's books which appeared posthumously were in fact edited compilations of his lecture notes, including: (1) his Carus lectures read at the American Philosophical Association in 1930, published as *The Philosophy of the Present* [PP] in 1932; (2) notes from his lectures in his course on social psychology held at the University of Chicago, published as *Mind, Self, and Society* [MSS] in 1934; (3) notes from his lectures in his course on "Movements of Thought in the Nineteenth Century" [MTNC] published under the same title in 1936; and (4) unpublished papers, supplemented by notes from lectures, published as *The Philosophy of the Act* [PA] in 1938. To this has now been added several edited collections of Mead's essays, both published and unpublished, including *George Herbert Mead on Social Psychology* in 1956, *Selected Writings: George Herbert Mead* [SW] in 1964, and *The Individual and the Social Self: Unpublished Work of George Herbert Mead* [ISS] in 1982.

Mead's Synthesis of American Philosophy

Throughout the present volume I attempt to clarify the central position which Mead occupies within the tradition of classical American philosophy, including both the movements of pragmatism and process cosmology. While a graduate student at Harvard University from 1887 to 1888, Mead was a student of both William James and Josiah Royce. Mead borrowed James's seminal notion of a *social self* along with its two components of "I" (the subjective self) and "Me" (the objectified self) and made it the cornerstone of his whole philosophical edifice. He also incorporated Royce's idea of achieving one's "greater social self" through an Ego-Alter dialectic in an intersubjective community of interpretation. Through Royce's later writings he learned of Peirce's theory of signs and thus came to develop a semiotic concept of self as constituted by a linguistic communication process of symbolic interaction using "significant symbols." Furthermore, Mead was a colleague of C. H. Cooley while an instructor at the University of Michican, and was influenced by the latter's "sociological pragmatism" based upon the concept of the twofold social self as an individual-society interaction. Also, Mead was the most intimate friend and colleague of John Dewey, first at University of Michigan, and then at the University of Chicago. Mead and Dewey influenced each other in many ways so that both developed a social concept of selfhood arising through open communication and mutual participation in a liberal democratic community. Finally, more than any other classical American thinker, Mead explicitly builds upon the organismic process cosmology of Alfred North Whitehead so as to develop a theory of the social and processual self which is grounded in the relational and temporal character of reality itself as a creative advance toward novelty. For this reason the social self theory and I-Me dialectic of Mead can be said to represent a creative synthesis of the whole tradition of classical American pragmatism including its extension into the organismic process cosmology of A. N. Whitehead. No less impressive is Mead's appropriation of the German intellectual heritage, including his social reformulation of Kant's universalist ethics, Hegel's self-other dialectic of mutual recognition, Dilthey's philosophical anthropology, Gestalt psychology, and Wundt's psychology of gestures. Against this background Mead has come to be regarded by many as the preeminent theorist of self-other relations after Hegel.

Aside from his brilliant theoretical synthesis of classical American philosophy, Mead has also played a central role in the history of pragmatism through his influence upon various intellectual movements associated with the University of Chicago. With John Dewey, James Tufts, James R. Angell, Edward Scribner Ames, and others, Mead was a principal founder of what has come to be known as the Chicago school of American pragmatism, which endeavored to apply the scientific experimental laboratory method toward the solution of moral and social problems. Futhermore, Mead was also a founding member of the Chicago school tradition of American sociology which includes such thinkers as John Dewey, C. H. Cooley, W. I. Thomas, Robert Park, Ernest W. Burgess, Ellsworth Faris, and Herbert Blumer. In particular, Mead's social-self theory and I-Me dialectic has been the major source of inspiration for the movement of "symbolic Interactionism" in American sociology developed by Herbert Blumer, Erving Goffman, and others. It is precisely this emphasis upon the social and moral dimensions of human selfhood as well as the effort to combine philosophy with the concepts and methods of the social sciences which characterizes the Meadian tradition of Chicago school pragmatism.

## Mead's Vision of the Social Self

Mead's entire philosophical and social scientific framework revolves around his central notion of the bipolar *social self* as a dialectic of *I* and *Me* or individuation and sociation. The philosophy of G. H. Mead designates a shift beyond the monological paradigm of self as an I or disembodied Cartesian subject to a dialogical paradigm of the social self arising through communicative interaction between the I and the Me, thus establishing a dialectical unity between the individual and the social, the subject and the object, the mind and the body, the organism and the environment. Mead thereby completely overturns the dualistic framework of Cartesian subjectivism for a nondual framework representing an intersubjective model of the social self as an individual-society interaction as well as a psychosomatic model of self as a body-mind interaction and an ecological model of self as a human-nature interaction. According to Mead's evolutionary process cosmology, the self is not only a *social self*, but also a *temporal self* and a *multiple self*, a series of emergent or discontinuous events wherein the creative, novel, and spontaneous I in the present responds to the deterministic social situation of the Me in the past, so that with each passing moment the old self is replaced by a partly new self in the ever-changing stream of consciousness. In the present work it is precisely what Habermas calls the "paradigm shift" in G. H. Mead to a new communicative-interaction model of the social self as an I-Me dialectic that is developed into an East-West intercultural framework to critically interpret the Japanese self, with a special focus on the Zen Buddhist concept of self as reformulated in twentieth-century Japanese philosophy.

For Mead the human self is neither a separate self nor an absolute self but a *social self* with two poles, the I pole representing *individuality* and the Me pole representing *sociality*. He asserts that the social self arises through an interaction between the I or individual organism and the Me or social environment including both human society and living nature. The self is not given at birth; it is something to be *realized* through a developmental process of communicative interaction with others. Mead provides a developmental account of how the individual is intersubjectively constituted as a social self through the mechanism of "role-taking" whereby the self gradually takes on the roles of others, finally taking on the roles of the *generalized other* representing the organization of attitudes of its entire community. According to Mead's evolutionary process cosmology, the human self is not only a social self as a field of interpersonal relationships, but also a *temporal self* as a sequence of emergent or discontinuous events which arise from the deterministic social situation inherited from the *past* as a Me and then respond with creativity, spontaneity, and novelty in the *present* as an I. The social, processual self is also a *multiple self,* a pluralistic field of selves which creates and recreates itself with each new social situation. From the standpoint of his Leibnizian cosmology of perspectives derived from A. N. Whitehead, the social self develops through perspective-taking whereby it enters into the emergent perspectives of others and then into the common perspective of the general other, thus to function as a mirror which reflects its entire community from a unique perspective as an individual microcosm of the social macrocosm. Sociality or the ability to enter into multiple perspectives is the basis for Mead's theory of socialization as well as his universalist ethics and political doctrine of a liberal democracy. Mead's communication theory of the social self also highlights the value-centrism of American philosophy wherein aesthetic, moral, and religious experience are analyzed as a function of sociality. Mead develops a pragmatic theory of self as an actor which underscores the nature of self as creative action, a creative problem-solver in experimental situations. It is this pragmatic understanding of the person as a creative actor which underlies his aesthetic view of self. In his aesthetics the self is depicted as a series of artistic, creative, and novel events wherein each event is a "social act" of communicative interaction which arises through the four stages of impulse, perception, manipulation, and consummation, the final or consummatory stage being characterized by the directly felt qualitative immediacy of aesthetic experience. Like Dewey, Mead understands each moment of the self as both instrumental and consummatory so as to constitute an ends-means continuum funded with pervasive aesthetic quality. Mead further establishes the basis for what Habermas terms a "communicative ethics" through a social reformulation of Kant's universalist ethics, whereupon the categorical imperative requiring universalization for all moral norms is no longer a monological procedure carried out in private minds, but a dialogical procedure conducted by a community through intersubjectively mounted public discourse. Although Mead formulates a completely secular account of the human self without any reference to a transcendent or supernatural principle, he nonetheless provides a naturalistic reformulation of Royce's philosophy of religion based on the notion of realizing a "greater social self" through membership in a community. Finally, Mead's whole framework is influenced by the pragmatism or experimentalism of C. S. Peirce which extends the scientific laboratory method to all fields of inquiry so that concepts are working hypotheses to be tested by experiment for their problem-solving ability. Mead's interdisciplinary account of the social self thus provides a unifying model for both philosophy and the social sciences which is empirically grounded in the scientific experimental method.

## The Significance of Mead's Thought

Mead's communicative-interaction model of the social self has been recognized as having profound if not revolutionary implications for both philosophy and the social sciences including sociology, social psychology, anthropology, and political science. John Dewey once described Mead as "the most original mind in philosophy in America of the last generation," adding: "I dislike to think what my own thinking might have been were it not for the seminal ideas which I derived from him" (1931, 310–11). Echoing Dewey's high appraisal of Mead's thought, A. N. Whitehead would later assert: "I regard the publication of the volumes containing the late Professor George Herbert Mead's researches as of the highest importance for philosophy. I entirely agree with John Dewey's estimate, a seminal mind of the very first order" (see D. L. Miller: 1973, ix). In *Symbolic Interactionism*, Herbert Blumer brought to light the value of Mead's symbolic interactionist notion of self as a theoretical basis for sociology, asserting: "We are indebted to George Herbert Mead for the most penetrating analysis of social interaction" (1986, 8). Moreover, the sociologist Peter L. Berger would later describe Mead's symbolic interactionist theory of the social self as the single greatest American contribution to social psychology and the social sciences. In Berger's words:

> [I]t is through the work of George Herbert Mead and the Meadian tradition of the 'symbolic-interactionist' school that a theoretically viable social psychology has been founded. Indeed, it may be maintained that in this achievement lies the most important *theoretical* contribution made to the social sciences in America. (1970, 373)

In *George Herbert Mead: A Unifying Theory for Sociology* (1986), John C. Baldwin argues that Mead's interdisciplinary model of the social self functions as the best "unifying theory" for sociology. Kathy E. Ferguson's *Self, Society and*

*Womankind* (1980) attempts to show how Mead's notion of the social self as a self-society interaction establishes the most adequate model for a feminist theory of selfhood as the basis for a sociological theory of women's liberation. Evaluating his significance for the history of philosophical anthropology, Hans Joas describes Mead as "the most important theorist of intersubjectivity between Feuerbach and Habermas" (1985, 2). Yet in recent years the significance G. H. Mead for both philosophy and the social sciences has especially been brought to widespread public attention by Jürgen Habermas's *The Theory of Communicative Action* (vol. 2: 1989, 1–112), which argues that Mead's framework represents no less than a major "paradigm shift" beyond the Cartesian philosophy of subject-centered consciousness to that of an intersubjective communication model of the social self based on the notion of linguistically mediated symbolic interaction between the individual and society. It is my intention that the present volume will further advance the positive reception of George Herbert Mead's work, not only insofar as it represents a creative synthesis of classical American pragmatism and process cosmology, a unifying theory for philosophy and the social sciences, and a paradigm shift to a new communicative-interaction model of the social self, but also as an *East-West transcultural framework* for the critical interpretation of Asian thought, including Confucianism, Zen Buddhism, and modern Japanese philosophy.

## The General Outline

Part One contains a general overview of various models of the social self which have been framed in modern Japanese thought, including the modern Japanese philosophy of Watsuji Tetsurō and Nishida Kitarō as well as the modern Japanese psychology of Doi Takeo. Chapter 1 examines the Zen/Confucian concept of Japanese personhood as *ningen* formulated by Watsuji Tetsurō (1889–1960), along with others who have been directly influenced by his thought such as Kimura Bin, Hamaguchi Eshun, and Kumon Shumpei. In his *Ethics* (*Rinrigaku*, 1937) Watsuji criticizes abstract Western concepts of the person based on "individualism" (*kojinshugi*) and develops a social, relational, and contextual notion of selfhood through a Heideggerian etymological analysis of the common Japanese term *ningen*, "person." Moreover, the two Sino-Japanese characters for *ningen* reveal the "double" or "twofold" (*futae*) structure of the person as an individual-society interaction. He further points out how the second of the two characters for *nin-gen*, which can also be pronounced *aida*, functions to disclose how the self exists in the *aidagara* or "betweenness" of persons. This understanding of the person as *ningen* is then grounded in the ontological concept of a *fūdo* or "climate" as the spatial locus for self-other relations. In this context Watsuji endeavors to work out a system of communitarian ethics based upon his *ningen* concept of selfhood as *hito to hito to no aidagara*, the "betweenness of person and person." Furthermore, the second of the two characters forming the word *ningen*, which as a literary and artistic term is also pronounced *ma*, signifies a traditional Japanese aesthetic ideal of negative space, or as it were, the space / and or time "in-between" all persons and events. From this standpoint Watsuji analyzes traditional Zen-influenced literary and artistic forms such as the tea ceremony (*chanoyu*) and linked-verse (*renga*) as a dialogical function of the *aida* (= *ma*) or "betweenness" of persons in a community. It is thus shown how Watsuji's social concept of the person as *ningen* designates a profoundly aesthetic as well as ethical mode of human existence. At the deeper theoretical levels of analysis, Watsuji's ethics and aesthetics based on the *ningen* model of Japanese personhood explicitly synthesizes the traditional Confucian idea of self as a center of social relationships governed by principles of *li* (J. *rei*) or "ritual propriety" with the traditional Zen Buddhist relational notion of self grounded upon the underlying concept of *kū* (Skt. *śūnyatā*) or "emptiness" as the dependent co-arising of individual and society. The Japanese ethics of Watsuji, like that of both traditional Confucianism and Zen Buddhism, is humanistic, secular, and naturalistic in that it is ultimately directed toward the goal of becoming a true person as *ningen* through interaction between an individual and its total surroundings. It can be said that Watsuji's Zen/Confucian model of personhood as *ningen* with its dialogical principle of betweenness (*aidagara*) and ontological notion of spatial climates (*fūdo*) altogether represents the classic analysis of the social self in modern Japanese philosophy.

In order to trace some of the more recent developments of Watsuji's philosophy, I then examine such works as *The Betweenness of Person and Person* (*Hito to hito to no aida*, 1972) and *Betweenness* (*Aida*, 1988) by psychiatrist Kimura Bin, who combines Watsuji's *ningen* model of personhood based on the *aida* principle of betweenness with the *amae* psychology of Doi Takeo, the "pure experience" of Nishida Kitarō, and traditional Zen Buddhist concepts of the self. Hamaguchi Eshun (1977, 1985) reformulates Watsuji's *ningen* model in terms of a sociological concept of *kanjin* or "contextual persons" wherein the characters of *ningen* (= individual + society) are now reversed and pronounced as *kanjin* (= society + individual), thereby to further underscore the primacy of social relationships over the individual in the Japanese notion of self. Based on a synthesis of the thought of Watsuji, Kimura, Hamaguchi, Doi, and others, Kumon Shumpei develops what he calls a "contextual" (*kanjin*) theory of the self as *ningen* representing a middle axiom between "individualist" and "collectivist" notions of personhood (1982). In this manner I clarify the development of the *ningen/kanjin* model of personhood articulated by Watsuji and others as a key to understanding the social character of the Japanese self and the groupism of Japanese household society.

Chapter 2 develops the Zen model of personhood worked out by Nishida Kitarō and his followers in the Kyoto school of modern Japanese philosophy. Nishida articulates a Zen model of personhood as a twofold social self (*shakaiteki jiko*) which is intersubjectively constituted by a dialectic of I and Thou (*ware to nanji*) in the *basho* or spatial locus of absolute Nothingness. In his first major work *A Study of Good* (*Zen no kenkyū*, 1911) Nishida works out his Jamesian notion of self as an egoless "pure experience" (*junsui keiken*) which is emptied of thought and devoid of subject-object dualism in the temporal stream of consciousness. He emphasizes that pure experience is a concrete whole that arises prior to the individual, and that it is from out of the original unity of pure experience that both the individual ego and the subject-object dichotomy come into existence through abstract mental reflection. Like James he rejects the notion of self as "substance" for the self as *process,* a series of events of pure experience in the ever-changing stream of consciousness with no underlying substantial identity. Moreover, like James, he describes the focus-field structure of pure experience wherein the self at each moment is characterized by a luminous focal region of consciousness which shades into a halo of darkness constituted by the "fringe of relationships" in the background field. Yet what has gone unnoticed is that in chapter 26 of this same work, Nishida formulates an explicit notion of a social self (*shakaiteki jiko*) as a way between the extremes of individualism (*kojinshugi*) and collectivism or cooperationism (*kyōdōshugi*). In his later philosophy Nishida introduces his Zen Buddhist notion of *basho*, or *topos*, the spatial "locus" (place, field, matrix) wherein the "true self" is revealed as a contradictory self-identity of I and Thou. At this point Nishida comes to argue that in the locus of *mu* or Nothingness, now understood as the locus of the social-historical world, the self is always a social self wherein the I is an I only by facing a Thou and a Thou is only a Thou by facing an I. Nishida's theory of the social self as a dialectic of I and Thou thereafter becomes a fundamental motif of his later philosophical writings. Nishida's thematization of the social self and I-Thou dialectic has been generally overlooked by scholars. Yet I attempt to establish that Nishida's social-self theory and correlate I-Thou dialectic of intersubjectivity is in fact a pervasive motif throughout his entire philosophical career, starting with his maiden work *A Study of Good* (*Zen no kenkyū*, 1911), and continuing up to his penultimate essay, "The Logic of Place and a Religious Worldview" (*Bashoteki ronri to shūkyōteki sekaikan*, 1945). I further examine the social dimensions underlying the *kenōsis/śūnyatā* or self-emptying model of personhood developed in the Christian-Buddhist inter-faith dialogue of Nishida and the Kyoto school. It is shown that in modern Japanese philosophy both Christian *kenōsis* and Buddhist *śūnyatā* are to be understood not only in mystical categories as an introspective act of empty-ing the mind into an imageless void, but also in social categories as a moral act of pouring out the self for others as exemplified by the self-emptying love of Jesus and the self-negating compassion of Buddha. Finally, I discuss the Zen model of selfhood elaborated by Ueda Shizuteru (1982), a leading mem-ber of the Kyoto school who uses the philosophy of Nishida to interpret the famous *Ten Oxherding Pictures* illustrating the Zen process of self-realization. Ueda's interpretation of the *Ten Oxherding Pictures* functions to illuminate the connection between the traditional Zen process of becoming a person and Nishida's developmental model of the social self as a threefold process of kenotic self-emptying, whereby the substantial ego-self at the eternalistic standpoint of Being (*u*), which is emptied into *muga* or no-self at the nihilistic standpoint of relative Nothingness (*sōtaiteki mu*), is then reconstituted as a relational self in the *between* of I and Thou at the middle way standpoint of absolute Nothingness (*zettai mu*).

Chapter 3 considers the *amae* or "dependency" model of Japanese selfhood developed in the social psychology of Doi Takeo. Doi formulates a social psychology by establishing *amae* (indulgent dependency) as an intra-psychic "drive," "motive," "wish," or "desire" which is more primary than the sexual and aggressive instincts in the individualistic psychology of Freud. While scholars like Nakane Chie show how the Japanese self is rooted in familial groups which are vertically organized by parent-child relations, Doi Takeo in turn shows how these relationships are psychologically invested with individual desire: that of *amae* or the infantile desire to be passively loved by others. From the standpoint of his *amae* psychology Doi analyzes Japa-nese selfhood as a nexus of infantile dependency relationships structured by a twofold private/public or *honne/tatemae* opposition. It is shown how Doi's psychological concept of *amae* or "dependency drive" as developed in *The Structure of Amae* (*Amae no kōzō*, 1972) was itself influenced by the philosophy of Kuki Shūzō, whose book *The Structure of Iki* (*Iki no kōzō*, 1930) analyzes the dynamics of intersexual relationships in Japanese group-consciousness by means of the Edo period aesthetic ideal of *iki* or "chic," understood as a tension between the positive element of *amami* (= *amae*) or "sweetness" which moves in the direction of establishing intimate human contact with others, and the negative element of *shibumi* or "elegant restraint" which function to establish distance from others. While Doi agrees with social scientists like

Nakane Chie (1970) who maintain that Japanese society is characterized by "groupism" and that these social groups are modelled after the *ie* or "family household" institution with a "vertical" (*tate*) structure of "parent-child" (*oyabun-kobun*) relations, he argues that these are to be explained in terms of his psychological principle of *amae*, "dependency drive." Furthermore, he argues that the Japanese contextualist model of personhood, including both the traditional Zen concept of self as a fusion of subject and object, as well as its modern reformulation in Nishida Kitarō's philosophy of pure experience, is to be critically analyzed as a psychological function of *amae*, the infantile dependency syndrome. It is thus demonstrated how in recent Japanese thought major representative figures like Watsuji Tetsurō and Nishida Kitarō in modern Japanese philosophy as well as Doi Takeo in modern Japanese psychology have all articulated a context-dependent model of personhood as a twofold social self based on a dialectic of self-other relations.

Part Two goes on to develop the intersubjective concept of personhood in the tradition of classical American pragmatism. Chapter 4 traces the evolution of the social self theory in American philosophy with sections on Charles S. Peirce, William James, Josiah Royce, Charles Horton Cooley, John Dewey, and Alfred North Whitehead. The intersubjective constitution of selfhood through communication in a community was first introduced as a central motif in American pragmatism by C. S. Peirce based upon his research into the relational function of "signs" in the process of interpretation. However, the notion of the social self along with its two components of "I" (the subjective self) and "Me" (the objectified self) were first introduced as technical terms by William James in chapter 10 of his pioneering work *Principles of Psychology* (1891). Under the influence of James and Dewey it was then Charles Horton Cooley who made widespread the notion of a social self in American sociology with the appearance of *Human Nature and the Social Order* in 1902. For Cooley, the individual and society are not separate entities but two sides of the same coin, the "distributive" and "collective" aspects of the social self in its wholeness. Through his famous notion of the "looking-glass self" Cooley explains how the self is a mirror which reflects the primary social groups to which it belongs. In *The World and the Individual* (1899) Josiah Royce describes the process of realizing one's "greater social self" through membership in a community. Citing the Bushidō ethics of the Samurai warrior in Japan, Royce's *The Philosophy of Loyalty* (1908) develops a moral system whereby individualism is overcome and community is established through "loyalty" to the suprapersonal cause of a social group. Throughout a series of works culminating in *Experience and Nature* (1925) John Dewey develops a concept of the "social individual" arising as an organism-environment interaction through open communication, cooperation, mutual participation, valuative transaction, and shared experience between individuals in a liberal democratic community. In *Process and Reality* (1929), Alfred North Whitehead elaborates an organismic process cosmology which endeavors to demonstrate how the social and processual nature of the human self as a society of interconnected events is grounded in the relational and temporal structure of reality itself.

Chapter 5 describes the social-self theory and the I-Me dialectic of George Herbert Mead. In the tradition of American pragmatism it was especially Mead who first systematically thematized the notion of a *social self* as a unifying concept for philosophy and the social sciences. The social self is a key technical term used throughout his major works like *The Philosophy of the Present* (1932), *Mind, Self, and Society* (1934), and *The Philosophy of the Act* (1938), and it is also the title of one of his important essays, "The Social Self" (SW 142–49). According to Mead the social self is not an atomic I or Cartesian subject but a dialectic of I and Me, which together represent the two interactive poles of subjectivity and objectivity, individuality and sociality, indeterminacy and determinacy. In his Whiteheadian evolutionary process cosmology of creative advance into novelty he further specifies the asymmetrical parameters of time's arrow underlying this dialectic of I and Me, whereby at each new moment the social self arises from its deterministic social context in the *past* as a Me to which it then reacts with creativity, spontaneity, and freedom in the *present* as an emergent I. It will thus be shown how Mead's communicative-interaction model of the bipolar social self as a dialectic of I and Me represents an original synthesis of the whole tradition of classical American pragmatism running through Peirce, James, Royce, Dewey, and Cooley, along with its visionary expansion into the organismic process cosmology of A. N. Whitehead.

Part Three introduces the social self as an intercultural theme for East-West comparative philosophy and interfaith dialogue with a focus upon the two major twentieth-century traditions outlined above: modern Japanese philosophy in the East and classical American pragmatism in the West. In particular G. H. Mead's communication model of the social self as an I-Me dialectic is applied to various models of selfhood formulated in modern Japanese thought, including Watsuji Tetsurō's Zen/Confucian *ningen* concept of self as an interpersonal "betweenness" (*aidagara*) of self and others, Nishida Kitarō's Zen Buddhist model of the "social self" as an I-Thou relation, and Doi Takeo's psychological "dependency" (*amae*) model of self as a dialectic of inside/outside. The *introduction* includes a brief synopsis of various comparative approaches to the Zen concept of self based on the underlying

principle of *śūnyatā* (J. *kū*) or "emptiness," alternatively construed by scholars in terms of such Western functional equivalents as *epoche* or "suspension
of judgment" in the ancient Greek skepticism of Sextus Empiricus, as "negativity" in the dialectical metaphysics of Hegel, as self-overcoming through
"[positive] nihilism" in the existentialist thought of Nietzsche, as "openness"
in the existential phenomenology of Heidegger, as the deconstruction of self-
identity through *différance* in the French poststructuralism of Derrida, as "universal relativity" in Whitehead's organic process cosmology, and as *kenōsis* or
"self-emptying" in Christian theology. However, I propose that the closest
parallel to the "true self" of Zen is Mead's concept of the "social self." I further suggest that the single best Western functional equivalent to the Zen
principle of *śūnyatā* or "emptiness" in its designated meaning as *pratītya-
samutpāda* or "interrelational existence" is what Mead calls his "principle of
sociality." If we render *śūnya* by "social" and *śūnyatā* by "sociality," it now
comes to designate that the human self and all phenomena in the continuum
of nature originate through social relations and are void or empty apart from
these relations. Both Mead and Zen have thus converged upon the same fundamental insight: that the self and all events are a function of *sociality*.

In Chapter 6 I briefly review the initial reception of Mead and American pragmatism in Japan through the efforts of Meiji and Taisho period intellectuals based at Waseda University like Tanaka Ōdō (1867–1932), who during the years between 1892 and 1897 became the first Japanese philosopher
to study directly under John Dewey, George Herbert Mead, James Tufts, James
R. Angell, Edward Scribner Ames, and others who together formed the
nucleus of Chicago school pragmatism. I point out that Mead's social-self
theory was first introduced to Japan as a form of totalitarianism wherein the
self is determined by its social environment, and then as a form of liberal
democratic individualism, such that there was a failure to understand his
concept of the social self as a contextualism establishing a middle axiom between individualism and collectivism.

Because the social concept of personhood developed in modern Japanese philosophy represents a syncretism of Confucian and Zen Buddhist value
systems, Mead's theory is first considered in chapter 7 with regard to the
Confucian idea of becoming a person as an expanding network of familial
relationships. Using the work of David Hall and Roger T. Ames (1987) it is
shown that Mead's genetic account of the social formation of selfhood through
internalization of the generalized other is in many ways parallel to the Confucian idea of person making whereby the self constitutes itself as a unity
through taking on the roles of other selves and combining them all in a communal self. Also, Mead's bipolar idea of a social self emerging through a dia-

lectic of I and Me is seen to have much in common with the Confucian idea of the self as arising through a dialectic of *yi* (creative response) and *li* (ritual propriety). Building on the work of Robert C. Neville (1987), it is then argued that like the Confucian ideal of a scholar-official, the social self of Mead is understood as arising through a valuative transaction between the individual organism and its social environment, thereby establishing a *continuity of thought and action* so as to exist within a continuum between the two poles of a private individual and public institutions. Referring to the work of Robert Munro (1977), I then demonstrate that there are significant points of contact between Mead's twofold *bio-social* theory of self and the concept of "bio-social man" developed by recent Confucian / Marxist-Maoist thinkers such as Liu Shao-ch'i in contemporary Chinese philosophy.

Chapter 8. The applicability of Mead's social self theory to both the traditional Japanese concept of self in general and the Zen concept of self in particular has been noted by scholars representing a broad spectrum of fields, including Van Meter Ames (1962) in philosophy, Charles Hartshorne (1984) in process cosmology, Kenneth Inada (1984) in buddhology, Peter L. Berger (1963), David L. Preston (1988), and Kuwayama Takami (1992) in sociology, Robert J. Smith (1983, 1985), Takie Sugiyama Lebra (1976, 1992), and David W. Plath (1980) in cultural anthropology, as well as Doi Takeo (1985) in social psychology. By systematically presenting these various applications I have attempted to establish a unified vision of Mead's social-self theory as an interdisciplinary transcultural framework by means of which to interpret the Japanese self. Kenneth Inada (1984, 76) maintains that Japanese Buddhism, like Peirce, James, Dewey, Whitehead, and Mead in American philosophy, conceives of selfhood as arising through an interaction between the individual organism and its entire social environment. R. J. Smith (1985, 39) criticizes the work of earlier Japanologists based on the individualistic psychology of Freud and asserts that the Japanese self and the Zen self can best be described through the social psychology of G. H. Mead. Takie Lebra (1992, 107) relates Mead's symbolic interactionist concept of self as an I-Me dialectic to the Japanese notion of self including the Zen relational self of nothingness as arising through interaction between the individual and *seken* or "society," pointing out how the Japanese notion of *seken* has something in common with both the Western concept of "reference group" and the "generalized other" of Mead. David W. Plath (1980/ 1992, 8) uses Mead's developmental account of the self as something which "blossoms" through social relations as a theoretical framework to interpret the Japanese archetype of growth into a social person through longtime engagements in the passage of time. Kuwayama Takami (1992, 130) analyzes the Japanese group-centered notion of self as a

self-other dialectic, whereupon he then relates this *other* constituting Japanese selfhood to Western "reference group" and "reference other orientation" theories in sociology, as well as their precursors in the writings of William James on the "social self," C. H. Cooley on the "looking-glass self," G. H.
Mead on the "generalized other," and Harry Stack Sullivan on the "significant other." Kuwayama (1992, 142) goes on to develop a reference other model
of Japanese selfhood as a relationship between the "self" of *jibun* and the
larger whole of society which Mead calls the "generalized other," whereupon he further subdivides these "others" into three distinct categories:
*mawari* (people around) or "immediate reference others," *hito* (people at large)
or "generalized reference others," and *seken* (society) or "reference society."

D. L. Preston (1988) criticizes the introspectionist psychological account
of Zen meditation popularized by Watts, Kapleau, and Suzuki and instead
works out a sociological interpretation from the Meadian tradition of symbolic interactionism wherein Zen theory and practice is now understood as
being oriented to the social reconstruction of a new self and society through
ritualized meditation practices within a community setting. The Chicago
school pragmatist Van Meter Ames (1962, 263) argues that Mead's concept
of the social self as an I-Me dialectic clarifies the two poles of "spontaneity"
and "sociality" represented by the Bodhisattva ideal of personhood in Zen
Buddhism. For Ames, the great accomplishment of Mead and Zen is that
both overcome dualism by accounting for the social formation of selfhood
without any reference to a transcendent or supernatural principle. The process philosopher Charles Hartshorne (1984) and the sociologist Peter Berger
(1963) both emphasize the resemblance between the frameworks of Mead
and Buddhism not only with regard to the "social" aspect of selfhood as a
network of interpersonal relationships, but also the *temporal* and *multiple* nature of the self as a series of emergent or discontinuous events which arise
and perish in the ever-changing stream of consciousness with no underlying
substantial identity. For Berger, this Meadian symbolic interactionist concept
of selfhood as a sequence of discontinuous moments is consonant with the
view of Buddhist psychology, wherein the self is compared to a long row of
candles, each of which lights the wick of its successor and is extinguished in
the same moment.

Taken altogether the scholars cited above suggest the enormous potential of Mead's social-self theory to function as an interdisciplinary model for
interpreting the Japanese self. However, up to this point scholars have for the
most part only made brief references to certain aspects of Mead's thought
and have not endeavored to systematically apply his framework as a whole
to the Japanese notion of self. Furthermore, scholars have thus far restricted

their applications of Mead only to the traditional Japanese concept of self and have not gone on to consider those major systematic theories of selfhood worked out in twentieth-century Japanese thought. Hence, in what follows Mead's communication theory of the social self is developed as an interdisciplinary unifying model for philosophy and the social sciences grounded in an organismic process cosmology which is then critically employed as an East-West transcultural framework to interpret modern Japanese concepts of self as formulated especially by Watsuji Tetsurō and Nishida Kitarō in modern Japanese philosophy and Doi Takeo in modern Japanese psychology.

Chapter 9. Mead's social-self theory and I-Me dialectic is now examined in relation to the syncretic Zen/Confucian concept of Japanese personhood as *ningen* based on the *aidagara* (betweenness) principle of self-other relations worked out by Watsuji Tetsurō and his followers like Kimura Bin, Hamaguchi Eshun, and Kumon Shumpei.[2] It is shown that like Mead's bipolar notion of the social self as an I-Me dialectic, the *ningen* model of Watsuji elucidates the twofold structure of selfhood as an individual-society interaction. Here I argue that both the social-self theory of Mead in American pragmatism and the *ningen/kanjin* model of personhood developed by modern Japanese thinkers like Watsuji, Kimura, Hamaguchi and Kumon, can together be subsumed under the Contexualist paradigm of selfhood as described by Stephen C. Pepper's typological classification scheme of world hypotheses and corresponding root metaphors.

Chapter 10. I next go on to examine the social-self theory and I-Me dialectic of Mead in relation to the Nishida Kitarō's Zen notion of personhood as a twofold "social self" (*shakaiteki jiko*) based on a dialectic of "I and Thou" (*ware to nanji*). As noted by Arisaka and Feenberg (1990, 195–96), Nishida's idea of *basho* or the *topos* of Nothingness represents a "social field theory" similar to that of G. H. Mead and others in the Western tradition of symbolic interactionism. From here I show that like Mead's idea of the social situation, Watsuji's idea of a *fūdo* or "climate" of lived space and Nishida's notion of the *basho* or spatial "locus" of Nothingness both represent a social field theory which functions as the ontological basis for a context-dependent concept of selfhood. Moreover, it is demonstrated that Mead and Nishida both underscore the *temporal* structure of the social self as a discontinuous continuity, that is, what Nishida refers to as a "continuity of discontinuity" (*hirenzoku no renzoku*). Both Mead and Nishida develop a process theory of the social self as a series of arising and perishing events, thereby to constitute the self in time as a continuity of discontinuity, so that with each passing moment the old self is replaced with a partly new self. Finally, I apply Mead's developmental psychology of the socialization process to the thought of Ueda

Shizuteru, who uses Nishida's philosophy to interpret the *Ten Oxherding Pictures* illustrating the Zen process of becoming a compassionate Bodhisattva articulated as a twofold selfless self in the *between* of I and Thou at the locus of absolute Nothingness.

Chapter 11. A significant advantage of Mead's symbolic interactionist framework of the social self is that it establishes a unifying model for both philosophy and the social sciences, including sociology, anthropology, social psychology, and political science, all of which are developed within the context of an organismic process cosmology based on the principle of sociality. As a social scientist Mead is above all else known for his contributions to social psychology. To repeat the words of Peter L. Berger, the social psychology of G. H. Mead can be regarded as "the most important theoretical contribution made to the social sciences in America" (1970, 373). Hence, in this section Mead's social psychology is used to clarify the Japanese *amae* psychology of Doi Takeo, who argues that the traditional Japanese model of selfhood, including both the Zen concept of self and its modern reformulation in the philosophy of Nishida Kitarō is to be understood as a function of *amae*, the dependency drive. In his book *Omote to ura* (Front and Back, 1985), which has now been translated into English as *The Anatomy of Self: The Individual Versus Society* (1986), Doi himself points out significant parallels between his *amae* concept of Japanese selfhood as a nexus of dependency relationships and the social self theories of William James, C. H. Cooley, and G. H. Mead. In this context, Doi (1985, 41–42) relates the distinction of *honne/tatemae* or "individual reactions/social institutions" defining the twofold structure of Japanese selfhood to the I-Me dialectic of self in the social psychology of Mead. In such a manner, the bipolar structure of Mead's communication model of the social self based on his I-Me dialectic of intersubjectivity is used to elucidate the twofold nature of human existence as an individual-society relationship in modern Japanese thought, including Watsuji Tetsurō's Zen/Confucian *ningen* model of personhood based on his *aidagara* theory of self-other relations, Nishida Kitarō's "social self" theory based on his I-Thou dialectic, and Doi Takeo's dependency (*amae*) model of Japanese selfhood based on the dialectic of *honne/tatemae*.

Chapter 12. For Mead the social self is always an embodied self understood as a body-mind unity. He asserts that the self is not a mere "I" or disembodied subject but a dialectic of "I and Me," thus representing the two interactive poles of subject and object, mind and body, mental and physical, or psychic and somatic. Mead's revolt against Cartesian subjectivism is seen not only in terms of his theoretical framework but also in terms of his method: that of "social behaviorism" based on a Wundtian psychology of *gestures*. The behavioristic psychology of Mead is an empirical method which abandons introspectivism and studies human consciousness, mind, and self through their external manifestation in the embodied gestures of observable human conduct. Mead's concept of the social self as a unity of body and mind provides a nondual framework to interpret the traditional Zen ideal of the true self as *shinjin ichinyo* or "oneness of body-mind" and its reformulations in twentieth-century Japanese philosophy. It is demonstrated that for both Mead and modern Japanese Buddhist philosophy the intersubjective model of the social self as an individual-society interaction also involves a psychosomatic model of the embodied self as a body-mind interaction. The parallels between Mead and modern Japanese Buddhist philosophers on the self as a bodymind unity are further clarified through the similarity of both to Merleau-Ponty's phenomenology of the "lived body."

Chapter 13. Mead's interdisciplinary approach to the social self provides a unifying model for the social sciences which integrates not only sociology, anthropology, social psychology, and political science at the micro level but also ecology at the macro level of analysis. His basic definition of the social self as arising through an *organism-environment interaction* unified by pervasive aesthetic quality functions to establish the continuity between the self and its total surroundings of human society and living nature. I demonstrate that the notion of self as a human-nature interaction is not only a basic theme of traditional Zen Buddhism but also twentieth-century Japanese philosophy as articulated through Watsuji Tetsurō's Zen/Confucian *ningen* model of self as located in a *fūdo* or spatial climate of nature, Nishida Kitarō's Zen concept of the social self as an I-Thou relation where the "Thou" which opposes the "I" includes both human society and the metaphysical society of nature, as well as Kimura Bin's concept of the Japanese self as a unity of *"mizukara* and *onozukara"* or "self and nature." It is therefore argued that both Mead and modern Japanese philosophers develop not only an intersubjective model of the social self as an individual-society interaction functioning to ground an interhuman ethics and aesthetics, but also an *ecological* model of self as a human-nature interaction which establishes the basis for an environmental ethics and conservation aesthetics.

Chapter 14. In this final chapter the model of a twofold social self as an I-Other relation developed by both Mead in American pragmatism as well as by Watsuji, Nishida, and others in modern Japanese philosophy is set in historical perspective from the standpoint of Martin Buber's overview of the history of philosophical anthropology. I point out that during his three years as a student in Germany from 1889 to 1891, Mead, like Buber, studied directly under W. Dilthey, the founder of the discipline of the history of philosophical

anthropology. As a result of Mead's study under Dilthey his own work adopts
a primarily anthropological orientation as a sustained inquiry into the human
self. Not unlike Feuerbach and others in the German tradition of *Anthropologie*,
Mead carries out an anthropological reduction which rejects the theological
approach and establishes the human self as the fundamental topic for philosophical reflection. In this context Mead's anthropological concept of
personhood as a bipolar social self in the between of I and Me is related to
Buber's bipolar concept of self in the between of I and Thou. Also, Mead's
concept of the social self as arising through *symbolic interaction* using "significant symbols" is developed in conjunction with the philosophical anthropology of Ernst Cassirer based upon his famous notion of man as an *animal
symbolicum*. I argue that Mead's notion of a "social self" arising through *symbolic interaction* functions to unify Cassirer's definition of self as a "symbolic
animal" with Aristotle's definition of self as a "social animal." Furthermore,
Mead's concept of the bipolar social self as an *I-Me relation* is juxtaposed with
John Macmurray's (1961, 1983) influential concept of self as an *I-You relation*
constituted by linguistic communication in a community of persons in relation. It is shown how Macmurray, like both Mead and Buber, has thematized
a bipolar concept of self as a relation of I and Other—what Macmurray calls
the relation of I and You, what Mead calls the relation of I and Me, and what
Buber calls the relation of I and Thou.

In *Between Man and Man* (1947, 1965) Buber traces the development of
various concepts of man, self, person, or human nature elaborated in the
history of philosophical anthropology throughout its various phases of individualism and collectivism, finally showing the turn from a monological to a
fully *dialogical* concept of personhood as an I-Thou relation in the landmark
work of Ludwig Feuerbach. Here I employ Buber's overview of the history
of philosophical anthropology to clarify what Jürgen Habermas calls the "paradigm shift" in Mead beyond Cartesian subjectivism and Hegelian absolutism
to an intersubjectivist communication theory of the social self as a conversation between I and Me. However, Buber's historical presentation of this turn
to a concept of man as a dialectic of I-Thou relationships clarifies the development of a twofold model of personhood articulated in all of the Eastern
and Western frameworks under consideration here, including not only the
bipolar structure of the social self as an I-Me dialectic elaborated by G. H.
Mead in American pragmatism, but also Watsuji Tetsurō's *ningen* concept of
the Japanese self as a self-other relation, Nishida Kitarō's concept of the social self as an I-Thou dialectic, and Doi Takeo's "dependency" (*amae*) model
of Japanese selfhood a dual consciousness of inside / outside. In particular it is
shown that both Nishida Kitarō in the East and Martin Buber in the West

independently worked out a dialogical concept of self based on Feuerbach's notion of personhood as an I-Thou relationship of intersubjectivity. The two-fold structure of the I-Thou dialogical self is further specified by Buber in terms of his ultimate category of "between" (*das Zwischen*) functioning as the ontological *place* in which both self and other arise through dialogue. At this point it is shown how in the tradition of American pragmatism, Buber's ontological category of the "between" functions similarly to G. H. Mead's principle of *sociality*, according to which the social self exists "betwixt and between" the deterministic system of the Me or social pole inherited from the past and the non-deterministic system of the I or individual pole emerging in the present. Just as for Buber the dialogical self exists in the betweenness of I and Thou, for Mead the social self is located in the betweenness of I and Me. In the tradition of modern Japanese philosophy, it is then demonstrated how Watsuji Tetsurō's principle of *aidagara* or "betweenness" is analogous to Buber's existential and ontological category of "between." Similarly, in the thought of Nishida Kitarō and the Kyoto school, especially as developed in the work of Ueda Shizuteru, the "true self" of Zen is analyzed as having the form of a twofold social self located in the *between* of I and Thou within the spatial locus of absolute Nothingness. Finally, it should be pointed out that like Martin Buber (1965, 163–75), modern Japanese philosophers such as Watsuji Tetsurō (1961, v–vi), Nishida Kitarō (NKZ VII, 179–80), and Takeuchi Yoshinori (1983, 122) have all argued that the German tradition of philosophical anthropology, leading up to and including Heidegger's analysis of man as *Mitsein* or "being-with," is ultimately committed to an individualistic notion of selfhood, and thus fails to achieve a truly dialogical concept of human existence as an I-Thou relationship of intersubjectivity. Arguing along similar lines, Jürgen Habermas (1987, 148–55), Ernst Tugendhat (1991, 169–200) and Hans Joas (1985, 41–42) maintain that what was not achieved by Heidegger and the German tradition of philosophical anthropology is at last realized in G. H. Mead's intersubjective communication model of the social self as a dialogical conversation between I and Me. Joas (1985, 2) therefore regards Mead as the most important philosopher of intersubjectivity standing between Feuerbach and Habermas. I argue that while on the surface there is a parallel between Zen and Heidegger in that for both the self is a nothingness or openness in which phenomena comes to presence, in fact Heidegger's idea of man is closed in self-being. In contrast, Mead develops a genuine concept of the open self whose openness is the unblocked communicative interaction between individual and society. Hence, from the standpoint of the history of philosophical anthropology, Martin Buber in European existentialism and G. H. Mead in American pragmatism, as well as representative thinkers like Watsuji Tetsurō and Nishida Kitarō in the tradition of modern Japanese philosophy, have converged upon a fully social concept of the person based on a dialectic of self-other relations and a dialogical principle of betweenness. I thus arrive at the fundamental thesis of this work: that in the twentieth century, both in the East and in the West, there has been a paradigm shift in the history of philosophical anthropology to an intersubjective communication model of personhood based on the concept of a bipolar social self which exists in the *between* of I and Other.

## Problematics of the "Social Self" Motif in East-West Dialogue

With this East-West paradigm shift to a new communication model of the social self as an I-Other relation of intersubjectivity there has emerged a corresponding set of problematics which must also be directly confronted. Hence, while on the one hand I attempt to establish a series of cross-cultural parallels between the social-self theory of Mead in American pragmatism and the Zen/Confucian concept of personhood in modern Japanese philosophy, on the other hand I address fundamental tensions arising between these East-West models of the self with respect to such problems as individualism versus collectivism, liberalism versus communitarianism, relativism versus universalism, and freedom versus determinism.

## Individualism versus Collectivism

Japanese culture is usually characterized as a form of "groupism." But such a one-sided description of Japanese society is an oversimplification which only shows a general trend, not the total situation. As Kuniko Miyanaga points out in *The Creative Edge: Emerging Individualism in Japan* (1991), Japanese society can be analyzed in terms of two sectors, the economic "mainstream" representing Japan Inc. or the world of large corporations as characterized by groupism, and the "periphery" representing the subculture of artists, religious seekers, dropouts, and so forth, which can be characterized by Individualism. Moreover, the mainstream of groupist culture and the periphery of individualist culture are always interacting in a dialectical way. Those in the modern technological culture of the economic mainstream dominated by large companies are the "situational selves," "contextual persons" or "ritual men" who have submitted to the established pattern of interaction rituals within the group. However there is also an increasing trend toward an *emerging individualism* on the periphery of Japanese society. From this perspective Kumiko Miyanaga analyzes those aspects of Japanese society being transformed in the direction of individualism so as to acquire the "creative edge," like the fashion industry, the art world, avant-garde designers, private entrepreneurs, self-made business owners, and so forth.

The structure of Japanese selfhood can likewise be analyzed in terms of two poles arising through a process of dialectical interaction, the individual pole and the social pole. While in the past there has been a priority accorded to the social over the individual poles of the self, since the advent of the Meiji Restoration period beginning in 1868 there has been an increased recognition of the "I" or individual aspect under to the influence of Western ization. Whereas earlier Japanese Buddhist models of selfhood tended to articulate human nature in negative terms as *muga* (Skt. *anātman*) or "no-self," the models formulated by twentieth-century Japanese thinkers have underscored the dialectical relation between the individual and social aspects of personhood. Hence, all the modern Japanese thinkers selected for inclusion in this volume have developed an explicit bipolar model of personhood as an I-Other relationship, including Nishida Kitarō's theory of the social self as an I-Thou dialectic, Watsuji Tetsurō's twofold *ningen* concept of the person as a "self-other" (*ji-ta*) dialectic, and Doi Takeo's "dependency" (*amae*) model of self as a dialectic of *honne-tatemae* or "individual reactions-social institutions." Watsuji Tetsurō (1937, 14–15) emphasizes that Japanese selfhood as *ningen* has a double nature insofar as it is both an individual and a part of society. Kumon Shumpei (1982, 18) argues that the *ningen* model of Japanese selfhood initially formulated by Watsuji Tetsurō and further developed by such thinkers as Kimura Bin and Hamaguchi Eshun represents a "contextualist" theory functioning to establish a middle axiom between "individualist" and "collectivist" notions of the person. Yet I argue that the *ningen* model worked out by Watsuji and his school fails to resolve the problem of individualism versus collectivism in that the individual aspect ultimately dissolves into the social aspect of the person. It may be said that Watsuji's *ningen* theory of man reflects the general pattern of group-centered Japanese culture based on the *ie* or "family" institution whereby social relationships come to supersede the individual, as is illustrated by the often-cited proverb: "The protruding nail is hammered down" (*Deru kugi wa utareru*). If Watsuji begins his analysis by emphasizing the double structure of the person as *ningen* insofar as it is both "individual" and "social," he ends by falling into a totalitarian ideology of what has been referred to as a form of "emperor system fascism" which deifies the state and advocates the militaristic ideal of self-sacrifice to the Japanese *kokutai* or national polity. Nishida's concept of the "social self" (*shakaiteki jiko*) based on a dialectic of I and Thou (*ware to nanji*) comes nearer to establishing a middle position between individualism and collectivism insofar as it underscores the irreducible self-creativity of the I or individual aspect as over against the absolute otherness of the Thou or social aspect. It is Nishida who most clearly works out the function of the I in the true self of Zen Buddhism. Nonetheless, the individualism and personalism of Nishida's social-self theory and I-Thou dialectic is undermined to the extent that he supports an "imperial ideology" of the emperor system in his political writings.

The problem of individualism versus collectivism is provided with a more adequate solution through the social-self theory and I-Me dialectic of G. H. Mead in American pragmatism. According to the evolutionary process cosmology of Mead the self arises through its relations to a social context in the past at the Me pole and then responds to it with emergent creativity, spontaneity, and novelty in the living present at the I pole. He further emphasizes that both the I and the Me are necessary phases of the social self in its wholeness. Since the I and Me are equal, reciprocal, and co-relative aspects of the social self, neither can be granted priority over the other. Through his analysis of the social self as an I-Me dialectic of intersubjectivity he thus establishes a true *via media* between possessive individualism and totalitarian collectivism.

## Liberalism versus Communitarianism

One of the major problems in contemporary social, moral, and political philosophy is that of liberalism versus communitarianism. In recent moral debates the autonomy-based framework of liberalism developed by John Rawls (1971) and others in Anglo-American social philosophy has been challenged by the commitment-based framework of communitarianism as developed by Alasdair MacIntyre (1981), Charles Taylor (1979), and Michael Sandel (1982). In the liberal position the moral agent is an "unencumbered self" which appears before society and then determines what constitutes the good through the self-legislative rationality of a Kantian transcendental ego. Society is formed in order to permit the the greatest possible freedom for unencumbered selves to choose their own conceptions of the good with minimal interference from others. However, the communitarians argue that the tradition of liberalism from Kant to Rawls is based on an implausible notion of self as a separate ego and an inadequate notion of community as a contractual association of atomic individuals. According to communitarianism the liberal position fails to understand that the self is intersubjectively constituted by its social relationships to others such that there is no self-identity prior to or apart from membership in a community. On the other side, proponents of liberalism emphasize that communitarianism is always in danger of collapsing the individual into society so as to fall into the extremes of social determinism, collectivism, and totalitarianism. Thus, most of those who take up the communitarian critique of liberal individualism do not argue for a one-sided communitarianism, but instead endeavor to bolster the rights-based framework of liberalism with the duty-based framework of communitarianism as grounded in a more social concept of the self and a stronger notion of community.

The communitarian/liberalism debate is a basic theme in the popular sociological critique of American individualism developed by Robert Bellah and others, in *Habits of the Heart* (1986). In this work Bellah and his colleagues question the American belief in individualism derived from the political philosophy of John Locke and the economic philosophy of Adam Smith, in both of which the individual is driven primarily by egocentric motivations of self-interest. Arguing from a communitarian position Bellah and others contributing to the volume argue that the traditional American emphasis on individualism and self-reliance "has led to the notion of pure, undetermined choice, free of tradition, obligation, or commitment, as the essence of the self" (1986, 152). This American individualistic concept of self is essentially a Cartesian subject or Kantian transcendental ego which tries to become completely "unencumbered" by freeing itself from all commitments to tradition and community. However, the alternative to American individualism selected by Bellah and his colleagues is an encumbered self arising through its membership in a "community of memory" (1986, 152). Like Alasdair MacIntyre's communitarian notion of a "narrative unity" of self as articulated in *After Virtue* (1981), and as further developed by Paul Ricoeur in *Oneself as Another* (1992, 158), Bellah and his colleagues describe the "community of memory" as having a narrative history—a unifying set of stories and traditions which are inherited by its all members. These narrative stories and traditions are said to "carry a context of meaning that can allow us to connect our aspirations . . . with the aspirations of a larger whole and see our our efforts as being, in part, contributions to a common good" (1986, 153).

In modern Japanese philosophy Watsuji Tetsurō develops a communitarian ethics of the family system based on his *ningen* concept of man which emphasizes the primacy of obligations, duties and commitments to one's social group. But like Hegel's philosophy of right in the West, the communitarian ethics of Watsuji slides into a totalitarian political ideology wherein the individual is collapsed into a function of the state. In recent social philosophy Jürgen Habermas has argued that a communication theory of the social self must be accompanied by a critical theory exposing the oppressive power relations of coercion, dominance, and authority that systematically distort the process of communicative interaction between individuals in society. As has been charged in the scathing ideology critiques leveled against Watsuji's *ningen* theory by Maruyama Masao, Ienaga Saburo, Arima Tatsuo, Tosaka Jun, and others in Japan, as well as by Robert Bellah, Gino Piovesana, Peter Dale, and others in the West, the form of communitarian ethics set forth by Watsuji and his followers privileges social solidarity over individual autonomy to the extent of falling into what has been rightly called a "totalitarian state ethics," an "emperor system fascism," and a "fascist ideology."

In contrast to the communitarian ethics of Watsuji, Mead works out a liberal democratic notion of selfhood based on the primacy of individual rights and liberties. While the social self theories of Watsuji and Nishida are used to support imperial ideology of the Emperor system, Mead's social-self theory instead functions as the groundwork for his political vision of a liberal democratic society based on the self-determination of free and equal individuals through open communication, cooperation, valuative transaction, shared experience, and public discourse. However, unlike the liberal tradition from Kant to Rawls which presupposes an individualistic notion of self as having an identity prior to its membership in a community, the liberal democracy of Mead is based on the concept of a bipolar social self arising through communicative interaction between the self and society. As emphasized in Habermas's interpretation of Mead, in contrast to liberalism wherein individuation precedes sociation, Mead was the first to clearly grasp that individuation and sociation are simultaneous interactive processes. For Mead, other selves in the community are not simply external but are part of one's own self. The self is constituted as a unity by taking on the perspectives of other selves in society so as to incorporate them as the "generalized other." While overcoming atomic individualism through his notion of a social self as an I-Me dialectic of intersubjectivity, the Chicago school pragmatism of Mead nonetheless stays within the American tradition of democratic liberalism in that *the social Me is always the servant of the individual I.* The self arises by taking on the roles of others in society as a Me to which it then responds with spontaneity and freedom as an I. The social self theory and I-Me dialectic of Mead thus represents a liberal democratic view of self which at the same time is bolstered by the values of communitarianism including both a social concept of self and a stronger notion of community. Mead (MSS 196) argues that since the social self has two component phases, the I or indeterminate phase and the Me or determinate phase, the I requires that we protect the rights and and freedoms of individuals as extolled by liberalism, while the Me imposes those moral duties, commitments, and obligations advocated by communitarianism. In this way Mead's social-self theory and I-Me dialectic functions to establish a new unifying model which integrates the autonomy-based framework of liberalism with the commitment-based framework of communitarianism.

However, at this point it is necessary to underscore the distinction between *norms* and *facts*, or between the "ideal" and the "real." At the *normative* level of analysis, both the twentieth-century Japanese and American philosophers under consideration here endeavor to articulate the *ideal* structure of personhood as a social self with two interacting poles, an individual pole and a social pole. Yet at the factual level of analysis the traditional Japanese self is no doubt more group-centered, in contrast to the American self, which is typically more ego-centered. Although Watsuji's concept of *ningen* functions normatively to represent an ideal mode of Japanese selfhood as existing in the *aidagara* or "betweenness" of the individual and society, in fact the Japanese character moves in the direction of collectivism, groupism, and sociocentrism. Likewise, while Mead's social-self theory and I-Me dialectic functions normatively to depict an ideal mode of human existence which balances individuality with sociality, in fact the American character moves in the direction of narcissism, egoism, and individualism. Hence, the time has now come for an expanded research program in the social sciences based on an East-West transcultural approach which combines the communicative-interaction model of the social self developed by G. H. Mead with the Zen/ Confucian concept of self as formulated by representative modern Japanese thinkers. In *Mind, Self, and Society* (1934), Mead remarks that through the growth of an international world community the East and the West are now exchanging their social roles, America taking on the perspectives of Asian culture and vice versa:

> Kipling says: "East is East and west is West, and never the twain shall meet"; but they are meeting. The assumption has been that the response of the East to the West and the West to the East are not comprehensible to each other. But, in fact, we find that we are awakening, and we are beginning to interchange roles. (MSS 271)

If Japanese communitarian thought and culture can teach America a deeper mode of social solidarity, cooperation and group harmony, then liberal American thought and culture can teach Japan a deeper mode of individual freedom, spontaneity, and creativity. Or in Meadian terms, if the Japanese educational system can teach America how to cultivate the Me or social pole of selfhood through internalization of the generalized other, then American education can teach Japan how to cultivate the I or individual pole through fostering creativity, originality and emergent novelty. It is such a turn or shift toward an intersubjectivist communication paradigm of the social self derived from a cross-cultural synthesis of classical American pragmatism in the West and modern Japanese philosophy in the East which can function to integrate both the rights-based liberal and the commitment-based communitarian value systems, thereby to forge a new *via media* between possessive individualism on the one side and totalitarian collectivism on the other.

## Relativism versus Universalism

Another fundamental problematic in social and moral philosophy which emerges here is that of the conflict between relativism versus universalism. Although popular romantic accounts of Zen Buddhism emphasize an ethics of universal "compassion" (*jihi*) for all living things, in the context of Japanese groupism it takes the form of a relativistic ethics of the *ie* or family household system wherein compassion is restricted to one's particular social group. Robert Bellah (1970), William Deal (1991) and other scholars have underscored the absence of any universal ethic and the consequent moral relativism and particularism which results from the family or group-centered value system of Japanese culture, including its expression in the Bushidō ethic of group loyalty and its restatement in the twentieth-century communitarian ethics of the family system developed by Watsuji Tetsurō. By contrast the moral philosophy articulated by G. H. Mead in such essays as "Fragments on Ethics" (MSS 379–89) and further developed by Jürgen Habermas in *Moral Consciousness and Communicative Action* (1990) endeavors to reformulate Kant's universalist ethics based on the categorical imperative in terms of an intersubjective communication paradigm of the social self. Kant's famous categorical imperative (1987, 49), which requires that the maxim by which one acts can be generalized into universal laws applicable to everyone, is no longer a "monological" procedure conducted by a solitary transcendental subject, but is now a *dialogical* procedure carried out by a social self in an intersubjective community through mutual participation and noncoercive open communication in public discourse. Hence, in opposition to the moral relativism of Japanese communitarian ethics whereby good and evil or right and wrong are defined in terms of one's particular social group as the primary frame of reference, in the communicative discourse ethics of Mead and Habermas they are instead defined in terms of universalizable or generalizable norms which transcend the group.

## Freedom versus Determinism

Closely related to the problems of individualism versus collectivism and liberalism versus communitarianism is that of freedom versus determinism. Insofar as Watsuji Tetsurō's *ningen* theory of personhood and communitarian ethics falls into a totalitarian collectivism it is also confronted with the problem of social determinism whereby the individual is oppressed by the coercive powers of the state. For Mead, however, the social self is analyzed has having two component processes, the I and the Me, representing the dual systems of indeterminacy and determinacy. The self arises from out of its deterministic social environment in the past at the Me pole and responds to it with creativity, novelty, and spontaneity in the present as an individual organism at the I pole. Again, the self is formed by incorporating the public institutions of society as a social Me while reconstructing those institutions through creative activity as an individual I. Mead's concept of the I accounts for the freedom of the acting self as an autonomous moral agent as well as the creativity of the artist, the inventor, and the scientist in the process of discovery.

Like Mead in American pragmatism, Nishida Kitarō develops an explicit theory of the social self based on an I-Other dialectic which overcomes Cartesian subjectivism while preserving the "I" of creative human agency and the acting self. Similar to the I-Me dialectic of Mead, the I-Thou dialectic of Nishida underscores the irreducible self-creativity and radical discontinuity of the individual I as over against the social determinism of the "Thou." However, at the political levels of analysis, it has been seen that whereas the social self and I-Thou dialectic of Nishida is used to support the emperor system, the social self and I-Me dialectic of Mead instead functions as the basis for a liberal democratic society.

Moreover, at the cosmological level of analysis, a debate emerges regarding the problem of freedom versus determinism. In a truly remarkable convergence of thought, both Mead and Nishida work out an explicit theory of the social self as an I-Other dialectic grounded in a Leibnizian cosmology of perspectives wherein the individual represents society in microcosm. However, I argue that while for Mead the social self is an emergent perspective which balances determinacy and indeterminacy, for Nishida the self is a total perspective which falls into social determinism. In his essay "Towards A Phi-losophy of Religion with the Concept of Pre-Established Harmony as a Guide" (1944), Nishida articulates a perspectivist model of selfhood which combines the perspectivism of Leibniz in the West and Kegon (Chinese: Hua-yen) Bud-dhism in the East. Citing Leibniz's perspectivist theory of monads, Nishida writes: "Our selves are 'creative points' of this world. Leibniz called the monad a metaphysical point, but I think of each individual self as a creative point of the historical world. It extends to the eternal future and to the eternal past as the point of self-determination of the absolute present" (NKZ XI, 135). Hence, like the jewels of Indra's net in Kegon Buddhism and the metaphysical points of Leibniz's monadology, for Nishida the self is a perspectival mirror which reflects past, present, and future in the bottomless depths of an eternal now. Similarly, in *The Philosophy of the Present* (1932) Mead asserts that what he finds to be of greatest value in A. N. Whitehead's cosmological framework is his "Leibnizian filiation, as it appears in his conception of the perspective as the mirroring in the event of all other events" (PP 164). But Mead's innova-tion is that he applies Whitehead's Leibnizian cosmology of perspectives to social psychology and the field of the social sciences (PP 164–65). In his devel-opmental theory of socialization, Mead converts Whitehead's cosmological theory of perspectives into his basic notion of "perspective-taking," whereby the individual is constituted as a social self by gradually *entering into the per-spectives* of others in the community to which it belongs, finally entering into the common perspective of the generalized other so as to replicate its whole society in miniature. Mead thus uses Whitehead's cosmological perspectivism as the basis for his social-self theory wherein each individual mirrors its com-munity from a unique perspective, just as for Leibniz each monad reflects its whole universe from a unique perspective (PP 201). It is this Whiteheadian/Leibnizian perspectivism which provides the deeper cosmological vision underlying Mead's social scientific theory of the human self.

It is precisely Mead's appropriation of Whitehead's Leibnizian cosmol-ogy of perspectives which establishes a relationship between the present vol-ume and my earlier book entitled *Process Metaphysics and Hua-Yen Buddhism* (1982).[3] In this earlier work I formulate a Whiteheadian process critique of Hua-Yen (J. Kegon) Buddhist modes of thought, including those schools based on the Kegon infrastructure like Zen and the modern Japanese philosophy of Nishida Kitarō. I argue that Whiteheadian process thought, like Kegon Buddhism and the modern Japanese philosophy of Nishida, has developed a cosmology of perspectives established through harmonious interpenetration of the many and the one so that each unifying event both contains and per-vades the whole continuum of nature as a microcosm of the macrocosm. Or as David Bohm asserts in his reworking of Whitehead's scientific cosmology (1980), each microcosmic-macrocosmic perspective functions like a *hologram* which enfolds the implicate order of unbroken wholeness in the dynamic holo-flux of nature. But while for Nishida, as for Leibniz and Kegon Buddhism, each perspectival self holographically mirrors past, present, and future within a symmeterical framework of causal relations so as to land in a form of determinism, for Whitehead, as for Mead, each perspectival self mirrors only its *past* within an asymmetrical framework of relations so as to allow for a fully open-ended universe as a temporal process of creative advance into novelty. Nishida argues that his cosmology of perspectives is different from the Leibnizian theory because as opposed to the "metaphysical points" of Leibniz, his own perspectives are to be regarded as "creative points" (*sōzō ten*). Nonetheless, insofar as for Nishida the self represents a *total perspective* mirroring all events of the past, present, and future alike it is inescapably deterministic and does not provide the metaphysical grounds for creativity, novelty, and freedom to be found in the American process thought of Whitehead and Mead. As opposed to Nishida's cosmology of total perspectives, the Whiteheadian process cosmology of Mead instead holds that the social self constitutes an *emergent perspective* arising in the temporal flux of nature as a creative advance toward novelty. While for Nishida the social self as an I-Thou dialectic is a total perspective mirroring past, present and future in the eternal now of absolute nothingness so as to land in determinism, for Mead the self as an I-Me dialectic is an emergent perspective which mirrors its social situation in the *past* as a Me and then responds with creativity, freedom, and novelty in the *present* as an I. Thus, Mead's bipolar concept of the social self as an I-Me dialectic has an asymmetrical, irreversible and cumulative time-structure which at once allows for both freedom and determinism, creativity and causation, or indeterminacy and determinacy.

## The Problem of Nihonjinron and the Myth of Japanese Uniqueness

A final problem arises here with respect to that field of scholarship which has come to be known as *nihonjinron*, the "study of Japanese identity." As pointed out by Peter Dale (1986), a problematic assumption of *nihonjinron* scholarship is its claim that Japanese are culturally, socially, and even racially homogeneous, despite historical evidence to the contrary. Also, it is claimed that the Japanese self and society differ radically from those of all other cultures, overlooking any commonalities which might be discerned through objective scholarship. For Dale, both of these unsubstantiated claims represent what he calls the "myth of Japanese uniqueness." The problem raised by *nihonjinron* scholarship is germane to our whole project of East-West dialogue insofar as its exaggerated claim for the absolute uniqueness of the Japanese self and society at once precludes any attempt to establish cross-cultural parallels.

Generally speaking, *nihonjinron* literature argues for an absolute uniqueness of the Japanese mind, self, and society as mirrored in (or constituted by) the unique structure of the Japanese language. This alleged uniqueness of traditional Japanese culture is especially defined in terms of the social nature of Japanese selfhood and the group-centered nature of Japanese household society. Japanese selfhood is thus repeatedly characterized by *ninhonjinron* scholarship through such notions as groupism, familism, contextualism, social relationism, collectivism, interpersonalism, cooperationism, sociocentrism, and so on. Or again, the Japanese self is said to be "social," "relational," "familial," "contextual," "interpersonal," "dialogical," "interactional," and so forth. *Nihonjinron* texts have developed an elaborate lexicon of key terms purporting to disclose the unique essence of Japaneseness (*nihonrashisa*), such as *ie* (family, household), *aida* (betweenness, relatedness), *ningen* (person), *amae* (dependency relationship), *wa* (harmony), *tate* (vertical relations), *kanjin* (contextual persons), *shūdanshugi* (groupism), *mono no aware* (sympathy with things), *ma* (space between), *iki* (chic), *kū* (emptiness of self), *muga* (selflessness), *shitashimi* (intimacy), and numerous others, all of which from various perspectives function to underscore the social character of Japanese selfhood and the groupism of Japanese society.

In his controversial study of *nihonjinron* theories entitled *The Myth of Japanese Uniqueness* (1986), Peter Dale argues that the claim for Japanese uniqueness carries with it the hidden agenda of establishing the absolute superiority of Japan. He maintains that the language of Japanese uniqueness can all too easily serve to mask an underlying right-wing political ideology characterized by elements of ultranationalism, cultural narcissism, ethnic chauvanism, militarism, racism, imperialism, and fascism. In this context Dale establishes a powerful and relentless if sometimes malicious and axe-grinding ideology critique of *nihonjinron* scholarship in its all its multivariate forms, arguing that Watsuji Tetsurō's *ningen* concept man, Nishida Kitarō's "pure experience" (*junsui keiken*), Doi Takeo's *amae* theory of dependency relationships, Kimura Bin's *aida* principle of social relationism, Hamaguchi Eshun's "contextualism," (*kanjinshugi*), Kumon Shumpei's "contextual" (*kanjin*) theory of Japanese selfhood, Nakane Chie's *ie* or "household" model of Japanese familial society, D. T. Suzuki's Zen Buddhist concept of self as *muga* or "selflessness," Motōri Norinaga's literary poetic of *mono no aware* or "sympathy with things," Kuki Shūzō's notion of *iki* (chic) as an aesthetic ideal of intersexual relationships, Nitobe Inazō's Bushidō warrior ethic of "self-sacrifice" and "group loyalty," and many similar notions, all function to conceal under the subterfuge of aesthetic, moral, and spiritual ideals a totalitarian state ethics and fascist political ideology based on a fusion of subject and object and dissolution of the individual into the whole.

In the recent proliferation of *nihonjinron* literature it has now become commonplace to characterize the Japanese communitarian notion of self as social, group-centered, and collectivistic, in direct opposition to the American liberal notion of self, which is by contrast said to be atomistic, egocentric, and individualistic. A classic example of this is to be found in the *Ethics* (1937) of Watsuji Tetsurō, which criticizes various Western concepts of the self based on "individualism" (*kojinshugi*), including *anthropos*, *homo*, man, *Mensch*, and even Heidegger's *Dasein*, arguing that among the world's languages only the unique Japanese word *ningen* functions to express the dual structure of selfhood as both "individual" and "social" in character. Furthermore, in ultranationalist essays like "The Way of the Subject in Japan" (*Nihon no shindō*), and "America's National Character" (*America no kokuminsei*), both released together in a wartime pamphlet dated July 1944, Watsuji argues for the complete superiority of traditional Japanese culture based on the ideal of "self-negation" (*jiko hitei*) over that of liberal democratic American society based on individualism, egocentrism, and utilitarianism (see Bellah: 1965, 578–79). In such works as *The Rediscovery of Japaneseness* ('Nihonrashisa' no saihakken, 1977), and *Japan—Society of Contextualism* (Kanjin-shugi no shakai nihon, 1982), and "A Contextual Model of the Japanese" (1985), Hamaguchi Eshun develops his own *nihonjinron* theory wherein the essence of Japaneseness (*nihonrashisa*) is to be found in his sociological principle of "contextualism" (*kanjin-shugi*), which he places in opposition to American "individualism" (*kojinshugi*). Peter Dale (1986) has argued that another master-text in the tradition of *nihonjinron* literature is psychiatrist Doi Takeo's *The Structure of Amae* (Amae no kōzō, 1971), which argues that the unique social character of Japanese selfhood is to be analyzed as a psychological function of *amae*, the infantile dependency syndrome. In *Omote to ura* (Front and Back, 1985), Doi uses the Sapir-Whorf hypothesis expressing the direct correlation between language and culture to support his conclusion that the unique structure of the Japanese language and especially the uniqueness of the Japanese word *amae* (dependency relationship) reflects the peculiarly social nature of the Japanese self. In his comparison of Eastern and Western notions of selfhood, Doi therefore

agrees with the often repeated generalization that Americans are "individualistic" (*kojinshugiteki*) and that the Japanese are characterized by "groupism"
(*shūdanshugi*) (1985, 53).

Hence, the fundamental assumption of *nihonjinron* scholarship is that
the Japanese self is absolutely unique and that the essence of Japanese uniqueness lies in its social or relational character. A further assumption is that while
the Japanese notion of self is defined by groupism, the Western notion of self
is defined by individualism. In particular the social concept of self in Zen and
traditional Japanese society is contrasted to the individualistic concept of self
in American liberal society. However, in direct opposition to *nihonjinron* theories it is my contention that an explicit concept of the social self constituted by
its relations to others in a community is in fact a central and pervasive motif
characterizing the whole tradition of classical American philosophy running
through Peirce, James, Royce, Dewey, Cooley, Whitehead, and Mead! Furthermore, it is my contention that G. H. Mead's communicative-interaction
model of the social self as an I-Me dialectic functions as the best transcultural
framework to elucidate both the Japanese self in general and the Zen self in
particular. This point has been emphatically made by Robert J. Smith, who
remarks: "In the mid–1930's George Herbert Mead . . . attempted to develop
a social psychology that fits almost perfectly what we are told is the peculiarly Japanese case" (1985, 39).

From what has been said above it can now be seen how there exists a
basic methodological difference between the transcultural *universalism* represented by Mead's theory of the social self versus the cultural *particularism*
represented by *nihonjinron* theories of Japanese self-identity. While *nihonjinron*
scholars argue for the uniquely social nature of Japanese selfhood in the peculiarly group-centered nature of Japanese culture, Mead instead argues that
*all* selves are necessarily "social" insofar as they are intersubjectively constituted through communicative interaction with others in society, although
each self reflects the particular social group from which it emerges. In the
words of Mead: "Any self is a social self, but it is restricted to the group whose
roles it assumes" (PP 194). Hence, it is my purpose to show that while the
communicative-interaction model of the social self developed by G. H. Mead
in classical American pragmatism functions to illuminate the profoundly social
character of Japanese selfhood and the groupism of Japanese society, at the
same time it dispels the "myth of Japanese uniqueness" by establishing a
more universal framework which clarifies how *every* self in *every* culture is a
social self in that it arises by taking on the roles of other selves in the social
group to which it belongs.

# I
## The Social Self
### in
## Modern Japanese Philosophy

Although Japan has had a long intellectual history rooted especially in Buddhist and Confucian modes of thought, modern academic "philosophy" (J. *tetsugaku*) arose only through the influence of Westernization with the Meiji Restoration period (1868–1912). The preeminent academic Japanese philosopher in the twentieth century is Nishida Kitarō (1870–1945), whose speculative writings are the major source of inspiration for the Kyoto school (*Kyōto-ha*), which includes such thinkers as Tanabe Hajime, Nishitani Keiji, Hisamatsu Shin'ichi, Ueda Shizuteru, Takeuchi Yoshinori, and Abe Masao, and in a more peripheral sense, Watsuji Tetsurō, Kuki Shūzō, and D. T. Suzuki. It is far beyond the scope of this work to attempt an exhaustive analysis of modern Japanese philosophy. Rather, my aim is to to provide an overview of various models of the social self in recent Japanese thought as developed by major representative figures like Watsuji Tetsurō and Nishida Kitarō in modern Japanese philosophy and Doi Takeo in modern Japanese psychology. First I consider Watsuji Tetsurō's Zen/Confucian *ningen* model of twofold Japanese personhood as a mutual emptying of the individual and society in *kū* or emptiness, along with its subsequent development by such thinkers as Kimura Bin, Hamaguchi Eshun, and Kumon Shumpei. Next I develop Nishida Kitarō's Zen Buddhist model of the true self of absolute Nothingness as a twofold "social self" (*shakaiteki jiko*) arising through an I-Thou dialectic of intersubjectivity in the social-historical world. Finally, I examine the *amae* psychology of Doi Takeo, which describes the social character of Japanese selfhood as a nexus of dependency relations with a polar opposition between *honne/tatemae* or "personal reactions/social institutions." It is thus shown how modern Japanese thinkers have arrived at the concept of the person as a twofold social self arising through an individual-society interaction.

# ∿ 1 ∿

## Watsuji Tetsurō's *Ningen* Model of Japanese Selfhood

Together with Nishida Kitarō, Tanabe Hajime (1885–1962), and Nishitani Keiji (1900–1991), Watsuji Tetsurō (1889–1960) stands out as among the premier representative thinkers of modern Japanese philosophy. Watsuji's *zenshū* ("complete works") in twenty volumes, published by Iwanami Shoten in 1963, contains a great variety of topics reflecting the diversity and breadth of his scholarship. Beginning at the age of twenty-four, Watsuji published his *Nietzschean Studies* (1913). In the second chapter of this book Watsuji makes insightful comparisons between Nietzsche's concept of self as will to power in the innocence of becoming with both Henri Bergson's idea of self as the flow of *élan vital* or vital life-impulse in creative evolution and William James's idea of self as an ever-changing stream of consciousness with no underlying substantial identity. This interest in James undoubtedly traces back to the ubiquitous influence of Nishida's *A Study of Good* (*Zen no kenkyū*, 1911), the first Japanese philosophical treatise to develop James's process theory of self as a series of events of pure experience in the stream of consciousness. Watsuji's book on Nietzsche was followed by *Soren Kierkegaard* (1915), and *Revival of Idols* (*Gūzō saikō*, 1918). At this point in his academic career, Watsuji underwent a radical "turn" (*tenkō*) whereupon he began a serious investigation into Asian and Japanese culture, including a study of Confucian and Buddhist modes of thought. Hence, in 1919 Watsuji published *Pilgrimage to Ancient Shrines*, followed by *Ancient Japanese Culture* (1920), *The Significance of Primitive Christianity in the History of World Culture* (1926), *Practical Philosophy of Primitive Buddhism* (1927), *Climate: An Anthropological Consideration* (1934), *Confucius* (1936), *Critique of Homer* (1946), and *The Ethics of the the Man of the Greek Polis* (1948), *National Seclusion: Japan's Tragedy* (1950), and *A Study of Japanese Arts* (1955). Among Watsuji's explorations of Japanese Buddhism, of special importance is his pioneering study of Dōgen (1200–1250), founder of the Sōtō sect of Zen Buddhism in Japan. Originally published as a series in two philosophical journals between 1920 and 1923, it was later included in a volume of *Studies on the Japanese Spirit* (*Nihon seishinshi kenkyū*, 1934; see WTZ IV, 156–246). Watsuji's study *Dōgen, the Novice* (*Shamon Dōgen*), is regarded as the work responsible for rediscovering the significance of Dōgen as the foremost original systematic thinker in traditional Japanese Zen Buddhism. However, Watsuji is above all recognized for his achievement in the field of ethics. Watsuji's book on *Confucius* (1936) provided the groundwork for the Confucian aspects of his moral philosophy based on the social idea of selfhood as a center of human relationships, just as his ground-breaking studies on Dōgen (1920–23) established a firm basis for the Zen Buddhist dimensions of his ethics, particularly his recurrent motif of overcoming egoism and attaining selflessness in the absolute negativity of *kū*, emptiness. In 1952, Watsuji's two-volume *History of Japanese Ethical Thought* (*Nihon rinri shisō-shi*) was published. Throughout these two volumes, Watsuji analyzes the Confucian and Buddhist elements of Japanese communitarian ethics, including the group-centered ethic of loyalty and self-sacrifice underlying Bushidō, the Way of the Samurai warrior. On the Western side, Watsuji's study with Heidegger in Germany during 1927–28 established the methodological basis for his phenomenological, existential, and hermeneutical approach to ethics. Although Watsuji's moral philosophy is to be found in many of his earlier writings, those works representing the statement of his own original and distinctive system of ethics include *Ethics as a Study of the Person* (*Ningengaku to shite no rinrigaku*, 1934), and especially his three-volume text *Ethics* (*Rinrigaku*), published in successive volumes in 1937, 1942, and 1949. In what follows I will focus particularly on Watsuji's concept of ethics as anthropology or a study of the person based upon his syncretic Zen/Confucian idea of Japanese selfhood as ningen (*person*) along with its correlate ideas of *aidagara* (betweenness) and *fūdo* (climate).

## Early Influences on Watsuji's Ethics

As pointed out by Robert N. Bellah (1965, 586) and James T. Kodera (1987, 6), it was upon reading the classic work by his teacher Nitobe Inazō, *Bushidō—The Soul of Japan* (1905), which first inspired Watsuji to take up the study of traditional Japanese culture in general and Japanese ethics in particular. From this book Watsuji became interested in Bushidō, the Way of the Samurai warrior, as an ethical system based upon the duty of loyalty to the group and the moral ideal of self-sacrifice to a cause. Watsuji develops Bushidō as a basis of traditional Japanese ethics in such works as his lengthy study called *The History of Japan's Ethical Thought* (*Nihon rinri shisōshi*, 1952). As pointed out by M. C. Collcutt in his historical survey of Bushidō, in contrast to Ienaga Saburo's view that the lord-vassal relationship was economic and contractual, Watsuji Tetsurō argues that the core of the medieval lord-vassal relationship was a "total, unconditional self-renunciation on the part of the follower to his lord" (1983, 222). Watsuji locates the moral value in Bushidō, as in Confucianism and Buddhism, in what he calls "the absolute negativity of the subject" (*shutai no zettaiteki hiteisei*) in which the totality is realized. That is to say, the Samurai warrior achieves moral perfection through "self-negation" (*jiko hitei*). Watsuji's understanding of Bushidō as an ethical system is important for a general understanding of his own original system of ethics. In general, Watsuji sees the traditional Bushidō ethic of self-sacrifice as representing a way beyond the standpoint of individualism characterizing Western moral theories and of establishing a group-centered communitarian ethics at the basis of true moral existence as a social being.

Watsuji's communitarian ethics of the Japanese family system based on his concept of the person as *ningen* and *aidagara* (betweenness) principle of self-other relationships was also strongly influenced by the writings of another of his teachers, Natsume Sōseki (1867–1916), the foremost novelist of modern Japan. For as is so often the case, technical philosophical categories have as their deeper source of inspiration the themes, images, and metaphors of great works of creative fiction produced by the literary imagination. In this case, fundamental motifs of Watsuji's ethics can be directly traced to the novels, essays, poems, and letters of Natsume Sōseki, whose mature works of fiction struggle with the basic problem of overcoming egoism. As summarized by D. A. Dilworth (1974, 7–11) and T. J. Kodera (1987, 6–7), during his earlier period of philosophical reflection Watsuji had adopted a standpoint of "romantic individualism" as expressed in his books on Nietzsche (1913) and Kierkegaard (1915). However, in his work *Revival of Idols* (*Gūzō Saikō*, 1918), under the heading "A Turning Point" (*tenkō*), Watsuji announced a radical turn in his thinking away from romantic individualism and aestheticism toward a socioethical standpoint (WTZ XVII, 20–21). This "turn" (*tenkō*) was in large part influenced by his *sensei* at Tokyo Imperial University, Natsume Sōseki. Watsuji met his teacher Sōseki in 1913, just when the latter was himself in the process of turning from the aesthetic individualism of his earlier period to a standpoint which fully transcends egoism. Sōseki expressed this standpoint which transcends the isolated ego-self with a four-character phrase used in his Chinese poems, *sokuten kyoshi*, "follow heaven and depart from the self." When Sōseki died three years later in 1916, Watsuji wrote a memorial essay about the novelist entitled *Sōseki sensei no tsuioku*, included in *Revival of*

*Idols* (WTZ XVII, 85–89). In this document Watsuji analyzes Sōseki's decisive shift from Western "individualism" (*kojinshugi*) and "egocentrism" (*rikoshugi*), to his later standpoint of "self-negation" (*jiko hitei*), whereby the latter finally returned to a more traditional Japanese Way of *sokuten kyoshi*. Watsuji here descibes how the later fiction of his teacher Sōseki focuses on exposing the bankruptcy of the isolated ego-self in modern individualism. In this context Watsuji makes special reference to Sōseki's novel *The Wayfarer* (*Kōjin*, 1913) as the work of fiction marking the turn away from egocentric individualism toward that of *sokuten kyoshi*, "following heaven and departing from the self." The protaganist of this novel, a man named Ichiro, suffers the painful alien-ation and loneliness of the isolated ego-self to the extent that he is psycho-logically cut off from all of his closest friends and relatives, including his wife Onao and his brother Jiro. He experiences the hell of egocentrism and mod-ern individualism to the point where he finally exclaims in the despair of his existential aloneness: "there is no bridge between individuals" (*hito to hito to no aida o tsunagu hashi wa nai*). The only solutions to this alienated existence of the isolated individual are seemingly madness, suicide, or faith in God, all three of which are rejected by Sōseki as individualistic alternatives to the problem. One year later Sōseki delivered lectures in which he underscored the necessity of completely transcending egocentric individualism and be-coming a true person (*ningen*) by establishing the essential "betweenness" (*aidagara*) of individuals. For Sōseki, the problem of egocentric individualism could be ultimately resolved only by following the selfless way of *sokuten kyoshi*. Yet this notion of "following heaven and departing from the self" did not mean to seek one's salvation in an otherworldly realm of some transcen-dent or supersensory beyond, but in and through the social relationships of everyday life. The way of *sokuten kyoshi* thereby designates for Sōseki the way of becoming fully human through concrete interpersonal relationships with others in society. Hence, in these writings by Natsume Sōseki is to be found some of the key themes and technical terms central to Watsuji's own later system of ethics based on the *ningen* concept of personhood as *hito to hito to no aidagara*, the "betweenness of person and person."

## Watsuji's Ethics as a Study of the Person

The title of the first chapter of Watsuji's work on ethics, *Ningen gaku to shite no rinrigaku no igi*, can be translated as "The Significance of Ethics as Anthropology," or alternatively, "The Significance of Ethics as a Study of the Person." For Watsuji, ethics must be based upon a study of philosophical anthropology, which takes as its primary subject matter the problem of the person or human self. He writes: "Thus, I must also clarify the idea of 'person' (*ningen*), which I have used vaguely up to now. This is especially needed in order to distinguish it from the 'philosophical anthropology' which has become popular in recent times" (1937, 7). He then goes on enumerate various archetypes of personhood which have been developed in the European and especially German history of philosophical anthropology running through such figures as Nietzsche, Kierkegaard, Dilthey, Scheler, and Heidegger, arguing that each of these archetypes represents an individualistic notion of self which abstracts individuals from social groups and attempts to grasp man as something independent or self-existing. At one point in his *Ethics*, Watsuji argues that even Heidegger's notion of *Dasein* (Being-there) is ultimately an individualistic concept of man (1937, 14–15). His polemic here is that Heidegger overemphasizes the individuality of *Dasein* over the sociality of *Mitsein* (Being-with). In the Preface to his book *A Climate* (1961, v–vi), Watsuji makes a similar criticism, arguing that while Heidegger focuses upon an existential-phenomenological description of "temporality" in order to underscore the individuality of *Dasein* as the basis for authentic existence, he neglects the aspect of *spatiality* which is precisely the context of social inter-relationships from which authentic selfhood emerges. That is to say, although Heidegger describes authentic existence as being-in-time and being-toward-death, he fails to underscore the importance of social existence within a climate (*fūdo*) of lived space. Watsuji argues that it is this one-sided privileging of the temporal over the spatial and the individual over the social which prevents Heidegger from developing an adequate concept of selfhood as the basis for an ethical system descriptive of persons in relation. In contrast Watsuji maintains that the double structure of the person as *ningen* can be arrived at only through a description of concrete human existence both in time and space. Watsuji supports his relational view of concrete human existence with an etymological analysis of the Japanese notion of being or existence as *sonzai*, a *kanji* compound having two characters standing for "time" (*son*) and "space" (*zai*), respectively (1937, 20–22).

According to Watsuji, then, Western philosophy has failed to produce a satisfactory system of ethics because of its premise of "individualism" (*kojin-shugi*). He then points out that Western terms for man like *anthropos*, *homo*, *man*, *Mensch*, and even Heidegger's *Dasein*, all designate abstract individuals. However, in contrast to Heidegger's individualistic notion of man based on the temporal structure of Being (G. *Sein*), the Japanese term *ningen* discloses the true nature of man as a social being anchored in the spatial-temporal structure of existence (J. *sonzai*). Not unlike the Sapir-Whorf hypothesis expressing the direct correlation between linguistic and cultural patterns, Watsuji holds that the unique structure of the Japanese language reflects the unique social structure of Japanese thought and culture itself. Using the Heideggerian method of etymological analysis Watsuji shows how the Japanese term *ningen* or "person" is composed of two *kanji* characters which function to reveal the double structure of human existence as both an individual and a part of society: "The concept of *ningen* (person) is therefore different from *anthropos*, in that it is defined through its twofold character (*nijū seikaku*) as both 'society' (*seken; yo no naka*) and the 'individual' (*hito*)" (1937, 14–15). For this reason he maintains that ethics (*rinri*) must now become a study of *ningen* (person, man, human being), which in contrast to Western terms instead expresses the double or twofold (*nijū, futae*) structure of selfhood as including both the "individual" (*hito, kojin*) and "society" (*shakai, seken, yo no naka*). It is this dialectical concept of personhood as *ningen*, conceived as a twofold individual-society relation, which is the basis for what he calls true "communal existence" (*kyōdō sonzai*) (1937, 15). In this context he writes:

> [S]uch words like *anthropos, homo, man,* and *Mensch* signify [only] the individual man . . . However, if man is essentially a social animal, such notions as betweenness or society cannot be divorced from man. A man must be able to exist both as an individual and as a social being. The word which best expresses this twofold character (*nijū seikaku*) is the word *ningen.* (1937, 9)

In this passage Watsuji asserts that the Japanese word *ningen* expresses Aristotle's view of man as a "social animal" (*shakaiteki dōbutsu*). Moreover, he further endeavors to clarify the "dialectical" (*benshōhōteki*) structure of the person as *ningen* in that it signifies the "twofold" (*futae, nijū*) structure of human existence as both individual and social:

> The Japanese language possesses a deeply significant term, *ningen.* We created the concept of *ningen* or person on the basis of the meaning of this word. *Ningen* is both "society" (*yo no naka*) and the "individual" (*hito*) who exists within it. Thus, it is not merely the "individual" (*hito*) and it is not merely "society" (*shakai*). This is the dialectical unity of the twofold character of *ningen.* (1937, 12)

He goes on the explain this twofold character of *ningen* in terms of a dialectic of "self-other" (*jita*) relations, arguing that while both the self and the other are absolutely other, they are nevertheless one in communal existence (1937,

12). According to Watsuji, it is precisely this dialectical unity between the "self" (*ji*) and the "other" (*ta*) which constitutes the double character of *ningen* in its essential wholeness as an individual-society relationship.

Watsuji next argues that the Japanese concept of personhood as *ningen* establishes the theoretical basis for a new system of communitarian ethics. He points out that the Japanese word for ethics, *rinri*, is itself composed of the two characters, *rin* (= *nakama*) or "compassionate association," and *ri* (= *koto-wari*) or "pattern," together signifying the "the study of the pattern of human relationships" (1937, 4–5). He then asserts that "ethics" (*rinrigaku*) must now be grounded upon this dialectical structure of the "twofold character" (*nijū seikaku*) of a person as *ningen*. Thus, at the outset of "The Significance of Ethics as Anthropology" constituting the first chapter of his book entitled *Ethics* (*Rinrigaku*), Watsuji states:

> The primary meaning of the effort to define ethics as a study of the person (*ningen*) is that it escapes from the error of the modern world which understands ethics (*rinri*) as only a problem of individual consciousness (*kojinishiki no mondai*). This error is founded on the individualistic view of man in the modern world . . . However, although individualism (*kojinshugi*) takes the individual as the totality of man, it is only one part of human existence . . . the standpoint of the isolated ego-self as the standpoint of the isolated ego self as the starting point of modern philosophy is also an example of this (1937, 1).

It is in this context that Watsuji elaborates the internal structure of *ningen* in terms of the idea of *aidagara*, "betweenness," or as it were, *hito to hito to no aidagara*, the "betweenness of person and person." The term *ningen* or "person" is a compound having two characters, *nin* (= *hito*) indicating "individual," and *gen* (= *aida*) meaning "betweenness" or "relatedness." Consequently the term *ningen* or person designates a "relatedness between individuals," whereupon the human self now becomes defined as both an individual and a part of society. For Watsuji, ethics thus consists essentially in the *aidagara* relationship between self and family, self and society, as well as self and nature. On this basis Watsuji argues in opposition to Western individualist ethics which he holds to be a consequence of bourgeois egoism and articulates a communitarian ethical system based on the notion of the *aidagara* or betweenness of persons. Watsuji asserts:

> The locus of ethical problems is not in the consciousness of the isolated individual but in the *betweenness of person and person* (*hito to hito to no*

*aidagara*). Therefore ethics is a study of the person (*ningen no gaku*). Except as problems of the betweenness of person and person, concepts such as good and evil of actions, duty, responsibility, and virtue cannot truly be understood. (1937, 2–3)

## Watsuji's Zen/Confucian Model of Japanese Selfhood as Ningen

Watsuji's *ningen* model of selfhood and *aidagara* theory of ethics is itself constituted by notions derived from both Confucian and Buddhist modes of thought. For this reason I refer to Watsuji's *ningen* theory as a syncretic Zen/Confucian model of the person. Watsuji's deep level of engagement with Confucian social ethics is seen by the fact that he published a work on *Confucius* in 1936. To begin with, he frames his ethical system in terms of the five cardinal relationships of Confucianism. In his *Ethics* he states: "In ancient China, the relationships between father-son, lord-vassal, husband-wife, older brother-younger brother, and friend-friend, were known as 'the great relationships of man' (*hito no tairin*)" (1937, 4). Like Confucian ethics, Watsuji understands the self as a center of human relationships, each of which is governed by a normative principle of *li* (J. *rei*) or "ritual propriety." He thus speaks of the Confucian theory of "the five constant relationships and the five cardinal virtues (*gorin gojo*)" (1937, 4). He further calls Confucianism the "Way of *ningen*" or the "Way of the person" (*ningen no michi*) (1937, 5), understood as a "Way of behavioral relationships" (*gōitekikankei no shikata*) (1937, 4). Watsuji thus appropriates the Confucian view of the self as an ever-expanding web of social relationships which embodies increasingly larger social groups including the family, the community, the village, society, and the nation. For Watsuji, this Confucian "Way of *ningen*" is conceived as being oriented toward the realization of "communal existence" (*kyōdō sonzai*). As opposed to a liberal ethics based on the primacy of individual rights, Watsuji thus establishes a communitarian ethics based upon the primacy of obligations, duties, and commitments within the family structured social group to which one belongs.

However, as emphasized in different ways by Piovesana (1969, 142), Nagami Isamu (1981), and LaFleur (1978, 244), Watsuji ultimately grounds his *ningen* theory of personhood and communiatrian ethics of the Japanese family system in a Buddhist framework based on the concept of *kū*, "emptiness." LaFleur argues that Watsuji's theory of human relationships underscores a "mutuality of dependence" more characteristic of Buddhism than the hierarchical theory of Confucianism (1978, 244). He also emphasizes

Watsuji's use of the Sino-Japanese character *kū* (Ch. *k'ung*), which in East Asia was used to represent the Indian Buddhist notion of *śūnyatā* or emptiness, as a basic term in his system. He adds: "[T]he very reason why man is both individual and social is because, according to Watsuji, the individuated dimension of existence 'empties' the social dimension and, conversely, the social dimension 'empties' the individuated one" (1978, 244). Pointing out the proximity of Watsuji's theory of emptiness not only to traditional Oriental Buddhism but also the modern Zen philosophy of Nishida Kitarō, Piovesana likewise writes:

> This Oriental tendency is even more evident in the first volume of *Ringrigaku* [*Ethics*, 1937], where a new stress is laid upon the negative aspects of morality. Moral laws are originated through the absolute negation (*zettaiteki hiteisei*) of the subject. The individual only through the negation of the self can join the whole of the nation. This absolute negation ends in the *kū* (the emptiness of self), in order to reach the "absolute totality," not dissimilar in purpose to Nishida's nothingness. (1968, 142)

This primacy accorded to Zen Buddhist *kū* or "emptiness" in Watsuji's *ningen* theory of personhood and communitarian system of ethics is clearly found through a textual analysis of Watsuji's own writings. To begin with, Watsuji's deep scholarly interest in various aspects of Buddhist philosophy are shown through his works like *Practical Philosophy of Primitive Buddhism* (*Genshi Bukkyō no jissen tetsugaku*), *Dōgen, The Novice* (*Shamon Dōgen*), and *Buddhism and the Japanese Literary Arts* (*Nihon no bungei to Bukkyō shisō*). Furthermore, in his major text on moral philosophy entitled *Ethics* (*Rinrigaku*, 1937), Watsuji uses a Zen Buddhist dialectic of mutual emptying in which both individual and group are negated in the absolute whole of emptiness or absolute negativity. Watsuji explicates the double structure of *ningen* as constituted by a dialectical process involving a double negation whereby the individual arises only as a negation of totality when the whole is emptied into the ego-self, just as the totality of man is established by the negation of individuality when the ego-self is emptied into the totality. He states:

> This twofold negation establishes the dual structure of man as *ningen* . . . Negation (*hitei*) develops into negation of negation (*hitei no hitei*). This is the movement of negation. Since human existence is fundamentally this movement of negation the origin of human existence can be nothing

other than that of *negation,* that is to say, *absolute negativity* (*zettaiteki hiteisei*). The individual (*kojin*) and the whole (*zentai*) are both in their true nature "empty" (*kū*), and this emptiness is itself the absolute totality (*zettaiteki zentaisei*). (1937, 26–27)

For Watsuji, the double negation or "negation of negation" (*hitei no hitei*) whereby the whole empties into the individual and the individual empties into the whole constitutes the twofold nature of "absolute negativity" (*zettaiteki hiteisei*). He finally calls this absolute negativity of Buddhist *kū* or emptiness the "absolute totality" (*zettaiteki zentaisei*). In such a manner, then, Watsuji's *ningen* theory of selfhood as an individual-society interaction is developed in terms of the Confucian Way of relationships, which is in turn finally rooted in an underlying Zen Buddhist framework whereby the person arises through the mutual emptying of the individual and society in the absolute negativity of *kū*, emptiness.

## The Person as Ningen and the Religio-Aesthetic Principle of Ma

Above it was shown how for Watsuji the Japanese word *ningen* reveals the double structure of human selfhood as both individual and social in nature. While the first of the two Sino-Japanese characters forming the word *ningen* signifies the individual, the second designates the relational, contextual, and social aspect of human existence. Watsuji further analyzes this double structure of the person as *ningen* through his category of *aidagara,* betweenness. The person as *ningen* is now conceived to exist in the *aidagara* or "betweenness" of its relationships to an embodied spatial "climate" (*fūdo*) of society and nature. For Watsuji, the double structure of the person as *ningen* understood in terms of the betweenness of persons is itself the basis upon which to construct an adequate theory of ethics. Yet for Watsuji not only ethics but all the value dimensions of human existence as *ningen* including art, morality, and religion, are to be analyzed as a function of *aidagara,* betweenness.

It should be pointed out that the second of the Sino-Japanese characters forming the word *ningen* or person is itself one of the key terms in the religio-aesthetic tradition of Japanese *geidō*—the "*tao* (or Way) of art." The character for *gen* (= *kan, aida, ma*), which as a religio-aesthetic ideal in the Japanese canons of taste is pronounced *ma,* denotes the idea of "negative space," the dimension of "betweenness." *Ma* refers to the opening, gap, blank, rupture, pause, hiatus, or void wherein comes to manifestation the empty space *between* all persons and events. As a religio-aesthetic ideal, *ma* therefore designates the space and or/time "in between." The principle of *ma* is concretely embodied in a wide variety of Zen-influenced arts and crafts in traditional Japanese Geidō, the Way of the artist, including the martial arts of Bushidō, the Way of the Samurai warrior. Richard Pilgrim (1986, 50) specifically relates the religio-aesthetic principle of *ma* in Zen Buddhist literature and art to Watsuji Tetsurō's *ningen* concept of personhood. He describes how the religio-aesthetic principle of *ma* is a cultural paradigm manifested in a wide range of Japanese artistic and literary forms developed under the aegis of Zen, including Noh drama, *haiku* poetry, *sumie* inkwash painting, calligraphy, landscape gardening, architecture, interior decorating, flower arrangement, the tea ceremony, and modern Japanese cinema, all of which function to create a plenary void expressing the fullness and openness of Zen emptiness or nothingness through a strategic display of the "space between." In all of these Zen-influenced artistic and literary forms, the beauty of *ma* or "betweenness" is manifested through the open continuum of empty blank space which stands *śūnyatā*-like in the middle way between the realms of being and nothingness, form and emptiness, or substantiality and nonsubstantiality. For instance, in traditional Zen *sumie* inkwash painting, *ma* is the *yohaku* or surplus void of enveloping pictorial space which always surrounds the objects presented in the foreground focus of attention. The plenary voids of *ma* are also found in the swirling patterns of blank white sand which encircle the stones of the famous rock garden at Ryōanji, thereby disclosing the inseparability of form and emptiness in the spatial locus of Nothingness. The *ma* principle of beauty is further seen in *chanoyu* or the tea ceremony, particularly in the empty blank spaces of the tea hut, thereby reflecting the artistic preference for simplicity, understatement, and austere rustic poverty expressed by such traditional Japanese aesthetic notions as *wabi, sabi,* and *shibui.*

In Noh drama, *ma* is displayed through silent moments of non-action (*senu-hima*) which gives the actor his charismatic stage presence. In Noh drama, as in *waka* poetry and other medieval Japanese arts, the aesthetic preference for *ma* or "negative space" is further communicated by evoking the beauty of *yūgen* or "profound mystery," whereby dark empty spaces are used to suggest the unfathomable depths of things as they fade into the surrounding background of openness or nothingness. Similarly, the modern cinematic expression of *ma* can be found in the characteristic silences and voids of an Ozu film. The religio-aesthetic principle of *ma* or "betweenness" is also a fundamental principle in the traditional Japanese martial arts of Bushidō, the Way of the Samurai warrior. Sadaharu Oh (1984), the greatest homerun hitter in the history of Japanese baseball, provides a fascinating account of his discovery of *ma* through a study of Aikidō with the legendary martial artist Ueshiba Morihei. In his autobiography Sadaharu Oh describes how he came to learn that a well-known *kabuki* actor had tried to incorporate Aikidō into his own discipline, adding that what he had sought from Aikidō was specifically the idea of *ma*, the space and / or time "in between." According to Sadaharu Oh, whereas in Aikidō the martial artist must abide in the *ma* or space between the martial artist and his or her opponent, in baseball one exists in the *ma* of the moment which arises between the pitcher and the batter. In this way the Zen Buddhist religio-aesthetic principle of *ma* representing the lived space and / or time "in-between" all events unfolds the profoundly artistic and spiritual dimension of human existence as *ningen* defined in terms of the *aida* or "betweenness" of persons.

There is a systematic character underlying Watsuji's thought in that his aesthetics and ethics are both developed in relation to his idea of personhood as *ningen*, which in turn is formulated in the context of a Zen Buddhist notion of *kū* or "emptiness" as interrelational existence. LaFleur (1978) points out how in essays like "Buddhism and the Japanese Literary Arts" (*Nihon no bungei to Bukkyō shisō*) Watsuji examines various Zen-influenced styles of art and literature, especially the tea ceremony (*chanoyu*) and linked verse (*renga*), because of the special way in which they express the *aida* or "betweenness" of the individual and society. Niether the tea ceremony nor linked verse are produced by individuals acting alone, but are instead paradigm examples of a social art form produced by several persons interacting together in a group. In other words, the aesthetic experience cultivated through the tea ceremony or linked verse is to be located not in the private minds of subjects or in the qualities of objects but in the experience of *aida* or "betweenness," including the betweenness of individuals and society as well as the betweenness of individuals and the encompassing spatial "climate" (*fūdo*) of nature. In his essay "Japanese Literary Arts and Buddhist Philosophy" (1971, 88–115), Watsuji asserts that Japanese literature and art influenced by Zen Buddhism is always characterized by a "moment of negation." In Watsuji's own words: "As arts under [Zen's] influence we can cite the Noh drama, gardening, tea ceremony, *sumie* painting, and so forth. Every one of these arts has a common point that the moment of negation lies at its core" (1971, 111). LaFleur (1978, 247) emphasizes that this "moment of negation" at the core of all Zen-influenced arts is not just the "negative expression" of prolonged silences and empty blank spaces, but a deeper ontological negation concerned with the Zen Buddhist notion of "emptiness" (*kū*) as *engi*, relatedness or dependent coorigination. Understood as the emptiness of dependent coorigination, the moment of negation at the core of Zen Buddhist aesthetics is therefore ultimately to be seen as expressing the *underlying relatedness* between all persons and events (1978, 248). In the philosophy of Watsuji, the empty center, sacred nothing, or moment of negation at the core of aesthetic experience reflects the *ningen* model of personhood as the relatedness or betweenness of self and others, which in turn rests upon the Zen Buddhist theory of emptiness as an existence which comprises both the individual and society through mutual negation. For Watsuji, then, the dialogical principle of *aida* (= *ma*) or "betweenness" constituting the twofold structure of man as *ningen* implies not only a moral, but also a profoundly religio-aesthetic mode of human existence.

The aesthetic value dimension underlying Watsuji's ethical concept of Japanese selfhood as a "betweenness" (*aidagara*) of persons in society can be further clarified through Dorinne Kondo's work *Crafting Selves* (1990). Kondo describes her anthropological field research at the Ethics Center (*Rinri Gakuen*) in Tokyo, which has developed a moral training program aimed at constructing ideal social selves. In this context she employs the traditional Japanese artisanal metaphor of "crafting" the self through interpersonal relations with others in the family, company, workplace, and other locations for the social construction of selfhood. Although Kondo does not make reference to the modern Japanese philosophy of Watsuji Tetsurō nor to the Confucian and Zen aspects of the Japanese self, her work nonetheless functions to illuminate several important elements of Watsuji's *ningen* theory of personhood. To begin with, her description of the Rinri Gakuen or Ethics Center in Tokyo clearly brings to light Watsuji's concept of ethics (*rinrigaku*) as a moral socialization process of achieving personhood as an ideal social self through forging relations with others in a community. Through this moral training program at the Ethics Center students learn to deconstruct their separate ego selves and to reconstruct new contextual selves which are *relationally defined* as social, decentered, multiple, fluid, open, shifting, and ever-changing. Just as Watsuji's *ningen* concept of personhood has a twofold structure as an individual-social interaction, Kondo describes how the Japanese relational self is located on a "sliding scale" of self and other (1990, 26). In her account of Japanese selfhood she then describes how the boundaries of self and other are fluid and constantly changing, depending on context, so that personhood is now relationally defined in terms of two *end points* of an open-ended continuum located between the "individual/social" or "private/public" sides of the self, which in Japanese is articulated by means of such distinctions as *honne/tatemae, uchi/soto,* and *ura/omote* (1990, 31). She further articulates this Japanese artisanal notion of *crafting selves* as a process of "creative self-realization through work," "aesthetic self-realization through work," and "polishing of the self through hardship." It has been seen how Watsuji's Zen/ Confucian *ningen* model of the twofold Japanese self represents not only a moral but also an aesthetic mode of human existence as an interpersonal "betweenness" (*aida, ma*) of self-other relationships. Kondo's artisanal model of Japanese selfhood can thus clarify the aesthetic dimensions of Watsuji's self-realization ethics as an artistic and creative process of *crafting* oneself into a person as an ideal social self by forging relations with others in the community.

## The Japanese Familial Self and the Ie (Household) System

Throughout his various writings Watsuji develops his idea of personhood as *ningen* and its underlying *aidagara* theory of self-other relationships in terms of the *ie* (family, household) system as the basis of traditional Japanese self and society. The fundamental idea here is that the Japanese self as *ningen* is not simply an "individual" (*kojin*) but always exists in relation to a social group having the internal structure and dynamics of an *ie* or family unit. In traditional Japanese household society the social context of one's family unit always takes priority over the individual, as seen by the fact that, as opposed to most Western societies, the larger whole precedes the part so that the family name comes first and the given name comes last.

The traditional Japanese *ie* or household institution, also referred to as the *kazoku-seido* or family system, originally designated the bloodline kinship unit which included the sacred ancestral lineage that provided continuity between the realm of the living and the realm of the dead. Yet in modern Japan the *ie* institution has been extended beyond its meaning of a kinship unit, to that of any social group which has been vertically organized in terms of *oyabun-kobun* or "parent-child" relations. In other words, the *ie* or family household became the model upon which all other social groups became patterned in modern Japanese society. As R. P. Dore notes in his study of the Japanese family system: "In Japan the habit of modelling the structure of social groups outside the family—occupational, educational, recreational, political, artistic, criminal—on the pattern of the family has been developed with a consistency rare in other societies" (1958, 94). Positions in these various social groups modelled on the pattern of an *ie* or household are formed by analogy with terms for positions in the family such as *oyabun* (parental part), *anikibun* (elder brother part), *iemoto* (family chief), and so forth. In modern Japanese society the paradigm case of a social organization patterned after the family structure having vertical parent-child relations is the *kaisha* or "company," with all of its employees as members of the household and the employer at its paternal head. When speaking to outsiders (*tanin*), members call their own work organization *uchi*, a colloquial term used for *ie* or family household. The tendency in Japan to model social groups on the family pattern such as corporate structures, management bodies, religious sects, or even criminal enterprizes like the *yakuza* crime families, is also discovered at the national level, as is expressed through the term *kokka* (state, country, nation), a two-*kanji* character compound literally meaning "nation-family," formed by the combination of *koku* (state, country, nation) plus *ka* (also pronounced *ie*, meaning home, house, family). Just as the father is the head of the family household, so the Emperor is the paternal head of the *kokka* or nation-family. At the sociopolitical level, the notion of *ie* or "family" is related to the Imperial Household, so that the cardinal virtue of filial piety (*koko*) to the father now becomes identified with the duty of loyalty (*chujitsu*) to the Emperor. The traditional *ie* institution therefore still continues in collective group-consciousness as the basis of contemporary Japanese social structure.

In her work *Japanese Society* (1970) anthropologist Nakane Chie provides a detailed account of the *ie* or family household as the pervasive structural element in Japanese groupism. Although Nakane's *Japanese Society* does not explicitly thematize the self, it has nonetheless become a classic source for the interpretation of Japanese selfhood as rooted in familial groups having the vertical parent-child structure of a household. Nakane writes: "The essence of this firmly rooted, latent group consciousness in Japanese society is expressed in the traditional and ubiquitous concept of *ie*, the household, a concept which penetrated every nook and cranny of Japanese society" (1970, 4). Nakane then goes on to argue that the household group organization of Japanese society reveals a "vertical" or "hierarchical" (*tate*) structural principle based on a complex system of ranking, the core of which is to be found in the basic social relationship between two individuals of upper and lower status. She adds: "This important relationship is expressed in the traditional terms *oyabun* and *kobun*. *Oyabun* means the person with the status of *oya* (parent) and *kobun* means with the status of *ko* (child)" (1970, 42). In other words, the interpersonal matrix of Japanese groupism is understood as constituting a "vertical society" (*tate shakai*) wherein various household groups in the *ie* family system are organized into a hierarchy of "parent-child" (*oyabun-kobun*) relationships. As will be discussed later, psychiatrist Doi Takeo (1972) goes on to argue that this vertical structure of parent-child relationships in the household system underlying the Japanese self and society is itself to be explained in terms of his psychological principle of *amae* (indulgent dependency), the infantile need to depend on others.

Watsuji Tetsurō's *ningen* concept of personhood is also to be understood as providing an account of the Japanese familial self in the collective group-consciousness of Japanese household society. That is to say, for Watsuji the person as *ningen* is always social by virtue of the fact that it is constituted by its relationships to others in a group having the structure of an *ie* or "household" unit. Watsuji develops his view of the family household system in terms of his key concepts of *ningen*, *aidagara*, and *fūdo* in his work entitled *A Climate* (*Fūdo*, 1961). In this work he describes how in modern European capitalism the person is seen as an individual and the family is only a gathering of atomic individuals to serve economic interests (1961, 139). By contrast, in Japanese culture, "Man is essentially social, or relational" (1961, 138). He therefore asserts that the family household in Japan represents a "structure of human relations" (1961, 145). Watsuji summarizes his view of the *ie* or family household institution as the basis for the Japanese self and traditional Japanese group-centered society as follows.

> Hence, the Japanese way of life regarded as that of a household is none other than the realization, through the family, of the distinctive relationship of Japan—the fusion of a calm passion and a martial selflessness . . . So the concept of "house" in Japan takes on the unique and important significance of, if you like, the community of all communities. This is the real essence of the Japanese way of life and the Japanese family system. (1961, 144)

Watsuji explains how the contrasts between Western individualism versus the groupism of the Japanese family system are reflected even by the differences in architectural design and use of space in the household structure. He writes: "A house in Europe is partitioned off into individual and independent rooms which are separated by thick walls and stout doors . . . The distinction between 'inside' and 'outside' as understood first and foremost as one of the heart of the individual is reflected in house construction" (1961, 146). Similarly, the intersubjective "betweenness" (*aidagara*) of contextual persons expressed by the social and familial concept of man as *ningen* is reflected in the architectural design of the Japanese home which provides a continuity between not only the self and others but also a continuity between the self and nature. In particular, the "betweenness" of persons can be seen in the open construction of the traditional Japanese house wherein unlocked sliding doors and paper screens divide without separating the various rooms into private compartments:

> [T]he house regarded as a structure of human relations is reflected in the layout of a house regarded simply as a building. Above all, the house exhibits an internal fusion that admits of no discrimination. None of the rooms are set off from each other by lock and key with a will to separation; in other words, there is no distinction between individual rooms. Even if there is a partitioning by *shoji* (sliding doors) or *fusuma* (screens), this is a division within a unity of mutual trust, and is not a sign of a desire for separation (1961, 145).

For Watsuji, then, the social, familial, and relational concept of Japanese selfhood as *ningen* is disclosed not only in the *ie* "household" institution as a mode of collective group-consciousness but even in the open-ended architectural design of the traditional Japanese house as a building, which is in turn contrasted to the idea of man as a private atomic individual with separate existence reflected in the compartmentalized structure of a traditional European home.

## Ideological Critiques of Watsuji's Social Philosophy

In his *Ethics* (1937) Watsuji uses a Zen Buddhist dialectic of "mutual emptying" in which both individual and group are negated in the absolute whole of *kū*, "emptiness." Watsuji (1937, 26) explicates the dual structure of *ningen* as constituted by a Zen dialectical process involving a double negation, or negation of negation, whereby the individual arises only as a negation of totality when the whole is "emptied" into the ego-self, whereupon the wholeness of man is then established by a negation of individuality when the ego-self is "emptied" into the totality. To repeat Watsuji's own words: "This two-fold negation establishes the dual structure of the person as *ningen* . . . The individual (*kojin*) and the whole (*zentai*) are both in their true nature empty (*kū*), and this emptiness is itself the absolute totality (*zettaiteki zentaisei*)" (1937, 26–27). For Watsuji the double negation or "negation of negation" (*hitei no hitei*) whereby the whole empties into the individual and the individual empties into the whole constitutes the twofold nature of "absolute negativity" (*zettaiteki hiteisei*). He finally calls this absolute negativity of Buddhist *kū* or emptiness the "absolute totality" (*zettaiteki zentaisei*), which in his political philosophy comes to represent nothing other than the deified Japanese state of the *kokutai* or National Polity, governed through the heavenly mandate of imperial rescript by the Divine Emperor and Imperial Household tracing its solar ancestry back to Amaterasu, the Sun Goddess enshrined at Ise.

Hence, at the level of political discourse, the danger of Watsuji's *aidagara* theory of communitarian ethics and *ningen* model of personhood based on a Zen logic of double negation between the individual and society is that it is all too easily applied in the direction of an ultranationalistic ideology which has been called by scholars a "totalitarian state ethics," "emperor system fascism," and a "fascist ideology." As T. James Kodera (1987) asserts in his study of Watsuji Tetsurō:

> [A]llegations of Watsuji's support for nationalism and the emperor system during the turbulent war years put Watsuji, after the war, in a position of decided disfavor in the popular mind. Watsuji's treatises on what he considered the distinct characteristics of Japanese history, culture, and ethical mores (in contradistinction to his writing on America) struck intellectuals and the populace alike as indicative of the "dangerous ideology" from which they sought to exorcise themselves and their nation. . . . At the same time, Watsuji's other works have been held suspect. (1987, 5)

Piovesana (1968) describes the dialectic of mutual emptying between the individual and society into an absolute negativity symbolizing the *kokutai* or National Polity of the Imperial Household as follows: "The individual only through the negation of the self can join the whole of the nation. This absolute negation ends in the *kū* (the emptiness of the self), in order to reach the 'absolute totality', not dissimilar in purpose to Nishida's nothingness" (1968, 142). He goes on to state that for Watsuji the social world is conceived as a dialectical development of self-denying units toward the great void which is social totality (1968, 143). Piovesana concludes that when we honestly confront the political implications of Watsuji's social relationism, it amounts to a "totalitarian state ethics" (1968, 143), adding that this aspect of his thought was to some extent corrected in the revised edition of postwar times.

In his critical analysis of the social-political dimensions of Watsuji's thought, Robert N. Bellah (1965) draws upon the ideological critiques directed against Watsuji as well as Nishida Kitarō and the "right-wing" (*uyoku*) of the Kyoto school, to which Watsuji was himself peripherally related, as formulated by Japanese thinkers like Maruyama Masao, Ienaga Saburo, Arima Tatsuo, and the Marxist philosopher Tosaka Jun. Bellah carefully examines not only Watsuji's *Ethics* (*Rinrigaku*, 1937) but also two notorious essays titled

"The Way of the Subject in Japan" (*Nihon no shindō*), and "America's National Character" (*America no kokuminsei*), both released together in a wartime pamphlet dated July 1944. These works argued for the complete superiority of traditional Japanese culture based on the ideal of "self-negation" (*jiko hitei*) and resolve to sacrifice oneself for the imperial sovereign over that of liberal democratic American society based on individualism, egocentrism, and utilitarianism (Bellah: 1965, 578–79). For Watsuji the moral basis of the Japanese spirit is to be found in an application of the Bushidō ideal of "the absolute negativity of the subject" (*shutai no zettaiteki hiteisei*) in which the concrete whole of the Japanese nation is realized. Bellah asserts that behind the cloak of Watsuji's thinking is concealed a pathological ideology of "emperor-system fascism" (1965, 593–94) which brought Japan to near total disaster in the twentieth century. Peter Dale (1986) echoes the view of Piovesana, asserting: "Little wonder that even sympathetic readings concede that in this form Watsuji's *aidagara* theory amounts to little more than a 'totalitarian state ethics'" (1986, 218). For Dale, Watsuji's *aidagara* theory reinforces the social relationism of Japanese group-consciousness which results in the fusion of subject-object and a complete submergence of the individual into society. According to Dale, the end result is that "Watsuji moves to a position which denies autonomy to private, individual consciousness itself" (1986, 217). In his relentless one-sided critique leveled against modern Japanese philosophy, Dale argues that although camouflaged under the subterfuge of various aesthetic, moral, and spiritual ideals, Watsuji's *ningen* concept of Japanese personhood and *aidagara* theory of social relationism ultimately represent a totalitarian state ethics and fascist ideology linked to Japanese right-wing militarism, ultranationalism, authoritarianism, ethnic chauvinism, and cultural narcissism.

Indeed, probing ideological critiques of Watsuji's sociopolitical philosophy developed by such writers as Maruyama Masao, Ienaga Saburo, Arima Tatsuo, Tosaka Jun, and others in Japan along with those of Robert Bellah, Gino Piovesana, Peter Dale, and others in the West, have made it abundantly clear that the form of communitarianism set forth by Watsuji and his followers, despite its profound moral and religio-aesthetic dimensions, nonetheless falls into an impossible totalitarianism which ultimately fails to preserve the integrity of the individual in relation to the state. In particular, such ideological critiques have clarified how Watsuji's communitarian ethics of the Japanese family household institution falls into a general pattern of totalitarianism based on a deification of the state and a correlate ethical ideal of complete self-sacrifice of loyal subjects to the imperial household as a unifying symbol of the Japanese *kokutai* or national polity. It has been seen how the above have characterized Watsuji's thought as a form of "totalitarian state ethics," "emperor-system fascism," and "fascist ideology." An examination of Watsuji's texts such as "Emperor Ideology and Its Heritage" (Sonnō shisō to sono dentō, 1943), "The Way of the Subject in Japan" (Nihon no shindō, 1944), and "America's National Heritage" (America no kokuminsei, 1944) support these ideological critiques leveled against Watsuji's thought. However, this should not lead to extreme reactions whereby antagonists reject Watsuji's system in toto and apologists deny or evade the problem altogether. As stated by Kodera (1987, 4–5), although we must subject the thought of Watsuji and other post-Meiji Japanese intellectuals to critical scrutiny as part of a broader critique of the Japanese wartime era, such an approach does not justify a categorical denunciation of his works as a whole.

## Recent Developments of Watsuji's Ningen Model of Personhood

Here I will examine Watsuji's ningen model of personhood as further developed by three recent Japanese thinkers: Kimura Bin, Hamaguchi Eshun, and Kumon Shumpei. All three are highly syncretic in that they combine Watsuji's ideas with various other Japanese writers in the areas of philosophy, religion, psychology, and the social sciences. Moreover, all three may be regarded as scholars of nihonjinron or "studies of Japanese self-identity," in that they attempt to describe the unique essence of Japaneseness, which they invariably find in the social, relational, and contextual nature of the Japanese self and the groupism of Japanese household society. Hence, each in their own way expands upon Watsuji's fundamental insights into the context-dependent structure of Japanese selfhood based on his concept of the person as ningen with its dialogical principle of "betweenness" (aidagara) and ontological theory of spatial "climates" (fūdo).

## Kimura Bin

In his work entitled Betweenness of Person and Person (Hito to hito to no aida, 1972), psychiatrist Kimura Bin has further elaborated upon Watsuji's basic principle of aida or "betweenness" in order to explicate the social character of Japanese selfhood and the groupism of Japanese society. At the outset of the first chapter Kimura clarifies the nature of group identity constituting the Japanese sense of selfhood, pointing out how Japanese people often refer to themselves as "we Japanese" (*ware ware nihonjin*). Kimura attempts to show that the phrase "we Japanese" stands for the Japanese group identity which is not on a personal level as in Western culture, but on a distinctively transpersonal level. Hence, like other writers in the tradition of *nihonjinron* studies, Kimura emphasizes the nature of Japanese self-identity as defined in terms of a collective group-centered "we" consciousness.

Kimura Bin's concept of Japanese personhood represents a synthesis of Watsuji Tetsurō's basic concepts of person (*ningen*), climate (*fūdo*) and be-tweenness (*aidagara*) with Doi Takeo's *amae* psychology, Nishida Kitarō's philosophy of "pure experience" (*junsui keiken*), and Dōgen's Zen Buddhist notion of self-realization through self-negation. Following Watsuji, Kimura emphasizes the social nature of the person as *ningen* in terms of the dialogi-cal principle of *aida*, "betweenness." The title and key notion of Kimura's book is of course derived from Watsuji's doctrinal formula, *hito to hito to no aida*, the "betweenness of man and man," or the "betweenness of person and person." In chapter 3, entitled "Climate and Personality," Kimura ex-presses special admiration for Watsuji's theory of climates (*fūdo*) as the social space for self-other relationships. He points out how according to Watsuji's climate theory of social space the person as *ningen* exists not only in the *aida* or "betweenness" of self and society, but also in the "betweenness" of self and nature. Hence, as will be discussed later, in his essay "The Japanese Concept of Nature" (1969), as well as in chapter 18 titled "Self and Nature" (*Mizukara to Onozukara*) from *Betweenness* (*Aida*, 1988), Kimura reformulates Watsuji's *ningen* concept of personhood as existing within a "climate" in terms of the traditional Japanese concept of personhood as a unity of *mizukara/ onozukara* or "self/nature," wherein the "self" (*mizukara*) and "nature" (*onozukara*) are the subjective and objective aspects of single field of reality.

Kimura, who is himself a distinguished psychiatrist in Japan, combines Watsuji's *ningen* theory of personhood with Doi's *amae* psychology. Although he is critical of certain aspects of Doi's theory, at the same he agrees that the notion of *amae* or "dependency drive" provides a psychological basis for ex-plaining the social character of Watsuji's *ningen* concept of Japanese selfhood as a "betweenness" of persons. Kimura thus writes: "The discovery of *amae* is a great contribution within the history of Japanese psychiatry" (1972, 147). Kimura (1972, 148) cites Doi's basic definition of *amae* as passive, dependency love, or the wish to be accepted and loved by others. Doi's formulation of *amae* as an intrapsychic "drive," "instinct," or "wish" is then summarized by Kimura through the following characteristics: (1) to wish to combine subjec-tivity and objectivity; (2) to wish to to feel inseparable with the other; (3) To wish to depend on somebody; (4) to wish to love somebody by being loved;

(5) to psychologically reject the separation between mother and child. For Kimura, then, Watsuji's *ningen* concept of Japanese personhood as the *aida* or "betweenness" of persons is itself to be comprehended as a psychological function of Doi's *amae* principle representing the infantile wish to fuse subject and object or the need to depend on others in a group.

Kimura goes on to integrate Watsuji's *ningen* theory of self as a "betweenness" (*aida*) of persons in an spatial "climate" (*fūdo*) of nature and Doi's *amae* theory of self as a nexus of dependency relations with Nishida Kitarō's early concept of self as a "pure experience" (*junsui keiken*). He strongly affirms Nishida's idea of "pure experience" (*junsui keiken*) as a unity of subject and object, stating that " 'pure experience' is a primary fact" (1972, 85). Like Doi, Kimura regards Nishida's idea of self as pure experience to be a function of *amae* as a "wish to fuse subject and object." Furthermore, he agrees with Nishida's ethics of self-realization whereby the achievement of the person is itself the greatest good. In this context he cites the words of Nishida from *A Study of Good* (1911): "In a word, goodness is the realization of one's personality" (Kimura: 1972, 55). Elsewhere in the text he goes on to synthesize the views of both Watsuji and Nishida on the self:

> Human beings find themselves through the climate and nature, no matter where and when they are . . . A person's view depends on how they find the self in the climate and nature. Nishida Kitarō says, "As the world realizes, the self realizes. As the self realizes, the world realizes. How we realize the self and how we realize the world means the same thing." (1972, 88)

Kimura's development of the Japanese *ningen* concept of personhood clearly represents an effort to integrate Watsuji's dialogical notion of *aida* or "betweenness" with Nishida's idea of *basho* or "locus" (*topos*, place, or field), thereby to underscore the character of "betweenness" as an ontological category. He writes:

> The "betweenness of person and person" (*hito to hito to no aida*) and "betweenness" (*aida*) do not signify merely a relationship between two individuals. The "betweenness of person and person" is the "locus" (*basho*) functioning as the source from out of which both I and others arise. (1972, 65)

Kimura further defines the concept of *aida*, "betweenness," or *hito to hito to no aida*, "the betweenness of person and person," through a dialectic of self and others. According to Kimura (1972, 14–18), the *aida* or "betweenness" of persons as a transpersonal *basho* or spatial "locus" is to be characterized as follows: (1) It is a locus which makes "self" and "non-self" exist at the same time; (2) It does not have any form; (3) It is the place of enables individuals to exists; (4) It is everywhere like energy and power; (5) It is similar to the *elan vital* or vital life-force in Henri Bergson's theory. Kimura's reworking of the Japanese *ningen* concept of personhood thus combines Watsuji's *aida* theory of self-other relations with Nishida's theory of selfhood as a dialectic of self and non-self. Kimura writes:

> To realize oneself as an individual, in other words, for a "self" to realize itself as a "self," it must be at the same time the "self" encounters something which is not the "self" itself. If a "self" could not find anything but "self" in this world, it could not find the "self." In short, a "self" should be always "self" against "non-self." But the "non-self" can be "non-self" only insofar as it is distinguished from the "self." Before the "self" becomes "self," the "non-self" could not be a "non-self." So the "self" and the "non-self" come into existence at the same time. Nishida Kitarō's famous words, "As the world realizes, our 'self' realizes; as 'self' realizes, the world realizes" refers to precisely this point. (1972, 14)

Hence, there are three fundamental points implicit in Kimura's idea of Japanese selfhood. (1) A "self" (*jiko*) needs a "non-self" (*jiko de nai mono*/*jikonarazu mono*) to realize the "self." (2) The "non-self" needs the "self" to be the "non-self." (3) The "self" and the "non-self" come into existence at the same time. He sums up his notion of personhood as a dialectic of self and non-self as follows:

> The simultaneity of the "self" and the "non-self" means that there should be something which makes these two emerge. The "self" does not make the "non-self" come into existence. At the same time the "self" encounters the the "non-self," the "self" and the "non-self" come into existence out of "something" like emitted sparks. Instantly the "non-self" is distinguished from the "self" . . . Then an individual comes into existence as his/her personality. An individual comes into existence out of the "something" when the "self" encounters the "non-self." The "some-thing" exists before existence of "self" and "non-self." (1972,14–15)

As Kimura goes on to clarify this "something" (*nanimono ka*) from which "self" and "non-self" emerge is precisely the "transpersonal" (*chōkojinteki na*) locus of reality which he terms, following Watsuji, *hito to hito to no aida*, the "betweenness of person and person" (1972, 15). Kimura regards *aida* or "betweenness" to be the transpersonal source from which the person as a dialectic of self and non-self emerges. He therefore states that for the Japanese, the existence of the transpersonal *basho* or "locus" of *hito to hito to no aida* is an ontological reality functioning like the existence of God for the Westerner. But while the Western idea of God is vertical, the Japanese idea of *basho* or locus as an *aida* or "betweenness" of persons is instead horizontal in structure. For Kimura, then, Japanese selfhood as a dialectic of self and non-self exists by virtue of this transpersonal locus of *hito to hito to no aida* (1972, 69).

In a more recent book entitled *Betweenness* (*Aida*, 1988), Kimura once again takes up his theme of *aida* as the key dialogical principle of Japanese selfhood. In the epilogue to this work, he writes:

> It has been 16 years since *The Betweenness of Person and Person* (*Hito to hito to no aida*, 1972) was published by Kobundo. Meanwhile I have discussed the topic of *"aida "* from many different aspects. *"Aida "* has become my trademark. When people ask me to give lectures, most of them want a topic about *aida*. (1988, 211)

In this later work Kimura now gives a precise definition of the self as a dialogical principle of *aida*, "betweenness." In Kimura's words: "The self is nothing but the principle of relation to the world in the betweenness (*aida*) of ourselves and the world" (1988, 104). Elsewhere in the same text he asserts: "The human being is an existence which includes *aida* (betweenness) physiologically and which exists in *aida*" (1988, 90). Throughout this work he emphasizes that in poetic terms, the concept of *aida* is equivalent to the traditional Japanese aesthetic principle of *ma*, "negative space." It can thus be said that Kimura Bin's definition of human selfhood as a dialogical principle of "betweenness" crystallizes the Japanese concept of the person as an intersubjective self-other relation which exists in the lived space and/or time "inbetween" all persons and events in the transpersonal locus of *aida* or *ma*.

## Hamaguchi Eshun

Another development of Watsuji's *ningen* concept of man is Hamaguchi Eshun's *kanjin* or "contexualist" theory of Japanese selfhood. In such works as *The Rediscovery of Japaneseness* ('*Nihonrashisa' no saihakken*, 1977), *Japan—*

*Society of Contextualism* (*Kanjin-shugi no shakai nihon*, 1982), and "A Contextual Model of the Japanese" (1985), Hamaguchi develops his own *nihonjinron* theory wherein the essence of "Japaneseness" (*nihonrashisa*) is to be found in the sociological principle of "contextualism" (*kanjinshugi*), which he turn opposes to the notion of Western "individualism" (*kojinshugi*). He emphasizes that while Western individualism aims toward self-fulfillment, the basic value of Japanese contextualism is the spirit of "harmony" (*wa*). For Hamaguchi, it is precisely this value placed on "harmony" in the group-oriented "contextualism" of Japanese management and company organization which constitutes its superiority over Western methods based on individualism: "Harmony in the work situation is a secondary matter for Westerners who believe in individualism . . . The outstanding efficiency of Japanese companies is the product of harmony, and the modernization of Japan depends on this group-orientation" (1982, 125–26).

Hamaguchi goes on to reformulate Watsuji's *ningen* concept of the person in terms of his own theory of Japanese selfhood based on the key notion of *kanjin* (= *nin-gen* with the original pronunciation of *jin-kan*, reversed to make *kan-jin*). While in the West the self is primarily an individual so that relationship to others is secondary, in Japan the self as *kanjin* is primarily a member of a social context, including the nation, society, the company, the village, and the family, and only in a secondary sense to be regarded as an individual. Defining his *kanjin* notion of Japanese selfhood in contextualist terms, he writes:

> [F]or the Japanese, "self" means the portion which is distributed to him, according to the situation he is in, from the living space shared between himself and the other person with whom he a has established a mutually dependent relationship. The reason why the self-consciousness of the Japanese is formed this way is because self and others are in a symbiotic relationship, and that they regard their own existence as largely depending on the existence of others. (1982, 142)

Hence, the innovation of Hamaguchi's *kanjin* model of Japanese personhood is that since the characters for *ningen* are reversed, the social aspect is now given even further priority over the individual aspect of the self.

In his essay "A Contextual Model," Hamaguchi again takes up his basic contrast between two alternative cultural models of human existence: the *kojin* or "individual" model of Euro-American society in the West versus the *kanjin* or "contextual" model of Japanese society in East Asia (1985, 299). Japanese contextualism is defined in contrast to Western individualism as follows: "Individualism can be characterized by (a) ego-centeredness, (b) self-reliance, and (c) regard of interpersonal relations as means to an end. Contextualism can be characterized by (a) mutual dependence, (b) mutual reliance, and (c) regard of interpersonal relations as an end in themselves" (1985, 318). He further develops this contrast through an "actor" (*shutai*) model of selfhood based on an opposition between the "individual actor" of Euro-American society versus the "relational actor" of East Asian society (1985, 297–98). Hamaguchi describes Japanese contextual persons (*kanjin*) as relational actors in opposition to the individual actors of Western models of the ego-centered self. He cites both Watsuji Tetsurō's *ningen* theory of Japanese selfhood and Kimura Bin's *aida* theory of Japanese selfhood as paradigm theories of Japanese contextual persons as relational actors. Hamaguchi writes:

> In contrast, a relational actor is established when relationships with other actors are objectified, emphasizing the co-existentiality (or complementarity) between the relationships and people. The relational actor represents a type of actor which is fundamentally different from the solipsistic individual actor. Both Watsuji's *ningen* (people "in between") who live in *jinkan* ("in between" people) and Kimura's *hito* (man) who exists in *hito to hito to no aida* (between man and man) corresponds to this type of actor. Let us use the term *kanjin* or "contextual," to conceptually distinguish the type of man who is a relational actor from the "individual" or *kojin*. (1985, 300)

Hamaguchi emphasizes the social character of Japanese contextual persons as relational actors who develop only through interpersonal relationships with others. He asserts that the Japanese *kanjin* or contextual person is always to be defined in terms of its *aidagara* or "social context" (1985, 307). Citing the work of Kimura Bin he points out that the Japanese word *jibun* (self) literally denotes "one's share" of something beyond oneself, or as it were, the "self part" of a greater social whole (1985, 302). According to Hamaguchi, the Japanese contextual person might be characterized as a "holon" insofar as it has a holistic structure which, looking inward, sees itself as a unique autonomous whole, and looking outward, as a dependent part in a higher-order system of social organization (1985, 320). He further underscores the temporal and multiple aspects of Japanese contextual persons, stating that "for the Japanese, selfness is not a constant like the ego but denotes a fluid concept which changes through time and situations according to interpersonal relationships" (1985, 302). Hence, in contrast to the fixed ego of

Western individualism, Hamaguchi maintains that Japanese contextual persons are socially defined selves which are relational, holistic, multiple, fluid, and always changing according to context.

## Kumon Shumpei

Kumon Shumpei (1982) develops his own context-dependent model of Japanese selfhood as *ningen/kanjin* through a synthesis of ideas derived from Watsuji Tetsurō along with Kimura Bin, Doi Takeo, Hamaguchi Eshun, and other thinkers. Kumon (1982, 19) suggests that while the term *aidagara* as initially formulated by Watsuji and later developed by Kimura is best translated as "context," Hamaguchi's basic notion of *kanjin* should be rendered as "contextual" (1982, 19). He thus states his intention to work out a *kanjin* or "contextual" model of Japanese selfhood which emphasizes that the "person" as *ningen* is always located in the wider relational system of an *aidagara* or "context."

First Kumon distinguishes two kinds of "things": *mono* and *koto*. While *mono* refers to the physical attributes of matter, *koto* refers to organizing relationships that connects various *mono* into a system. He then relates these two kinds of things to the spatial notions of *ma* and *aida* which represent coordinates. Thus *ma* is a place in the coordinate space where a *mono* lies, while *aida* is a relation that connects different *ma* to produce *aidagara*, which he translates as "context" (1982, 11). He next asserts that Watsuji's contextualist idea of the person as *ningen* is to be analyzed through its location within this coordinate system of social relationships between *ma* and *aida*. Explaining Watsuji's *ningen* theory of the context-dependent self, he now writes:

> At this juncture let me refer to a Japanese word which has most intriguing connotations. This word is now pronounced *ningen* as a composite of *nin* (or *hito*, meaning people) and *gen* (or *ma* or *aida*). But it was originally pronounced as *jinkan* (*jin* + *kan*, which is people + *aida*) and meant this world or society. (1982, 11)

Kumon then proceeds to distinguish between three meanings of the word *ningen* : (1) A human being placed in a *ma*, (2) a group of people embedded in a social field (*aidagara*), and (3) the social field as an abstract relation. He adds that it is these multiple meanings of the single word *ningen* that makes it a key concept in his Japanese contextualist model of selfhood (1982, 12).

At this point the *ningen* theory of Watsuji is now further analyzed by Kumon in terms of its reformulation by Hamaguchi Eshun, wherein the characters for *ningen* are reversed to further underscore the social, relational, and contextual aspects of selfhood:

> Hamaguchi Eshun (1977) of Osaka University first coined the expression *kanjin*, which I think beautifully describes people (*jin*) who belong to a certain *kan* (*aidagara*). I thought it would be appropriate to translate *kanjin* into English as "contextual" while translating *aidagara* as "context." (1982, 19)

In his discussion of Hamaguchi's *kanjin* contextual model of Japanese selfhood, Kumon points out that like the Chinese and Koreans, "the Japanese say their family name first and given name last, with the whole or larger framework preceding the parts or elements" (1982, 12). Kumon thereby clarifies how the enveloping context of one's *ie* or family household always takes priority over the individual in Japanese society.

The *ningen/kanjin* model of Japanese contextual persons developed by Kumon Shumpei is said to represent a standpoint between "individualism" on the one side and "collectivism" on the other. Kumon cites the work of Yoshida Tamito, a Japanese sociologist, who distinguishes three different kinds of personal identity or selfhood: *individualism, collectivism,* and *contextualism* (1982, 17). While the individualist identifies himself as just what he is, the collectivist and the contextualist transcend their limited selves by going outward, looking for larger social contexts which they can join or with which they can identify themselves. However, while the *individualist* separates from society by going inside to identify with the ego-self, and the *collectivist* loses the inner self almost totally by becoming identified with society, the *contextualist* occupies a middle position between both individualism and collectivism. Kumon asserts: "In contrast to both individualist and collectivist, a contextualist . . . identifies himself both in terms of the social relation or context (*aidagara*) to which he belongs and in terms of his personal self" (1982, 18).

It has been seen that ideology critiques leveled against Watsuji's *ningen* theory of personhood show how the individual is finally dissolved into the collective whole of society so as to collapse into a mode of totalitarian collectivism. This movement of Watsuji's framework toward the direction of collectivism, totalitarianism, and social determinism is made further explicit by Hamaguchi Eshun's *kanjin* (society + individuality) model of Japanese contextual persons wherein the characters of *ningen* (individual + society) are now reversed in order to give an additional priority to social relationships over the individual. However, Kumon Shumpei demonstrates that, at least in principle, the *ningen/kanjin* model of Japanese contextual persons is meant to establish the theoretical basis for an ideal social self which occupies a *via media* between the extremes of abstract individualism on the one side and abstract collectivism on the other. In such a manner, then, Watsuji Tetsurō, along with Kimura Bin, Hamaguchi Eshun, Kumon Shumpei, and others have attempted to explicate the social nature of the Japanese self and the groupism of Japanese society through a *ningen/kanjin* contextualist model of personhood based on a dialogical principle of "betweenness" (*aidagara*) and an ontological theory of spatial "climates" (*fūdo*) as the transpersonal locus for self-other relationships.

# ∴2∴

# The Social Self and J-Thou Dialectic of Nishida Kitarō

## Nishida Kitarō and the Kyoto School

Nishida Kitarō (1870–1945), whose "collected works" (*zenshū*) amount to nineteen volumes, is widely regarded as the founder of modern Japanese philosophy. Much of twentieth-century Japanese philosophy centers around the development of, and critical reaction against, the thought of Nishida, whose prolific writings inspired the formation of what has come to be known as the Kyoto school (*Kyōto-ha*), including such luminary figures as Tanabe Hajime, Nishitani Keiji, Hisamatsu Shin'ichi, Ueda Shizuteru, Takeuchi Yoshinori, and Abe Masao. Watsuji Tetsurō, who is the leading figure in modern Japanese ethics, and Kuki Shūzō, who has produced the most creative work in modern Japanese aesthetics, are among those regarded as being "peripherally" related to the Kyoto school, in that while they were called by Nishida to teach in the Department of Philosophy at Kyoto University, and to some extent were influenced by his thought, at the same time they elaborated their own highly original and distinctive philosophical schemes. D. T. Suzuki, widely known for having spread Zen Buddhist philosophy throughout America, was Nishida's most intimate life-long friend since their childhood days in Kanazawa, and is yet another prominent Japanese thinker considered as being peripheral to the Kyoto school. Finally, it should be mentioned that Tosaka Jun (1900–45) and Miki Kiyoshi (1897–1945), two of Nishida's former students at Kyoto University, led the development of Marxist philosophy in Japan, which elaborated a strong ideological critique of Nishida Kitarō and the Kyoto school.

Nishida Kitarō, like Nishitani Keiji, Hisamatsu Shin'ichi, Ueda Shizuteru, Abe Masao, and D. T. Suzuki, may be said to have adopted a primarily Zen Buddhist orientation based on thinkers like Dōgen (1200–53), wherein the true self of absolute Nothingness is directly apprehended in an immediate experience through the "self-power" (*jiriki*) method of intuitive contemplation as a function of will. However, others in the Kyoto school like Tanabe Hajime and Takeuchi Yoshinori have instead taken up the position of True Pure Land (Jōdo Shinshū) Buddhism based on the teachings of Shinran (1174–1262), wherein Nothingness now becomes understood as the transformative grace of absolute "Other-power" (tariki) which breaks in upon the self from without through the operation of faith. The great achievement of Nishida Kitarō and the Kyoto school is to have formulated an East-West comparative philosophy and Buddhist-Christian interfaith dialogue within an overall Mahāyāna Buddhist framework of Nothingness (mu).

Nishida received instant acclaim in Japan with the publication of his maiden work, Zen no kenkyū (1911), first translated into English by Valdo Viglielmo as A Study of Good (1960), and later retranslated by the Kyoto school philosopher Abe Masao as An Inquiry into the Good (1990). In the opening chapter of this work Nishida articulates a concept of "pure experience" (junsui keiken) devoid of subject-object dualism and empty of thought which has clearly been influenced by William James in American pragmatism. However, it is widely held that Nishida reformulates James's "pure experience" in terms of his own study and practice of Zen Buddhism. Nishida subsequently reworked his original idea of pure experience through such notions as self-consciousness, absolute will, acting intuition, locus, absolute Nothingness, and the social-historical world. The major shift in Nishida's thought comes in his work From the Acting to the Seeing (1927), wherein he now reformulates pure experience through his Zen Buddhist notion of basho, or topos, the "place" (locus, field, matrix) of absolute Nothingness, conceived as the spatial locus wherein the "true self" is revealed as a self-identity of absolute contradictions. He then goes on to apply his notion of basho to the social-historical world as the spatial topos of absolute Nothingness in which the self is intersubjectively constituted as a contradictory self-identity of I and Thou. In his penultimate essay "The Logic of Place and a Religious Worldview" (1945), Nishida works out a comparative philosophy of religion based on the "self-negation" of both self and God in the spatial basho of absolute Nothingness. It is in this context that he develops a Christian-Buddhist interfaith dialogue based on parallels between the idea of kenōsis or "self-emptying" in Christianity and the idea of śūnyatā (J. kū) or emptiness in Zen Buddhism.

In the following presentation I endeavor to bring to light one of the most significant yet at the same time one of the most overlooked concepts in Nishida's philosophical thought: namely, his idea of the true self as a "social self" (shakaiteki jiko) arising through a dialectic of I and Thou (ware to nanji) in the basho or spatial "locus" of absolute Nothingness. Nishida's thematization of the social self as an I-Thou relation of intersubjectivity has been almost

entirely neglected by Japanese and Western scholars alike. An example of
this is to be found in Nishitani Keiji's recently translated book, *Nishida Kitarō*
(1991), which provides a detailed analysis of Nishida's theory of selfhood, yet
never enters into a discussion of his pervasive theme of the social self as an I-
Thou relationship. Nishitani, like other scholars, focuses on Nishida's early
idea of self as pure experience and his later idea of self as absolute Nothingness, while failing to articulate his concept of the social self as an I-Thou
relation. However, it is my contention that Nishida's social-self theory is in
fact a central and recurrent motif running throughout his entire philosophical
career in its various phases of development, starting with its original formulation in his maiden work *An Inquiry into the Good (Zen no kenkyū*, 1911), to
brief discussions of the I-Thou relation in *Art and Morality (Geijutsu to dōtoku*,
1923), to its first major expression in a chapter entitled "I and Thou" from
*Self-Conscious Determination of Nothingness (Mu no jikakuteki gentei*, 1932),
to its detailed treatment in *Fundamental Problems of Philosophy (Tetsugaku no
kompon mondai*, 2 vols. 1933–34), and continuing up until his penultimate
essay, "The Logic of Place and a Religious Worldview" (*Bashoteki ronri to
shūkyōteki sekaikan*, 1945).

## Nishida Kitarō's Zen Concept of the Self as Pure Experience

In his first major work, *An Inquiry into the Good (Zen no kenkyū*, 1911),
Nishida formulates his Jamesian idea of the self as an egoless "pure experience" (*junsui keiken*), which arises prior to the subject-object distinction and
anterior to cognitive reflection. He says that pure experience means to abandon the self and perceive events just as they are without the least addition of
thought or reflection. Pure experience is therefore "direct experience" or
"immediate experience" (*chokusetsu keiken*). For Nishida, as for James, this nondual model of selfhood understood as a pure experience devoid of subject-object
dualism at once undercuts the notion of an independent Cartesian subject or
isolated ego-self. For Nishida, pure experience is defined as the "oneness of
subject and object" (*shukaku gōitsu*). He emphasizes that pure experience is a
unified, concrete whole that exists prior to the individual. There is no individual which "has" pure experience; rather, it is from pure experience in its
concrete wholeness that the abstract individual and the subject-object dichotomy later arise through a process of reflection. Throughout this work Nishida
develops pure experience as the basis for value in art, morality, and religion.
The unified wholeness of events of pure experience is repeatedly clarified

through analogies to the aesthetic intuition of artists and poets. The realization of the person as a unity of subject and object or self and world in pure experience is also the supreme goal of ethics. Ultimately, pure experience is identified with the religious experience of God, understood as the *unifying* power of consciousness.

In Nishida's first chapter of *An Inquiry into the Good* it is clear that he has been profoundly influenced by William James's relational, temporal concept of the self developed in the context of a doctrine of pure experience. Nishida, like James, abandons the notion of self as "substance" with permanent existence and instead adopts a process view that regards the self as a series of events of "pure experience" in the ever-changing stream of consciousness with no underlying substantial identity. Moreover, like James he rejects the notion of self as substance in its meaning as separate existence and instead adopts a field model of the self based on the "focus-field" structure of pure experience in which the self discriminated in the foreground focus of attention is surrounded at each moment by a fringe of causal relationships located in the background field. In later works Nishida clarifies that the *basho* or spatial locus of absolute Nothingness is to be understood precisely as the "fringe of consciousness" which gives bottomless depths to the self in the immediacy of pure experience. As Nishida writes in *Fundamental Problems of Philosophy*: "William James wrote of a 'fringe of consciousness,' but the world of the present has an infinite fringe. Therein lies the world of infinite nothingness" (NKZ VII, 330). Hence, the true self is a concentrated focus point for the whole field of absolute Nothingness, wherein the luminous consciousness of the focal self in the foreground is surrounded by a halo of darkness of bottomless Nothingness constituted by the infinite fringe of consciousness in the background.

Although in his earliest work Nishida does not himself explicitly relate "pure experience" to Zen Buddhism, his followers in the Kyoto school all invariably equate pure experience with awakening to the true self in Zen Buddhism. Like the *satori* of Zen, "pure experience" is an egoless state in the immediate flux of the present which is empty of thought and devoid of subject-object bifurcation wherein the self is abandoned and events are seen just as they are in their concrete qualitative suchness. Valdo Viglielmo's pioneering translation of Nishida's 1911 work *Zen no kenkyū* (*A Study of Good*, 1960) is accompanied by an introduction by D. T. Suzuki, who underscores the connection of Zen Buddhism to both Nishida's pure experience and its later development in terms of absolute nothingness: "Nishida's philosophy of absolute nothingness or his logic of the self-identity of absolute contradictions is difficult to understand, I believe, unless one is passably acquainted with Zen experience. . . . He thought it was his mission to make Zen intelligible to the West" (Nishida 1960, iii). Viglielmo's translation also includes an overview of Nishida's philosophy by Shimomura Torataro, who likewise states: "[T]hat which particularly constituted the foundation of his [Nishida's] entire thought and his basic motive was Zen intuition . . . Pure experience as well, which is the basic concept of *A Study of Good*, as stated above, was already a thing possessing a character which in its foundation was originally linked with Zen intuition" (Nishida 1960, 206). In the introduction to his retranslation of Nishida's *Zen no kenkyū*, now rendered as *An Inquiry into the Good* (1990), Abe Masao emphasizes that while Nishida's "pure experience" cannot simply be equated with Zen philosophy, it has its roots in Zen, and can be characterized as representing a mutual transformation between philosophy and Zen: "An Inquiry into the Good stands upon this mutual transformation of Zen and philosophy. As both a philosopher and a Zen Buddhist, Nishida transformed Zen into philosophy for the first time in the history of this religious tradition" (Nishida 1990, xii). Nishida's eminent disciple Nishitani Keiji associates the former's idea of pure experience with Zen intuition when he writes: "The standpoint of pure experience that we have just seen in Nishida's philosophy incorporated a position that overcame the one-sidedness into which materialism and existentialism had fallen. . . . And the intuition constituting the basic formative power of this philosophical standpoint was provided by Zen Buddhism" (1991, 92). The Kyoto school philosopher Takeuchi Yoshinori similarly asserts: "The concept of pure experience . . . is the Western philosophical mold into which Nishida poured his own religious experience cultivated by his Zen training" (1982, 182). Ueda Shizuteru, another leading representative of the Kyoto school of modern Japanese philosophy writes: "As a philosopher, Nishida was at the same time a practicer of Zen; and as practicer of Zen, at the same time a philosopher" (1982, 167). In Yuasa Yasuo's work *The Body* (1987), wherein he develops the Japanese concept of the somatic self as a bodymind unity, he connects Nishida's "pure experience" (*junsui keiken*) to Zen meditation, pointing out that Nishida designates "experience" not only by the Japanese term *keiken*, but also by *taiken* (body experience), which indicates that lived experience is always physical or embodied experience using both the mind and body as an integral whole. In this context he remarks: "It is said that the philosophy of Nishida Kitarō was based on his lived experience (*taiken*) within seated meditation (*zazen*)" (Yuasa: 1987, 49). The Japanese psychiatrist Doi Takeo underscores the influence of Zen on Nishida's idea of pure experience as a fusion of subject and object, both of which he interprets as expressions of *amae* or the intrapsychic dependency drive. "It is interesting in this connection that the Nishida philosophy that won such a following in prewar Japan should, in its emphasis on the pure experience in which subject and object merge, have been so obviously been influenced by Zen, since Nishida himself was so obviously convinced that his philosophy, while inspired by the traditions of Western philosophy, was rooted in the Japanese experience" (1973, 83; 1971, 92). Hence, as the above citations clearly demonstrate, Nishida's definition of self in terms of an egoless pure experience as a fusion of subject and object has been understood by those within the tradition of twentieth-century Japanese thought as representing a modern reformulation of the Zen Buddhist notion of the true self as realized through *satori* or enlightenment.

## Nishida's Personalism

One of the most striking aspects of Nishida's maiden work *An Inquiry into the Good* is his emphasis that the highest good is to be found in the realization of "personality" (*jinkaku*). Moreover, he argues that the true self is precisely that of a "personal self" (*jinkakuteki jiko*). Influenced by Western personalism and individualism Nishida thus develops a self-realization ethics wherein the ultimate moral good is to become a person. The "personalism" (*jinkaku-shugi*) of Nishida's early philosophy of pure experience has been highlighted in *Zen and the Birds of Appetite* (1968) by Thomas Merton. In a chapter titled "Nishida: A Zen Philosopher," Merton describes Nishida's concept of self as pure experience devoid of subject-object dualism as a modern restatement of the Zen Buddhist notion of the true self. He starts by analyzing the difference between Nishida's nondualistic Zen philosophy of pure experience and Cartesian subjectivism: "The starting point of Nishida is a 'pure experience,' a 'direct experience' of undifferentiated unity which is quite the opposite to the starting point of Descartes in his *cogito*" (1968, 67). While Descartes finds his basic intuition in the reflexive self-awareness of the individual thinking subject which stands outside of and apart from its objects, for Nishida what comes first is the intuition into the fundamental unity of subject and object. The starting point of philosophical reflection is thus not the "I think" of *cogito ergo sum*, but a unified pure experience which itself arises prior to the subject-object discrimination. To this extent, Nishida's idea of pure experience seems to be a reformulation of the Zen Buddhist concept of *muga* (Skt. *anātman*) or "no-self." However, at the same time, Merton regards the most innovative aspect of Nishida theory of pure experience to be its personalism: "Perhaps the most original, indeed the most revolutionary aspect of Nishida's thought, at least from the Buddhist viewpoint, is his personalism. The conclusion of his

*A Study of Good* is that, in fact, the highest good is the good of the person"
(1968, 68). Merton goes on to argue that Nishida's personalism may seem at
first sight to be a direct contradiction of the basic tenets of Buddhism insofar
as Buddha taught that all evil is rooted in the ignorance which makes us take
our individual ego as our true self. But as Merton then points out, Nishida is
not confusing the "person" with the individual ego-self of Cartesian subjectivism, but instead understands human personality as unification of subject
and object in the concrete immediacy of pure experience (1968, 69).

In his book *Nishida Kitarō*, Nishitani Keiji asserts that the central topic
of Nishida's book *An Inquiry into the Good* is that of the realization of the self
or person. Nishitani states: "Nishida speaks of *self-* development and *self-*
initiating activity. Indeed we might even say that the standpoint of his book is
mirrored in that single world *self-*" (1991, 104). In this context he cites Nishida's
passage from *An Inquiry into Good*: "the realization of personality is for us the
absolute good" (cited in Nishitani 1991, 122). He underscores Nishida's idea
of the self as the unifying power of consciousness wherein subject and object
or self and world are fused (1991, 118). However, like nearly all other com-
mentators on the thought of Nishida Kitarō, his disciple Nishitani Keiji fails
to even mention Nishida's doctrine of the social self and its later reformulation in terms of a dialectic of I-Thou relationships in the social-historical world.
Yet as will now be demonstrated, the social self is fundamental to Nishida's
thought from his first book *An Inquiry into the Good* (1911) to his penultimate
essay "The Logic of Place and a Religious Worldview" (1945).

## Nishida's Initial Formulation of the Social Self

What has been overlooked by scholars of Nishida Kitarō is that in his book
*An Inquiry into Good*, Nishida not only borrows William James's notion of the
self as "pure experience" in the stream of consciousness, but also his idea of
the "social self." For Nishida, as for James, the social self is an extension of
the focus-field model of selfhood as a "pure experience" in which the focal
self is at each moment surrounded by a fringe of social relationships in the
felt background of experiential immediacy which constitutes each moment
as a felt whole and confers upon it boundless depths with intrinsic value.
Nishida explicitly introduces his concept of the "social self" (*shakaiteki jiko*)
in the chapter of *An Inquiry into the Good* entitled "The Goal of the Good (The
Content of Good)." It is significant that Nishida introduces this notion here
since the overall purpose of his book is that of an inquiry into the "good,"
(*zen*), and the social self is at this point identified as the very content of the

good. In this chapter he maintains that the social self is a way to surmount the false alternatives of "individualism" (*kojinshugi*) and "collectivism" (*kyōdōshugi*). Nishida argues that individualism and collectivism coincide insofar as the individual and society are always correlative functions: "Individualism and collectivism are said to be diametrically opposed to each other, but I think they coincide. It is only when individuals in society fully engage in action and express their innate abilities that society can progress. A society that ignores the individual can never be a healthy one" (1984, 196). Nishida then asserts individualism and collectivism can only be said to coincide in what he variously refers to as the "social self" (*shakaiteki jiko*), the "social animal" (*shakaiteki dōbutsu*) and "social consciousness" (*shakaiteki ishiki*). It can thus be said that when Nishida holds that the highest good is the achievement of the person and the development of personality, he specifically means that the supreme value of concrete human existence is the realization of the "social self" as a middle axiom between abstract individualism and abstract collectivism.

## Nishida Kitarō's I-Thou Dialectic of the Social Self

It has become commonplace to characterize Nishida's theory of selfhood in terms of his idea of "pure experience" (*junsui keiken*) understood as a "oneness of subject and object" (*shukaku gōitsu*). Moreover, criticism of Nishida's philosophy is often based on this same characterization of the self as pure experience. In his work *The Structure of Amae* (*Amae no kōzō*, 1971), psychiatarist Doi Takeo states his view that Nishida's "pure experience" is a modern reformulation of Zen *satori* or enlightenment, both understood as the fusion of subject and object into a primordial unity. From the psychological standpoint Doi (1971, 92) criticizes both Zen *satori* and Nishida's "pure experience" as expressions of the Japanese *amae* mentality, the infantile dependency syndrome. Based on similar premises, Peter Dale (1986) develops an ideology critique of Nishida's pure experience, arguing that it is a metaphysical disguise for a totalitarian state ethics and fascist ideology based on the fusion of subject and object and dissolution of the individual into the whole. However, these criticisms are unfair to Nishida to the extent that they fail to take into account his mature conception of personhood as a twofold social self constituted as an I-Thou relation of intersubjectivity in the social-historical world.

In *From the Acting to the Seeing* (*Hataraku mono kara miru mono e*, 1927), Nishida introduces his new Zen Buddhist concept of *basho*, or *topos*, the spatial "locus" (place, field, matrix) of absolute Nothingness wherein the "true self"
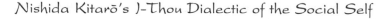

is revealed as a no-self or selfless self. In still later works he develops his no-tion of the *basho* or locus of Nothingness as the social-historical world. It is clarified that the "true self" disclosed in the locus of absolute Nothingness is precisely the "social self" (*shakaiteki jiko*), now understood as a contradictory self-identity of "I and Thou" (*ware to nanji*). The individualistic ego-self at the standpoint of Being (*u*) which is then negated into *muga* or no-self at the nihilistic standpoint of relative Nothingness (*sōtaiteki mu*) is now reaffirmed as a twofold social self intersubjectively constituted through a dialectic of I and Thou at the middle way standpoint of emptiness (*kū*) or absolute Nothing-ness (*zettaiteki mu*). Although Nishida describes this I-Thou dialectic as early as his book *Art and Morality* (*Geijutsu to dōtoku*, 1923), the chapters of which appeared even prior to this in serialized form, he first explicitly thematizes this idea in a chapter entitled "I and Thou" from *Self-Conscious Determination of Nothingness* (*Mu no jikakuteki gentei*, 1932), followed by a continual rework-ing of this same idea through a series of philosophical writings up until his penultimate essay, "The Logic of Place and a Religious Worldview" (*Bashoteki ronri to shūkyōteki sekaikan*, 1945). Nishida himself points out that his essay "I and Thou" published in 1932 represents a critical juncture in the develop-ment of his philosophical thought (NKZ VI, 341 fn). This dialectical I-Thou relation of intersubjectivity thereafter becomes a recurrent and central mo-tif in the writings of Nishida. The I-Thou relationship of intersubjectivity thematized in modern Japanese philosophy by Nishida Kitarō has been taken up in various ways by subsequent members of the Kyoto school including Nishitani Keiji (1982), Ueda Shizuteru (1982), Takeuchi Yoshinori (1982, 122) and Abe Masao (1985). It is significant that Nishida's idea of the social self as an I-Thou relation appears not to have been in any way derived from Martin Buber's celebrated treatise entitled *I and Thou* (*Ich und Du*, 1923), but rather both of these thinkers were influenced by Ludwig Feuerbach's seminal notion of man as a unity of I and Thou which he outlined in *Principles of the Philosophy of the Future* (*Grundsatze der Philosophie der Zukunft*, 1843). Furthermore, both Nishida and Buber understand the self as being intersubjectively constituted by I-Thou relations in three spheres: self with self, self with nature, and self with God. Hence, as will be further examined in the concluding section of this work, both Nishida Kitarō in Japan and Martin Buber in the West inde-pendently and simultaneously developed a philosophical anthropology based upon a social concept of selfhood as an I-Thou relation of intersubjectivity.

In his essay "I and Thou" (*Ware to nanji*, 1932), Nishida clarifies that the self is always a social self which arises through an intersubjective relation between the I (*ware*) and the Thou (*nanji*), the self (*jiko*) and the other (*ta*), or the individual (*kobutsu*) and the environment (*kankyō*). Hence, the social self

is no longer a mere fusion of subject and object in the unity of pure experience, but a contradictory self-identity of I and Thou. That is to say, for Nishida,
the social self is always intersubjectively constituted by an I in relation to an
"absolute other" (*zettai no ta*) at the inmost "bottom" (*soko, kontei*) of the self.

> A self must include an absolute other in itself. It is not that a self becomes
> other and other becomes the self through a medium. But the self
> becomes the other through the bottom of itself. Because there is the
> other at the bottom of the self's existence and there is the self at the
> bottom of the other's existence. I and Thou are absolute others. There
> is no general thing which includes I and Thou. But I am I by
> acknowledging Thou, and Thou are Thou by acknowledging me. There
> is a Thou at my bottom, and my I at Thy bottom. I unite with you
> through my bottom, and the Thou unites with with me through Thy
> bottom. Because they are absolute others, they unite with each other
> inside of themselves. (NKZ VI, 381–2)

A fundamental concept throughout Nishida's entire philosophy is his notion
of *jikaku*, variously translated as "self-consciousness," "self-awareness" or "self-
awakening." Marxist writers like Tosaka Jun and Miki Kiyoshi developed
ideology critiques of Nishida's philosophy of pure experience, arguing that it
represents an idealistic theory of pure "self-consciousness" which is disengaged
from those material, economic, social, moral, and political concerns essential
for transformation of the public sphere. However, Nishida's shift to a social
concept of self based on an intersubjective dialectic of I-Thou relationships
in the social-historical world signifies a turn from a psychologistic and idealistic notion of man as *homo interior* to that of *homo exterior*. Hence, in his essay
"I and Thou" Nishida specifies that "self-consciousness" is always a social
consciousness of *spatial relationships* between persons in society, or as it were,
a social consciousness of dialectical relations between the I and the Thou:

> True self-consciousness should be social and based on the spatial relation
> between people. I and Thou stand on this dialectical relation. Therefore,
> I acknowledge Thou through the reflection of my personal conduct,
> and Thou must acknowledge me through the reflection of Thy personal
> conduct. We acknowledge absolute others at the bottom of each other.
> That is what we regard as real consciousness of personal conduct. In
> short, I and Thou know each other through the response of each other's
> conduct. (NKZ VI, 392)

Taking as his departure point the concept of selfhood as a social consciousness of I-Thou relations, he asserts that the individual always has its origins in society: "Originally our self does not start from the individual. As we can find through various native tribes, it starts from the sense of the common. The individual is born in society" (NKZ VI, 350). The individual I understood as a response to the social Thou allows for the constant reconstruction of history and society: "Our personal self can be thought of as an ultimate limitation of the social and the historical, but has creativity to limit history and change society . . . A great figure can be thought of as a focus of social consciousness" (NKZ VI, 368).

Of special interest to the "linguistic turn" in contemporary philosophy is Nishida's idea of the I-Thou relation as a function of *language*. Due to Nishida's early characterization of "pure experience" as a "direct experience" or "immediate experience" (*chokusetsu keiken*) of events just as they are in their suchness wherein no thought or reflection is added, it might be said that Nishida holds a skeptical distrust of language and the faculty of thought. Yet in the section on Thought from the Pure Experience chapter of *An Inquiry into the Good*, Nishida then clarifies that "thought" can itself be regarded as a mode of pure experience as the unity of emotion, volition, and conception in the stream of consciousness. Moreover, in his later work Nishida further emphasizes that the I and Thou cannot interact directly, but only through communication using the intersubjective medium of *language*. In Nishida's words: "Yesterday's I and today's I are united directly. But I cannot know directly what other people think. I and others understand each other through what is called written and spoken language. I and Thou cannot be united directly" (NKZ VI, 347). Again, he states: "I and Thou belong to the physical world having bodies . . . I and Thou communicate not by mere air vibration, but by language" (NKZ VI, 372). According to Nishida, then, the human self is not confined to immediacy in pure experience insofar as reflexive self-consciousness arises through linguistically mediated communicative interaction between an I and a Thou in the locus of absolute Nothingness.

Nishida ends his essay called "I and Thou" by developing the concept of Christian *agape*, self-giving love, as distinguished from *eros*, personal desire for an object:

> Once I distinguished the love toward human beings from the desire toward objects. I distinguished the true love of *agape* from *eros*. True love is not love become of some value, but love of person for person. If you love some people for some goal, no matter how important the

goal is, this love is not true love. True love is to see I through the absolute
other. (NKZ VI, 423)

According to Nishida, whereas individualism is grounded in *eros* or the desire
for objects, the dialectical relation between I and Thou at the bottom of the
"personal self" *(jinkakuteki jiko)* is based upon *agape* or selfless love, in other
words, a love of neighbor as ourself in imitation of the *agape* or selfless love
of God: "We can be personal because we love our neighbor as ourselves following God's *agape*" (NKZ VI, 425). He adds:

> In *agape* we do not love human beings but we love human beings
> through God's love. I and Thou are God's creation limited by history,
> and exist in the same history. I, as God's creation, love Thee, as God's
> creation, like myself. I and Thou must have certain meaning as God's
> creation in the historical world, because I and Thou exist through *agape*.
> (NKZ VI, 427)

Following his initial thematization of the I-Thou relation in *Self-Conscious Determination of Nothingness* (1932), he then goes on to further elaborate the logical foundation of this idea in his next book called *Fundamental
Problems of Philosophy* (*Tetsugaku no kompon mondai*). In the preface to this
latter volume he thus asserts: "In this work, I think that I have provided a
logical basis for the notions of my *Self-Conscious Determination of Nothingness*,
especially those contained in the chapter of that work called 'I and Thou'"
(NKZ VII, 3). Using his paradoxical Zen logic of emptiness or absolute Nothingness he now defines the acting self in the social-historical world as a "self-
identity of absolute contradictions" (*zettaimujunteki jikodōitsu*). Hence, the
attainment of personhood is to be regarded as an absolute paradox which is
logically defined as an absolutely contradictory self-identity of one and many,
subject and object, self and other, or I and Thou. Again, using his Zen logic
of absolute paradox, he conceives of the person as a "continuity of discontinuity" (*hirenzoku no renzoku*), so that concrete acting self at the bottom of the
locus of Nothingness is neither simply continuous nor simply discontinuous
with the other to which it stands in opposition, but is instead a *discontinuous
continuity* of I and Thou.

This latter work now attempts to elaborate what he calls "the social-
historical world of the I and the Thou" (NKZ VII, 303). Nishida now emphasizes that the person is to be understood as a social being: "The person (*ningen*)
must be social; a mere individual (*kojin*) cannot exist" (NKZ VII, 329). For
Nishida, the idea of a separate individual is merely an abstraction from the

whole person understood as a concrete *social self* which is intersubjectively constituted by a self-other dialectic of I-Thou relationships: "The I is an I by facing a Thou, and the individual is an individual by facing other individuals. The self must be social" (NKZ VII, 382). To become a person the self must always stand over against an "absolute other" (*zettai no ta*), just as an *I* must always stand over against a *Thou*. In Nishida's words: "My concept of the person does not mean simply an abstract individual. The true personal self exists when the absolute other is seen in the self and the self in the absolute other, as was said in my essay '*I and Thou*'" (NKZ VII, 75). Again, he writes: "As I said in part five of 'The Self and the World' [from *Fundamental Problems of Philosophy*], the active self must always be social and not merely a solitary self . . . Thus, the acting self must be social and historical. The I and Thou are to be thought of as socially and historically determined." In this context Nishida criticizes the standpoint of Descartes's *cogito ergo sum*, "I think therefore I am," which results merely in the concept of an abstract I or isolated ego-self and thereby fails to arrive at the notion of a social self comprehended as a dialectical relationship of I and Thou (NKZ VII, 173–74).

One of the most significant aspects of Nishida theory of "self-consciousness" (*jikaku*) as a social consciousness of linguistically mediated I-Thou relations is his dialectic of mutual recognition. For Nishida, as for Hegel in German idealism, reflexive self-consciousness emerges only through a self-other dialectic of intersubjectivity. Moreover, this self-other relation involves a dialectic of *mutual recognition* whereby self-consciousness arises only through recognition of the other and recognition by the other. Nishida describes this dialectic of "recognition" (*mitomeru*) between self and other or I and Thou as follows: "When it is thought that the I becomes an I by recognition of a Thou, and that an individual is determined by its relations to other individuals, personal action comes to have the meaning of something determined by a world of circular determination" (NKZ VII, 139). Again, he writes:

> The I becomes an I only through recognition by a Thou, just as a Thou becomes a Thou only through recognition by an I. There is no merely solitary self. This is the meaning of the determination of the individual-as-environment and of the environment-as-individual. (NKZ VII, 169)

In the context of formulating a dialectic of recognition between I and Thou, Nishida here introduces his notion of the "mutual determination" (*sōgo gentei*) of individuals in the locus of Nothingness. Moreover, Nishida describes this process as a mutual determination of individual and environment. He thereby articulates the I-Thou dialectic of the social self in terms of an organism-environment interaction, expressed here in terms of his idea of "determination of the individual-as-environment" (*kobutsuteki gentei soku kankyōteki gentei*).

As indicated by his doctrine of mutual determination between individual and environment, Nishida understands the I-Thou dialectic as applying not only to the relation of self with self but also to the relation of self with living nature. This is clearly expressed when he writes:

> There must be a relation of I and Thou between individual and individual. In the concrete world there must be the an I-Thou relation between thing and thing. That which faces the I must have the meaning of a Thou. I and Thou does not mean simply a relation between individual and individual . . . everything which stands against the I, including the mountains, rivers, trees, and stones, has the meaning of a Thou. It is in this sense that the concrete world may be thought of as a metaphysical society. (NKZ VII, 59)

Moreover, the I-Thou relations of self with self and with self and nature is also extended over into the relation of man with God. That is to say, the social self is constituted by its I-thou relationships not only with other persons in the human community as well as the mountains, rivers, trees, and stones in the metaphysical society of nature, but also by its I-Thou relationship with an immanently transcendent God as the absolute Other and eternal Thou. In this context he emphasizes that the Christian must always refer to God as *Thou*. However, a fundamental distinction must be made, says Nishida, between the divine *Thou* used to address God, and the interhuman *thou* used when we call our neighbor a *thou*. In the former case, the divine *Thou* must rather be called Father or Lord. Therefore, even loving one's neighbor as oneself by means of an interpersonal I-Thou relation based on *agape* is itself divine communion with God (NKZ VII, 210). In his penultimate essay "The Logic of Place and a Religious Worldview" (*Bashoteki ronri to shūkyōteki sekaikan,* 1945), Nishida goes on to develop a Buddhist-Christian interfaith dialogue based on analogies between the Christian idea of *kenōsis,* "self-emptying," and the Zen Buddhist idea of *śūnyatā* (J. *kū*), "emptiness" (NKZ XI, 399). Just as in Christianity true selfhood is achieved by emptying oneself into relations with others out of *agape* or divine love, in Buddhism it is realized by making oneself empty out of divine compassion. In this context he interprets both the self-emptying love of Christian *kenōsis* and the self-negating compassion of Buddhist *śūnyatā* in terms of his social concept of self as a dialectic of I and Thou. The self and God are not simply identical as in mysticism but are instead related as a contradictory self-identity of I and Thou in the locus of absolute Nothingness. Hence, even up until his last major writing Nishida continued to develop in various contexts his thematization of the I-Thou relation of intersubjectivity.

## The Zen Model of Selfhood
## Illustrated by the Ten Oxherding Pictures

Nishida's concept of the twofold social self as an I-Thou relationship in the social-historical world has been further developed by Ueda Shizuteru (b. 1926), a long time disciple of Nishitani Keiji and his successor as head of the Kyoto school of modern Japanese philosophy. In his essay "Emptiness and Fullness: Śūnyatā in Mahāyāna Buddhism" (1982), Ueda graphically illustrates the Zen process of becoming a person through the famous *Ten Oxherding Pictures* as interpreted through the paradoxical logic of Nothingness developed by Nishida and the Kyoto school. Ueda understands the *Ten Oxherding Pictures* as illustrating the process whereby the self dies and is reborn in "absolute Nothingness," comprehended in Zen Buddhism as a plenary void of boundless openness wherein emptiness is fullness and fullness is emptiness. In this context he explains the Zen oxherding series as a pictorial illustration of the developmental stages of self-realization whereby one moves from the ego-self at the eternalistic standpoint of Being to the non-ego at the nihilistic standpoint of relative Nothingness and finally to the true self of a compassionate Bodhisattva at the middle way position of absolute Nothingness. According to Ueda's Zen Buddhist developmental model of personhood, this true self of absolute Nothingness disclosed in the final picture of the oxherding series designates precisely the *betweenness* of I-Thou intersubjectivity. The emptied self or selfless self of Zen is an *ecstatic* self which stands out into the boundless openness of absolute Nothingness as the *betweenness* of I and the Thou. This I-Thou relational self of Zen Buddhism represents a "middle way" between the extreme views of a substantial self of Being as posited by eternalism and of a mere no-self of Nothing as held by nihilism. Ueda's essay on the *Ten Oxherding Pictures* thereby functions not only as a splendid introduction to the Zen Buddhist philosophy of the middle way based on the principle of *śūnyatā* or emptiness but also as a primer to the paradoxical logic of Nothingness formulated by Nishida and the Kyoto school of modern Japanese philosophy. Moreover, Ueda's understanding of the tenth and final oxherding picture representing the true self of Zen Buddhism clearly synthesizes Nishida's fundamental idea of the social self as constituted by an I-Thou relation of intersubjectivity in the *basho* of absolute Nothingness and

The *Ten Oxherding Pictures* by Shūbun

7. The Ox Forgotten, the Self Alone.

8. The Ox and the Self Forgotten.

9. Returning to the Origin, Back to the Source.

10. Entering the Marketplace with Helping Hands.

Watsuji's *ningen* model of personhood according to which the self is spatially located in the the *aidagara* or "betweenness" of individuals within the absolute negativity of *kū*, emptiness. Finally, it is shown how in another essay titled "Meister Eckhart and Zen Buddhism" (1982), Ueda argues that the breakthrough to the level of an I-Thou relational self at the standpoint of absolute Nothingness through Zen Buddhist contemplation in the East also has its counterpart in the kenotic path of *via negativa* Christian mysticism represented by Meister Eckhart in the West.

## The Ten Oxherding Pictures

Scholars point out that as early as the Southern Sung period (1127–1297), Chan/Zen monks used a series of inkwash paintings to depict the analogy between stages of oxherding and the stages of self-realization leading to Buddhahood. This has generally become known as the *Ten Oxherding Pictures* (Ch. *shih-niu t'u*; J. *jūgyū-zu*). In the middle of the twelfth century Kuo-an Shih-yuan (c. 1150), a master of the Lin-chi (Rinzai) school of Ch'an, wrote short poems and prose comments on the ten stages of self-realization disclosed in a series of ten pictures drawn in the form of circle or *ensō* diagrams. Yet in his preface he refers to another earlier Chan master who used a series of five pictures in which, to illustrate the developing stages of self-realization, a black ox became progressively whiter and finally vanished altogether into an blank circle of void empty space. Other early versions of this motif employed six, eight or ten pictures, also ending in a blank circle of void empty space. Kuo-an, however, pushed the teaching to a deeper level, ending not with the blank space of an empty circle representing nihilistic Nothingness, but with two more additional pictures showing the awakened Bodhisattva's return to the beauty of nature and then to the everyday social world out of compassion others. This version, reproduced in Chinese books, was brought by Japanese monks to Japan, where it found widespread popularity during the fourteenth and fifteenth centuries. It is generally agreed that the greatest version of the *Ten Oxherding Pictures* based on Kuo-an's prototype is a Japanese handscroll with ten *sumie* inkwash paintings owned by Shokoku-ji temple and attributed to the renowned fifteenth-century Zen Buddhist artist-monk Shūbun (active ca. 1423–60). In the Japanese Buddhist religio-aesthetic tradition of *geidō* or the Way of the artist, the inkwash paintings of the *Ten Oxherding Pictures* came to be used as a kind of "skillful means" (Skt. *upāya*; J. *hōben*) for transmitting the various stages of self-realization leading to Buddhahood and their corresponding degrees of enlightenment.

*Ueda Shizuteru on the Ten Oxherding Pictures*

In his essay, "Emptiness and Fullness: Śūnyatā in Mahāyāna Buddhism" (1982), Ueda Shizuteru endeavors to articulate the traditional Zen Buddhist model of selfhood as presented by the famous *Ten Oxherding Pictures* using the paradoxical logic of Nothingness developed by Nishida Kitarō, Nishitani Keiji, D. T. Suzuki, and other thinkers related to the Kyoto school. In this context he interprets the *Ten Oxherding Pictures* as depicting a threefold negative dialectic or emptying process wherein the separate ego-self at the level of substantial Being empties into *muga* or selflessness at the level of relative Nothingness which in turn empties into the true self of Zen Buddhism at the *basho* or locus of absolute Nothingness. These three moments in the negative dialectic of the *Ten Oxherding Pictures* can be summarized as follows. (1) The first seven developmental stages represent the separate ego-self at various levels at the standpoint of Being as posited by eternalism. (2) The decisive leap that breaks through to the void which empties the self of all substantiality occurs at the eighth stage depicted simply by an empty circle. Yet the eighth stage is also transitional insofar as it represents the no-self or non-ego at the standpoint of relative Nothingness as posited by nihilism. Ueda emphasizes that this Zen Buddhist Nothingness that desubstantializes the ego-self must not be adhered to as a Nothingness but must itself be emptied through a deeper realization of the Nothingness of Nothingness. (3) The ninth and tenth stages depict the true self in the locus of absolute Nothingness, the middle way of emptiness between eternalism and nihilism. The self and all phenomena reified by substance thinking at the standpoint of eternalism which are then negated or emptied at the standpoint of nihilism are now affirmed just as they are in their true suchness at the locus of absolute Nothingness, understood as a boundless openness, wherein emptiness is fullness and fullness is emptiness.

In terms of the dialectic of double negation characterizing the paradoxical logic of *śūnyatā* elaborated by Nishida and the Kyoto school, Ueda (1982, 15) asserts that while the first seven pictures in the Zen oxherding series designate the standpoint of self-affirmation, and picture 8 signifies the standpoint of radical self-negation, pictures 9 and 10 represent the standpoint of complete self-affirmation achieved by a double negation, or as it were, a negation of negation. This kind of negative dialectic illustrated by the *Ten Oxherding Pictures* can be further elucidated through Nishida's logic of *śūnyatā* as translated into his paradoxical logic of *soku hi*, "is and yet is not." While the first seven pictures represent the level of presence, affirmation, or being, and the eighth picture represents the level of absence, negation, or non-being, the ninth and tenth pictures signify the level of contradictory self-identity between presence and absence, affirmation and negation, or being and non-being, thereby constituting a *via media* between eternalism and nihilism. Hence, in the last two pictures as comprehended through Nishida's Zen logic of *soku hi*, the self is both present yet absent, absent yet present, both there and somehow not there at all in the locus of absolute Nothingness. That is to say, in the locus of absolute Nothingness the self "is not" in that it is devoid of any substantial Being; yet this does not mean nihilistic Nothingness, because the self still "is" in the sense of possessing a contingent relational existence through dependent co-arising. Nishida's Zen logic of *soku hi* is therefore illustrated very clearly in the Zen oxherding series, according to which pictures 1–7 show how the self "is" at the eternalistic standpoint of eternal Being and picture 8 shows how the self "is not" at the nihilistic standpoint of relative Nothingness, while pictures 9 and 10 reveal how the self paradoxically both "is" and "is not" at the middle way standpoint of absolute Nothingness.

To the extent that the paradoxical logic of Nothingness formulated by Nishida and the Kyoto school has appropriated the negative dialectics of Tendai, Kegon, and Zen Buddhism, the *Ten Oxherding Pictures* illustrate the three moments of the emptying process operating in the texts of both traditional and modern Japanese Buddhist philosophy based upon the teachings of the middle way and its underlying principle of *śūnyatā*, emptiness. In terms of the traditional Zen Buddhist dialectic of form and emptiness, the first moment represented by pictures 1–7 shows the world of form, and the second moment represented by picture 8 is the world of formless emptiness, leading finally to the third moment of the middle way represented by pictures 9 and 10, the world in which form is emptiness and emptiness is form as proclaimed by the *śūnyatā* tradition running through the thought of Nāgārjuna, the *Heart Sutra*, the *Prajñāpāramitā* texts, the Chan/Zen teachings, and the Kyoto school of modern Japanese philosophy. Again, in terms of the famous *kōan* given by Chan/Zen master Ch'ing-yuan Wei-shin (J. Seigen Ishin) of the T'ang Dynasty, whereas the first moment of pictures 1–7 is the level in which "Mountains are Mountains, Waters are Waters," and the second moment of picture 8 is the level in which "Mountains are *not* Mountains, Waters are *not* Waters," the third moment of pictures 9 and 10 is the level in which "Mountains are *really* Mountains, Waters are *really* Waters" (see Abe: 1985, 4). Or in terms of the dialectics of Kegon (Ch. Hua-yen) Buddhism, pictures 1–7 is the realm of particulars (*ji*), the world of the Many, and picture 8 is the realm of the universal (*ri*), the world of the One, while pictures 9 and 10 show the realm of harmonious interfusion between the particular and the universal (*riji muge*), the unobstructed mutual penetration between the Many and the One. Moreover, in terms of Tendai Buddhist dialectics as expressed through the doctrine of the "three truths" (*santai*), while the first seven pictures show the truth of conventional existence (*ketai*), and the eighth picture discloses the truth of emptiness (*kūtai*), the ninth and tenth pictures reveal the truth of the middle way (*chūtai*) between eternalism and nihilism. However, in the case of the Kyoto school of modern Japanese philosophy this same threefold emptying process has been codified in a dialectical logic of negations whereby "Being" (*u*), empties into *muga* or selflessness in the locus of "relative Nothingness" (*sōtaiteki mu*), which in turn empties into the true self in the locus of "absolute Nothingness" (*zettaiteki mu*), that is, the standpoint of *śūnyatā* (*kū*), where emptiness and fullness are the same. Ueda's essay thus functions to demonstrate how the *Ten Oxherding Pictures* of Zen Buddhism is a skillful means for imaginatively vizualizing this threefold dialectical process of self-realization which moves from Being to relative Nothingness to absolute Nothingness at the heart of the Kyoto school strategy for overcoming both eternalism and nihilism at the standpoint of the middle way.

From the standpoint of the existentialist orientation of modern Japanese philosophy as developed by the Kyoto school, the most significant feature of the oxherding series is that it does not end with merely an empty circle depicting the complete absence of self in a nihilistic void of relative Nothingness. Rather, it adds a ninth and tenth picture representing the standpoint of absolute Nothingness in its sense as a fully positive emptiness or boundless openness which affirms the self and all things in their concrete immediate suchness. Ueda argues that the realization of absolute Nothingness as shown by these last two pictures in the oxherding series involves an understanding of the fundamental Mahāyāna Buddhist principles of *śūnyatā* (emptiness), *anātman* (no-self), and *pratītya-samutpāda* (dependent coorigination), all of which function to underscore the primacy of *relationships* over the category of "substance." In this context he writes: "In contrast to the concept of substantial being, Buddhism recognizes only the category of 'relation' . . . Everything that is, only is in relation to other things, in a relationship of mutual conditioning among beings" (1982, 24). Whereas the ninth picture shows the aesthetic continuum of nature in which the individual exists through its relationship with the surrounding environment, the tenth picture discloses the moral realm of self-emptying compassion in which the individual exists through its relationships with others in society. Ueda (1982, 28) emphasizes that the ninth picture showing the aesthetic continuum of nature in its concrete immediacy corresponds to the level which Nishida Kitarō refers to in the opening chapter of *A Study of Good* as "pure experience" (*junsui keiken*), the unifying moment of awareness emerging prior to cognitive reflection and anterior to the subject-object dichotomy. However, in the tenth and final picture this pure experience of subject-object unity deepens into to the moral realization of what Nishida calls the social self constituted by its I-Thou relations of intersubjectivity. The tenth and final picture of the oxherding series thus leads to the moral wisdom of a Bodhisattva that Nothingness is great compassion (1982, 19).

Ueda's essay on the *Ten Oxherding Pictures* further describes the locus of emptiness or absolute Nothingness as the realm of "between." This category of *between* designates the "middle way" position of Buddhist philosophy based upon the principle of *kū* or emptiness according to which all things exist *śūnyatā*-like at the intersection of Being (*u*) and non-Being (*mu*). The true self of Zen Buddhism exists precisely in the *betweenness* of all persons and events in the locus of Nothingness, including both the "betweenness" of man and nature as shown by picture 9, and the "betweenness" of man and man as revealed by picture 10. However, for Ueda the *Ten Oxherding Pictures* culminate in the betweenness of persons in human society. For in the tenth and final oxherding picture, the ego-self which dies in the nihilum of relative Nothingness signified by the eighth picture showing an empty void is now reborn in the boundless openness of absolute Nothingness as an emptied self, ecstatic self, or selfless self existing in the betweenness of self and other. Ueda thus writes: "The matter treated expressly in the tenth and final state concerns the encounter between human individuals. Here the true self resurrected from nothingness is at work between individuals, or comes into play there, as a selfless dynamic of the 'between'" (1982, 20). For this reason, absolute Nothingness, now understood as the *betweenness* of persons, is to be further comprehended as the locus of I-Thou intersubjectivity. The true self of Zen existing in this realm of the "between" at the standpoint of absolute Nothingness is not a Cartesian subject in the sense of an atomic I or separate ego-self but is always a *double self* constituted by an intersubjective unity of I and Thou. Ueda continues:

> This "between" is here the self's own domain, its inner playground. In other words, the self, cut open by absolute nothingness and laid bare, unfolds as this "between" . . . This communion in a common life is the second resurrection body of the selfless self. I am "I and thou," "I and thou" is I. The self is seen as a double self in virtue of selflessness. This is the . . . model of "emptiness and fullness." (1982, 20–21)

Hence, in opposition to the nihilistic understanding of Zen *muga* as a mere selflessness wherein the individual is merely extinguished in a void of relative

Nothingness, in this more positive understanding the idea of *muga* disclosed at the standpoint of absolute Nothingness hereby comes to be understood as representing a double or twofold I-Thou relational self existing in the "between" of self and other:

> In the tenth station of the Oxherding Pictures we saw two men meeting on a road. In the context of self-becoming as understood by Zen and as the accompanying text explains, it is an image of the true self in its aspect of a double self grounded on selflessness in nothingness. Split open by absolute nothingness the self spreads out and unfolds itself selflessly into the *between* where the other in its otherness belongs to the selflessness of the self. . . . It is [thus] able to present what is characteristic with regard to the problem of "I and Thou." (1982, 34–35)

In this way Ueda's Zen model of personhood as illustrated by the developmental stages of the *Ten Oxherding Pictures* may be said to represent a synthesis of Nishida's social self as a dialectic of I and Thou in the locus of absolute Nothingness and Watsuji's *ningen* theory of self based upon the key principle of *aidagara* or "betweenness" of persons in the absolute negativity of *kū*, emptiness. If analyzed through the dialectics of the Kyoto school, the atomic ego-self reified at the eternalistic standpoint of substantial Being (*u*) which dies in the nihilistic standpoint of relative Nothingness (*sōtaiteki mu*) is finally resurrected at the standpoint of the middle way as an ecstatic self held out suspended in the boundless openness of absolute Nothingness (*zettaiteki mu*), understood now as a social self arising through I-Thou relations of intersubjectivity. Or in terms of Watsuji's *ningen* model of personhood, while the first seven oxherding pictures show the abstract individual, and picture 8 portrays the no-self, the last two pictures manifest the double structure of *ningen* or the true person as being contextually located in an encompassing spatial "climate" (*fūdo*), which includes both the "betweenness" (*aidagara*) of the person and living nature shown in picture 9 and the "betweenness" of persons in human society shown in picture 10. The tenth and final oxherding picture represents Watsuji's twofold *ningen* concept of personhood as an individual-society interaction based on the Buddhist notion of *kū* or "emptiness" and Zen logic of double negation whereby society is "emptied" into the individual and the individual is "emptied" into society. The Mahāyāna Buddhist intersubjectivist paradigm of selfhood as reformulated by Ueda Shizuteru in the tradition of modern Japanese philosophy thus functions as a corrective to overly mystical interpretations of Zen which view it only as a contemplative mode of introspectionism such as is symbolized by the eighth picture in the Oxherding series, or even as a kind of nature aestheticism as is shown by the ninth picture, but instead clarifies how the ultimate break-through to a selfless self of absolute Nothingness revealed in the tenth and final picture is a social self dwelling in the *between* of I and Thou.

## The Kenōsis/Sūnyatâ Ideal of Personhood as Self-Emptying Love

In his final essay Nishida Kitarō (NKZ XI, 399) articulates an interfaith dialogue based on an an explicit comparison between the Buddhist concept of *śūnyatā* or emptiness of self and the Christian idea of *kenōsis*, "self-empty-ing."[4] For Nishida both Christian *kenōsis* and Buddhist *śūnyatā* are to be un-derstood as cross-cultural variants of his paradoxical Zen logic wherein the true self is realized by an act of total self-negation in absolute nothingness. Nishida's use of the *kenōsis/śūnyatā* motif as a basis for Christian-Buddhist dialogue has been further developed by subsequent members of the Kyoto school including Tanabe Hajime, Nishitani Keiji, Ueda Shizuteru, and Abe Masao. In the Kyoto school of modern Japanese philosophy, both the Chris-tian *kenōsis* and Buddhist *śūnyatā* traditions have converged upon the ideal of selfhood as act of "making oneself nothing" whereby total self-fulfillment is achieved only through total self-emptying.

The self-emptying of Christ, like the self-negation of Buddha, is most often interpreted in mystical terms as an introspective act of emptying the mind of all thoughts and symbols into an imageless void so as to be filled by the peace, light, and joy of the divine. In *Zen and the Birds of Appetite* (1968) the great contemplative monk Thomas Merton writes:

> The "mind of Christ" as described by St. Paul in Philippians 2 may be theologically worlds apart from the "mind of Buddha" . . . But the utter "self-emptying" of Christ—and the self-emptying which makes the disciple one with Christ in His *kenōsis*—can be understood and has been understood in a very Zen-like sense as far as psychology and experience are concerned. (1968, 8)

He further explains how the *kenōsis* or self-emptyng of Christ described in Philippians 2:5–11 represents "a kenotic transformation, an emptying of all the contents of the ego-consciousness to become a void in which the light of

God or the glory of God . . . are manifested" (1968, 75). The kenotic self-emptying of Christ is in turn compared to Zen Buddhism wherein "the highest development of consciousness is that by which the individual ego is completely emptied and becomes identified with the enlightened Buddha" (1968, 76). For Merton, both the Christian *kenōsis* and Buddhist *śūnyatā* traditions represent the *via negativa* path of apophatic contemplation wherein the pleroma of fullness is realized by self-emptying into nothingness. The problem here is that Merton, like most others, interprets both Christian *kenōsis* and Buddhist *śūnyatā* in mystical terms as a form of absorptionism based upon an individualistic psychology. However, while this contemplative understanding of Christian *kenōsis* and Buddhist *śūnyatā* is profound it does not represent the final stage of self-emptying. My contention here is that in the Buddhist-Christian dialogue formulated by Nishida and the Kyoto school the kenotic self or emptied self is ultimately to be understood as the social self constituted by I-Thou relations in absolute Nothingness. The kenotic self is not to be understood simply in mystical terms as an introspective process of emptying the mind into an imageless void, but in social and moral terms as a process of emptying the self into relationships with others in the community. The social dimensions of Nishida's kenotic self theory is highlighted by the Christian-Buddhist dialogue of Ueda Shizuteru (1982), who employs the *Ten Oxherding Pictures* to illustrate how for both Zen and the *via negativa* Christian mysticism the ego undergoes death or negation in Nothingness at the eighth stage only to be resurrected as a relational self located in the *between* of I and Thou at the tenth and final stage. Nishitani Keiji further develops the social implication of this kenotic model of personhood through his notion of "making oneself into a nothingness in the service of all things" (*mizukara o mu ni shite arayuru mono ni tsukaeru koto*) (1961, 315; 1982, 285). In the thought of Tanabe Hajime the social and moral aspects of this kenotic self theory is brought to light with his argument that the self-negating love represented by God's *kenōsis*-exaltation pattern of Christian salvation corresponds to the Pure Land Buddhist idea of *ōsō-gensō*, or "going to" the Pure Land and then "returning to" the world from the Pure Land as a function of Love-qua-Nothingness. The Buddhist-Christian dialogue of Nishida and the Kyoto school thus rejects the substantialistic ideal of divine / human perfection as "self-sufficiency" for the ideal of "self-negation" as exemplified by the self-emptying compassion of a Bodhisattva in Buddhism and the self-emptying love of Jesus in Christianity. Hence, both the Buddhist *śūnyatā* and Christian *kenōsis* traditions have envisaged the ideal of human perfection as an act of pouring out the self for others.

## Nishida's Kenotic Model of Personhood as Self-Emptying Love

Nishida Kitarō, like others in the Kyoto school, continually resorts to negative expressions in order to articulate a Zen Buddhist theory of the true self as *muga* or "no-self" in the locus of absolute Nothingness, including "self-negation" (*jiko hitei*), "self-abandonment" (*jiko suteru*), "self-sacrifice" (*jiko gisei*), "self-emptying" (*jiko o munashiku shite*), "self-forgetting" (*jiko o wasureru*), "self-transcendence" (*jiko o koe*), and so forth. Hence, for Nishida and the Kyoto school, the "true self" of Zen Buddhism is to be understood as a function of self-negation in the locus of absolute Nothingness. In terms of Nishida paradoxical Zen logic of *soku/hi* or affirmation/negation, self-realization can only be achieved by an act of total self-negation. To illustrate this Zen logic of paradox Nishida and other Kyoto school thinkers often quote a famous verse from the *Genjōkōan* chapter of the *Shōbōgenzō* written by Zen master Dōgen, founder of the Sōtō sect of Zen Buddhism: "To study the way of the Buddha is to study the self, and to study the self is to forget the self; and to forget the self is to be enlightened by all things."

In one of his very earliest essays titled *"An Explanation of Beauty"* (*Bi no setsumei*, 1900), written eleven years before the publication of *An Inquiry into the Good* (1911), Nishida defines not only the experience of beauty, but also that of art, morality and religion as all based on the immediate experience of *muga* (Skt. *anātman*), a term with strong Zen Buddhist associations meaning no-self, selflessness, non-ego or ecstasy. He summarizes his views in the concluding passage of this essay, which I have elsewhere translated in full (see Nishida 1987), stating: "If I may summarize what has been said above, the feeling of beauty is the feeling of *muga* (no-self) . . . beauty can be explained as the discarding of the world of discrimination and the being one with the Great Way of *muga;* it therefore is really of the same kind as religion" (1987, 217). Nishida's conclusion in *"An Explanation of Beauty"* is that while art, religion, and morality differ by degree, thereby establishing a hierarchy of values, they all have their ultimate source in the experience of *muga*, "no-self."

Nishida's early concept of selfhood as *muga* or no-self, along with his value theory wherein art, morality, and religion are all analyzed as a function of self-negation, is subsequently developed in his maiden work *An Inquiry into the Good* (1911) in terms of his Jamesian notion of an egoless "pure experience" (*junsui keiken*) devoid of subject-object bifurcation and empty of all thought. For Nishida, pure experience is the original concrete whole in the flowing stream of consciousness from which the abstract individual and the subject-object distinction later emerge through mental reflection. As such, pure experience is essentially a positive description of *muga* or no-self. Even in the famous opening passage from *An Inquiry into the Good,* wherein Nishida defines his concept of a "pure experience" devoid of subject-object duality, he uses this characteristic language of self-negation, stating that pure experience means to "completely throw away the artifices of the self" (*mataku jiko no saiku o suteru*) (NKZ I, 9). In his book *Nishida Kitarō* (1991), Nishitani Keiji argues that the key to Nishida's entire theory of the person as "pure experience" lies precisely in this fundamental concept of self-negation: "Throughout *An Inquiry into the Good* phrases like 'abolishing the self,' 'doing away with the self,' 'forgetting the self,' and 'oblivious of oneself and things' appear again and again" (1991, 118). He cites Nishida's statement that "the true person appears where the [subject] self has been forgotten" (cited by Nishitani 1991, 122). Also, he points out that the basis for Nishida's Christian-Buddhist interfaith dialogue formulated in *An Inquiry into the Good* is grounded in this notion of a pure experience where the ego-self has been abolished. He again cites from Nishida's work: "The reason Sakyamuni and Christ still have the power to move people after thousands of years is that theirs was a highly objective spirit. Egoless persons, those who have abolished the self, are the greatest" (cited by Nishitani 1991, 94).

In his pivotal work *From the Acting to the Seeing* (*Hataraku mono kara miru mono e,* 1927), Nishida then introduces his new Zen Buddhist concept of *basho,* or *topos,* the "locus" of absolute Nothingness understood as the spatial horizon of disclosure wherein the "true self" is revealed as *muga* or no-self. Here Nishida makes explicit an idea present in his thought since the outset, that the true self is the no-self, selfless self, or emptied self of absolute Nothingness, a self-identity of absolute contradictions wherein self-affirmation is only achieved through self-negation. Nishida's continual reworking of this theme finally culminates in his penultimate essay, "The Logic of Place and a Religious Worldview" (*Bashoteki ronri to shūkyōteki sekaikan,* 1945), wherein he now develops an existential philosophy of religion based upon the self-negation of both God and self in the locus of Nothingness. For Nishida, self-negation is the fundamental concept of all religion.

It is precisely in the context of developing an existential philosophy of religion based on the concept of "self-negation" (*jiko hitei*) that Nishida (NKZ XI, 399) goes on to introduce his Christian-Buddhist interfaith dialogue rooted in parallels between the Christian idea of *kenōsis* or "self-emptying" and Buddhist *śūnyatā* (J. *kū*), "emptiness." For both the Christian *kenōsis* and Buddhist *śūnyatā* traditions, religious salvation is conceived as a function of complete self-negation. Just as for Christianity human/divine perfection is attained through *kenōsis* or self-emptying love, in Zen Buddhism it is achieved through *śūnyatā*, self-negating compassion. According to Nishida, both the Christian *kenōsis* and Buddhist *śūnyatā* traditions articulate the ultimate paradox of religious salvation whereby self-realization is achieved only through the act of complete self-negation. For both the Christian *kenōsis* and Buddhist *śūnyatā* traditions, salvation is attained by realizing the contradictory nature of the self wherein to be empty is to be full, just as to be poor is to be rich, to humble oneself is to exalt oneself, to abandon the self is to find the self, and to give up one's life for God is to save it. He argues that in Buddhism this paradox of salvation is expressed through the Zen logic of *soku/hi* meaning "is/is not" or "affirmation/negation." Nishida illustrates this paradoxical Zen logic of *soku/hi* with a famous verse from the *Diamond Sutra* which propounds: "Because there is no Buddha, there is Buddha, and because there are not sentient beings, there are sentient beings" (NKZ XI, 398–99). Shortly thereafter Nishida goes on to develop the Christian variant of his paradoxical logic of absolute Nothingness. It is at this point in this text where Nishida first makes an explicit reference to the Christian idea of the divine *kenōsis* or self-emptying of God:

> A God who is simply self-sufficient is not the true God. In one aspect God must empty Himself through *kenōsis*. A God that is both thoroughly transcendent and thoroughly immanent, both thoroughly immanent and thoroughly transcendent, is a truly dialectical God. If it is said that God has created the world from love, then God's absolute love must be essential to the absolute self-negation of God and is not *opus ad extra*. (NKZ XI, 399)

In this passage Nishida emphasizes that a merely transcendent and self-sufficient God is not truly God; for God is only God when in one aspect He "empties Himself" through *agape* or self-giving love, thereby pouring out his total transcendence into total immanence in the bottomless depths of absolute Nothingness. The *kenōsis* or self-emptying love of God thus functions to establish a paradoxical identity of transcendence and immanence, or what Nishida otherwise refers to as the doctrine "immanent transcendence" (*naizaiteki chōetsu*). Divine/human perfection is now conceived, not in terms of the Aristotelian/Scholastic ideal of "self-sufficiency," but in terms of the *kenōsis/śūnyatā* ideal of "self-emptying." Moreover, just as God must "empty Himself" out of *agape* in the act of creation, so the self attains salvation through *kenōsis* or self-emptying love. In this context Nishida once again takes up his recurrent theme of I and Thou. In the *topos* of absolute Nothingness the true self is related to other selves, to nature, and to God as an I in relation to a Thou or absolute Other as an expression of *agape,* divine love. The kenotic ideal of an "emptied self" or "selfless self" is therefore ultimately to be regarded in moral terms as a social self constituted by an I-Thou dialectic of intersubjectivity.

## Ueda Shizuteru

In his essay "Emptiness and Fullness: Śūnyatā in Mahāyāna Buddhism" (1982), Ueda Shizuteru of the Kyoto school employs the *Ten Oxherding Pictures* in order to illustrate the Zen process of becoming a person, arguing that the tenth and final picture represents the level of a compassionate Bodhisattva existing in the *between* of I and Thou at the standpoint of absolute Nothingness. In another essay titled "'Nothingness' in Meister Eckhart and Zen Buddhism" (1982, 162–63), Ueda again uses the *Ten Oxherding Pictures* to clarify the Zen concept of selfhood as an I-Thou relationship, now with the aim of establishing the basis for a Christian-Buddhist interfaith dialogue. Describing the selfless self of absolute Nothingness depicted by this last diagram of the Zen oxherding series, he writes, "there appears the selfless self, which by its very selflessness, takes the hyphenated 'between' of the I-Thou, as its own existential inner realm of activity" (1982, 162). In this context he adds: "The self, cut open and disclosed through absolute nothingness, unfolds itself as the 'between.' I am 'I and Thou,' and 'I and Thou' are I. What we have here is the self seen as a double self grounded on selflessness in nothingness." (1982, 162–63)

According to Ueda, the last diagram in the *Ten Oxherding Pictures* illustrating the breakthrough to an I-Thou relational self of absolute Nothingness in Zen Buddhism also has its counterpart in the kenotic tradition of *via negativa* Christian apophatic mysticism represented by Meister Eckhart. For Ueda, the spiritual kinship between Zen Buddhism and the Christian mysticism of Meister Eckhart appears when the latter speaks of a "breakthrough to the nothingness of the godhead" (cited by Ueda 1982, 158). Moreover, he asserts that "Eckhart's thought exhibits a gradual ascent to this nothingness of the godhead" (1982, 158). The highest stage of this process of self-emptying into the Nothingness of godhead is then described by Ueda as follows:

Eckhart links this "beyond" in the "godless" life directly to the *vita activa* of the everyday reality of the world. In unison with the movement "away from God to the nothingness of the godhead" goes a movement "away from God to the reality of the world." . . . He points the way to overcoming the *unio mystica* and to arriving at a non-religious religiosity. (1982, 159)

Hence, like the Zen Buddhist process of becoming a person as illustrated by the *Ten Oxherding Pictures,* Eckhart describes the Christian kenotic practice of self-emptying as a developmental process which occurs in a hierarchy of stages, at last culminating in a breakthrough to the godhead of Nothingness beyond the transcendent God. However, for Ueda the most significant aspect of this parallel between Zen and the *via negativa* Christian mysticism of Eckhart is that both involve a "non-religious religiosity" through a dialectical negation of holiness which emphasizes that the breakthrough to absolute Nothingness of the godhead beyond God itself designates a return to the everyday social world of relationships between I and Thou.

## Nishitani Keiji

In his work *Shūkyō to wa nanika* (What is Religion?, 1961), now translated into English under the title *Religion and Nothingness* (1982), Nishitani Keiji (1900–91) further develops Nishida's kenotic model of personhood as an emptied self or selfless self of absolute Nothingness. The innovation of Nishitani's work is that he applies the *kenōsis/śūnyatā* motif toward the end of overcoming the problem of *nihilism* as described especially by Nietzsche and Heidegger in Western existentialism. For Nishitani, the problem of nihilism can only be overcome by shifting from the "self-centered" mode of existence as represented by egocentrism or theocentrism toward the standpoint of "self-emptying" as represented by both the Christian *kenōsis* and Buddhist *śūnyatā* traditions. Nishitani's general strategy for overcoming nihilism is worked out in terms of Nishida's Zen Buddhist logic of Nothingness as a threefold emptying process which moves from Being to relative Nothingness to absolute Nothingness. While Sartre develops the relationship between the human self and the category of the nothing, he sets up a dualism of Being versus Nothingness, and so is still at the level of relative Nothingness. Nietzsche's idea of the overman who endures the nihility without God, and Heidegger's idea of man as being "held out suspended in nothing," both develop a more positive concept of Nothingness wherein Being and Nothing are the same. In this way both Nietzsche and Heidegger move closer to the Zen standpoint of *śūnyatā* developed in positive terms as the boundless openness of an absolute Nothingness wherein emptiness is fullness and fullness is emptiness. However, for Nishitani, as for Nishida, the Zen standpoint of emptiness or absolute Nothingness is most closely approximated by the Christian idea of *kenōsis*, "self-emptying" or "making oneself nothing." According to Nishitani, nihility (*kyomu*), or relative Nothingness, can only be overcome by being radicalized to Emptiness, or absolute Nothingness, as is realized by the Christian *kenōsis* tradition on the one side and the Buddhist *śūnyatā* tradition on the other. The isolated ego-self reified at the eternalistic standpoint of Being (*u*) is emptied into a void of *muga* or no-self at the nihilistic standpoint of relative Nothingness (*sōtaiteki mu*), finally being emptied out for the sake of others at the middle way standpoint of absolute Nothingness (*zettaiteki mu*), the boundless openness wherein emptiness is fullness and fullness is emptiness so that all things are affirmed in their particular suchness.

Nishitani develops the Christian idea of *kenōsis* as self-emptying out of *agape* or non-discriminating love from the standpoint of a Buddhist metaphysic of absolute Nothingness, with its correlate principles of emptiness (*kū*), non-ego (*muga*) and compassion (*jihi*). He argues that both the Christian *kenōsis* and Buddhist *śūnyatā* traditions conceive of divine perfection as consisting of self-emptying and ego-negating love. This is summarized when he writes. "[T]hroughout the basic thought of Buddhology, especially in the Mahāyāna tradition, the concepts of emptiness, compassion and non-ego are seen to be inseparably connected. The Buddhist way of life as well as its way of thought are permeated with *kenōsis* and *ekkenōsis*" (1982, 288 fn.). Nishitani's most sustained treatment of the *kenōsis*/*śūnyatā* motif is in the second chapter of *Religion and Nothingness* entitled "The Impersonal and the Personal in Religion." Here Nishitani introduces the concept of *kenōsis* in the context of analyzing the Christian idea of *agape* or non-discriminating love expressed in Matthew 5:43–48.

> What is it like, this nondifferentiating love, this *agape*, that loves even enemies? In a word, it is "making oneself empty." In the case of Christ, it meant taking the form of a man and becoming a servant, in accordance with the will of God, who is the origin of the *ekkenōsis* or "making himself empty" of Christ. . . . What is *ekkenōsis* for the Son is *kenōsis* for the father. In the East, this would be called *anātman*, or non-ego. (1982, 60; 1961, 69)

In this passage Nishitani seeks to define the Christian idea of divine perfection in terms of the Greek notion of *kenōsis*, which he translates into Japanese as *onore o munashiku suru koto*, "making oneself empty" (1961, 69). This divine perfection of *kenōsis* is then equated with the Greek ideal of *agape*, which he defines in Japanese as *musabetsu no ai*, "non-discriminating love" (1961, 69). In this context Nishitani establishes his doctrine according to which the *ekkenōsis* of Christ has its source in the original *kenōsis* of God. His polemic here is that although self-emptying out of non-discriminating love is the fundamental characteristic of divine perfection, *kenōsis* or the condition of being self-emptied is essentially entailed from the beginning in the idea of the perfection of God, while *ekkenōsis* or the activity of self-emptying love as typified by Christ and commanded of man is the embodiment of that perfection. Just as the self-emptying compassion of Buddha rooted in the original emptiness and non-ego of the Buddha-nature is the paradigm for enlightenment in Buddhism, the *ekkenōsis* or self-emptying love of Christ based on the original *kenōsis* of God is the model of salvation in Christianity. He asserts that the self-emptying of Christ has its source in the original self-emptying of God in order to underscore the fact that *kenōsis* is ontological in nature. Not only Christ but the aboriginal God is kenotic in Nishitani's view. The *ekkenōsis* or self-emptying of Christ is a revelation of the divine *kenōsis* of God himself, just as the self-emptying of Buddha is a disclosure of the emptiness, compassion, and non-ego of the Buddha-nature. Nishitani thus goes on identify the Christian idea of *kenōsis/ekkenōsis* with the Buddhist notion of *anātman* (J. *muga*), or non-ego, which in Mahāyāna Buddhist philosophy is equated with *śūnyatā* (*kū*), emptiness. Moreover, he correlates Christian *kenōsis* and *agape* with Buddhist emptiness, non-ego and compassion in the context of developing his notion of "impersonal personality" or "personal impersonality." Nishitani's idea of self-emptying as impersonal personality is meant to function as a corrective both to the "impersonalism" of traditional Buddhist *anātman* or "no-self" theory as well as the "personalism" of traditional Christianity.

Nishitani concludes his book with a discussion of the kenotic motif in relation to his notion of the standpoint of *śūnyatā* as a field of relationships wherein "the self serves others and makes itself a nothingness" (*jiko o mu ni shite ta ni hoshisuru*) (1961, 313; 1982, 284). In this field of relationships which opens up at the standpoint of *śūnyatā*, true freedom is achieved through a complete liberation from all "self-centered" (*jiko chūshinteki*) modes of being, which is itself realized by "making oneself into a nothingness in the service of all things" (*mizukara o mu ni shite arayuru mono ni tsukaeru koto*) (1961, 315; 1982, 285). Both the transcendent God of theocentrism and the private subject of egocentrism are emptied out into a field of relationships with others in the locus of Nothingness. In the final analysis Nishitani finds the ultimate meaning of Buddhist *śūnyatā* and Christian *kenōsis* in this fundamental notion of "making oneself into a nothingness in the service of all things." Hence, for Nishitani both the Buddhist *śūnyatā* and Christian *kenōsis* traditions culminate in the ideal of human perfection as self-emptying love—the pouring out of self for others.

## Abe Masao

Abe Masao's famous essay on "Kenotic God and Dynamic Sunyata" now included in a volume called *The Emptying God* (1990) with theological responses and a rejoinder, has stimulated much discussion and debate in the area of Buddhist-Christian interfaith dialogue. Following Nishida and Nishitani, Abe maintains that the Christian idea of a kenotic God is the functional equivalent to the Zen Buddhist notion of *śūnyatā*, which he translates in the verb form of "self-emptying" instead of the noun form of emptiness. In his analysis of the kenotic God he begins his discussion with a direct reference to the *kenōsis* hymn from Paul's Epistle to the Philippians (2: 5–8):

> Have this mind in you, which was also in Christ Jesus, who, existing in the form of God, counted not the being on an equality with God a thing to be grasped, but emptied himself, taking the form of a servant, being made in the likeness of man; and being found in fashion as a man, he humbled himself, becoming obedient even unto death, yea, the death of the cross. (cited by Abe 1990, 9)

He goes on to provide a Zen Buddhist interpretation of this passage which underscores that the *kenōsis* of Christ is rooted in the *kenōsis* of God, so that the self-emptying of the Son of God is an ontological revelation of the self-emptying of God the Father. From the standpoint of a Zen Buddhist paradoxical logic of *soku/hi* or "is/is not" he then formulates the concept of contradictory self-identity implied by *kenōsis* or self-emptying in relation to God as well to both Christ and the human self. First, God is not God because he negates or empties himself into otherness out of love; precisely because he is not God he is God because his nature is self-emptying love (1990, 16). Next, the Son of God is not the Son of God for he is essentially self-emptying; precisely because he is not the Son of God he is the Son of God, for he works as Christ in his salvational function of self-emptying (1990, 12). And in relation to the human self, he likewise asserts: "Self is not self (for the old self must be crucified with Christ); precisely because it is not, self is truly self (for the new self resurrects with Christ)" (1990, 12). In this way Abe employs the Zen logic of contradictory self-identity to express the Christian paradox of salvation whereby self-realization is a function of self-negation, self-fulfillment is a function of self-emptying, and self-exaltation is a function of self-abasement.

In his treatment of Zen Buddhism, Abe emphasizes that the true self of Zen Buddhism is dynamic *śūnyatā*: "That is to say, true Sunyata is nothing but the true self and the true self is nothing but true Sunyata" (1990, 28). Insofar as dynamic Sunyata is the Buddhist correlate to the kenotic God of Christianity, Abe (1990, 29–32) then goes on to enumerate 5 points summarizing the positive meanings of what he calls dynamic Sunyata: (1) First, in Sunyata, everything is realized as it is in its *suchness* or "is-ness"; (2) Sunyata is *boundless openness* without any fixed "center," including egocentrism, anthropocentrism, theocentrism and cosmocentrism; (3) Sunyata is *jinen* meaning "things as they are," "spontaneity," or "naturalness"; (4) Sunyata is interdependence and interpenetration of all events; and (5) Sunyata contains the two characteristics of wisdom and compassion. All of this is summarized by saying that true Sunyata is not static but *dynamic*, an unceasing function of self-emptying, making self and others manifest their suchness (1990, 60). It is the compassionate aspect of Sunyata which establishes its function of dynamic self-emptying (1990, 59). Through the aspect of compassion Sunyata completely empties everything, including itself (1990, 26). Abe concludes that when we realize the kenotic God of Christianity and dynamic Sunyata of Zen Buddhism we discover a common basis at a deeper dimension without eliminating the distinctiveness of each religion (1990, 61).

While Abe's analysis of both the kenotic God and dynamic Sunyata functions to illuminate many aspects of the Christian-Buddhist dialogue, it does not make fully explicit the notion that the kenotic self is the social self. Yet this idea is there by implication in that both kenotic God and dynamic Sunyata represent a ceaseless process of self-emptying into otherness out of compassion. Also, in that dynamic Sunyata is a boundless openness free of all fixed metaphysical centers it deconstructs both the self-centered standpoint of egocentrism and the God-centered standpoint of theocentrism. In its aspect of interdependence and interpenetration the self-emptying function of dynamic Sunyata establishes the interrelatedness of all persons and events. As Abe states in his essay, "the freedom of the Buddhist is found in the awakening to the nonsubstantiality and the interdependence of everything in the universe" (1990, 31). Abe thus make clear the positive aspects of dynamic Sunyata as the boundless openness of absolute Nothingness wherein emptiness is fullness and fullness is emptiness, thereby to provide a standpoint to overcome the problem of nihilism and other religion-negating ideologies prevailing in contemporary society.

Katherine Keller's powerful feminist process critique of Abe's essay contained in the same volume titled *The Emptying God* (1990, 102–15) serves to clarify the need to make further explicit the social or relational aspects of his kenotic theory of Zen selfhood as dynamic self-emptying. Keller holds that the common denominator of both Christian *kenōsis* and Buddhist *śūnyatā* is their patriarchalism. She affirms that Abe's reading of Biblical *kenōsis* (Phil. 2: 5–11) in terms of *agape* and his focus on the self-sacrificing, self-humbling, and obedient aspects of *agape* is continuous with the heritage of Christian hermeneutics, and that the text itself unfolds the meaning or Christ's incarnational self-emptying in terms of the motifs of servanthood, self-humbling, and obedience unto death (1990, 105). But Keller then points out the oppressive use of the Christian rhetoric of self-sacrifice and humble service to keep women in their place (1990, 105). In a social situation of women's subordination, when the male preachers exhort the predominantly female flock to deny themselves by practicing obedience, self-abasement, and kenotic humility, they reinforce woman's already unhealthy lack of selfhood as well as their dependency on men for their own identity. Keller holds that while men err in the direction of a "separative self" or masculine ego which is cut off from relationships, women err in the opposite and complementary direction of a "soluble self" which dissolves into its feelings and relationships. The call to agapic self-sacrifice may provide the corrective to the masculine ego; but women sin in the reverse direction—the underdevelopment of the self. If the "separate self" of men is in need of kenotic self-emptying, the "soluble self" of women instead requires self-development. Women need to have a self before they can empty it. She therefore cites a feminist dictum set down in capital letters: SELF-DEVELOPMENT IS A HIGHER DUTY THAN SELF-SACRIFICE (1990, 105).

As for the juxtaposition of Christian *kenōsis* with Buddhist *śūnyatā*, Keller asserts: "I fear that Masao Abe's coupling of Christian self-sacrifice with the Buddhist *anatta* [no-self] attenuates the problem. Will the Christian-Buddhist dialogue offer the worst of both worlds to women?" (1990, 106). For Keller the Buddhist self-awakening to the interdependence of everything in the universe can add to the feminist effort to develop an ontology of relationships and a relational concept of self. However, she argues that while the Buddhist metaphysic elucidates the relational interdependency of the self, there are tensions between the feminist pursuit of a relational self and the Buddhist pursuit of a nonself whose relationality discloses its emptiness of any own-being (1990, 107). Whereas for Buddhism interdependency functions as a radically deconstructive analysis, for feminism it functions as the basis for a reconstructive vision. Thus, in her book *From a Broken Web* (1986) Keller elaborates a systematic feminist ontology of relationships and a feminist view of relational selfhood based on the tradition of American process cosmology including William James, G. H. Mead, and especially A. N. Whitehead.

## Tanabe Hajime

Tanabe Hajime (1885–1962) became Nishida Kitarō's most famous successor to the chair of philosophy at Kyoto University. Like Nishida Kitarō, Nishitani Keiji, Abe Masao, and other Kyoto school thinkers, Tanabe has explicitly discussed the relation of Christian *kenōsis* to a Japanese Buddhist philosophy of emptiness or absolute Nothingness. However, whereas Nishida, Nishitani and Abe generally write from the *jiriki* or "self-power" standpoint of Zen Buddhism, Tanabe, like Takeuchi Yoshinori, writes from the *tariki* or "Other-power" standpoint of Jōdo-Shinshū, the True Pure Land sect of Japanese Buddhism founded by Shinran (1173–1262). Tanabe follows traditional Japanese Buddhism as well as the modern Japanese philosophy of Nishida Kitarō and the Kyoto school in characterizing both the self and ultimate reality as "absolute Nothingness." However, against Zen Buddhism and the philosophy of Nishida, Tanabe argues that absolute Nothingness can never be immediately grasped in a pure experience through the *jiriki* or "self-power" activity of intuitive contemplation, but instead asserts that true absolute Nothingness is the transcendent ground of a transformative grace that breaks in upon the self from without as *tariki* or "Other-power."

At the outset of *Philosophy as Metanoetics*, Tanabe introduces "metanoetics" (*zangedō*) or metanoesis (*zange*) as the master concept of his philosophical system. By the term "metanoesis" Tanabe means the salvific experience of repentance, conversion, awakening, and transformation through faith in the grace of absolute "Other-power." Repentance is the negative aspect of *zange* which signifies the moment of death or self-negation, while conversion is the positive aspect of *zange* which designates the moment of resurrection or self-affirmation. The repentance of *zange* involves an existential encounter with the evil and sin which negates the ego's right to exist at its very core, leading to metanoia as a discipline of death that lets go of the self. Yet, this experience of complete self-negation which arises in the negative aspect of *zange* as repentance is itself followed by its positive aspect as conversion or awakening, wherein the ego is brought by the transformative grace of absolute Other-power to undergo total death-and-resurrection in order to be restored to its real yet nonsubstantial existence as "Being-qua-Nothingness" (*u-soku-mu*), or what he also terms "emptied being" (*kū-u*). Hence, for Tanabe, as for Nishida, the transformation and enlightenment of metanoesis is achieved through a kenotic act of self-emptying into absolute Nothingness. However, while Nishida sees the self-emptying of Christian *kenōsis* and Buddhist *śūnyatā* in terms of the Zen notion of *jiriki* or self-power, Tanabe views the act of self-emptying as being prompted from without by the transformative grace of *tariki*, absolute Other-power. That is to say, while for Nishida the kenotic act of self-emptying into Nothingness is a function of intuitive contemplation grounded in the will, for Tanabe the act of making oneself nothing is a function of existential faith grounded in the operation of divine grace.

Tanabe continuously underscores the moral-social dimensions of metanoetics through his use of the two Pure Land Buddhist categories of *ōsō* or "going toward" the Pure Land, and *gensō*, "returning to" the world from the Pure Land. Tanabe's polemic here is that while Zen Buddhism, Nishida philosophy, and other forms of ordinary mysticism based on intuitive contemplation emphasize *ōsō* or the aspect of "going toward" the Pure Land, his own philosophy of metanoetics follows the True Pure Land Buddhism of Shinran in focusing upon the aspect of *gensō*, "returning to" this world from the Pure Land as a result of the self-negating function of *mu-soku-ai* or Love-qua-Nothingness (PM 3). It is precisely this doctrine of *gensō* or "returning to" this world from the Pure Land as a result of the self-negating function of Love-qua-Nothingness which ultimately establishes the social and moral dimensions in Tanabe's philosophy of metanoetics. Hence, Tanabe argues that his philosophy of metanoetics based upon the Buddhist idea of absolute Nothingness is the basis for a new social philosophy. In Tanabe's words:

> With the development of the Bodhisattva-ideal in the Mahayana-tradition, Buddhism developed the ideal of "benefiting oneself-*qua*-benefiting-others." This evolution culminates in the Shin doctrine of *gensō*. Strange as it may seem, this process is but the natural unfolding of the essential Buddhist teaching of *muga*—that there is no self or ego in all reality—which is the principle of absolute nothingness . . . Under the guidance of Shinran's attitude of total *zange*, metanoetics is thus able to develop a social doctrine inaccessible by way of Western philosophy alone.' (PM, 270)

Tanabe uses a dialectical logic of "absolute mediative self-negation" (*zettai baikaiteki jiko-hiteisei*) in order to reinterpret Christianity's mythologized conception of a personal God as well as the Buddhist notion of of Amida Buddha and the Pure Land in terms of his own Buddhist principle of Love-qua-Nothingness. It is in this context that he first brings under consideration the Christian idea of divine *kenōsis* as it relates to the self-negating operation of love implied by Amida's Original Vow. Tanabe's explicit discussion of the *kenōsis/śūnyatā* motif is to be found in his essay titled "Christianity, Marxism, and Japanese Buddhism" which was added as an appendix to his work *The Dialectic of Christianity* (*Kirisutokyō no benshōhō*, 1948; see *Tanabe Hajime zenshū*, 1963, Vol. 10, 300–1). Tanabe describes religious self-awareness as a Love-qua-Nothingness expressed in both the *ōsō-gensō* Pure Land myth of the Bodhisattva, as well as the Christian myth of the *kenōsis* or self-emptying of God in Christ. The dialectical pattern in both of these myths is that of descent and reascent, self-negation and self-affirmation, death and resurrection, or *kenōsis* and exaltation. The True Pure Land Buddhist mythological teachings are transformed into logical teachings as the reciprocal mediation of *ōsō* and *gensō*. In this way Amida's Original Vow can be understood as saving all sentient being through the self-negating compassion of "Love-qua-Nothingness" (*mu soku ai*), which corresponds to God's *kenōsis* or self-emptying love in Christ. What is significant here is that Tanabe relates the *kenōsis* of God in Christ not to the *jiriki* or self-power teachings of Zen, but to the *tariki* or Other-power teachings of the True Pure Land sect of Japanese Buddhism founded by Shinran. The self-emptying love through which Christ descends to save the world corresponds to the self-negating compassion and grace expressed by Amida's Original Vow (*hongan*), whereby he descends from the Pure Land to save all sentient beings in the realm of samsara. In other words, the self-negating love typified by God's *kenōsis*- exaltation pattern of Christian salvation corresponds to the Pure Land Buddhist idea of *ōsō-genso*, or "going to" the Pure Land and then "returning to" the world from the Pure Land out of Love-qua-Nothingness. Moreover, human salvation is also to be conceived through the *kenōsis* -exaltation pattern whereby the moment of death and self-negation is followed by resurrection as "emptied being" (*kū-u*) or Being-qua-Nothingness (*u-soku-mu*). But again, unlike the Zen Buddhist model of personhood adopted by Nishida and his followers wherein *kenōsis* is achieved through "self-power" (*jiriki*) techniques of meditation on absolute Nothingness as a function of will, the Pure Land Buddhist model of Tanabe Hajime instead regards the salvific act of kenotic self-negation into Being-qua-Nothingness as arising through the divine grace of absolute Other-power (*tariki*) which breaks upon the self from without by the existential operation of passionate inward subjective faith.

## Mutō Kazuo

Mutō Kazuo is another recent Japanese thinker who has set forth a kenotic model of personhood as self-emptying love which combines elements of both the Zen Buddhist thought of Nishida Kitarō and Nishitani Keiji with the Pure Land Buddhist thought of Tanabe Hajime. However, while Nishida, Nishitani, and Tanabe are writing as philosophers based more in the tradition of Japanese Buddhism, Mutō is a Protestant minister writing from the standpoint of Christian theology. Mutō develops the self-emptying motif as an intercultural theme for comparative philosophy of religion and Buddhist-Christian dialogue especially in chapter 2 entitled "Christianity and the Idea of Nothingness" of *New Possibilities in the Philosophy of Religion* (*Shūkyō tetsugaku no atarashii kanōsei*, 1974). He writes:

> Various points about the idea of Nothingness (*mu*) in Christianity have thus far been considered. Moreover, I think one should pay attention to two or three points concerning this problem, mainly based on the New Testament. I need not say but self-sacrifice and self-negation are included in the love called *agape*. . . . In the New Testament it says "Love your enemies as yourself" (Mark 22:39) but in order to "Love your neighbor like yourself," on the other side, means paradoxically that you must abandon the self. Therefore, the operation of that kind of love is something which means the operation of Nothingness that empties the self and transcends the self. (1974, 51)

In this passage, as elsewhere throughout his essay, Mutō describes Christian *agape* in such negative terms as "self-sacrifice" (*jiko gisei*), "self-negation" (*jiko hitei*), "self-abandonment" (*jiko o suteru*), "self-emptying" (*jiko o munashiku*), and "self-transcendence" (*jiko o koe*). Moreover, following the thought of Nishida Kitarō, Nishitani Keiji, and Tanabe Hajime, he emphasizes that the self-emptying love of *agape* must be understood in Buddhist terms as the function of *mu*, Nothingness. He thus adds:

> Love must be the making empty and the negation of the self-centered ego. In other words, love must be to surrender body and mind to the

function of Nothingness (*mu*), which makes love be self-effacing. Love of one's neighbor is the realization of the love of God as "Love-qua-Nothingness" by turning the self toward others. (1974, 51)

Mutō argues that the basic function of Christian *agape* as described in the New Testament teachings concering "love of one's neighbor" is that of a "making empty" (*kūka*) and "negation" (*hitei*) of the self-centered ego. Again, he asserts that the self-negating and self-emptying function of Christian *agape* corresponds to the operation of Buddhist *mu* or Nothingness. In this context he goes on to specifically relate the self-negating and self-emptying function of Christian *agape* or divine love to Tanabe Hajime's fundamental Buddhist idea of "Love-qua-Nothingness" (*mu-soku-ai*) as developed in *Philosophy as Metanoetics* and other major works. For Mutō, as for Tanabe, the notion of "Love-qua-Nothingness" functions to underscore the social and moral dimensions of self-emptying love as an act of "turning the self toward others."

Although Mutō argues that Tanabe's idea of Love-qua-Nothingness is illustrated by the self-negating love of *agape* as found in various passages of the New Testament, above all else, he holds that it manifested in the *kenōsis* hymn in Paul's Letter to the Philippians. That is to say, the divine *kenōsis* whereby Christ "made himself empty" or "made himself nothing" out of *agape* as self-negating love directly corresponds to Tanabe's key notion of Love-qua-Nothingness, which in classical Mahāyāna Buddhist terms signifies the "indivisibility of emptiness and compassion" (*śūnyatā-karunā-bhinnam*). In Mutō's words: "However, the character of the love of God as 'Love-qua-Nothingness' is best exhibited by Phil 2:6–11" (1974, 51). He adds:

> Therefore, the self-identity of Christ's divine nature can exist by self-abandonment as an emptying or negation, or as it were, as "Being-qua-Nothingness." Moreover, the *kenōsis* whereby he "emptied himself into the form of a servant" includes *tapeinōsis*, or humility, that is, "making himself lowly." . . . The life of Christ is the way of the cross (*via crucis*) as the manifestation of Love-qua-Nothingness as an expression of *tapeinōsis*. (1974, 53)

As Mutō shows in this passage, the self-identity of Christ's divine nature must be understood in paradoxical terms as "Being-qua-Nothingness" (*mu-soku-u*), since it is a self-identity constituted precisely by a kenotic act of self-emptying or self-negation. The *kenōsis* whereby Christ emptied himself into the form of a servant furthermore includes within itself the idea of *tapeinōsis*, humility, or "making oneself lowly" (*jiko o hiku suru koto*). For Mutō, Christ's life of *kenōsis, agape,* and *tapeinōsis* as a *via crucis* or way of the cross is itself the supreme expression of Buddhist Love-qua-Nothingness. It is this "making oneself nothing" and "making oneself lowly" out of self-negating love whereby Jesus emptied himself into the servant form for the sake of others. From the Buddhist standpoint of Love-qua-Nothingness, then, Christian *kenōsis, agape,* and *tapeinōsis* altogether designate a radical conversion from egocentric existence rooted in self-centeredness to that of an existence-for-others based on divine self-emptying.

## Japanese Kenoticism

The kenotic model of selfhood developed by Nishida and the Kyoto school has many points in common with what has been called the "new kenoticism" of Anglican theology as articulated by Bishop Robinson in *Honest to God* (1963). The fundamental idea which Robinson's kenotic theory brings into question throughout *Honest to God* is that of a transcendent God who is literally "up there" or "out there." In this context he states his intention to apply Bultmann's program of "demythologizing" to the whole question of a God "out there" so as to abandon the entire conception of a supernatural order (1963, 24). Toward this end Robinson utilizes elements from the critique of "transcendence" developed in the kenotic theories of both Tillich and Bonhoeffer. In this treatment of Tillich he underscores the former's notion that God is not a projection "out there," a transcendent Other beyond the skies, but the depth and ground of our very existence. He describes Tillich's view that it is because Jesus completely emptied himself or made himself nothing that he was able to become transparent to the depth and ground of Being-itself and thereby become a bearer of final revelation (1963, 73). Robinson further argues that it was toward some such form of kenotic Christology which Bonhoeffer was working in his "Outline for a Book" in *Letters and Papers from Prison.* Bonhoeffer's idea of "religionless Christianity" based on a secular understanding of transcendence takes on a profound social and ethical character as summarized by his idea of Jesus as the "man for others" (cited by Robinson 1963, 76). In Bonhoeffer's words: "This concern of Jesus for others is the experience of transcendence" (cited by Robinson 1963, 76). According to Bonhoeffer, our relation to God is not a relationship to a supreme Being, which is a false concept of transcendence, but a new life for others.

There are several points at which the "new kenoticism" described by Robinson provides a key to understanding the East-West encounter theology of Nishida and the Kyoto school based on the *kenōsis/śūnyatā* model of personhood as self-emptying love. To begin with, *kenōsis* does not signify a mere "self-concealing" (*krypsis*) of the glory of God in the person of Jesus as is held by the medieval patristic theory of *occultatio Dei*, nor is it a mere "self-divesting" (*Selbstentaeusserung*) of divine attributes to make the Incarnation possible as said by Thomasius and the ninteenth-century German theologians, but a real and literal "self-emptying" out of agapic love. The new kenoticism rejects those negative interpretations of *kenōsis* in older kenotic theories as a concealment, limitation, or reduction of the divine nature and instead emphasizes a positive understanding of the concept whereby *kenōsis* or self-emptying is *plerōsis*, self-fulfillment. Just as for the new kenoticism it is said that *kenōsis* = *plerōsis* and *plerōsis* = *kenōsis*, for Nishida and the Kyoto school *kenōsis* is interpreted in positive terms as Buddhist *śūnyatā*, the boundless openness of absolute Nothingness wherein emptiness is fullness and fullness is emptiness. Moreover, the new kenoticism of Robinson is based on a synthesis of Tillich's view of transcendence as the depth and ground of human existence and Bonhoeffer's idea of transcendence as "existence for others" through participation in the life of Christ as the "man for others." Similarly, in the kenotic self theory of Nishida and the Kyoto school, transcendence goes not in the direction of an other-worldly beyond but in the direction of bottomless depths—what Nishida calls "immanent transcendence" (*naizaiteki chōetsu*). Or in the words of Nishitani, there is not a transcendence on the yonder shore of the far side, but a transcendence on the hither shore of the *this* side. Hence, like the new kenoticism of recent Western theology, the Japanese kenoticism of Nishida and the Kyoto school is characterized by a reinterpretation of achieving divine transcendence through self-emptying love, first in existential-ontological terms as signifying the "depths" of life in the everyday world, and second, in social-moral terms as denoting a new life of "existence-for-others."

In the Western tradition of theology the concept of *kenōsis* understood as "self-emptying" or "making oneself nothing" has always conflicted with the ancient Greek substance metaphysics of self-sufficient Being which came to support the Christian faith through a Hellenization of the Gospels. However, I would argue that this reinterpretion of Christian *kenōsis* from the standpoint of Buddhism represents a whole new phase in the history of kenotic theology. Just as historians of Christianity speak of different phases in the development of kenotic theology, including German, British, and Russian kenoticism, or the "new kenoticism" of Bishop Robinson and the Anglicans, we might now speak of a "Japanese kenoticism," characterized by the effort to reinterpret Christian *kenōsis* in terms of Buddhist *śūnyatā* (J. *kū*), empti-

ness of self. This parallel between the Christian *kenōsis* and Buddhist *śūnyatā*
traditions was initially worked out by the founder of modern Japanese philosophy, Nishida Kitarō. It is probably Nishida's introduction of the *kenōsis/
śūnyatā* or "self-emptying" motif as a basis for Buddhist-Christian interfaith
dialogue and East-West encounter theology which will remain his most lasting contribution to speculative thought. The kenotic self theory worked out
by Nishida and other modern Japanese thinkers opens up new directions for
theology by reformulating the Christian ideas of *kenōsis* (self-empying) and
*agape* (self-giving love) in terms of a Buddhist metaphysics of *mu* or Nothingness, with its correlate principles of emptiness of self (*kū*), non-ego (*muga*),
compassion (*jihi*), and interrelational existence (*engi*). Generally speaking,
the kenotic model of self formulated by the Kyoto school rejects any
substantialistic notion of an independent ego based on self-centered or self-
sufficient existence for that of a social, relational, and dialogical concept of
personhood based on the notion of self-emptying love. From the Buddhist
standpoint of modern Japanese kenoticism the achievement of the true self
through an act of *kenōsis* or self-emptying love in absolute Nothingness does
not mean dissolution into a nihilistic void, but a social and moral act of emptying oneself into relationships with others in the community. Or to repeat
the words of Nishitani Keiji, when Christian *kenōsis* is conceived from the
perspective of Buddhist *śūnyatā*, it now becomes a process of "making oneself into a nothingness in the service of all things" (*mizukara o mu ni shite arayuru mono ni tsukaeru koto*) (1961, 315; 1982, 285). According to the Buddhist-
Christian interfaith dialogue of Nishida and the Kyoto school, then, while in
negative terms the kenotic ideal of personhood signifies the realization of
no-self, selfless self, or non-ego at the transitional level of relative Nothingness, it is ultimately to be comprehended in positive terms as the achievement of a twofold social self existing in the *between* of I-Thou relations at the
level of absolute Nothingness.

　　In what I have referred to as the period of "Japanese kenoticism" inau-
gurated by Nishida Kitarō, the *kenōsis/śūnyatā* motif is a pervasive theme to
be found in the writings of such diverse thinkers as Tanabe Hajime, Nishitani
Keiji, Ueda Shizuteru, and Abe Masao in modern Japanese philosophy, Mutō
Kazuo, Kitamori Kazō, Doi Masatoshi, and Koyama Kosuke in modern Japanese theology, and even the fiction of Endō Shūsaku in modern Japanese
literature. According to Nishida Kitarō, Japan's most influential philosopher,
God is not a transcendent Lord but an immanently transcending God of love
who like a compassionate Buddha "empties Himself" through *kenōsis* into a
dialectical interpenetration of transcendence and immanence, *nirvāna* and
*samsāra*, the sacred and the profane, the absolute and the relative. *Theology of*

*the Pain of God* (*Kami no itami no shingaku*) and other works by Kitamori Kazō, Japan's most influential Christian theologian, describe not a transcendent deity but an immanent God of love who undergoes *kenōsis* or self-emptying into the world, analogous to the compassionate Bodhisattva that pours himself out into *samsāra* to save others by taking on their suffering as his own. In *Silence* (*Chinmoku*) and other Christian religious novels by Endō Shūsaku, one of Japan's most influential contemporary novelists, the uniquely Japanese image of Jesus Christ refashioned in the image of a compassionate Bodhisattva appears on the *fumie* (plaques of Jesus upon which suspected illegal Christians in Japan were made to trample), which show not the transcendent Christ in Glory, but the Humiliated Christ, the kenotic Christ emptied of glory who has poured himself out for the sake of others. If in the Zen Buddhist *śūnyatā* tradition this ideal of personhood as self-emptying love is visualized through the iconographic image of a compassionate Bodhisattva in fellowship with others as shown in the tenth and final Oxherding picture, in the Christian *kenōsis* tradition it is depicted through Bonhoeffer's inspired kenotic vision of Jesus as the "man for others," or the image of the kenotic Christ poured out for others depicted on the *fumie* as graphically described in the Japanese novels of Endō Shūsaku. Hence, like the Zen Buddhist ideal of self-negating compassion, the Christian kenotic ideal of self-emptying love is to be understood in social and moral terms as an act of *pouring out of self for others*.

# ᴖ·3·ᴖ

## The Dependency Self Model of
## Doi Takeo's Amae Psychology

### The Social Psychology of Doi Takeo

In *Amae no kōzō* (*The Structure of Amae*, 1971) and *Omote to Ura* (*Outside and Inside*, 1985), the distinguished Japanese psychiatrist Dr. Doi Takeo argues that the social character of Japanese selfhood, the group-centered structure of Japanese society, and the interpersonal dynamics of Japanese communication are all to be analyzed as a function of *amae* (indulgent dependency), defined as "the need of an individual to be loved and cherished or the prerogative to presume and depend upon the benevolence of another." As discussed by psychiatrist Frank A. Johnson (1993, 200) in his recent study of Doi's psychology, entitled *Dependency and Japanese Socialization*, Doi's principle of *amae* is articulated not only in behavioral terms as describing a pattern of interaction between persons in Japanese culture; it is also developed in *intrapsychic* terms as a fundamental "drive," "motive," "need," "wish," "trait," "disposition," or "desire" to depend on others. Freud has argued that there are two intrapsychic drives which he identified as the primal id-instincts of sex and aggression, both of which are socialized in the early developmental stages through the repressive mechanism of the superego by the internalization of parental norms. However, Doi argues that *amae*, the drive to depend on others, is itself coequal to if not more primary than the libidinous and aggressive instincts postulated by Freud. That is to say, *amae* represents a nonlibidinous instinct to seek human affiliation with others in a group. As an intrapsychic "drive," *amae* thus represents the primary need to be loved, cherished, indulged, and cared for, or the desire for intimacy, physical contact, support, warmth, protection, and nurturing. The notion of *amae* or "dependency drive" hereby comes to establish the theoretical grounds for an other-directed *social psychology* in contrast to Freud's self-directed individualistic psychology. Furthermore, based on this intrapsychic disposition of *amae* or "dependency drive" he formulates a social, interactional, and contextual model of the Japanese self as a nexus of infantile dependency relations. In his efforts to articulate the social nature, origin, and development of the Japanese self grounded in the notion of an underlying dependency drive it can thus be said that Doi stands within the great tradition of social psychology pioneered by such thinkers as Alfred J. Adler, George Herbert Mead, and Harry Stack Sullivan in the West.

Doi variously defines the noun *amae* as "dependency wish," "drive to dependence," or "passive object love." Again, *amae* is conceived by Doi as "the ability and prerogative of an individual to presume or depend upon the benevolence of another." The noun form of *amae* is also related to the adjectival form of *amai* (sweet), indicating the characteristic sweetness and permissiveness of typical *amae* behavior. Furthermore, the verb *amaeru* means "to coax," "to presume upon another's love," "to play the baby," "to behave like a spoiled child," or "to take advantage of another's kindness." The prototype of *amae* behavior lies in the psychology of the infant in its relationship to its mother. *Amae* mentality represents the infant's desire to be close to its mother, or as it were, it is the infant's attempt to psychologically deny the fact of separation from the mother and thereby to obliterate the pain of that separation. Hence, while Doi points to *amae* as the fundamental drive to dependence underlying social relationships in Japanese group-centered society, at the same time he underscores the infantile, regressive, and pathological nature of these relationships.

While children *amaeru* or play the baby to their mother, their mothers in turn *amayakasu* or "spoil" their children. That is to say, Japanese mothers indulge, pamper, baby, or coddle their children in the sense that they allow their infants to *amaeru* them without constraint. In order for *amae* (indulgent dependency) to occur there must be a mutual tacit agreement to suspend the conventional normative restraints of *enryō*, defined as "ritualized hesitation or deference." For this reason, scholars like T. S. Lebra (1976), Kumagai Hisa (1981), and F. A. Johnson (1993) have emphasized the reciprocal character of *amae* as a two-way "*amaeru*/*amayakasu* transaction" which involves a codependent relation between two participants, the one who displays *amaeru* and the one who provides *amayakasu*. Kumagai Hisa criticizes Doi's definition of *amae* as "passive love" and clarifies the underlying *strategic activity* involved in seeking indulgent dependency, enumerating various examples of strategic interactions like "asking favors," "feigning helplessness," or "expressing anger." Thus, *amae* is at once a profoundly social concept in that it always presupposes an interaction between at least two persons in the form of an *amaeru*/*amayakasu* relationship.

In his comparative analysis of Eastern and Western concepts of selfhood, Doi states that he frankly agrees with the generalization that Americans are "individualistic" (*kojinshugiteki*) and that the Japanese are characterized by "groupism" (*shūdanshugi*) (1985, 53). He goes on to say, "*amae* is the psychology underlying Japanese groupism" (1985, 55). Thus, for Doi the principle of *amae* is the psychological key to the Japanese mind, self, and society insofar as it explains the structure and dynamic of Japanese "groupism," or what he also refers to as the phenomenon of "Japanese group-consciousness" (*nihon no shūdan-ishiki*) (1985, 55). He agrees with many other scholars that the Japanese self is social, relational, contextual, interactional, familial, collective, sociocentric, dependent, and so forth. From the standpoint of philosophy and religion some scholars have explained the interdependent, interconnected and interrelational character of Japanese selfhood by emphasizing the influence of the Zen concept of self as emptiness based on the metaphysical principle of *engi* or "dependent coorigination," as well as the Confucian notion of self as a center of familial relationships. Again, scholars representing the social sciences have clarified the interdependent character of Japanese selfhood through its genesis by "household" and "village" principles of organization. However, Doi's great contribution is to have identified the underlying psychological mechanism of Japanese selfhood through the principle of *amae*. That is to say, for Doi both the social character of Japanese selfhood and the group-centered familial structure of Japanese society are to be understood as a psychological function of *amae*, the infantile dependency syndrome. For Doi, *amae* is the psychological "glue," so to speak, which binds together the person as *ningen* into relationships with others in intimate social groups.

## The Amae Principle and Japanese "Household" (Ie) Society

With cultural anthropologist Nakane Chie (1970), Doi understands Japanese society through the notion of *ie* or "family household" in its wider meaning as a symbol of collective group-consciousness defined by the "vertical" (*tate*) structure of its "parent-child" (*oyabun-kobun*) relationships. Yet for Doi, all parent-child relationships characterizing the family household structure of group-formation in Japanese society are again to be understood as a function of *amae* mentality. In other words, for Doi the *amae* syndrome is the basic psychological mechanism which establishes the drive toward infantile dependency relationships within various social groups modeled on the pattern of a traditional Japanese family household unit. As such, this infantile *amae* mentality is not confined to the social interaction between a baby and its mother during childhood, but also extends into all aspects of adult behavior in Japanese society, including such *oyabun-kobun* or "parent-child" relations like husband and wife in the marriage situation, student and teacher at school, employee and employer at the company office, preceptor and disciple in the religious organization, or leader and follower in various other social groups organized on the basis of a familial household structure.

## Doi's Critique of Morita Therapy

As a psychiatrist and medical physician, Doi is also concerned with the more concrete application of his *amae* principle to psychotherapeutic theory and practice. In particular, Doi is concerned with the practical diagnosis, treatment and cure of patients whose impulse to *amaeru* or depend on others becomes exaggerated to the point of manifesting a clinically pathological condition of infantile *over-dependency*. While discussing the pathology of *amae*, Doi praises Morita Shoma (1874–1938) for his analysis of "nervousness" (*shinkeishitsu*) and "preoccupation" or "obsessiveness" (*toraware*) as the basis of what has come to be known as Morita Therapy. Yet if Doi praises Morita for his account of neurosis and obsession as primary symptoms of mental disorder, he at the same time criticizes the latter's failure to locate their underlying cause. In particular Doi criticizes Morita's Zen-influenced "quiet therapy" based on methods of introspection, solitude, and tranquility to the extent that it treats only the symptoms and not the underlying root cause of mental conflict. In Doi's own psychotherapy, "obsession" and "nervousness" arise through "resentment" (*uramu*) which is caused by frustration of *amae* as the drive toward indulgent dependency relations. For this reason, says Doi, neurotic, compulsive, and obsessive behavior cannot be effectively cured until one overcomes the underlying problem rooted in *amae*, the infantile dependency syndrome.

## Doi's Critique of Zen, Nishida Philosophy, and Japanese Culture

In his work *The Structure of Amae*, Doi (1971) uses his key psychological notion of *amae* ("coaxing" in dependency relationships) as a generalized explanatory principle functioning to interpret not only Japanese groupism but also the whole spectrum of traditional Japanese culture, including the art, literature, and aesthetics of Japan. Doi defines the structure of *amae* as follows: "*Amae* is essentially a matter of dependence on the object, a desire for the identification of subject and object" (1971,114; 1973, 99). According to Doi, it is precisely this infantile wish to depend on an object or to identify subject and object, typical of *amae* mentality, which characterizes the general pattern of social interaction in Japanese group-consciousness. He then proceeds to interpret the Japanese sense of beauty as an example of the *amae* mentality in that aesthetic experience also merges the subject with the object: "Let us now consider the Japanese aesthetic sense. Here also the *amae* sensibility is an important factor. What is called beauty usually indicates that an object pleases the senses, such that the one who enjoys the beauty of the object becomes one with it through that experience" (1971, 87). In this context Doi applies his *amae* principle to various traditional ideals of beauty which have emerged in the canons of taste throughout the history of Japanese aesthetics, including *mono no aware* (the "pathos" of things), *wabi* (rustic poverty), *sabi* (solitariness), *shibui* (elegant restraint), and *iki* (chic), all being defined as functions of *amae* in its meaning as the desire to fuse subject and object (1971, 91).

Doi then goes on to criticize the Zen Buddhist ideal of fusion between subject and object in the nondual experience of *satori* or "enlightenment," as well as Nishida Kitarō's concept of "pure experience" (*junsui keiken*) based on the notion of *shukaku gōitsu*, "oneness of subject and object" (1971, 92; 1973, 83). For Doi, both the Zen Buddhist experience of *satori* and its modern reformulation in the East-West philosophy of Nishida Kitarō as a kind of Jamesian "pure experience" are expressions of Japanese *amae* mentality with its underlying dependency wish for an identification of subject and object. Doi thus writes: "In this regard it is interesting that the Nishida philosophy which became so popular in prewar Japan, with its notion of a pure experience in which subject and object fuse, has clearly received an influence from Zen" (1971, 92). Here Doi's criticism of Zen *satori* and Nishida's pure experience as variants of *amae* mentality is in certain respects reminiscent of Freud's psychoanalytic critique of the "oceanic feeling" characterizing mystical experience as representing an infantile regression and fixation to the pre-ego state, a pathological return to the maternal womb as a defensive mechanism against the pressures of adulthood. For Doi, symptoms of mental disorder like "nervousness" (*shinkeishitsu*) and "obsession" (*toraware*) cannot be removed simply by a return to Nishida's "pure experience" devoid of the subject-object distinction as achieved through the practice of traditional Zen meditation or its modern psychotherapeutic form of Morita Therapy, but only by transcending the regressive infantile dependency wishes of the *amae* syndrome, along with the "resentment" (*urami*) which is caused by frustration of the *amae* impulse, and thereby to achieve true personhood through relationships with others. Hence, Doi concludes: "The aim from now on, surely, must be to overcome *amae*. Nor will it do simply to return to the Zen world of identity between subject and object; to discover, in other words the person" (1971, 93–94; 1973, 84).

## Kimura's Synthesis of Amae Psychology and Japanese Philosophy

More recently, another eminent psychiatrist Kimura Bin has further developed Doi's *amae* theory. In a section entitled "On *Amae*" from his book *The Betweenness of Person and Person* (*Hito to hito to no aida*, 1972), Kimura expresses his deep appreciation for Doi's *amae* psychology as follows:

> I would like to consider the notion of *amae* which has lately become a topic of such great interest to people. According to Dr. Doi Takeo, a psychoanalyst, one cannot find any proper translation of this word among the Western languages. This is an original Japanese word. Because it is the key notion in understanding the structure of Japanese human nature, it is a notion which is the center of Dr. Doi's psychotherapy. The discovery of the *amae* principle is a great contribution in the history of Japanese psychiatry. (1972, 147)

Kimura goes on to combine the *amae* psychology of Doi Takeo with Watsuji Tetsurō's *ningen* concept of personhood defined through the notion of *hito to hito to no aida*, the "betweenness of person and person." Kimura's analysis clarifies how Watsuji's *ningen* theory of personhood as the *aida* or "betweenness" of persons in society is to be understood as a psychological function of *amae*. He further argues that *amae* mentality is closely related to Watsuji's notion of *fūdo*, "climate." Kimura regards Watsuji's idea of a *fūdo* or "climate" of lived space as functioning similarly to Nishida's *basho* or "place," the spatial locus wherein both self and others arise through mutual encounter. When a person lives safely in the Japanese climate, he "depends on" (*amae-te-iru*) the surrounding climate of living nature. Like Watsuji's concepts of *ningen* (person) and *aidagara* (betweenness, relation), his idea of *fūdo* (climate) is thus also to be understood as a function of the *amae* principle. For Kimura, then, Doi's concept of *amae* provides a psychological framework for understanding Nishida's concept of *basho* or "place" as the spatial locus wherein the true self is revealed as a self-other relation along with Watsuji's basic philosophical notion of Japanese personhood as *ningen* existing in the *aida* or interpersonal "betweenness" of a *fūdo* or "climate" of space.

## Doi Takeo's Amae Psychology and Kuki Shūzō's Aesthetic of Iki

Doi Takeo (1971, 89) points out that his *amae* psychology has been directly influenced by the aesthetics of *iki* (chic) formulated by the modern Japanese philosopher Kuki Shūzō (1888–1941). The very title of Doi's book *The Structure of Amae* (*Amae no kōzō*, 1971) at once reflects the title of Kuki's major work, *The Structure of Iki* (*Iki no kōzō*, 1930). In particular, Doi's idea that the social nature of Japanese selfhood is a function of *amae* can itself be traced back to Kuki's (1930, 50–57) much earlier hermeneutic analysis of such linguistically overlapping terms as *amae*, *amaeru*, and *amami* in their relation to the Edo period aesthetic ideal of *iki*. It will be seen that Kuki elucidates the structure of his aesthetic ideal of *iki* or "chic" in terms of a polar contrast between two opposing value qualities, *amami* (sweetness) and *shibumi* (astringency), whereby *shibumi* designates a "negative" value moving in the direction of elegant restraint in avoidance of social contact, and *amami* / *amae* is a "positive" value moving in the direction of interpersonal relationships. The upshot is that for Kuki, as later for Doi, the notion of *amami* / *amae* is established as the basic explanatory principle underlying Japanese group-consciousness. But while Kuki highlights primarily the aesthetic and erotic dimensions of *amae* in the course of analyzing the structure of *iki* as a norm for intersexual relationships, Doi instead brings to light the psychological content of *amae* as an infantile dependency drive.

Born into a wealthy aristocratic family, "Count Kuki" traveled to Germany in 1922 where he studied philosophy under Edmund Husserl and Martin Heidegger, afterwards going to Paris where he hired the young Jean Paul Sartre as his private language tutor while also studying modern French philosophy with Henri Bergson, finally returning to Japan in 1927, at which time he joined Nishida Kitarō as a professor in the Department of Philosophy at Kyoto University. In 1926, while still living in France, Kuki finished a manuscript entitled *The Essence of Iki* (*Iki no honshitsu*), the rough draft of what would later become his highly original work *The Structure of Iki* (*Iki no kōzō*), first published in 1930. Kuki's *The Structure of Iki*, like Doi's *The Structure of Amae* (*Amae no kōzō*, 1971), has become one of the standard *nihonjinron* texts purporting to disclose the fundamental characteristic of Japanese uniqueness and identity. Just as some have discerned the essence of "Japaneseness" (*nihonrashisa*) in *amae* (dependency), *aware* (pathos), *aidagara* (relationship, betweenness), *ningen* (person), *kanjin* (contextuality), *tate* (verticality), *ma* (interval, space), *ie* (family, household), *ki* (spirit, mood, feeling), *wa* (harmony), *sunao* (gentleness), or *shitashimi* (intimacy), so Kuki sees the quintessence of Japaneseness in his concept of *iki* (chic). Like other key terms in the literature of *nihonjinron*, including Doi's concept of *amae*, Kuki's notion of *iki* underscores the social, relational, and contextual nature of selfhood in Japanese group-consciousness. However, Kuki's aesthetic notion of *iki* is distinguished by virtue of the fact that it specifically focuses upon the erotic character of "intersexual" (*iseiteki*) relationships between persons in society. For while traditional Japanese aesthetic ideals like *yūgen* (mystery), *wabi* (poverty), *sabi* (aloneness), and *shibui* (elegant restraint) are embodied by the contemplative Zen hermit in the tranquil solitude of nature, Kuki's moral-aesthetic ideal of *iki* is instead embodied by the amorous *geisha*, the flirtatious courtesan (*tayu*), and the sophisticated dandy (*tsūjin*) who inhabited the urban "floating world" (*ukiyo*) of the sprawling Yoshiwara pleasure quarters during Edo period bordello culture, although his characterizations are no less apposite with regard to the "love motel," "sex *manga*," "water trade" (*mizu shōbai*), and "soap land / *Turko* bath" culture of present-day Tokyo.

While in the second chapter Kuki (1930, 28) analyzes the triadic structure of *iki* in terms of seductive coquetry (*bitai*), the gallant's pride (*ikuji*), and detached resignation (*akirame*), in chapter 3 he further goes on to clarify the dyadic structure of *iki* in terms of a series of paired antonyms, including *shibumi* (astringency) / *amami* (sweetness); *jōhin* (refinement) / *gehin* (crudeness); and *jimi* (plain) / *hade* (gaudy). Especially in a section entitled "*Shibumi / Amami*" (1930, 50–57) he proceeds to underscore the paradoxical structure of *iki* as an aesthetic, moral, and existential lifestyle which is mediated by two formerly opposed values, "astringency" (*shibumi*) and "sweetness" (*amami*). As clarified by Kuki's schematic chart on the structure of *iki* appearing in the same section, while the sweetness of *amami* is a "positive" (*sekkyokuteki*) value directed toward the "gaudy" (*hade*), the astringency of *shibumi* is a "negative" (*shōkyokuteki*) value of "elegant restraint" directed toward the "plain" and "somber" (*jimi*) (1930, 57).

In his own book called *The Structure of Amae*, psychiatrist Doi Takeo provides an extensive discussion on the nature of *amae* mentality in relation to the dyadic *amami / shibumi* or "sweetness / astringency" tension constitutive of *iki* as described by Kuki Shūzō's work *The Structure of Iki*. Doi writes:

In *Iki no kōzō*, an excellent work by Kuki Shūzō which analyzes *iki* in detail, the author defines *iki* as "sophisticated" and then established its relationship to *amae* mentality. . . . He explains that *iki*, along with *amami* and *shibumi*, are special intersexual modes of existence . . . considering *amami* as the normal state, one finally arrives, by means of *iki*, at the point of *shibumi*, whereupon one then exercises restraint in relationships with others. (1971, 89)

As further clarified by Doi, the word *amae*, which is etymologically related to both the adjective *amai* or "sweet," and the noun *amami* or "sweetness," is itself a nominative meaning "dependency wish" or "drive to dependence." The verbal form, *amaeru*, means "to play the baby to," "to act like a spoiled child," "to coax," or "to indulge upon another's love." In terms of the *amami/ shibumi* contrast, while *shibumi* is a "negative" quality which moves in the direction of restraint in order to avoid social contact, *amami* or *amae* is a "positive" quality which moves in the direction of establishing interpersonal communication within the intimacy of a social group. Kuki writes: "*Amami* (sweetness) expresses the positive quality in this contrast in that between a person being indulged (*amaeru-sha*) and a person indulging (*amaerareru-sha*), there is always a positive communication opened up" (1930, 51). For Kuki, *amae* or *amami* functions similarly to the *bitai* component of *iki* insofar as it denotes a sweet, flirtatious, and seductive type of coquettish behavior associated especially with intimate amorous relations between the sexes. As an example he cites various colloquial expressions using *amae* in an erotic sense like "A woman is most desirable when she *amaerus*" (*amaeru sugata iro fukashi*) (1930, 53). According to Kuki, then, there is an inner tension within the polarized structure of *iki* : on the one side, *shibumi*, like *akirame*, has a negative value which moves towards detachment from an object or person; whereas on the other side, *amae* and *amami*, like *bitai*, have a positive value which moves towards an intimate union with an object or person. In the social psychology of Doi Takeo, it is precisely this *amae/amami* aspect of *iki* which comes to function as the psychological key to interpersonal communication in Japan just as it is the basic explanatory mechanism for the social character of Japanese selfhood and the group-centered nature of Japanese culture. However, while the *amami* component in Kuki's aesthetic principle of *iki* emphasizes the specifically erotic, amorous, and sexual nature of interpersonal relationships in Japanese group-consciousness, Doi's psychological principle of *amae* or "dependency drive" focuses upon the infantile, compulsive, and regressive character of social interaction in various *oyabun-kobun* or "parent-

child" relations operating within the "familial household" (ie) structure of
Japanese groupism. Hence, with its complex of aesthetic, erotic, and infantile
overtones, the principle of *amae* is understood by Doi as the wish to depend
upon an object or the desire to identify subject and object, thereby functioning as the basic psychological drive for dependence upon others in society.

## Amae and the Twofold Structure of Japanese Selfhood

In his sequel work entitled *Omote to Ura* (Front and Back,1985), which
has since been translated into English as *The Anatomy of Self: The Individual
Versus Society* (1986), Doi Takeo further develops his *amae* model of the Japanese self in terms of the dual aspects of inward human feelings (*honne, ura,
uchi, ninjō*) versus the outer aspect of social norms (*tatemae, omote, soto, giri*),
both of which correspond to the directional coordinates of the "individual"
versus "society." First of all, he develops the Japanese self through the polar
categories of *omote* and *ura*, meaning "front" and "back," or in its Latin equivalents, *recto* and *verso*. According to Doi, the *omote-ura* or "front-back" distinction can also be understood in terms of the *soto-uchi* or "outside-inside": "I
think it can be said that *omote* and *ura* correspond to the distinction between
*soto* and *uchi* that is understood in Japan especially in the consciousness of
human relationships" (1985, 11). Doi then goes on to restate the *omote-ura*
(front-back) or *soto-uchi* (outside-inside) structure of Japanese selfhood in terms
of the distinction of *tatemae-honne* (front-stage/back-stage), defined as the
split between "personal reactions" and "social institutions" (1985, 25–42). The
opposition between *giri-ninjō* or "social obligation" and "human feeling" in
Japanese social ethics is also understood by Doi in terms of this "outside-
inside" model of Japanese selfhood. Hence the Japanese self described as a
nexus of infantile dependency relations in *The Structure of Amae* is now revealed as having a "dual consciousness" articulated through such well-known
contrastive terms like *omote-ura, soto-uchi*, and *tatemae-honne*, all of which
generally signify the distinction between "public-private." Again, he states
that such distinctions as *omote-ura, soto-uchi*, and *tatemae-honne* all represent
the "double-sidedness" (*nimensei*), or as it were, the "twofold" (*futae, nijū*)
aspect of the Japanese self in its dependency relationships with others (1985,
17). The *omote* and *ura* or front and back sides of the Japanese self are meta-
phorically located in the heart and face, as expressed by Doi when he writes:
"It should also be stated that in classical Japanese *omote* (front) signifies *kao*

(face) and *ura* (back) denotes *kokoro* (heart)" (1985, 11). While *omote* (front) symbolized by the face represents the social self on the outside, *ura* (back) symbolized by *kokoro* or the heart signifies the emotional self on the inside of the twofold Japanese self.

Finally, it should be clarified just how the twofold structure of Japanese selfhood is related to Doi's key psychological principle of *amae*. According to Doi, the Japanese self is divided into "front" (*omote*) and "back" (*ura*), "outside" (*soto*) and "inside" (*uchi*), or "personal feeling" (*honne*) and "social institutions" (*tatemae*) according to the restraint verses expression of *amae*, the infantile dependency wish. Doi concisely explains Japanese selfhood as a dual consciousness of "outside/inside" (*omote/ura*) in relation to his *amae* principle as follows: "For example, when it is said that to presume upon others through *amae* on the outside (*soto*) is not good but that it is acceptable if one is inside (*uchi*), this is the logic of *omote* and *ura*" (1985, 19). Thus, the Japanese self in its relation to others has two sides, *soto* or "outside" where the dependency needs of *amae* are subject to the constraints of social rituals, conventions, and institutions, and *uchi* or "inside" where *amae* can be freely expressed in the privacy of one's home with family and friends. That is to say, while the infantile coaxing attitude of *amae* or the prerogative to presume and depend upon the benevolence of others is appropriate on the "inside" (*uchi*), on the "outside" (*soto*) one must instead conform to the established social norms of restraint as expressed by the term *enryō* (reserve), meaning "ritualized hesitation or deference." Competent social navigation in Japanese culture therefore requires the basic skill called *kejime* (discrimination), the ability to "discriminate" between that behavior which is appropriate to outside versus inside, front versus back, or public versus private. It can be said that Doi's articulation of the twofold outside/inside (*omote/ura*) structure of Japanese interpersonal selfhood in relation to the restraint versus expression of *amae* has itself been significantly influenced by Kuki Shūzō's (1930, 50–57) dyadic analysis of the intersexual aesthetic ideal of *iki* (chic) in terms of the polar tension between *amami* (sweetness) as a positive value which seeks intimate human communication with others, and *shibumi* (astringency) or the negative value of "elegant restraint" which functions to establish distance from others. However, as will be shown in the final comparative sections of this work, Doi's psychological model of the twofold Japanese self as a dialectic between *honne* (personal reactions) and *tatemae* (social institutions) has also been directly influenced by G. H. Mead's communication model of the bipolar social self as a dialectic between the I or individual pole and the Me or institutional pole.

## Summary

While in modern Japanese philosophy Watsuji Tetsurō has developed a model of the twofold Japanese self as *ningen* through a "self-other" (*ji-ta*) dialectic based on his *aidagara* principle of interpersonal "betweenness," and Nishida Kitarō has articulated a twofold model of the Japanese "social self" (*shakaiteki jiko*) through a dialectic of "I and Thou" based on his principle of *basho* or "place" as the spatial locus of self-other relations, so in modern Japanese psychology Doi Takeo has set forth an explicit twofold model of Japanese selfhood through a dialectic between "inside/outside" (*uchi/soto*) based on his underlying principle of *amae*, the intrapsychic "dependency drive." It has also been seen how psychiatrist Kimura Bin (1972) has attempted to synthesize the social psychology of Doi with modern Japanese philosophy so that Watsuji's Zen/Confucian *ningen* model of self as a "betweenness" (*aida*) of persons in a *fūdo* or spatial climate, and Nishida's Zen idea of the true self in a *basho* or spatial locus where both self and other arise through mutual encounter, are now to be understood as a psychological function of Doi's *amae* principle of dependency relationships. In the final analysis it can be said that the general aim of all the various theories described above is to undercut the conventional dichotomy of individual versus society and to clarify the nondual structure of Japanese selfhood as a twofold individual-society interaction.

# II
## The Social Self in G. H. Mead and American Philosophy

The concept of a twofold social self arising through an individual-community interaction which was thematized in the tradition of classical American philosophy begins with C. S. Peirce's semiotic notion of selfhood as a web of signs constituted by linguistic communication in an intersubjective community. Peirce writes: "To be a self is to be a possible member of some community" (CP 5.402 n. 2). In chapter 10 of *The Principles of Psychology*, William James introduces the notion of a social self, which he defines as follows: "*A man's Social Self* is the recognition which he gets from his mates" (1981, 281). Josiah Royce asserts that the individual must overcome the isolation of egocentrism through membership in a community, thereby to realize his or her "greater social self" (1959, vol. I, 55). Describing the social self by means of his famous notion of a looking-glass self which reflects its primary social group, Charles Horton Cooley states: "A social self of this sort might be called the reflected or looking-glass self" (1964, 84–85). Similarly, John Dewey writes: "The individual is always a social individual" (1971–72: vol. 5, 55–6). Alfred North Whitehead affirms the ancient notion of man as a "social animal" (PR 204). Making the social self the key notion of his whole philosophical system, George Herbert Mead likewise propounds, "Any self is a social self" (SW 292). The technical notion of a social self which is intersubjectively constituted by its relations to others in a community thus became established as a central and recurrent theme in the American philosophical tradition.

The American thinkers have developed the "social" not only as a characteristic of human selfhood but as an ultimate metaphysical category representing a generic trait of all existence. In *The Problem of Christianity*, Josiah Royce declares, "The universe . . . is a realm which is through and through dominated by social categories" (1913, vol. 2, lecture 8, 49; 1981, 300); John Dewey writes in *Philosophy and Civilization* that the "social" is *the* inclusive philosophic idea (1931, 86); Alfred North Whitehead asserts in *Process and Reality* that not only is man a "social animal," but that by analogy "every actual occasion is social" (PR 204); and G. H. Mead states in *Philosophy of the Present* that the social character of human mind and self is "only the culmination of that sociality which is found throughout the universe" (PP 86). This generalization of the "social" into a universal metaphysical category is most clearly expressed by what G. H. Mead has termed the *principle of sociality*

whereby the self and all phenomena are constituted by their social relationships to others in a community. In such a manner the classical American
thinkers underscore the "social" as an ultimate metaphysical category
whereby the social character of human selfhood is grounded in the social
character of reality itself.

Hence, from out of the golden age of classical American pragmatism
there has emerged one of the great themes of twentieth-century philosophy:
that of *the social construction of human selfhood through communication in a community.* American philosophers have endeavored to articulate the social character of the self not only in the sense that a person "co-exists" together with
others, but in the deeper ontological sense whereby a person is intersubjectively *constituted* through his or her relationships with others in a community. The social construction of self in community is a pervasive motif to be
found in the whole tradition of classical American philosophy running through
Peirce, James, Royce, Cooley, Dewey, Whitehead, and Mead, as well as more
recent American philosophers like Justus Buchler and Charles Hartshorne.
Yet it was especially G. H. Mead who first thematized and problematized the
notion of a social self. The framework of Mead provides an empirically based
genetic account of the social nature, origin, and development of the self
through a gradual process of "role-taking" wherein the individual becomes a
social self with reflexive self-consciousness by taking on the roles of the *generalized other* representing the whole community to which it belongs. However,
Mead's social-self theory overcomes atomic individualism without falling
into absolutism, collectivism, or social determinism by means of his ingenious
I-Me dialectic of intersubjectivity. For Mead the self is not an isolated I or
Cartesian subject but a dialectic between I and Me. Through his bipolar model
of the social self as an I-Me dialectic he clarifies how the self arises by taking
on the roles of others at the Me or internalized social pole and then by reacting
with emergent creativity, spontaneity, and novelty at the I or individual pole.
The two aspects of I and Me or *individuality* and *sociality* are therefore both
given equal weight in Mead's concept of self. Yet his social-self theory supports the classical American vision of liberal democratic individualism in that
the public aspect of the social Me is always the servant of the private aspect
of the individual I. Mead's social-self theory and I-Me dialectic establishes a
creative synthesis of the whole tradition of American pragmatism along with
its extension into the organismic process cosmology of A. N. Whitehead.
Also, Mead's interdisciplinary approach to the social self provides a unifying
model for philosophy and the various social sciences including sociology,
anthropology, and social psychology at the micro level and ecology at the
macro level, all of which are grounded in an organic process cosmology of

emergent evolution and creative advance into novelty. In Mead's process cosmology it is clarified that the self is not only "social" as a field of relationships but also *temporal* and *multiple* as a series of emergent or discontinuous events which arise and perish in the creative advance of nature. Like others in the tradition of American philosophy, Mead formulates a value-centric theory which underscores the aesthetic, moral, and religious dimensions of human existence as a social self arising through communication with others in a community. Along with Peirce, Bergson, and Whitehead, Mead has developed an aesthetic creationist paradigm of the social self based on the root metaphor of a creative act such as that of an artist, inventor or imaginative scientist. Following Jürgen Habermas it will be emphasized that Mead's framework represents a "paradigm shift" beyond Cartesian subjectivism and Hegelian absolutism to a new communication model of the social self based on linguistically mediated symbolic interaction between the individual and society. I would now like to examine the development of the "social self" as a central motif in classical American pragmatism, finally arriving at its full crystallization in the philosophy and social science framework of G. H. Mead.

# ༀ4ༀ

## The Social Self in Classical American Philosophy

### Charles Sanders Peirce

Charles Sanders Peirce (1839–1914), the founder of the American philosophical movement known as pragmatism, is widely held to be the most original, versatile, and comprehensive thinker in classical American philosophy. It was Peirce who developed *pragmatism,* or as he would later call it, "pragmaticism," as a generalized extension of the scientific experimental method to all branches of knowledge. In Peirce's laboratory method of pragmatism or experimentalism, a concept is not a fixed and dogmatic "truth," but a provisional, tentative, and fallible *hypothesis* which is empirically tested for its ability to solve problems through ongoing self-corrective inquiry conducted by an unlimited intersubjective community. Peirce endeavored to completely abandon the dualistic model of Cartesian subjectivism based on the individualistic method of intuitionism with its appeal to private verification through an intuitive knowledge of objects, for that of an *intersubjective* model based on the modern scientific experimental method, which instead requires *public verification* by the "community of inquirers." It is precisely through his key notion of community that Peirce came to replace the idea of an isolated Cartesian subject with that of a fully social, relational, and dialogical concept of the person. In this context he formulates a semiotic notion of personhood as intersubjectively constituted by a sign process of linguistic communication in a community. Peirce's fundamental theme of community as articulated in terms of the scientific community of inquirers was thereafter to become a recurrent motif in American pragmatism, later being developed by Royce as the community of interpretation, by Dewey and Mead as the secular liberal democratic community, and by A. N. Whitehead as the metaphysical community of harmonic interpenetration between the many and the one. Furthermore, the concept of a social self thematized in American pragmatism also traces back to its origins in C. S. Peirce's semiotic vision of personhood as a relational web of signs constituted through linguistic communication in an intersubjective community.

## Peirce's Phenomenological Categories: Firstness, Secondness, and Thirdness

In order to understand Peirce's semiotic communication model of personhood based on the theory of signs it is necessary to view it in relation to his philosophic system as a whole. Peirce based the threefold architectonic structure of his overall philosophical framework upon the discipline of phenomenology (or phaneroscopy), defined as the description of "all that is any way or in any sense present to the mind, quite regardless of whether it corresponds to any real thing or not" (1955, 74). The three fundamental categories of Peirce's phenomenology are what he called *Firstness*, *Secondness*, and *Thirdness*, or Quality, Force, and Connection. Again, in psychological terms he states that Firstness, Secondness and Thirdness correspond to Feeling, Willing and Knowing. These three phenomenological categories are further reflected in Peirce's pragmatic theory of valuation as expressed in his "Hierarchy of the Normative Sciences" (1955, 62), whereby Logic (= Thirdness) or the control of thought, depends on Ethics (= Secondness) or the control of action, which in turn depends on Aesthetics (= Firstness) or that which is admirable for its own sake without reference to anything else. According to Peirce, all three categories must be present in each and every phenomenon which manifests itself to consciousness. Firstness is the directly felt aesthetic quality of an event in immediate experience just as it is in its *qualitās* or "suchness," or in terms of his logic of relations, it is the *monadic* aspect of a thing considered in and of itself. Firstness also represents the creativity, spontaneity, freedom, unpredictability, and novelty intrinsic to all events in their qualitative immediacy. It can be said that by means of his category of Firstness, Peirce accounts for that ineffable dimension of directly felt qualitative immediacy of events in their unanalyzed wholeness as emphasized by Zen Buddhism in the East or various schools of mysticism, romanticism, and intuitionism in the West based on the primacy of aesthetic feeling. Secondness is the brute causal interaction between things in their *dyadic* opposition. The category of Secondness is emphasized by existentialism, voluntarism, and other positions based on the priority of will. However, each event in nature also has its *triadic* element of Thirdness, the logical component of meaning and intelligibility. Thirdness is prominent in the ideas of betweenness, mediation, relatedness, representation, communication, community, generality, regularity, continuity, cognition, and abstraction. The category of Thirdness is underscored by idealistic theories which accord a priority to mind, consciousness, or thought. According to Peirce's theory of semiotics, it is in its cognitive or logical aspect of Thirdness that an event is said to function as a linguistic *sign* which invites continuous interpretation by the future community of inquirers. While Peirce's category of Firstness celebrates the directly felt aesthetic quality of phenomena in their unique ineffable suchness, at the same time it is emphasized that Firstness gives us only immediate experience, *not* immediate knowledge. In the pragmatism of Peirce, knowledge, truth, and meaning are always a function of *signs* as represented by the category of Thirdness, and in that signs point to other signs which in turn point to other signs, they always require continuous interpretation by an unlimited future community of inquirers. It is precisely this relational character of signs as pointing beyond themselves to other signs which led to Peirce's emphasis on both the significance of community and the social or intersubjective nature of human selfhood.

## Peirce's Semiotic Vision of Community

Peirce argues that the human self cannot be defined with reference to a private mind but only by reference to a community. In Peirce's words: "To be a self is to be a possible member of some community" (CP 5.402 n. 2). Yet Peirce's themes of community and the intersubjective nature of selfhood are themselves arrived at by his pragmatic theory of meaning as well as his doctrine of semiotics based on the relational nature of linguistic signs. Peirce intended pragmatism to function as theory of *meaning*, a way to make our ideas clear, and as such, held that it required a philosophy of communication—what he called "semiotics" or a general theory of *signs*. Peirce defines semiotics as "the doctrine of the essential nature and fundamental varieties of possible semiosis" (CP 5.488). He further explains that the process of semiosis involves a "triadic relation of Sign-Object-Interpretant" (CP 8.361). This triadic relation is further clarified as follows: "A sign, or *representamen*, is something which stands to somebody for something in some respect or capacity" (CP 2.228). Again, using his threefold phenomenological categories of Firstness, Secondness, and Thirdness, he says that a sign "is a First which stands in a genuine triadic relation to a Second, called its Object, as to be capable of determining a Third, called its Interpretant" (CP 2.274). That is to say, for Pierce, a sign is a triadic relation which always involves (1) an indication of (2) something to (3) someone. For Peirce, a sign is a fallible hypothesis, a matter of inference, an invitation to further inquiry, which can be ramified by other signs *ad infinitum*. Every sign representing an object has an interpretant, which in turn has its own interpretant, and so on, such that the meaning of signs gradually exfoliates through an unlimited community of interpreters. According to the pragmatism of Peirce, the meaning of a sign can never be a self-evident truth which has absolute certainty, exactitude, or universality within an apodictic present, but instead always lies in the future, insofar as it is a provisional, tentative, fallible hypothesis which needs to be empirically tested and verified in the context of an ongoing process of self-corrective inquiry. The upshot of Peirce's concept of semiosis is that the meaning of a sign is never located within the private mind of a solitary individual but is always intersubjectively constituted by a *community* of interpreters. Hence, the meaning of a sign cannot be conceived in monological terms as something which abides in an solitary mind, but is instead something which unfolds through a dialogical process of linguistic communication in an intersubjective community. Through his semiotic investigations Peirce thereby discovered that the self and all phenomena function as signs making reference to other signs without end, thereby arriving at an insight into the relational structure of all existence, including the social character of human selfhood, the centrality of communication, and the significance of community.

## Peirce's Semiotic Vision of Selfhood

According to Peirce's semiotic concept of selfhood the person is itself a "sign." While in its Firstness the self is a spontaneous and unique individual which is directly felt in its qualitative immediacy, and in its Secondess it both acts and is acted upon by others, in its Thirdness it functions as a relational *sign* which makes reference to other signs in an endless semiotic web. In that a sign always points to other signs which in turn points to still other signs in an interpretive process extending *ad infinitum*, the fictitious unity of the substantial self becomes deconstructed into a centerless web of continuous sign-relations with no fixed essence, inner core, or intrinsic nature. Peirce's theory of the human self as a "man-sign" constituted by a process of semiosis is explicitly developed in his essay "Some Consequences of Four Incapacities," originally published in the *Journal of Speculative Philosophy* as early as 1868. First he argues that the contents of consciousness is always a sign: "the contents of consciousness, the entire phenomenal manifestation of mind, is a sign resulting from inference" (1955, 248). Hence, the mind is itself a semiotic process of ramifying signs in the stream of consciousness: "the mind is a sign developing according to the laws of inference" (1955, 248). Peirce then argues that not only the contents but also the very subject of consciousness is itself a semiotic process, so that the self is also to be regarded as a linguistic sign: "the word or sign which man uses is the man himself. For, as the fact that every thought is a sign, taken in conjunction with the fact that life is a train of thought, proves that man is a sign. . . . Thus my language is the sum total of myself; for the man is the thought" (1955, 249; also, CP 5.314). Peirce then goes on to demonstrate how the semiotic concept of the person as an ongoing sign-process points a way out of Cartesian subjectivism with its idea of an independent *cogito*, toward an intersubjective concept of self as social, dialogical, and relational. He attempts to show how the idea that man is a relational network of linguistic signs involves a fundamental shift from the standpoint of individualism whereby meaning is determined by an isolated human subject, to that of an intersubjective model of selfhood in which meaning and truth are always determined by the *community*. For Peirce, the immediate contents of consciousness, whether a feeling, sensation, image, or thought, always functions through its logical aspect of Thirdness as a relational "sign" which invites ongoing future inquiry conducted by an unlimited community of interpreters. He writes: "We individually cannot reasonably hope to attain the ultimate philosophy which we pursue; we can only seek it, therefore, for the *community* of philosophers" (1955, 299). This semiotic view of the self developed in relation to the pragmatic idea of meaning "involves the notion of a COMMUNITY, without definite limits, and capable of a definite increase of knowledge" (1955, 247). He ends this essay by arguing that the concept of selfhood as a sign leads to the negation of a separate ego-self in favor of the view that the individual is always inseparable from the future community of interpretation:

Finally . . . reality depends on the ultimate decision of the community . . . In this way, the existence of thought now, depends on what is to be hereafter; so that it has only a potential existence, dependent on the future thought of the community. The individual man, since his separate existence is manifested by ignorance and error, so far as he is anything apart from his fellows . . . is only a negation. (1955, 250)

In his article "What Pragmatism Is," originally published in *The Monist* in 1905, Peirce explicitly formulates a semiotic model of the social self as follows:

Two things here are all-important to assure oneself and to remember. The first is that a person is not absolutely an individual. His thoughts are what he is 'saying to himself,' that is saying to that other self that is just coming into life in the flow of time. When one reasons, it is that critical self that one is trying to persuade; and all thought whatsoever is a sign, and is mostly of the nature of language. The second thing to remember is that the man's circle of society (however widely or narrowly this phrase may be understood) is a sort of loosely compacted person, in some respects of higher rank than the person of an individual organism. (CP 5.421)

Hence, in the context of clarifying his view of pragmatism, Peirce begins by rejecting the standpoint of Cartesian subjectivism wherein the person is regarded as a mere individual. He then asserts that the self is not a static entity but a dynamic sign activity or semiosis process in the flow of time. In this context he develops his social concept of thinking as a kind of inner conversation or internal dialogue with the use of linguistic signs. The social dimensions of selfhood are especially brought into focus with his above remark that "the circle of a man's society . . . is a sort of loosely compacted person." This results in a fully organic view of selfhood whereby the social group is a person in macrocosm and the person is the social group in microcosm.

Peirce's semiotic vision of the self as a relational web of signs has especially been clarified by V. M. Colapietro in his work *Peirce's Approach to the Self: A Semiotic Perspective on Human Subjectivity*. Colapietro writes: "Semiotic promises a way out of this subjectivism, for in granting priority to signs over ideas it shifts the focus from what occurs within a finite individual consciousness to what occurs between social beings within a common framework of experience and action" (1989, 27). He argues that Peirce's semiotic account of the self goes beyond the approach of Cartesian subjectivism in which an isolated and disembodied human subject is regarded as the ultimate locus of meaning and truth, to that of an intersubjectivist approach, in which some human community functions as the fundamental source of both meaning and truth (1989, 27). The human subject thereby is discovered to be a "network of relations" enmeshed in the "semiotic web" (1989, 28). Summarizing Peirce's semiotic model of personhood through a contrast between the communicative self versus the solitary self, Colapietro writes: "For Peirce, then, the individual self is, in its innermost being, not a private sphere but a communicative agent . . . The solitary self is the illusory self, a being who has its basis in selfishness; the communicative self is the authentic self, a being who has its roots in agape" (1989, 79). Hence, in this way Colapietro indicates the deeper cosmological aspects of Peirce's semiotic vision of personhood, which abandons the subjectivist notion of a solitary self acting out of greed or self-interest for a social theory of the communicative self rooted in *agapism* or the doctrine of "evolutionary love."

## Justus Buchler on Peirce's Semiotic Concept of Selfhood

In his editor's Introduction to *Philosophical Writings of Peirce*, Justus Buchler explains how Peirce's pragmatic notion of meaning and semiotic theory of communication involves a thoroughly social concept of human selfhood as a relational web of signs:

> Peirceian pragmatism (pragmaticism) . . . is the first deliberate theory of meaning in modern times, and it offers a logical technique for the clarification of ideas . . . Peirce maintains that in so far as thought is cognitive it must be linguistic or symbolical in character—that is, it must presuppose communication. Communication takes place by means of signs, and Peirce's theory, in its investigation of the nature and conditions of the sign-relation, endows with a new and vital significance the old truth that man is a social animal. (Peirce 1955, xi–xii)

As Buchler then goes on to argue, according to the pragmatic definition, truth, knowledge, and meaning cannot be determined by individual reaction or private sensation, as is the case with feeling, intuition, or immediate experience, all of which are incommunicable, but only by that which is public, social, communal, and general—a linguistic *sign*. In opposition to atomistic psychology, Peirce demonstrates that no thought or mental sign is "simple" but is a *complex* to be ramified by future interpretations into a "web of continuously related signs" (Buchler 1955, xii). According to Buchler, then, Peirce's semiotic communication theory of human selfhood as a relational web of signs offers a modern reformulation of Aristotle's concept of man as a *social animal*.

Justus Buchler, who should be recognized as one of the greatest philosophers to have emerged in the more recent period of American speculative metaphysics, initially distinguishing himself as one of the foremost scholars of C. S. Peirce, after which he then proceeded to formulate his own highly original system called the "metaphysics of natural complexes." Buchler reformulates Peirce's semiotic communication theory of self in order to achieve a higher degree of metaphysical generalization, thereby pointing out the limitation of Peirce's view while at the same time drawing out its wider implications. The strategic agenda governing Buchler's entire philosophical enterprise is to critically undermine the principle of "ontological primacy" whereby certain discriminanda are privileged over all others, for the alternative principle of *ontological parity*, whereby all discriminanda are assigned equal ontological status within their own respective orders or relational contexts. Buchler deconstructs all absolutes, ultimates, or simples assigned ontological primacy by showing how anything regarded as an onto-logical simple is really a "natural complex" which can be factored into other natural complexes, and so on without end. In this context Buchler articu-lates what he calls a metaphysics of the human process, which establishes a fully social, relational, and multiple concept of the communicative self, understood as a "natural complex" located in a plurality of "orders" (per-spectives, contexts, or spheres of relatedness), each with their own "integ-rity," yet interconnected within the overall "contour" of a total identity. In *Nature and Judgment* Buchler describes his relational concept of self as a natu-ral complex when he writes: "An individual is a natural complex contingently associated with, affecting, and affected by, other natural complexes" (1985, 118). Buchler's metaphysics of the human process involves a general theory of human utterance based on the centrality of communication with signs as conceived by C. S. Peirce and other classical American philosophers: "The sign-studies of Peirce, Royce, and Mead, together with the powerful work of Dewey, have done much to invigorate the study of human utterance by suggesting the centrality of communication" (1985, 9). Building upon the general theory of signs developed by Peirce and other classical American philosophers, Buchler works out his own social concept of man based on a semiotic communication theory of human selfhood that deconstructs the substantial ego-self into an inexhaustible web of sign-relations, wherein each sign is a natural complex which can be factored into other sign-relations, and so forth, *ad infinitum*. Describing his relationally defined notion of a commu-nicative self, Buchler speaks of "the extended nature of individuality, its com-municative essence, and the indefinite bounds of relatedness" (1985, 106). Using the vocabulary of G. H. Mead, Buchler argues that since the commu-nicative self is a function of "sociality," it has an extended scope, a relational spread in time and space by virtue of its ordinal location in a multiplicity of contexts: "The human self, as some philosophers have recognized, is spread out in space as well as in time . . . The self's spread, its relatedness, is the basis of sociality" (1985, 56).

Although Buchler adopts Peirce's semiotic concept of the self as a social animal constituted by a "web of continuously related signs," at the same time Buchler's sign theory differs significantly from that of Peirce in that he endeavors to overcome the cognitive bias of the latter whereby the "sign" is given a primarily *mental* connotation. While Peirce underscores the role of community and communication in the intersubjective constitution of a social self, he focuses upon the "community of inquirers," and thus understands the communicative self in intellectualistic terms as an *inquirer* who ramifies cognitive signs by means of *logical judgements* through *scientific inquiry*. In contrast, Buchler subordinates the notion of "inquiry" to the more general category of *query*. For Buchler, "Query is the genus of which inquiry is a species" (1985, 7). Whereas inquiry ramifies judgments only in the assertive or cognitive mode, query instead signifies the ramification of judgments in *three* modes: the assertive (cognitive), active (volitional), and exhibitive (valuative). In Buchler's semiotic communication model of personhood the three modes of judgment including the (i) assertive, (ii) active and (iii) exhibitive, respectively correspond to the three human spheres of (i) saying, (ii) doing, and (iii) making, which in turn correspond to the three fields of (i) science, (ii) morality, and (iii) art. "Communication" is a generic trait of the human self so that what he calls societized man always communicates through its manipulation and interpretation of signs in at least one of these three modes of judgment. As Buchler clarifies in *Nature and Judgment*, the three modes of human production, doing, making, and saying, are three modes of judgment designated respectively as active, exhibitive, and assertive (1985, 20). Moreover, "The modes of judgment are also modes of communication. We communicate by acting and by making no less than by stating" (1985, 30). He further argues that the three modes of production and the three modes of judgment are all modes of communication in that judgments in all three modes can function as *signs*: "The fact that all three modes of judgment may be efficacious in communication follows in part . . . from a philosophic truth suggested in modern philosophy by Berkeley and generalized by Peirce and Royce, namely, that anything whatever may function as a sign" (1985, 30). He adds that "Judgments in any mode may consequently function as signs" (1985, 30). Hence, the innovation of Buchler's semiotics is that it enlarges and generalizes the meaning of a "sign," so that it now comes to designate "a means of further judgment" (1985, 156), or "an instrument fostering judgment" (1985, 157). A "sign" is any natural complex that invites further interpretation in any of the three modes of judgment, including assertive, active, and exhibitive judgments. The communicative self thus ramifies signs by means of aesthetic and moral judgments as well as by logical judgments.

Buchler's methodological notion of "query" as the systematic ramification of judgments in three modes is itself derived from Peirce's three phenomenological categories of Firstness (= exhibitive judgment), Secondness (= active judgment) and Thirdness (= assertive judgment). But while Peirce inconsistently privileges the category of Thirdness so as to understand the communicative self as one who ramifies cognitive signs in the assertive mode of logical judgment through scientific inquiry, Buchler draws out the wider implications of Peirce's categories so as to formulate a more inclusive and general concept of the communicative self as a being who ramifies sign-relations in all three modes of judgment through science, ethics, and aesthetics. Although it was Peirce himself who suggested that anything can function as a sign, whether qualities of feeling (Firstness), volitional actions (Secondness), or logical thoughts (Thirdness), he nonetheless privileged the cognitive aspect of Thirdness as the basis for inquiry. Buchler's polemic is that Peirce's theory of signs is not general enough to function as a metaphysics of human utterance insofar as it privileges the cognitive over other possible modes of communication. Hence, through the greater degree of generalization achieved by his principle of ontological parity, Buchler redefines the Peirceian idea of a communicative self as an agent who ramifies, interprets, and communicates with signs by means of query in all three fundamental modes of judgment, the assertive, the active, and the exhibitive, as conducted through the three corresponding fields of science, morality, and art.

## The Semiotic Model of Decentered Selfhood in Peirce and French Poststructuralism

Here I would briefly like to consider Peirce's concept of self as a sign-process in relation to the semiotic theory of decentered selfhood which has been developed by French poststructuralist thinkers like Derrida, Barthes, Foucault, and others based on the sign theory of Ferdinand de Saussure. In his *Course on General Linguistics* Saussure defines semiology as an aspect of social psychology, stating: "A science that studies the life of signs within society is conceivable; it would be part of social psychology and consequently of general psychology; I shall call it semiology (from Greek *semeion* 'sign')" (1966, 16). He further suggests that semiology can function as the basis of all other disciplines, now understood as the study of various sign-systems. Saussure goes on to define language as a "differential," or *relational* system of signs in which there are no positive entities, in that the meaning of each sign is determined only by virtue of its relationships to other signs. On the basis of Saussure's semiology, Jacques Derrida and other French poststructuralists have undertaken the deconstructive project of decentering all modes of "self-identity" into *différance*, the differential play of signs. Derrida and others in the movement of French poststructuralism endeavor to deconstruct all absolute metaphysical "centers" functioning as a Transcendental Signified, including both the human-centered standpoint of egocentrism and the God-centered stand-point of theocentrism. The semiology of Saussure thereby developed into the deconstructionist theme of the "disappearance of the self" through the complete decentering of the self-identical Cartesian subject into a differential or relational network of empty traces and floating signifiers with no positive, substantial entities. This dissolution of man or decentering of the human subject in French deconstructionism based on the semiology of Saussure has been concisely summarized in *The Pursuit of Signs* by Jonathan Culler (1981, 32–35), who cites the often repeated dictum from Levi-Strauss's *The Savage Mind*: "The goal of the human sciences is not to constitute man but to dis-solve him." Again, he cites from Foucault's *The Archaeology of Knowledge*: "The researches of psychoanalysis, of linguistics, of anthropology have 'decentered' the subject in relation to the laws of its desire, the forms of its language, the rules of its actions, or the play of its mythical and imaginative discourse." As Culler's discussion clarifies, what has been discovered in postmodern semiotic theory is not "man" but *signs*. No longer man-centered, the human sciences now become understood as semiotics: semiotics of the unconscious for Lacan, semiotics of the codes of kinship and myth for Levi-Strauss, semiotics of the relations and contradictions in society for Althusser, semiotics of literary texts for Barthes and Genette, a semiotics of historical discourse for Foucault, and a philosophical theory of semiotics for Derrida. The total dissolution of the human subject into a centerless web of sign-relationships thus becomes the ultimate effect of a semiotic approach to selfhood in French deconstructionism and poststructuralism.

It has now been seen that a semiotic model of decentered selfhood has been developed both in classical American pragmatism and French poststructuralism. While the American model is based on the semiotics of C. S. Peirce, the French model is based on the semiology of Ferdinand de Saussure. Like the semiotic view of personhood developed in recent French poststructuralism, Peirce attempts to decenter the Cartesian subject into a "semiotic web" (Colapietro 1989, 28), or a "web of continuously related signs" (Buchler 1955, xii). American pragmatism and French poststructuralism have both developed a semiotic notion of personhood which replaces the notion of self as substance with a relationally defined self which is decentered, open, multiple, fluid, shifting, and ever-changing. The semiotic concept of self developed in both American pragmatism and French poststructuralism therefore functions to deconstruct the substantial ego-self into a centerless web of sign-relationships with no fixed core, essence, or nature. However, it should be pointed out that the semiotic communication model of the social self articulated by C. S. Peirce as worked out in such essays as "Some Consequences of

Four Incapacities," originally published in the *Journal of Speculative Philosophy* as early as 1868, was developed well before the semiology of Ferdinand de Saussure, whose *Course on General Linguistics* was published in 1915. Moreover, there are profound differences between the semiotic models of personhood developed by Peirce in American pragmatism and those of French poststructuralism. Based on Saussure's notion of language as a relational or differential network of signs with no positive entities, French poststructuralism deconstructs the human subject into a play of signifiers to the extent of nihilism, thus resulting in an anti-humanist position whereby there is a total loss of self or disappearance of man, the complete dissolution of the human subject. The semiotic notion of decentered selfhood formulated in French poststructuralism thus fails to account for the creative agency and self-reflexivity of an acting subject in human experience. Among recent social thinkers this nihilism in the French model of decentered selfhood has been strongly criticized by Anthony Giddens. In *The Constitution of Society* (1984), Giddens develops his theory of *structuration*, in which the whole "individual/society" dualism is abandoned and replaced by what he calls the "duality of structure." He emphasizes that while in his theory of structuration the "decentering" of the subject is fundamental, unlike the movements of semiotics and deconstruction on the Continent, the acting subject or the I of human agency cannot be dissolved into a differential play of signs. In the words of Giddens: "I acknowledge the call for a decentring of the subject and regard this as basic to structuration theory. But I do not accept that this implies the evaporation of subjectivity into an empty universe of signs" (1984, xxii). Elsewhere, Giddens (1979, 47) similarly asserts that while the theme of "decentring of the subject" is of essential importance to social theory insofar as it implies an escape from Cartesian subjectivism, this should not lead to the total disappearance of the reflexive components of human conduct.

V. M. Colapietro's *Peirce's Approach to the Self: A Semiotic Perspective on Human Subjectivity* argues for the advantage of Peirce's semiotic notion of personhood over that of the antihumanist theory of French deconstructionism precisely in that the former view achieves a decentering of the Cartesian ego into a web of sign-relations without the complete liquidation of human agency:

> Peirce's general theory of signs, insofar as it is a normative account of reasoning, entails a commonsensical understanding of human agency. . . . His refusal to eliminate the acting subject along with the Cartesian *cogito* is one of the important respects in which Peirce's semiotic vision is superior to the antihumanist orientation of Saussure's structuralist and poststructuralist offspring. For these offspring, the decentering of the subject amounts to nothing less than the liquidation

of the agent. . . . Here is a difference that surely makes a difference. (1989, xix)

Hence, a vital difference between the Continental tradition based on the semiology of Saussure and the American tradition based on the semiotics of Peirce is that while the former deconstructs the self-identity of the ego-centric Cartesian subject into a web of multiple sign relations to the extent that there is a complete "loss of self" or "disappearance of the subject," thereby falling into nihilism and antihumanism, in the latter tradition there is an effort to decenter the subject while at the same time preserving the creative element of human agency and the reflexive aspects of the I or acting self. It should be further pointed out that the French poststructuralist theory of semiotics leads to the conclusion of relativism whereas Peirce's semiotics does not. This relativism of French poststructuralists derives from an understanding of signs as they function primarily in literary texts, where the meaning of a sign disseminates into irreducible multiplicity, openness, and indeterminacy. For Peirce, however, the understanding of signs is based on their function as fallible hypotheses in a scientific experiment, wherein the veracity of an hypothesis is tested through its predictive power and problem-solving ability in the ongoing process of self-corrective inquiry. Hence, while the semiotics of French deconstructionists falls into relativism, Peirce instead develops a sign theory based on the nonfoundationalist scientific experimental laboratory method which counters relativism and allows for progress in knowledge. The semiotic communication model of the social self formulated by C. S. Peirce and subsequently developed by other American pragmatists like Royce, Mead, Dewey, and Buchler, thus establishes a significant alternative to the tradition of French deconstructionism on the Continent.

## William James

Although William James (1842–1910) obtained his Ph.D. in medicine from Harvard Medical School in 1869, and opened the first experimental laboratory in psychology in America while teaching physiology and anatomy at Harvard during the 1880s, he went on to become one of the central figures in classical American philosophy. His father, Henry James Sr., was the friend of such famous New England literary figures as Ralph Waldo Emerson, Henry David Thoreau, and Nathaniel Hawthorne, who frequently visited the family household. William James's brother was Henry James, Jr., the great novelist who is regarded as one of the forerunners of the psychological "stream of consciousness" novel. Willliam James was the most intimate friend of Charles

Sanders Peirce, and it was James who first popularized his "pragmatism." James was also the closest friend and colleague of Josiah Royce in the Department of Philosophy at Harvard University. James thus lived in the very midst of the intellectual renaissance during the golden age of classical American philosophy.

In his writings on philosophy and psychology James undermines the tradition of Cartesian subjectivism with his notion of self as a "pure experience" arising prior to the subject-object bifurcation and anterior to all reflective judgement. James rejects all substantialistic concepts of self, whether an aggregate of material substances as posited by atomism, or a single absolute substance as posited by monism, and instead formulates a process theory of self as a series of drops of pure experience in the ever-changing stream of consciousness with no underlying substantial identity. He also develops a field model of self wherein each drop of pure experience is characterized by its focus/field structure having a luminous focal region of consciousness in the foreground which is surrounded by a vague subconscious fringe of dimly felt causal relationships in the background of the perceptual field. At the same time he describes the creative dimensions of the self in that the focus-fringe pattern of its perceptual field is actively constructed by the power of selective attention as governed by teleological interests, goals, and aims. Furthermore, James introduces an explicit theory of the social self. Although the concept of a social self and its two component phases of I and Me is especially associated with the social psychology of George Herbert Mead and the Meadian tradition of symbolic interactionism, in fact, as is the case with so many other seminal ideas of twentieth-century philosophical thought, the source of these terms is to be found in the writings of James. In addition, Mead's important notion that the social self constitutes a *multiple self* was also inspired by James.

## James's Process Theory of Selfhood

In 1890, when he was forty-eight years of age, James published his monumental two-volume work, *The Principles of Psychology*. A primary feature of James psychology is that it rejects both monism and atomism based on the category of substance and instead works out a *process* theory of the self as a "stream of thought." James uses his process theory of self to criticize the various substantialist psychologies prevalent at the time, especially the "mind-stuff theory," the "associationist theory," and the "transcendentalist theory," all of which held to some belief in the existence of a psychic or mental substance. James repudiates all transcendentalist theories such as the Platonic/

Judeo-Christian idea of an immortal soul, the Cartesian *cogito*, Kant's Transcendental Ego, and Hegel's Spirit, all of which regard the self as a single substance or permanent, self-sufficient entity that requires nothing other than itself in order to exist. While transcendentalist theories represent a form of monism in which the self is held to be a single absolute substance, "mind-stuff" and "associationist" theories represent versions of atomism whereby the self is a collection of discrete unrelated substances. In his chapter entitled "Personal Identity" from *Treatise on Human Nature*, David Hume develops an associationist psychology according to which the self is described as a bundle or collection of discrete atomic perceptions which succeed each other with inconceivable rapidity and are in perpetual flux with no underlying substance. According to the empiricism of Hume all our distinct perceptions are distinct existences, and the mind never perceives any real connection among distinct existences. Thus, by Hume's empiricism there is no way to account for personal identity except for as a "habit of thought." Kant would later agree with Hume's conclusion that we do not directly experience a necessary connection between separate moments, but then attempts to account for causal relationships as a "form of thought," an *a priori* category of the understanding imposed on the manifold of sensations as a necessary precondition of experience. However, the radical empiricism of James rejects both the conclusion of Hume and Kant. James asserts that the self is not just a "succession of feelings" as said by Hume, but also a *feeling of succession* which constitutes the continuity of selfhood from one moment to the next in the flowing stream of thought. According to James's process theory of self, each thought in the stream of consciousness is private, separate, and insulated, yet at the same time *fringed* so as to include the experience of "felt relations," or what he otherwise calls the datum of *felt transitions, feelings of transition*, or *feelings of causation*. A moment is not a "knife-edge" but instead occupies the temporal span of a *duration* or "specious present" with both a backward-going fringe of memory and a forward-going fringe of anticipation. The process model of self as a stream of thought views personal identity as constituted by a succession of transitory selves in which each past self is replaced with a new self whereupon the sum total of the person is increased with each passing moment. Hence, for the radical empiricism of James, as for the empiricism of Hume, the permanent substantial self of absolutism is deconstructed into a flux of temporal becoming; but while for Hume the self in flux is a chain of discrete moments with no relations between them, for James the self is a ever-flowing stream of consciousness in which each momentary self is separate yet overlapping with its past and future selves through the datum of felt transitions.

## James's Focus-Field Model of Self

In his work *Essays in Radical Empiricism* (1912) James goes on to develop his celebrated theory of "pure experience," defined as immediate experience in the instant field of the present which arises prior to the division of subject and object and anterior to all reflective judgement. Accordingly, the self is now comprehended as a sequence of drops of pure experience devoid of any subject-object dualism in the stream of consciousness. As stated before, the radical empiricism of James is a philosophical method which, in opposition to the empiricism of David Hume, recognizes the existence of continuities, causal transmissions, and conjunctive relations as directly felt in immediate experience, or what Hume otherwise refers to as datum of "necessary connection." According to James, the empiricism of Hume does not go far enough to the extent that it fails to discover "transitions" and "fringes" constituting the connective tissue in the flux of immediate experience. An event of pure experience comprising the self at any given moment is phenomenologically described by James as an immediately felt whole characterized by its "focus-field" or "focus-fringe" structure in which focal awareness discriminated in the foreground focus of attention through an act of selective interest is always surrounded by a fringe of dimly felt causal relationships located in the background of the perceptual field. Although we usually identify our self with only the focal region of consciousness, our true self is co-extensive with the whole field of causal relations from which it has emerged. In his essay "The Continuity of Experience" James explicitly articulates his field model of the self as follows: "My present field of consciousness is a centre surrounded by a fringe that shades insensibly into a subconscious more . . . What we conceptually identify with and say we are thinking of at any time is the centre; but *our full self is the whole field.*" Due to this focus-fringe structure of pure experience the context-dependent self in its wholeness is therefore always located within a flowing "stream" of time and an encompassing "field" of space. In this way the pure experience of James represents a focus-field model of personhood designating a shift from the separative self to the connective self. James rejects Hume's atomic self which has no causal connection to others, just as he rejects Kant's transcendental-constitutive self wherein causal connection is an *a priori* category of the understanding. Yet he also rejects the absolute self of Hegel, Bradley, and Royce, for whom the self is causally related to everything else in the universe as a single organic system. While for James the self is encircled by a relational fringe in the felt background of immediate experience which

constitutes it as a felt whole, it is not a felt totality as described in the absolute idealism of Bradley. As opposed to the atomic self of Hume which recognizes only external relationships, or the absolute self of Hegel, Bradley, and
Royce which recognizes only internal relationships, the radical empiricism
of James supports a contextualist model of selfhood whereby the background
fringe of relationships encompassing the focal self at any moment is constituted by both internal and external relations, both conjunctions and disjunc-
tions, both continuities and discontinuities in a pluralistic multivariate field
of confluent experiences. In contrast to the atomism of Hume wherein there
are only separate facts with no causal relations between them, or the monism
of idealist thinkers like Bradley wherein the multiplicity of selves ultimately
dissolves into a single absolute self, in the metaphysical pluralism of James
there is an irreducible multiplicity of insulated selves which are at the same
time overlapping, interpenetrating, and continuous at their outermost
"fringes" in the felt background of immediate experience. James's relational,
temporal self based on the focus-field structure of pure experience thus
represents a contextualist model of personhood establishing a *via media* between the atomic self of abstract individualism and the absolute self of abstract
collectivism.

Some characteristic features in James's process theory of selfhood may
now be enumerated as follows: First, the self is not a substance but a series of
pure experiences in the *stream of thought*. As such, the self of immediate experience is not something already made but *in-the-making*. Each momentary
self is replaced by a new self with every passing moment. Consequently, the
sum total of events in the stream of consciousness is always *increasing*. Every
experience in the stream of consciousness is separate yet related by *felt transitions*. The self is not only described by James in temporal categories as an
ever-flowing stream of consciousness grounded by the datum of felt transitions; it is also described in terms of spatial categories as a focus/fringe
pattern grounded by the datum of felt wholeness. To begin with a transitory
moment of pure experience is devoid of subject-object bifurcation and anterior to reflection. Also, pure experience is characterized by a focus/fringe
structure wherein the foreground focus of attention is surrounded by a background field or fringe of causal relationships. The focus-field structure is not
fixed or given but *constituted* by acts of selective attention which are teleologically governed by pragmatic human interests, goals and ends. Although
we identify our focal self with the center, *our full self is the whole field*. Every
momentary self is private yet is *fringed* with relations, including both conjunctive and disjunctive relations. There are an *irreducible plurality* of selves,

all private yet overlapping and copenetrating with the others through their relational fringes. Finally, individuals are continuous with other selves and God in the *subconscious more* located at the margins in the background field of pure experience.

James's "focus-field" model of self exerted a profound influence on the American process thought of Dewey, Mead, and Whitehead, who all describe the "foreground-background" structure of a situation as the basic unit of immediate experience. Dewey, Mead, and Whitehead develop a social concept of self as a foreground-background situation whereby each individual organism in the foreground is dependent for its existence on the wider social environment located in the background of the perceptual field. In their doctrines of aesthetic experience they further emphasize that this irreducible contrast between the foreground focus and and background field characterizing a moment of immediate experience is the basic structure of beauty. The function of art is to elicit hidden depths by raising into clarity this background field of dimly felt causal relationships which forever surrounds those objects presented for clear awareness in the foreground focus of attention. Moreover, James's focus-field model of self was reformulated in terms of the point-horizon or figure-ground *Gestalt* contexture of the perceptual field in the movement of Continental phenomenology running through Husserl, Heidegger, and Merleau-Ponty. Like the radical empiricism of James, Husserlian phenomenology clarifies how the focus-field structure of primordial perception in the stream of internal time-consciousness is not fixed or given but is instead *constituted* by intentional acts of selective attention. The modern Japanese philosopher Nishida Kitarō also develops a theory of selfhood in terms of the focus-field structure of pure experience in the stream of consciousness under the influence of James. It is no exaggeration to claim that James's focus-field model of self represents one of the most significant contributions to the concept of personhood in twentieth-century thought.

## The Social Self Theory of William James

In addition to his process model of self as a series of drops of pure experience in the stream of consciousness, and his focus-field model of self as encompassed by a fringe of causal relationships in the felt background of immediate experience, James also worked out a theory of the social self with its two components of I and Me. Throughout *The Principles of Psychology* James develops what is in certain respects an individualistic concept of selfhood based on an introspective method as he analyzes those psychological categories of conception, attention, memory, perception, sensation, instincts, emotions and will. Nonetheless, in chapter 10 entitled "The Consciousness of Self" he articulates an explicit theory of the social self. Analyzing the self into its constituent parts, James (1981, 280) first distinguishes what he calls the material self, the social self, the spiritual self, and the pure ego. The primary importance which James assigns to his notion of the social self is then stated as follows: "Of all these wider, more potential selves, *the potential social self* is the most interesting . . . by reason of its connection with our moral and religious life" (1981, 300). Clarifying his reflexive view of the social self, he writes: "*A man's Social Self* is the recognition which he gets from his mates" (1981, 281). James underscores the fact that one's self-image depends on recognition by others in society, while at the same time emphasizing that each individual in fact possesses *many social selves*: "Properly speaking, *a man has as many social selves as there are individuals who recognize him* and carry an image of him in their mind" (1981, 281–82). In this way James can be said to have deconstructed the Cartesian ego into a plurality of social selves. For James, then, the social self is also a *multiple self.*

The distinction between the I and the Me as two abstract phases of the social self, made famous by G. H. Mead and the movement of symbolic interactionism in American sociology, is also to be traced back to this same text by James. Throughout his discussion concerning the consciousness of self he shows that while the subjective I is in certain respects analogous to Kant's pure ego, the "I think" which accompanies all of our representations as the transcendental unity of apperception, the objectified Me is akin to what Kant terms the empirical self. This Kantian distinction between the I or pure ego and Me or empirical self is explained by James when he writes: "The only self we know anything positive about, he thinks, is the empirical *me*, not the pure *I*" (1981, 343). James then goes on to announce the introduction of the I and the Me as specialized technical terms denoting the subjective and objective aspects of self: "*Hereafter let us use the words* ME *and* I *for the empirical person and the judging Thought*" (1981, 350). Finally, in the summary to this chapter James depicts the consciousness of self as involving a "stream of thought" constituted by the dialectic of I and Me (1981, 378–79). Both the similarities and differences with Kant's notion of the self are made clear by James in the following statement:

> This me is an empirical aggregate of things objectively known. The *I*
> which knows them cannot itself be an aggregate; neither for

> psychological purposes need it be considered to be an unchanging
> metaphysical entity like the Soul, or a principle like the pure Ego, viewed
> as 'out of time.' It is a *Thought,* at each moment different from that of
> the last moment, but *appropriative* of the latter, together with all that
> the latter called its own. (1981, 379)

Hence, in this work James adumbrates a process theory of the social self
whereby the unity of the self is constituted by virtue of an internal dialectic
between the unifying acts of a subjective *I* and the empirical content of an
objectified *Me.* However, while James's distinction between I and Me is in
certain respects derived from Kant, at the same time, he clarifies that the I is
not to be conceived in substantialist terms as an unchanging Transcendental
Ego, but in process terms as a momentary idea which arises and perishes in
the "stream of thought." For James the I is located in the stream of consciousness itself rather than a transcendental ego which stands outside the
temporal flow of experience in order to organize it. In summary, it can be
said that while James pointed the way toward the construction of a fully
relational and temporal concept of the self, he did not truly develop a social
psychology which explains the social origin and formation of the self within
an intersubjective community.

## Charles Horton Cooley

Although Charles Horton Cooley (1864–1929) spent his entire academic
career at the University of Michigan, he is still generally associated with the
Chicago school of sociology, which included among its founding members
both John Dewey and George Herbert Mead. Along with Peirce, James,
Dewey, and Mead, C. H. Cooley is regarded as one of the main inspirations
for the "symbolic interactionist" school of sociology in America. A student
of John Dewey and heavily influenced by the psychology of William James,
Cooley regarded his own position as representing a form of "social pragmatism" or "sociological pragmatism." Today he is best remembered for his
concepts of "the primary group" and the "looking-glass self" as formulated
in his three major works: *Human Nature and the Social Order* (1902), *Social
Organization* (1909), and *Social Process* (1918). However, he was also the first
thinker to systematically develop the notion of a social self in American sociology. As noted by M. J. Cohen: "Though the term 'social self' had a wide
circulation in the philosophical circles of the 1890's, Cooley was the first sociologist to incorporate it into a coherent social theory" (1982, 124).

## Cooley's Theory of the Social Self as an Individual-Society Relation

Cooley introduced the idea of a social self in his first major work entitled *Human Nature and the Social Order* (1902). This work begins with Cooley's analysis of the relation between the individual and society, which provides a sharp contrast to earlier sociological theories. Unlike Spencerian individualism, he did not see the individual as basic and the group as the sum total of parts, nor did he see the collective consciousness of the group as having primacy over individuals, as Durkheim did. Instead, for Cooley, society and the individual are to be understood as "collective" and "distributive" aspects of the same phenomenon as an organic whole with two aspects. By this view both "individual" and "society" are not to be regarded as separate systems but as two sides of the same coin. He writes:

> A separate individual is an abstraction unknown to experience, and so likewise is society when regarded as something apart from individuals. . . . In other words, "society" and "individuals" do not denote separable phenomena, but are simply collective and distributive aspects of the same thing. (1964 [1902], 36–37)

Cooley goes on to develop a systematic critique of all theories that regard society and the individual as opposing or antithetical entities. Unlike the Freudians, Cooley does not see the individual and society as being in conflict. He therefore asserts: "I think, then, that the antithesis, society *versus* the individual, is false and hollow whenever used as a general or philosophical statement of human relations" (1964, 41–42). In opposition to such theories Cooley views the social self as a product arising from the dynamic interdependence between society and the individual. The social self of Cooley can therefore be said to represent the first effort in sociology to construct a *via media* between various theories of one-sided individualism and one-sided collectivism prevalent at the time.

Just as Cooley's ideas on the individual and society were influenced by his teacher John Dewey, so his idea of the social self was influenced by the psychological views of William James and James Baldwin. Above all else, he attributes his concept of the social self to William James as developed in the latter's work, *The Principles of Psychology*. Cooley writes:

> This idea that social persons are not mutually exclusive but composed largely of common elements is implied in Professor William James's

doctrine of the Social Self and set forth at more length in Professor James Mark Baldwin's *Social and Ethical Interpretations of Mental Development*. Like other students of social psychology I have received much instruction and and even more helpful provocation from the latter brilliant and original work. To Professor James my obligation is perhaps greater still. (1964 [1902], 125 fn)

Yet in his Journals he also criticizes James's idea of the social self as falling short to the extent that it is developed within the overall framework of an individualistic psychology, and for this reason, it fails to realize the ideal of a "social pragmatism." In this context, he states:

> Although William James had insight into the social nature of the self he did not develop this into a really organic conception of the relation of the individual to the social whole. His conceptions are intensely individualistic. . . . He saw men as separate individuals, not as, in any intelligible sense, members one of another. A social, or perhaps I should say a sociological, pragmatism remains to be worked out. (Journal, XXII, 1921, 47–48; cited in M. J. Cohen 1982, 139 fn.)

## Cooley's Theory of the "Looking-Glass Self"

Cooley's idea of the social self is especially developed in chapters 4 and 5 of *Human Nature and the Social Order*. In this section of his work he emphasizes the development of a social self through interaction between the individual and society by means of *communication*. For Cooley, "communication" is the very stuff of which the social self is made. He writes: "The social self is simply any idea, or system of ideas, drawn from the communicative life, that the mind cherishes as its own" (1964, 179). Thus, like Peirce, Dewey, and Mead, Cooley articulates a communication paradigm of the social self based on dialogical interaction between the individual and society. Cooley then proceeds to introduce the idea for which he best known, the idea of the *social self* as reformulated in terms of what he calls the "looking-glass self," whereby the individual is conceived to be a mirror reflecting its primary social group:

> A social self of this sort might be called the reflected or looking-glass self . . . As we see our face, figure, and dress in the glass . . . so in imagination we perceive in another's mind some thought of our

appearance, manners, aims, deeds, character, friends, and so on, and are variously affected by it. (1964, 84–85)

Cooley's theory of the "looking-glass self" partly derives inspiration from William James's reflexive notion of the social self according to which a person's self-image depends on the images other members of society have of him. For Cooley the development of the individual into a social self requires an ability to both view and judge himself as he imagines others do. That is to say, individuals gain a view of themselves by imaginatively entering into the position of others in the primary social groups to which they belong. Cooley next asserts that a social person's self-image has three principal elements: "The imagination of our appearance to the other person; the imagination of his judgment of that appearance, and some sort of self-feeling, such as pride or mortification" (1964, 184). It is on the basis of his idea of the person as a looking-glass self whereby he arrived at his view that one's imagination of others constitutes the basic social facts for sociological theory. In Cooley's own words: "I conclude, therefore, that the imaginations which people have of one another are the *solid facts* of society, and that to observe and interpret these must be a chief aim of sociology" (1964, 121). Cooley's sociology has also clearly been influenced on this point by Adam Smith's looking-glass theory of self. Adam Smith argued that in the economic world, the seller must look at himself from the standpoint of the buyer, and vice versa. Or as Cooley asserts, in social conduct we can use "sympathetic imagination" to look at ourselves from the point of view of others in society. According to Cooley's looking glass notion of the social self, then, people imagine their own appearance from the standpoint of others, thereby developing reflexive self-consciousness by seeing themselves reflected in the community as if looking into a mirror.

## Josiah Royce

During the golden age of American pragmatism, Josiah Royce (1855–1916) was teaching in the Department of Philosophy at Harvard University together with William James and George Santayana. Yet unlike other leading thinkers in the tradition of classical American philosophy, Josiah Royce was to the end of his career an absolute idealist in the neo-Hegelian tradition who conceived of ultimate reality in religious terms as an absolute Mind, Consciousness, or Spirit. According to the characterization of James, while his own position designates a radical pluralism based on the image of a "multi-

verse," the idealism of Royce instead represents a form of monism or absolutism based on the image of a "block universe." In his famous refutation of
Royce's position, James once exclaimed: "I say, Royce, damn the Absolute!"
Nevertheless, Royce considered himself to be a pragmatist, and his own position as that of an absolute pragmatism. As Royce states in his *Lectures on
Modern Idealism,* "I assert that personally I am both a pragmatist and an absolutist" (1919, 258). It is significant that although Royce, James, and Santayana
were the best of friends and colleagues, they nonetheless carried out an ongoing philosophical debate at the highest level of discourse in the spirit of
mutual criticism. Thus, while Royce, James, Santayana and others at Harvard
University did not form a "school" based on a common doctrine in the same
sense as the Chicago school of Dewey and Mead, they nonetheless formed a
*community of inquirers* based on the ideals of open communication, cooperation, and public discourse.

The fundamental concept in the philosophy of Josiah Royce is that of
community. From the standpoint of his metaphysics of absolute idealism
Royce works out the social nature, origin, and development of the self within
a community. For an individual to develop into a social self with full self-
consciousness, he must necessarily belong to a community. Royce argues
that it is only by entering into a community that an individual can overcome
separation from others and realize his "greater social self." The self must
therefore always be understood in relation to a community and vice versa.
Among the various kinds of communities described by Royce are the community of loyalty, the community of interpretation, the community of inquirers,
the beloved community of the church, and the great community or world
community. In a metaphysical idealism there is a constant danger of the individual disappearing into the community or the self disappearing into the
absolute as a mere cell in the social organism. However, for Royce the unique
individuality of a person is accounted for by his concept of the individual as a
"plan," "purpose," or "project." An individual is defined not in terms of an
underlying soul-substance but in terms of a "life-plan," and is thus a *purpose
to be fulfilled* or a *task to be performed.* Throughout his works Royce is concerned with overcoming the problem of individualism versus collectivism,
which he in turn relates to the metaphysical problem of the many and the
one. While the position of individualism represents a many without a real
one, that of collectivism represents a one without a real many. For Royce,
the notion of community functions to resolve this problem in that it signifies
the unity of both a real many and a real one. Against the background of
German idealism Royce develops his idea of the self as an Ego-Alter dialectic
within the community. Inspired by the Japanese Bushidō ethic of loyalty and

self-sacrifice he then articulates his idea of both self and community as a function of "loyalty" to a supra-individual cause. In his later writings Royce develops a Christian soteriology based on his theme of religious salvation through the community. Finally, Royce goes on to use Peirce's semiotics or general theory of signs as the philosophical basis for a dialogical theory of the social self in a community of interpretation. It can thus be said that the pervasive theme unifying the various stages in the development of Royce's philosophy is that of self-realization in the community.

## Royce's Ego-Alter Dialectic of the Social Self and the Principle of Betweenness

In his work *The World and the Individual* (1901), Royce sets forth an explicit notion of the social self. It is through communication with others in an intersubjective community that an individual overcomes the isolation of ego-centrism and develops what he calls the "greater social self" (1959, vol. 1, 55). It is only through membership in a community that an individual realizes its "greater social self," whereupon the community becomes the individual in macrocosm and the individual becomes the community in microcosm. For Royce, the community is thus to be regarded as a larger unit of the self-conscious individual.

Royce further articulates his notion of the "greater social self" in terms of an Ego-Alter dialectic of intersubjectivity. He argues that the individual begins to achieve reflexive self-consciousness through the act of *imitation*. Through imitation the child develops self-consciousness by learning the distinction between the self and the not-self, or what he otherwise calls the "contrast-effects" between Ego and Alter. Royce asserts that "empirical self-consciousness, from moment to moment, depends upon a series of contrast-effects, whose psychological origin lies in our literal social life" (1901, 260). And again: "In literal social life, the Ego is always known as in contrast to the Alter" (1901, 264). In this context, Royce asserts that the unity of the Ego-Alter or self/not-self dialectic constituting human selfhood is based upon the key psychological principle that the self has a "predominantly Social origin." Royce thus states:

> But there still does remain *one psychological principle* running through all these countless facts, and explaining, in general, both why they vary, and why yet we always suppose, despite the chaos of experiences, that the Self of our inner and outer life preserves a genuine, although to us

hidden unity. This psychological principle is the simple one that, in us men, the distinction between between Self and Not-Self has a predominantly *Social origin*, and implies a more or less obviously present contrast between . . . an Alter, and the life, which by contrast with that of the Alter, is just then viewed as the life of the present Ego. (1901, 260)

Throughout his work *The World and the Individual*, Royce develops his concept of "the *between*" as a fundamental social category expressing the triadic intermediary relation between self and not-self or Ego and Alter. For Royce, any two facts which one discriminates in experience, whether these are two physical objects or the two aspects of the Ego and the Alter constituting human selfhood, must always be connected by a third element (Peirce's Thirdness): namely, the interval of space which stands *between* them: "If I discriminate attentively between two facts in space . . . I observe, in general, that there is something *between* these two discriminated objects, and also that there are regions of space *between which* these two distinguished objects are to be found" (1901, 66). Influenced by Peirce's semiotic theory of sign-relations whereby a "sign" is a First which stands in a genuine triadic relation to a Second, called its Object, as to be capable of determining a Third, called its Interpretant, Royce emphasizes that the space *between* any two objects represents "a triadic relation" (1901, 80). Hence, the Self is a triadic relation located in the interspace *between* the Ego and the Alter.

## Royce's Community as a Function of Loyalty and the Influence of Bushidō

One of the most fundamental theories in the moral philosophy of Royce is that both the community and the social nature of self are a function of loyalty. In *The Philosophy of Loyalty* (1908), Royce defines loyalty as the "willing and practical and thoroughgoing devotion of a person to a cause" (1908, 16f). For Royce, loyalty is always devotion to a cause, and in that a cause has a superindividual character, it functions to bind the many individual selves who are loyal to it together into an intersubjective community. The various kinds of communities described by Royce are therefore all to be understood as a function of the sustained loyalty of its members to the cause or goal for which it exists. The "community of inquirers" requires that its members be loyal to the cause of truth as the common goal toward which the scientific community strives, just as the "beloved community" of the church requires that its members be devoted to God as the supreme goal of the religious community, and the "great community" of all mankind is commited to international cooperation as the goal of the world community. It is thus only by loyalty to the superindividual cause underlying the formation of a community that one can overcome egoism and realize one's "greater social self." Royce illustrates the spirit of loyalty by reference to both the European medieval tradition of knighthood based on the ethical code of chivalry, and the Japanese Zen-inspired tradition of the Samurai based on the ethical code of Bushidō. Royce became interested in the duty-based ethics of loyalty at the heart of Bushidō, the Way of the Samurai warrior, upon reading Nitobe Inazō's book entitled *Bushidō—The Soul of Japan* (1905). For Royce, the Japanese ethics of Bushidō offers a paradigm case of social selves united together in a community by virtue of their steadfast loyalty to the same cause (1908, 72–77, 98). When the Samurai warrior acts out of devotion to a cause, his actions are not ego-centered, but are instead group-centered. Moreover, Royce uses the Bushidō ethic in order to illustrate that loyalty to a cause is the basis of not only "community," but also of true *individualism*. For Royce, the individual is defined not by virtue of some underlying soul-substance but rather in terms a unifying "life-plan," a *purpose* which no one else can decide and that no one else can realize. Thus, by choosing one's cause as a purpose to be fulfilled or a task to be performed, one becomes a true individual. He writes: "There is only one way to be an ethical individual. That is, to choose your cause, and then to serve, as the Samurai his feudal chief, as the ideal knight of romantic story his lady,—in the spirit of all the loyal" (1908, 98). Elsewhere in the same text Royce describes how the duty-based ethics of loyalty in Bushidō combined both personal and social elements so as to synthesize the virtues of self-sacrifice and self-effacement on the one hand with those of self-assertion and interior self-possession on the other:

> Now, Bushidō did indeed involve many anti-individualistic features. But it never meant to those who believed in it any sort of mere slavishness. The loyal Japanese Samurai, as he is described to us by those who know, never lacked his own sort of self-assertion . . . Chinese sages, as well as Buddhistic traditions, influenced his views of the cultivation of this interior self-possession and serenity of soul. And yet he was also a man of the world, a warrior, an avenger of insults to his honor; and above all, he was loyal. His loyalty, in fact, consisted of all these personal and social virtues together. (1908, 72)

Royce then argues that in the Way of the Samurai warrior the achievement of spiritual fulfillment and serenity amidst strife is also a consequence of loyalty to a cause. In Royce's words: "the finding of one's rest and spiritual fulfillment even in one's very life of toil itself,—this state is precisely the state of the loyal, in so far as their loyalty gets full control of their emotional nature. . . . The truly serene of spirit are to be found at their best among the loyal" (1908, 98). From the standpoint of East-West comparative philosophy, Royce's discussion of community and the social nature of self as a function of loyalty in relation to the Way of the Samurai warrior and the duty-based ethics of Bushidō is the most significant case of direct influence from the Japanese tradition among any of the classical thinkers of American pragmatism.

## Royce's Semiotic Concept of Self and the Community of Interpretation

The most innovative aspect of Royce's work *The Problem of Christianity* is his pragmatic reformulation of self and community in terms of Peirce's semiotics or general theory of signs. Royce was thus the first thinker to use Peirce's sign theory as the philosophical basis for a social concept of selfhood. In this context Royce reworks his earlier notion of self in Peircean semiotic terms as interpreter of a continuous web of sign-relations and the church to which it belongs as the community of interpretation. He writes: "And if, in ideal, we aim to conceive the divine nature, how better can we conceive it than in the form of the *Community of Interpretation*, and above all, in the form of the Interpreter, who interprets all to all, and each individual to the world, and the world of spirits to each individual" (1913, vol. 2, 219). Based on Peirce's holistic analysis of semiotic communication as involving *triadic* sign-relations, Royce holds that when A interprets B to C, the three constitute a community of interpretation. The goal of interpretation is therefore always the establishment of a community. For Royce, the social nature of man consists in that he is now to be understood as an interpreter of sign-relations, the individual self interpreting other selves to one another through communication, and also interpreting himself to himself through the internal conversation of thinking. For Royce, the community of interpretation is not a static block universe, but is instead to be regarded as a "time-process" (1913, 2, 37) wherein its members share a common interpretation of both its origins in the past and a common interpretation of its goals for the future. The self also depends on interpretation and is therefore, like the community, a time-process whereby a present self interprets its past self to a future self in a never ending chain of interpretive acts. Royce thus asserts, "my idea of myself is an interpretation of my past,—linked also with an interpretation of my hopes and intentions as to to my future" (1913, II, 42). Royce summarizes his semiotic notion of self and community as a chain of interpretive acts when he writes:

> Interpretation, as we have seen in our general discussion of the cognitive process in question, demands that at least an infinite series of distinct individual acts of interpretation shall take place. . . . If, then, the real world contains the Community of Interpretation just characterized, this community of interpretation expresses its life in an infinite series of individual interpretations, each of which occupies its own place in a perfectly real order of time. (1913, 2, 270ff.)

Royce thus provides the concept of an extended self as an infinite series of interpretations wherein all interpretations are themselves signs which require their own interpretation, and so on, into the indefinite future. While Royce's discussion of the absolute in terms of Peirce's sign theory is at times admittedly vague, in terms of its general orientation it clearly sets forth a social concept of man whereby the community and the self are now both understood as products of a dialogical communication process of interpretation. It can be said that Royce's semiotic idea of the self as a continuous series of interpretations within the infinite system of a community of interpretation is the culmination of his effort to reformulate an idealist metaphysics in terms of what he called an "absolute pragmatism."

## Royce's Theory of Salvation as Self-Realization through the Community

Throughout *The Problem of Christianity* (1913) Royce argues that reality is dominated by *social* categories such that the self, the community, and the universe are all to be comprehended as social in nature. Furthermore, this social basis of the self, the community, and the universe is due to the fact that all have the nature of a sign or a system of signs. In this context he underscores the social character of Christianity and argues that this interpretation accords with the very essence of Pauline thought. He now endeavors to reinterpret Christianity as salvation of the individual self through membership in a community: namely, what he refers to as the beloved community of the church. Royce considers the three central Christian ideas as those of sin, atonement, and community. While original sin or the "moral burden" of humanity is understood as isolation, brought about by rebellion against the community which developed its self-consciousness, atonement is conceived as achieving salvation by membership to a community. That is to say, sin is separation from the community, and atonement is reconciliation with the community. *Salvation in community* thus becomes the unifying theme in the later moral and religious philosophy of Royce. Moreover, it is *loyalty* to the super-personal cause whereby one finds salvation in community. But in his christology, Royce emphasizes that salvation does not occur through loyalty to *any* community; spiritual redemption is specifically a function of loyalty to the beloved community of the church understood as the body of Christ. He writes: "Paul and his apostolic Christians were not content with family loyalty, or with clan loyalty, or with a love for any community that they conceived as merely natural in its origin. A miracle, as they held, had created the body of Christ" (1913, 1, 170). Again linking his doctrine of loyalty with the theme of salvation through the community, he writes: "For the new life of loyalty, if it appears at all, will arise as a bond linking many highly self-conscious and mutually estranged social individuals in one" (1913, 1, 185). Royce here emphasizes that it was Paul who was the first to accurately interpret the salvific function of the beloved community as the body of Christ: "We know how Paul conceives the beginning of the new life wherein Christian salvation is found . . . On earth he called into this community its first members. He suffered and died that it might have life. *He is now identical with the spirit of this community.* This, according to Paul, was the divine grace which began the process of salvation for man" (1913, 1, 186–87). For Royce, as for Paul, Jesus Christ is the suffering servant who gave up his life on the cross so as to give birth to the redemptive community, and now lives on as the continuing body and spirit of that community. The Pauline doctrine that Christ has been resurrected as the body and spirit of the redemptive community also accords with the words of Jesus, who said: "For where two or three are gathered together in my name, there am I in the midst of them" (Matthew 18:20). According to Royce's understanding of the Pauline doctrine, then, the body and spirit of Christ is now identical with his community of loyal believers, and salvation through Christ is therefore achieved only by becoming a member of the beloved community as the embodied spirit of Jesus Christ.

## John Dewey

John Dewey (1859–1952) is widely regarded as the leading representative of American pragmatism. At the conclusion of his 1930 essay called "The Philosophies of Royce, James, and Dewey in their American Setting," G. H. Mead has asserted: "In the profoundest sense John Dewey is the philosopher of America" (SW 391). Born in New England, he attended the University of Vermont and Johns Hopkins University, afterwards taking up his lifelong career as a professor at the Universities of Michigan, Minnesota, and Chicago, and, from 1904 until his retirement in 1930, Columbia University. Dewey's pragmatism is called *experimentalism* in that it represents an extension of the scientific experimental method to all fields of knowledge, whereupon concepts are regarded as "working hypotheses" to be tested for their ability to solve problems. His pragmatic theory of inquiry is characterized by *fallibilism* or *nonfoundationalism* in that it abandons the "quest for certainty" and replaces the dogmatic notion of "truth" with that of *warranted assertability*. According to Richard Rorty (1979), Dewey's nonfoundationalist approach to truth as "warranted assertability" functions to deconstruct the picture of mind as a mirror of nature wherein truth is regarded as correspondence and knowledge as accuracy of reflection. Dewey's pragmatism is also referred as *instrumentalism* in that all hypotheses are instruments used by an organism trying to adjust or adapt to its environment in a problematic situation. Again, his position is sometimes called *naturalism* in that it rejects the notion of a transcendent or supernatural principle and regards all transactions as evolving from within the continuum of nature. However, labels such as pragmatism, experimentalism, instrumentalism, fallibilism, nonfoundationalism, and naturalism fail to encompass the whole of Dewey's thought. After he turned sixty, the philosophy of Dewey took a more speculative turn, at which time he produced his greatest works, including *Experience and Nature* (1925), *The Quest for Certainty* (1929), *Art as Experience* (1934), and *Logic: The Theory of Inquiry* (1938). His book *Experience and Nature* (1925) undermines the category of substance and formulates a naturalistic process metaphysics describing the "generic traits" of immediate experience, which he characterizes as being precarious or changing, continuous, holistic, qualitative, aesthetic, and social. He defines immediate experience as arising through a process of interaction between organism and environment in a situation unified by aesthetic quality. A "situation" pervaded by immediately felt aesthetic quality now becomes the basic unit of immediate experience and all dualisms like subject-object or mind-matter are regarded as functional distinctions within a situation instituted for certain purposes of analysis. In *Art as Experience* (1934), often regarded as the greatest twentieth-century work on aesthetics in the English language, Dewey further emphasizes the aesthetic, valuative, and consummatory dimensions of immediate experience as an ends-means continuum. He criticizes the museum concept of beauty whereby art is compartmentalized apart from society and argues that all immediate experience has pervasive aesthetic quality which makes it a whole and funds it with value. According to Dewey, then, although experience is "pragmatic" and "instrumental," a *means* to something else, in its directly felt qualitative immediacy it is also "consummatory," an *end* in itself. While Dewey was a prolific author who wrote on a vast range of topics, it can be said that his notions of inquiry, experience, nature, quality, art, morality, religion, science, democracy, education, and so forth, are all understood from the standpoint of his fundamental concept: namely, the category of the *social*. Hence, a distinctive feature of Dewey's pragmatism is that it establishes the "social" as the ultimate category of human experience.

## The Social as an Ultimate Category

In *Philosophy and Civilization* (1931), Dewey argues that the "social" is *the* inclusive philosophic idea, and that the physical, organic, mental, and individual are all functional distinctions to be included within the social aspect of experience. He writes: "Now of the mental as of the physical and organic it may be said that it operates as an included factor within *social* phenomena, since the mental is empirically discernable only where association is manifested in the form of *participation* and *communication*" (1931, 86; italics added). The various organism-environment transactions which occur in nature culminate at the level of human experience with the emergence of social transactions involving language, communication, and participation. He therefore states that the category of the *social* is "the richest, fullest, and most delicately subtle" of all natural transactions (1931, 80). By establishing the social as the ultimate philosophical category, Dewey thus came to underscore the intersubjective nature of self, the significance of community, and the centrality of communication in human experience.

Dewey's emphasis upon the social as an ultimate metaphysical category or generic trait of human existence led to his focus upon related social issues like morality, democracy, and education. Together with G. H. Mead, J. H. Tufts, James Angell, Edward Scribner Ames, and others at the University of Chicago, Dewey established what came to be dubbed by William James the "Chicago school" of American pragmatism, which endeavored to apply the experimental laboratory method of science to the solution of concrete social and moral problems. Dewey has perhaps exerted the most impact both in America and throughout the world by his pedagogical theories and is associated with the educational movement referred to as "progressive education." While at the University of Chicago, Dewey was chairman of the Department of Philosophy, Psychology, and Education, at which time he founded and directed the "Dewey School" of Chicago, also known as the Experimental School or Laboratory School. He lectured widely on education throughout the world including Japan in 1919, and then for two years in China, followed by tours in Turkey, Mexico, and the Soviet Union. Dewey argues that the educational process is the basic vehicle for establishing a liberal democratic society. Moreover, education is the basis for achieving personhood through both the individualization and socialization of the self. For Dewey, then, it is primarily by means of education that one cultivates personhood as a social individual through a process of communication, interaction, participation, and sharing in an intersubjective community.

## Early Psychological Basis for the Social Self

In their collaborations together at University of Chicago from 1894 to 1904, Dewey and Mead together developed a bio-social concept of self based on a revolutionary approach to social psychology developed in critical reaction to the reductionistic S-R (stimulus-response) behaviorism. Dewey prepared the foundation in his landmark article "The Reflex Arc Concept in Psychology" (1896) while Mead further refined the theory, making it the psychological basis for his concept of the "social act" of communicative interaction. In "The Reflex Arc Concept in Psychology" Dewey undermines the traditional dualism of stimulus-response in favor of what he calls "circuit co-ordination" or "organic interaction." The idea of organic interaction now becomes the basic unit of behavior. Dewey criticizes the dualistic interpretation of "stimulus-response" by showing how the S-R relation is not a mechanistic connection between two atomic events, but a directed, holistic, and organic process of mutually coordinated interaction. It is only the whole "circuit" of the reflex arc which converts the initial phase into a stimulus and the last phase into a response. Or as he clarifies in his later works, the relation of subject and object, organism and environment, or individual and society is not so much an "interaction" between two separate aspects, but a *transaction* in which both arise as functional distinctions within the whole. The stimulus-response relation of the reflex arc is therefore always situational, contextual, and trans-actional in nature. Experience is always an organic coordination or transac-tional whole in which the parts functionally interrelate to create some value. Dewey's early works on psychology which analyze human behavior as a ho-listic circuit of organic interaction between stimulus-response later came to function as the underlying theoretical basis for his other philosophical notions, including his reconstruction of immediate experience as a subject-object transaction, his concept of self as a individual-society transaction, and his naturalistic metaphysics of contextual situations arising through an organism-environment transaction.

## Dewey's Concept of the Social Individual

The social dimensions of Dewey's theory of selfhood are most fully worked out in *Experience and Nature* (1925). In this work he maintains that the person or self arises out of its organic and social interactions with its surrounding context: "Personality, selfhood, subjectivity are eventual functions that emerge with complexly organized interactions, organic and social" (1985, 208). For Dewey, the self is social in that it arises through a dynamic process of inter-action between an individual organism and its whole social environment within an ontological situation, field, or context. Or as he emphasizes in his later work, immediate experience is not an "interaction" between separate parts but a holistic and organic *transaction* in which the parts functionally interrelate to produce some value. Dewey's pragmatism endeavors to under-cut all the traditional dualisms of Western substance philosophy and to re-place them with the principle of *continuity*. All dualisms like subject-object, organism-environment, mind-matter, individual-society, foreground-back-ground, or experience-nature are functional distinctions within a trans-actional situation characterized by the internal continuity of its parts. He asserts that the self emerges through a "valuative transaction" between an organism and its total environment so as to produce a foreground/back-ground situation pervaded by a unifying aesthetic quality which constitutes its wholeness and funds it with value. It is this concept of personhood as an organism-environment transaction pervaded by immediately felt aesthetic quality which functions to establish an unbroken continuity between the individual and his total surroundings of both human society and living nature.

Like Hegel and Royce, John Dewey formulates a philosophy of *self-realization* through organic interaction between the individual and his sur-roundings. However, while the concept of self-realization worked out by Hegel and Royce is committed to a monistic doctrine of absolutism, Dewey is instead committed to a pluralistic doctrine of contextualism. Hence, whereas for Hegel and Royce self-realization occurs through relationships between the individual and the absolute whole, for Dewey self-realization occurs through interaction between the individual and his surrounding context of society and nature. Dewey's concept of the social individual as a transactional situation is intended to function as a middle axiom between atomistic and monistic theories of selfhood. In Dewey's own words: "[T]he theory of experiential situations . . . is by its very nature a *via media* between extreme atomistic pluralism and block universe monisms" (1939, 544). With his idea of personhood as a transactional situation, Dewey attempts to overcome the tradition of Cartesian subjectivism based on the idea of self as an atomic individual without falling into the opposite extreme of collectivism based on the Hegelian notion of an absolute self. The contextualist idea of a plurality of transactional situations preserves the Hegelian concept of organic inter-dependence without dissolving the self into a block universe wherein all is related in a single organic system. Dewey's notion of a transactional situation as the whole in which the individual and society are functional distinctions thus represents a contextualist theory of selfhood which establishes a *via media* between atomism and monism, individualism and collectivism, or Cartesian subjectivism and Hegelian absolutism.

Critics have sometimes charged that Dewey emphasizes community and the social to the point that he fails to account for the individual. Although it is true that Dewey focuses especially upon the social dimensions of experience, at the same time he attempts to work out a concept of the person which allows for both real individualism and real community. In his *Ethics*, Dewey articulates an ethics of self-realization whereby one enlarges the self through relations with others in the community: "The kind of self which is formed through action which is faithful to relations with others will be a fuller and broader self than one which is cultivated in isolation from or in opposition to the purposes and needs of others" (1908, 335). Yet his ethical theory further emphasizes the two-sided nature of the self as what he calls the "social individual," thus assigning equal importance to examining human activity from the perspective of individuals and that of society, asserting that either viewpoint describes the same organic process:

> All ethical theory is two faced. Society is always a society of individuals, and *the individual is always a social individual*. . . . But we can state one and the same process (as, for example, telling the truth) either from the standpoint of what it effects in society as a whole or with reference to the particular individual concerned. (1971–72: vol. 5, 55–56; emphasis added)

Dewey's ethical concept of the "social individual" thus articulates the double structure of personhood whereby the self is understood to exist on a continuum between two aspects, the private aspect of the individual and the public aspect of society.

Dewey's Communication Theory of the Social Self

Above all else, Dewey emphasizes the centrality of *communication* in human experience. Dewey argues that the social nature of human selfhood is itself a function of communication or communicative interaction through language, signs and symbols. The central role of linguistic communication in the social constitution of human selfhood is especially elucidated in an important chapter from *Experience and Nature* entitled "Nature, Communication and Meaning," where he propounds: "Of all affairs, communication is the most wonderful . . . the fruit of communication should be participation, sharing is a wonder by the side of which transubstantiation pales" (1958, 166). Hence, communication, participation, and sharing are three fundamental elements in Dewey's category of the "social," including his concept of self-in-society as well as related social issues of morality, community, democracy, and education. In accord with the "linguistic turn" of twentieth-century philosophy, Dewey underscores the central role of *language* in the social construction of human selfhood. However, he rejects the idea of language as an "expression" of subjective mental states, and instead argues that its essence lies in communication: "The heart of language is not 'expression' of something . . . It is communication" (1958, 179). In another famous statement, Dewey asserts: "Shared experience is the greatest of human goods" (1958, 166). For Dewey, the cultivation of shared experience through social communication and mutual participation is itself the supreme moral good and the most profound dimension of human existence. Furthermore, in accord with his idea of the *ends-means continuum*, social communication is something which is both instrumental and consummatory. He writes: "Communication is uniquely instrumental and uniquely final" (1958, 204). As "instrumental," communication is a *means*, an exchange which produces something wanted, while as "consummatory," it is an *end*, an immediate qualitative enhancement of life, enjoyed for its own sake (1958, 183). He writes: "When instrumental and final functions of communication live together in experience, there exists . . . a society worthy to command affection, admiration, and loyalty" (1958, 205). The consummatory, aesthetic, and valuative aspects of communication are further clarified through the communicative dimensions of art. In *Art as Experience* (1934) Dewey emphasizes that the function of art is to foster communication in an intersubjective community: "In the end, works of art are the only media of complete and unhindered communication between man and man that can occur in a world full of gulfs and walls that limit community of experience" (1934, 105). Dewey thus formulates a communication theory of selfhood whereby the social individual develops through a process of open communicative interaction, mutual participation, shared experience, cooperation, and valuative transaction in a liberal democratic community.

## Alfred North Whitehead

In the twentieth-century Western tradition of philosophy, the most profound system of speculative metaphysics has no doubt been set forth by the great Anglo-American thinker Alfred North Whitehead (1861–1948). Although he was born in England and spent the first part of his life as a Professor of Mathematics in Cambridge and London, upon retirement at the age of sixty-three he began a new career teaching philosophy at Harvard University. After having produced important works in logic, mathematics, and the philosophy of science while in England, in America he went on to formulate a speculative philosophy, culminating in his epoch-making cosmological work, *Process and Reality* (1929). Whitehead is generally considered an American philosopher because his major philosophical books were written at Harvard University, and also, his influence has also been largely in America. Moreover, in his later work on speculative metaphysics produced while teaching at Harvard University, Whitehead aligned himself with the tradition of American pragmatism as developed especially by William James and John Dewey. Whitehead's categoreal scheme is an extension of pragmatism in that it applies the scientific laboratory method to speculative metaphysics so as to be characterized by fallibilism, experimentalism, and nonfoundationalism. In contrast to the dogmatic character of earlier metaphysics based upon absolute foundations, Whitehead's antifoundationalist scheme is presented as an open system of metaphysical categories having the status of fallible hypotheses to be continually revised through self-corrective inquiry. Although Whitehead's organismic process cosmology of events is partly derived through a method of "imaginative generalization" from working hypotheses in modern physics and the other natural sciences, at the same time he follows the radical empiricism of William James wherein all concepts must be carved from and returned to the primordial flux of immediate experience.

According to Whitehead's process philosophy the human self is not a permanent substance undergoing change, but a sequence of arising and perishing events with a personal order. Whitehead's philosophy of organism further characterizes the self as a serially ordered "society" of occasions, each of which arises through its social relations to other occasions in the metaphysical community of one in many and many in one. He abandons the notion of "substance" or independent self-existence for a social theory of existence as relational in character. Like others in the tradition of classical American philosophy, Whitehead emphasizes the *social* as an ultimate philosophical category. Similar to both Dewey and Mead, Whitehead conceives of the self as social in that it arises through a dynamic process of interaction between an individual organism and its social environment. Or in terms of the focus-field model of immediate experience, each occasion of experience is social in that an individual organism located in the foreground focus of attention is always dependent for its existence on a wider social environment in the background field. Whitehead generalizes such notions as the "social," "community," and "society" into metaphysical categories which apply not only to the human self but to all events in the aesthetic continuum of nature. In such a manner Whitehead develops an organismic process metaphysics in which the social and processual character of the human self is grounded in the relational and temporal character of nature itself.

## Whitehead's Category of the Ultimate

Throughout the history of Western metaphysics various ideas have been selected as the first principle or ultimate category such as substance, matter, form, being, and so forth. However, Whitehead was the first to explicitly propose "creativity" as the first principle governing his categoreal scheme: namely, what he calls the Category of the Ultimate (PR 21), with its three interlocked notions of creativity, many, and one. The ultimate metaphysical principle is that of creativity or creative synthesis whereby the many become one and are increased by one, thus constituting the nature of reality as a creative advance into novelty. The principle of creativity is defined as follows:

> Creativity is the principle of novelty. An actual occasion is a novel entity diverse from any entity in the "many" which it unifies. Thus, "creativity" introduces novelty into the content of the many, which are the universe disjunctively. . . . The ultimate metaphysical principle is the advance from disjunction to conjunction, creating a novel entity other than the entities given in disjunction. (PR 21)

According to Whitehead's Category of the Ultimate, creativity is an act of emergent synthesis whereby each occasion of experience includes all previous actual occasions as elements in its own constitution. An actual occasion is a center of social relationships which emerges into actuality through the creative synthesis of manyness into oneness, multiplicity into unity, or disjunction into conjunction, so that the macrocosm becomes a microcosm. Yet for Whitehead the creative process is asymmetrical in that it is always an emergent creative synthesis which unifies only the *past* many into a new one in the production of novel togetherness.

While the Category of the Ultimate articulates the relational or social character of all events, at the same time it avoids the problem of social determinism by also establishing the *self-creativity* of events. That is to say, although for Whitehead each occasion constituting the self arises through its felt relations to other occasions, it is not determined by its relations because it is a *creative synthesis* of those social relationships into a novel and aesthetic unity. Each occasion arises out of its social relationships to other events and then unifies them all with an emergent act of creative synthesis in the production of novel togetherness. This dialectic between self-creativity and causal determination is further clarified by Whitehead in terms of the *bipolar* nature of all occasions. Each occasion of experience is "bipolar" (PR 108) in that it arises from its multiplicity of social relationships from the past at the "physical pole" and then synthesizes them into a novel and aesthetic unity through a creative act at the "mental pole." For Whitehead, then, the self is not a permanent substance with simple location, but a series of self-creative, aesthetic, and novel events, each of which arises out of its inherited social relations to every other event so as to both contain and pervade the whole continuum of nature as a microcosm of the macrocosm.

As discussed earlier, in his typology of four world hypotheses (formism, mechanism, organicism, contextualism) based on four root hypotheses (forms, machines, organisms, events) Stephen Pepper held that Whitehead was an eclectic who had conflated the various paradigms. Charles Hartshorne (1942, 73–74) criticized Pepper's view, arguing that Whitehead had in fact developed a new root metaphor very different than the traditional alternatives. Hartshorne, in accord with his own philosophical commitments, identified the new root metaphor originated by Whitehead as *social* in character so that reality is a social process in which the self is constituted by societies of events, each of which is constituted by its social relations to other events. Hence, in his later work (1961) Pepper goes on to suggest that Whitehead's organic process metaphysics represents a distinctive world hypothesis based upon a new root metaphor of the *creative act* such as that of an artist, inventor, or imaginative scientist (1961, 86). Hartshorne (1987, 369) describes Whitehead along with Peirce and Bergson as having converged upon a new paradigm of "aesthetic creationism" insofar as they all make self-creativity and its aesthetic character the center of their process metaphysics. For Hartshorne the paradigm of aesthetic creationism is a view wherein the self

is a series of momentary events or occasions, each of which are characterized as self-creative experience constitutive of its own novel and aesthetic
unity. Yet as Hartshorne emphasizes throughout his writings, the creativity
of experience is itself the sociality of experience insofar as each occasion of
experience arises through a *creative synthesis* of its social relations to other
occasions. In Hartshorne's words: "Sharing of creativity is the social character
of experience, its aspect of sympathy, participation, identification with others"
(1983, 8). Similarly, David Hall (1982) has developed a metatheoretical classification scheme which subsumes Whitehead's process metaphysics under the
paradigm of aesthetic creationism based on the primary analog of self-creative
aesthetic events which are novel, transitory, and finite. Furthermore, Hall
(1982, 212) goes on to make cross-cultural applications of this scheme, arguing that Whitehead's aesthetic creationism is the most adequate paradigm
for interpreting Chinese modes of thought such as Confucianism, Taoism,
and Buddhism. Just as for Whitehead aesthetic occasions are not produced
externally through the divine creation of God but through emergent acts of
self-creativity, so for Taoism all events create themselves in the *tao* or
primordial creativeness of nature. Indeed, Whitehead's notion of self-creativity
might be used to illuminate the first principles underlying a wide range of
Asian systems, including the first hexagram entitled "Creativity" in the *Book
of Changes*, the *tao* of Taoism, the *tsu-jan* (Japanese: *shizen/jinen*) or spon-
taneousness of Chan/Zen Buddhism, the *tai-ch'i* or great ultimate of neo-
Confucianism, and even the *yi* or responsiveness as over against the *li* or
ritual actions of classical Confucianism. It can be said that by setting forth
creativity as the first principle of his categoreal scheme, Whitehead has crystallized the aesthetic creationist paradigm of the social self whereby at each and
every moment the self is an artist which creates itself as a novel and aesthetic
occasion of experience.

## Whitehead's Principle of Relativity

In Whitehead's categoreal scheme the social or relational character of the
self and all occasions is formally expressed by his "principle of relativity." The
principle of relativity states that each actual occasion can be defined only by
virtue of its social relationships to other occasions. The principle of relativity
asserts that "every item of the universe including all other actual entities, are
constituents in the constitution of any one actual entity" (PR 148). Again, the
principle of relativity stipulates that "every item in the universe is involved in
each concrescence" (PR 22). The principle of relativity states that through

concrescence or the process of becoming an actual occasion, an event arises through its social relationships to every other event in the cosmos. Whitehead's principle of relativity involves the rejection of Aristotle's notion of "substance" in its meaning as separate, permanent, and simply located existence, for the alternate notion of interconnected spatiotemporal events which momentarily arise through their social relations to other events and therefore include each other as elements within their own internal constitution. He writes:

> The principle of universal relativity directly traverses Aristotle's dictum: 'A substance is not present in a subject.' On the contrary according to this principle an actual entity *is* present in other actual entities. . . . Every actual entity is present in every other actual entity. The philosophy of organism is mainly devoted to the task of making clear the notion of 'being present in another entity.' (PR 50)

The principle of relativity thus functions in Whitehead's categoreal scheme as a universal principle of social relatedness, or as it were, a generalized metaphysical category expressing the interconnectedness, interdependence, and interpenetration of everything in the universe.

Whitehead's organismic process metaphysics based upon the "principle of relativity" at once bears a deep structural resemblance to the Buddhist metaphysics based upon the principle of *śūnyatā* in its translation by "relativity." The Buddhist principle of *śūnyatā* has been translated as "relativity" and even "universal relativity" by the pioneering Russian Buddhologist Th. Stcherbatsky. In *The Conception of Buddhist Nirvana*, first published in 1927 Stcherbatsky explains the basis for his translation of *śūnyatā* by "relativity" and *śūnya* by "relative," stating:

> The central conception of Mahayana was their relativity (*śūnyatā*). Since we use the terms 'relative' to describe the fact that a thing can be identified only by mentioning its relations to something else, and becomes meaningless without these relations . . . we safely, for want of a better solution, can translate the word *śūnya* by relative or contingent, and the term *śūnyatā* by relativity or contingency. (1927, 42)

The advantage of Stcherbatsky's translation of *śūnyatā* by "relativity" is that it functions to underscore the relational character of the self and all events in Buddhist metaphysics according to which every event is constituted by its social relations to other events, and it utterly "empty," "void," or "nothing" in itself apart from these relationships. The translation of *śūnyatā* by "relativity" also functions to underscore its basic philosophical meaning as *pratītya-samutpāda*, variously rendered as "dependent coorigination," "interrelational existence," or "relationality." Thus, in its negative, deconstructive aspects as *anātman* (non-ego) and *nihsvabhāvata* (nonsubstantiality), the relativity of Buddhist *śūnyatā* designates the abandonment of "substance" with independent existence, while in its constructive and positive aspect as *pratītya-samutpāda* (relationality), it signifies the interrelational character of the self and all events.

Indeed, Whitehead's organismic process metaphysics based upon the principle of relativity is at once reminiscent of the Buddhist metaphysics based upon the principle of *śūnyatā* in its translation by "relativity" or "universal relativity." The principle of relativity underlying Whitehead's speculative framework especially functions to illuminate the Buddhist category of *śūnyatā* in terms of its standard definition of *pratītya-samutapāda*, "relationality." The Kyoto school philosopher Abe Masao remarks on this striking parallel between Whitehead's principle of universal relativity and the Buddhist notion of *pratītya-samutpāda* in his book *Zen and Western Thought*:

> Whitehead's idea of the relatedness of actual entities is surely stikingly similar to the Buddhist idea of *pratītya-samutpāda*, which may be translated as 'dependent coorigination,' 'relationality,' 'conditioned coproduction' or 'dependent co-arising.' . . . It is not hard to see a parallel between Whitehead's principle of universal relativity and the Buddhist idea of 'dependent co-origination.' (1989, 152–53)

Hence, Whitehead's principle of relativity, like Buddhist *śūnyatā* and its correlate principle of *pratītya-samutpāda*, designates that the self and all events can only be defined by virtue of their social relationships to other events, and are meaningless apart from these relations. However, unlike the Zen Buddhist view of symmetrical relationships wherein events are internally related to all other events of past, present, and future in the all-embracing matrix of Indra's net, Whitehead instead articulates a theory of asymmetrical relationships wherein events are internally related to only all past events while being externally related to present and future events. Hence, while for Buddhism there is a simultaneous mutual containment of events, for Whitehead each event contains its predecessors but neither its contemporaries nor its successors. Also, while for Buddhism it is said that that one is many and many is one, for Whitehead the many become one and are *increased* by one. Whereas Buddhism emphasizes how the self is empty or void insofar as it can be exhaustively factored into its social relationships, Whitehead instead argues that the self is at each new moment a *creative synthesis* of its social relations to other events. It is precisely Whitehead's understanding of the social self as an emergent creative synthesis of the past many into a new one that preserves the asymmetrical, irreversible, and evolutionary structure of "time's arrow" in the creative advance toward novelty.

## The Ontology of Social Events and the Metaphysical Community

In *Religion and the Making*, Whitehead articulates his social vision of the universe as a metaphysical community of interrelated occasions:

> The actual temporal world can be analyzed into a multiplicity of occasions . . . Call each such occasion an "epochal occasion." Then the actual world is a community of epochal occasions. . . . The epochal occasions are the primary units of the actual community, and the community is composed of the units. But each unit has in its nature a reference to every other member of the community, so that each unit is a microcosm representing in itself the entire all-inclusive universe. (RM 88–89)

Just as others in the tradition of classical American philosophy have developed theories of the social self in relation to various forms of community, including the scientific community of inquirers (Peirce), the religious community of loyalty (Royce), and the secular liberal democratic community (Dewey, Mead), in this passage Whitehead underscores the social character of the self and all events through his notion of a metaphysical community of "epochal occasions" which arise through their social relationships to every other event in the community. For Whitehead the metaphysical community is constituted by harmonic penetration of many into one and one into many in the undivided aesthetic continuum of nature. He emphasizes that insofar as each epochal occasion makes reference to every other occasion in the community, it represents a microcosm of the macrocosm. Whitehead's metaphysics is a modern reformulation of the monadology of Leibniz based on the notion of *perspectivism*. He develops a Leibnizian cosmology of perspectives which abandons the idea of self as a substance with "simple location" and instead views the self as a living mirror which reflects the whole antecedent universe from a unique perspective as an individual microcosm of the social macrocosm in the metaphysical community of occasions.

## Whitehead's Social Concept of the Self and Nature

Whitehead fully accepts the ancient Aristotelian notion that man is a "social animal" (PR 204). Moreover, in his effort to work out a metaphysics expressing those ultimate notions of the highest generality at the base of actuality, his philosophy of organism argues not only for the social nature of the human self, but for the social nature of *all* actual occasions. That is to say, Whitehead argues by analogy from the social nature of man so as to extend "the social" into a generic trait characterizing each and every occasion of experience in the aesthetic continuum of nature.

> [T]he philosophy of organism appears as an enlargement of the premise in ethical discussions that man is a social animal. *Analogously, every actual occasion is social*, so that when we have presumed the existence of any persistent type of actual occasions, we have thereby made presumptions as to types of societies comprised in its environment. (PR 204; emphasis added)

Whitehead's generalization of the "social" into an ultimate metaphysical category is made further explicit in *Religion in the Making*, where he states that "every entity is in its essence social and requires the society in order to exist" (RM 18).

Similarly, the idea of "society" is generalized into a metaphysical category which applies not only to human societies, but all occasions of experience without exception. Since every occasion arises through an emergent creative synthesis of the "many" into the "one" it is a *society* of all other actual occasions. For Whitehead the self is not only "social": it is is a serially ordered "society" of occasions, each of which is also social by virtue of its relations to other occasions. Indeed, for Whitehead, the human self is not only a "society" of occasions with a personal order, but a "society of societies," and even a "society of societies of societies." As a society of societies, the personal unity of the human self is composed of a multiplicity of arising and perishing epochal occasions, each of which is also a society of societies, and so forth, without end. In *Adventures of Ideas*, he thus writes:

> [The] Universe achieves its value by reason of its co-ordination into societies of societies, and into societies of societies of societies. Thus an army is a society of regiments, and regiments are societies of men, and men are societies of cells, and of blood and bones, together with the dominant society of personal human experience, and cells are

societies of smaller physical entities such as protons, and so on, and so on. (AI, 264)

Again, in *Symbolism*, Whitehead argues that his concept of society applies equally to human societies as well as by subhuman group interrelations, so that human societies exhibit the same principles as societies of occasions:

> Communities with geographical unity constitute the primary type of communities which we find in the world. Indeed the lower we go in the scale of being, the more necessary is geographical unity for that close interaction of individuals which constitutes society. Societies of the higher animals, of insects, of molecules, all possess geographical unity. A rock is nothing else than a society of molecules . . . I draw attention to this lowly form of society in order to dispel the notion that social life is a peculiarity of the higher organisms. The contrary is the case. (S 76)

According to Whitehead, every society requires an environment; there is no society in isolation (PR 90). Each individual organism in the foreground requires for its existence a social environment in the background. The universe is to be conceived in terms of increasingly larger social orders in which the wider and more general societies provide the necessary character presupposed by the more specialized societies. Charles Hartshorne brings to light the central role of "society" as a generic trait pertaining to the self and all events in Whitehead's categoreal scheme when he remarks: "Whitehead's 'philosophy of organism' might perhaps better have been called 'the societal philosophy,' for 'society' is a more central technical term in it than 'organism'" (1972, 131). For this reason Hartshorne has characterized Whitehead's concept of reality as "socially structured process" (1972, 111). It can be said that Whitehead thus achieves a fully social concept of the human self defined as a society of occasions emerging through social relations to other occasions in the metaphysical community of nature.

## Human Perception in the Mode of Symbolic Reference

It has now been seen that based on his principles of relativity and creativity expressing the universal relatedness of events, Whitehead extends such notions as "the social," "community," and "society" into metaphysical categories so that they become generic traits characterizing all occasions of experience in the interconnected continuum of nature. Hence, for Whitehead, sociality is not in itself the distinguishing trait of human selfhood. The *differentia* of the human self is instead to be found elsewhere: namely, in his theory of "symbolic reference." In his chapter on symbolic reference from *Process and Reality* (1929), and in his book *Symbolism: Its Meaning and Effect* (1927), Whitehead formulates his theory of perception in three modes, including (i) causal efficacy, (ii) presentational immediacy, and (iii) symbolic reference. All occasions are social insofar as they arise through dim feelings of causal relationship to every other occasion at the level of perception in the mode of causal efficacy. At the higher phases of experience organisms enjoy the clear and distinct sense data of colors, sounds, and scents at the level of perception in the mode of presentational immediacy. However, human experience is characterized by the evolutionary development of perception in the mode of symbolic reference, the mixed mode of perception wherein the sense data of presentational immediacy function as symbols making reference to the dim, vague, and obscure feelings of relationships arising in causal efficacy. Whitehead does not say that symbolic reference is exclusive to human occasions but he does argue that it is the characteristic mode of human experience. Thus, similar to Ernst Cassirer's definition of man as an *animal symbolicum* or "symbolic animal" and G. H. Mead's symbolic interactionist concept of the social self, Whitehead argues that the characteristic trait of human selfhood is perception in the mode of symbolic reference.

# ↞5↠

## The Social Self and I-Me Dialectic
## of G. H. Mead

### Mead's Creative Synthesis of
### Classical American Philosophy

The social-self theory of G. H. Mead represents a creative synthesis of the whole tradition of classical American philosophy running through Peirce, James, Royce, Dewey, Cooley, and Whitehead. Fundamental motifs in the American philosophical heritage such as the social construction of self in society, the significance of community, the centrality of communication, and the value dimensions of social existence are all integrated into Mead's notion of the bipolar social self as an I-Me dialectic of intersubjectivity. Mead's communication model of the social self incorporates the insights of Peirce's semiotic notion of personhood as a relational web of signs in an intersubjective community of inquirers, James's idea of the social self with its two phases of I and Me in the stream of consciousness, Royce's notion of realizing one's larger social self in a community of interpretation, Dewey's notion of the social individual as an organism-environment transaction arising through communication in a liberal democratic community, Cooley's looking-glass notion of the social self as an individual-community interaction, and Whitehead's process theory of self as a sequence of emergent perspectives which mirror the whole community as an individual microcosm of the social macrocosm. It can be said that Mead's social-self theory and I-Me dialectic represents one of the crowning achievements of classical American pragmatism.

### Mead and Peirce

Mead is known to have met Peirce on at least one occasion, and was to some extent familiar with the thought of Peirce, as shown when he discusses

187

"Peirce's laboratory habit of mind" in his classic essay on American pragmatism, "The Philosophies of Royce, James, and Dewey in Their American Setting" (SW 385, 389). Mead was above all else influenced by Peirce's pragmatic methodology understood as an application of the scientific experimental laboratory method to all fields of inquiry. In his 1929 essay "A Pragmatic Theory of Truth," Mead writes: "Pragmatic doctrine is a logical generalization of scientific method" (SW 334). Following the pragmatism of Peirce, Mead regards all concepts as "working hypotheses" (SW 330) which are to be tested by the community of inquirers for their *problem-solving* abilities. As emphasized by Jürgen Habermas, Cartesian subjectivism was attacked at the turn of the century by analytic philosophy of language and behavioristic psychology, both of which are indebted to the pragmatism of C. S. Peirce, who conceived of action and knowledge in terms of observable, shared practices. Habermas (1989, 3) further asserts that these two Peirceian disciplines of linguistic philosophy and behavioristic psychology were first integrated into a unified framework in the symbolic interactionism of G. H Mead. While Mead defines the social self in terms of linguistically mediated communicative interaction, this is restated in his behavioristic psychology as a "conversation of *gestures*" or a "language of *gestures*" wherein each physical, verbal, and significant or symbolic gesture is *publicly observable* by a community of inquirers. Hence, by describing symbolic interaction in behavioristic terms as a language of significant gestures, Mead at once combines the Peirceian disciplines of language philosophy and behavioristic psychology into a single framework.

Aside from their similarities with regard to the laboratory method of pragmatism or experimentalism, both Peirce and Mead develop a semiotic communication model of selfhood. Mead, like Peirce, can be said to have abandoned the notion of a "separate self" for that of a "communicative self." Mead's idea of selfhood as arising through symbolic communication using "significant symbols" was indirectly yet decisively influenced by Peirce's semiotics or general theory of signs as reformulated in Josiah Royce's doctrine of the community of interpretation. As stated by Hans Joas: "The influence unquestionably exercised by Peirce's theory of signs on Mead's conception of the significant symbol was indirect, and came to Mead via Royce's later writings" (1985, 37). Similarly, Beth J. Singer has observed: "While he uses different terminology than Peirce, Mead's concept of the nature and basis of meaning is also derived from the Peirceian concept of interpretation" (1983, 105). Colapietro (1989, xix) has argued that although both Peirce and French poststructuralism develop a semiotic view of self as a web of signs, whereas the latter results in nihilism and antihumanism through the total dissolution of man, Peirce instead decenters the Cartesian subject without liquidating human agency. Likewise, Mead's symbolic communication model of the social self is articulated in terms of an I-Me dialectic wherein the Me or generalized other represents the Peirceian "community of interpretation," and the I represents the creative agency of the acting self. Mead's concept of the social self as an I-Me dialectic functions to decenter the Cartesian subject into a semiotic web of linguistic signs or significant symbols as a Me while retaining the creativity, individuality, and freedom of human agency as an I. Peirce's semiotic vision of a decentered self which is intersubjectively constituted by linguistic communication in a community is thereby fully crystallized in Mead's concept of the social self as symbolically mediated communicative interaction between the individual and the community.

## Mead and James

Mead was a student of both William James and Josiah Royce during his graduate student years at Harvard.[5] It is known that starting in the autumn of 1887, Mead actually lived in the home of James as the private tutor of his children. Mead's concept of the social self as an individual-society interaction arising within an organism/environment situation is phenomenologically rooted in the "focus/field" model of immediate experience articulated by James in his psychology of perception, according to which the focal self is always surrounded by an encompassing *fringe* or *field* of social relationships within a flowing stream of consciousness. Also, like James's psychology of perception, Mead rejects the view of psychological determinism based on the passive spectator model of experience, and instead analyzes those autonomous constitutive *acts* whereby the foreground/background structure of the perceptual field is spontaneously organized by the selective power of attention as teleologically governed by human ends, goals, interests, and aims. In Mead's words: "Our attention enables us to organize the field in which we are going to act. Here we have the organism as acting and determining its environment" (MSS 25). Moreover, from James he borrowed the concept of the social self as well as its two component phases of I and Me to represent the subjective and objective aspects of self. He was further influenced by James's idea that the social self is a "multiple self" which reflects all the other selves in the community. However, even though James sketched out a doctrine of the social self, he otherwise develops an individualistic account of selfhood based on an introspective psychology which underscores the "insulation" of one self from other selves. For James, the "social self" was only one among several selves, understood as the social mirroring of the self, to which he attributes influence, but not a constitutive function. Mead (MSS 173) rejects these individualist assumptions underlying James's introspective psychology, arguing that the latter fails to provide a genetic account of how the self arises from its social context, and therefore assumes that the self can exist prior to or apart from its social interactions with others in a group. Thus, even though Mead adopts the terminology of James, he at the same time radically transforms its function and meaning in terms of his own theory concerning the social nature, origin, and formation of the human self. Mead thereby wholly reformulates James's notion of the social self along with its two aspects of I and Me within the context of a thoroughgoing social psychology.

## Mead and Royce

While a graduate student at Harvard University Mead was especially interested in the absolute idealist metaphysics of his teacher Josiah Royce. Mead derived from Royce his strong interest in German idealism, especially Hegel's self-other dialectic of mutual recognition. Also, Mead was deeply influenced by Royce's doctrines of self-realization through the community of interpretation, the individual-world dialectic, the theory of the social nature and origin of the human self, the Ego-Alter dialectic of the self, and the category of *between* as expressing the triadic intermediary relation between self and other. Hence, there are many important points of similarity between the philosophical systems of Royce and Mead. Both Mead and Royce agree that no self is complete in itself apart from a community, and that the self always requires a community in order to develop. For both thinkers, self-consciousness and personality development require a self-other dialectic between Ego and Alter. They assert that the self exists only in relation to society and vice versa. Both emphasize the category of *betweenness* as an intermediary principle between self and other. In terms of their respective moral theories, both maintain that rights and duties are social concepts entailing each other, so that no one has a right except insofar as he also has an obligation. Just as for Royce the individual realizes his "greater social self" through membership in a community, for Mead the individual is constituted as a social self by taking on the roles of the generalized other representing the universalized human community. They each regard the community as a kind of larger unit of the self-conscious individual. For both Mead and Royce the individual realizes his larger social self by incorporating the community whereupon the community becomes the individual in macrocosm and the individual becomes the community in microcosm.

Yet a fundamental difference between them is that Royce founded his ethical system on the Christian religious belief that man is born into a fixed and predetermined moral order established by a transcendent God or the Absolute, while the moral order according to Mead is to be found only in social institutions which arise from the human community and are therefore continually subject to change. Mead directly criticizes Royce's commitment to a preestablished moral order based on a metaphysics of absolute idealism as follows:

> But the Western world has been obsessed with the conception of a given moral order with which the individual will must accord if the individual is to be moral. . . . And it was out of attempted solution of the relation of the individual will and its purpose to a given all-inclusive aim of the absolute will that Royce's idealism arose. (SW 379)

The similarities and differences between these two thinkers can also be seen in terms of their development of a Peircean semiotic theory of self. The great innovation of Royce's absolute idealism is his pragmatic reformulation of the absolute in terms of Peirce's semiotic notion of a community of inter-pretation, so that now the self is understood as an interpreter of sign-relations whereby each individual self interprets other selves to one another through intercommunication, and also interprets itself to itself through the internal communication of thinking. For Royce both the self and community are produced by a dialogical communication process of interpretation. In Mead's social-self theory, the counterpart to Royce's community of interpretation is the *Me* or "generalized other," which arises by internalizing the social institutions of the community to which it belongs through role-taking. As David L. Miller remarks, "Royce's 'Community of Interpretation' is similar to Mead's generalized other" (1975, 69). However, Royce, after Peirce, held that every sign calls for an interpretation, which itself calls for an interpreta-tion, endlessly, so that the meaning or the interpretant of every sign is still another sign. Royce therefore understands the self and the community in purely idealistic terms such that interpretation is always a mental act estab-lishing a relation between minds. Mead, on the other hand, defines the social act of linguistic communication in behavioristic terms as embodied in a "con-versation of gestures," wherein the observable gesture is a stimulus calling out for an observable response which is the "meaning" of that gesture. Mead defines a linguistic "sign" or "significant symbol" in behaviorist terms as a *sig-nificant gesture*, so that the meaning of a sign is ultimately not another sign, but rather an adjustive *response*, thereby to emphasize the pragmatic, behavioristic, and embodied aspects of Peirce's sign theory as a doctrine of intersubjective praxis. Like the absolute idealism of Royce, the pragmatism of Mead is directed toward the goal of self-realization through an intersubjective community of interpretation. But Royce's Christian religious ideal of self and society based on a metaphysics of absolute idealism is reformulated by Mead in terms of a wholly secular, naturalistic, and humanistic model of the social sciences which eliminates all dualism by providing a genetic account of the social nature, origin, and development of the self without any reference to a transcendent or supernatural principle.

## Mead and Cooley

While teaching at the University of Michigan from 1891 to 1893, Mead was the colleague of Charles Horton Cooley, who adopted James's notion of a social self as a fundamental doctrine in his sociological framework (see Cooley 1964, 125 fn.). Cooley was therefore instrumental in Mead's own development of a social-self theory which could function as a unifying model for sociology and the other social sciences. Mead was influenced by Cooley's holistic and functional analysis of the individual-society relation as the "distributive" and "collective" aspects of the social self in its organic unity. Mead, like Cooley, holds that the individual and society are not two separate systems but two aspects of the social self in its integrated wholeness. For Mead, as for Cooley, the individual and society are understood as two sides of the same coin. He was also influenced by Cooley's notion of the "looking-glass self," according to which people imagine their own appearance from the standpoint of others, thereby developing reflexive self-consciousness by seeing themselves reflected in the community as if looking into a mirror. Cooley's doctrine that reflexiveness is acquired by viewing oneself from the standpoint of others through the mechanism of "sympathetic imagination" was transformed by Mead into his doctrine of "taking the role of the other." At the same time Mead (MSS 224 fn.) was extremely critical of Cooley's position, arguing that the latter's so-called social psychology was in fact introspective and individualistic in its basic assumptions. According to Mead, since for Cooley all social interactions depend upon the imaginations of the individuals concerned, and because society therefore has no existence other than in the privacy of an individual's mind, his social psychology falls into complete solipsism. In other words, if society has its locus only in the mind, the social process itself is necessarily a consequence of individual minds. Mead further argues that Cooley's analysis of how reflexive self-consciousness is formed by the imaginations which people have of each other already presupposes the existence of an individual mind or consciousness, and thus, on this basis he criticizes Cooley for his failure to develop a genetic account of the social origin and formation of consciousness itself (MSS 224 fn.). Also, in that for Cooley the process by which selves arise is internal and individual rather than external and social, Mead argues that his psychology is committed to a subjectivistic and idealistic, rather than an objectivistic and naturalistic metaphysics (MSS 224 fn.).

## Mead and Dewey

Mead's relationship to John Dewey is particularly interesting. Throughout his life Mead was the most intimate friend of Dewey, as well as his colleague for extended periods at the University of Michigan, where Mead was an instructor from 1891 to 1893, and then at the University of Chicago, where he taught from 1894 until his death in 1931. It was especially Mead and Dewey who together formed the axis for the Chicago school of American pragmatism, which endeavored to apply the scientific experimental method to social and moral issues. Also, both Mead and Dewey were instrumental in forming the Chicago school of American sociology. Both thinkers made a "pragmatic turn" from Hegelianism to experimentalism, thus rejecting the absolutist paradigm for a contextualist theory standing between individualist and collectivist models of self. These two thinkers influenced each other in many ways, and it can be said that in most important respects the philosophy of Mead is in essential agreement with the pragmatism of Dewey. Beginning with his early writings on psychology, Dewey's famous analysis of the *reflex arc*, developed in collaboration with Mead, criticizes the dualistic interpretation of "stimulus-response," by showing how the S-R (stimulus-response) relation is not a mechanistic connection between two atomic events, but a situational, contextual, and transactional process of mutually coordinated organic interaction. It is only the whole "circuit" of the reflex arc which converts the initial phase into a stimulus and the last phase into a response. Mead went on to further refine Dewey's notion of organic interaction as the basic unit of behavior so as to make it the basis for his own analysis of the "social act," according to which the anticipation of the response of the other gives one's own gesture (the stimulus) its meaning. Stimulus (= gesture) and response (= meaning) are therefore analyzed as functional distinctions within the organic unity of a social act of communicative interaction. This organic, functional account of the reflex arc model for S-R relations as developed in the psychology of Dewey and Mead also serves as the basis for their general understanding of the "social self" as a holistic individual-society interaction. The locus of the social self is neither the individual nor society but a "social situation," an organic whole in which both the individual and society are functional distinctions or two abstract phases of the same process. Moreover, this same holistic analysis of the reflex arc model is further extended into the naturalistic metaphysics of Mead and Dewey, according to which the social self arises as an organism-environment interaction. The locus of the social self is therefore neither in the subject nor in the object but in a "situation" unified by pervasive aesthetic quality arising through the valuative transaction between organism and environment. Both thinkers underscore the aesthetic, valuative, and consummatory dimensions of social experience in the community. Furthermore, for both thinkers each moment in the social constitution of selfhood is both instrumental and consummatory, both a *means* toward a goal and an *end* in itself, so that the temporal process is an "ends-means continuum" funded throughout by pervasive aesthetic quality. In general, both Dewey and Mead emphasize open communication, mutual participation, cooperation, valuative transaction, and shared experience as basic elements in their articulation of a social concept of personhood in a secular liberal democratic community.

However, there is a vital difference between Dewey and Mead in their respective treatments of the self. As Richard J. Bernstein writes at the conclusion of his study entitled *John Dewey*: "I think that the weakest part of Dewey's philosophy is his analysis of the self" (1966, 176). While Dewey formulates a social concept of self as an element in his philosophy, it is not thematized to the extent found in the philosophy of Mead. Also, while Dewey often fails to clarify the role of the individual in his social concept of self, Mead balances the relation between the individual and society through his bipolar concept of the social self as a dialectic of I and Me. While Dewey emphasizes the social dimensions of experience to the point that the individual seems to become a mere cell in the social organism, for Mead the freedom, spontaneity, and creativeness of human agency is clearly established as a function of the I or individual pole of the social self. Mead, like Dewey defines the self in evolutionary terms as an organism-environment interaction. But while Dewey conceives of this process in more Darwinian evolutionary terms as an "adaptation" of organism to environment, Mead instead develops a theory of emergent evolution whereby the self arises through a *spontaneous response* of an individual organism at the I pole to the deterministic social environment at the Me pole in the creative advance of nature. Hence, while there is much in common between the frameworks of these two thinkers, the special achievement of Mead was to have explicitly thematized the concept of a social self and its underlying dialectic of I and Me.

## Mead and Whitehead

Finally, it should be pointed out that more than any other classical American thinker, Mead explicitly builds upon the organismic process cosmology developed by Alfred North Whitehead. It is known that at least on one occasion Mead and Whitehead both attended a conference together in 1926 at Harvard University.[6] Mead's whole symbolic interactionist framework of the social self, including both his philosophy and his social scientific research program, is grounded in a Whiteheadian process cosmology of creative advance toward novelty. The framework of Mead can be classified together with A. N. Whitehead's aesthetic creationist paradigm based on the new root metaphor of a creative purposive act such as that of an artist, inventor, or imaginative scientist. Both Mead and Whitehead have thereby converged upon an aesthetic creationist paradigm of the social self as a series of self-creative events which are novel, aesthetic and transitory. Like Whitehead's *principle of relativity* (PR 148), Mead's *principle of sociality* (PP 86) functions to generalize the "social" into a universal metaphysical category so that not only the human self but *all* events in the continuum of nature are social insofar as they are ontologically constituted by their relationships to others in a community. Like Whitehead, Mead endeavors to show how the social and processual character of the human self is grounded in the relational and temporal character of reality itself. Although Mead's symbolic interactionist theory of the social self has exerted a strong influence upon both sociology and social psychology in America, most scholars writing from the standpoint of the social sciences have focused almost exclusively on *Mind, Self, and Society* (1934). However, in his more speculative works like *The Philosophy of the Present* (1932) and *The Philosophy of the Act* (1936), Mead provides an extensive treatment of Whitehead's organismic process cosmology of emergent evolution and creative advance into novelty. Mead was especially influenced by Whitehead's earlier works, including *The Principles of Natural Knowledge, The Concept of Nature*, and *Science in the Modern World* (see Mead PP 10 fn.). For Mead, as for Whitehead, the basic unit of existence is an "emergent event" (PP 3), which is located in a "present" (PP 1), and is characterized by its "becoming and disappearing" (PP 1). Both thinkers reject the notion of self as unchanging substance and formulate a process model of self as a series of creative, novel, and aesthetic events which arise and perish in the stream of consciousness with no underlying substantial identity. Both Mead and Whitehead underscore the fact that an emergent event in the creative advance is discontinuous so that at each new moment the old self is replaced with a new self which is numerically nonidentical with its predecessors. Similar to Whitehead's genetic analysis of the concrescence of events into stages resulting in an aesthetic experience of "satisfaction," Mead describes each event comprising the self at any moment as a "social act" which arises through the perceptive, manipulative, and consummatory stages, whereby the consummatory stage has the character of aesthetic experience. Following Whitehead, Mead rejects the notion of self as a substance with "simple location" and argues that because the self is a function of sociality its locus is coextensive with the whole field of social relationships by which it has been constituted. Elsewhere, Mead takes up Whitehead's arguments against the *bifurcation of nature* into an inner world of subjective qualities and an outer world of spatiotemporal extension as well as the *fallacy of simple location* whereby the aesthetic qualities of experience can be located either in the organism or in the environment: "If we abandon with Whitehead the bifurcation of nature, the colors, sounds, tastes, odors, and temperatures are there in nature quite as genuinely as spatiotemporal extension" (PA 337). Hence, for Mead, as for Whitehead, there is a continuity between the subjective world of human experience and the objective world of living nature so that the immediately felt aesthetic qualities of experience *are* the aesthetic qualities of nature. As Mead clarifies in *The Philosophy of the Present*, he was particularly influenced by Whitehead's cosmology of "objective perspectives" (PP 163), wherein each momentary event is akin to a Leibnizian monad which mirrors its universe as an individual microcosm of the social macrocosm. For Mead, the social self frames an objective perspective of the social group to which it belongs, thereby functioning as a mirror which reflects, if not the whole universe, at least its entire community, so that each individual mind and self represents society in microcosm. Also, like the process cosmology of Whitehead, Mead rejects the idea of a single absolute perspective and instead works out a doctrine of emergent temporal perspectives which constitute the "creative advance of nature" (PP 172).

It should further be explained how both Whitehead and Mead have clarified the *bipolar* structure of the social self. Both thinkers show how the human self is located on a continuum between two poles, the social, relational, causal pole on the one side and the individual, private, and autonomous pole on the other. In Whitehead's pluralistic event cosmology each actual occasion of immediate experience constituting the self as social process is said to be *bipolar*, having both a "mental pole" and a "physical pole" (PR 108). The *physical pole* is the conformal phase of "concrescence" or the process of unifying the many into one whereby each momentary occasion reproduces the causal conditions of the past, while the *mental pole* is the supplemental phase introducing the elements of creativity, spontaneity, and novelty. Mead's distinction between the two poles of the social self, the I pole and the Me pole, essentially corresponds to the bipolar structure of Whitehead's actual occasion, the mental pole and the physical pole. In Mead's theory of the social self, while the Me corresponds to the physical pole of an actual occasion, the aspect whereby a momentary event arises through its social relationships to other actual occasions, the I corresponds to the mental pole which introduces creativity, novelty, and spontaneity. Or in terms of the asymmetrical theory of time as creative advance underlying Mead's I-Me dialectic of the social self, the Me represents the physical pole as the aspect of causal continuity with the *past*, while the I represents the mental pole as the aspect of novel emergence or radical discontinuity in the *present*. Again, the social self arises from its deterministic social environment inherited from the past at the Me pole to which it then responds with creativity, originality, and freedom as an individual organism emerging in the present at the I pole. The mental and physical poles of an actual occasion in Whitehead's pluralistic event cosmology, like the I and Me poles of the social self in Mead's philosophy, thus represent the dual aspects of freedom and causation, indeterminacy and determinacy, or discontinuity and continuity.

It has been seen that in his chapter on symbolic reference from *Process and Reality* (1929), and in his book *Symbolism: Its Meaning and Effect* (1927), Whitehead argues that while all living organisms enjoy perception in the mode of "causal efficacy" and while the higher animals develop sense experience or perception in the mode of "presentational immediacy," human experience is characterized by perception in the mode of "symbolic reference." Whitehead's emphasis on the symbolic nature of human perception is characteristic of the whole movement of classical American philosophy. Peirce, Royce, Dewey, and Mead have all underscored the social character of human selfhood in terms of a semiotic communication process using language, signs, and symbols. However, the symbolic character of self has especially been clarified by the *symbolic interactionism* of George Herbert Mead. Similar to Whitehead's principle of relativity, Mead's principle of sociality asserts that each event in nature is constituted by its social relationships to other events. Furthermore, like Whitehead, Mead locates the *differentia* between man and the other animals in the symbolic character of human social experience. Just as for Whitehead the higher phases of human experience are distinguished by the development of perception in the mode of "symbolic reference," for Mead the distinguishing trait of human selfhood is symbolically mediated communicative interaction using "significant symbols." For this reason the social self model of G. H. Mead is to be described as representing a creative synthesis of the whole tradition of classical American pragmatism, including its extension into the organismic process cosmology of A. N. Whitehead.

## Mead's Concept of the Social Self

In the tradition of American pragmatism it was especially Mead who first thematized the notion of a "social self" as a unifying principle for both philosophy and the social sciences. For Mead the human self is neither a substantial self nor an absolute self but a relational, interactional, and dialogical self, or what he otherwise terms the social self. He rejects the Cartesian idea of a substantial ego which requires nothing than itself in order to exist and maintains that the self is always a social self which is intersubjectively constituted by its relationships to others in a community. In Mead's words: "Any self is a social self" (SW 292). The materialistic concept of a physical self over against a physical object is always "an abstraction from a social self" (PA 429). The "social self" is a key technical term used throughout Mead's writings, and it is also the title of one of his most significant essays, "The Social Self," first published in 1913, and now reprinted in *Selected Writings of George Herbert Mead* (SW 142–49). Mead adopts James's notion of a social self with its two component phases of I and Me and makes it the cornerstone of his entire philosophical edifice. But at the same time Mead completely reformulates the Jamesian concept of the social self in the context of a social psychology which describes the social nature, origin, and formation of the self through communicative interaction.

Mead rejects the Cartesian notion of a private subject and argues that the self is socially constituted by its relations to others in the community to which it belongs: "Selves can only exist in definite relationships to other selves. No hard-and-fast line can be drawn between our own selves and the selves of others . . . The individual possesses a self only in relation to the selves of the other members of his social group" (MSS 164). Like the self, the mind is a field of relationships which cannot be localized in the body or the brain but extends throughout the whole field: "If mind is socially constituted, then the field or locus of any given individual mind must extend as far as the social activity or apparatus of social relations which constitutes it extends" (MSS 223n.). Similarly, in that consciousness arises through social interaction between an organism and the environment, it cannot be localized in either but permeates the whole situation which contains both at once: "Consciousness

as such refers to both the organism and its environment and cannot be located simply in either" (MSS 332). For Mead, the self, mind, and consciousness
are all a function of sociality, and thus have a relational spread in both space
and time. In other words, because the human self is a function of sociality its
locus is coextensive with the whole field of social relationship by which it has
been constituted. Justus Buchler clearly expresses the sociality of the human
self as a relational field when he writes: "The human self, as some philosophers have recognized, is spread out in space as well as in time. . . . The self's
spread, its relatedness, is the basis of sociality" (1955, 56).

One of Mead's fundamental notions is that the "social self" is something which must be *realized* through a developmental process. Mead's concept of the social self fully clarifies how one becomes a human self only by
means of communicative interaction with others in society through the
intersubjective medium of language. Famous cases such as the wolf girl of
India and the savage child of Aveyron demonstrate that if an individual is
somehow prevented in their infancy from growing up through the socializ-
ing influences of language and culture in a society then he or she will not
become a human but will end up as an animal, even losing the capacity for
language acquisition. Mead discusses the well-know case of Hellen Keller,
who was both deaf and blind since birth, thereby reduced to living in a the
most primitive animal state, and in fact could not develop a human mind or
self until a method of symbolic communication was discovered by means of
touch. He writes:

> What is essential to communication is that the symbol should arouse
> in one's self what it arouses in the other individual. . . . With a blind
> person such as Helen Keller, it is a contact experience that could be
> given to another as it is given to herself. It is out of that sort of language
> that the mind of Hellen Keller was built up. As she has recognized, it
> was not until she could get into communication with other persons
> through symbols which could arouse in herself the responses they
> arouse in other people that she could get what we terms a mental
> content, or a self. (MSS 149)

The dramatic case of Hellen Keller or those rare instances of children being
raised by animals from birth function to clarify Mead's basic point that the
self is something which develops through social relations. For Mead the self
is not only social in its nature but in its origin and development: "And hence
the origin and foundations of the self, like those of thinking, are social" (MSS
173). He repudiates any notion of a self as existing prior to or apart from its

social relations with others, stating: "It is the social process itself that is responsible for the appearance of the self; it is not there as a self apart from this type of experience" (MSS 142). The self is not something that exists first and then enters into relationship with others, but is itself constituted by its social relations (MSS 182). In opposition to the assumption of Cartesian subjectivism that individuation precedes sociation, Mead's theory of the social self as a dialectic of I and Me clarifies how individuation and sociation occur together. Mead argues that the social self is not something given at birth, but is instead an *achievement* which requires a developmental process of socialization: "The self is something which has a development; it is not initially there, at birth, but arises in the process of social experience" (MSS 135). He therefore claims that the individual realizes itself as a social self only through its relations to other selves. "Since it is a *social self*, it is a self that is realized in its relationship to others" (MSS 204; italics added). At the same time Mead underscores the fact that the intersubjective constitution of the social self in society in no way entails the loss of "personality" (MSS 324). Hence, Mead's framework is ultimately directed to the goal of becoming a person or unique personality as an ideal social self through communicative interaction with others in a community.

## Mead's Bipolar Model of the Social Self as a Dialectic of I and Me

According to Mead, the self is not an isolated I or Cartesian subject but a relation of I and Me. He thereby develops a *bipolar* model of selfhood wherein the I represents the pole of *individuality* and the Me represents the pole of *sociality*. Mead asserts the social self is dialogically constituted through a "conversation of the 'I' and the 'me'" (MSS 179). This is then restated in behavioristic terms, "The 'I' and the 'me' belong to the conversation of gestures" (MSS 182). Again, he writes: "The self is both the 'I' and the 'me'; the 'me' setting the situation to which the 'I' responds" (MSS 277). While the I refers to the individual, the Me is the *generalized other* representing the internalization of the organized attitudes of the whole community: "This process can be characterized in a certain sense in terms of the 'I' and the 'me,' the 'me' being that group of organized attitudes to which the individual responds as an 'I'" (MSS 186). Or in a similar formulation: "The 'I' reacts to the self which arises through the taking of the attitudes of others. Through taking those attitudes we have introduced the 'me' and we react to it as an 'I'" (MSS 174). The mechanism of role-taking whereby the I takes on the organized attitudes of the Me or generalized other is regarded by Mead as analogous to the internalization of parental authority by the superego or moral conscience which exercises social control over primal id-impulses rooted in the biological instincts according to Freudian psychology (MSS 210, 255 n.). Mead's social self model and I-Me dialectic therefore represents a *biosocial* theory of man as having two poles, the I or biological pole and the Me or the social pole. Or as Mead elsewhere states, the I is the "physiological pole" while the Me is the "institutional pole" (MSS 230). In this way Mead's bipolar model of the social self as an I-Me dialectic has crystallized the twofold character of human existence as an individual-society interaction.

The basic theme of Mead's philosophy is the social construction of mind and self in society. His social scientific research program is an effort to clarify that "minds and selves are essentially social products" (MSS 1). Yet he avoids the problem of social determinism through his I-Me dialectic of intersubjectivity. The self arises from its social situation as a Me and then responds with creativity, spontaneity, and novelty as an I. Mead often points out the I is the source of the emergence of novelty (MSS 177, 197, 198, 209). "The 'I' gives the sense of freedom, of initiative" (MSS 177). The I which reacts to the conservative and habitual Me is said to be found in the creative attitude of the artist, the inventor, and the scientist in his process of discovery (MSS 214). He states that "In the artist's attitude, where there is artistic creation, the emphasis upon the element of novelty is carried to the limit" (MSS 209). It is precisely this creativity of the I over against the determinisms of the Me which places Mead's view of self within an aesthetic creationist paradigm based on the root metaphor of a purposive creative act such as that of an artist or imaginative scientist. This dialectic of I and Me functions to deconstruct the substantial Cartesian ego into a network of social relationships at the Me pole while retaining the creative agency of the acting self at the I pole. In his ethics the I-Me dialectic provides a way for the rights-based framework of liberalism to be bolstered by the commitment-based framework of communitarianism. Mead (MSS 214) propounds that insofar as the social self is both I and Me, the I requires that we protect the rights and and freedoms of individuals, while the Me imposes those moral duties and obligations to others as members of society. Both the individuality of the I and the sociality of the Me are therefore necessary phases of the self in its wholeness. In the words of Mead: "Both aspects of the 'I' and 'me' are essential to the self in its full expression" (MSS 198). Thus, for Mead the social self is made up of two component processes, the I and the Me, which represent dual systems of nondeterminacy and determinacy. Mead's bipolar concept of the social self as a dialectic of I and Me thereby provides a via media between one-sided positions like individualism and collectivism, atomism and monism, liberalism and communitarianism, freedom and determinism.

In his essay, "The Definition of the Psychical" (1903) Mead points out the tendency to privilege the Me pole over the I pole: "There is nothing that has suffered more through loss of dignity of content in modern positivistic psychology than the 'I' . . . the greatest loss is the constant drain from the 'I' to the 'me'" (SW 47). He explains the difficulty in empirically discovering the forever elusive I by stating that as soon as the inner subjective content at the I pole is made out it is projected into the objective world at the Me pole (SW 47). For the I to be observed it must be an object; however the I is both nonobjectified and nonobjectifiable, for as soon as it becomes an object, it is no longer the I but the Me. In another essay called "The Social Self" (1913), he again makes this point, arguing that "the self cannot appear in consciousness as an 'I,' that it is always an object, i.e., a 'me,'" (SW 142). Yet the Me is inconceivable apart from the I, a subject for which it is an object. Since the I cannot be given as a direct presentation of consciousness, it must therefore be a presupposition (SW 142). In this way Mead endeavors to articulate the social dimensions of the objectified self as a Me while at the same time fully accounting for the interior subjectivity of the self as an unreified and unreifiable I. Mead's followers in sociology and the social sciences have tended to focus almost exclusively upon the function of the Me or generalized other as the expense of the I or creative individual in order to emphasize the social construction of the human self. In his book *Symbolic Interactionism*, J. M. Charon clearly expresses the priority of the Me phase over the I phase of the self as follows: "Self as object is usually referred to as the 'me.' However, Mead and other symbolic interactionists also describe another aspect of the self called the 'I.' *This part of the self is not nearly as important as the 'me'*" (1989, 85; italics added). He even goes so far as to just identify the self with the Me phase, adding: "Indeed, unless I note otherwise, I will use the term 'self' to mean the 'me,' the self as object" (1989, 85). J. D. Lewis (see Aboulafia 1991, 112) provides a good overview on the primacy of the Me over the I in the Meadian tradition of social behaviorism, citing those who maintain that the I has only a *remedial* function in Mead's framework insofar as it has been added on to what is an otherwise deterministic theory of the self as a product of its social environment. Others hold to the residual interpretation whereby Mead is seen as advocating an essentially social deterministic concept of behavior and that the I is irrelevant to the core explanatory theory (Aboulafia 1991, 112–13). But against the "remedial" and "residual" interpretation of the I component in Mead's I-Me dialectic of the social self it must be emphasized that Mead's social scientific framework and method of social behaviorism are developed within the overall context of an evolutionary process philosophy influenced by the emergent evolution of L. Morgan and S. Alexander, the creative evolution of H. Bergson, and the process cosmology of creative advance toward novelty worked out by A. N. Whitehead. It is completely irresponsible for social scientists to focus on Mead's social behaviorism developed in *Mind, Self, and Society* in complete abstraction from his Whiteheadian process cosmology of creative advance to novelty articulated in other works like *The Philosophy of the Present* and *The Philosophy of the Act*. According to Whitehead's process cosmology of creative advance each emergent event comprising the self is "bipolar" (PR 108), wherein the "physical pole" is the causal determination of the past and the "mental pole" is the creative novelty of the present. Likewise, Mead's evolutionary process cosmology is based on an asymmetrical theory of time as creative advance wherein the bipolar social self is constituted by a series of emergent or discontinuous events, each of which arises from its deterministic social environment inherited from the past at the Me pole and then reacts with creativity, novelty, and freedom in the present at the I pole. Mead's concept of the I is neither remedial nor residual but is in fact central and integral to his temporal concept of the social self as developed in the context an evolutionary process cosmology of creative advance into novelty.

## Mead's Neo-Hegelian "Self-Other" Dialectic of Mutual Recognition

As has been emphasized by H. Joas (1985) and more recently by M. Aboulafia (1991), Mead's notion of the social self as an I-Me dialectic of intersubjectivity requires a knowledge of its background in the dialectical thought of German idealism, and especially, G. W. F. Hegel's dialectic of self-other relationships. Hegel rejected liberal individualism and instead developed a communitarian theory of personhood whereby an individual is fulfilled only in and through totalizing social structures of the nation-state. In *Philosophy of Right*, Hegel argues that the state is "mind objectified" and that only as a member of this political state does the individual become a true person with an ethical life. The liberal notion of self as an isolated, atomic individual whose membership to a state or other social group is optional such as is held by social contract theories is regarded by Hegel as a complete abstraction. In this way Hegel provides a wholly social definition of the self. However, as many critics have charged, Hegel's concept of the social order repudiates the abstract in-dividuality of liberalism only at the expense of their subordination to a col-lectivity, thereby giving rise to a form of totalitarian statism.

One of the most striking aspects of Hegel's social concept of the per-son is his self-other dialectic of mutual recognition. According to Hegel's metaphysics of absolute idealism, the notion of Spirit (*Geist*) is that of achiev-ing self-realization by means of a threefold dialectical process whereby pure subjective consciousness of Spirit in the first moment of *thesis* empties itself into objectified Spirit as the community of others in the second moment of *antithesis*, finally returning to itself out of alienation as absolute Spirit through the recognition of self in the other in the third moment of *synthesis*. Accord-ing to Hegel, it is only through the dialectic of recognition whereupon one attains complete reflexive self-consciousness by becoming an object to one-self. For Hegel, then, reflexive self-consciousness is achieved by being recog-nized by another self-consciousness. One's self-consciousness exists "in and for itself" only insofar as it "exists for another." By the Hegelian view, self-consciousness cannot be a solitary Cartesian subject which is transparent to itself through intuition but is instead a social process of realizing itself in otherness. That is to say, Hegel's dialectic of mutual recognition is the pro-cess whereby reflexive self-consciousness is achieved precisely through rec-ognition of the other and recognition by the other in the community or state as the realm of objectified Spirit. At this moment of the dialectic, says Hegel, "They recognize themselves as mutually recognizing one another" (1977, 112). Hegel finally explains the culmination of this self-other dialectic of mutual recognition when he says, "What lies ahead for consciousness is the experience of what Spirit is . . . 'I' that is 'We' and 'We' that is 'I.'" (1977, 110)

This neo-Hegelian element of dialectical thought first came to G. H. Mead through the influence of Josiah Royce in the Department of Philoso-phy at Harvard University, where the former began graduate study in 1887. Furthermore, Mead studied with W. Wundt, W. Dilthey and others in Ger-many where he stayed from 1888 to 1891. The direct influence of German idealism can be especially seen in Mead's discussions of Fichte, Schelling, and Hegel in his work *Movements of Thought in the Nineteenth Century* (1936). In these lectures Mead clearly exhibits his interest in the post-Kantian German idealist theme concerning the realization of the self by means of the non-self. Mead's neo-Hegelian dialectical orientation first becomes apparent within his own thought system in an essay published in 1900 called "Suggestions Toward a Theory of the Philosophical Disciplines," wherein he attempts to unify metaphysics, psychology, ethics, aesthetics, and logic within a "dialec-tic within the act" (SW 7). He further specifies that "the general theory of the intelligent act as a whole would fall within that of logic as treated in works such as that of Hegel" (SW 8).

In his later thinking Mead develops Hegel's "dialectic of recognition" whereby one comes to self-realization only through the other. The Hegelian self-other dialectic of mutual recognition is articulated in *Mind, Self, and Society* in the course of explaining how the social self arises through a dialectic between the I and the Me. He first asserts that the contents which go to make up the social self are the I and the Other, or as he also says, the I and the Me, whereby the Me is that organized set of attitudes of the whole community represented by the generalized other (MSS 194). In this context he states:

> We cannot realize ourselves except in so far as we can recognize the other in his relationship to us. It is as he takes the attitude of the other that the individual is able to realize himself as a self. (MSS 194)

And again:

> There are various ways in which we can realize that self. Since it is a social self, it is a self that is realized in its relationship to others. It must be recognized by others to have the very values which we want to have belong to it. (MSS 194)

Hence, for Mead, as for Hegel, self-realization is acquired through a dialectical process of *mutual recognition*. Self-consciousness is constituted only through recognition of the other and recognition by the other. Furthermore, it is only through recognition of the other by adopting the attitude, role or perspective of the other that the self becomes an object to itself, and thereby attains complete reflexive self-consciousness. In Mead's words, "to be self-conscious is essentially to become an object to one's self in virtue of one's social relations to other individuals" (MSS 172).

More than anyone after Hegel, it is Mead who has gone furthest in clarifying the achievement of reflexive self-consciousness through self-other relations and the dialectic of mutual recognition. Yet the disparity between Hegel and Mead can finally be characterized precisely in terms of their respective formulations of this dialectic. The framework of Mead, like that of Dewey, must be understood as in part being an effort to *naturalize* Hegel's organismic worldview based on a shift from absolutism to experimentalism. Thus, while Hegel's self-other relation is grounded in a monistic theory of absolute idealism, Mead instead conceives of the dialectic of self and other in terms of a pluralistic theory based on a metaphysical naturalism. Again, whereas the self-other dialectic of Hegel is comprehended from the standpoint of idealism as a dialectic between the individual and the totality within the predetermined historical unfolding of an absolute Spirit, the self-other relation of Mead is instead naturalistically conceived as a dialectical interaction between organism and environment which produces novel events in the creative advance of nature seen as a process of emergent evolution.

Hegel propounds that the ultimate goal of this self-other dialectic of mutual recognition is the realization of Spirit as "'I' that is 'We' and 'We' that is 'I'" (1977, 110). In the case of Mead (MSS 194) this self-other dialectic of mutual recognition is directed toward the realization of the social self as a relation of I and Me. Hence, just as for Hegel the absolute Self is defined an *I-We relationship,* for Mead the social self is defined as an *I-Me relationship.* Both Hegel and Mead argue that the self is not an isolated I but is instead a dialectical relation of I and Other—what Mead calls the relation of I and Me and what Hegel calls the relation of I and We. The difference is that for Hegel the individual I is submerged into the collective We so as to collapse into a totalitarian statism. But for Mead the self arises out of its deterministic social situation in the past at the Me pole, to which it then responds with creativity, novelty, and freedom in the present at the I pole. Mead thereby corrects the deterministic basis of Hegel's self-other dialectic by means of balancing the social determinism of the Me with the freedom and creative agency of the I.

## Self-Development, Role-Taking and the Generalized Other

The "generalized other" is no doubt the most famous neologism in Mead's lexicon of technical terms. In Mead's socialization theory the individual becomes a social self by incorporating the Me or "generalized other" representing the organization of attitudes of its whole community. The self takes on the roles of the generalized other as a Me and then responds to it with creativity as an I. Mead defines the generalized other as follows: "The organized community or social group which gives to the individual his unity of self may be called 'the generalized other.' The attitude of the generalized other is the attitude of the whole community" (MSS 154). It is only by internalizing the attitudes of the community represented by the "generalized other" through the mechanism of role-taking that the unity of the self is constituted (MSS 155).

In Mead's developmental psychology it is only by taking on the roles of the generalized other and viewing oneself as an object from the standpoint of the generalized other that one becomes a social self with reflexive self-consciousness and personal identity. Or in terms of his Whiteheadian theory of objective perspectives, the individual acquires reflexivity by entering into the perspectives of others in the community, thereby to view itself from the *common perspective* of the generalized other: "He is able then to become a generalized other in addressing himself in the attitude of the group or the community . . . This is the common perspective" (PP 168). Mead's concept of the "generalized other" has clearly been influenced on this point by William James's reflexive notion of the social self according to which a person's self-image depends on the images other members of society have of him, as well as by C. H. Cooley's notion of the "looking-glass self" wherein the self develops reflexivity by imagining its own appearance from the standpoint of others in the primary social group to which it belongs. Like James's reflexive notion of the social self and Cooley's notion of the looking-glass self, Mead argues that the generalized other is the basic frame of reference for self-appraisal and attitude formation. Hence, one becomes a social self with reflexive self-consciousness only by taking the attitude of the general other toward itself.

Mead's concept of the generalized other also designates the repository of social norms which the individual inherits from the community and tradition to which he belongs. He points out the analogy between his notion of the general other and Freud's superego, the judicial branch of the psyche functioning as the moral conscience or censorship mechanism which takes on the norms, values, and ideals of society through the internalization of parental authority. Taking on the roles of the generalized other means to internalize the organized attitude of the group, the norms of society, the parental controls of the family, the rules of the game, the laws of the state, the social institutions of the community, the rituals, rites, and ceremonies of the church, the values, ideals, and customs of tradition, and so on. In his moral philosophy Mead argues that the universalizibility of moral norms required by the categorical imperative of Kant's universalist ethics or the golden rule of Christian ethics is made possible only if we take the attitude of the generalized other as the universalized human community (MSS 379). The generalized other is thus the basis for all norm-governed rational thought and moral action in human experience.

Mead's genetic account of how the individual is constituted as a social self by taking on the roles of the generalized other is a secular reformulation of Royce's theme of achieving one's greater social self through the religious community of interpretation. As pointed out by David L. Miller, "Royce's 'Community of Interpretation' is similar to Mead's generalized other" (1975, 69). However, in contrast to Royce's theological notion of community, the "generalized other" of Mead has no connotation of a metaphysical absolute or religious ultimate but is understood in wholly secular and naturalistic terms as the *universalized human community* which is internalized by the individual through the socialization process. Miller also clarifies how Mead's generalized other functions analogously to William James's concept of an *ideal social self* as the judge guiding norm-governed thought and action. He quotes James (*Principles of Psychology*, I, 315–16) as asserting: "The ideal social self which I thus seek . . . is the true, the intimate, the ultimate, the permanent Me which I seek. This judge is God, the Absolute Mind, the 'Great Companion'" (cited by Miller 1975, 49). Miller then relates the ideal social self of James to the generalized other of Mead as follows: "I mention James's view in order to make it clear that for Mead the 'Great Companion' is the generalized other . . . But there is no place in Mead's system . . . for a transcendent mind apart from minds of individual men" (1975, 49). In this context it should be further pointed out how the generalized other of Mead functions similarly to the concept of God in A. N. Whitehead's process theology. At the conclusion of *Process and Reality*, Whitehead states: "God is the great companion" (PR 351). For Whitehead, the primordial nature of God is the source of norms, values, and ideals which "ingress" into the creative advance of nature. Also, in his consequent nature God is the divine memory which preserves the values achieved in creative process. For Mead the "great companion" is again to be understood as the generalized other. Like Whitehead's idea of God as the great companion, Mead's generalized other is judge functioning as the source of norms, values and ideals governing the social self as well as the collective memory of human society. However, as emphasized by Miller, there is no place in Mead's system for a transcendent or supernatural principle. Thus, in contrast to the dipolar God of Whitehead, the generalized other of Mead develops from out of the social process itself and has no transcendent existence apart from or prior to the social process.

Mead's doctrine of the "generalized other" can further be clarified through Justus Buchler's notion of the "reflexive community." Influenced by thinkers like Peirce, Dewey, and Mead, the American philosopher Justus Buchler develops a notion of the social self as a reflexive community which reproduces its entire social community through a semiotic process of communication. In his work entitled *Toward a General Theory of Human Judgment*, Buchler writes:

> The Individual in himself constitutes a community, the reflexive or pro-
> ceptive community. Logically and genetically, the reflexive community
> presupposes a social community . . . Reflexive communication
> actualizes the reflexive community. This community is the final court
> of appeal in all issues concerning reason and belief. (1959, 39–40)

Hence, the "reflexive community" described by Buchler functions in essentially the same way as the "generalized other" of Mead. Mead's account of
how the social self internalizes the attitudes of its community by taking on
the roles of the generalized other is described by Buchler as a communication process whereby the "social community" at the macro level is replicated
by the "reflexive community" at the micro level. Both the generalized other
of Mead and the reflexive community of Buchler therefore represent the community as incorporated into the self. In both Mead's notion of the generalized
other and Buchler's concept of the reflexive community the self is constituted as a social self by reproducing its entire community so that the individual represents the community in microcosm. Furthermore, Buchler's
notion of the reflexive community carries out the same normative function
as Mead's concept of the generalized other. Just as for Buchler the reflexive
community is "the final court of appeal" in the making of normative judgments, for Mead the generalized other is the impartial judge or jury which
legislates for all norm-governed rational thought and moral conduct.

   According to Mead's developmental account there is a progression of
stages through which the individual is constituted as a social self by taking
on the roles of other selves, first taking on the roles of individual selves at the
play stage, then taking on small groups or teams of selves at the game stage,
finally taking on the roles of all selves in the abstract community at more
advanced stages of socialization by entering into the common perspective of
the generalized other. Herbert Blumer summarizes the developmental stages
whereby an individual attains reflexive self-consciousness through role-taking
as follows:

> Like other objects, the self-object emerges from the process of social
> interaction . . . Mead has traced the way in which this occurs in his
> discussion of role-taking. He points out that in order to become an
> object to himself a person has to see himself from the outside. One can
> do this only by placing himself in the position of others and viewing
> himself or acting towards himself from that position. The roles the
> person takes range from that of discrete individuals (the "play stage"),

through that of discrete groups (the "game stage") to that of the abstract community (the "generalized other"). (1986, 12–13)

Mead writes that children use the mechanism of role-taking "in building a self" (MSS 150). For an individual in early childhood to "build a self" or to develop reflexive self-consciousness, one must take the roles of others and view oneself from the perspective of others, thus to become a social object to oneself. Mead (MSS 144–46) describes several stages in the development of the social self through role-taking in early childhood, including: (1) the early use of significant symbols and linguistic gestures, (2) play, and (3) games. Mead argues that as soon as the child uses "significant symbols" with shared meanings he or she at once begins to take on the attitudes, roles, and perspective of others. He asserts that by using significant symbols, "We are unconsciously putting ourselves in the place of others and acting as others act" (MSS 69). Since a significant symbol has the same meaning for both the listener and the speaker it establishes a common perspective and thus makes possible the achievement of consensus and mutual understanding through communicative interaction. Hence, using significant symbols through linguistic and vocal gestures is the basic mechanism of role-taking whereby one enters the perspectives of others so as to develop a social self with reflexive self-consciousness (MSS 69). Both play and games involve role-taking by unconsciously entering the perspectives of others or putting oneself in the place of others. The basic difference between play and games is that games have rules, whereas play does not, and is therefore a simpler mechanism of role-taking (MSS 152). Through the creative activity of play the developing self takes on the roles of specific individuals like parents, teachers, and friends, so that the child begins acquiring the roles of those who belong to his society (SW 285). A more complex form of role-taking occurs through the rule-organized structure of games. Games with teams are especially important for internalizing the "generalized other" as an organization of the whole community of players. Mead argues that each member of a team playing a game such as baseball must internalize the attitudes of every other member of the team, which as a composite together form the generalized other (MSS 154). He says that, "In the game we get an organized other, a generalized other" (MSS 160). The child then moves beyond the role-taking of play and games to appropriate the generalized other of society as a whole, thereby to internalize the institutions, laws, traditions, customs, and rituals of the entire community to which it belongs. In Mead's political philosophy the example is given how an adult takes on the generalized other into which it has entered, thereby to take on the organized attitudes of that entire party toward the rest of a social community the problems which confront the party within the given social situation (MSS 156). Thus, in the later stages of development one becomes a full self constituted not only by the organization of particular individual attitudes, or what H. S. Sullivan calls "significant others," but also by an organization of the social attitudes of the *generalized other* or the social group as a whole to which it belongs (MSS 158).

## Mead's Theory of Multiple Selfhood

For Mead, as for James, the "social self" is also a decentered *multiple self*, that is, it is irreducibly plural. In Mead's words, "We are all persons of multiple selves" (1974, 71). Mead's position is influenced by James's theory of multiple selfhood as stated in *Principles of Psychology* (1890), according to which "*a man has as many social selves as there are individuals who recognize him* and carry an image of him in their mind" (1981, 281–82). It also shows the influence of Josiah Royce, who in the Preface to *The World and the Individual* (1901) argues for the natural existence of "multiple personality" on the basis that the self can only be understood as arising under social conditions, so that various selves are interwoven in complex ways (1959, xii). Mead describes the social self as a plural or multiple self when he writes: "We divide ourselves up in all sorts of different selves with reference to our acquaintances. . . . There are all sorts of different selves answering to all sorts of different social reactions" (MSS 142). Rather than underscore only the negative or pathological aspects of multiple personality, Mead instead asserts: "A multiple personality is in a certain sense normal" (1934, 142). Hence, like Nietzsche who decenters the unified Cartesian ego into a "soul of subject-multiplicity," arguing that the *psyche* or soul is not an eternal oneness but an irreducible plurality of images, so Mead holds that that the social self is constituted by a reflection of all the selves in the community as the primary social group from which it has its genesis. However, while Nietzsche's idea of the *psyche* as a subject-multiplicity soul is based on a depth psychology which reveals the self to be a plurality of psychical images, it fails to develop a social psychology. Consequently, while Nietzsche formulates a doctrine of the multiple self, he does not develop a theory of the social self, but instead falls into a kind of radical individualism. By contrast, Mead formulates a theory of multiple selfhood within the context of a thoroughgoing social psychology which provides an empirically based genetic account of how the plurality of selves emerges through the socialization process of role-taking. Again, Mead's theory of multiple selfhood resembles the position of French poststructuralism which deconstructs the notion of self-identity into an irreducible play of signs with no fixed center, essence, or core. The unitary self of Cartesian subjectivism is thereby replaced by a relational self which is multiple, decentered, open, fluid, and ever-changing. However, Mead decenters the unity of the Cartesian subject with his notion of the Me while at the same time retaining the creative agency of the acting self with his notion of the I or unique individual. For Mead, the social self is a multivariate *field of selves* which gets built up by taking on the roles, attitudes, and perspectives of other selves of the Me or generalized other. He thus states: "The unity of the self involves an organization of all the other selves" (ISS 164). Elsewhere, he speaks of "the various elementary selves which constitute, or are organized into, a complete self" (MSS 144). From this point of view, the social self arises as an organization of all the other selves in the community as a Me and then responds to it with creative novelty as an individual I. The Me or "generalized other" is therefore a sort of corporate individual, a composite image built up from all the other members of the community. Both the I and the Me are necessary phases of the social self in its multiplicity and in its wholeness. The phenomenon of disso-ciation of personality as manifested in the split personality or multiple per-sonality syndrome is caused by a breaking up of the complete, unitary self into the component selves of which it is composed (MSS 144). As Mead writes in *The Individual and the Social Self* (1974):

> When the situation is healthy, these may be merged into a single personality. When they are not merged, we have a disassociation of selves, and the cure involves bringing them together. . . . We are all persons of multiple selves, but all of these have their relation to the organic fundamental self. (ISS 71)

The multiple-self theory of Mead has been appropriated as a funda-mental principle of symbolic interactionism in American sociology. In his book *Symbolic Interactionism*, J. M. Charon summarizes Mead's decentered multiple-self theory as follows: "The human has many *selves*, each related to the interaction he or she is involved with, and each constantly being changed in the process of interaction" (1979, 29). Similarly, in his work *Invitation to Sociology* (1963, 106–7), Peter L. Berger asserts that Mead's psychological theory of multiple selfhood as a kaleidoscope of roles and identities clarifies how the self is not an unchanging substantial entity with a fixed essence, but a temporal process whereby a person is re-created in each new social situation. Mead's genetic account of the development of multiple selfhood through the mechanism of role-taking has been further developed into the "dramaturgical model" of self-presentation worked out by Erving Goffman and other symbolic interactionists related to the Chicago school of sociology. In his influential book *The Presentation of Self in Everyday Life* (1956), Goffman emphasizes that the presentation of the self occurs through the dramatic performance of a multiplicity of social roles, thus constituting the self as a plurality of alternate identities. By this view, the concept of the "person" is understood in terms of its theatrical etymology as derived from the Latin word *persona* (the technical term given to the actors' masks in classical theater), so that the self is now perceived as a repertoire of social roles governed by interaction rituals, each with its own identity. According to this dramaturgical model of the self based on Mead's notion of role-taking, the person is a multiplicity of selves insofar as he or she is likened to an actor playing a variety of roles as presented through a series of social masks worn during the dramatic performance of everyday life. This dramaturgical model of the decentered multiple self developed by symbolic interactionism again calls for a comparison with Nietzsche, who fractures the unitary Cartesian subject into a plurality of actors, roles, and masks. Yet, as Meltzer, Petras, and Reynolds show in their book *Symbolic Interactionism*, among symbolic interactionists there has arisen a "multiple self versus unitary self debate" (1975, 95). Whereas all symbolic interactionists follow Mead in analyzing the social self as a symbolically mediated individual-society interaction, one side focuses upon the self as a unitary entity while the other side focuses upon the self as a multiple phenomenon. This multiple self versus unitary self debate in the Meadian tradition of symbolic interactionism is analogous to the monotheistic psyche versus polytheistic psyche debate in current depth psychology. While the monotheistic psychology of C. G. Jung underscores the aim of self-realization as a quest for wholeness through an integration of archetypal images from the collective unconscious with ego consciousness, neo-Jungians like James Hillman instead argue for a more polytheistic, polycentric, and polymorphic vision of the psyche as an irreducible plurality of psychic images. For Jung the process of individuation culminates with the integration of the Self-archetypes or God-images (*imago Dei*) projected from the collective unconscious representing images of wholeness establishing psychic totality through a union of opposites; while for Hillman it culminates in the shattering of the ego into an irreducible plurality of images so as to incarnate the multiple forces and values represented by the whole polytheistic pantheon of deities from the underworld depicted in the ancient myths as collective dreams of the human soul. Like Jung, Mead focuses upon the nature of self-realization as a quest for wholeness in which the self is constituted as a unity by taking on the normative roles of the generalized other. However, at the same time

Mead recognizes the inherent multiplicity of the generalized other as a pluralistic field of selves. Mead thereby shows how the social self as an I-Me dialectic is to be comprehended both in terms of its wholeness and its multiplicity. To repeat Mead's words as cited above: "We are all persons of multiple selves, *but all of these have their relation to the organic fundamental self*" (ISS, 71; italics added). Mead's theory of decentered multiple selfhood thus constitutes one of the most profound and suggestive aspects of his intersubjective communication model of the social self as a dialectic of I and Me.

## The Social Psychology of G. H. Mead

Mead's symbolic interactionist model of the social self functions to provide a unifying theory which combines philosophy with the social sciences. Whereas on the side of philosophy Mead develops the tradition of American pragmatism as grounded in a process cosmology, on the side of the social sciences he above all else focuses upon the discipline of social psychology. As noted by Charles Morris in his Introduction to Mead's work, *Mind, Self, and Society*: "Philosophically, Mead was a pragmatist; scientifically, he was a social psychologist" (MSS ix). At the very outset of this work, Mead defines the field of social psychology as follows: "Social psychology is especially interested in the effect which the social group has in the determination of the experience and conduct of the individual members" (MSS 1). Mead then argues throughout his work that the self is not a separate individual but must always be defined by reference to a social group, that the self is socially constructed by communicative interaction with others in its group, that the group provides the basic frame of reference for attitude formation and self-evaluation, that the self develops reflexivity or self-awareness by taking the attitude of others in the group toward itself, that to be a self requires membership in a group and that the self cannot exist prior to or apart from the group. Yet Mead never allows the individual to be submerged into a collective group-consciousness; for the self is constituted as a unity by internalizing the social group as a Me to which it then responds with creativity, novelty, and freedom as an I.

The social psychology of Mead was itself deeply influenced by the psychological theories of other American pragmatists including James, Cooley, and Dewey. It should be recalled that from the very start, his key notion of a social, processual self was influenced by his teacher William James's pioneering work, *Principles of Psychology*. From James's psychology Mead inherited not only his basic idea of a social self with its two components of I and Me, but also the notion of a decentered *multiple self.* (MSS 142–44). Yet it has been seen that for James the social self is only one out of several selves to which he attributes influence but not a constitutive function. Mead (MSS 173) thus criticizes both James's introspective method in psychology as well as his individualistic presupposition that the self can exist apart from its relations to others in a group. He was further influenced by the social psychology of his colleague Charles Horton Cooley, which provides a holistic and functional analysis of the individual-society relation as the "distributive" and "collective" aspects of the social self in its integral unity, thus representing two sides of the same coin. Mead was inspired by Cooley's notion of the "looking-glass self," according to which people imagine their own appearance from the standpoint of others, thereby developing reflexive self-consciousness by seeing themselves reflected in the primary social group to which they belong. Nevertheless, Mead strongly criticizes what he regards as those individualistic, solipsistic, and subjectivistic elements of Cooley's position, asserting: "Cooley's social psychology, as found in his *Human Nature and the Social Order,* is hence inevitably introspective" (MSS 224 fn.). He was strongly influenced by his close friend and colleague John Dewey's early psychological essays culminating in "The Reflex Arc Concept in Psychology" (1896), which itself became the basis for Mead's holistic understanding of the "social act" as the basic unit of human experience arising through coordinated interaction between gesture (stimulus) and response (meaning). It should be noted that Mead (MSS 37, 38, 129) was also influenced by fundamental notions of *Gestalt* psychology, wherein human perception is understood in holistic terms as a value-laden figure/ground gestalt configuration organized by acts of attention.

Like John Watson, Mead rejects the introspective method of psychology and instead adopts a form of "psychological behaviorism" as the science of overt conduct. For Mead, behavioristic psychology studies "the experience of the individual from the point of view of his conduct, particularly, but not exclusively, the conduct as it is observable by others (MSS 2). But Mead (MSS 8) strongly criticizes Watson's approach on two counts, arguing that it is *reductionistic* insofar as it denies the existence of internal contents (feelings, sensations, images, etc.) which are not manifest in overt behavior, as well as *individualistic* in that it focuses only upon the conduct of isolated individuals apart from their relation to others in a social situation. Thus, in contrast to Watson's reductionistic form of behaviorism which rejects the existence of images, Mead (MSS 190fn.) underscores the constitutive role of mental images in the act of social communication. Similar to the depth psychology of Freud and Jung, the psychology of Mead recognizes that all experience is conditioned by mental images. Also, in contrast to the individualistic behaviorism of Watson, Mead's psychology represents a form of "social behaviorism" (MSS 6). In addition, Mead (MSS 42) adopts Wundt's social psychology of the *gesture*, including physical, vocal, and linguistic gestures, thereby to overcome introspectionist psychology through a behavioristic account of mind and self based on overt gestures which are publicly observable by a community of inquirers. He combines Wundt's psychology of social gestures with the S-R analysis of behaviorism, whereupon the publicly observable "gesture" now becomes the *stimulus* and the publicly observable *response* becomes the "meaning" of the gesture. Mead describes the intersubjective constitution of the human mind and self in society through social acts of symbolically mediated communicative interaction, defined through his behavioristic psychology as a "conversation of significant gestures." The "gesture" is therefore not to be conceived in individualistic terms as an expression of inner feelings but in social terms as a stimulus which calls out for a response from others in a social act of communication. Finally, one should not overlook the indirect but profound influence of C. S. Peirce on Mead's behavioristic social psychology. As pointed out by Jürgen Habermas (1989, 3), early in the twentieth century Cartesian subjectivism was assaulted on two fronts, by philosophy of language and behavioristic psychology, both of which are indebted to the pragmatism of C. S. Peirce, who conceived of action and knowledge in terms of *observable, shared practices*. According to Habermas (1989, 3), the two disciplines of linguistic analysis and behavioristic psychology were first combined in the symbolic interactionist framework of social psychology developed by G. H. Mead.

Mead (MSS 210, 255n) points out certain analogies between his own psychological theory of "bio-social man" as a dialectic between the I or instinctual pole and the Me or internalized social pole and Freud's concept of the human psyche as an interaction between the primal instincts of the id and the internalized social controls of the superego. However, Mead's process theory of self rejects the notion that there is any fixed content or essence determining human nature and thus replaces Freud's substantialistic idea of "instincts" with the more plastic notion of *impulses* which change through the process of social evolution. Also, Mead's orientation is fundamentally different from the psychology of Freud in that it is social rather than individualistic. In contrast to Freudian psychology which emphasizes the self-directed narcissism of unconscious infantile instincts, Mead is closer to social psychologists like Alfred Adler, Karen Horney, Eric Fromm, and Harry Stack Sullivan, who instead underscore the other-directed aspect of interpersonal communication rooted in the primary nature of man as a social being. Mead's analysis of the "inferiority complex," and its opposite attitude, the "superiority complex," as they both function in the development of the social self through a dialectic of mutual recognition, at once approximates the psychology of Alfred Adler as presented in *Understanding Human Nature* (1927) and other works. Mead writes:

> Since it is a *social self*, it is a self that is realized in its relationship to others. It must be recognized by others to have the very values which we want to have belong to it. It realizes itself in some sense through its *superiority* to others, as it recognizes its *inferiorities* in comparison with others. The *inferiority complexes* are the reverse situations to those *feelings of superiority* which we entertain with reference to ourselves as over against the people about us. (MSS 204; italics added)

The social psychology of Mead, like that of Adler, aims to overcome social maladjustments rooted in the fundamental problem of egocentricity by the achievement of a social self, understood as the *via media* between those pathological extremes of an "inferiority complex" based upon feelings of inadequacy on the one side and of a "superiority complex" based upon feelings of self-aggrandizement on the other. Just as for Adler the inferiority and superiority complexes can only be overcome through the cultivation of "social feeling," for Mead they are resolved by the formation of a "social self."

It has been seen that Mead also articulates a developmental psychology in some respects similar to that of Piaget which clarifies how individual minds and selves arise in progressive stage-structures through the basic internalization mechanism of "perspective-taking," thereby taking on the attitudes of the whole community represented by the Me or generalized other. He clarifies how the self emerges through the development of reflexive self-consciousness by entering into the perspective of others in the community, thus to become an object to itself by seeing itself from the common perspective of the generalized other. Mead's developmental psychology of the social self based on progressive stages of perspective-taking has exerted a major influence upon Kohlberg's developmental stages of moral socialization as well as Habermas's developmental stages of communicative competence. Hence, one of Mead's greatest contributions to the social sciences has been his articulation of a comprehensive *social psychology* which provides an empirically based genetic account of the social nature, origin, and development of the self through communicative interaction with others in the community.

## The Social Construction of Self through Language

The framework of Mead at once represents part of what Richard Rorty has termed the "linguistic turn" characterizing twentieth-century philosophy. To begin with, Mead emphasizes what he calls "the social context of language" (MSS 69). Elsewhere he states, "Language is a social process and grows out of gesture" (ISS 36). Similar to the later Wittgenstein, Mead holds that there can be no private language, that the meaning of a word is its use in a social context, and that language is always a social affair involving communication using symbols with a shared meaning. For Mead the self is always a social self precisely because it is socially constructed by the intersubjective medium of language. Through the influence of Josiah Royce he was influenced by C. S. Peirce's semiotic doctrine that "my language is the sum total of myself" (Peirce 1955, 249; also, *Collected Papers*, 5.314). But Mead avoids the idealistic conclusions of Royce wherein the self and the world are pure language, thought, and signs within the mind in that he defines language in behaviorist terms as a gestural language or conversation of gestures functioning as significant symbols which call out the same meaning in oneself as to others: "Language as a set of significant symbols is simply the set of gestures which the organism employs in calling out the response of others" (MSS 335).

According to Mead, because the self is a social self it is not simply given but is something which requires development through linguistically mediated communicative interaction with others in a community. First of all the human self or person can only arise through a developmental process of socialization and language is the intersubjective medium through which socialization occurs: "Such is the process by which a personality arises. I have spoken of this as a process in which a child takes the role of the other, and said that it takes place essentially through the use of language" (MSS 160). It is only by linguistically mediated communicative interaction using significant symbols with a shared meaning that the developing individual can take the role of others and thereby develop a self with reflexive awareness. The central role of language in the social constitution of the self is elsewhere articulated as follows: "The self is something which has a development; it is not initially there, at birth, but arises in the process of social experience" (MSS 135). In this context he adds, "the language process is essential for the development of the self" (MSS 135). Like the human self, the mind is also socially constituted by language: "Out of language emerges the field of mind" (MSS 133). Again, he writes: "Language as made up of significant symbols is what we mean by mind" (MSS 190 n.). Not only the human self and mind but also the objects of human perception are socially constituted through the inter-subjective medium of language. He states: "Language does not simply symbolize a situation or object which is already there in advance; it makes possible the existence or the appearance of that situation or object, for it is a part of the mechanism whereby that situation or object is created" (MSS 78). Mead was therefore among the first to clearly recognize and to explicitly articulate the full extent to which the human self, mind, consciousness, and field of perception are socially constituted through symbolic communication with language.

## Mead's Communication Model of the Social Self

The social-self theory of Mead brings into focus a recurrent theme to be found in Peirce, Royce, Dewey, and Cooley: namely, the centrality of *communication* in human experience. As Dewey proclaims in *Experience and Nature*, "Of all affairs, communication is the most wonderful" (1958, 166). In *Human Nature and the Social Order*, C. H. Cooley writes: "The social self is simply any idea . . . drawn from the communicative life, that the mind cherishes as its own" (1964, 179). Similarly, in *Mind, Self, and Society*, Mead asserts that the self is constructed through a process of "communicative interaction" (MSS 158). Elsewhere, he asserts: "[T]he individual reaches his self only through communication with others" (MSS 233). And again: "A self can arise only where there is a social process . . . For that process, the communication and participation to which I have referred is essential" (SW 42). For Mead, as for Peirce, Royce, Dewey, and Cooley, the "social self" is therefore a *communicative self*. The semiotic communication theory of self as a web of signs in a community of interpretation worked out by Peirce and Royce is restated by Mead in terms of his idea of the social self arising through symbolically mediated communicative interaction between the individual and the community.

In accord with the linguistic turn of twentieth-century philosophy Mead describes the emergence of the social self through progressive stages of development by means of communicative interaction using language, signs, and symbols. There is no self existing prior to or apart from linguistically mediated communicative interaction with others in society. The social constitution of the self in a community through the intersubjective medium of symbolic or linguistic communication is the basic theme underlying Mead's entire philosophy. For Mead symbolic interaction through the social act of communication using "significant gestures" or "significant symbols" with a shared meaning is a necessary precondition for the development of individual minds and selves. As stated by Herbert Blumer in *Symbolic Interactionism* (1969), "We are indebted to George Herbert Mead for the most penetrating analysis of social interaction" (1986, 8). Blumer goes on to clarify that Mead identifies two levels of social or communicative interaction in human society, "the conversation of gestures," or nonsymbolic communication, and "the use of significant symbols," or symbolic interaction (1986, 8). While animals communicate through the conversation of gestures at the nonsymbolic level, only the human self communicates with significant gestures having shared meanings at the symbolic level so as to develop a social self with reflexive self-consciousness. Through significant symbols one evokes the same response in oneself as in others. Insofar as lower animals communicate only through non-significant gestures, Mead argues that they cannot develop a self: "We have no reason to assume, for example, that in lower animals there are such entities as selves" (PS 42). The ability to communicate with significant symbols or significant gestures having a shared meaning which is identified by Mead as the "outstanding characteristic in human communication" (PS 38). Hence, like Ernst Cassirer's notion of man as an *animal symbolicum* (1944, 26), Peirce's semiotic understanding of personhood as a network of linguistic signs, and Whitehead's notion of human perception in the mode of "symbolic reference," Mead argues that the human self is distinguished by virtue of the fact that it arises through a communicative process of symbolic interaction using significant symbols.

## Communication, Significant Symbols, and Meaning

Mead's understanding of how the self arises through symbolic communication using significant symbols or signs can further be analyzed in terms of his theory of *meaning*. Like Dewey, Mead understands "meaning" to be a function of symbolic communication with others. Citing Dewey's chapter entitled "Nature, Communication and Meaning" from from *Experience and Nature,* Mead asserts: "Dewey says that meaning arises through communication" (MSS 79). For both Dewey and Mead, "meaning" is not a fixed content but instead emerges within the social act of communicative interaction between individuals in the flow of conversation itself. Influenced by Wundt's psychology, Mead analyzes the nature of "meaning" within communicative interaction by focusing on the dynamics of the *gesture.* He tells us that animals gesture to one another and thereby communicate. By this view a gesture is understood as a stimulus that calls out a response, the meaning of the gesture. The innovation of Mead's behavioristic approach is that he defines a publicly observable gesture in functional terms as the "stimulus" and its *meaning* as the "response" it evokes. In Mead's words: "The gesture stands for a certain resultant of the social act . . . so that the meaning is given or stated in terms of response" (MSS 76). Hence, in contrast to introspective psychology which analyzes the nature of meaning as a function of private minds, Mead formulates a behavioristic psychology which analyzes meaning as a function of publicly observable "gestures" within the social act of communication. The definition of meaning in behaviorist terms as a publicly observable response to a stimulus or publicly observable gesture thereby functions to get meanings *out in the open.*

According to Mead the social act of linguistically mediated communicative interaction is to be defined in behaviorist terms as a "conversation of gestures," including bodily, vocal, and linguistic gestures. He also distinguishes between animal communication through a conversation of nonsignificant gestures at the nonsymbolic level, and "significant gestures," or "significant symbols" at the symbolic level of communicative interaction. The origin of language is found in the conversation of gestures, whereupon gestures become significant symbols which evoke the same meaning in oneself as for others. Influenced by the semiotic communication theory of self developed by Peirce and Royce, Mead also sometimes refers to significant symbols as *signs,* for instance, when he asserts: "Conscious communication—conscious conversation of gestures—arises when gestures become signs" (MSS 69 n.). For Mead, significant symbols or signs allow us to be aware of meaning. Furthermore, meaning is defined in functional terms—in terms of the *similarity of responses* called out by a gesture. One of his deepest insights is that if an individual, by his gesture, calls out in himself the same response that he evokes in another through a social act, then that gesture is a "significant gesture" or "significant symbol," by virtue of having a shared or common meaning to both the one who makes it and to the other. That is to say, a significant symbol calls out the same response in the speaker as to the listener. When a gesture calls up the same meanings in both the speaker and the listener, Mead defines it as a "significant gesture" as it has the same significance or functionally identical meaning for both self and other (MSS 67). It is from the use of significant symbols in social acts the individual minds and selves with reflexive self-consciousness emerge. The social self arises through a process of "role-taking" or "perspective-taking" which takes place by communication with others in society through the shared meanings of signs or significant symbols. It is by role-taking through communication with significant symbols that the individual can get outside of himself, so to speak, and see himself as an object from the standpoint of others, thereby to develop into a social self with reflexive self-consciousness: "Only by social means—only by taking the attitudes of others toward himself—is [a person] able to become an object to himself" (MSS 226). Because a significant symbol has a shared meaning for both the speaker and the listener it opens up a common perspective which makes possible the achievement of consensus and mutual understanding through communicative interaction. It is the shared meaning or common perspective of significant symbols that allows one to put themselves in the perspective of others and view themselves as an object from the perspective of others, thereby to acquire reflexivity. Of special importance for the development of a social self is communication with significant symbols having shared meanings through vocal gestures: "We hear our own vocal gestures as others hear them" (SW 387). In his universal pragmatics, Jürgen Habermas thus develops Mead's notion of the "social act" in terms of the *speech act* of linguistically mediated communicative interaction through a conversation of vocal gestures as significant symbols evoking the functionally identical response in the speaker and the listener. Moreover, the social act of communication through a conversation of significant symbols occurs not through external conversation with others, but also through the "inner conversation" whereby an individual communicates with himself in the process of *thinking*. "The mechanism of thought, insofar as thought uses symbols which are used in social intercourse, is but an inner conversation" (SW 243). And elsewhere: "The internalization in our experience of the external conversations of gestures which we carry on with other individuals in the social process is the essence of thinking" (MSS 47). In this way Mead develops a thoroughgoing social psychology which explicates the social nature of the self through symbolic communication, including both external conversation with others through vocal gestures and the inner conversation with the generalized other carried on through the social process of thinking. Thus, by means of communication through the shared meanings of signs or significant symbols, both internally and externally, the individual takes on the attitudes, roles, and perspectives of others in society and thereby develops a social self.

Mead and Dewey together worked out an organic and holistic account of "meaning" through social acts of symbolic communication between self and other. Mead's idea of the "social act" is a refinement of Dewey's notion of organic interaction as the basic unit of behavior, which he uses to replace the dualistic stimulus-response model of the *reflex arc*. The *act* or "social act" is the basic unit of communicative interaction which stretches beyond the dualism of subject and object, thus to include both the gestural stimulus and the meaningful response it calls out in another. Dewey undermines the dualistic concept of S-R as a mechanistic connection between two external events and shows how the S-R relation is a directed, holistic, and organic process of mutually coordinated interaction. The "social act" of linguistically mediated communicative interaction including both gesture (stimulus) and response (meaning) is defined as situational, contextual, and transactional in character. It is only the whole "circuit" of the reflex arc which transforms the initial phase into a "stimulus" and the last phase into a "response." Likewise, the social act is a holistic and organic process of intercommunication between self and other wherein the anticipation of the "response" of another gives one's original gesture, the "stimulus," its meaning. He thus writes: "In other words, the relationship between a given stimulus—as a gesture—and the later phases of the social act for which it is an early (if not the initial) phase constitutes the field within which meaning originates and exists" (MSS 76).

Mead (MSS 75–82) goes on to analyze the logical structure of meaning within a social act of communicative interaction in terms of a triadic relation which at once reveals the influence of the semiotics of C. S. Peirce and its development by Josiah Royce. According to Mead, the triadic structure of meaning within a social act consists of (1) an individual's "gesture," the *stimulus,* (2) a second individual's adjustive *response,* the "meaning," and (3) the *consequence* of the interaction. "The logical structure of meaning . . . is to be found in the threefold relationship of gesture to adjustive response and the resultant of the given social act" (MSS 80). The triadic structure of meaning thus consists of the "relation of the gesture of one organism to the adjustive response of another organism . . . to the completion of the given act" (MSS 76). He summarizes this triadic structure of meaning as follows: "This threefold or triadic relation between gesture, adjustive response, and resultant of the social act . . . is the basis of meaning" (MSS 80). The upshot of Mead's threefold account of meaning is that language is not a medium for communicating the inner emotions or thoughts of a subjective consciousness, but is instead a vehicle for eliciting *responses* from others within the unity of a social act. "Meaning" is not a fixed content but something that arises through a *spontaneous adjustive response* to a gestural stimulus within the living flow of communication, dialogue, and conversation. The social act is therefore to be understood in organic, holistic terms as a situational or transactional unit of meaning which stretches across the dualism of stimulus-response so as to include the entire "circuit" of gesture, response, and completion.

## The Constitutive Function of Mental Images in Communicative Interaction

Mead's theory of the social self underscores the constitutive role of *mental images* in the social act of communicative interaction. In her book *The Self Imagined: Philosophical Reflections on the Social Character of Psyche*, Karen Hanson argues that the functioning of imagination and mental imagery are the key factors implicit in Mead's theory of the social constitution of human selfhood, stating: "I would like to suggest that Mead's view of the development of the self in fact depends on the organism's imaginative capacity, that it is only in and through imaginative identification with the other that one can become an object to himself" (1986, 39). Although Mead adopts a form of behaviorist psychology, his focus on the mental imagery of imagination stands in direct opposition to Watson's reductionistic approach to psychological behaviorism which attempts to explain human selfhood solely in terms of observable conduct without reference to any internal contents like feelings, sensations, and images. Since Watson finds no behavioral manifestation of mental imagery, he goes so far as to deny the very existence of images and the faculty of imagination. Mead, on the other hand, asserts that imagery cannot by dismissed as Watson did simply because it is difficult to reconcile with behaviorism. At one point, he states: "The content of our minds is (1) inner conversation . . . [and] (2) . . . imagery" (MSS 190fn.). According to Mead, images are constitutive of the objects of perception: "a considerable part of our perceptual world, the world existing 'out there,' as we say, is made up out of mental images . . . These images actually go to make up objects we see and feel" (MTNC 398). To begin with, mental images are constitutive of the initial phase of the social act so as to shape the "selective character of attention" which selects the appropriate stimulus where an impulse seeks expression (MSS 337–38). Furthermore, "Imagery may be found at any place in the act" (MSS 346). Hence, mental images can contribute to the organization of all phases of a social act including impulse, perception, manipulation, and consummation. It has been seen that in Mead's analysis of the social act as a coordinated interaction between gesture and response in an organic circuit of behavior, the anticipation of the "response" of another gives one's original gesture, the "stimulus," its meaning. However, it is only by forming an image of the adjustive response to our gesture that meaning arises in a social act of communicative interaction. This is shown clearly by the following passage:

> As long as one individual responds to the gesture of another by the appropriate response, there is no necessary consciousness of meaning. . . . It

is not until an image arises of the response, which the gesture of one form will bring out in another, that a consciousness of meaning can attach to his own gesture. The meaning can appear only imaging the consequence of the gesture. (SW 111)

Mead's social psychology therefore represents a holistic and nonreductionistic form of behaviorism which analyzes human selfhood in terms of publicly observable conduct while at the same time elucidating the primary function of mental images produced by creative imagination within the social act of communication between self and other. Hence, the symbolic images of creative imagination play a normative role in determining the social construction of the self through a dialectic between I and Me. However, for Mead the process of sympathetic imagination by means of which the self is constituted through identification with the generalized other occurs through the cognitive mechanism of internalization which he calls "taking the role of the other."

## Mead's Perspectivist Model of Selfhood

Mead's social-self theory and unified social science framework is based on a doctrine of "objective perspectives" derived primarily from the Leibnizian cosmology of perspectives reformulated by A. N. Whitehead. Mead states: "What I wish to pick out of Professor Whitehead's philosophy of nature is this conception of nature as an organization of perspectives, which are there in nature" (PP 163). He adds that he intends to focus on Whitehead's "Leibnizian filiation, as it appears in his conception of the perspective as the mirroring in the event of all other events" (PP 164). As Whitehead argues in *Science and the Modern World*, his events are to be understood as being similar to Leibniz's monads, each of which is said to be a living mirror reflecting its entire universe from a unique perspectival locus in nature. For Whitehead the self is a Leibnizian mirror which reflects events occurring *there* and *then* from the perspective defining a new event occurring *here* and *now*. According to this Leibnizian perspectivist model of nature developed by Mead and Whitehead, each organism is conceived to be a living mirror which reflects its whole environment from a unique perspective so as to constitute an individual microcosm of the social macrocosm. Each perspective in the continuum of nature constitutes the prehensive unity of an individual organism with its entire social environment, as expressed by Mead when he speaks of "the organism and environment in the perspective" (PP 173). When Mead's theory of selfhood is understood in terms of his Whiteheadian theory of perspectives, each individual organism constitutes a perspectival mirror which reflects its entire social environment including not only the human community but the whole of nature. For Mead, the social self is akin to a Leibnizian monad or Whiteheadian event which mirrors, if not the whole universe, at least the whole community from its own unique perspective, thereby to constitute an individual microcosm of the social macrocosm. Mead writes that "each individual self within that social process, while it reflects in its organized structure the behavior pattern of that [social] process as a whole, it does so from its own particular and unique standpoint . . . just as every monad in the Leibnizian universe mirrors that universe from a different point of view, and thus mirrors a different aspect or perspective of that universe" (PP 201). He emphasizes that Whitehead's perspectivism is an aspect of his abandonment of *simple location,* according to which each event mirrors every other event from a perspective, so that "it is possible to conceive of the same body of events as organized into an indefinite number of different perspectives" (PP 164). According to the Leibnizian perspectivism of Whitehead and Mead, the concept of simple location is replaced with that of *multiple location,* in that each event both mirrors and is mirrored by every other event from multiple perspectives. Mead thus uses the Whitehead-Leibniz perspectivist model of selfhood as the metaphysical basis for his sociological theory of the "looking-glass self" derived from C. H. Cooley wherein the social self is conceived as a mirror which reflects the primary social group to which it belongs.

One of the most significant features of Mead's social-self theory is that it is grounded within the speculative framework of a Whiteheadian process cosmology based upon the doctrine of emergent social and temporal perspectives. Yet the great innovation of Mead's social-self theory is that it appropriates Whitehead's concept of nature as an organization of perspectives and then applies it to the *social sciences* including sociology, social psychology, and anthropology at the micro level and ecology at the macro level. He therefore states, "I wish to consider the conception of a body of events as the organization of different perspectives of these events, from the standpoint of the field of social science, and that of behavioristic psychology" (PP 164–65). He adds, "My suggestion was that we find in society and social experience, interpreted in terms of a behavioristic psychology an instance of that organization of perspectives . . . of Professor Whitehead's philosophy" (PP 171). Mead's conception of the pragmatic method of inquiry arrived at through an extension of the scientific experimental method is itself based on his concept of objective, shared or common perspectives. The experimental method of science consists in formulating and testing a tentative hypothesis, which results in a common perspective that is sharable by the whole community of inquirers. He writes that "the critical scientist is only replacing the narrower social perspectives of other communities by that of a more highly organized and hence more universal community" (PP 166). Mead sums up his application of the theory of objective perspectives to the social sciences when he writes:

> The social perspective exists in the experience of the individual in so far as it is intelligible, and its intelligibility that is the condition of the individual entering into the perspectives of others, especially of the group. In the field of any social science the objective data are those experiences of the individuals in which they take the attitude of the community, i.e., in which they enter into the perspectives of the other members of the community. (PP 166)

In his developmental psychology Mead argues that the social and multiple self emerges by taking on the perspectives, roles, and attitudes of all the other selves in its social group. He thus writes that "the individual enters into the perspective of others, in so far as he is able to take their attitude or occupy their point of view" (PP 165). Again, he states: "It is only in so far as the individual acts not only in his own perspective but also in the perspective of others, especially in his the common perspective of a group, that a society arises. The imitation of social organization is to be found in the inability of individuals to place themselves in the perspectives of others, to take their points of view" (PP165). Perspective-taking, the process of entering the perspectives of others in society, is therefore the basic mechanism whereby an individual goes outside of himself and sees himself as an object from the standpoint of others, thereby to develop a multiple and social self with reflexive self-consciousness and personal identity. Mead's idea of "perspective-taking" or "role-taking" according to which the self develops through entering into the perspectives of others is also the basis of his moral philosophy, wherein he endeavors to reformulate Kant's universalist ethics in the context of an intersubjectivist communication paradigm of the social self. Furthermore, it is Mead's idea of perspective-taking which became the basis of L. Kohlberg's developmental scheme of moral socialization as well as Jürgen Habermas's developmental stages of communicative competence. For Kohlberg and Habermas, as for Mead, it is only by the ability of the self to take on the perspective of others and to see things from their point of view which can serve as the basis for a procedure which establishes impartial, fair, and universal norms as the basis for moral conduct. Sociality is thus developed through perspective-taking.

Mead's universalist ethics based upon the capacity of the self to enter into the objective perpectives of others attempts to overturn the moral relativism of other perspectivist theories. However, Mead's perspectivism is developed not so much in opposition to the theory of relativism as it is an effort to combine both relativism and objectivism in a third alternative: namely the concept of *objective perspectives*. Mead refers to the objectivity of perspectives as "an aspect of the philosophy of relativism which Professor Whitehead has presented" (PP 162). In his Introduction to *Mind, Self, and Society*, Charles W. Morris summarizes Mead's theory of objective perspectives based on the modern scientific theory of relativity with the term "objective relativism" (MSS xix). In contrast to the moral and epistemological relativism associated with Nietzsche's perspectivism and its development in French poststructuralism, according to which there are no facts but only perspectival interpretations, Mead argues for a theory of the objectivity of perspectives, which instead asserts that while all meanings are relative to a context, nonetheless each point of view incorporates a shared or common perspective, that is, a social perspective. The objectivity of perspectives is thus constituted by their sociality, sharability, and generalizability. According to Mead's genetic acount of the social self, the individual perspective always emerges from a community perspective: "It is the relation of the individual perspective to the common perspective that is of importance" (PP 167). It is a distinctive trait of the human self that it can enter into multiple perspectives by taking on the social roles of others in the community. Adopting a shared or common perspective by taking on the role of the other happens when the individual is able to evoke in himself through his own behavior (gesture) the same functionally identical response that his behavior evokes in another. "He is able then to become a generalized other in addressing himself in the attitude of the group or the community... This is the common perspective" (PP 168). He adds, "It is then such a coincidence of the perspective of the individual organism with the pattern of the whole ... that constitutes the objectivity of the perspective" (PP 174–75). Richard Bernstein (1988) has argued that the current philosophical era is to be conceived as an effort to advance beyond relativism and objectivism. It can thus be said that Mead's theory of "objective relativism" based on the objectivity of shared perspectives represents one of the major efforts in twentieth-century social philosophy to move beyond the extremes of relativism on the one side and objectivism on the other.

## Mead's Evolutionary Process Cosmology of Emergent Perspectives

Like other American pragmatists and process thinkers, G. H. Mead formulates a concept of self under the influence of Darwinian evolutionism wherein the self develops through organism-environment interactions in problematic situations. However, in contrast to Dewey's emphasis on the "adaptation" or "adjustment" of an individual to its surroundings, Mead describes the self as arising through a *creative response* of organism to environment in the evolutionary process. Thus, while Dewey presents a more Darwinian view, Mead instead works out an emergent and creative evolutionary model of the self. In his first published work entitled *The Philosophy of the Present* (1932) Mead develops his theory of the social self (PP 194) within the overall context of an evolutionary process cosmology influenced by the emergent evolution (PP 43) of L. Morgan and S. Alexander, the creative evolution of H. Bergson (PP 21), and especially the process cosmology of creative advance toward novelty (PP 161) of A. N. Whitehead. The basic unit in the creative advance of nature is that of "emergent events" (PP 3), wherein each emergent event is said to be located in a "present" (PP 1) as characterized by "its becoming and its disappearing" (PP 1). Indeed, Mead's emergent evolutionism is radical to the extent that he argues for "new pasts arising with emergent events" (PP 46). As a result, Mead understands the self not as a permanent substance with a fixed essence but as a flux of "emergent events" which forever arise and perish in an evolving temporal process of creative advance toward novelty. In general it can be said that Mead locates the human self within temporal process of emergent evolution at every level, including both the wider evolutionary and historical processes at the macro level as well as the developmental and socialization processess at the micro level.

Like Whitehead, Mead rejects the idea of an "absolute perspective" developed by Hegel, Bradley, and Royce, since it undermines the reality of finite temporal perspectives in the creative advance toward novelty. In Mead's words:

> The grandiose undertaking of Absolute Idealism to bring the whole of reality within experience failed. It failed because it left the perspective of the finite ego hopelessly infected with subjectivity and consequently unreal. From its point of view the theoretical and practical life of the individual had no part in the creative advance of nature. (PP 161)

For the process theory of Mead, as for that of Whitehead, each perspective in nature is not only "social" but also *temporal*. Similar to Whitehead's "epochal" theory of time based on the photonic character of space-time events in quantum physics, Mead rejects the idea an "absolute perspective" as held by absolute idealism, and argues that each objective perspective in nature is *emergent*, that is, a discrete creative act of unification which is temporal, discontinuous, and novel. It is this emergent or discontinuous character of temporal perspectives which constitute nature as a creative advance into novelty. Again citing the authority of Whitehead, he asserts: "In Professor Whitehead's phrase, in so far as nature is patient of an organism, it is stratified into perspectives, whose intersections consititute the creative advance of nature" (PP 163). Mead summarizes his Whiteheadian concept of nature as a creative advance into novelty based on a theory of emergent temporal perspectives when he writes: "What I am suggesting is that this process, in which . . . new common perspectives arise, is an instance of the organization of perspectives in nature, of the creative advance of nature . . . Nature in its relationship to the organism, and including the organism, is a perspective that is there" (PP 172).

For Mead, then, the self is an ever-changing temporal process of emergent evolution in the creative advance of nature. Mead describes the emergence of the human "mind" and "self" as a new and more advanced form of *sociality* which has developed in the evolutionary process: "I have wished to present mind as an evolution in nature, in which culminates that sociality which is the principle and form of emergence" (PP 85). He adds: "I wish to emphasize the fact that the appearance of mind is only the culmination of that sociality which is found throughout the universe, its culmination lying in the fact that the organism by occupying the attitudes of others can occupy its own attitude in the role of others" (PP 86–87). It is further clarified that human mind and self with reflexive self-awareness which have emerged from out of the evolutionary process is a culmination of the universal principle of sociality in that it involves the development of communication by "symbols" (PP 87), what he elsewhere terms significant symbols or significant gestures. Through the emergence of "mind" in the evolutionary process of creative advance there has been an upward development of sociality beyond the subhuman level of nonsymbolic communication through a language of nonsignificant gestures to that of the human level of symbolic communication through a language of significant gestures functioning as significant symbols with a shared or common meaning. According to Mead's evolutionary cosmology, then, the emergence of human mind and self represents an evolution of sociality to a higher mode of communicative competence through symbolic interaction using significant symbols, just as for Whitehead the emergence of human mind designates an evolution beyond perception in the modes of causal feeling and sense experience to perception in the higher mode of symbolic reference.

Mead does not predict any future emergents which might appear in the process of evolution. He discusses the emergent evolutionism of S. Alexander wherein a sequence of progressive qualities "emerges" from the space-time matrix, including matter, life, mind, and ultimately, that of deity: "Alexander presented space and time as such an environment out of which emerged matter, qualities, life, mind and deity. His philosophy was that of an emergent evolution, as the biologist Morgan presented it" (PP 43). While Alexander's emergent evolutionism is directed toward the future emergence of "deity," Mead, like Whitehead, formulates a process cosmology of emergent evolution which is not grounded upon an *arché*, nor is it governed by any grand meta-narrative, nor is it directed toward any final *telos*, *eschaton*, or omega-point, but is a fully open-ended process driven by an appetition for aesthetic experience, emergent novelty and creative advance without end. Yet Mead clearly views the development of a "social self" with reflexive self-awareness through symbolic communication as the culmination of sociality which has thus far emerged through the evolutionary process and the creative advance of nature. If there is a futural stage of emergent evolution suggested by Mead it is his visionary notion of "universal discourse" (MSS 327), an ideal of undistorted communicative interaction "carried through and made perfect" as "the formal ideal of communication" (MSS 327) and "the ideal of human society" (MSS 328). For Mead the emergence of universal discourse wherein there is unrestrained open communication between all members of the ideal communication community would function as the basis for the establishment of an ideal democratic society wherein each self can enter into the perspective of all the other selves in the community in the formation of universalized democratic principles, laws, and moral norms (MSS 328). Thus, not unlike Peirce's agapistic evolution, Mead's process of emergent creative evolution aims at *universal discourse* as the futuristic utopian ideal for a norm-governed democratic human society of unlimited open communication in a community of social selves.

## Aesthetic, Moral and Religious Dimensions of the Social Self

Interpretations of Mead's thought developed by specialists in the social sciences typically fail to engage the axiological and value-centric basis for his social-self theory. But for Mead the social self is always an organism understood as a whole in which the parts are functionally interrelated to realize some aim, purpose, or value. Like the organismic process cosmology of A. N. Whitehead, Mead envisions the social self as a temporal sequence of creative, novel, and aesthetic events, wherein each event is a "social act" arising in stages, the perceptive, manipulatory and consummatory stages, the final consummatory stage having the character of aesthetic experience. In his aesthetics, especially influenced by Dewey, he regards the process of communicative interaction as an end-means continuum wherein each moment is both instrumental and consummatory so as to be funded throughout with immediately felt pervasive aesthetic quality. His moral philosophy, especially influenced by the universalist ethics of Kant, regards the capacity for taking the role of the generalized other as the basis for establishing impartial, universalizable, and generalizable norms as required by the categorical imperative or the golden rule of Christian ethics. And in his philosophy of religion, especially influenced by Royce, realizing the larger social self by joining with others in the fellowship of community is the essence of the religious spirit. Mead's fundamental insight is that aesthetic, moral, and religious values are to be analyzed as a function of *sociality*. The achievement of a social self through communicative interaction with others in the community is therefore a profoundly aesthetic, religious, and ethical mode of existence in the value philosophy of Mead.

Earlier it was pointed out how in his 1900 essay called "Suggestions Toward a Theory of the Philosophical Disciplines," Mead (SW 7) undertakes the ambitious neo-Hegelian effort to unify metaphysics, psychology, logic, ethics, and aesthetics by means of a "dialectic within the act". And in his 1905 essay titled "The Philosophical Basis of Ethics" Mead (SW 85) similarly asserts that for the movement of pragmatism, various aesthetic, ethical, metaphysical, intellectual, and perceptual processes exist only as functions of an "act" which is the fundamental unit of communicative interaction. What Mead terms "the act" or the "social act" is otherwise called "experience," "field," "situation," "context," "perspective," and various other double-barreled holistic terms used to designate the event of communicative interaction between self and other within a group. The main point for Mead is that "the social act" is the basic unit of communicative interaction which stretches across such ordinary dualisms as stimulus-response, subject-object, organism-environment, I-Me, self-other, or individual-society. Mead analyzes the social act as arising by means of a valuative transaction between organism and environment in the creation of an emergent whole whose parts functionally interrelate to produce some value. In his analysis of the various phases of the social act he speaks of the perceptual, manipulative, and consummatory phases. This "consummatory phase" of the social act of communication indicates the immediate quality of aesthetic value achieved by each interaction between organism and environment. One of the most suggestive aspects of Mead's value theory is that aesthetic, moral, religious, and other modes of value experience are interpreted as a *fusion* of the I and Me poles which together constitute the twofold nature of the social self (MSS 273–81). Hence, for Mead all value experience, including artistic, religious, and moral experience, is to be understood as a dynamic function of the social self which arises through the fusion of the I and the Me.

## Aesthetic Experience as a Function of Sociality

Speaking of the emotional exaltation characterizing aesthetic experience as well as religious myths, rites, and rituals, Mead characterizes the enjoyment of aesthetic delight as a fusion between the I and the Me poles of the social self: "The idea of the fusion of the 'I' and the 'me' gives a very adequate basis for the explanation of this exaltation. I think behavioristic psychology provides just the opportunity for such development of aesthetic theory" (MSS 280). In his essay "The Nature of Aesthetic Experience" (SW 294–305), which is clearly inspired by John Dewey's two works, *Experience and Nature* and *Art as Experience,* Mead goes on to further articulate his theory of aesthetic enjoyment as a function of the social nature of human selfhood. Mead (SW 300) quotes Dewey's famous assertion that "shared experience is the greatest of human goods," clarifying that among these modes of shared experience is the aesthetic. He adds: "Whether this form of the enjoyed result has an aesthetic function or not," depends on whether a work of literature or art serves to convey the "shared experience of the community of which he feels himself to be a part" (SW 302). An experience thus has an aesthetic function when "it serves to give the man the gratification of his experience as shared by the community to which he belongs" (SW 302). In this context Mead argues that the nature of the aesthetic and consummatory experience in the creative process "belongs to coordinated efforts of man, when the role of the other in production is aroused in each worker at the common task, when the sense of team play, *esprit de corps,* inspires interrelated activities" (SW 299).

Dewey criticizes the museum concept of art as the beauty parlor of civilization, that is, what he terms the "compartmentalization" of art from society, and instead holds that all creative processes should be saturated throughout by pervasive aesthetic quality including both the activities of the artist and the common labor of the artisan. In his social theory of art Dewey thus argues that each moment of social experience is both an immediately enjoyed quality, an end in itself, as well as a means toward the consummatory act, so that the whole process is funded with intrinsic value as an "ends-means continuum." Similarly, in his analysis of the "social act" as the fundamental unit of existence, Mead emphasizes that the act is can be analyzed into the perceptive, manipulatory and consummatory stages. The social act thus always culminates in a consummatory stage of aesthetic enjoyment. However, the consummatory stage of a social act comes not only at the end but is anticipated throughout each and every moment of the entire creative process in shared aesthetic experience: "I have presented aesthetic experience as a part of the attempt to interpret complex social life in terms of the goals toward which our efforts run" (SW 296–97). He adds, "Normal aesthetic delight in creation is the recovery of the sense of the final outcome in the partial achievement and gives assurance to the interest of creation" (SW 299). This social theory of art understood as an ends-means continuum is exemplified by Mead when he then writes: "[I]n the words of Professor Dewey 'shared experience is the greatest of human goods,' and if out of the drudgery that men put through together there arises a social end in which they are interested, achieving this end will have its delight, and insofar as this end can involve the tasks themselves, the dignity and delight of the social realization will suffuse the tasks" (SW 300). For Mead, as for Dewey, aesthetic experience is a function of the social nature of selfhood as arising through open communication, mutual participation, shared experience, cooperation, and valuative transaction between individuals in society. Moreover, both Dewey and Mead develop a pragmatic theory of valuation according to which each moment of the creative process is both an end in itself and a means toward a common goal, such the whole ends-means continuum is pervaded throughout by aesthetic quality. The pragmatism of Dewey and Mead is often characterized merely as "instrumentalism" in that thought is regarded as an instrument whereby an individual organism can adjust to its social environment in a problematic situation. Yet both thinkers underscore not only the "instrumental" but also the *consummatory* nature of events. In such a manner, then, both Mead and Dewey emphasize the aesthetic, the valuative, and the consummatory dimensions of the social self as an individual-society interaction.

## Religion as Self-Realization through Community

Mead is strongly critical of the dogmatic attitude of institutionalized religions, particularly of the Christian church. He therefore speaks of "Oppressive, stereo-typed, and ultra-conservative social institutions—like the church which by their rigid and inflexible unprogressiveness crush or blot out individuality" (MSS 262). However, at the same time, Mead undertakes the interpretation of mystical experience and the religious dimensions of human existence in terms of his themes of community, communication, and the social nature of the self. On the social character of religious experience, he says: "The conception of the religious life is itself a social conception; it gathers about the idea of the community" (MSS 385). With his teacher Josiah Royce he thus holds that religious salvation does not lie in an individual's private relation to a transcendent beyond, but in a social being's relation to the community (PA 475–78). Like Royce, Mead argues that salvation occurs not merely by the mystical ecstasy of a solitary being, but through membership in a community.

> There is need for salvation—not the salvation of the individual but the salvation of the self as a social being. I think that side of it rather than the mystic attitude is of the greatest importance . . . Our religious experiences come back to that possibility of the development of society so as to realize those values which belong to social beings." (PA 476)

Mead does not reject the notion of mystical experience per se, but argues that its salvific function is that it leads to "the sense of the relation of man to his society" (PA 478). In other words, the ecstasy of mystical experience is now to be understood as a fusion of the I and the Me poles of the social self: "It is where the 'I' and the 'me' can in some sense fuse that there arises the peculiar sense of exaltation which belongs to the religious and patriotic attitudes" (MSS 273). Similarly, he understands the phenomenon of religious conversion as an "enlarged experience" brought about by the fusion of the I and the Me poles of the social self, whereupon the individual develops a sense of belongingness to the new community into which it has entered:

> This enlarged experience has a profound influence. It is the sort of experience which the neophyte has in conversion. It is the sense of belonging to the community, of having an intimate relationship with an indefinite number of individuals who belong to the same group . . . The person has entered into the universal community of the church, and the resulting experience is the expression of the sense of identification of one's self with everyone else in the community. (MSS 219)

For Mead, the religious genius of Jesus lies in the fact that he "generalized the conception of the community in terms of the family" (MSS 216). He adds

that the religious doctrines of Jesus and the Buddha both emphasize the relation of the individual to the community: "Take the religious genius, such as
Jesus or Buddha. . . . What has given them their unique importance is that
they have taken the attitude of living with reference to a larger society" (MSS
217). Mead thus develops a wholly social concept of religious experience in
which conversion, mystical exaltation, and salvation are all to be interpreted
as overturning the separate ego-self by realizing one's true nature as a social
self through membership in a community. His understanding of religious
experience can be understood as a development of Royce's theme of *self-
realization through community*. In the final analysis, Mead's philosophy of religion is based on Royce's idea of realizing the "greater social self" through
membership in a community, but as as reformulated within a secular framework devoid of any reference to a transcendent or supernatural principle.


## The Communicative Discourse Ethics of Mead

Mead, like Dewey, develops a pragmatist ethics which holds that ethical theory
is reflection on the practical procedure for solving moral problems involving
the adjustment of an individual organism to its social environment. Ethical
problems are thus always thoroughly social in character. Mead writes that
"ethical problems arise for individual members of any given human society
whenever they are individually confronted with a social situation to which
they cannot readily adjust and adapt themselves" (MSS 319). Also, like Dewey,
ethics is to be understood as the application of the scientific experimental
method to the solution of moral problem-situations. It is clear that Mead's
pragmatist ethics based on the experimental method and the problem-solving
approach to moral problems has itself been deeply influenced by the *Ethics*
(1908) co-authored by Dewey and Tufts, a work directly cited by Mead in his
"Fragments on Ethics" (MSS 384). At the same time, Mead works out his
own highly innovative moral theory based on an intersubjectivist communication model of the social self which emphasizes *universality* in ethics more
strongly than Dewey. Indeed, his social reformulation of Kant's universalist
ethics resulting in what Habermas terms a "communicative discourse ethics"
signifies one of Mead's single greatest contributions to philosophy.
    Like art and religion, morality is understood by Mead to be a function
of the social self as an individual-society interaction. Concerning the social
basis of morality, he states: "As human nature is essentially social in character, moral ends must be also social in their nature" (PA 385). Again, in Mead's
essay called "The Social Self" (1913), wherein his analysis of the social nature

of selfhood passes over into a discussion on the social nature of ethics, he affirms "the essentially social character of the ethical end" (SW 148). It can be said that in his moral philosophy, Mead works out a kind of self-realization theory of ethics. However, Mead asserts that the self to be achieved through moral development cannot be "the self whose realization is the goal of the ethics of Green and his ilk" (SW46). He clarifies that it is not a self-realization ethics in pursuit of an absolute self as formulated by the Oxford school of absolute idealism including T. H. Green, Bernard Bosanquet, Edward Caird, and others in the neo-Hegelian tradition (SW 46 n.). Rather, the moral philosophy of Mead is a self-realization ethics aimed toward realizing one's true human nature as a twofold social self arising through an I-Me dialectic of intersubjectivity. Thus, is his "Fragments on Ethics," Mead states that "those ends are good which lead to the realization of the self as a social being" (MSS 385).

According to Mead, ethical conduct is to be understood as a mode of intersubjective praxis in which there occurs a *fusion* of the I and Me poles constituting the social self. He explains, "The self under these circumstances is the action of the 'I' in harmony with taking the role of others in the 'me'" (MSS 277). Mead argues that this capacity of the I pole for "taking the role of others" at the Me pole representing the general other is the basis of making impartial moral judgments regarding the suitability of a norm to function as a universal validity claim in ethics. That is to say, one can determine if a contestable norm is right, fair, and just in a problematic moral situation only by putting oneself into the position of others in the community, that is, by taking the role of the generalized other. In recent moral philosophy, Lawrence Kohlberg and Jürgen Habermas have developed Mead's seminal notion of "ideal role-taking" or "perspective-taking" as a formal procedure for moral-practical decisions having such features as impartiality, universalizability, reversibility, and prescriptivity. Of special interest is the work of Jürgen Habermas and Karl-Otto Apel, who build upon the insights of American pragmatism in an effort to reformulate Kant's universalist ethics by grounding moral norms in the dialogical process of intersubjective communication, thereby arriving at what they term a communicative ethics or discourse ethics. However, while Apel is influenced more by Peirce's doctrine of the intersubjective community as the basis for establishing ethical norms, Habermas instead focuses upon the communication theory of Mead. In the communicative discourse ethics formulated by Mead and further developed by Habermas, the categorical imperative of Kant which demands universality for moral norms cannot be a monological procedure conducted by a solitary transcendental subject, but must instead be carried out as a dialogical procedure through communication and public discourse by an intersubjective community. While the communicative discourse ethics of Habermas has of late received much attention by scholars in the field, the tendency has been to neglect the origins of his theory in the work of Mead. Hence, in what follows I will explicate Kant's universalist ethics based on the categorical imperative, followed by an account of recent efforts to reconstruct his theory by Mead, Kohlberg, Habermas, and Rawls.

Immanuel Kant established a Copernican revolution in moral philosophy through the formulation of a duty-based (deontological) universalist ethics as codified in terms of his famous "categorical imperative." According to Kant, an action has moral value when it is performed, not out of private inclination or a selfish desire for some end, but out of a sense of "duty." According to Kant's deontological ethics, all moral conduct is based on *duty for duty's sake* without regard for the consequences of those actions. Moreover, one's duty is prescribed by a moral law or categorical imperative which is itself determined by the autonomous functioning of self-legislative practical reason. In his *Fundamental Principles of the Metaphysics of Morals* (1785), the categorical imperative is set forth by Kant as follows: "*Act only on that maxim whereby thou canst at the same time will that it should become a universal law*" (1987, 49). The categorical imperative is developed by Kant as a formal procedure in ethics whereby *universalizability* functions as the rational criterion or principle of justification for discriminating between valid and invalid norms. A norm for moral governing conduct is acceptable only if it can be *universalized* as a law applicable to everyone without exception. In another brilliant move, Kant then goes on to establish the *autonomy* of moral subjects with regard to the moral law as categorical imperative. Kant propounds that the categorical imperative brings us to "the idea of *the will of every rational being as a universally legislative will*" (1987, 60). The will of a rational being is not merely subject to the law since it must also be regarded *as itself giving the law* by means of the universalization procedure stipulated by the categorical imperative. Consequently, as autonomous rational beings we each prescribe the moral law to ourselves through the self-legislative function of practical reason.

One of the most significant and innovative features of Mead's ethical philosophy is the effort to reinterpret Kant's universalist ethics grounded in the categorical imperative by means of his intersubjectivist communication theory based on the social nature, origin, and development of the self. In other words, Mead attempts to reformulate Kant's categorical imperative by means of his own principle of sociality. Mead writes:

> It is possible to build up an ethical theory on a social basis, in terms of our social theory of the origin, development, nature, and structure of

the self. Thus, for example, Kant's categorical imperative may be socially stated or formulated or interpreted in these terms, that is, give its social equivalent. (MSS 379)

Mead goes on to argue that the rational nature of ethical conduct owing to the categorical imperative is due to the social nature of the self arising through its ability to take the role, attitude, or perspective of the generalized other, and that the requirement of universality placed upon all ethical acts is therefore to be understood in terms of the principle of sociality.

> Man is a rational being because he is a social being. The universality of our judgments, upon which Kant places so much stress, is a universality that arises from the fact that we take the attitude of the entire community, of all rational beings. We are what we are through our relationship to others. . . . Sociality gives the universality of our ethical judgments. (MSS 379)

With Kant, Mead holds that the maxim by which one acts must be universalizable if it is to have moral worth. In contrast to Kant, however, Mead explains that universality arises out of a social process of communication using significant symbols. As emphasized by Mead in this passage, ethical universality such as is required by the categorical imperative can be grounded only in sociality, since only by sociality is it made possible: "Sociality gives the universality of ethical judgements" (MSS 379). Hence, while Mead agrees with Kant that an act has moral worth when it is based upon a sense of duty, and that duty is itself determined by a universalizable maxim, he at the same time emphasizes that the sense of duty arises through taking on the attitudes of the generalized other and that moral conduct is thoroughly social in nature. In Mead's words: "The sense which the individual self has of his dependence upon the organized society or social community to which he belongs is the basis and origin, in short, of his sense of duty . . . ethical and unethical behavior can be defined essentially in social terms" (MSS 320). Furthermore, Mead attempts to reconcile Kant's duty ethics based on motives or intentions without regard for consequences, and utilitarianism based on ends without concern for motives. He argues that if regard for consequences is understood as directed toward social ends rather that hedonistic states of subjective pleasure, it combines both the the universalism of Kant and the utilitarianism of Bentham and Mill.

The capacity for making impartial, universal, and objective judgments guaranteed by the categorical imperative is accomplished in Mead's framework by taking on the social attitudes of the generalized other. Mead himself points out the relation between the generalized other and Freud's notion of the superego, the moral conscience or censorship mechanism arising through the internalization of parental authority. Similarly, for Mead the individual becomes a social self by taking on the roles, attitudes, and perspectives of the generalized other and judging itself with impartiality from the standpoint of that other. While for Freud the biological instincts of the id are controlled by the censorship mechanism of the superego or conscience, for Mead the impulses arising at the I or instinctual pole of the biosocial self are regulated by the generalized other at the Me or internalized social pole. As said by H. R. Niebuhr in *The Responsible Self,* Mead's generalized other is the equivalent of Adam Smith's impartial spectator (1963, 76–77). Adam Smith asserted that the self judges itself by regarding itself from the point of view of an impartial spectator. Mead replaces this notion of an impartial spectator with his concept of the generalized other, which as the universalized human community becomes the impartial jury legislating for all norm-governed rational thought and moral conduct.

Mead's communicative discourse ethics based on the intersubjectivist principle of sociality can also be explained through his perspectivism, what he otherwise calls his theory of "objective perspectives." As described above, Mead adopts the Leibnizian perspectivism of A. N. Whitehead as the basis for his social science framework. For Mead, *perspectivism* means the ability of an autonomous rational subject to take the role of others, or as it were, to enter into the perspective of others in the community. From the standpoint of this social perspectivism he thus recommends that ethical conduct be regulated by a procedure that he calls "role-taking." This procedure requires that any free rational agent making an ethical judgment put himself into the position of all who would be affected if a particular norm were to take effect within a given problematic situation. For Mead, then, the ability of a moral agent to act in accordance with intersubjectively valid norms as prescribed by the categorical imperative of Kant's universalist ethics and the golden rule of Christian ethics is itself due to the human capacity for perspective-taking or role-taking. In a word, the generalizability or universality of the categorical imperative is a function of perspectivism, the ability to put oneself in the other person's shoes. It can be said that through Mead's dialogical reinterpretation of Kant's categorical imperative and the golden rule of Christian ethics with a notion of perspective-taking he was at the same time reworking the ethical imperative of his teacher Josiah Royce. In his first published book *The Religious Aspect of Philosophy* (1885), Royce articulates his own Christianized version of Kant's ethical imperative as follows: "In so far as in thee lies, act as if thou wert at once thy neighbor and thyself. Treat these two lives as one" (1885, 149). Mead, who was forever engaged in the project of secularizing the Christian religious and moral themes of Royce, develops precisely this same ethical imperative in terms of his concept of perspective-taking, so that it might now take the form: "Act so as to take on the perspective of thy neighbor as if it were thine own." That is to say, the Christian morality of loving thy neighbor as thyself now assumes the form of putting oneself in another's perspective as the procedural basis for a communicative discourse ethics.

Mead agrees with Kant that the sense of "duty" or the moral "ought" expressed by such formal procedures as the categorical imperative and the golden rule must be grounded in a principle of universalization (MSS 380). Only a free rational agent could give universal form to his act and therefore be able to generalize the maxim of his act into a law of nature applicable to all persons in the community without exception. However, while Mead shares Kant's universalist approach to ethics, he rejects Kant's individualist assumptions and instead argues for the social formation of the self and human rationality. Explaining the individualism underlying Kant's version of the universalization principle, Mead continues: "Kant approached that universality from the assumption of the rationality of the individual, and said that if his ends, or the form of his acts, were universal, then society could arise. He conceived of the individual first of all as rational and as a condition for society" (MSS 379). In opposition to Kant's subjectivist approach to the categorical imperative based upon a methodological individualism, Mead argues that rationality is a social concept and that the principle of universalization must therefore be understood in terms of an intersubjectivist model of ethics. Contrary to Kant's view no solitary individual can will the maxim of an act to become a universal law in accord with the categorical imperative. Rationality and the self-legislative function of moral reason is not innate within the individual but only emerges through a socialization process of incorporating the generalized other, which is the organized set of responses of that community or social group to which one belongs. Rationality, like thinking, is social in that it is a communicative process of taking on the attitudes of the community represented by the generalized other and of controlling conduct by virtue of these attitudes (MSS 334). Consequently, the universal norms governing the moral conduct of rational agents cannot be rooted in Kant's transcendental subject which stands outside the community, but is instead due to the function of what Mead calls role-taking, the ability of a social self to take on the role, attitude, or perspective of the generalized other through open communication and universal discourse. Hence, the upshot of Mead's attempt to reformulate the categorical imperative in terms of his own principle of sociality is that he shifts the frame of reference from Kant's solitary moral agent based upon a theory of subject-centered consciousness to that of an intersubjective community based upon a communication model of the social self.

Mead's project of reconstructing Kant's universalist ethics based on the categorical imperative from the standpoint of an intersubjectivist communication paradigm has inspired a major new direction in contemporary moral philosophy, notably the moral socialization theory of Lawrence Kohlberg (1981), and the communicative discourse ethics of Jürgen Habermas (1990). Furthermore, Mead's social-self theory and I-Me dialectic is a primary inspiration for the Christian social ethics of responsibility formulated by H. Richard Niebuhr in his work *The Responsible Self: An Essay in Christian Moral Philosophy* (1963). To begin with, in his intersubjectivist theory of ethics Mead develops the stages in the social formation of the self as stages in moral development, and also as stages in the development of society to freedom from domination. Directly influenced by Mead's ethics, L. Kohlberg has gone on to work out in detail the various stage-structures of moral consciousness as they develop through the socialization process of "role-taking" or "perspective-taking." And as has been emphasized elsewhere in the present work, Jürgen Habermas's communication theory as developed especially in *The Theory of Communicative Action* fully takes into account the "paradigm shift" in Mead's thought from Cartesian subjectivism to an intersubjective model of the social self as symbolically mediated interaction between the individual and society (1987, 1–111). In *Moral Consciousness and Communicative Action* (1990) Habermas proceeds to clarify the implications of his theory of communicative action for moral philosophy. Throughout this latter work he systematically articulates a communicative discourse ethics which builds upon the moral socialization theories of both Mead and Kohlberg. The socio-scientific research program of Habermas as articulated in these and other works sets forth a general theory of communication, what he also calls a universal pragmatics, which itself serves as the foundation for a theory of socialization explaining the developmental stages whereby a rational subject gradually acquires communicative competence through symbolic interaction. In this context Habermas combines the approaches of moral philosophy and developmental psychology into a hierarchical model of levels of communicative competence which integrates L. Kohlberg's stages of moral consciousness with other developmental schemes like J. Piaget's stages of cognition, J. Loevinger's stages of ego development, and R. Selman's stages of interpersonal relations. This hierarchy of levels of communicative competence reflects a developmental logic which occurs through progressive stages of role-taking or perspective-taking that begins with the narrow egocentric perspective of individualism, and gradually unfolds through increasingly complex I-Thou perspectives, finally culminating in the decentered, nonegocentric worldview represented by the intersubjective paradigm of a social self in a norm-governed ideal communication community. The stages of perspective-taking are thus correlated with the stages of moralization and then organized hierarchically by means of a developmental logic according to which the higher stages incorporate the socio-moral perspectives of the lower stages but not vice versa.

In recent moral theory the two most significant efforts to reformulate Kant's universalist ethics based on the categorical imperative are no doubt Rawls's theory of justice as fairness and Habermas's communication ethics. In *A Theory of Justice*, Rawls underscores the Kantian basis for his ethical theory of justice as fairness through his description of the original position as a "procedural representation" (1971, 256) of the categorical imperative. The universalizability of Kant's categorical imperative as a procedure for testing moral norms is achieved in Rawls's original position by lowering a "veil of ignorance" over all participants in the original choice situation so that they are deprived of any specific information regarding status, personal commitments, familial and religious ties, and the like, or of any particular conception of the good, so that all persons reflect Kant's moral conception of the person as a free and equal member of a Kingdom of Ends. For Rawls it is this legislative procedure of imposing a "veil of ignorance" which ensures the impartial selection of principles of justice acceptable to all participants in the original choice situation. However, communitarians like Michael J. Sandel (1982) have strongly criticized the liberalism of Rawls, arguing that it presupposes an individualistic notion of self as having an identity prior to its membership in a community and prior to its attachments to any social ends. According to Sandel, Rawls's theory is flawed not only by its inadequate notion of self as an atomic individual but also by its inadequate notion of community.

In contrast to the Kantian universalist ethic of Rawls which remains commited to an individualistic notion of selfhood, the discourse ethics of Habermas instead builds on G. H. Mead's project of transforming Kant's universalist ethics grounded in the categorical imperative through a communication model of the social self. For Kant, the categorical imperative constitutes a private thought experiment which each rational agent can conduct as a solitary individual or transcendental subject so that each person asks if he or she can will a norm to be a universal law applicable to everyone. But for Habermas, as for Kohlberg and Mead, the test is instead whether or not a contested norm is acceptable to all who are affected by that norm, so that the maxim by which one acts satisfies the interests of all participants in public discourse. Seyla Benhabib provides a lucid explanation of communicative discourse ethics when she writes:

> Discourse ethics . . . requires that controversies over the validity of contested norms be settled through an argumentative process in which the consensus of all concerned decides upon the legitimacy the controversial norm. Participation precedes universalizability. The old adage, 'no taxation without representation', is now reformulated as 'no universalizability without participation.' (1986,315)

For Habermas, whether or not a contested norm can meet the approval of all participants can be determined only through what in the social perspectivism of Mead is referred to as "role-taking," the ability to put one-self in the position of others. He points out that when Kohlberg develops the notion of "ideal role-taking" as an appropriate procedure for moral-practical decisions, he is being guided by Kantian intuitions that have been reinter-preted from the pragmatist theories of Peirce and Mead to mean participa-tion in a "universal discourse" (1990, 36). He adds that Kohlberg finds in John Rawls's theory of justice as fairness the same basic intuition that valid norms have to find universal assent, so that a just solution to a moral problem is a solution acceptable to all parties. Explaining the principles underlying his communicative discourse ethics in relation to the notion of ideal role-taking as articulated by Mead and Kohlberg, Habermas asserts:

> While its *universalization principle* [U] furnishes a rule of argumentation, the *principle of discourse ethics* (D) expresses the fundamental idea of moral theory that Kohlberg borrowed from G. H. Mead's communication theory as the notion of "ideal role taking." This principle postulates the following: (D) Every valid norm would meet the approval of all concerned if they could take part in a practical discourse. (1990, 121)

He goes on to cite with approval Kohlberg's perspectivist theory derived from Mead according to which impartial moral judgments must always have the features of reversibility, universality, and reciprocity: complete *reversibility* of the perspectives from which participants produce their arguments; *universality* as the inclusion of all perspectives concerned; and *reciprocity* or equal recog-nition of the perspective of each participant by all others (1990, 122).

Habermas refers to one of the hierarchical stages in Lawrence Kohlberg's developmental scheme for moral socialization based upon Mead's idea of "perspective-taking," wherein the person transcends the narrow egocentric perspectives of the lower stages and achieves an intersubjective perspective expressed by the golden rule—"Do unto others as you would have them do unto you." In the words of Kohlberg: "This stage takes the perspective of the individual in relationship to other individuals. . . . The person relates points of view through the 'concrete Golden Rule,' putting oneself in the other person's shoes" (cited by Habermas 1990, 128). That is to say, the Golden Rule requires that one frame a universally valid ethical norm by entering the perspective of the other. In the communication model of ethics outlined by Mead and further developed by Kohlberg and Habermas, the formulation of impartial, universally valid norms through a dialogical procedure of public discourse and noncoercive open communication such as is required by the golden rule or the categorical imperative involves the capacity of a social self to adopt the perspectives of all participants so as to embody an interest common to all affected by the moral judgment.

In the communicative ethics of Habermas and Mead, ethical norms of autonomous rational agents are said to be universal if they are social, shareable, and generalizable. According to Habermas and Mead, then, justifiable moral norms or universal validity claims established by the categorical imperative are ones which incorporate *generalizable interests* which can be communicatively shared by all participants in discourse. As Mead states: "One should act with reference to all of the interests that are involved: that is what we would call a 'categorical imperative'" (MSS 386). Similarly, in Habermas's communicative discourse ethics a norm is right when it corresponds to a general or generalizable interest so that the interest of any particular individual can be accepted without coercion by all those involved in the consensus-formation process of open dialogue. Again citing Mead as his primary source of inspiration, Habermas writes:

> The principle of universalization is intended to compel the universal exchange of roles that G. H. Mead called "ideal role taking" or "universal discourse." Thus every valid norm has to fulfill the following condition: (U) All affected can accept the consequences and the side effects its *general* observance can be anticipated to have for the satisfaction of *everyone's* interests. . . . (D) Only those norms can be valid that meet (or could meet) with the approval of all affected in their capacity as participants in a practical discourse. (1990, 65–66)

Hence, while for Kant the categorical imperative which asks for universal validity in ethics is a *monological* process as conceived through a subjectivist model of rationality and an individualistic notion of self, for Habermas,

Kohlberg, and Mead it is a *dialogical* process understood through an intersubjectivist paradigm of communicative rationality and a social notion of self, whereupon the norm by which one acts must now satisfy the generalizable interests that are shared by all participants involved in a given problematic moral situation. In the words of Habermas:

> [D]iscourse ethics rejects the monological approach of Kant, who assumed an individual tests his maxims of action *foro interno* or, as Husserl put it, in the loneliness of his soul. . . . Discourse ethics prefers to view shared understanding about the generalizability of interests as the *result* of an intersubjectively mounted *public discourse*. (1990, 203)

It can therefore be said that Habermas and Mead both accept Kant's notion of *universalizability* as the rationalist principle of justification which discriminates between valid and invalid norms for ethical conduct. Yet the communicative ethics of Habermas, like that of Mead, replaces the monological procedure of Kant's categorical imperative with that of a dialogical procedure of justification whereby intersubjectively valid norms are negotiated through reasoned agreement among participants in practical discourse.

For Habermas, the meta-norm underlying the condition for the possibility of a communicative ethics is established through Mead's notion of *universal discourse,* or what in the universal pragmatics of Habermas is called the "ideal speech situation" and the "ideal communication community." In *The Theory of Communicative Action* (1989), Habermas asserts: "Mead develops the basic assumptions of a communicative ethics. . . . The basic theoretical concept of the ethics of communication is 'universal discourse,' the formal ideal of mutual understanding in language" (1989, 96). As further emphasized by Habermas (1989, 96), Mead supports his notion of universal discourse as the formal ideal of communication by the spread of democratic ideals. In his universal pragmatics Habermas develops Mead's notion of universal discourse into an "ideal speech situation" characterized as pure intersubjectivity or unrestrained communication as the precondition for mutual understanding and rational consensus through dialogue as well as for justifying all normative validity claims raised by communication through speech acts. Mead himself clearly describes this ideal of universal discourse presupposed by norm-governed rational thought and moral conduct as follows:

> If that system of communication could be made theoretically perfect, the individual would affect himself as he affects others in every way.

That would be the ideal of communication, an ideal attained in logical discourse wherever it is understood. The meaning of that which is said is here the same to one as it is to everybody else. Universal discourse is then the formal ideal of communication. If communication can be carried through and made perfect,then there would exist the kind of democracy to which we have just referred. (MSS 327)

This utopian concept of universal discourse as an ideal communication community of undistorted open communication where consensus is communicatively achieved in language is itself the ultimate condition for the possibility of a communicative discourse ethics in both Mead and Habermas, including the formation of all universalizable principles of norm-governed conduct, all democratic principles of will-formation, and all universalistic principles of law in the modern state.

## Mead's Theory as a Unifying Model for Sociology

It is especially in the field of sociology that Mead's ideas have thus far exerted the most significant influence. In addition to being one of the founders of the Chicago school of pragmatism in classical American philosophy, Mead was also a principal founder of the Chicago school tradition of American sociology which includes such thinkers as John Dewey, C. H. Cooley, W. I. Thomas, Robert Park, Ernest W. Burgess, Ellsworth Faris, and Herbert Blumer (see L. R. Kurtz 1984). Underscoring the major contribution which Mead's symbolic interactionist theory has made to sociology and the social sciences in America, Peter Berger writes:

[I]t is through the work of George Herbert Mead and the Meadian tradition of the "symbolic-interactionist" school that a theoretically viable social psychology has been founded. Indeed, it may be maintained that in this achievement lies the most important theoretical contribution to the social sciences in America. (1970, 373)

John C. Baldwin's work *George Herbert Mead: A Unifying Theory for Sociology* (1986) has argued that insofar as it establishes a nondualistic theory that unifies data on mind and body, subject and object, micro and macro society, along with other related factors, the social self model of Mead represents the single most adequate unifying paradigm for sociology and the other social sciences. Historically speaking, *The Nature of Human Nature* (1937) by Ellsworth

Faris of the Chicago school was the first major sociological treatment of Mead's thought. *The Social Psychology of George Herbert Mead* (1959) by Bernard N. Meltzer was among the next important sociological interpretations of Mead's social philosophy and psychology. However, the sociological aspects of Mead's pragmatic philosophy and social psychology have above all else been adapted by the movement of "symbolic interactionism" as developed especially by Herbert Blumer (1969), who originally coined the term. Blumer's work entitled *Symbolic Interactionism* (1969) remains a classic statement on the sociological dimensions of Mead's framework. Although the perspective of symbolic interactionism has also been profoundly influenced by C. S. Peirce, William James, and John Dewey in American pragmatism as well as by the pragmatic theories of W. I. Thomas and C. H. Cooley in American sociology, it traces its principal origins to the social-self model of G. H. Mead as formulated especially in *Mind, Self and Society* (1934). Symbolic interactionism and the Chicago school tradition of sociology have been influenced by Mead's pragmatic philosophy of intersubjective praxis which emphasizes the dialectical relationships between thought and action, theory and practice, the self and society. Symbolic interactionists have adopted Mead's understanding of the pragmatic theory of inquiry as an extension of the scientific experimental method to all areas of knowledge, including the social sciences of sociology, psychology, and anthropology. Mead's seminal notions like the "social self," the "I-Me dialectic," the "generalized other," the "significant symbol," and "role-taking" (or "perspective-taking"), have now become standard doctrines in symbolic interactionism. The fundamental idea which symbolic interactionism derives from Mead is the social understanding of selfhood as a dynamic individual-society interaction. Symbolic interactionism is based on Mead's genetic and developmental model of the social self according to which both mind and self arise through internalizing the public institutions of society. The mind and self reproduce society through a socialization process which occurs by the internalizing mechanism of "role-taking," wherein the individual becomes a social self by progressively taking on the roles of the community or generalized other. By this view the social self arises through a communicative process of symbolic interaction between the I or individual pole and the Me or internalized social pole, so that the individual and society are now regarded as inseparable units. The self is always a social self because mind, self, and society are ontogenetically coterminous. Hence, individual minds and selves represent society in microcosm. The concept of a social self as a twofold individual-society interaction developed by Mead and symbolic interactionism thus undercuts the traditional dualism of self/society and regards both "individual" and "society" as two sides of the same coin.

Many sociologists have pointed out that a limitation in Mead's theory of selfhood is that it emphasizes the harmonious interaction between individual and society while neglecting the element of *conflict*. As opposed to the harmony model of individual-society interaction worked out by Mead, the conflict model of Freud, Weber, and Marx explicates the dynamics of struggle between the individual versus society through a description of coercive power relations. While the Freudian tradition clarifies the internal repression of primal id-instincts through the social control mechanisms of the superego, the Marxian tradition elucidates the external oppression of the individual by economic forces in society. To correct this deficiency there has been an ambitious effort on the part of various thinkers to integrate Mead's symbolic interactionist concept of the social self as a twofold individual-society relation with other major sociological theories. *The Social Construction of Reality* (1966) by Peter L. Berger and Thomas Luckman has become a classic work on the sociology of knowledge which combines the symbolic interactionism of Mead with the sociological theories of Durkheim, Marx, Freud, Schutz and others. In this work the co-authors argue for the "social construction of reality" based upon Marx's premise that man's consciousness is determined by his social being, combined with Durkheim's notion of collective consciousness, and the thesis that selfhood develops through the internalization of social reality as held by the Meadian school of symbolic interactionism. Berger and Luckman have clarified and expanded Mead's analysis of the dialectic of self-society interaction by means of the threefold processes of *externalization, objectification* and *internalization*. Through "externalization," society is established as a human product; through "objectification," society is reified as an objective reality, apart from the individuals within it, thereby functioning as the source of alienation; and through "internalization," the objectified world reenters consciousness through socialization, as human beings are seen as social products as well as social producers. In *Rethinking Sociology* (1973) Irving Zeitlin recommends a synthesis of the sociological views of Mead with those of Marx and Freud (*via* Marcuse) in order to arrive at a more complete version of the social self which accounts for the of the coercive power relationships of both internal repression (Freud) and external oppression (Marx). Zeitlin argues that Mead does not provide an adequate analysis of the element of conflict in self-other relations, thereby failing to clarify the effect of domination and coercion on the individual which occurs through obeying those social control mechanisms of the Me or generalized other. He thus advocates an integration of Mead, Marx, and Freud in order to develop the idea of repression that he finds implicit in Mead's own writings.

In her book *From A Broken Web: Separation, Sexism, and Self* (1986), Catherine Keller provides an excellent account of how the American process cosmology of A. N. Whitehead and G. H. Mead provides the basis for a feminist concept of personhood based on the image of a social, relational, and connective self which functions to liberate women from the dominant and repressive masculine image of an independent ego-self. Keller argues that Mead's notion of the social self as an I-Me relationship establishes a liberating alternative to both the ego-centric "separative self" of men who are cut off from human relationships as well as the self-effacing "soluble self" of women who instead make the opposite error of dissolving into their relationships. In *Self, Society, and Womankind* (1980), Kathy E. Ferguson has developed a more sociological approach to Mead's social-self model as the basis for a feminist theory of women's liberation. According to Ferguson, Mead's theory of the social and processual self as an I-Me dialectic provides the most adequate conception of selfhood for political and social theory in that it allows for both individual freedom and social community. However, building up on the thought of sociologist like Luckman, Berger, and Zeitlin she argues that Mead's analysis of self as an individual-society interaction does not consider the exercise of coercive power relationships because he considers only interactions among *equals*. In criticism of previous theories attempting to combine symbolic interactionism with an ideology critique of power relations she points out that Zeitlin's effort to merge Mead and Freud suffers from a failure to recognize how the basic emphasis on process and sociality in Mead is incompatible with Freud's reductionistic view of an instinctual, substantive self with fixed drives. Although there is a basic analogy between Mead's biosocial theory of self as an I-Me relation whereby the I corresponds to Freud's id and the Me corresponds to the internalized social controls of the superego, Mead rejects the view that there is a primary content to the human being and opts instead for the notion that selfhood is characterized by an ever-changing temporal process that is fundamentally social in character. Similarly, the attempt to integrate Mead and Marx fails in that Marx's concept of human nature based on an image of the *producing* individual is inconsistent with Mead's process theory of self which denies that there is any fixed nature, content or essence defining human existence. Also, while Mead ignores the influence of power relations and views all social interactions as equal, Marx takes another extreme position and identifies labor as the most basic form of human activity, thereby to single out economic relations as the only source of power. Ferguson argues that a complete account of self-other interaction must deal with all forms of dominance/subordinance relations without reducing them to any one activity. In an effort to develop a feminist theory of women's liberation she thus combines Mead's sociological concept of selfhood as an individual-society interaction with an ideology critique of dominance/subordinance relations in American society within the four dimensions of sex, race, class, and bureaucratic hierarchy whereby men have power over women, whites over blacks, employers over employees, social workers over poor people, as well as public officials and bureaucrats over citizens.

The synthesis of Mead with Freud, Marx, Weber, Durkheim, and other sociologist has now been most fully realized in the comprehensive social scientific research program of Jürgen Habermas (1989). He agrees with other sociologists who maintain that a shortcoming of Mead's own social-self theory is that it tends to overemphasize cooperative interaction without due attention to elements of *conflict* in the individual-society relation. Hence, the critical theory of Habermas influenced by the Frankfurt school undertakes an ideology critique of all power relations which systematically distort communicative interaction, thereby to supplement the harmony model of G. H. Mead with the conflict model of sociology in the tradition of Marx, Weber, and Freud. Through an integration of Mead's genetic account of the self through perspective-taking with insights drawn from modern developmental psychology Habermas establishes a general theory of communication which itself serves as the foundation for a theory of moral socialization explaining the hierarchy of stage-structures whereby a rational subject gradually acquires "communicative competence" through symbolic interaction. From the standpoint of his critical theory Habermas then integrates Mead's communication theory with the Enlightenment theme of *emancipation*, so that the developing stages of communicative competence represent a gradual liberation from "ideology," understood as those coercive power relations which function as blocks to open communication. By combining Mead's communication theory with the emancipatory aims of an ideological critique, the ultimate goal of Habermas's social scientific research program becomes that of a progressive liberation from all power relations, thus to arrive at a norm-governed ideal communication community wherein the social self achieves mutual understanding with others through open communication and unconstrained public dialogue free of all internal repressive (Freud) and external oppressive (Marx) forces of coercion, dominance, and authority. Moreover, like Richard Rorty, Habermas establishes points of contact between American pragmatism and various twentieth-century movements of Continental philosophy including linguistic analysis, hermeneutics, phenomenology, and deconstructionism. Habermas sees a convergence between Mead's theory of communicative interaction and the Continental tradition of hermeneutics developed by Gadamer, in that both regard meaning as a function of dialogue, communication, and conversation with the goal of establishing mutual understanding. Yet he argues that a theory of hermeneutics must always be accompanied by a critical theory which exposes those coercive power relations functioning to systematically distort the communication process of dialogue leading to a forced consensus. The writings of Habermas, like those of Rorty, have done much to revitalize interest in the tradition of American pragmatism. However, while Rorty focuses almost exclusively upon the "antifoundationalism" of pragmatist thought so that it moves in the direction of deconstructionism with its consequences of relativism and nihilism, Habermas instead follows Mead in the direction of universalism and objectivism in order to provide normative grounds for ethical conduct and a basis for progress in knowledge through experimental inquiry.

## Mead's Paradigm Shift to a Communicative Interaction Model of the Social Self

Among contemporary social philosophers no one has better recognized the epoch-making significance of Mead's thought than Jürgen Habermas. It has already been seen that in his work *Moral Consciousness and Communicative Action* (1990) Habermas applies Mead's developmental psychology of the social self based on perspective-taking to reformulate Kant's universalist ethics as expressed through the categorical imperative so that it now becomes a dialogical procedure for establishing universally valid ethical norms which meet the approval of all participants in public discourse. For Habermas, Mead's social reconstruction of Kant's categorical imperative constitutes a turn in the history of moral philosophy to the extent that it prepares the foundations for a communicative discourse ethics. He states that Mead develops the basis for a communicative ethics based on "universal discourse," or what in the universal pragmatics of Habermas is called the "ideal speech situation" and the "ideal communication community," the formal ideal of mutual understanding and agreement in language through undistorted open communication. Furthermore, in *The Theory of Communicative Action* (1989) and other recent works, Habermas propounds that Mead's thought represents no less than a "paradigm shift"[7] beyond Cartesian subject-centered consciousness to a new intersubjective communication model of the social self as linguistically mediated symbolic interaction between the individual and society. Habermas (1989, 3–4) argues that the main defect of the Cartesian philosophy of subject-centered consciousness is its location of the original source of valuation and cognition in an isolated ego, thereby ignoring the primary significance of the speech act of communicative interaction. He maintains that Cartesian subjectivism was attacked at the turn of the century by analytic philosophy of language and behavioristic psychology, both of which are indebted to the pragmatism of Charles Sanders Peirce, who conceived of action and knowledge in terms of observable, shared practices. Habermas (1989, 3) maintains that these two disciplines were first integrated within a single unified framework in the symbolic interactionist perspective of G. H. Mead. For Habermas the fundamental insight of Mead is that an individual can achieve selfhood only through intersubjective communication by means of language, signs, and symbols. He makes reference to Mead's (MSS 233) assertion that "the individual reaches his self only through communication with others" (cited by Habermas 1989, 43). The central notion for Habermas's communication theory now becomes the concept of the social self arising through what Mead calls the process of "communicative interaction" (MSS 158). He further contends that Mead was the first to clearly grasp the realization of selfhood as an achievement of socialization through individualization by means of linguistic communication (1989, 41). Elsewhere he asserts that the mediation between individual and society is best achieved in G. H. Mead's paradigm shift to an intersubjectivist communication model of the social self, according to which "we understand the process of socialization itself as one of individuation" (1987, 334). In a more recent essay called "Peirce and Communication" Habermas writes: "George Herbert Mead, a pragmatist of the second generation, was the first to conceive language as a medium that socializes communicative actors only insofar as it individualizes them" (1992, 110). Again, in an essay titled "Individuation through Socialization: On George Herbert Mead's Theory of Subjectivity," he asserts: "The only promising attempt to grasp the entire significance of social individualization in concepts is, I believe, initiated in the social psychology of George Herbert Mead" (1992, 151). In opposition to the Cartesian model of subject-centered consciousness wherein individuation precedes socialization, Mead was thereby the first to elucidate the shift to a communication model of the social self wherein individuation and socialization now take place concurrently through the intersubjective medium of language.

For Habermas, Mead's analysis of the social constitution of the self represents a fundamental "paradigm shift"; namely, a turn from Cartesian subjectivist theories of consciousness which situate the locus of personhood in an isolated ego-self, toward that of an intersubjective model of the social self which situates the locus of personhood in a speech act of symbolically mediated communicative interaction. Following Habermas, another German philosopher Hans Joas (1993, 24) has described this paradigm shift from a subjective to an intersubjective model of self as the "social turn" initiated by the pragmatism of Mead and the Meadian tradition of symbolic interactionism. Habermas underscores this paradigm shift in Mead's thought especially in Section V of *The Theory of Communicative Action* (vol. 2), which is aptly titled, "The Paradigm Shift in Mead and Durkheim: From Purposive Activity to Communicative Action" (1989, 1–112). In this context he says, "The paradigm shift prepared by Mead's social psychology interests us here because it clears the way for a communication concept of rationality" (1989, 5). Later, while summarizing his notion of a paradigm shift in Mead, Habermas writes: "Following the thread of Mead's theory of action, we have traced the paradigm shift from purposive rationality to communicative action to a point at which the theme of intersubjectivity and self-preservation again comes to the fore" (1989, 113). Habermas combines Mead's *ontogenetic* analysis of the "social self" emerging from a communicative process of symbolic interaction between the "I" and the "Me" with Emile Durkheim's *phylogenetic* analysis of a "collective consciousness" which arises from the sacred foundations of morality in the ritually preserved fund of social solidarity (1989, 1–112). He thus states: "[T]he paradigm shift from purposive activity to communicative action was prepared by George Herbert Mead and Emile Durkheim . . . Mead with his communication-theoretic foundation of sociology, Durkheim with a theory of social solidarity connecting social integration to system integration" (1989, 1). Comparing the notions of personhood of these two thinkers, Habermas states: "Mead conceives of personal identity exactly as Durkheim does—as a structure that results from taking over socially generalized expectations" (1989, 58). While Mead is significant because of his communication theory of the social self, Durkheim explains the social origins of the sacred in collective consciousness and the genesis of ethical norms through the secularization of sacred rites. Hence, while Mead prepares the basis for a theory of communicative interaction, Durkheim establishes the foundation for a theory of norm-regulated ethical conduct. For Habermas, Mead's ontogenetic theory of the social constitution of the self through communicative interaction and Durkheim's phylogenetic theory of the evolutionary transformation of "rites" from the sacred to the secular together provide the twofold basis for a new unifying theory of sociology and the social sciences.[8] It is in such a manner that Habermas has brought to light the paradigm shift in Mead beyond Cartesian subjectivism to an intersubjective communication model of the social self based on symbolic interaction between the individual and the community.

# III

## The Social Self

### in

## Japanese and American Philosophy

Here we enter into the core of this study: namely, the development of the social self as an intercultural theme for East-West comparative philosophy. Part one examined various models of the social self in twentieth-century Japanese thought, focusing on representative figures such as Watsuji Tetsurō and Nishida Kitarō in modern Japanese philosophy and Doi Takeo in modern Japanese psychology. In part two it was shown that the social nature of selfhood is also a recurrent motif in classical American pragmatism including Peirce, James, Royce, Cooley, Dewey, Whitehead, and Mead. It was demonstrated how those insights into the intersubjective nature of personhood, the primacy of communication, the significance of community, the normative dimensions of interpersonal conduct and the aesthetic value dimensions of social experience as articulated in American philosophy have been crystallized in the social-self model and I-Me dialectic of George Herbert Mead. Furthermore, it has been argued that Mead's interdisciplinary model of the social self can function as a unifying theory for both philosophy and the social sciences whereby social psychology, sociology, anthropology, and other fields of inquiry can all be integrated into a coherent framework developed in accord with the modern experimental method. Following Jürgen Habermas, it has been emphasized that the social science framework of Mead represents a paradigm shift beyond subject-centered consciousness to an intersubjective communication model of the social self based on linguistically mediated symbolic interaction between the individual and society. Altogether this paradigm shift to an intersubjectivist model of selfhood has been summed up by Hans Joas as constituting the social turn in American pragmatism initiated by Mead and the Meadian tradition of symbolic interactionism.

In part three an effort will now be made to systematically apply Mead's communication model of the social self to East Asian modes of thought, with a special emphasis on Zen Buddhist concepts of the person in modern Japanese philosophy. After considering the social-self paradigm of Mead in relation to traditional Confucian and Zen notions of the person I then proceed to examine the syncretic models of selfhood formulated in twentieth-century Japanese thought. The social-self paradigm and I-Me dialectic of Mead is now employed to critically analyze Watsuji Tetsurō's Zen/Confucian *ningen* model of Japanese contextual persons based on the dialogical principle of *aidagara* or "betweenness" and the doctrine of *fūdo* or "climate" as the spatial locus for self-other relations. This is followed by an examination of Mead's framework in relation to Nishida Kitarō's concept of the "social self" (*shakaiteki jiko*) based on the dialectic of I and Thou (*ware to nanji*) and the doctrine of *basho* as the spatial locus in which the person arises through the mutual encounter between self and other. Parallels between Mead's developmental model of the social self and the Zen process of becoming a person are examined from the standpoint of Ueda Shizuteru, a leading scholar of Nishida's philosophy and a representative thinker of the Kyoto school, whose interpretation of the *Ten Oxherding Pictures* articulates how the individual ego at the eternalistic level of substantial Being, which is emptied into a no-self at the nihilistic level of relative Nothingness, is then emptied into the form of a relational self existing in the *betweenness* of I and Thou at the middle way position of emptiness or absolute Nothingness. Furthermore, Mead's social psychology is considered in relation to the *amae* psychology of Doi Takeo, whose dependency model of Japanese selfhood as a dialectic of *honne* (personal reaction) and *tatemae* (social institutions) has been directly influenced by Mead's symbolic interactionist framework of the social self as a dialectic of the I or individual pole and the Me or institutional pole. In the following chapter I then clarify how like the social-self theory of Mead, the Zen/Confucian concept of personhood in modern Japanese philosophy rejects the Cartesian dualism of body and mind in favor of a psychosomatic theory of the *embodied self* as a unified body-mind experience. Next, I argue that both Mead and modern Japanese philosophy have developed not only a sociological model of the self arising through an individual-society interaction as the basis for interhuman ethics and aesthetics, but also an *ecological* model of the self constituted by a human-nature relation as the ground for an environmental ethics and conservation aesthetics. The concept of a social self is thus hereby introduced as a transcultural motif for East-West comparative philosophy and interreligious dialogue.

## The Zen Self in Western Perspective

In the early twentieth century Zen/Chan Buddhism was disseminated throughout America by D. T. Suzuki, an intimate friend of Nishida Kitarō and a peripheral member of the Kyoto school of modern Japanese philosophy. Yet it was Jack Kerouac's novel *Dharma Bums* (1958) that triggered the "Zen boom" in America, combining the Square Zen from Japan with American counterculture in the formation of an East-West kind of "Beat Zen." Zen Buddhist meditation, philosophy and aesthetics was then further popularized by such influential writers as Kapleau, Merton, and Watts. Through its integration into American thought and culture traditional Zen Buddhism has since undergone many transformations. In the field of transpersonal psychology, the Zen cultivation of selfhood has been variously seen by A. H. Maslow as a self-actualization process of ego-transcendence leading to peak experience, by Reichians as the release of all psychosomatic blocks of bioenergentic current leading to full orgastic potency, by Jungians as a quest for psychic wholeness through a descent into the collective unconscious, by Ken Wilbur 's transpersonal psychology as an ascent up the spectrum of altered states to superconsciousness, by Bucke as a mystical expansion into cosmic consciousness, by the Gestalt therapy of Fritz Pearls as the total sensory awareness of a holistic figure/ground gestalt consciousness, by John C. Lilly as reprogramming the human bio-computer to achieve multidimensional consciousness. The proliferation of New Age literature has explored the Zen achievement of a true self in *satori* or sudden enlightenment through a wide variety of mind-altering technologies for the induction of trance states, ranging from self-hypnosis, crystals, and psychedelics to isolation float tanks, polygraph meters, and biofeedback devices, while the new Cyberpunk generation envisages a futuristic mode of computerized high-tech Zen through cyberspace virtual reality decks, biochemistry, and genetic engineering. From traditional Square Zen in Japan to 1950s Beat Zen to 1960s Hippie Zen to 1970s New Age Zen to 1980s Cyberpunk Zen, the Wheel of Dharma has turned once again with the coming of age of Buddhism in America.

East-West comparative philosophers have viewed the Zen self of *mu* or Nothingness from the standpoint of Hegel's dialectical consciousness of absolute negation, Nietzsche's overman who dwells in the abyss of nihility without God, Sartre's phenomenology of consciousness as an egoless, transparent Nothingness which stands over against objectified Being, Heidegger's *Dasein* who exists held out suspended into the openness of Nothingness, Meister Eckhart's *via negativa* apophatic mysticism of emptying into the godhead of Nothingness, the Christian theology of *kenōsis* or "making oneself nothing," and the Kabbalistic *Ain Soph Aur,* Infinite Boundless Nothingness. Again, the Zen concept of a temporal, dynamic, and nonsubstantial self as "impermanence-Buddha-nature" (*mujō-busshō*) in the flux of "being-time" (*uji*) has been alternatively understood in terms of Nietzsche's positive self-overcoming of nihilism through affirmation of the innocence of becoming, Husserl's presencing of internal time-consciousness, Heidegger's authentic human existence as a being-in-time and being-toward-death, Bergson's direct intuitive grasping of real duration as the continuous flow of vital-force in creative evolution, James's notion of self as the felt transitions of pure experience in the ever-changing stream of consciousness, and Whitehead's process theory of self as a perpetual perishing of momentary events in the creative advance toward novelty.

From the standpoint of comparative philosophy scholars have further attempted to clarify the Zen Buddhist notion of a true self as śūnyatā (J. kū) or "emptiness" in terms of various Western functional equivalents such as the kenōsis or "self-emptying" of Christianity, the "openness" of Continental phenomenology, the différance of French deconstructionism, the epoche or "suspension of judgment" of ancient Greek skepticism, the "principle of relativity" in Whiteheadian process metaphysics, and so forth. Each of these Western functional equivalents to Buddhist śūnyatā brings to light another dimension of the Zen concept of selfhood: interpreted as Christian kenōsis it clarifies human / divine perfection as an act of compassionate "self-emptying"; as the "openness" of Heideggerian phenomenology it explains human existence as standing out through ek-stasis into nothingness or openness; as the différance of Derrida and French poststructuralism it signifies the deconstruction of "self-identity" into a play of differences; as the therapeutic epoche of Sextus Empiricus in ancient Greek skepticism it designates a "suspension of judgement" leading to the state of ataraxia or "mental tranquility"; and as the "relativity" of Whitehead's process metaphysics it denotes the interrelatedness of the self and all events in nature.

However, it is my position that the single most adequate framework for interpreting the true self of Zen Buddhism is the communicative interaction model of the social self formulated by G. H. Mead. To restate the thesis here, both Mead in American pragmatism and the Zen tradition of modern Japanese philosophy have taken a social turn in the direction of a communication theory of the social self as an I-Other dialectic, including an intersubjective model of the self as an individual-society interaction as well as an ecological model of self as a human-nature interaction and a psychosomatic model of self as a body-mind interaction. At the most generalized level of discourse a comparison between the Zen model of personhood and Mead's idea of the social self is ultimately based on an analogy of the first principles governing their two respective systems: namely, the Zen principle of śūnyatā (J. kū) or "emptiness" and the Meadian "principle of sociality" (see Mead PP 47–67). The conventional translation of śūnyatā by such nihilistic terms as "emptiness" or "voidness" is for the purpose of breaking attachments to contingent phenomena and often fails to convey the positive content of the Buddhist term as pratītya-samutpāda (J. engi), "interrelational existence." But if we render the Buddhist concept of śūnyatā by "sociality" and śūnya by "social," it functions to clarify the social nature, origin, and development of all phenomena emerging through dependent coorigination. The reformulation of Buddhist *śūnyatā* in terms of the "sociality" of Mead designates that the self and all events are constituted by their social relationships to other events and are void or empty apart from these relationships. Furthermore, the principle of sociality describes the temporal structure of the social self as existing "betwixt and between" the old system of the Me derived from the *past* and the new system of the I emerging in the *present*. Mead's principle of sociality thus functions to illuminate not only the "social" character of Zen selfhood as arising out of a field of interpersonal relationships but also its temporal as well as multiple character as a series of emergent or discontinuous events which arise and perish in the stream of becoming. It is thus proposed that while the closest Western parallel to the "true self" of Zen is the "social self" of Mead, the best Western functional equivalent to the Zen principle of *śūnyatā* is the Meadian *principle of sociality*.

The social nature of the Japanese self and the groupism of Japanese society have become one of the most important topics of discourse in recent Japanese Studies, especially in the field of the social sciences. Moreover, the profound resemblance between Mead's notion of the social self and the Japanese sense of self has been noted by Japanologists and comparative scholars representing a wide range of disciplines such as philosophy, buddhology, anthropology, sociology, psychology, education, and political science. This can be explained by the fact that one of Mead's foremost accomplishments was to have framed an *interdisciplinary* model of the social self which establishes a unifying framework for both philosophy and the social sciences, all of which is set within the context of an organismic process cosmology. Mead's interdisciplinary theory of the bipolar social self as a dialectic I and Me thus provides a unifying model which can elucidate a broad spectrum of notions employed to characterize the Japanese self by Japanologists in the social sciences, including psychiatrist Doi Takeo's *amae* theory of the dependent self with its two sides of private and public, anthropologist Nakane Chie's familial self rooted in vertically structured household (*ie*) groups, Takie Sugiyama Lebra's interactional self arising through social interaction between Ego and Alter, sociologist Hamaguchi Eshun's contextual self (*kanjin*), Kumon Shumpei's contextual (*kanjin*) model of self as a person (*ningen*) located in its social context (*aidagara*), Kuwayama Takami's reference other model of self as a relation between the I and its concentrically ordered reference groups, Makino Seiichi's extended ego (*kakudai ego*), Kimura Bin's self as a unity of *mizukara* and *onozukara* or self and nature, D. Kondo's artisanal model of the crafted self forged through social relations in the workplace; and in philosophy, Nakamura Hajime's relational self based on the Zen principle of interrelational existence, Watsuji Tetsurō's Zen/Confucian concept of *ningen* as an individual-society relation in *kū* or emptiness, Nishida Kitarō's Zen model of the social self as an I-Thou relation in the locus of *mu* or nothingness, Ueda Shizuteru's Zen model of the compassionate Bodhisattva as a twofold selfless self in the between of I and Thou, Izutsu Toshihiko's field model of the Zen self as a concentrated focus point of the whole field, and Yuasa Yasuo's Japanese Buddhist model of the somatic self as a body-mind unity. It is thus a primary aim of this work to demonstrate how Mead's interdisciplinary model of the social self can function as an East-West transcultural framework by means of which to articulate a unified vision of the Japanese self in its multivariate aspects—as social, relational, dialogical, interactional, contextual, unsubstantial, temporal, multiple, embodied, communicative, creative, aesthetic, fluid, open, decentered, shifting, and ever-changing.

One of the first comparative philosophical works to underscore the context-dependent nature of Japanese personhood in general and Zen personhood in particular was *Zen Action/Zen Person* (1982) by T. P. Kasulis. Through an analysis of the Japanese word *ningen* or "person" Kasulis describes how the Zen self is always defined in relation to its surrounding context. From the Western side he then interprets the Zen contextualist notion of selfhood in terms of a Husserlian phenomenology of "presence." Based on his phenomenological rendering of Dōgen's idea of *genjōkōan* as the "presence of things as they are," he articulates the Zen concept of personhood as the realization of "presence." Kasulis writes: "Thus, the person returns to the source of his or her experience: the immediate situation of the presence of things as they are (*genjōkōan*)" (1981, 100). Just as he characterizes Dōgen's concept of the person as "presence" (1981, 87–103), he states that "presence" is the sole content of *zazen* (1981, 89), and the function of *haiku* poetry is to express the "presence" of events of *genjōkōan* (1981, 124).

The relational nature of Zen selfhood is further developed from the standpoint of French deconstructionism in *Derrida on the Mend* (1984) by Robert Magliola. While Kasulis articulates the Zen concept of self in phenomenological terms as the realization of an event of *genjōkōan* or "the presence of things as they are," Magliola instead understands Zen personhood in deconstructionist terms through Derrida's semiotic idea of linguistic *trace*, "the interplay of presence and absence." According to Magliola, the best Western functional equivalent to the Zen principle of *śūnyatā* (J. *kū*) is the *différance* of Derrida in French deconstructionism. In the words of Magliola: "I shall argue that Nāgārjuna's *śūnyatā* (devoidness) is Derrida's *différance*, and is the absolute negation which absolutely deconstitutes but which constitutes directional trace" (1984, 89). Like the *śūnyatā* of Nāgārjuna and Zen/Chan Buddhism, the *différance* of Derrida represents a critical deconstruction of the principle of "self-identity," that is, what in Buddhist discourse takes the form of deconstituting all substantialist modes of "own-being" or "self-existence" (*svabhāva*). Through Derrida's strategies for deconstruction all metaphysical "centers" understood as a mode of absolute self-identity are disseminated into a network of differential sign relationships in which there are no positive entities. Magliola writes that "differential Zen, like Nāgārjuna's Madhyamika, disclaims 'centered' experience of any kind" (1984, 104). When this deconstructive logic of acentric Zen Buddhism is applied to personhood the unity of the fictive self disseminates into a play of linguistic signs devoid of any fixed center or inner core. For Derrida, the Husserlian idea of "presence," like the notions of substance, matter, God, ego, consciousness, and various other Western philosophical notions, functions as a kind of reified metaphysical Center or Transcendental Signified with an absolute self-identity. He thus deconstructs Husserl's notion of "presence" with his semiotic notion of linguistic trace, understood as the interplay of presencing and absencing, identity and difference, or being and nothingness. According to Magliola (1984, 88), Derrida's semiotic understanding of decentered selfhood as a linguistic trace arising through the interplay of presence and absence best accords with the *via media* established by Nāgārjuna and acentric Zen Buddhism wherein the self abides in the Middle Way between the "it is" of eternalism and the "it is not" of nihilism. Hence, the phenomenological interpretation of the Zen self as "presence" is for Magliola a form of "centric Zen," as opposed to the differential logic of acentric Zen whereby the self is at the same time both absent while present and present while absent.

The French postmodernist interpretation of acentric Zen Buddhism based on the analogy of *śūnyatā* and *différance* is one of the most significant Western frameworks for deconstructing the substantial identity of the Cartesian ego-self while at the same time clarifying the differential or relational character of the decentered self. In an essay titled "Derrida and the Decentered Universe of Zen Buddhism" (1990), I have considered at length the application of French deconstructionism to the Japanese decentered model of self and society. After examining Magliola's comparison of *śūnyatā* and *différance*, I further show how in the philosophical writings of Nishida Kitarō and the Kyoto school, Zen Buddhist *śūnyatā* or emptiness is to be comprehended as the infinite openness of an absolute nothingness devoid of all fixed metaphysical centers, including both the theocentric (*kami-chūshinteki*) and anthropocentric (*ningen-chūshinteki*) standpoints of Western substance philosophy. Nishida's Buddhist logic of *śūnyatā* or "emptiness," which he reformulates in terms of a paradoxical Zen logic of *soku/hi* or "is/is not," and again as a logic of "absolutely contradictory self-identity," is shown to have a close structural proximity to Derrida's deconstructive logic whereby all self-identity is shattered into a differential play of presencing and absencing. In his book *Empire of Signs* (1982) Rolland Barthes gives a deconstructionist reading of the Japanese cultural "text" as a decentered sign systems understood as a differential or relational network of floating signifiers in which there is a complete absence of a fixed metaphysical center, including both the transcendent God of theocentrism and the individual subject of egocentrism. I then show how after Barthes's work various scholars have come to read Japanese self and society in light of a postmodern semiotics as a radically dislocated and uncentered text constituted by empty signs wherein the meaning of the signified is always infinitely deferred through a freeplay of signifiers. Against the background of the differential logic underlying critical deconstructionist strategies of acentric Zen Buddhism, the art, literature, cinema, and other sign systems in the Japanese cultural text have been analyzed as a fractured semiotic field with no fixed center. In this way scholars influenced by French deconstructionism have arrived at a fully postmodern vision of Japan as a decentered text wherein each sign is emptied into a chain of differential traces and floating signifiers—without closure, without origin, and without a privileged center.

The application of French deconstructionism to the social and relational nature of Japanese selfhood has been especially developed by Dorine K. Kondo in her book entitled *Crafting Selves* (1990). In this work Kondo endeavors to clarify how in Japanese corporate society the self is socially constructed through webs of relationships and matrices of power in families, companies, schools, and other community settings. Kondo's work is in part based on anthropological field research during her stay at the Ethics School (*Rinri Gakuen*) in Tokyo, which provides a rigorous moral training program aiming to cultivate ideal social selves through relations with others in society. In order to interpret this social concept of self in Japanese corporate society, Kondo relies primarily upon the French deconstructionist strategies of poststructuralism, wherein an individualistic and egocentric notion of personhood as a self-identical substance with a fixed essence is abandoned for a relationally defined self which is fluid, shifting, open, decentered, and multiple in nature. Kondo further employs the logic of French poststructuralism to deconstruct the fixed binary between self/society, private/public, or interior/exterior as a key motif in the critique of individualism (1990, 24). In contrast to the rigid self/society binary reinforced by Western narrative conventions, the relationally defined Japanese self is described as being on a "sliding scale" of self and other (1990, 26). The boundaries of self and other are fluid and constantly changing, depending on context, so that personhood is now understood in terms of two *end points* of an open-ended continuum located between the individual/social or private/public sides of the self, which in Japanese is articulated by means of such distinctions as *honne/tatemae, uchi/soto,* and *ura/omote* (1990, 31). The artisanal metaphor of "crafting" ideal social selves is employed by Kondo in order to underscore the traditional Japanese aesthetic concept of personhood as an artistic creative process whereby the self is forged through interpersonal relationships with others in ever-shifting contexts of power.

However, as discussed in part two of this work, classical American pragmatists like Charles Sanders Peirce, Josiah Royce, and George Herbert Mead, and more recent American thinkers like Justus Buchler, have also articulated a semiotic vision of personhood which functions to decenter the absolute self-identity of the Cartesian subject into a fluid and ever-shifting linguistic web of multiple sign-relationships. A semiotic concept of decentered personhood is again to be found in the American "neo-pragmatism" of Richard Rorty, who in *Contingency, Irony, and Solidarity* (1989) describes the contingent self as a web of desire and belief devoid of a fixed center, core, or essence. It was seen that Peirce's theory of the human self as a semiotic communication process was developed in such essays as "Some Consequences of Four Incapacities," originally published in the *Journal of Speculative Philosophy* as early as 1868, wherein he states that "man is a sign" and that "my language is the sum total of myself" (1955, 249; also 5.314). Justus Buchler characterizes Peirce's semiotic notion of selfhood as a "web of continuously related signs" (1955, xii), adding that this gives a new significance to that old truth that man is a "social animal" (1955, xi–xii). In *Peirce's Approach to the Self: A Semiotic Perspective on Human Subjectivity,* V. M. Colapietro similarly describes Peirce's semiotic account of self as a "network of relations" enmeshed in the "semiotic web" (1989, 28). Based on Peirce's theory of man as a web of signs-relations, Royce worked out his theory of self-realization through the community of interpretation. After learning of Peirce's sign theory from the later works of Royce, G. H. Mead then went on to develop his intersubjective communication model of the social self as linguistically mediated symbolic interaction using "significant symbols."

Colapietro (1989, xix) emphasizes that a major problem with the semiotic model of self worked out by French poststructuralism is that it decenters the Cartesian ego by deconstructing self-identity into an endless play of signs to the extent that there is a total dissolution of the human self, thereby ending in nihilism, relativism, and antihumanism. The radical antihumanist position of the deconstructionists results in the complete "disappearance of man" or "dissolution of self"—the total evaporation of the human subject! Colapietro persuasively argues that the great advantage of Peirce's semiotic notion of personhood over French deconstructionism is that it decenters the Cartesian subject into a continuous web of sign-relations *without* liquidating the creative agency of an acting self. It can be said that this is is even more clearly achieved through G. H. Mead's semiotic communication theory of the bipolar social self as an I-Me dialectic of intersubjectivity. For Mead the self is constituted as a social self through communicative interaction using "signs" (MSS 69) or "significant symbols" (MSS 68). Mead's dialectic of I and Me functions to decenter the Cartesian subject into the linguistic network of signs and symbols constituting the self as a socialized Me while still preserving the creative agency of the acting self as an individualized I. Also, no less than French postmodernism, Mead emphasizes that the "social self" is at the same time a decentered *multiple self,* an irreducible plurality of roles, identities, and selves in the ever-changing stream of consciousness with no underlying substantial identity. But while French deconstructionism shatters all self-identity into a multiple play of differences with no unity, Mead instead shows how the multiple self arises by taking on the social roles of others in the community at the Me pole while having a source of unity and individuality at the I pole. While for French deconstructionism the self is a centerless web of signs in which the meaning of a sign is always another sign, for Mead the meaning of a sign is always a creative and spontaneous *adjustive response* to a significant gesture in a social act of communicative interaction, thus bringing out the behavioristic, embodied, dialogical, and pragmatic aspects of semiosis. Mead's symbolic interactionist model of the social self based on the sign theories of Peirce, Royce, and others in American pragmatism thus represents a significant alternative to French deconstructionism as a semiotic framework for elucidating the Zen self as a differential web or relational net of signs which is multiple, open, fluid, shifting, and wholly devoid of a fixed center.

# ∿6∿

## Tanaka Ōdō and the Initial Reception of American Pragmatism in Japan

Prior to examining the application of Mead's communication paradigm of the social self to Japanese notions of personhood I would first like to briefly survey the initial reception of American pragmatism by the Japanese intelligentsia during the late Meiji Restoration (1868–1912) and early Taisho (1912–26) periods. Of particular significance is the role which American philosophy came to play in the thought of Nishida Kitarō (1870–1945), widely recognized as Japan's premier modern philosopher. It has already been discussed at some length how Nishida's early notion of selfhood was deeply influenced by William James's idea of the self as "pure experience" (*junsui keiken*) anterior to the subject-object distinction as well as the self-world dialectic of Josiah Royce. Hence, the American philosophy of both James and Royce became a key factor in the pioneering East-West synthesis of Nishida Kitarō.

As summarized by G. K. Piovesana (1969, 62–69), Motora Yujiro presented the psychology of John Dewey and William James's pragmatism as early as 1888 in the journal *Rikugo zasshi*. Translations then began to appear, including James's *Principles of Psychology* as translated by Motora Yujiro and Fukumoto Kazuo in 1902, followed by *Pragmatism* in 1910. Shortly thereafter Nakajima Rikizo of Tokyo University introduced John Dewey's *Outlines of Critical Theory of Ethics*. However, in modern Japanese philosophy the current of twentieth-century American pragmatism was disseminated primarily by Taisho-period intellectuals based at Waseda University in Tokyo. In part this connection with American pragmatism is to be explained by the fact that, in contrast to the more conservative government regulated Imperial Universities, Waseda University was a private institution whose relative independence enabled it to become the leading center of the "Taisho democracy," a liberal democratic movement which flourished before the Showa period that gave rise to the wartime climate of authoritarianism, militarism, ultranationalism, and totalitarianism in Japan. The introduction of American pragmatism in

Taisho-period Japan was above all else due to the work of Tanaka Ōdō (1867–1932), a philosophy professor at Waseda University who spent nearly a decade in the United States studying at the University of Chicago. During the years between 1892 and 1897 Tanaka studied under the direct tutelage of John Dewey, George Herbert Mead, James Tufts, James R. Angell, and Edward Scribner Ames, who together formed the nucleus of the Chicago school of pragmatism. Through the efforts of Tanaka and his many students, including future prime minister Ishibashi Tanzan, Waseda University became the base for liberal democratic individualism as developed by the Chicago school pragmatists.

The assimilation of Chicago school pragmatism by Tanaka Ōdō and other modern Japanese liberal thinkers based at Waseda University is discussed at length by Sharon N. Nolte in her work entitled *Liberalism in Modern Japan* (1987). As explained by Nolte, the pragmatism of Tanaka was commited to the spread of liberal democratic ideals in modern Japanese society, including the freedom of individuals, the pluralistic structure of social institutions, equality for women, combating state censorship, progressive educational reform, and the reconstruction of society. Tanaka implicitly challenged the ideology of the Meiji Restoration founded on the concept of the *kokutai* (national polity), the idea of the imperial family-state, and the emperor system in light of the concepts of individualism, participation, communication, democracy, and liberalism extolled by the Chicago pragmatists. Tanaka's pragmatism, instrumentalism, functionalism, and naturalism, which above all else reflects the ideas of John Dewey, is developed in such essays as *Tettei kojinshugi* (Radical Individualism, 1918). Tanaka describes his pragmatism as "naturalistic" in opposition to any mystical, religious, or supernatural conception of life. The pragmatism of Tanaka is further expressed through his notion of "experimentalism" (*jikken-shugi*), according to which life should be lived experimentally as one progresses toward a higher and more organic unity of the self in the functional adjustment of an organism to its environment (see Piovesana: 1968, 68). For Tanaka, the scientific experimental method propounded by Chicago school pragmatism is the best instrument for the constant reconstruction of self and society. Tanaka's pragmatism located society's potential for communication and cooperation within the experience of individuals who internalized and then reconstructed existing social institutions. The emphasis on progressive educational reforms in Tanaka's pragmatism was especially influenced by Dewey's pedagogical theories. Yet in her study of modern Japanese liberalism, Nolte points out the central importance of Mead's social self theory for Dewey's philosophy of education, stating:

Dewey's progressive educational theory relied heavily on George Herbert Mead's conception of the *social self*, which recognized the extent to which the self was formed by society and suggested that a new type of individual who would remold the larger society could be nurtured by control of the society of young children, especially in the schools. (1987, 81; italics added)

With regard to our present study it is of special interest to observe that the social-self model formulated by G. H. Mead and the Chicago school pragmatists was developed by Japanese Taisho-period intellectuals in the extremist directions of both totalitarianism and individualism. Yashushi Adachi (1969, 29) points out that G. H. Mead's *Mind, Self, and Society* (1934) was first published in Japan in 1941 as part of a series on "Theories of Totalitarianism." Mead's social-self theory was therefore initially understood by Japanese scholars as representing a totalitarian concept of personhood based on a notion of social determinism wherein the individual organism is entirely a product of its social environment. At the other extreme, Tanaka Ōdō developed Chicago school pragmatism in the direction of a "radical individualism" as expressed in his essay *Tettei kojinshugi* (Radical Individualism, 1918). As Nolte (1987, 58–59) asserts in her study of modern Japanese liberalism, the pragmatic philosophy of Tanaka based on the idea of "radical individualism" differs significantly from the Chicago school pramatism of Dewey and Mead, which instead gives equal emphasis to both the individual and social aspects of the self. She writes:

> Tanaka's radical individualism . . . differed from from the Chicago pragmatism. Dewey, for example, assigned equal importance to examining human activity from the point of view of individuals and that of society, insisting that either viewpoint described the same process . . . Similarly, Mead posited the group as prior to the formation of the individual self through the medium of language, and he also noted that any institution (such as science) could be described as the activities of individual persons making discoveries, sharing and communicating them. (1987, 58)

Hence, on the one side Tanaka's "radical individualism" came to play a significant role in the early dissemination of liberal democratic values during the formative years of modern Japanese social and political thought. Insofar as Tanaka was reacting to the collectivism of Japanese society it was natural that he should emphasize the liberal democratic individualism of Chicago school pragmatism. Yet on the other side it must be said that the bipolar social-self model of G. H. Mead and the Chicago school pragmatists was not correctly grasped by Tanaka and other Taisho period Japanese scholars as a contextualist model of personhood which aims to establish a middle ground between individualist and collectivist theories of the self. For this reason it is now time to reevaluate the potential application of Chicago school pragmatism to the Japanese concept of personhood based on a more thorough understanding of Mead's paradigm shift to a new intersubjectivist communication model of the bipolar social self based on a dialectic of I and Me.

# ∴7∴

## The Social Self in Mead and Confucianism

Mead's social concept of the person shares much in common with the Confucian view of man as unity of self and society. Both Mead and Confucianism work out a program for constructing an ideal social self through relationships with others in the community. Illuminating parallels between the social-self paradigm of G. H. Mead and others in American pragmatism in relation to the Chinese Confucian model of personhood have been pointed out by coauthors David L. Hall and Roger T. Ames (1987), as well by as Robert C. Neville (1987). This parallel between Confucianism and the American pragmatism of Mead assumes a special importance for our study, not only because of the extent to which both Confucianism and Buddhism have influenced patterns of behavior institutionalized at the cultural levels of Japanese society, including the Bushidō ethics of the Samurai warrior and ritualized aesthetic traditions such as *chanoyu* or the tea ceremony, but also in light of the fact that the Confucian and Buddhist theoretical models of selfhood have been fully incorporated by Watsuji Tetsurō, Nishida Kitarō, and others in the tradition of modern Japanese philosophy.

At the most general level of analysis I would argue that the Confucian vision of man as a nexus of ever-expanding social relationships governed by normative principles of *li* (J. *rei*) or "ritual action" can be understood through the Meadian tradition of symbolic interactionism in American sociology as developed particularly by Erving Goffman in *Interaction Ritual* (1967) as contextual selves conforming to the established pattern of "interaction rituals" in a social group. Although she discusses neither the Confucian background of Japanese ritual action nor the Meadian background of Goffman's concept of interaction ritual, Miyanaga Kuniko nevertheless makes this same observation when she writes: "In the case of the Japanese, the goal of a close relationship is perfect mutual understanding, achieved through an interaction similar to what Erving Goffman conceptualized as 'interaction ritual' in North American relationships" (1991, 84). She further points out that relationships

271

between Japanese "contextual persons" (*kanjin*) in a social group are carefully controlled by interaction rituals at both the verbal and nonverbal levels of communication, including the full range of body language such as physical gestures, tone of voice, degree or avoidance of eye contact, laughter, smiles, serious expressions, and so forth. A person failing to act in accordance with these standardized interaction rituals will be judged as "blunt" or "dull" if they are seen as being unreceptive to cues, "impolite" if they are seen as deliberately choosing to miss cues, or as *gaijin mitai*, "like a foreigner" (1991, 8). It is my suggestion that the whole spectrum of Confucian ritual actions pervading traditional Japanese patterns of behavior, ranging from the simple *ojigi* or ritualized "bow" of everyday greetings, to the ritual expressions of "filial piety" (*kōkō*) towards parents and elders, ritual acts of "loyalty" (*chūjitsu*) in Bushidō, the highly aestheticized *temae* or ritual procedures of the tea ceremony (*chanoyu*), rituals of ancestor worship before the household *ihai* or memorial tablets, as well as countless other everyday secular rites of propriety governing verbal and nonverbal communication between contextual persons in various social groups, can all be regarded as what Goffman terms "interaction rituals" in the Meadian sociological tradition of symbolic interactionism.

### The I–Me Dialectic of Mead and the Yi–Li Dialectic of Confucianism

An application of the framework of G. H. Mead to the tradition of classical Confucianism is to be found in *Thinking Through Confucius* (1987) by David L. Hall and Roger T. Ames. In this work the authors develop Confucian social ethics as involving the process of becoming a person, or as it were, an activity of "person making." While they point out interesting common features between concepts of personhood in both Western existentialism and Chinese Confucianism, they assert, "the fatal disadvantage of existentialism is its individualistic presuppositions," adding that "Pragmatism provides a corrective to the individualism of the existentialist" (1987, 79). For this reason they state that it is "the pragmatic philosophies associated with Peirce, James, Dewey, and Mead, and extended toward a process philosophy such as that of A. N. Whitehead, that can serve as the best resource for philosophical concepts and doctrines permitting responsible access to Confucius' thought" (1987, 15). Of special interest here is their comparative analysis between the activity of person making in Confucianism and the social psychology of G. H. Mead. According to Hall and Ames, "The fact that Mead begins in the most radical manner with the concept of society renders his analysis of the emergence of the self within its social context extremely valuable as a resource for reflecting upon Confucius' understanding of person making" (1987, 80). They go on to characterize the Confucian process of person making as follows: "Authoritative personhood is a calculus of 'taking in' the selves of others and exercising one's own judgment in trying to effect what is most appropriate for all concerned" (1987, 119). This is in turn related to Mead's social psychology, wherein the person achieves unity as a self by virtue of internalizing the attitude of the "generalized other" and then by responding to it. Hence, for Mead, as for Confucianism, the self is a *field of selves* that results from "taking in" other selves and making them all a part of our communal self (1987, 119).

However, at the heart of their comparative analysis is a striking juxtaposition of the I-Me dialectic of Mead's developmental psychology with the *yi-li* dialectic in the Confucian theory of person making. Following a brief exposition of Mead's idea of the social self as constituted by a dialectic of I and Me (1987, 79–83), they proceed to formulate a highly innovative account of the "authoritative person" (*jen*) in Confucian social ethics in terms of a parallel dialectic of *yi* (signification) and *li* (ritual acts). They approach their subject through a critique of H. Fingarette's thesis articulated in *Confucius: The Secular as Sacred* (1972), which argues for the primacy of *li* or "ritual action" in Chinese culture. Fingarette develops Confucianism as the *tao* or Way of following institutionalized rites of *li*, understood as those prescriptive ethical norms governing the basic human relationships of mankind, including parent-child, lord-subject, husband-wife, friend-friend, brother-brother, and other cardinal relationships. By Fingarrete's account, *li* or ritual action is the basic mechanism for constituting both self and society in Confucian thought and culture. With great insight he uses the metaphor of alchemical transformation to show how mundane ceremonial acts of *li* such as the simple act of bowing out of reverence for others functions to transmute the "secular" into the "sacred," thereby leading to the consecration and transfiguration of the everyday, commonplace world. Fingarette has best appreciated the functioning of custom, ritual, and tradition in Confucian thought, but concentrates on rites of *li* as the forms through which the benevolence of *jen* is expressed, thereby focusing almost exclusively upon the stabilizing and harmonizing aspects of *li*. According to Hall and Ames, what is missing in Fingarette's account of *li* is overcoming *inertia of the past*. Their polemic here is that the inertia of *li* as a formula for repetition must be supplemented by the creative acts of *yi* which introduce novelty into the social order. An act of *yi* is understood as "context-dependent" (1987, 102), or the "appropriateness" of a self to its surrounding context. Also, an act of *yi* requires more than the application of an antecedently existing principle, so that it is always "at least to some degree spontaneous, novel, and creative" (1987, 102). That is to say, acts of *yi* cannot be simply a matter of applying some externally derived norm in that persons must exercise their own moral judgement in response to the uniqueness of a particular situation. By this view, the spontaneous, novel, and creative acts of *yi* are codified in the embodied heritage of social customs, traditions, laws, institutions, and rituals of *li*. In this way, the rites of *li* are understood as reifications of *yi*, the spontaneous, novel, and creative acts of aesthetic/moral insight springing from the authoritative person as a self-in-context. Ritual acts of *li* without the spontaneous acts of *yi* exaggerate its normative force at the expense of creativity, thus reinforcing the idea of Confucianism as a conservative, backward-looking, and an order-imposing system. In opposition to this conservative view of Confucian social ethics, Hall and Ames argue for a mutuality, reciprocity, or co-relativity of *yi* and *li*. When this dialectical interplay between the Confucian categories of *li* and *yi* are considered from the standpoint G. H. Mead's philosophy, it becomes clear that while *li* corresponds to the Me, the internalization of society with its ritually preserved fund of traditional values, *yi* corresponds to the I, the spontaneous, novel, and creative response of a unique individual to its social context. The critique framed by Hall and Ames overturns the privileging of *li* over *yi* and instead establishes parity between the two in the worldview of Confucianism. Just as the Confucian ideal of an authoritative person emerges through a dialectic of *yi* and *li*, so the social self of Mead arises through a dialectic of I and the Me.

## The Bipolar Model of the Social Self in Mead and Confucianism

In his work *The Puritan Smile: A Look Toward Moral Reflection* (1987), Robert C. Neville makes a significant application of both American pragmatism and American Puritanism to the tradition of Chinese Confucianism, including both the classical tradition of Confucius and Mencius as well as the neo-Confucianism of Chu Hsi and Wang-yang Ming. Like Hall and Ames, Neville underscores the manner in which both Chinese Confucianism and American pragmatism develop a social concept of self wherein the person is analyzed in terms of a dialectical interaction between the two poles of the private individual and the public institutions of society. First, he attempts to circumvent the liberalism-Marxism dialectic which has dominated moral philosophy in the recent past with the Confucian/Puritan emphasis on personal responsibility and the social definition of the individual. The need for tolerance and liberty is asserted by Neville in order to offset the tendencies toward dogmatism and totalitarianism which he sees as being inherent within both the Puritan and Confucian frameworks. Altogether he tries to integrate a Puritan sense of social participation with a Confucian sense of moral obligation and a liberal appreciation of freedom and tolerance.

In this context Neville draws further illuminating parallels between Confucianism and American pragmatism. Neville asserts that, "By 'pragmatism' I mean the classical positions of Charles Peirce, William James, John Dewey, George Herbert Mead, and the neighboring position of Alfred North Whitehead" (1987, 226 fn.). He adds that his parallels with Chinese philosophy do not hold plausibly for the epistemological pragmatism of Nelson Goodman or Willard Quine, nor for the rhetorical neopragmatism recently popularized by Richard Rorty (1987, 226 fn.). The first aspect of Neville's comparative analysis which I would like to focus upon here is that according to the worldviews of both Chinese Confucianism and American pragmatism, there is a *continuity of thought and action* so that the self is to be understood as being located in a *continuum between two poles*, the private individual and public institutions, the inner world of the subject and the outer world of the object, or the individual organism and the social environment. Neville observes:

> The first great virtue of the Confucian moral mode is its insistence on the continuity of thought and action. Expressed as early as the doctrine of the Mean, any personal event is located on a continuum between two poles. One is the absolute center of pure tranquility and readiness-to-respond-but-not-yet-responding. The other is the objective realm of other things as unrelated to the person. Both of the poles are abstractions, according to the Confucian belief. (1987, 28)

Neville then points out that some representatives of liberal individualism in American moral philosophy such as Robert Nozick have gone so far as to suggest that the relation between a person and his or her social roles is external. However, in contrast to this stands the Confucian concept of selfhood typified by the ideal of the scholar-official. Since the person in Confucianism is a self-in-context who exists in the continuum between the two poles of private individual and public institutions, the self is now understood to be internally related to its social roles. Neville thus writes:

> The modern Western assumptions about the externality of role to person are not shared by the sense of publicness in the Confucian ideal of the scholar-official. Precisely because a person's nature is located on

the continuum between abstract inner core and abstractly external things, the person is internally related to the social roles of the context. (1987, 33)

Another aspect of Neville's comparison between Confucianism and pragmatism which I would like to elaborate upon is the axiological or value-centric basis for all interaction between the individual and his or her social environment. Just as American pragmatism underscores the inseparability of theory and praxis or the continuity of thought and action, neo-Confucians like Chu Hsi hold that thought is the beginning of action while action is the completion of thought. Neville articulates the Confucian/pragmatist notion of "the continuity of thought and action" by emphasizing its *valuative* dimension in explicitly pragmatic terms, focusing especially on John Dewey's key notion of "valuative transaction"(1987, 29). For Dewey, Mead, and other American pragmatists, the self is understood to be a situation pervaded by aesthetic quality which arises through a "valuative interaction" between an individual organism and its social environment. From the standpoint of this pragmatic theory of valuation, Neville writes: "From Mencius's doctrine of the Four Beginnings to Wang Yang-ming's theory of heart-mind, the Confucian tradition interpreted experience and personal reality as a valuative transaction" (1987, 29). He again takes the Confucian ideal of the scholar-official located on the continuum between two abstract poles of private core and public institutions as the paradigm case for "valuative transaction" between an individual and society (1987, 30).

While Neville draws upon the whole tradition of American pragmatism to elucidate the nature of personhood in Confucianism, I would emphasize that it is especially G. H. Mead who thematizes the notion of a social self as well as the *bipolar* structure of the self as an individual-society interaction, articulated in dialectical terms as a conversation between I and Me. It is the symbolic interactionist communication framework of Mead which best explains how the social self is located in a continuum between two poles, the I or private individual pole and the Me or public institutional pole. At the same time Mead points out that the two poles of I and Me are not substantial entities but only abstract phases or functional distinctions within the self as social process instituted for purposes of analysis. Like the Confucian process of becoming a person, Mead's developmental psychology explains how the person constitutes itself as a unity by taking on the roles of the generalized other, such that the self is now understood as being internally related to its social roles. The Confucian ideal of personhood embodied by the scholar-official who exhibits a continuity of thought and action through valuative transactions between the individual and society, thereby to exist in a continuum between two poles of a private inner core and public institutions, may thus be said to represent a paradigmatic example of the social self and I-Me dialectic formulated by G. H. Mead in American pragmatism.

## Bio-Social Man in Mead and Modern Chinese Philosophy

Finally, I would like to consider the potential application of G. H. Mead's social-self model to the Confucian/Marxist concept of personhood as a twofold *"bio-social* man" articulated by leading Maoist thinkers in twentieth-century Chinese philosophy. In his work, *The Concept of Man in Contemporary China* (1977), Donald J. Munro examines the social nature of man formulated by Maoist thinkers in contemporary China against the background of Confucian and neo-Confucian theories of the self in ancient China, on the one side, and of Marxist theories of the self, both in Germany and the Soviet Union, on the other. He in turn contrasts the Confucian/Maoist-Marxist theory of man as social in contemporary China with the liberal democratic concept of man as developed by John Rawls in the tradition of American individualism.

Munro points out that in Confucianism, the social nature of man included innate tendencies to behave in certain ways toward other people, including the tendency to feel and behave compassionately toward kin and others out of *jen* or human heartedness, the inclination to act respectfully to elders, and the tendency to form social organizations (1977, 15). Mencius drew the distinction between the "social" and "biological" natures by speaking of the social aspect as the greater part of the self or the Heavenly nature while the biological or animal aspect was the lesser part of the self (1977, 15). Munro goes on to argue that Marx also made an implicit distinction between man's "social" and "biological" natures, whereby the biological nature is the trivial aspect and the social nature is the nontrivial aspect of the self. In this context he cites Marx's classic statement concerning the social nature of the human essence as contained in his *Sixth Thesis on Feuerbach*, according to which "the human essence is no abstraction inherent in each single individual. In its reality it is the ensemble of social relations" (1977, 9). Munro hereby presents the twofold bio-social concept of man in contemporary China as forming through a synthesis of the Confucian and Marxist theories of the self. The classic Chinese Maoist-Marxist statement on man's social nature is contained in an essay by Liu Shao-ch'i entitled "Man's Class Nature" (1941), translated by Munro as follows: "Man has two essences: one is man's nature essence (*pen-neng*), including his physical constitution, cleverness, state of health, instinctive capacities, and so forth . . . the other is man's social essence" (1977, 16). In Munro's exegesis of this famous passage by Liu Shao-ch'i, he points out that while the Confucian/Marxist idea of bio-social man presented by Maoist thinkers is said to have two natures, the biological and the social, it is the "social nature" (*she-hui-hsing*) which is alone unique to man, while the biological nature is shared with the animals. Munro states:

> Ever since Liu's essay contemporary Chinese philosophers and psychologists have differentiated between man's biological and social nature. Bifurcation is a convenient device for assigning to the trivial biological dimension central to the liberal democratic concept of man. The distinguishing characteristic is the social nature (*she-hui-hsing*). (1977, 16)

As indicated above, the Chinese concept of a twofold bio-social man is regarded as being in direct opposition to the American liberal democratic notion wherein man is understood to be a separate and atomic individual with a private inner core. For this reason Munro states that "the American conception of human nature conflicts directly with the central dimensions of the Chinese idea . . . The primacy of natural man, not social man, is clear; and a place in the psyche is made for the private self." (1977, 8) In contrast to the American liberal democratic concept of man as an atomic individual, classical German and Soviet writings in Marxist theory claim that man's essential nature is social and that the idea of a natural man apart from social relations is nonsensical (1977, 8–9).

However, an explicit twofold theory of the person as bio-social man has in fact also been set forth by G. H. Mead in twentieth-century American pragmatism. Mead clearly distinguishes between the "biological" and the "social" aspects of the self arising within an organism-environment situation when he writes: "I assume that the objects of immediate experience exist in relationship to the *biological* and *social* individuals whose environments they make up" (SW 240; italics added). Hence, as has been emphasized by David L. Miller (1987, xvi; also 3–24), Mead's concept of the social self represents what is essentially a twofold *bio-social* theory of the person. That is to say, Mead's idea of a bipolar social self constituted by a dialectic of I and Me can be summarized by the notion of bio-social man. Based on Mead's own comments (MSS 210, 255), it has become common among pragmatists and symbolic interactionists to understand the two components of Mead's social self, the I and the Me, or the biological pole and the social pole, as roughly corresponding to Freud's notions of id and superego. In a chapter entitled "Bio-Social Man" from his book *George Herbert Mead,* Miller writes: "We may say that the Freudian id correspond to the Meadian I, and the superego corresponds to Mead's generalized other. . . . In Freudian terms, Mead holds that the id and the superego (the I and the Me) are essential components of the self and that neither could exist apart from the other" (1973, 6). Accordingly, the I component of Mead's social self corresponds to the biological instincts which Freud called the id, while the "Me" component signifies the censorship mechanism or moral conscience of the superego developed through the internalization of parental authority and other social controls. Thus, in Mead's theory of bio-social man, the I or individual pole represents the impulsive aspect of the self rooted in the biological instincts, while the Me or institutional pole represents the social aspect of the self arising from an internalization of the community functioning as the generalized other.

Although there are fascinating similarities between the bio-social concepts of man as developed by G. H. Mead in American pragmatism and Confucian/Maoist-Marxist thinkers like Liu Shao-ch'i in modern Chinese philosophy, nonetheless, there also exists a crucial disparity between these two models of the self. While the Confucian/Marxist paradigm of bio-social man is regarded as having two essences, the biological and the social, the social essence is always privileged over and above the biological essence. According to Munro's account, for Mencius in classical Confucianism the social essence is the greater part of the self or the Heavenly nature, while the biological essence is the lesser part of the self or the animal nature. For Marx the biological nature is the trivial aspect while the social nature is the nontrivial aspect of the self. Whereas in the synthesis of Confucian and Marxist notions of selfhood developed by recent Maoist thinkers like Liu Shao-ch'i, the biological nature is shared with the animals while only the "social nature" (*she-hui-hsing*) is unique to man. In contrast to the Confucian/Maoist-Marxist theory of man stands the bio-social concept of personhood developed by G. H. Mead in American pragmatism. According to Mead's notion of bio-social man, both the "biological" aspect of the I pole and the "social" aspect of the Me pole are necessary phases of the twofold social self in its wholeness. For Mead, the impulsive I and the socialized Me are equal and co-relative aspects of the self so that neither aspect can be accorded priority over the other. Moreover, for Mead the impulsive I is not simply the primitive instinctual aspect of the bio-social man; it is also the source of creativity, novelty, and freedom in the evolutionary process whereby an individual organism makes a spontaneous adjustment to the deterministic social environment. As bio-social man with a double nature, the self emerges from its deterministic social environment as a Me and then responds to it with creativity, spontaneity, and freedom as an emergent I. Mead asserts that the impulsive and spontaneous I which reacts to the social controls of the Me is essential to the creative attitude of the artist, the inventor, and the scientist in his process of discovery (MSS 214). Also, it is the spontaneous response of the impulsive I over against the habitual and conservative Me which militates against the reification of existing social institutions through a constant "reconstruction of society" (MSS 214). The social self develops by internalizing the public institutions of society at the Me pole and then by constantly reconstructing those institutions through the creative activity at the I pole. In summary, then, both G. H. Mead in American pragmatism and the Confucian/Maoist-Marxist thinkers in contemporary Chinese philosophy can be said to have converged upon a *bio-social* concept of man with two essences, the "biological" and the "social." But while the Confucian/Maoist-Marxist concept of bio-social man always privileges the social aspect while relegating the biological aspect to the status of primitive animal nature, the bipolar social-self paradigm of Mead places equal weight on both the biological and social components of the self through a dialectical interaction between the I and the Me.

## ~:8:~
## The Social Self in Mead, Zen, and Japanese Society

Throughout this work it has been emphasized that G. H. Mead's broad interdisciplinary approach to the social self provides a unifying framework for both philosophy and the social sciences, including sociology, anthropology, and social psychology. For this reason, the applicability of Mead's framework to various aspects of Zen Buddhism and the traditional Japanese notion of personhood in general has been noted by scholars representing a wide variety of disciplines such as Doi Takeo (1985), Kenneth Inada (1984), Charles Hartshorne (1984), Peter L. Berger (1963), Robert J. Smith (1985), Takie Sugiyama Lebra (1976, 1992), David W. Plath (1980), Kuwayama Takami (1992), David L. Preston (1988), and Van Meter Ames (1962). To begin with, the *amae* psychology of Doi Takeo (1985, 41–42;1986, 46–47) establishes an analogy between the bipolar I-Me structure of the social self in the social psychology of Mead and the *honne/tatemae* or "private reaction/social institution" contrast in the double structure of traditional Japanese selfhood as a nexus of dependency relations. Kenneth Inada (1984, 76) mentions the close resemblance of Japanese Buddhist *śūnyatā* (J. *kū*) or "emptiness" in its meaning as "interrelational existence" to the organismic worldview articulated by the movement of American philosophy including Peirce, James, Dewey, Whitehead, Mead, and others who understand human experience in terms of the dynamic relationship between man and his total surroundings.

Charles Hartshorne remarks that the social process theory of selfhood developed by G. H. Mead, according to which the self is at each present moment constituted by the spontaneous, emergent, and ever partly new I responding to the objectified Me, is close to the "Buddhist-Whiteheadian view of the momentary self as numerically non-identical with its predecessors" (1984,126). For Zen Buddhism in the East as for both the process cosmology of Mead and Whitehead in the West, the self is a series of transitory events wherein at each moment the old self is replaced by a new self which is partly continuous with and partly discontinuous with its antecedents. Hartshorne's insight thus functions to accentuate the structural resemblance between the frameworks of Mead, Whitehead, and Buddhism not only with regard to the "social" aspect of selfhood as constituted by a network of causal relationships, but also the *temporal* nature of the emergent self as a series of discontinunous momentary quantum events which perpetually arise and perish whole in the stream of becoming.

In his work *Invitation to Sociology* (1963, 106–7), sociologist Peter L. Berger makes a similar comparison between the Buddhist and Meadian views of self as a temporal stream of discontinuous moments. For Berger (1963, 106), Mead's psychological theory of *multiple selfhood* as a kaleidoscope of roles and identities clarifies how the self is not an unchanging substantial entity with a fixed essence, but a temporal process whereby a person is continuously created and re-created in each new social situation, held together only by the slender thread of memory. He then relates this Meadian concept of selfhood with the view of Buddhist psychology, wherein the self is compared to a long row of candles, each of which lights the wick of its neighbor and is extinguished in that moment (1963, 107). Hence, like Charles Hartshorne, Berger has recognized how both Mead in the West and Buddhism in the East have articulated the social and processual dimensions of the self as a discontinuous continuity of emergent moments which perpetually appear and disappear in the temporal stream of consciousness with no underlying substantial identity.

Berger's focus on Mead's insights into the *multiple* nature of selfhood accords with a fundamental trait of Japanese personhood highlighted in a recent collection of valuable essays published under the title, *Japanese Sense of Self* (1992). At the end of her editor's introduction, Nancy Rosenberger points out that in contrast to Western notions of selfhood, the Japanese self includes elements of *multiplity, change, and interaction:*

> In conclusion, the essays in this volume present a view of Japanese self as multiple and moving which urges a reconsideraton of concepts of self in other societies as well. . . . It is hoped that these studies of Japanese self will expand Western-trained scholars' conceptions of self to include multiplicity, change, and interaction with others, not only in non-Western societies such as Japan, but in Western cultures as well. (1992, 16)

However, it must be emphasized that in Western philosophy a fully systematic view of the self which includes the factors of multiplicity, change, and interaction has *already* been set forth in the communication model of the social self developed by G. H. Mead and others in the Meadian tradition of symbolic interactionism. In part two of this study it has already been discussed at length how Mead's symbolic interactionist framework of the social and temporal self also entails a doctrine of a multiple self. To repeat Mead's own words: "We are all persons of multiple selves" (1974, 71). Again, he states: "We divide ourselves up in all sorts of different selves. . . . There are all sorts of different selves answering to all sorts of different social reactions" (MSS 142). And elsewhere, "A multiple personality is in a certain sense normal" (MSS 142). The developmental psychology of Mead explains how the social self is constituted through communicative interaction by taking on the roles of other selves so as to combine them all in a field of selves. When Berger (1963, 106) describes Mead's social, processual self as "a kaleidoscope of roles and identities" he is therefore bringing to light Mead's pluralistic concept of a decentered multiple self constituted by a series of discontinuous events in the ever-changing stream of consciousness devoid of any underlying substantial identity. Hence, like the Japanese self, the Meadian self is a relationally defined social self which is multiple, decentered, changing, open, and variable.

In his work *Japanese Society: Tradition, Self and the Social Order* (1983), Robert J. Smith propounds that a fundamental problem with Japanology has been that scholars have attempted to analyze the Japanese self from the standpoint of Freudian individualistic psychology instead of the Meadian symbolic interactionist tradition of social psychology. He states that

> if over the past thirty-five years research had been conducted in the framework of the interactionist social psychology of figures like George Herbert Mead and Henry Stack Sullivan [*sic*], rather than the individual psychology of Freud and others who provided the framework that was in fact employed. Had the intellectual influences been different, we should long since have had an eminently plausible picture of the Japanese conception of the self. (1983, 74)

For Smith, the social psychology of Mead clarifies not only the social, relational, and interactional character of the Japanese self; it also also illumines the *decentered* character of the Japanese self as a nexus of social relations with no fixed center. As Smith writes, "there is no fixed center from which . . . the individual asserts a noncontingent existence" (1983, 81).

In his study of the *ie* or "family household" institution of traditional Japanese society, Smith (1985, 39) points out that Americans are likely to find the Japanese to be excessively group-oriented, far too willing to submerge the self in the collectivity, and possessed of weak ego boundaries. To this, he comments: "But our own restricted view of the matter causes us to overlook the high priority the Japanese assign to the growth of human beings as *social persons*" (1985, 39; also see 1983, 73). Smith examines the various accounts of Japanologists in philosophy and the social sciences regarding the social nature of the Japanese self. However, against the claim of scholars in the tradition of *nihonjinron* that social selfhood is a unique characteristic of Zen Buddhism or traditional Japanese society, Smith argues (1985, 39) that the social nature of self in Japan can in fact be best understood through the writings of someone who was not himself a Zen master, a Japanese, or even a Japanologist: namely, the social psychology of G. H. Mead in American pragmatism! He therefore states: "In the mid-1930s George Herbert Mead . . . attempted to develop a social psychology that fits almost perfectly what we are told is the peculiarly Japanese case." (1985, 39) After citing three passages on the social self from the works of Mead, Smith adds: "Taken together these three statement seem to me to offer one of the best summaries I know of how the self comes to be formed and how it operates in Japanese society" (1985, 39). Smith goes on to emphasize that for Mead, the self is always a social self by virtue of the fact that it emerges from its social context through interaction with others. He thus asserts:

> Mead would have been puzzled by much of the current debate about the nature of the self in Japan, at least to the extent it appears that to imply there is something unusual about it, for in his view the individual selves of all the members of all societies are the products of the groups within which they interact and live out their lives. (1985, 40)

Hence, while Mead's social psychology no doubt provides us with a penetrating insight into the social nature of the Japanese self, at the same time it offers a more universal account of the genetic development of social selves in every culture. Smith concludes that from the standpoint of Mead's social psychology, what is unusual about Japanese society is not that there is a high degree of group orientedness or that family household and village principles organize it, but rather that the acknowledgment of interdependence is so open and the importance of group affiliation is made so thoroughly explicit (1985, 40).

Takie Sugiyama Lebra (1976, xviii) acknowledges the strong intellectual debt which she owes to G. H. Mead and the American sociological movement of symbolic interactionism in her analysis of the Ego-Alter dialectic constituting the social character of selfhood in traditional Japanese group-centered society as developed in her now standard work, *Japanese Patterns of Behavior*. At the outset of her recent essay titled "Self in Japanese Culture" (1992), Lebra once again expresses the influence of G. H. Mead's thought upon her own analysis of Japanese selfhood

> This essay takes as its point of departure the universalistic thesis on self which is credited to G. H. Mead (1934) and Hallowell (1955). The most essential feature of self, according to these and other scholars, is self-awareness, which is variously worded such as reflexivity, self-objectification, self as an object to itself, self as at once subject and object, "I" and "me," and so on. The same thesis postulates that self-awareness is generated and fostered through self-other interaction on the one hand and the symbolic processing of information on the other. (1992, 105)

Based partly on Mead's social-self theory and I-Me dialectic of intersubjectivity, Lebra next elucidates the structure of Japanese personhood in three dimensions: the "interactional self," the "inner self" and the "boundless self" (1992, 105). Like the social self of Mead, the interactional self of Japanese personhood refers to "the awareness of self as defined, sustained, enhanced, or blemished through social interaction" (1992, 106). According to Lebra, "The interactional self is what occupies Japanese most of the time" (1992, 111). Insofar as all selves are products of social interaction, this dimension of self is said by Lebra to be found most commonly across cultural groups. The socially constructed interactional self is further subdivided into two polar orientations, the "presentational self" and the "empathetic self." The presentational self is defined in terms of Goffman's (1959) symbolic interactionist dramaturgical analogy of self-presentation as an actor performing roles before an audience within the social theater. In the context of Japanese society, Lebra states that this dramaturgical world of audience is called *seken*, "society." (1992, 106–7). She adds that the Japanese concept of *seken* as here conceived is analogous to both "reference group" theory and Mead's idea of the "generalized other": "While the *seken* has something in common with the Western concept of 'reference group' (Inoue 1977), or with 'the generalized other' of Mead, I identify it as the generalized audience or jury surrounding the self in an inescapable way" (1992, 107). The second orientation of the interactional self, which is continuous with, but conceptually distinct from the presentational self, is the "empathetic self," understood by Lebra to denote an awareness of self as an insider of a group or network of social relationships. Empathy thus ties in with Doi Takeo's concept of *amae*, the desire for being endulged or the

wish to depend upon another (1992, 107–8). These two aspects of the interactional self, the presentational self and the empathetic self, are said to be in
opposition in that the former presupposes social or psychological distance
between self and other to the point of self-defense and other-avoidance while
the latter minimizes such distance (1992, 110). Because the interactional self
is forever shifting in accord with its relational contexts it is also to be conceived as a *multiple self*. In Lebras's words: "As long as one stays in the interactional world, multiple and variable self-identification seems necessary. A
multiple and variable self like this ultimately boils down to 'non-self' as symbolized by the zero form" (1992, 110).

In contrast to the socially constituted "interactional self" is what Lebra
calls the "inner self." This basic contrast between the "interactional self" and
the "inner self" in turn corresponds to the common distinction (*kejime*) between the private world of inner feeling and the public world of social relations: "As much as the social world is divided into outside and inside (*soto*
versus *uchi*), or front and back (*omote* versus *ura*), and others into outsiders
and insiders, so is self divided into outwardly (socially) involved and the in-
wardly oriented realms" (1992, 112). While the interactional self is characterized as being "relative, multiple, and variable" in accordance with how self
stands vis-à-vis other, the inner self represents a "less relative, more stable,
fixed self—the world of pure subjectivity" (1992, 115). Although Lebra's analysis of the twofold structure of Japanese personhood in terms of the interactional and inner dimensions of self accords with Mead's general analysis of
achieving reflexive self-consciousness through a dialectic of self-other relations,
at the same time she goes beyond the limits of Mead's theory when she posits
a "boundless self." The boundless self is meant to offer "an alternative goal
or strategy that can be mobilized to disengage one from the socially or in-
wardly obsessed or entrapped self" (1992, 116). She relates her notion of the
"boundless self" to the traditional Japanese Zen Buddhist notions of an empty
self, non-self, or self of nothingness (*muga, mushin, mu*, etc.). Yet she also
points out that there seems to be a correspondence between a boundless
"Zen person" of nothingness and a secular, social person with respect to the
ultimate significance of relationality (1992, 116). Hence, the boundless self of
Zen does not reject or replace the socially bounded relative self.

Like Robert J. Smith (1983, 1985) and Takie S. Lebra (1976, 1992), David
W. Plath is a cultural anthropologist whose analysis of Japanese self and society
has been significantly influenced by the symbolic interactionism of G. H. Mead.
Plath's *Long Engagements: Maturity in Modern Japan* (1980 / 1992) is an ethnolog-
ical field study of lifespan development, maturation, aging, and mass longevity
in Japan. For Plath the East-West dialogue on maturity is complicated by the

fact that America emphasizes the growth of unique monadic individuals while Japan emphasizes the development of "social persons," so that each side misperceives the other's archetype of growth (1992, 215–16). Thus, from the Western standpoint of individualism the Japanese are characterized in terms of collectivism, sociocentrism, and anti-individualism, whereupon the Japanese are said to have "weak and permeable ego boundaries," a "submerged self," or no "real" sense of self at all (1992, 216). Americans often take the view that the Japanese are collectivistic whereas we are individualistic, and see the Japanese as peculiarly attuned to hierarchy or seniority in social relations whereas we are said to favor equality. Plath agrees that these East-West stereotypes have an element of truth and function to point out certain differences in concepts of the self and the nature of social relations (1992, 4). At the same time he argues against such clichés about American individualism versus Japanese collectivism, claiming that the Japanese archetype of growth is not "sociocentric" or bound to abstract roles and social structures, but "people-centered" in that it focuses upon the development of personality as a capacity for human relationships (1992, 217). In the Japanese archetype of growth, "The lifelong struggle is to carry out one's responsibilities to others without diminishing one's playful responsiveness toward them" (1992, 217).

For Plath, G. H. Mead's symbolic interactionist account of how individuals develop into a social self through relationships with others in a community provides a Western theoretical framework for interpreting the Japanese archetype of growth. Plath states, "It was George Herbert Mead who gave twentieth-century human science a vision of society as the product of collective discourse" (1992, 223). Also, he employs E. Goffman's dramaturgical model of symbolic interactionism to describe the Japanese "presentation of self" through the performance of social roles before an audience of others (1992, 226). He further makes reference to Charles H. Cooley's "primary group," Harry Stack Sullivan's "significant others," Jules Henry's "personal community," and Helen Perlman's "vital role others" to describe the primary function of the *nuturing other* and the closeness of core personal relations in the Japanese archetype of growth into social persons (1992, 225). He adds that while he has been influenced by Mead and other symbolic interactionists, it is from Kenneth Burke and Hugh Duncan that he specifically derives his notions of long engagements of maturity (1992, 223). The symbolic interactionist view of development into a social self through personal relations with significant others needs to be supplemented with the elements of duration and cumulation, the *time-depth* needed for those long mutual engagements that maturity requires (1992, 225). In this context Plath characterizes the Meadian symbolic interactionist notion of self as follows: "The interactionist self is a kind of blossom that appears in social relations. As reflexive (self-aware) beings we must constantly integrate our subjective and objective sides, reconcile the 'I' and the 'me'" (1980, 8). By means of his poetic analogy he points out that like a flower which blossoms over time, in Mead's symbolic interactionism the self is not merely given at birth but is something which requires development through social relations with others. Hence, through the personal narratives of four life histories and their reflection in four modern Japanese novels, Plath endeavors to portray just how the Japanese self "blossoms" through webs of ever-deepening long-term social engagements as they change across the years and seasons with the passage of time.

In his essay "The Reference Other Orientation" (1992), Kuwayama Takami follows Smith, Plath, and Lebra in an effort to interpret Japanese selfhood through the social-self theory of Mead and other symbolic interactionists. He particularly makes reference to Smith's (1983, 73) assertion that in contrast to Western individualism, "the Japanese assign a high priority to the growth of human beings as social persons" (cited by Kuwayama: 1992, 132). He further cites Smith's (1983, 74) view that a basic error of Japanologists has been their failure to interpret the Japanese self in terms of the framework of the symbolic interactionist social psychology of George Herbert Mead rather than the individualist psychology of Freud (cited by Kuwayama: 1992, 132). Kuwayama affirms the social constructionist view of Japanese selfhood, writing: "The Japanese self has variously been described as 'relational,' 'interactional,' 'interdependent,' 'particularistic,' 'situational,' 'contextual,' 'relative,' 'collective,' 'group-oriented,' and 'sociocentric'" (1992, 121). He then attempts to interpret the social nature of Japanese selfhood and the groupism of Japanese society in terms of the "reference group," "reference other orientation" theories of modern sociology. "Reference group theory" is based on the recognition that people are not individuals with separate existence but can only defined by reference to "others," and that these others provide the frames of reference for self-appraisal and attitude formation. The "reference other orientation" derives from "reference group theory" and is based on the recognition that people often orient themselves to groups *other than their own* in shaping their attitudes and evaluations. However, he further clarifies that the theory of reference groups traces its origins back to the earlier symbolic interactionist movement of social psychology in classical American thought running through James, Cooley, and Mead, as well as the later work of Harry Stack Sullivan:

> Although it was only in the early 1940s that the theory of reference groups emerged, the concept itself is undoubtedly old, finding

immediate precursors in the works of William James (1950 [1890]) on the "social self," Charles H. Cooley (1983 [1902]) on the "looking-glass self," George H. Mead (1934) on the "generalized other," and those of other scholars associated with the early school of symbolic interactionism. Also, the psychiatrist Harry Stack Sullivan's notion of the "significant other" (1945, 1970) is closely related to this school's orientation. (1992, 129–30)

In this context Kuwayama articulates what he calls his *reference other model* of Japanese selfhood wherein the "Other" is interpreted in terms of the social self of James, the looking-glass self of Cooley, the generalized other of Mead, and the significant other of H. S. Sullivan, along with more recent developments of this symbolic interactionist perspective in the "reference group" and "reference other orientation" theories. The main purport of all such theories is that "others" exert great influence on the self and provide the basic frames of reference for self-appraisal and attitude formation whereby social persons develop reflexive self-awareness.

For Kuwayama the Japanese self is to be understood in symbolic interactionist terms as a self-other relation or self-society interaction, which is expressed in terms of the Japanese categories of *jibun* (self) and *seken* (society). It should be noted here that the word for self in Japanese is *jibun*, which literally means "self part," indicating that the *self is a part of some larger social whole* that consists of various reference other groups. The "reference other model" of Kuwayama explicates how *jibun* or the "self part" arises through interaction with *seken* or "society" in its function as the "generalized other." Kuwayama's analysis here in part accords with Takie Lebra's view that, "*seken* has something in common with the Western concept of 'reference group' . . . or with 'the generalized other' of Mead" (Lebra: 1992, 107). Thus, Lebra and Kuwayama both analyze the social construction of the Japanese "self" through its interaction with *seken* or "society," while also pointing out the resemblance of the Japanese notion of *seken* to "reference group" theory and Mead's concept of the "generalized other."

However, Kuwayama's main contribution has been to further specify the distinct subcategories which go to make up this "other" or "generalized other" within the particular reference other orientation of Japanese groupism:

> The question to be asked at this point is: who are these others? More specifically, are there any categories of people who serve as a point of reference for the Japanese self? . . . I discovered that the Japanese relationship between the self and others is expressed systematically as

*jibun* (I) versus *mawari* (people around), *hito* (people at large), and *seken*
(society). (1992, 142)

Hence, according to Kuwayama's reference other model, there are three distinct categories of "others" in Japan, *mawari* (people around), *hito* (people at
large), and *seken* (society), which are concentrically related to the I or self
(*jibun*) at the center. Moreover, in accordance with their proximity to the self
(*jibun*), and in view of the fact that they provide the self with important points
of reference, he terms these three categories of others "immediate reference
others," "general reference others," and "reference society," respectively (1992,
142–43). While *mawari* (immediate reference others) would correspond to
Harry Stack Sullivan's "significant others" or the intimate nurturing others
like parents, family members, friends, and teachers, *hito* (generalized reference
others) and *seken* (reference society) are two subdivisions in the universalized
community of Mead's "generalized other." Whereas *hito* (general reference
others) are the primary reference groups which influence the self as the basic
frame of reference of attitude formation and self-evaluation, *seken* or "reference society" designates the wider sphere of reference other groups beyond
one's own. Kuwayama argues that his *reference other model* of Japanese selfhood
differs from the now standard *uchi-soto* or inside-outside model which has
dominated Japanese studies in at least two significant respects. First, whereas
the place of the I or self is ambiguous in the *uchi-soto* model, it is clearly
indicated by the term *jibun* in the reference other model. Second, the reference other model can show the interaction of the self and others in more
concrete terms than the *uchi-soto* model to the extent that the others are
classified into three categories of *mawari*, *hito* and *seken* in accordance with
their proximity to the self or *jibun*, instead of the two opposing categories of
inside and outside (1992, 144–46).

In his work *The Social Organization of Zen Practice*, David L. Preston (1988)
interprets Zen Buddhism from the standpoint of symbolic interactionism in
American sociology in order to explicate the social construction of selfhood
through ritual meditation practices. Preston goes on to suggest that the "true
self" achieved through Zen meditation can be described in terms of the symbolic interactionist perspective of G. H. Mead as "that part of the social self
called the 'I' (Mead, 1934) in contrast to the 'Me' that is more clearly reflexive
and limited to, and by, the more mundane processes of everyday life" (1988,
135). For Mead the I is that nonobjectified awareness which can never be
objectified without at once becoming the Me. In contrast to those symbolic
interactionist who accord priority to the Me pole of the social self, Preston
underscores the importance of the spontaneous I pole to articulate the

unreified and unreifiable subjectivity of the true self achieved through Zen meditation.

While the standard works on Zen meditation practice by D. T. Suzuki, A. Watts, P. Kapleau, and others take an individualistic psychological approach in order to understand the inner functioning of mind, Preston instead draws upon the recent sociological theories of symbolic interactionism, ethnomethodology, and lifeworld phenomenology so as to explicate the social construction of reality through Zen meditation. This social constructionist view of symbolic interactionism became widespread especially through an influential work by Peter L. Berger and Thomas Luckmann, which is aptly entitled *The Social Construction of Reality* (1966). It is this kind of social constructionist view of symbolic interactionism which Preston applies to *zazen* meditation practice in the Zen community setting. First he emphasizes that "The kind of Zen practice that has been developing in the United States is a community practice" (1988, 29). Preston here underscores the fact that Zen meditation is not an insulated practice conducted by solitary individuals but is in fact a highly ritualized mode of symbolic interaction which occurs within the social context of a community. The community setting of a Zen *sesshin* or intensive retreat is socially organized by formalized procedures of meditative rituals in such a way as to facilitate a shared sense of reality anchored in collective consciousness and social solidarity. Among the normatively prescribed body-mind rituals of a Zen *sesshin* he includes sitting meditation (*zazen*), interviews with a teacher (*dokusan*), walking meditation (*kinhin*), formal meals (*oryoki*), ritual strikes with the awakening stick (*kyōsaku*), and various ceremonial gestures like bowing (*ojigi*) or the folded hands posture (*gassho*). Although Zen meditation is often regarded as an introspective psychological technique of absorptionism, the social, dialogical, and intersubjective dimension of *zazen* are clearly brought out in the Rinzai tradition by means of its practice of ritual meditation on the *kōan*, meaning "public cases," which typically consist of dialogues occurring in moments of encounter between Zen masters and their disciples. Also, a disciple's mastery of a particular *kōan* or "public case" is tested by the dialogical process of *dokusan*, an interview with the Roshi supervising a Zen *sesshin*, thus further underscoring the social, embodied, and ritual aspects of Zen practice. The Sōtō Zen technique of *shikantaza* or "sitting-only" also represents a highly ritualized meditation practice which emphasizes adherence to the correct *form* of upright sitting posture based on Dōgen's notion of the unity of body-mind. Such highly formalized ritual meditation practices function to produce a heightened collective consciousness of social solidarity when a group of people concentrate their attention upon a common symbolic object with a shared meaning.

Conversion involves a resocialization process whereby through ritual interaction with believers in a community the recruit comes to share their
worldview leading to the social construction of a new reality. From the standpoint of a sociology of religion, then, Preston attempts to show how Zen
Buddhist meditation is not merely a system of inward contemplation based
on introspective techniques for producing interior states of ecstasy, but is
rather to be understood in terms of the social construction of a new self and
society through symbolic ritual interaction in a communal setting.

Going beyond the scope of Preston's study, I would argue that a social
constructionist theory of symbolic interactionism should be applied to all
the spiritual technologies of "self-cultivation" (*shugyō*) which have emerged
in traditional Japanese Buddhism. The ritual *zazen* (seated meditation) exercises of Zen Buddhism, including both the paradoxical *kōan* meditation of
Rinzai Zen and the silent illumination technique of *shikantaza* or sitting-only
in Sōtō Zen, the Zen-inspired arts and crafts of Geidō or the Way of aesthetics,
the *kata* or ritual combat exercises in the Zen-influenced martial arts of
Bushidō or the Way of the samurai warrior, the *goma* fire ceremony and other
symbolic rituals of Shingon and Tendai Esoteric (Mikkyō) Buddhism, the
*nembutsu* ("*Namu Amida Butsu* ") or ritual invocation of Amida's Other-power
grace in Pure Land Buddhism, the ritual incantation of *daimoku* ("*Namu Myōhō
Renge Kyō*") before the *gohonzon* or object of worship in Nichiren Buddhism,
and even the shamanic *okiyome* (*jōrei, mahikari no waza*) technique of ritual
healing, purification, and exorcism by radiating divine light from the palm as
taught in "new religions" (*shin-shūkyō*) based on Shinto-Buddhist syncretism
like Mahikari, can all be understood as methodologies for the social reconstruction of a new self and society through symbolic interaction rituals between contextual persons in a community setting. Furthermore, the practice
of compassionate self-emptying for the sake of others in both the Christian
*kenōsis* and Buddhist *śūnyatā* traditions as developed in the interreligious dialogue of Nishida Kitarō and the Kyoto school of modern Japanese philosophy
can likewise be interpreted from the standpoint of symbolic interactionism
as aiming toward the social reconstruction of self as an I-Thou relation of
intersubjectivity. From the standpoint of Mead's symbolic interactionism,
then, both "meditation" and "enlightenment" are to be understood in Japanese Buddhism as functions of *sociality*. By this view the various contemplative
practices of Japanese Buddhism are now to be conceived as symbolic interaction rituals which aim toward the production of an ideal social self. The
Meadian tradition of symbolic interactionism thus carries us beyond the
mystical interpretation of Japanese Buddhism based on introspectionism and
brings us to the great theme of the social sciences: namely, the social con-

struction of the human self through communicative interaction with others in a community.

In his book entitled *Zen and American Thought,* Van Meter Ames examines the close structural proximity of traditional Japanese Zen Buddhism to the whole tradition of American philosophy which he regards as culminating in the naturalism of G. H. Mead. According to Ames: "The affinity between Mead and Zen is striking" (1962, 274). He says that "Readers of Mead can confirm and supplement Zen. His students had with him something like the relationship in Zen between beginner and master" (1962, 15). This reference to a similarity between the profound teacher-student relationship enjoyed by those attending the lectures of Mead and the traditional master-disciple relationship of Zen assumes a deeper significance in light of the fact that, as pointed out by David L. Miller (1973, xxx), Van Meter Ames attended no less than thirteen different courses and seminars taught by Mead at the University of Chicago during the 1920s. Ames points out how Mead's I-Me dialectic of the social self clarifies the double nature of an enlightened Bodhisattva with the two poles of *spontaneity* and *sociality:* "The social and spontaneous self of Mead is the sense of Zen, and the basis of the *bodhisattva* ideal" (1962, 263). The two poles of Buddhahood are then expressed in somewhat different terms when he asserts that the I represents the *aloneness* and the Me represents the *sociality* of the twofold social self: "There is the social and the alone come together in the social self, its civilized 'me' guiding the aboriginal 'I'" (1962, 278). Ames rightly points out that both Zen Buddhism and the social psychology of Mead reject the concept of a separate ego so as to argue that true selfhood is achieved only through relationships with others in a community (1962, 263). He adds that both Zen and Mead understand how in the developmental process of self-realization, individuation is achieved through socialization and *vice versa:* "The self is a process of becoming more personal and more social at the same time. The Zen men saw the fact. . . . They had the insight that human nature is Buddha-nature. They anticipated Mead and he justified them" (1962, 288). Emphasizing the centrality of pervasive aesthetic experience in both Zen Buddhism and the American pragmatism he asserts: "It is finally in aesthetic experience that East and West meet" (1962, 258). Mead's analysis of the "social act," wherein the consummatory stage not only comes last but is anticipated throughout in the aesthetic experience of qualitative immediacy characterizing the wholeness of each and every moment, is said by Ames to render the Zen joy of aesthetic experience more accessible (1962, 258–59). For Ames, the social formation of selfhood in both Confucianism and Zen Buddhism is scientifically restated by Mead's genetic account of the self as it grows from taking the roles of others to joining them in a generalized other (1962, 278). Suggesting a broader application of Mead's pragmatism to the three great traditions of East Asian philosophy, he writes: "So, in Mead, the scientific West arrives at something like a fusion of the Confucian cultivation of virtue through the bonds of family and community, Taoist *laissez faire* and yearning for Nature, and Buddhist compassion for man's need of Nirvana" (1962, 278). Ames then underscores the central importance of Mead within the tradition of American philosophy as well as the similarity between the naturalistic framework of Mead and nondualistic worldview of Zen in that both account for the social formation of self without any reference to a transcendent or supernatural principle:

> The striking thing about Zen, to an American, is that it is a religion, or a way of life in place of religion, which denies the dualism associated with religion in the West, and is entirely naturalistic. In America, a similar position was finally reached most clearly and convincingly by the Chicago philosopher George Herbert Mead (1863–1931). He disposed of dualism by accounting for the human self without any transcendent or supernatural principle. The whole course of American thought leads up to his achievement. (1962, 5)

A significant limitation of Van Meter Ames's study, as for all the other scholars examined above, is that he applies the framework of Mead and American pragmatism to only the traditional Zen concept of self without considering the major systematic theories of Zen selfhood which have emerged with the renaissance of speculative thought in twentieth-century Japanese philosophy. By restricting his comparison only to traditional Zen Buddhist formulations of the self as negatively expressed in terms of *muga* (Skt. *anātman*) or "selflessness," Ames is finally led to the erroneous conclusion: "Yet, the importance of the self, for Mead, seems to stand in contrast to the 'selflessness' aimed at by all branches of Buddhism" (1962, 287). Indeed, by ending his comparative study with the conclusion that Mead's ideal of the social self stands in contrast to the Zen ideal of "selflessness," Ames has undermined his own thesis that there is a striking parallel between the two! However, a distinctive trait of twentieth-century Japanese philosophy is the effort to overcome nihilistic concepts of selfhood expressed simply in negative terms as *muga* or "no-self" for a more positive idea of the person as an ideal social self arising through a dialectic of self-other relations. For Watsuji Tetsurō the goal of human existence is to become a "person" (*ningen*) while for Nishida Kitarō the highest good is the achievement of "personality" (*jinkaku*). Watsuji clarifies how Japanese personhood as *ningen* has two aspects, the "individual" and the "social," while Nishida describes the double structure of personhood as a social self (*shakaiteki jiko*) arising through a dialectic of I and Thou (*ware to nanji*). Thus, while the notion of a social self with the two poles of individuality and sociality was implicit in traditional Zen Buddhist discourse, it becomes explicitly thematized only in the writings of twentieth-century Japanese philosophy.

In the preceding discussion I have summarized applications of Mead's framework to Confucian, Zen, and Japanese concepts of self made by scholars representing a wide variety of disciplines ranging from philosophy, theology, and cosmology to sociology, anthropology, and social psychology. From this has emerged a more unified vision of how Mead's social-self theory and I-Me dialectic can function as an interdisciplinary transcultural framework by means of which to interpret the Japanese self in its multidimensional aspects. However, in what follows I would like to open up a new area for comparative studies: the application of G. H. Mead's communicative interaction theory of self to those fully explicit models of the social self which have been formulated in modern Japanese thought, including Watsuji Tetsurō and Nishida Kitarō in modern Japanese philosophy and Doi Takeo in modern Japanese psychology.

# ॒9॰

## The Social Self in Mead and Watsuji

### Mead's Social Self Theory and
### the Ningen Model of Watsuji Tetsurō

Even at first glance it is evident that both G. H. Mead in American pragmatism and Watsuji Tetsurō in modern Japanese philosophy have independently converged upon an intersubjective communication model of the social self based on a dialectic of self-other relations. It should first be pointed out that Watsuji's radical "turn" (tenkō) from romantic individualism to a socio-ethical standpoint is to be understood as corresponding to what Hans Joas (1993, 24) has aptly called the "social turn" in the Meadian tradition of American pragmatism. Also, Mead's notion of the social self at once suggests a fascinating parallel to Watsuji's Zen/Confucian concept of Japanese personhood as ningen. Both thinkers establish the social character of the human self. Mead writes that "Any self is a social self" (SW 292). Similarly, Watsuji asserts: "Man is essentially social, or relational" (1961,138). Watsuji's clarification of the double nature of human existence as ningen based on the aidagara theory of self-other relations functions to illuminate the bipolar structure of Mead's social self as an I-Me dialectic and vice versa. Just as Watsuji's analysis of the two Sino-Japanese characters making up the word ningen reveals the person to have a twofold nature insofar as it is both an individual and a part of society, so for Mead the social self has a bipolar structure constituted through a dialogical conversation between the I or individual pole and the Me or internalized social pole: "The self is both the 'I' and the 'me'; the 'me' setting the situation to which the 'I' responds" (MSS 227). Again, he asserts: "Both aspects of the 'I' and 'me' are essential to the self in its full expression" (MSS 199). Likewise, in his Ethics (Rinrigaku, 1937) Watsuji explains the double structure of ningen as both "individual" and "social" when he writes: "The concept of ningen (person) is therefore different from anthropos, in that it is defined through its twofold character (*nijū seikaku*) as both 'society' (*yo no naka*) and the 'individual' (*hito*)" (1937, 14–15). And elsewhere in the same text he states; "A man must be able to exist both as an individual and as a social being. The word which best expresses this twofold character (*nijū seikaku*) is the word *ningen*" (1937, 9). The two pictographs standing for the "individual" and "society" which together compose the Japanese term *ningen* or "person" at once enables us to clearly visualize the Meadian concept of a social self with its two components of I and Me. Conversely, Mead's bipolar notion of the social self provides the best Western framework for understanding Watsuji's twofold *ningen* concept of the person. Like Mead's idea of the social self as an I-Me dialectic, Watsuji's *ningen* concept of man undercuts the conventional dualism of self/society and elucidates the twofold nature of personhood as an individual-society interaction.

The parallel between Mead's social self-theory and Watsuji's *ningen* model of personhood can be further elucidated through its reconstruction in terms of a concept of Japanese selfhood as *kanjin* or "contextual persons" developed by the sociologist Hamaguchi Eshun (1977, 1985) and Kumon Shumpei (1982). Peter N. Dale has dismissed Hamaguchi's idea of *kanjin* as being tantamount to a mere play of words, or as it were, a "trick of semantic juggling which presumes to make an advance on Watsuji's formulation of *ningen* as *hito no aida*" (1986, 220). Yet Hamaguchi's *kanjin* theory of Japanese personhood is in at least one respect similar to the social psychology of Mead. It should be recalled that Hamaguchi endeavors to reformulate Watsuji's idea of *ningen* in terms of his own sociological theory of Japanese contextual persons wherein the order of the two characters of *ningen* (= individual + society) are reversed to make *gennin*, originally pronounced *kanjin* (= society + individual), thereby to accord a stronger priority of social relations over the individual. According to Hamaguchi, the *kanjin* theory of selfhood explicates how the context of one's *ie* or family household unit always takes priority over the individual in Japanese society, as seen by the fact that the Japanese say their family name first and their given name last, the whole always preceding the parts. Similarly, in *Mind, Self, and Society*, Mead asserts: "For social psychology, the whole (society) is prior to the part (the individual), not the part to the whole; and the part is explained in terms of the whole, not the whole in terms of the part" (MSS 7). Although the social self of Mead, like the *ningen* concept of personhood developed by Watsuji, conceives the self as an individual-society nexus, there is an important sense in which a primacy is accorded to society over the individual. W. C. Tremmel asserts: "In this kind of thinking Mead is an innovator. . . . The thinkers who preceded him generally conceived of society as a group of interrelated individuals. Mead everywhere insists on the primacy of society. An individual is merely an abstraction from a social group" (1957, 12). Bernard Meltzer (1972, 11) argues that Mead's book *Mind, Self, and Society* (1934) should really be entitled *Society, Self, and Mind*, since individuals are always born into a society, and that is what gives them such human characteristics as self and mind. Meltzer's suggestion that the title of Mead's work should be reversed in order to express the primacy of society over individual minds and selves is thus consonant with Hamaguchi's notion of *kanjin*, which likewise reverses Watsuji's *ningen* concept of personhood so as to underscore the primacy of the social over the individual aspects of the human self. At the same time it should be emphasized that for Mead, society has priority over the individual only in the *genetic sense*, insofar as the latter always emerges from out of the former and not vice versa. Yet at the dialectical level of analysis, the I and the Me are co-relative terms so that there is a full parity between the individual and the social components of the social self. Again, Mead constructs a liberal democratic theory of selfhood wherein the social Me is always the servant of the individual I. While the self emerges from out of its deterministic social environment inherited from the past as a Me, it then responds to this situation in the present with spontaneity, creativity, and freedom as an I. Hence, in this sense Mead ultimately accords a priority of the individual freedom of the I over the social determinism of the Me in his bipolar model of the human self.

One of the most significant parallels is that both Watsuji and Mead underscore the idea of "betweenness" as a basic category of the social self. Watsuji clarifies that the second of the Sino-Japanese characters making up the word *ningen* or person, that of *gen*, can also be pronounced *aida*, meaning "betweenness." In terms of the structural resemblance of Mead's social-self theory to the framework of Martin Buber discussed by such thinkers as Paul Pfuetze (1973), it becomes clear that for both Mead and Buber in the West, selfhood is to be found precisely in the *betweenness* of I and Other, what for Buber is the between of I and Thou and what for Mead is the between of I and Me. It has been seen that the counterpart to Watsuji's dialogical principle of *aida* or "betweenness" in Mead's theory is what the latter refers to as his "principle of sociality," defined in *Philosophy of the Present* (1932, 47) as the stage of "betwixt and between" the old system of the social environment as represented by the deterministic Me pole and the new system of the emergent individual as represented by the spontaneous I pole. Watsuji locates the self neither in the individual nor in society but in the *aidagara* or "betweenness" of persons. Similarly, instead of focusing on individual personality or on how the deterministic social situation causes individual behavior, the social psychology of Mead focuses on the dynamic process of *interaction* which occurs "between" persons in the social act of communication itself. As J. M. Charon (1989, 22) asserts in his book *Symbolic Interactionism*, this focus on the process of "interaction" between the individual and society is a distinguishing characteristic of the Meadian tradition of symbolic interactionism in American sociology. It can be said that this focus on communicative interaction between persons through an analysis of what Mead calls the interspace of "betwixt and between" and what Watsuji calls the interspace of *aidagara* or "between-ness" initiates a whole new orientation for the study of the human self in philosophy and the social sciences. For both Watsuji and Mead, then, human existence is located on a continuum between two poles, for Watsuji between the individual and social poles of the person as *ningen*, and for Mead between the I and Me poles of the social self as an individual-society interaction.

Finally, both Mead and Watsuji clarify not only the social nature of the self but also the social origin and formation of the self through a developmental process. For both Watsuji and Mead, the social self is not given at birth; it is as an *achievement* which is realized through a developmental process of moral socialization. Similar to Watsuji's Zen/Confucian *ningen* model whereby the self develops by gradually incorporating various familial and social groups so as to embody an ever-expanding web of human relationships in the process of achieving true personhood, for Mead the individual becomes a social self only by taking on the multiple roles, attitudes, and perspectives of the Me or generalized other, which means to enter into the perspective of the family, the community, and other social groups, thereby to internalize the norm-governed behavior of society, the laws and institutions of the state, the customs and rituals of tradition, the rules of the game, and so forth. The Confucian idea of self-development adopted by Watsuji is scientifically restated by Mead's empirically based genetic account of the social formation of selfhood in progressive stages through the mechanism of role-taking. Both Watsuji and Mead develop a nondualistic framework which accounts for the social nature, origin, and development of selfhood without any reference to a transcendent or supernatural principle. Just as in the humanistic Zen/Confucian framework of Watsuji the aim is to overcome individualism and become a true person as *ningen*, in the naturalistic and secular framework of Mead the goal of the developmental process is to become a social self by taking on the roles of others in the community. Hence, both Mead's social psychology and Watsuji's Zen/Confucian framework are ultimately directed toward the end of becoming fully human as an ideal social self which arises through communication with others in society.

## An East-West Contextualist Paradigm
### of the Social Self

At the most general level of analysis, both G. H. Mead and Watsuji Tetsurō have framed a "contextualist" model of personhood based on an underlying root metaphor of the "social act." In the West, Stephen C. Pepper has classified American pragmatism under the contextualist paradigm, while in Japan, the *ningen* concept of Japanese personhood, first explicated by Watsuji Tetsurō and then further developed by such thinkers as Kimura Bin, Hamaguchi Eshun, and Kumon Shumpei, has also been frequently described as a form of "contextualism" (*kanjinshugi*). The contextualist model of self, both in its American and Japanese philosophical variants, argues that the self is not a separate ego with independent existence, but is always to be understood in terms of the relationships between an individual and its social context. Mead's contextualist model of the social self is rooted in his principle of "sociality," just as Watsuji's contextualist model of the person as *ningen* is grounded in the Buddhist principle of *śūnyatā* (J. *kū*) or "emptiness" as dependent co-arising. As I suggest elsewhere in this work, Mead's principle of sociality is a Western functional equivalent to the Buddhist principle of *śūnyatā*, whereupon the self and all phenomena arise through their social relations to others and are void or empty apart from these relations.

According to Stephen Pepper's typological classification scheme as developed in *World Hypotheses* (1942), there are four basic "world hypotheses": (1) formism (Aristotle, Plato, Scholasticism); (2) mechanism (Descartes, Locke, Hume); (3) contextualism (Peirce, James, Bergson, Dewey, Mead); and (4) organicism (Hegel, Bradley, Royce). These four world hypotheses are in turn correlated with four underlying "root metaphors": (1) similarity; (2) the machine; (3) the act; and (4) organicism. The root metaphor underlying the contextualist paradigm is identitfied by Pepper as "the historic event," otherwised termed *the act*. Pepper states: "We may call it an 'act' . . . it is an act in and with its setting, an act in its context" (142, 232). The basic categories of contextualism are identified by Pepper in process terms as those of *change* and *novelty* (1942, 235). When further specified these categories are exhibited as details within other categories which he terms quality and texture. The quality of a context is its *felt wholeness*, the "fusion" of its details into a novel and emergent unity, whereas the texture is the details and relations which make up its qualitative wholeness (1942, 238). Pepper explicitly places Mead and the other American pragmatists in the contextualist paradigm: "Contextualism is commonly called 'pragmatism.' It is associated with Peirce, James, Bergson, Dewey, Mead" (1942, 141). Evaluating the achievements of the individual pragmatists, he then asserts: "Peirce and James intuited the pragmatic, or contextualistic, root metaphor . . . As pragmatists their cognitive achievements were probably inferior to those of Dewey and Mead, though as creative thinkers they were probably superior" (142, 107). Mead himself argues that insofar as mind and self arise through a social act of communication with others in society, an individual is always to be defined in terms of his relation to social context. In Mead's words: "Mind arises through communication by a conversation of gestures in a social process or *context* of experience" (MSS 50; italics added). Furthermore, what Pepper identifies as the underlying root metaphor of contextualism, "the act," is the basic unit of human experience in Mead's pragmatism. As Mead writes in *The Philosophy of the Act*: "the unit of existence in human experience is the act" (PA 66). Again, he terms his basic unit the "social act" (PA 446). Mead calls the *act* or *social act* the "unit of existence," adding that "the act stretches beyond the stimulus to the response" (PA 65). Hence, for Mead the basic unit of human existence is a "social act," or as it were, an *act in context*, wherein all dualisms like stimulus-response, subject-object, organism-environment, or individual-society are to be regarded as functional distinctions within the present moment of immediate experience.

The Zen Buddhist model of personhood can also be be placed within the contextualist paradigm of selfhood. In accord with the Mahāyāna Buddhist philosophy of the Middle Way tracing back to Nāgārjuna, and ultimately to the Buddha himself, Zen Buddhism argues that the true self is neither an independent ego with atomic existence, nor an absolute self with eternal Being, but is instead a *relational self* which is always dependent for its existence upon a surrounding context, including society, nature, and the cosmos. As stated by T. P. Kasulis in *Zen Action/Zen Person* (1974), Zen Buddhism in Japan abandons the notion of self as an "individual" (*kojin*) for a Japanese notion of personhood as *ningen*, wherein the self is always related to its social context:

> *Ningen* is also a popular equivalent for "human being" or "man." . . . Following our analysis of the constituent characters [of *ningen* ], when the Japanese see someone as an "individual" (*kojin*), they see him or her as one object among many, but when they see someone as a "human being" (*ningen*), they see that person in a context. From the Japanese point of view . . . the person is *always* in a context, in a necessary relationship with what is around him or her. (1974, 6)

Similarly, in the twentieth century, the *ningen/kanjin* model of personhood formulated by Watsuji Tetsurō (1934), Kimura Bin (1972),

Hamaguchi Eshun (1977), Kumon Shumpei (1982), and other modern Japanese thinkers may also be classified under the world hypothesis of contextualism based on the root metaphor of a social act. Like Mead's idea of "contexts," "acts," or "situations," both Nishida's *basho* or spatial "locus" and Watsuji's *fūdo* or spatial "climates" have been seen to represent an ontology of social fields as the basis for a context-dependent model of selfhood. Hamaguchi Eshun articulates an explicit theory of Japanese selfhood based on the notion of *kanjin* or "contextual persons" governed by ritual interactions in social groups. In his book *Japan—Society of Contextualism (Kanjin-shugi no shakai nihon*, 1982), he develops a *nihonjinron* theory wherein the essence of "Japaneseness" (*nihonrashisa*) is to be found in the sociological principle of "contextualism" (*kanjinshugi*), which he posits in strong opposition to the Western concept of "individualism" (*kojinshugi*). Likewise, in "A Contextual Model of the Japanese" (1985, 299), he establishes a contrast between the Euro-American egocentric model of self as an "individual" (*kojin*) versus the Japanese model of self as "contextual" (*kanjin*). Hamaguchi cites both Watsuji Tetsurō's *ningen* theory and Kimura Bin's *aida* theory as exemplifications of this Japanese model of *kanjin* or contextual persons functioning as relational agents in society, whereupon he adds: "Let us use the term *kanjin* or 'contextual,' to conceptually distinguish the type of man who is a relational actor from the 'individual' or *kojin*" (1985, 300). Kumon Shumpei has also explicitly classified the *ningen/kanjin* model of personhood and its underlying principle of *aidagara* (= *aida*) as that of "contextualism." While Kumon translates Watsuji's notion of *aidagara* into English as "context," he translates Hamaguchi's term *kanjin* into English as "contextual" (1982, 19). Kumon points out that "the first author who made a systematic analysis of and theorized on the concept of 'context' (*aidagara*) on the basis of Watsuji's pioneering work (Watsuji, 1934) was Kimura Bin." Through a synthesis of Watsuji Tetsurō, Kimura Bin, Hamaguchi Eshun, Doi Takeo, and other modern Japanese authors, Kumon Shumpei formulates a "contextual" (*kanjin*) theory of the self in the Japanese *ie* or family household society based on the *ningen* model of personhood which emphasizes that the human being is always located within a surrounding "context" (*aidagara*). Kumon also refers to the "contextual" (*kanjin*) theory of personhood as a form of "Japanese pragmatism" (1982, 14). Like the Meadian concept of *multiple selfhood* as an ever-shifting plurality of roles and identities, Kumon's theory of Japanese contextual persons recognizes that the self is not an unchanging substantial entity, but a temporal process whereby a person is always created and recreated in each new social context into which it enters. Kumon therefore asserts: "A contextualist changes his identity depending upon the context he is in or who his companions are within a given context" (1982, 23). He further maintains that the Japanese contextualist model of selfhood represents a middle axiom between the individualist and collectivist positions. To repeat Kumon's words: "In contrast to both individualist and collectivist, a contextualist . . . identifies himself both in terms of the social relation or context (*aidagara*) to which he belongs and in terms of his personal self" (1982, 18). From the standpoint of an East-West comparative typology of the human self, then, both the "social self" theory of G. H. Mead in American pragmatism and the *ningen/kanjin* model of Japanese personhood can be subsumed under Pepper's world hypothesis of contextualism based on an underlying root metaphor of the "social act," wherein the person is always to be defined in terms of its relation to context.

Stephen Pepper (1969, 324) has further expanded his meta-philosophical taxonomy of world hypotheses and correlate root metaphors into a typological classification scheme for aesthetic theories of art and beauty. According to Pepper there are four world hypotheses in aesthetics: (1) formism, (2) hedonism, (3) organicism, and (4) contextualism. Each world hypothesis in aesthetics in turn has its own criterion of beauty: (1) similarity to type, (2) degree of pleasure, (3) organic unity, and (4) vividness of quality. Hence, in his philosophy of art Pepper has also developed contextualism as a world hypothesis in which the criterion for beauty is "aesthetic quality," that is, the immediately felt wholeness of a social context prior to subject-object dualism. Moreover, Pepper has extended the world hypothesis of contextualism into a cross-cultural paradigm of beauty under which he subsumes both the aesthetics of American pragmatism in the West and Zen Buddhism in the East (1969, 325). Zen Buddhism in Japan celebrates the natural aesthetic qualities of contextual events immediately experienced in their concrete "suchness" as expressed by the Zen understanding of *satori* or enlightenment as the realization that "willows are green, flowers are red." The return to the pervasive aesthetic qualities of immediate experience is likewise a recurrent motif in the tradition of American philosophy, including Peirce, James, Santayana, Dewey, Mead, Whitehead, and Hartshorne. Thus, just as the Zen tradition emphasizes the concrete, aesthetic immediacy of phenomena in their qualitative "suchness," the American philosophical tradition underscores the aesthetic experience of contextual events as directly felt in their qualitative immediacy.

In the construction of a cross-cultural typology of selfhood both Mead in American pragmatism and Watsuji in modern Japanese philosophy can be subsumed under the contextualist paradigm based on the root metaphor of the "social act," as well as the contextualist paradigm of beauty based on the criterion of "aesthetic quality." Just as Mead's social-self theory fits into the contextualist paradigm insofar as it signifies a context-dependent notion of personhood grounded in a root metaphor of the "social act," the consummatory phase of which is characterized by the aesthetic experience of qualitative immediacy, so Watsuji's *ningen* theory accords with the contextualist paradigm in that it is based on the principle of *aida* or "context," which pronounced as *ma* signifies a contextualist notion of beauty. At the level of value theory it has been seen that for both Mead and Watsuji all qualitative aesthetic experience is analyzed as a function of *sociality*, or the interaction between an individual and his entire social context of human society and living nature. Watsuji analyzes traditional Zen-inspired Japanese social art forms like the tea ceremony (*chanoyu*) and linked verse (*renga*) in which the aesthetic experience of beauty is co-created and shared together by a group of interacting persons. Also, it has been pointed out that the second of the Sino-Japanese characters making up the word "person" as *ningen* can also be pronounced as *ma* (= *gen, kan, aida*), which in the Zen tradition of Geidō or the religio-aesthetic Way of the artist is among the foremost principles of beauty in the traditional Japanese canons of taste. The Zen Buddhist religio-aesthetic principle of *ma* representing the space and/or time "in-between" all things and events unfolds the profoundly aesthetic dimension of human existence as *ningen* defined in terms of the *aida* or "betweenness" of persons. In modern Japanese philosophy Kumon Shumpei (1982, 19) explicitly translates the Watsuji's notion of *aida* (= *ma*) as "context." Building upon the thesis of Pepper, the Zen Buddhist *ma* aesthetic developed by modern Japanese thinkers like Watsuji Tetsurō, Kimura Bin, and Kumon Shumpei can be placed together with the pragmatists under the contextualist paradigm of beauty. Just as Watsuji underscores the religio-aesthetic mode of human existence as *ningen* through an analysis of traditional Japanese art and literary forms which express the interdependence of individuals and society, so Mead highlights the aesthetic, qualitative, and consummatory dimensions of the social self arising through a valuative transaction between an individual organism and its social environment. In the contextualist model of personhood developed by Dewey and Mead, the social self as an organism-environment transaction is always dependent for its existence upon a surrounding context, situation, or field of social relationships unified by an immediately felt pervasive aesthetic quality which makes it a unique whole and funds it with intrinsic value. For Mead (PA 3–25), the social self arises through an "act" of communicative interaction, with its four distinguishable phases of impulse, perception, manipulation, and consummation, the final or consummatory phase of which is an aesthetic experience characterized by qualitative immediacy. As A. J. Reck states: "The consummatory phase of the act has the immediate qualitative character of aesthetic experience" (see Mead SW, xxii). An "act" of social communication is therefore not just *instrumental*, a "means" to something else, but also *consummatory*, an "end" in and of itself. Mead's analysis of aesthetic delight as a "shared experience" arising through cooperation and mutual participation in a community, wherein the final consummatory experience comes not only at the end but pervades the whole creative process with the aesthetic enjoyment of immediate quality as an ends-means continuum, is itself one of the best perspectives by which to understand the Zen aesthetic of the tea ceremony and other social art forms analyzed by Watsuji in his classic studies of traditional Japanese culture. This emphasis upon the aesthetic or qualitative dimension of immediate experience rooted in the social, relational, and contextual nature of selfhood is characteristic of the whole tradition of American pragmatism as well as of Japanese thought and culture in general. Hence, like Mead's communication model of the bipolar social self, Watsuji's twofold *ningen* model of Japanese personhood represents a profoundly aesthetic mode of human existence wherein aesthetic quality arises through an interaction between the individual and its social context. Both Mead and Watsuji have thereby arrived at a contextualist model of selfhood as a *betweenness* of individual and its social context unified by a pervasive aesthetic quality.

This aesthetic value dimension of our East-West contextualist model of the social self can be encapsulated by means of the striking artisanal metaphor of "crafting" oneself which has been so skillfully employed by Dorine K. Kondo in her characterization of traditional Japanese selfhood. It should be recalled that in her book entitled *Crafting Selves* (1990), Kondo describes her field research at the Ethics School (*Rinri Gakuen*) in Tokyo which has developed a moral training program with the aim of "crafting" ideal social selves through relations with others. In this context she also speaks of "aesthetic self-realization in work," "creative self-realization through work," "polishing the self through hardship," and similar expressions which convey the Japanese artisanal notion of "crafting" a relationally defined self which is fluid, open, decentered, shifting, and multiple. It can likewise be said that the East-West Contextualist model of self exemplified by the frameworks of Watsuji Tetsurō in modern Japanese philosophy and G. H. Mead in American pragmatism is ultimately directed toward the goal of achieving personhood through the artistic process of "crafting" an ideal social self as an aesthetic unity of relationships between the individual and its surrounding context of society and nature.

## Individualism versus Collectivism in Mead and Watsuji

While there are many significant parallels between the social-self theories of Watsuji and Mead, the conflict between their respective frameworks is equally profound. Upon evaluating Watsuji's version of the contextualist paradigm from the perspective of Mead's social-self model, supplemented by an ideology critique of oppressive power relations as is carried out in the communication theory of Jürgen Habermas, vital questions arise with regard to individualism versus collectivism, liberalism versus communitarianism, freedom versus determinism, and relativism versus universalism. Insofar as Watsuji and Mead attempt to work out a Contextualist paradigm of the bipolar social self as an individual-society interaction they have both endeavored to forge a *via media* between the extreme positions of individualism and collectivism. In particular Kumon Shumpei (1982, 18) has emphasized how Watsuji's *ningen* concept of personhood represents a "contextualist" theory standing between the individualist and collectivist positions. But if Watsuji's *ningen* theory begins with an effort to balance the "individual" and "collective" aspects of personhood, it ends by falling into one-sided collectivism wherein the individual is all but completely submerged into the Japanese *kokutai* or national polity.

The reason why the views of Watsuji and Mead can both be located within the contextualist model of selfhood and yet still manifest this fundamental tension between individualism versus collectivism can be explained within the framework of Stephen Pepper's own meta-theoretical classification scheme of world hypotheses and root metaphors. According to Pepper (1942), while the world hypotheses of formism and mechanism are analytic and reductionistic in character, those of contextualism and organicism are synthetic and holistic. Moreover, he argues that although there is much in common between contextualism and organicism, they are to be distinguished by virtue of the fact that while the former is "dispersive" the later is "integrative." That is to say, while both contextualism and organicism elucidate the unity, wholeness, and connectedness of things and to this extent are synthetic paradigms, the contextualist moves in the direction of pluralism whereas the organicist instead moves in the opposite direction of monism. Pepper asserts that some thinkers ambiguously conflate the two paradigms and even cites John Dewey as an example of one whose philosophy sometimes inconsistently alternates between contextualism and organicism. From this standpoint it can be said that while the frameworks of Mead and Watsuji have been classified together under the Contextualist model of the social self as a twofold individual-society interaction, Mead emphasizes the creativity, spontaneity, and freedom of the individual so as to retain the pluralistic features of a genuine contextualism, while the latter instead underscores the aspect of sociality, collectivity, and group solidarity so as to approximate the monistic position of organicism or absolutism.

It should be added that in a latter essay Stephen Pepper (1961) expands his typological classification scheme to include a fifth root metaphor which better fits the position of A. N. Whitehead. Although previously Pepper regarded Whitehead as an eclectic thinker who oscillates between paradigms, in this essay he now suggests that Whitehead's organismic process philosophy instead represents a distinctive world hypothesis based on a new root metaphor; that of the *creative purposive act* of aesthetic events. Pepper writes that Whitehead takes as his ultimate model "a creative purposive act such as that of an artist, inventor or imaginative scientist" (1961, 86). For Whitehead, as for other classical American thinkers, the self is defined in contextualist terms as a sequence of historical events arising through an organism-environment interaction unified by an immediately felt aesthetic quality. Although there are many elements in common between the paradigms of contextualism and aesthetic creationism, the difference is that in the latter view the self is not constituted just by a mechanistic "adjustment" or "adaptation," but through a *creative response* of an individual organism to its social context in the self-creation of a novel and aesthetic occasion of experience. This fifth paradigm of aesthetic creationism based on the new root metaphor of a creative purposive act no doubt fits the thought of G. H. Mead better too. As emphasized by Hans Joas, the "'social' or 'intersubjective' turn" (1993, 250) of Mead's pragmatism represents the effort to formulate a new model of self as *creative action*, which is itself based on a new guiding metaphor of *creative problem-solving acts* in an experiment (1993, 247–48). The social-self models of both Zen and Mead can be subsumed together under the contextualist paradigm insofar the individual is defined by social context. Yet it will now be seen how in contrast to American thinkers like Mead and Whitehead, the Zen tradition of modern Japanese philosophy does not arrive at the paradigm of aesthetic creationism, whereby selfhood arises through the *creative responsiveness* of individuals to their social context.

In his book *Ways of Thinking of Eastern Peoples*, Nakamura Hajime clarifies how social context predominates over the individual in the traditional Japanese model of selfhood when he writes:

> Due to the stress on social proprieties in Japan another characteristic of its culture appears—the tendency of social relationships to supersede

or take precedence over the individual. . . . When this type of thinking is predominant, consciousness of the individual as an entity appears always in the wider sphere of consciousness of social relationships, although the significance of the individual is still recognized (1954, 409).

According to Nakamura, while both the individual and the social aspects of selfhood are recognized in the Japanese concept of selfhood, there is always a tendency for social relations to take priority over the individual. Moreover, he asserts that the Japanese tendency to privilege society over the individual is especially seen in their practice of rules of propriety (1964, 407). He views this Japanese system of proprieties governing all human relationships as being manifested in the strict monastic rules of the Sōtō Zen sect established by Dōgen, as well as the Confucian system of morality based on the principle of li or "ritual propriety" (1964, 408).

In *Zen Action/Zen Person*, T. P. Kasulis (1981, 1–9) also discusses the context-dependent model of the person in Zen Buddhism and traditional Japanese culture, analyzing the dual structure of selfhood based on the concept of *ningen* as signifying a relationship between individuals and their surrounding context. Kasulis rightly argues that from the Japanese point of view, the person as *ningen* is not primarily an "individual" (*kojin*) but is always located in a wider context. Expressing his essential agreement with Nakamura's account of the contextual nature of self in Japanese society, Kasulis writes:

> Nakamura's analysis agrees with our observation that while the "individual" (*kojin*) is a real entity, one most fully becomes a "human being" (*ningen*) when one is in relationship to one's surroundings. (1981, 9)

Kasulis further agrees with Nakamura that social context is accorded a definite priority over the individual in the Japanese *ningen* model of personhood. He thus asserts: "This brief investigation of Japanese linguistic and communicative modes leads the conclusion that in Japan the context is given primacy over the individual: the context defines and elaborates the individual rather than vice versa" (1981, 8).

This tendency to privilege the social over the individual is also clearly to be found in the Zen/Confucian *ningen* model of personhood articulated by Watsuji Tetsurō in modern Japanese philosophy. Although in Watsuji's *ningen* theory both the "individual" and "social" aspects of self are recognized, the individual is finally subordinated to its context of social relationships. Despite his effort to establish a contextualist paradigm representing a Buddhist "middle way" between extreme positions of individualism and collectivism, in the final analysis, the *ningen* model of personhood emphasizes the aspect of collective group-consciousness to the extent that the individual is submerged into the community. The *ningen* model privileges social solidarity over individual autonomy so that liberal values are collapsed into a communitarian framework. This tendency to subordinate the individual to the social group in Watsuji's *ningen* (individual + society) theory becomes even more evident through its reformulation by Hamaguchi Eshun in terms of a doctrine of *kanjin* (society = individual) or "contextual persons," in that the Sino-Japanese characters making up *ningen* are now reversed so as to further emphasize the priority of society over the individual.

In Robert Bellah's ideology critique of Watsuji's social philosophy he concludes that Watsuji's ethics highlights crucial problematics underlying Japanese culture in general:

> Watsuji's characterization . . . points to a crucial aspect of the problem of Japan's cultural identity. . . Individuals are defined fundamentally as group members and have no identity independent of the group. It is then our hypothesis that it is this tendency for the individual to identify with his role, his group, and his culture in a relatively undifferentiated way which accounts for the cultural particularism which was described at the beginning of this paper. (1965, 592)

According to Bellah, then, Watsuji's ethics reflects the general tendency of Japanese culture itself, wherein individuals are defined as group members and lack individual autonomy outside of the group.

It is precisely this direction of Watsuji's communitarian ethics of the Japanese family system based on the *ningen* model of personhood whereby the totality of social relations come to finally supersede the autonomy of individuals which can be rectified by Mead's Contextualist paradigm of the social self. In contrast to Watsuji *ningen* model whereby the individual eventually gets submerged into society, Mead's social-self theory preserves both the individual and social aspects of personhood through a dialectic of I and Me. While for Watsuji the individual aspect becomes subordinated to the social aspect of personhood, for Mead the individual "I" and social "Me" are irreducible functions of the social self in its wholeness. As held by R. N. Bellah (1965, 592), Watsuji's ethics points to certain problems of Japanese cultural in general, wherein individuals identify with their social roles to the degree that the self merges in collective group-consciousness. By contrast, Mead argues that while self arises by taking on the social roles of its group constituting the Me or generalized other, it then makes a spontaneous adjustive response as an I. The self incorporates the public institutions of society at the Me pole while continually reconstructing these institutions through creative activity at the I pole. It has been argued that Watsuji's dialogical principle of *aidagara* or "betweenness" is in certain respects analogous with Mead's principle of sociality, defined as the "betwixt and between" of the I and the Me. Yet the sociality of Mead is not only a relational principle of "betweenness" but also a principle of *adjustment*. In contrast to Watsuji's *aidagara* principle whereby the individual is dissolved into its context of social relationships, Mead's principle of sociality involves the spontaneous adjustment of the I or individual organism to the Me or social environment. According to Mead the individual arises from his deterministic social context as a Me and then reacts to it with spontaneity, creativity, and freedom as an individual I. In this way Mead's social-self theory overcomes the standpoint of Cartesian subjectivism without losing the creative agency of the I or unique individual.

Both Mead and Watsuji can be said to have developed a model of the social self based on communicative interaction between the individual and society. Yet as Habermas points out, a communication model of the social self must always be accompanied by a critical theory which aims toward the goal of emancipation from authority by undertaking an ideology critique of all oppressive power relations which systematically distort the process of communicative interaction. It has been seen how the scathing ideological critiques developed by such writers as Maruyama Masao, Ienaga Saburo, Arima Tatsuo, Tosaka Jun, and others in Japan along with those of Robert Bellah, Gino Piovesana, Peter Dale, and others in the West, have all argued that Watsuji's *ningen* model ultimately collapses into an impossible totalitarianism wherein the individual is oppressed by the coercive powers of the state. Watsuji's political thought has been characterized as an "emperor-system fascism" by Bellah (1965, 593–94) as well as a "totalitarian state ethics" by Piovesana (1968, 143)" and Dale (1986, 218). According to critics like Dale, Watsuji's moral system based on the *ningen* concept of man as a "totalitarian state ethics" and "fascist ideology" wherein subject and object are merged and the individual is dissolved into the greater whole of the nation. Watsuji's ethics of the Japanese *ie* or "family household" system is developed in ultra-nationalistic terms so that filial piety or reverence for parents is now identified with loyalty to the Emperor. The individual is emptied into increasingly larger household groups, finally being emptied into the imperial household of the Japanese nation-family (*kokka*). Watsuji uses the Bushidō warrior ethic based on ideals of "self-negation" (*jiko hitei*) and "the absolute negativity of the subject" (*shutai no zettaiteki hiteisei*), wherein the Japanese soldier resolves to sacrifice his life for the sake of the imperial sovereign out of loyalty to the

Japanese *kokutai* or national polity. His *ningen* concept of personhood and ethics of the Japanese family system is ultimately grounded in a Buddhist metaphysic of *kū* or "emptiness" with its Zen logic of double negation. To repeat Watsuji's own words from the *Ethics*: "This twofold negation establishes the dual structure of the person as *ningen* . . . The individual (*kojin*) and the whole (*zentai*) are both in their true nature empty (*kū*), and this emptiness is itself the absolute totality (*zettaiteki zentaisei*)" (1937, 26–27). The person as *ningen* is both individual and social in nature precisely due to this self-negating function of *kū* or emptiness, the "absolute negativity" (*zettaiteki hiteisei*) or movement of double negation whereby society and the individual are both "emptied" into the "absolute totality" (*zettaiteki zentaisei*) (1937, 26–27). It is through this mutual emptying of self and society whereby the individual is finally "emptied" into the whole of the *kokutai* or national polity of the Japanese state.

While the *ningen* theory of Watsuji is used to support a totalitarian state ethics of the emperor system based on an ideology of the Japanese *kokutai*, Mead's social-self theory is instead used as the basis for his political theory of a liberal democratic society. Mead (MSS 281–89; 327–28), like Dewey and others in the Chicago school of American pragmatism has developed a social-self theory as the groundwork for a political vision of a liberal democratic society based on the self-determination of free and equal individuals through open communication and public discourse which has been emancipated from all oppressive power relations of coercion, dominance, and authority. Mead's political doctrine of a liberal democracy, like his discourse ethics, is built upon his communication theory of the social self based on the notion of *perspectivism* or "perspective-taking." Through communicative interaction the social individual is able to put himself itself into the multiple perspectives, attitudes, and roles of every other participant in the legislative process, thereby to meet the *general interests* of all in the community. The democratic society envisioned by Mead is based on his utopian ideal of "universal discourse" (MSS 327), or what in the universal pragmatics of Habermas (1989, 96) is called the ideal speech situation and ideal communication community based on ideal perspective-taking, the system of communication carried through and made theoretically perfect in which each person can enter the perspective of all other selves in the formation of universalizable principles of democracy, laws, and ethical norms. Mead is critical of American liberal democracy in its present form insofar as it has yet to realize this ideal level of open communication through perspective-taking: "As democracy now exists, there is not this development of communication so that individuals can put themselves into the attitudes of those whom they affect" (MSS 328). He adds,

"If communication can be carried through and made perfect then there would exist the kind of democracy to which we have referred" (MSS 327). Mead's concept of a liberal democratic society overcomes the problem of abstract individualism, not by the subordination of its members to a collectivity, but through a democratic process of mutual participation, valuative transaction, universal discourse, cooperation, shared experience, and communicative interaction between individuals in an open society. Mead asserts that the liberal democratic consensus-formation process whereby agreement is achieved requires that each participant always consider the meaning of an issue both to themselves as an individual and to the collective whole of society: "This is what democratic government means, for the issue does not actually exist as such, until the members of the community realize something of what it means to them *individually* and *collectively*" (SW 257; italics added). Mead's political ideal of a liberal democracy thus aims to provide a standpoint for overcoming the extreme positions of both abstract individualism and abstract collectivism.

It should further be emphasized that Mead's notion of liberal democracy repudiates any concept of a fixed political order grounded in an absolute source of authority, whether it be the God of Christianity or the divine emperor and imperial household descended from the Sun Goddess, holding instead that all political and social institutions arise through the secular human community and are therefore always subject to constant change and reconstruction through the self-corrective experimental method of science. Or in terms of his I-Me dialectic of intersubjectivity, the social self arises by internalizing the public institutions of society at the Me pole, and then continually reconstructs those institutions through creative adjustments at the I pole. Hence, in Mead's liberal democratic vision of man, the Me or social pole is always to be understood as a servant of the I or individual pole of the social self.

## Liberalism versus Communitarianism in Mead and Watsuji

Closely related to the individualism versus collectivism problem is the liberalism versus communitarianism debate. Communitarians like Alistair MacIntyre, Michael J. Sandel, and Charles S. Taylor argue that the tradition of liberalism from Kant to Rawls is based on an overly individualistic notion of selfhood and an inadequate notion of community as a mere contractual association of atomic individuals. In terms of this latter issue it can be said that while both Watsuji and Mead have developed a social concept of personhood, the *ningen* theory of Watsuji stands on the side of communitarianism while the social-self theory of Mead stands on the side of liberalism. As asserted by Gino Piovesana (1969, 137), Watsuji's moral thought essentially represents a system of "communitarian ethics," while at the same time expressing a strong bias against "individualistic ethics," which he held to be a result of bourgeois egoism. In the *Ethics* Watsuji argues that his moral theory based on the *ningen* concept of personhood is oriented to a form of "communal existence" (*kyōdō sonzai*) (1937, 5). As opposed to a liberal ethics based on the primacy of individual rights, Watsuji thus establishes a communitarian ethics of the Japanese *ie* or household system based upon the primacy of obligations, duties, and commitments within the family-structured social group to which one belongs.

In *Fūdo* (WTZ VIII, 7) Watsuji defines the relational existence of *ningen* in a climate of social space in terms of "I as a We and We as an I" (*wareware de aru tokoro no ware, ware de aru tokoro no wareware de aru*). The basic unit of the Japanese self is therefore "We" (*wareware*). Watsuji's definition of the Japanese self as grounded in a We-consciousness is of course a mere restatement of Hegel's (1977, 110) definition of absolute Spirit as "'I' that is 'We' and 'We' that is 'I'" (*Ich, das Wir, und Wir, das Ich ist*). It is clear that both Mead and Watsuji have been influenced by Hegel's social concept of self as a dialectic of self-other relations. Just as for Mead the social-self is defined as an *I-Me relation*, for Watsuji and Hegel the social self is an *I-We relationship*. But as argued by Dale (1986, 221), both Watsuji Tetsurō's idea of *ningen* as an I-We relation and the Hegelian concept from which it was derived represent a deterministic theory of totalitarian state ethics. For Watsuji no less than for Hegel the individual I is submerged into the collective We so as to collapse into a totalitarian statism.

In contrast to the communitarianism of both Hegel in the West and Watsuji in the East, Mead along with Dewey and other Chicago school pragmatists stands within the tradition of American democratic liberalism emphasizing the primacy of individual rights. However, while Mead's thought can be said to represent a political theory of democratic liberal individualism, it is not an *abstract* individualism, or the notion of atomic individuals bound to others only through a legalistic social contract. As opposed to the abstract liberal notion of an atomic individual who enters into a social contract with others motivated solely out of considerations of "self-interest" (Hobbes), or "natural rights" to self-preservation and private property (Locke), the liberal democratic notion of personhood developed by Mead involves a fully social concept of self as an I-Me dialectic of intersubjectivity. Mead's liberal democratic notion of the social self also stands in contrast to the liberal individualism of John Rawls. In *Liberalism and the Limits of Justice* (1982) Michael J. Sandel argues that the liberalism of Rawls as developed in the latter's *A Theory of Justice* (1971) is based on a set of implausible metaphysical views about the self. Sandel criticizes Rawls's liberal individualism from the standpoint of what he calls the *sociological objection*, which claims that liberalism is wrong because "It misunderstands the fundamentally 'social' nature of man, the fact that we are conditioned beings" (1982, 11). Sandel's communitarian critique holds that Rawls's liberal theory of justice as fairness is self-contradictory in that it implicitly relies on an "intersubjective" and "social" concept of self which he officially rejects in favor of an individualistic notion of personhood (1982, 80). He furthermore questions Rawls's individualistic Kantian view of an "unencumbered self" or "disembodied subject" as possessing an identity prior to its membership in a community and prior to its socially given roles, ends, and relationships, arguing instead the self is always contextually embedded in its social roles.

One of the best overviews of this debate, "Assessing the Communitarian Critique of Liberalism" (1988) by Allen E. Buchanan, clarifies that while the liberal notion of selfhood tends to fall into an atomic individualism, the communitarian notion of selfhood typically collapses into a variety of social determinism or totalitarian collectivism. As Buchanan (1988, 853) further points out, a fundamental criticism which communitarianism levels against liberalism is that the latter devalues or neglects community, and community is a fundamental ingredient in the good life. Also, liberalism overemphasizes individual rights and liberties to the point that it fails to provide an adequate account of the importance of certain types of obligations, duties, and commitments, such as familial obligations and duties to support one's community or country. Liberalism wrongly exalts *justice* as being the "the first virtue of social institutions," failing to see that, at best, justice is a remedial virtue, needed only in circumstances in which the higher virtue of *community* has broken down. And most important for our present study, liberalism presupposes a defective conception of the self as a separate, atomic individual, failing to recognize that the self is partly constituted by its social relationships, ends, and commitments. On the other side, proponents of liberalism emphasize that communitarianism is always in danger of collapsing the individual into society so as to fall into the extremes of political statism, social determinism, and totalitarian collectivism. Buchanan asserts, "contemporary communitarians, like Hegel before them, run the risk of obliterating autonomy entirely and of dissolving the self into a concatenation of unreflective roles imposed by one's social position" (1988, 871). Thus, most of those who take up the communitarian critique of liberal individualism do not argue for a one-sided communitarianism, but instead endeavor to bolster the rights-based framework of liberalism with the duty-based framework of communitarianism based on a more intersubjective or social concept of the self. Buchanan argues for a position that would represent "a fruitful convergence of what is best in liberalism and communitarianism, not a victory of the one over the other" (1988, 882). Similarly, Amy Gutman (1985, 320) holds that "Communitarianism has the potential for helping us discover a politics that combines community with a commitment to basic liberal values" (1985, 320).

It can be said that while the moral theory of Rawls typifies the tendency for liberalism to fall into a one-sided individualism, the ethics of Hegel in the West and Watsuji in the East reveal the tendency for communitarianism to fall into a one-sided collectivism. However, Mead's social-self theory and I-Me dialectic provides a way beyond the impasse between liberal and communitarian views of selfhood. While the spontaneous I of the social self places a requirement upon us to protect those freedoms, liberties, and rights of unique individuals advocated by liberalism, the Me imposes those moral duties, commitments and obligations upon us as members of a social group emphasized by communitarianism. Mead therefore asserts: "Over against the 'me' is the 'I.' The individual not only has rights, but he has duties; he is not only a citizen, a member of the community, but he is one who reacts to this community" (MSS 196). Mead argues that the social self arises by taking on the roles of others in the community at the Me pole and then by reacting with spontaneity, creativity, and freedom at the I pole. In this way Mead's I-Me dialectic of intersubjectivity functions to bolster the autonomy-based framework of liberalism with the commitment-based framework of communitarianism. His account of how the self is constituted as a unity by taking on the attitudes of its whole community represented by the Me or generalized other provides for both a more social concept of self and a stronger theory of community as required by the communitarian position of Hegel and neo-Hegelians like Charles Taylor in the West or Watsuji Tetsurō in Japan. Yet as a representative of American liberal democratic individualism Mead holds that the Me or social aspect is always in the service of the I or individual aspect of the self. In this way Mead's bipolar concept of the social self as a dialectic of I and Me functions to overcome the liberal excesses of possessive individualism without going over into the opposite extreme of totalitarian collectivism. It is thus suggested here that Mead's idea of the social self as an I-Me dialectic provides a unifying model in which both liberal and communitarian values can be integrated, thereby establishing a true *via media* between possessive individualism on the one side and totalitarian collectivism on the other.

## Relativism versus Universalism in Mead and Watsuji

Another fundamental problematic in social and moral philosophy which emerges here is that of the conflict between relativism versus universalism, or as it were, relativism versus objectivism. It has been seen that Watsuji has been influenced by the Zen/Confucian ethics of Bushidō based on the ideal of "the absolute negativity of the subject" (*shutai no zettaiteki hiteisei*). As asserted by M. C. Collcutt (1983, 222) Watsuji argues that the core of the medieval lord-vassal relationship in the tradition of Japanese Bushidō was a "total, unconditional self-renunciation on the part of the follower to his lord." But like many Japanese wartime intellectuals, Watsuji makes an ultranationalistic application of this Bushidō ethic so that it now takes the form of self-sacrifice to the Emperor and the duty of loyalty to the Japanese *kokutai* or national polity. Bellah points out that in his political essay "The Way of the Subject in Japan" (*Nihon no shindō*, 1944), Watsuji begins by citing a standard definition of the Japanese military spirit: "to die happily for the sake of one's lord" (cited by Bellah: 1965, 579). By this application of the Bushidō ethic, the Japanese soldier is the self-effacing subject—the vassal or loyal retainer whose moral perfection lies in a resolution to sacrifice oneself for the sake of the Emperor and imperial household. Bellah thus asserts: "For Watsuji the core of ethical value in the Japanese tradition and the reason for its superiority to other traditions lies in the Way of Reverence for the Emperor" (1965, 579). Watsuji's group-centered communitarian ethics of the Japanese family system is therefore based on loyalty to the imperial household so that the virtue of "filial piety" is now identified with loyalty to the Emperor as supreme ruler of the Japanese "nation-family" (*kokka*). The Japanese familial or group-centered value system and Zen/Confucian Bushidō ethics of group loyalty adopted by Watsuji Tetsurō is in certain respects a form of *deontological* or "duty-based" ethics. In American pragmatism, G. H. Mead has also developed a revised Kantian theory of duty-based ethics. However, the problematic which emerges here is that while the Japanese Bushidō ethic based on the duty of loyalty, and the Kantian tradition of ethics adopted by Mead, can both be classified as a variety of a duty-based ethics, while the former moves in the direction of *moral relativism*, the latter instead signifies a position of *moral universalism*.

From the standpoint of an East-West comparative ethics it can be said that like the deontological ethics of Kant, and the Hindu ethics of *dharma* or "duty" expounded by the *Bhagavad Gita* in India, the Zen/Confucian warrior tradition of Bushidō represents a form of "duty-based" ethics. For the deontological ethics of Kant, moral worth is determined by acting on the basis of duty for its own sake without regard for the consequences of one's acts. Similarly, in chapter two of the *Bhagavad Gita*, Krishna instructs Arjuna that spiritual "liberation" (*moksa*) can be attained by the way of *karma yoga* or the "yoga of action," which involves acting in accordance with one's *dharma* or "duty" without attachment to the "fruits" (*phalam*) of one's actions. The Bushidō tradition of Japan is in some respects a virtue-based ethics which, like the Western tradition of Aristotle, Aquinas, and MacIntyre, aims to cultivate "virtues" or moral dispositions to act in ways that constitute human excellence such as courage, valour, fortitude, loyalty, and so forth. Yet in essence Bushidō represents a duty-based ethics wherein moral perfection is understood as acting in accordance with the social obligations of *giri* or "duty" as over against the private inclinations of *ninjō* or "human feeling." In his influential book entitled *Bushidō—The Soul of Japan*, originally published as an English work in 1905, Nitobe Inazō emphasizes the central role of *giri* or "duty" in the Japanese Zen/Confucian ethics of Bushidō, and above all else, the primacy accorded to the "duty of loyalty" (1969, 82–93). He points out that while the term *giri* literally means "right reason," it has come to mean "duty." Nitobe writes:

> I speak of *Giri*, literally the Right Reason, which came in time to mean a vague sense of duty . . . it meant duty, pure and simple,—hence, we speak of the *Giri* we owe to parents, to superiors, to inferiors, to society at large, and so forth. In these instances *Giri* is duty; for what else is duty than what Right Reason demands and commands us to do? Should not Right Reason be our categorical imperative? (1969, 25–26)

In this passage Nitobe suggests that the moral obligations of *giri* functions as a categorical imperative, a sense of duty which is determined not by self-interest or by private inclination but only by "right reason," thereby implying a parallel between the duty-based ethics of Bushidō and the deontological ethics of Kant. However, it must be emphasized that in contrast to the deontological ethics of Kant, according to which one's moral duty is prescribed by the universal principles of self-legislative reason carried out by autonomous agents, for Bushidō one's duty of loyalty is always relative to one's particular social group.

R. N. Bellah (1970) has underscored the absence of any universal ethic and consequent moral relativism which results from the family and group-centered value system of Japanese culture. Bellah asserts that in Japan, "Ethics consists mainly in acting as one should in one's group; there is no universal ethic" (1970, 117). Bellah elsewhere develops this moral relativism underlying Japanese groupism in terms of the concept of "particularism" (1965, 592). Despite the rhetoric of universal "compassion" (*jihi*) symbolized by the Bodhisattva ideal in romantic accounts of Zen Buddhist ethics, as it functions in Japanese groupism this compassion does not extend beyond members of a social group. The idea of compassion is therefore not universal but restricted to the particular social group to which one belongs. The sociologist Talcott Parsons clarified this point with his term *particularism,* and was subsequently applied to the relativistic Japanese group-centered value system by Bellah.

Commenting on Bellah's study, William Deal (1991) points out that Japanese ethics defines good and evil or right and wrong in terms of the social group as the primary frame of reference, not in terms of universal principles transcending the group, thereby falling into a dangerous position of moral relativism:

> The fact that values are recognized and realized in groups makes the ethical problem of good and evil a *relative* one for the Japanese. The *ronin* [masterless Samurai] acted in terms of their group context, not out of some underlying notion of absolute good or evil. . . . This is not to imply that the Japanese have no concept of good and evil or right and wrong, but rather that these are defined in terms of the group as the frame of reference, not as principle transcending the group. (1991, 239; emphasis added)

As the primary example of this kind of moral relativism implicit in the Japanese communitarian group-centered value system, Deal cites the Japanese Zen/Confucian Bushidō ethic of the Samurai warrior tradition, wherein the cardinal virtue is that of "loyalty" (*chūjitsu*) to one's particular social group. To illustrate the relativism underlying this kind of group-centered loyalty, Deal recounts the seventeenth-century incident which became the basis for a famous play, *The Forty-Seven Ronin.* A feudal lord angered by the humiliation he suffered at the hands of a government official, drew his sword in Edo castle. This act resulted in the lord's forced suicide. The lord's retainers, now *ronin* or "masterless Samurai," vindicated the death of their lord by assassinating the government official involved. The *ronin* themselves were forced to commit suicide because of their act, but not before proving their intense group loyalty. Upon evaluating the moral issues raised by this celebrated tale, Deal (1991, 239) remarks that these Samurai had no universal principle by which to judge whether their lord's action was itself right or wrong, but that their own sense of proper action was focused only by their group loyalty. He adds that this relativistic Samurai ethic of group loyalty was impressed upon the world by the unquestioning loyalty to the nation and emperor that led the World War II *kamikaze* pilots on their suicidal missions.

The ethical principle of Bushidō is the duty of loyalty as defined in existentialist terms by the "death resolve." That is to say, for the Samurai warrior tradition, moral worth is determined by the resolution to die for one's cause out of a duty of loyalty to the group. This resolution to die underlying Japanese Bushidō ethics has been concisely summarized by Roger T. Ames as follows: "The resolution to die of *Bushidō* can therefore be seen as a constant while the cause it serves is a historical variable. . . . The 'resolution' of *Bushidō* is ultimately mobile and neutral. It can be attached to any cause or purpose, no matter how trivial or contrary that might be to prevailing morality" (1980, 68). Hence, while the *resolution to die* underlying the Japanese Bushidō ethic is a constant, the *cause* to which it is applied has been an historical variable, ranging from medieval Samurai defending their warlords during the Tokugawa feudal period, to the *kamikaze* pilots of World War II, activists of the Red Army, extreme political factions, Japanese militarism, loyalty to the Emperor, and to this should be added, members of Yakuza crime families. The "death resolve" of Bushidō warrior ethics is therefore a neutral principle which can be applied to any cause whatsoever. In this way the standards for right and wrong or good and evil in the duty-based moral code of the Samurai tradition rooted in the underlying principle of a "death resolve" comes to be defined entirely *relative to one's social group* so as to lack any universally valid ethical norm which transcends that group.

Like Watsuji Tetsurō in Japan, the American pragmatist Josiah Royce became interested in the Bushidō duty-based ethic of loyalty and self-sacrifice as the basis of an idealist system communitarian ethics. Van Meter Ames (1962, 176n.) has pointed out that the source of Royce's interest in Bushidō was Nitobe Inazō's book titled *Bushidō—The Soul of Japan*, (1905), which appeared several years prior to the publication of Royce's *The Philosophy of Loyalty* (1908). R. N. Bellah (1965, 586) notes that it was upon reading this same work on *Bushidō* by Nitobe, who was among Watsuji's own teachers, which inspired the latter to take up his life-long investigation of traditional Japanese ethics. J. T. Kodera also makes this point, stating: "Nitobe's book on *Bushidō, The Soul of Japan*, began to awaken [Watsuji] Tetsurō not only to the Eastern heritage but also to the study of ethics" (1987, 6). However, whereas the Japanese Bushidō ethic of loyalty is relativistic in that it always has the family or group as its basic frame of reference, Royce's religious ethic of group loyalty is based on a universal moral order established by God, the Absolute. Watsuji's moral philosophy finally ends with a communitarian ethics of the

Japanese family system in which filial piety is equated with loyalty to the Emperor as supreme patriarch of the imperial household, whereas Royce instead develops a Christian universalist ethic based on the duty of loyalty to Jesus Christ and the embodiment of His presence in the Church as the beloved community. Royce maintains that the original sin of man is isolation, brought about by rebellion against the community which developed his reflexive self-consciousness, while atonement and salvation of the individual occurs through membership in a community. But for Royce, salvation does not arise from membership in any social group, including the military clans of the Samurai warrior; it comes only through belonging to the soteric community of the Church as the body and spirit of Jesus Christ. Hence, Royce's view might be compared to the Japanese Christian thinker Uchimura Kanzō (see Furukawa Tesshi: 1967, 237), and the novel entitled *Samurai* by Endō Shūsaku, insofar as both identify the spirit of Bushido with loyalty to Christ.

A universalist duty-based ethic has also been formulated by Royce's student G. H. Mead. But in contrast to the universalist Christian ethics of Royce, wherein an individual is born into a predetermined and eternally fixed moral order established by the absolute will of God, in the naturalistic, secular, and humanistic framework of Mead, the moral order is only found in social institutions arising from the human community, which are therefore always subject to change and reconstruction. Mead (SW 378–79) explicitly undermines this closed and dogmatic nature of Royce's universalist Christian ethics grounded in the metaphysics of absolute idealism in his essay, "The Philosophies of Royce, James, and Dewey in their American Setting." In contrast to Royce, the moral philosophy worked out by Mead in his essay "Fragments on Ethics" (1934, 379–89) and further developed by Jürgen Habermas in *Moral Consciousness and Communicative Action* (1990), endeavors to reformulate Kant's universalist ethics based on the categorical imperative in terms of an intersubjective communication paradigm of the social self. Kant's categorical imperative, which requires that the maxim by which one acts can be generalized into universal laws applicable to everyone, is no longer a monological procedure conducted by a solitary transcendental subject detached from society, but is now a *dialogical* procedure carried out by a social self within an intersubjective community through mutual participation and noncoercive open communication in public discourse. For Mead, as later for Habermas, the requirements for ethical conduct placed upon us by the categorical imperative can be fulfilled only through a developmental process of perspective-taking, wherein the individual perspective of the I goes outside itself by entering into the decentered social perspective of the Me or generalized other, and then by objectively evaluating a problematic moral situation from the standpoint of that other. Hence, in opposition to the moral relativism and particularism of the Japanese communitarian ethics of the family system whereby good and evil or right and wrong are defined in terms of the group as the frame of reference, in the "communicative discourse ethics" of Mead and Habermas they are instead defined in terms of *universalizable* or *generalizable* norms which transcend the group.

In conclusion, the fundamental problem facing an East-West transcultural paradigm of deontological ethics is that of establishing *normative grounds* for duty-based conduct. Although the *Bhagavad Gita* of India teaches a deontological ethic insofar as it is based on doing one's *dharma* or "duty" without attachment to the "fruit" (*phalam*) of one's acts, it lacks any universally binding legislative procedure for grounding those norms. For the *Bhagavad Gita*, "duty" is instead prescribed by the particular caste into which one has been born through the cause-effect law of *karma*. Since Arjuna is a member of the *kshatria* or warrior caste, he is told by Krishna that it is therefore his moral duty to take up arms against the opposing clan. And besides, we are told, since the *Ātman* or soul is eternal and imperishable, no one is really killed anyway! Both early Indian Buddhism and Jainism have severely criticized the Hindu caste system underlying the duty-ethic propounded by the *Bhagavad Gita*. It is significant that G. H. Mead has also criticized the caste system of India, stating: "The development of the democratic community implies the removal of castes" (SW 318). He argues that the caste system is a group-centered ethic, and that "hostility toward the person outside the group is essential to the development of the caste" (SW 318 fn.). In particular, he analyzes the warrior caste of India as a group which emerged from military conquest (SW 318–19). Hence, arguing from the standpoint of a liberal democratic vision of free and equal persons, he rejects the notion of caste as a basis for establishing universally valid normative grounds.

It has been seen that the Japanese Bushidō ethic is also a form of deontological ethics based on acting in accord with the social obligations of *giri* or "duty" as opposed to merely following the private inclination and self-interest of *ninjō* or "human feelings." However, the Bushidō warrior ethic of duty is grounded on loyalty to one's particular family or social group so as to lack any procedural justification for establishing universally valid norms as the basis of action. Bushidō therefore falls into moral relativism or particularism in that duty is always prescribed by membership in a group such as to lack universal principles transcending that group. In the West, it was Kant who articulated the first great system of deontological ethics wherein moral worth is determined by acting out of duty for its own sake without regard for private inclinations, self-interests, or the desired consequences of one's

The *Ningen* Paradigm of Selfhood of Watsuji Tetsurō

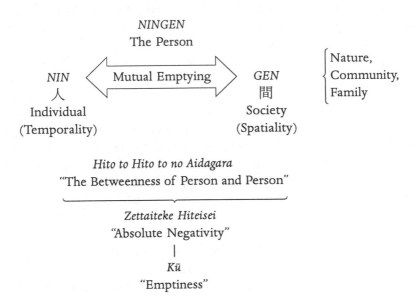

NINGEN
The Person

NIN     Mutual Emptying     GEN     Nature,
人                     間     Community,
Individual           Society     Family
(Temporality)       (Spatiality)

*Hito to Hito to no Aidagara*
"The Betweenness of Person and Person"

*Zettaiteke Hiteisei*
"Absolute Negativity"
|
*Kū*
"Emptiness"

The "Social Self" Paradigm of G. H. Mead
THE SELF AS SOCIAL PROCESS

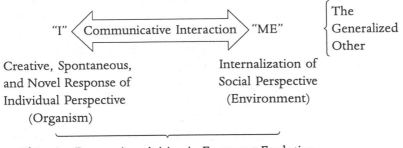

"I"   Communicative Interaction   "ME"     The
                                    Generalized
                                    Other
Creative, Spontaneous,     Internalization of
and Novel Response of     Social Perspective
Individual Perspective     (Environment)
(Organism)

Objective Perspectives Arising in Emergent Evolution
of Nature as Creative Advance

An East-West Contextualist Paradigm of the Social Self

acts. However, unlike the *Bhagavad Gita* in India or Bushidō in Japan, Kant provides a procedural justification for determining the normative grounds of duty, not by virtue of one's birth into particular caste or membership to a particular social group, but by the self-legislative reason of autonomous subjects who follow laws they give to themselves. In this context Kant sets forth his categorical imperative as a test procedure for moral norms based upon the criterion of *universalizability*. In recent American moral philosophy John Rawls (1971, 256) underscores the Kantian basis for his liberal theory of justice as fairness through his description of the original position as a "procedural representation" of the categorical imperative, wherein universalizability and impartiality as a test for moral norms is achieved by lowering a "veil of ignorance" over all participants in the original choice situation. But as pointed out by Michael J. Sandel (1982), a major problem in the liberalism of Rawls is that it is based on an individualistic concept of self which possesses an identity prior to its membership in any community and prior to its attachment to any specific ends.

By contrast, the discourse ethics of Mead and Habermas attempts to reconstruct Kant's categorical imperative as a test procedure for moral norms which is instead based on a fully social concept of selfhood and a strong theory of community. Mead agrees that the best procedure for establishing normative grounds is "Kant's rigorous but empty categorical imperative" (SW 379). Mead, followed by Habermas, works out a communicative discourse ethics based on a social reformulation of Kant's categorical imperative, whereupon it is transformed from the monological procedure of a transcendental subject to a dialogical procedure conducted by a social self which through perspective-taking enters into the position of all who would be affected if a given norm were put into action. Mead's attempt to work out a Kantian universalist ethics based on the categorical imperative within the context of his communication model of the social self thus presents a formidable challenge to the moral relativism characterizing the Japanese group-centered value system, including both the traditional duty-based Zen/Confucian warrior ethics of Bushidō and its modern restatement in Watsuji's communitarian ethics of the Japanese family system.

# ~:10:~

## The Social Self in Mead and Nishida

### Common Sources of Mead and Nishida

There is no question that significant parallels exist between G. H. Mead representing the Chicago school of American pragmatism and Nishida Kitarō representing the Kyoto school of modern Japanese philosophy. Nishida's recognition of Feuerbach's epoch-making turn from a monological to a dialogical concept of self as an I-Thou relationship can be said to correspond to the social turn initiated by Mead in classical American pragmatism. The *social turn* of Nishida in Japan and Mead in America is especially to be seen in the fact that both thinkers have independently converged upon an explicit theory of the social self based on a dialectic of I-Other relationships. These parallels between the respective social-self theories of Mead and Nishida can to some extent be accounted for in terms of those common sources which influenced both thinkers. Mead was a student of William James and Josiah Royce during his graduate years at Harvard University. Furthermore, Mead's social-self theory and self-other dialectic synthesizes fundamental notions derived from both James and Royce. While from James he adopted the concept of a social self with its two aspects of I and Me, from Royce he acquired his idea of the social self as an Ego-Alter dialectic and correlate theory of self-realization through the community. However, as was discussed previously, Nishida Kitarō has also been profoundly influenced by James and Royce in American pragmatism. Thus, from the very outset there has been a fundamental connection between modern Japanese philosophy and classical American pragmatism.

In his maiden work *A Study of Good* (*Zen no kenkyū*, 1911) Nishida developed his process theory of selfhood as a sequence of appearing and disappearing momentary events of "pure experience" (*junsui keiken*) devoid of subject-object dualism in the stream of consciousness under the influence of James. Like James, Nishida works out a focus-field model of the self. James describes his focus-field model of selfhood when he writes: "My present field of consciousness is a centre surrounded by a fringe that shades insensibly into a subconscious more . . . What we conceptually identify with and say we are thinking of at any time is the centre; but *our full self is the whole field*" (1966, 296; italics added). Here James clarifies that the self is not to be identified with the clear light of "consciousness" in the foreground focus of attention but in large part is constituted by the vague darkness of the *subconscious more* at the outermost fringes of the background field. Nishida follows James's analysis of the specious present which is not a knife-edge, but a saddle back which has both a rearward-going fringe of memory and a forward-going fringe of anticipation, thus constituting the continuity of self in a stream of consciousness. In his later work entitled *Fundamental Problems of Philosophy*, Nishida clarifies that what James calls the "fringe of consciousness" is in fact the locus of Nothingness located in the felt background of experiential immediacy: "William James wrote of a 'relational fringe of consciousness,' but the world of the present has an infinite fringe. Therein exists the word of infinite nothingness" (NKZ VII, 330). Nishida repeatedly uses the mystical image of self as a center surrounded by an infinite circumference to illustrate his idea of consciousness encircled by a boundless fringe of relationships. For Nishida, as for James, although we often identify the self with only the center, the true self is the whole field of causal relationships from which it has emerged. In his essay "The Philosophy of Nishida," Takeuchi Yoshinori writes: "According to Nishida . . . The self ultimately finds itself in the abyss of darkness. . . . The self is thus haloed with a luminous darkness" (1982, 183). Nishida, like James, thus describes the self as encompassed by a relational fringe, characterized as a halo of darkness in the background field which forever surrounds the luminous region of consciousness in the foreground focus of attention. Moreover, like James in American philosophy, Nishida goes on to explicate the social dimensions of this focus-field model of self, whereby the individual organism in the foreground focus is surrounded by a fringe of social relationships in the background field. While James introduces his notion of the social self in chapter 10 of *Principles of Psychology*, Nishida works out a doctrine of the social self (*shakaiteki jiko*) in *A Study of Good*. Just as William James regards his contextualist theory of self to represent a golden mean between atomism and monism, in chapter 26 of *A Study of Good*, Nishida develops a contextualist model of the social self as a middle position between "individualism" (*kojinshugi*) and "collectivism" (*kyōdōshugi*). Since it was through James that the notion of a social self acquired currency in twentieth-century philosophy, psychology, and sociology, I have suggested that Nishida not only borrowed James's notion of "pure experience," but also his concept of the social self.

As pointed out by Ha Tai Kim in his essay "Nishida and Royce" (1952), in *A Study of Good* Nishida not only works out a Jamesian notion of selfhood as a "pure experience," but also Royce's Hegelian idealistic concept of the person as a self-developing whole. Kim (1952, 20) further emphasizes that the very title of Nishida's book, *A Study of Good*, was itself inspired by the title of Royce's work, *Studies of Good and Evil*. Nishida's first public announcement of his indebtedness to Royce appears in the preface of his second major book, *Intuition and Reflection in Self-Consciousness* (*Jikaku ni okeru chokkan to hansei*, 1917), wherein moments of pure experience are now conceived of as voluntaristic acts of pure "self-consciousness" (*jikaku*). In this text Nishida works out Royce's idea of the "self-conscious individual" in terms of what he calls the "self-conscious system" (*jikakuteki taikei*) (Kim: 1952, 20). Similar to Royce's theory, Nishida argues that pure self-consciousness (*jikaku*) is a concept which accounts for the inner relationship between "intuition" (*chokkan*) and "reflection" (*hansei*). According to Nishida, "intuition" is an immediate consciousness of pure experience in which subject and object are not yet divided, while "reflection" is an ongoing consciousness looking upon itself as an object from outside this process (see Kim: 1952, 22). Both Mead and Nishida were thus influenced by Royce's idea of developing reflexive self-consciousness through a dialectical process between subject and object, what for Nishida becomes a dialectic between intuition and reflection, and what for Mead becomes a dialectic between I and Me. In addition to their common interest in the American pragmatism of James and Royce, both Mead and Nishida were also deeply influenced by the thought of various German social thinkers, including Hegel's self-other dialectic of mutual recognition, Dilthey's philosophical anthropology, and the social psychology of Wundt. It is against this common background that both Mead in American pragmatism and Nishida in modern Japanese philosophy came to work out their own cross-cultural variants of a social-self theory based upon a dialectic of I-Other relationships.

## The Social Self as an I-Other Dialectic in Mead and Nishida

For both Mead and Nishida the self is not merely given but is something which needs to be constructed through a developmental process of self-realization. Also, for both thinkers the process of self-realization is directed to the actualization of *personality*. In Nishida's *An Inquiry into the Good* he states, "The good is the actualization of personality" (1990, 142). He thus clarifies that the supreme good is the achievement of "personality" (*jinkaku*) and that personality is something which requires a process of "realization" or "actualization" (*jitsugen*). Likewise, it has been seen that for Mead "The self is something which has a development" (MSS 135). He further asserts that the developmental process of self-realization through linguistic communication is "the process by which a personality arises" (MSS 160). And as described below, for both Mead and Nishida the self-actualization of personality occurs precisely through the formation of a twofold social self by constantly reconciling the I and the Other, thus to integrate the individual and social, the subjective and objective, the mental and physical.

Both Mead and Nishida have abandoned the idea of an abstract individual Cartesian ego as posited by the philosophy of subject-centered consciousness for that of an intersubjectivist communication paradigm based on the idea of a social self. It has now been demonstrated that the social self is a technical term in the lexicon of both thinkers. Nishida first introduces his explicit notion of the social self (*shakaiteki jiko*) in his maiden work *An Inquiry into the Good* (1911), while Mead frequently uses the "social self" or "social selves" as the key notion of his entire philosophical system (see PP 194; MSS 204, 324; PA 429; SW 292, 357–59), and it is also the title of one of his most important essays, "The Social Self," first published in 1913, and now reprinted in *Selected Writings of George Herbert Mead* (SW 142–49).

Like Mead, Nishida understands the "social self" as arising through a process of interaction between the organism and the environment within a situational context, or what Nishida refers to as the "mutual determination" (*sōgo gentei*) of individual and environment in the locus of Nothingness, understood as the "determination of the individual-as-environment and the environment-as-individual" (NKZ VII, 169). Moreover, both Mead and Nishida have articulated the double structure of the social self as constituted by I-Other relations of intersubjectivity. "The I is an I by facing a Thou, and the individual is an individual by facing other individuals. The self must be social" (NKZ VII, 382). They reject the individualistic model of self as an atomic I or Cartesian subject for an intersubjective model of the social self as a relation of "I and Other," what Mead calls the relation of "I and Me" and what Nishida calls the relation of "I and Thou." Just as the social self of Nishida is intersubjectively constituted by a dialectical relation between I and Thou, so the social self of Mead (MSS 192–200) is described as arising through a dialectic between I and Me. Moreover, both Mead (MSS 162) and Nishida (NKZ VI, 347) argue that the interaction between self and other occurs through the intersubjective medium of language. Also, for both Mead (MSS 204) and Nishida (NKZ VII, 139) the person attains reflexive self-consciousness only through a Hegelian self-other dialectic of mutual recognition. This parallel between the bipolar social self and I-Me dialectic of Mead and the twofold social self and I-Thou dialectic of Nishida surely represents one of the most significant points of contact for East-West dialogue between American pragmatism and modern Japanese philosophy.

## The Social Field Theory of Existence in Mead, Nishida, and Watsuji

Another important parallel is to be found between Nishida's key notion of *basho* or "place" (field, locus, matrix, *topos*) and Mead's idea of an organism / environment "situation," or what he alternatively refers to through such holistic notions as the "social situation," "act," "context," "locus," "matrix," and "field." For Mead, as for Dewey and Whitehead, the social self arises through a process of valuative transaction between organism and environment within a holistic situation, context, or field of relations unified by pervasive aesthetic quality. In terms of the focus-field model of selfhood, the individual organism in the foreground focus and the social environment in the background field are pervaded throughout by a single unifying aesthetic quality which make the situation a whole and funds it with value. For Mead and the other American thinkers a "situation" is the basic unit of immediate experience which stretches beyond all dualisms like subject-object, organism-environment, individual-society, or foreground-background. Mead explains his concept of a social situation as an ontological field of relationships when he writes: "All living organisms are bound up in a general social environment or situation, in a complex of social interrelations and interactions upon which their continued existence depends" (MSS 228). The idea of a situation is what elsewhere Mead describes as the concept of social field or locus, stating: "If mind is socially constituted, then the field or locus of any given individual mind must extend as far as the . . . social relations which constitutes it extends" (MSS 223 n.). Hence, for Mead, as for Whitehead, the self cannot be "simply located" in that it both contains and pervades the whole spatio-temporal field of social relationships by which it has been constituted.

In his work *Toward a Philosophy of Zen Buddhism*, Izutsu Toshihiko explicates the "Zen image of man" in ontological terms as expressing the field structure of ultimate reality, whereby "The 'I' is a subjective crystallization of the entire Field" (1977, 51). Izutsu further states that according to the Zen image of personhood an individual is "a total actualization of the Field of Reality . . . a concentration point of the entire energy of the Field" (1977, 55). An individual articulated in the foreground focus of attention is always surrounded by a nonarticulated whole of Nothingness in the background field. Moreover, the subject-object dualism is to be understood as an abstraction or functional relation within this holistic field structure of the Zen self (1977, 54). It is precisely this ontology of fields which underlies Nishida's Zen concept of self in modern Japanese philosophy. In his later thought Nishida reformulates his idea of pure experience in terms of his Zen Buddhist notion of *basho*, or *topos*, the spatial field of Nothingness in which the "true self" is revealed. He goes on to apply the idea of *basho* to the social-historical world, whereupon it now comes to be understood as a spatial *topos*, the field of social relationships in which the self is intersubjectively constituted through the mutual determination of I and Thou. The "I" or individual organism in the foreground is determined by its relation to a "Thou" or the social environment in the background field. The close proximity of Mead to Nishida in this regard has been noted in passing by Arisaka and Feenberg (1990), who refer to Nishida's idea of *basho* or the *topos* of Nothingness as a "social field theory" (1990, 195), adding that "Social field theories appear increasingly in modern sociology, beginning with George Herbert Mead" (1990, 196). Just as for Mead the social self arises through communicative interaction between I and Me within a situational context, so for Nishida the social self emerges through mutual determination of I and Thou within the social field of a *basho* or spatial locus. Again, Nishida's idea of self as "the determination of the individual-as-environment" (*kobutsuteki gentei soku kankyōteki gentei*) (NKZ VII, 169) within the topos of Nothingness is reminiscent of Mead's notion of the social self as an organism-environment situation. Mead argues that the communicative interaction whereby the social self is constituted presupposes a contextual situation as the matrix of relationships in which such interaction can occur, while Nishida maintains that the mutual determination between individuals presupposes the locus for their mutual determination. Both the "situation" of Mead and the *basho* of Nishida represent a medium in which the social self arises as an individual-society interaction. By this view, ontological primacy is accorded neither to the individual as assumed by methodological individualism, nor to society as asserted by Hegel and Marx, but rather to the *social field* of relationships in which both the individual and society arise through mutual encounter.

This analogy between Mead's concept of the "social situation" and Nishida's idea of a spatial *basho* can be extended to the ontological notion of a *fūdo* or "climate" in Watsuji's social theory of existence. As pointed out by Dilworth (1974,14), Nishida's concept of the *basho* of Nothingness as the place of I-Thou relations worked out between 1927 and 1934 seems to have exerted some direct influence upon Watsuji's notion of a *fūdo* or "climate" as the spatial locus wherein the person as *ningen* arises through relationships between the individual and society. Among recent Japanese thinkers, Watsuji's theory of *fūdo* or "climates" has also been directly related to Nishida's concept of *basho* or spatial locus by Kimura Bin, especially in chapter 3 on "Climate and Human Nature" (*Fūdo to ningensei*, pp. 81–128) from his work entitled *The Betweenness of Person and Person* (*Hito to hito to no aida*, 1972), as well as by Yuasa Yasuo in his work *The Body* (1972, 65). Furthermore, the principle of *aidagara* or "betweenness" underlying Watsuji's *ningen* model of Japanese contextual persons and theory of *fūdo* or "climates" has been explicitly formulated by at least one scholar as a "social field" theory of human existence. Kumon Shumpei (1982, 12) specifies that Watsuji's concept of the person as *ningen* (individual + society) has as one of its basic meanings that of a human being or group of people "embedded in a social field (*aidagara*)." For Kumon, then, the person as *ningen* is always to be located in the "social field" of *aidagara*, a term which he otherwise translates as "context" (1982, 19). It should also be remembered that Watsuji's notion of the *aidagara* or "betweenness" of persons in a social field or context has been explicitly identified with with Nishida's idea of *basho* or the spatial locus for I-Other relations by scholars like Kimura Bin (1972, 65) and Yuasa Yasuo (1987, 38). Thus, by extending our comparative analysis yet further, it can be said that just as for Nishida the social self exists between the mutual determination of individuals within the spatial locus of a *basho*, and for Watsuji the person as *ningen* exists in the *aidagara* (context, social field) as an intersubjective "betweenness" of self and other within an encompassing *fūdo* or "climate," so according to Mead's principle of sociality the self exists "betwixt and between" the I and the Me within a relational field, context, or situation. The social situation of Mead, the *basho* of Nishida, and the *fūdo* or climate of Watsuji all function similarly to the extent that they signify the concept of a transpersonal locus in which the person arises through the mutual encounter between self and other. Hence, like Mead's concept of "situation," Nishida's idea of *basho* or "locus" and Watsuji's idea of *fūdo* or "climate" designate a social field theory of existence as the ontological basis for a contextualist model of selfhood.

## The Developmental Psychology of Zen and Mead

The application of G. H. Mead's communication theory of the social self and I-Me dialectic to both the traditional Zen concept of selfhood as well as its reformulation in the social-self theory and I-Thou dialectic worked out by Nishida Kitarō in modern Japanese philosophy can further be clarified through Ueda Shizuteru's interpretation of the *Ten Oxherding Pictures*. It has been seen that Ueda Shizuteru (1982), a leading scholar of Nishida Kitarō and a representative thinker of the Kyoto school, uses the famous *Ten Oxherding Pictures* to graphically illustrate the developmental stages in the Zen path of becoming a person culminating in the realization of a social self as an I-Thou relationship in the spatial *basho* or "place" of absolute Nothingness. According to Ueda's interpretation of the *Ten Oxherding Pictures*, diagrams 1–7 portray the ego-self at the standpoint of eternalistic Being (*u*), diagram 8 shows the negation or emptying of the substantial ego into *muga* or no-self at the nihilistic standpoint of relative Nothingness (*sōtaiteki mu*), whereas pictures 9 and 10 reveal the true self or selfless self of the compassionate Bodhisattva at the middle way standpoint of absolute Nothingness (*zettaiteki mu*). He further clarifies that the highest stage in the Zen path to enlightenment is not the dissolution of the substantial ego and breakthrough to the clear light of the void represented by the eighth picture, nor is it an aesthetic experience of unity between the self and nature represented by the ninth picture, but the realization of personhood as a twofold social self located in the *betweenness* of I and Thou within an intersubjective community as represented by the tenth and final picture.

It is my contention that Mead's developmental psychology of the social self, which explains how the social self arises through progressive stages of perspective-taking, is the best explanatory scheme by means of which to illuminate the development of the true self represented by the Bodhisattva ideal in Zen Buddhism as portrayed by the *Ten Oxherding Pictures*. The tenth and final picture of the Zen oxherding series as interpreted by Ueda in terms of Nishida's social-self theory and I-Thou dialectic is best understood in terms of the communication model of personhood articulated by the tradition of American pragmatism, especially Mead's concept of the social self as a conversation between I and Me. Nishida, like Watsuji, is influenced not only by the Zen concept of self as a field of relationships but also by the Confucian idea of self as an ever-expanding network of familial ties which embodies increasing larger social groups. Mead's developmental psychology based on the notion of role-taking clarifies not only the Zen process of becoming a person but also the Confucian idea of person making whereby the unity of the self is constituted by gradually taking on the roles of other selves and combining them all in a field of selves. In *Mind, Self and Society*, Mead argues that the "social self" is not given, but is instead something which requires a developmental process of socialization: "The self is something which has a development; it is not initially there, at birth, but arises in the process of social experience" (MSS 135). In his social psychology Mead works out an empirically based genetic account of the social nature, origin, and development of the self. He thereby shows the progressive stage-structures whereby an individual becomes a social self through gradually taking on the roles, attitudes, and perspectives of others in the community. Mead's developmental psychology of the social self based on the mechanism of "perspective-taking" or "role-taking" has exerted a significant influence on both L. Kohlberg's developmental stages of moral socialization as well as Jürgen Habermas's developmental stages of communicative competence. Habermas has worked out a general theory of communication based on a hierarchical model of levels of communicative competence which combines Mead's genetic account of the social self through perspective-taking with insights derived from more recent advances in developmental psychology, including L. Kohlberg's stages of moral consciousness, J. Piaget's stages of cognition, J. Loevinger's stages of ego development, and R. Selman's stages of interpersonal relations. This hierarchy of levels of communicative competence reflects progressive stages of perspective-taking that begin with the narrow egocentric perspective of individualism, and gradually unfold through increasingly complex I-Thou perspectives, finally culminating in the decentered or nonegocentric worldview represented by Mead's intersubjective paradigm of a social self in a norm-governed ideal communication community.

If viewed in a comparative light, the *Ten Oxherding Pictures* of Zen Buddhism as interpreted by the Kyoto school of modern Japanese philosophy may be seen as a fascinating pictorial analog to the hierarchy of evolving stage-structures whereby one achieves personhood through the moral socialization process as formulated by Mead's developmental psychology of the social self and its expansion into the communication theory of Habermas. Like Mead, the *Ten Oxherding Pictures* clarify that the self is not given but requires a developmental process of moral socialization. Also, similar to Mead the ninth oxherding picture shows the unity of individual and environment in the undivided aesthetic continuum of nature through the realization of pervasive aesthetic quality or suchness at the level of immediate experience. However, like Mead's developmental psychology, the *Ten Oxherding Pictures* culminate in the achievement of a decentered social self located in the *betweenness* of I and Other. Mead's developmental psychology, like the Zen process of becoming a person, the Confucian idea of person making, and their synthesis in modern Japanese thought, is ultimately directed toward the realization of one's true human nature as a twofold social self through a dialectic of I-Other relations. Hence, the present volume may be regarded as an effort to provide an interpretation of the Zen concept of personhood in modern Japanese philosophy as illustrated by the the *Ten Oxherding Pictures* from the standpoint of G. H. Mead's intersubjective communication theory of the social self based on a dialectic of I and Me.

## Individualism versus Collectivism

As is the case in our comparison of Mead and Watsuji, the parallel between Mead and Nishida raises a constellation of problems such as individualism versus collectivism and freedom versus determinism. With regard to the question of individualism versus collectivism there are certain respects in which Nishida's theory of selfhood more closely approximates Mead's concept of the social self than does the *ningen* model of Watsuji. Previously it was shown that although Watsuji begins with an effort to forge a middle way between individualism and collectivism with his twofold *ningen* concept of personhood located in the "betweenness" (*aidagara*) of the individual and society, it nevertheless ends by falling into a totalitarian statism wherein the individual is ultimately submerged into the collective whole of the Japanese *kokutai* or national polity. Nishida moves closer to overcoming the problem of individualism versus collectivism with his I-Thou dialectic of intersubjectivity. For Nishida, the "I" and the "Thou" are co-relative aspects of the social self in such a way that the individual and society are accorded an equal status. Furthermore, Nishida goes on to underscore the autonomy, the radical discontinuity, and the irreducible self-creativity of the individual "I" as over against the social "Thou" in the intersubjective constitution of selfhood. Thus, in contrast to Watsuji's *ningen* model of personhood, Nishida's social-self theory and I-Thou dialectic includes an element of *individualism*. This "individualism" (*kobutsushugi*) in Nishida's more personalistic account of selfhood has been emphasized by Kosaka Kunitsugu in his recent book *A Study of Nishida Philosophy* (*Nishida tetsugaku no kenkyū*, 1991). As pointed out by Kosaka (1991, 28), a critical essay by Tanabe Hajime on the thought of Nishida Kitarō ("*Nishida sensei no oshie o aogu*," 1930) even goes so far as to characterize at least one phase of Nishida's philosophy as a form of "absolute individualism" (*zettaiteki kobutsushugi*).

It has been seen that both Mead and Nishida develop an explicit theory of the "social self" which is intersubjectively constituted by a dialectic of I and Other, what Mead calls the dialectic of I and Me and what Nishida calls the dialectic of I and Thou. Furthermore, just as Mead articulates the creativity, novelty, and spontaneity of the I or individual pole in relation to the Me or social pole, Nishida underscores the self-creativity of the I in relation to the Thou. As will be discussed later, both Mead and Nishida ground their

I-Other dialectic of selfhood in a process theory of time as creative advance wherein at each new moment the self arises through a creative act of synthesizing the many into the one so as to constitute its unity as a continuity of discontinuity. In order to avoid the problem of social determinism, both Nishida and Mead hold that the social self arises through a "mutual determination" of the individual organism and the social environment within the locus of an ontological context, field, or situation. Hence, from the standpoint of Mead's communication model of the social self, it can be said that Nishida's theory of selfhood has established a more balanced relation between the individual and society than the *ningen* model of Watsuji. Yet at the political level of discourse there is nevertheless a major discrepancy arising between Mead and Nishida which must now also be directly confronted.

While members of the Kyoto school emphasize only Nishida's philosophy of religion and Christian-Buddhist dialogue with its theory of pure experience and metaphysics of Nothingness, Japanese Marxist thinkers have developed strong ideology critiques exposing the ultranationalism of Nishida's political thought. In his ideology critique of *nihonjinron* theories Peter Dale (1986, 220–23) regards both Nishida's "pure experience" (*junsui keiken*) and Watsuji's *ningen* theory of personhood as masking a totalitarian state ethics and fascist emperor ideology based on a fusion of subject-object and dissolution of the individual into the whole. Others have pointed out that there is much in common between Nishida's idea of selfhood grounded in a metaphysics of "absolute Nothingness" (*zettai mu*) and Watsuji's *ningen* theory grounded in "emptiness" (*kū*) or "absolute negativity" (*zettaiteki hiteisei*) based on a Zen logic of double negation whereby society "empties" into the individual and the individual "empties" into society. To repeat Piovesana's characterization of the *kū* or "emptiness" of Watsuji in relation to the *mu* or "nothingness" of Nishida: "The individual only through the negation of the self can join the whole of the nation. This absolute negation ends in the *kū* (the emptiness of the self), in order to reach the 'absolute totality,' not dissimilar in purpose to Nishida's nothingness" (1968, 142). Marxists and other political thinkers have leveled probing ideology critiques against both Watsuji and Nishida, charging that they employ a religious metaphysics of absolute Nothingness in order to support an "imperial ideology" (*Tennō ideorogi*) based on the an ultra-nationalist doctrine of the *kokutai*—the national polity, national entity, or national body, uniquely created by the *kami* or Shinto gods and ruled through imperial rescript by the divine Emperor of the imperial household who in an unbroken ancient solar lineage descends from Amaterasu, the Sun Goddess enshrined at Ise. According to the paradoxical Zen Buddhist logic of emptiness used by Nishida and Watsuji, there is a double negation of the individual and society whereby both are emptied into the totality of absolute Nothingness, a vacant center at the heart of the Japanese nation, which is in fact occupied by the divine Emperor and the imperial household functioning as the dialectical source of unity for Japan's cultural and historical diversity. The Japanese "nation-family" (*kokka*) now becomes a vast political household in which the Emperor is the father and the subjects of the nation are his children, so that loyalty to the Emperor and filial piety to the father are one and the same virtue.

Nishida Kitarō is to be assessed as a philosophical if not spiritual genius who was the very first to construct a fully developed East-West comparative philosophy and interfaith dialogue. Nonetheless, he is to be strongly criticized for his allegiance to the Emperor system during the critical prewar years. Nishida's support of imperial ideology and absolutization of the Japanese state is very clearly expressed in such ultranationalistic political essays as "The Problems of Japanese Culture" (*Nihon bunka no mondai*, 1940; NKZ XII, 274–94) and "The Problems of the Reason of the State" (*Kokka riyū no mondai*, 1941; NKZ, X, 265–332), as well as "Principles of the New World Order" (*Sekai shinchitsujo no genri*, 1943) and "The National Polity" (*Kokutai*, 1944), these latter two having now been combined under the title *Tetsugaku ronbunshu daiyon hoi* (NKZ, XII, 397–492). Throughout these and other essays Nishida continually articulates his concept of Japanese selfhood in relation to imperial ideology supporting the Emperor system, arguing that the true self is a self-identity of absolute contradictions as an individual-qua-totality with the imperial household at its center. The imperial household of the *kokutai*, or national polity, is repeatedly identified with the absolute Nothingness functioning as the dialectical source of unity for all contradictory opposites like self and other, subject and object, individual and totality, or one and many. As Nishida writes in his essay *Kokutai* (1944):

> As I have said in *Nihon bunka no mondai* (Problems of Japanese Culture, 1940), in the *kokutai* (National Polity) of our nation the Imperial Household is the beginning and end of the world. The essence our our *kokutai* is that in it the Imperial Household . . . is a complete historical and formative realization of the Individual-qua-Totality and the Totality-qua-Individual. (NKZ XII, 409)

Nishida goes on to argue that the Japanese *kokutai* establishes the order of world history itself, adding: "This is the essence of our *kokutai*, that as the self-determination of the eternal present all things arise from the imperial household and all things return to it" (NKZ XII, 417). Nishida's philosophy of history therefore includes an eschatology of the Japanese *Tennō* (Emperor) system, whereby in ancient times world history began with the establishment of the imperial household and in the future is destined to return to it, now to establish the "New World Order" (*sekai shinchitsujo*) based on the unifying principle, "Eight Corners, One Roof" (*Hakko ichiu*). Elsewhere he very specifically asserts that not only all of Asia, but also America and England are destined to submit to the Japanese *kokutai* (NKZ XII, 434). It should be emphasized that not only Nishida Kitarō but various others related to the right-wing of the Kyoto school (*Kyōto-ha*) have also supported this ultra-nationalistic political orientation based on imperial ideology, in some cases to a far more extreme degree, including Tanabe Hajime, Nishitani Keiji, Kosaka Maasaki, Koyama Iwao, and Suzuki Naritaka, not to mention Watsuji Tetsuro, along with those who further developed Nishida's view of world history based on an eschatology of the Emperor system like Hiraizumi Kiyoshi and Kihira Masami (see Piovesana:191–97).

One of the outstanding achievements of both G. H. Mead in American pragmatism and Nishida Kitarō in modern Japanese philosophy is their formulation of an explicit theory of the social self based on a dialectic of I-Other relations and ontology of social fields in an effort to overcome the isolated Cartesian subject *without* losing the creative agency of the I or unique individual. Yet the disparity between the social-self theories of Mead and Nishida can now be clearly discerned in terms of their radically divergent political orientations. As opposed to Nishida and the Kyoto school of modern Japanese philosophy, G. H. Mead (MSS 281–89; 327–28) and other Chicago school pragmatists have developed a liberal democratic theory of the self. It has been emphasized that Nishida's social-self theory represents a significant advance over Watsuji's *ningen* concept of Japanese personhood insofar as it underscores the individual creativity of the I as over against the social determinism of the Thou. However, despite the ingenious dialectic of I-Thou relationships upon which his social-self theory is constructed, in the final analysis, Nishida, like Watsuji, falls into a version of totalitarian statism where the self as an individual-qua-totality is emptied into the great void of the Japanese *kokutai* with the Emperor and imperial household as its absolute center. Thus, while Nishida's social-self theory and I-Thou dialectic functions to support an ultranationalistic imperial ideology of the Japanese *kokutai*, Mead's social-self theory and I-Me dialectic instead serves as the groundwork for his political vision of a liberal democratic society based on the self-determination of free and equal individuals through open communication and universal discourse.

## The Temporal Structure of Selfhood as Discontinuous Continuity

The problem of individualism versus collectivism in Nishida and Mead can be further examined at the metaphysical level of discourse in terms of the related problem of freedom versus determinism or discontinuity versus continuity. For Nishida, as for Mead and Whitehead, the self is both *social* and *processual*, that is, both relational and temporal. Moreover, for the Zen Buddhist philosophy of Nishida, as for the process philosophy of Mead and Whitehead, the temporal structure of the social self is described as a *discontinuous continuity*. Nishida, Whitehead, and Mead thus all endeavor to challenge the presupposition of substance philosophy that there is an unbroken continuity of the self by recasting personal identity as a continuous temporal stream of momentary events which are radically discontinuous in character. Hence, like Mead's I-Me dialectic of the social self, the I-Thou dialectic of Nishida attempts to reconcile the aspect of freedom or causal discontinuity with that of determinism or causal continuity.

A. N. Whitehead describes the unity of the self as a discontinuous continuity which develops as a temporal process of creative advance from the many to the one. While in his earlier writings like *An Enquiry Concerning the Principles of Natural Knowledge* Whitehead emphasizes the temporal continuity of the self, in his later writings he shifts to a theory of "temporal atomicity": namely, what he calls his "epochal" theory of time. As Lewis Ford asserts, "The adoption of temporal atomism marked a fundamental reorientation of his [Whitehead's] metaphysical thinking" (1984, 5), adding elsewhere that "this doctrine of temporal atomicity directly contravenes Whitehead's earlier emphasis upon temporal continuity" (1984, 3). Whereas the early Whitehead describes the temporal structure of selfhood as a pure "continuity" in order to accentuate the flow of causal transmission in the stream of consciousness, the later Whitehead breaks with this model and develops an "epochal" theory of time as discontinuous continuity, thereby reconstructing his process cosmology in accord with the insights of quantum physics. Thus, in *Science and the Modern World* he argues that the revolutionary discovery of "discontinuous existence" or the quantum jump compels us to "revise all our notions of the ultimate character of material existence" (SMW 35). Moreover, in his chapter entitled "The Quantum Theory" from the same work he states: "The discontinuities introduced by the quantum theory require revision of physical concepts in order to meet them. In particular, it has been pointed out that some theory of discontinuous existence is required" (SMW 135). Whitehead's epochal theory of time as a discontinuous continuity is brought to culmination in his masterpiece on cosmology, *Process and Reality*, wherein he articulates an epochal model of the self as a series of atomic occasions of experience which become and perish whole in quantum jumps. He now argues that due to the radical discontinuity or quantum characteristic of each becoming and perishing occasion of experience, the temporal passage of the concrete self as a creative advance from many into one involves, not a "continuity of becoming," but a *"becoming of continuity"* (PR 35; emphasis added). In other words, there is a "creation of continuity" within each *discontinuous* occasion of experience. Each self-actualizing occasion of experience constituting the unity of the person at a given moment is "continuous" with its predecessors in that it arises through antecedent causal conditions, yet is "discontinuous" as a spontaneous *creative act* with emergent novelty in the present moment of actuality. Each concrescence or process of becoming an occasion of experience is an indivisible creative act and so the temporal advance of the self is not continuous but discrete. Yet, the "temporal atomicity" of Whitehead's later process cosmology which displaces his earlier emphasis on "temporal continuity" must in no way be confused for a theory of material atoms based on the premise of "simple location"; for each atomic occasion of experience is an indivisible quantum field arising as a creative synthesis of the many into the one so as to both pervade and contain the entire universe as a microcosm of the macrocosm: "Thus the ultimate metaphysical truth is atomism. The creatures are atomic. In the present cosmic epoch there is a creation of continuity. . . . But atomism does not exclude complexity and universal relativity. Each atom is a system of all things" (PR 35). Hence, Whitehead abandons the notion of selfhood as an enduring substance undergoing change for that of a process model of the self as a series of becoming and perishing epochal occasions, each of which atomizes the whole space-time continuum as a one-in-many and a many-in-one. At the existential level of discourse, Whitehead describes the immediate experience of discontinuous continuity as "perpetual perishing" (PR 340). Moreover, since each atomic occasion of experience constituting the unity of the self must perish immediately upon its arising, he elsewhere refers to this existential experience of perpetual perishing as "the sense of tragedy" (AI 294).

The process cosmology of G. H. Mead, like that of A. N. Whitehead, also conceives of the temporal structure of human selfhood in terms of a discontinuous continuity. At the cosmological level of analysis, Mead's doctrine of the radical discontinuity of the social self is connected to his theory of *emergence* which he derived from the emergent evolutionism of Lloyd Morgan and Samuel Alexander, the creative evolutionism of Henri Bergson, and especially, the process theory of time as creative advance developed by

A. N. Whitehead. As Mead clarifies in his essay "The Nature of the Past," the main problem for philosophy is to reconcile the element of *continuity* or causal determination of the past with that of *discontinuity* or the emergent novelty of the present (SW 345–54). In *The Philosophy of the Present* Mead likewise asserts: "It is the task of the philosophy of today to bring into congruence with each other this universality of determination which is the text of modern science, and the emergence of the novel" (PP 14). Mead argues that the solution to this problem of continuity versus discontinuity rests upon an adequate theory of time which can integrate the factors of causal conditioning with emergent novelty. Similar to the emphasis on *immediate experience* in the process cosmology of Whitehead, Mead argues that "Reality exists in a present" (PP 1). That is to say, for Mead and Whitehead, a present is always the concrete locus of reality and the self. Just as for Whitehead the present consists of arising and perishing epochal occasions of immediate experience, Mead states, "That which marks a present is its becoming and its disappearing" (PP 1). The becoming and perishing of each present moment is what Mead otherwise refers to as an "emergent event" (PP 3). Mead's theory of emergence is so radical that he goes so far as to argue for a theory according to which there are "new pasts arising with emergent events" (PP 46). That is to say, the past is actually recreated anew from the unique perspective of each novel and emergent event in the present moment of immediate experience. Like Whitehead, Mead argues that while each present moment is continuous with the past insofar as it arises through causal conditions, it is at the same time a creative act or emergent event which is novel, unique, and discontinuous. As Mead puts it, "There is a continuity of experience, which is a continuity of presents" (SW 346), while "The discontinuous is the novel" (SW 347). Whitehead maintains that each actual occasion is "bipolar" (PR 108), having both a "physical pole" which reproduces the causal conditions of the past, and a "mental pole" which introduces creativity, novelty, and spontaneity into the present. Likewise, Mead describes the self as having two poles, the Me pole representing the aspect of continuity or causal conditioning from the past, and the I pole representing the aspect of discontinuity or novel emergence in the present moment of immediate experience. Mead integrates the continuity and discontinuity of the self with his "principle of sociality" (PP 47), according to which the social self exists "betwixt and between" the old system of the Me representing the aspect of causal continuity with the past and the new system of the I representing the new system of emergent novelty in the present. He thus writes: "I have also called emergence an expression of sociality" (PP 70). In this way both Whitehead and Mead have arrived at a dynamic theory of selfhood as temporal process according to which the social self is neither a chain of atomic moments with no causal continuity between them as for Hume, nor a continuous being with a fixed essence as for the metaphysics of substance, but a continuous stream of discontinuous events, each of which is only partly identical to its predecessors.

In his book *Invitation to Sociology*, Peter L. Berger describes Mead's genetic account of multiple selfhood through role-taking and the further development of role theory into the dramaturgical model of self as an irreducible plurality of social masks worked out by Erving Goffman and other symbolic interactionists. Berger then goes on to clarify how Mead's theory of social and multiple selfhood understood as a "kaleidoscope of roles and identities" also involves a notion of "the *discontinuity* of the self" (1963, 106; emphasis added). Berger writes:

> Such a sociological view of personality . . . challenges radically one of the fondest presuppositions about the self—its *continuity*. Looked at sociologically, the self is no longer a solid, given entity that moves from one situation to another. It is rather a process, continuously created and re-created in each social situation that one enters, held together by the slender thread of memory. (1963, 106; emphasis added)

For Mead and other symbolic interactionists, then, the self is not a permanent substance with unbroken continuity, but a discontinuous temporal process arising through social interactions which is perpetually created and recreated by the ever-changing relationships of each new social situation from which it emerges.

Berger goes on to relate this Meadian concept of selfhood as a discontinuous continuity with the view of Buddhist psychology, "in which the self was compared to a long row of candles, each of which lights the wick of its neighbor and is extinguished in that moment" (1963, 107). He adds that the Buddhist psychologists used this image of radical discontinuity to undermine the Hindu notion of transmigration of an eternal soul with continuous being or permanent existence, in that there is no substantial entity which passes from one candle to another. According to Berger, the Buddhist picture of the self as a row of candles each lighting their successor is equally valid for the sociological model of selfhood developed by Mead and others in the tradition of symbolic interactionism. Complementing the view of Berger, Charles Hartshorne remarks that the social process theory of selfhood developed by Mead, according to which the self is at each present moment constituted by the spontaneous, emergent, and ever partly new I responding to the objectified Me, is close to the "Buddhist-Whiteheadian view of the momentary self as numerically non-identical with its predecessors" (1984,126). Hartshorne thus describes how both Mead and Whitehead in the West as well as Buddhism in the East have articulated a social, processual concept of self as a continuous stream of discontinuous events in the creative advance toward novelty.

Building upon the comparative insights of Berger and Hartshorne I would further point out that this radically temporal concept of the social self as a continuous stream of discontinuous events formulated by A. N. Whitehead and G. H. Mead in American process cosmology is the single most adequate framework for interpreting the temporal structure of human selfhood developed in Japan, including both traditional Japanese Zen Buddhism and its reformulation in the modern Japanese philosophy of Nishida Kitarō. Recent scholarship in East-West comparative philosophy has emphasized the parallel between the temporal model of selfhood based on the notion of *uji* or "being-time" in the Zen Buddhism of Dōgen and the existentialism of Martin Heidegger as worked out in *Being and Time* (1927). By this analogy, just as for Dōgen one realizes the true self through the constant remembrance of impermanence and death, for Heidegger authentic selfhood is achieved by realizing that one is a "being-in-time" and a "being-toward-death." Both Dōgen and Heidegger thereby overturn all substance and eternalistic ontology derived from static now-time while establishing a basis for the dynamism, continuity, and nonsubstantiality of primordial time. Yet Heidegger's existential-phenomenological analysis of temporal human existence is in at least one important respect inadequate to articulate the Zen theory of time and self in that it underscores the aspect of temporal continuity while completely neglecting the aspect of temporal discontinuity (see Odin 1985). Leading scholars of Zen Buddhism have emphasized that the element of radical discontinuity is primary in the concepts of "impermanence" (*mujō*) and "being-time" (*uji*) at the core of the doctrine of temporality established by Dōgen. In his work *Dōgen Kigen—Mystical Realist*, Hee-jin Kim asserts that there is an "ultimacy of discontinuity" in Dōgen's Zen Buddhist theory of being-time (1975, 213). As Kim explains, for Dōgen each discontinuous "dharma-position" (*ju-hōi*) constitutes the whole of "being-time" (*uji*) as an "absolute now" (*nikon*), comprehended as the self-actualization of the total presence of the Buddha-nature. Kim further elaborates: "This is a radical rejection of the flow of time, or the stream of consciousness, or any other conception of time based on the idea of continuity or duration. That is, time is absolutely discrete and discontinuous. This characteristic is *primary* in Dōgen's thought" (1975, 202). In *Zen and Western Thought*, Abe Masao of the Kyoto school also emphasizes the radical discontinuity of being-time in Dōgen's theory of *mujō-busshō* or "impermanence-Buddha-nature," asserting: "Dōgen denies continuity of time and emphasizes the independence of each point of time" (1985, 63). He adds: "Only by the realization of the complete discontinuity of time and of the independent moment . . . does time become real time" (1985, 65). Yet in Dōgen's concept of *uji* or being-time, primordial temporality is not merely discontinuous, since it also flows continuously as is denoted by the concept of *kyōryaku*, "continuous passage." For this reason, Abe further asserts: "However, in spite of the complete discontinuity of time and the independent moment, time flows. This is *kyōryaku*, i.e., seriatim passage" (1985, 65). Hence, for Dōgen there is a profound sense in which the true self of being-time in the flux of impermanence-Buddha-nature, comprehended as a unity of *nikon* (the absolute now) and *kyōryaku* (continuous passage), is both discontinuous and continuous at the same time.

Like Mead and Whitehead in American process cosmology, and like Dōgen in traditional Zen Buddhism, the leading twentieth-century Japanese philosopher Nishida Kitarō underscores the radically temporal character of the self. Moreover, like Mead and Whitehead in the West and Dōgen in the East, Nishida emphasizes that the self of pure experience always exists in the instant field of the *present* ; namely, what he continually refers to as the "absolute present" (*zettaiteki genzai*). Pure experience is always an immediate experience of the eternal now or absolute present in the flowing stream of consciousness. Indeed, Mead's constant emphasis on immediate experience in the present as the locus of the self is one of the most significant points of convergence with the Zen model of temporal selfhood, including both Dōgen's idea of the self-actualization of impermanence-Buddha-nature in the absolute now (*nikon*) of being-time and Nishida's idea of the true self in the absolute present (*zettaiteki genzai*). For Nishida, as for Whitehead and Mead, the unity of the self is constituted by a series of appearing and disappearing events of immediate experience so that each momentary self in the absolute present is replaced with a new self which is numerically nonidentical with its predecessors. Similar to Whitehead's description of the self as a discontinuous continuity which develops as a temporal process of creative advance from the many to the one, Nishida develops a Zen Buddhist model of the "true self" as a "continuity of discontinuity" (*hirenzoku no renzoku*), formulated in terms of a temporal process which moves "from the created to the creating" (*tsukurareta mono kara tsukuru mono e*) as constituted through the "contradictory self-identity of the many and the one" (*ta to ichi to no mujunteki jikodōitsu*) (NKZ IX, 149). Nishida, like Whitehead, underscores the *unifying* power of self as an emergent creative act which at each new moment synthesizes the many into the one, thereby constituting the unity of the self as a continuity of discontinuity. Nishida writes:

> The process of many becoming one does not create a unity without specific distinctions as is usually thought. The individual becomes an individual when it becomes one by negating itself. A continuity of discontinuity as the self-determination of the dialectical universal must exist . . . A continuity of discontinuity is not simply a continuity, nor is it simply a discontinuity; and again, neither is it simply a jump from individual to individual; also, it does not mean that there is no connection between them. (NKZ VII, 257)

In this passage Nishida refutes the position held by traditional Western substance philosophy which conceives of the temporal structure of selfhood as a series of discrete now-points characterized by pure "discontinuity" (*hirenzoku*); yet, he also repudiates the concept of time having the form of pure "continuity" (*renzoku*) as held by philosophers like Husserl or Heidegger. Instead, the unity of time constituting the true self as a creative advance from many into one can only be described as a "discontinuous continuity," or as it were, a "continuity of discontinuity" (*hirenzoku no renzoku*). Thus, later in the same text Nishida writes:

> As I have said before, the unity of the individual cannot be thought of as simply a continuity, rather, it must be a continuity of discontinuity, so as to constitute the unity of independent beings with every step. Each moment of time passes into the next moment by negating itself, hence establishing the unity of time. (NKZ VII, 268)

Moreover, Nishida describes the existential realization of discontinuous continuity in the absolute present as "living by dying" (*shisuru koto ni yotte ikiru*) (NKZ VII, 295). Hence, at the existential level of analysis, just as for Whitehead the realization that the self appears and disappears at every instant is felt as a tragic sense of "perpetual perishing," for Nishida it is this discontinuous continuity of creative advance whereby the true self negates itself and enters into Nothingness at each and every present moment which constitutes human selfhood as a temporal process of "living by dying." Consequently, authentic selfhood is not realized by the "futural anticipation" of oncoming death as is the case for Heidegger, but through the existential realization of "living by dying" or "perpetual perishing" which occurs in the *present* moment of immediate experience. The organismic process model of selfhood developed by Mead and Whitehead thus converges with the Zen model of selfhood postulated by Nishida Kitarō not only in that it articulates the "social" character of the self as a dialectical interaction between the I and the Other, but also clarifies the radically *temporal* dimensions of the self as a continuity of discontinuity wherein creative advance from many to one is constituted by a sequence of transitory events forever arising and perishing whole in the present moment of the stream of becoming.

## The Perspectivist Models of Self in Mead, Whitehead, and Nishida

In his essay "Towards A Philosophy of Religion with the Concept of Pre-Established Harmony as a Guide," Nishida articulates a perspectivist model of selfhood which combines the perspectivism of Leibniz in the West and Kegon (Chi. *Hua-yen*) Buddhism in the East. Nishida writes: "Our selves are 'creative points' of this world. Leibniz called the monad a metaphysical point, but I think of each individual self as a creative point of the historical world. It extends to the eternal future and to the eternal past as the point of self-determination of the absolute present" (NKZ XI, 135). Nishida here argues that the individual self is like the "metaphysical point" or "monad" of Leibniz's *Monodology*, wherein each monad is conceived to be a living mirror which reflects the whole universe from its own perspective as a microcosm of the macrocosm. Moreover, Nishida's notion of self is at once reminiscent of the perspectivism of Kegon Buddhism, with its striking image of the jewel net of Indra describing the continuum of nature as a vast web or net of dynamic causal relationships in which at each point of intersection there is a brilliant jewel reflecting all the other jewels and the whole net from its own unique perspective as a many in one and a one in many. Again, Kegon Buddhism illustrates this perspectivist cosmology through the hall of mirrors wherein a golden statue of Buddha lit by a torch is reflected from every possible standpoint in a gallery of mirrors. Nishida cites the well-known doctrinal formulas expressing this perspectivism of Kegon Buddhism: *riji muge*, "interfusion between particular and whole," and *jiji muge*, "interfusion of particular and particular." Like the perspectivist models of self articulated by both Leibniz and Kegon Buddhism, Nishida's perspectivist cosmology holds that the self functions to reflect past, present, and future in an eternal now or absolute present. However, unlike Leibniz and Kegon, Nishida underscores the creative element in his perspectivist notion of self. In contrast to the "metaphysical point" of Leibniz, the self is now conceived as a "creative point" (*sōzōten*) of the social-historical world in the *basho* or locus of absolute Nothingness.

Similarly, G. H. Mead develops a Leibnizian perspectivist model of self derived from A. N. Whitehead's theory of perspectives as worked out in the latter's *Science and the Modern World* (1925). In an essay called "The Objective Reality of Perspectives" included in *Philosophy of the Present* (1932) Mead describes his interest in the perspectivism of Whitehead as follows: "What I wish to pick out of Professor Whitehead's philosophy of nature is this conception of nature as an organization of perspectives" (1932, 163). Mead adds that his own cosmology focuses upon Whitehead's "Leibnizian filiation, as it appears in his conception of the perspective as the mirroring in the event of all other events" (1932, 164). For Mead, the social self is akin to a Leibnizian monad or Whiteheadian event in that it mirrors, if not the whole universe, at least the whole community from its own unique perspective, thereby to constitute an individual microcosm of the social macrocosm. Mead writes that "each individual self within that social process, while it reflects in its organized structure the behavior pattern of that [social] process as a whole, it does so from its own particular and unique standpoint . . . just as every monad in the Leibnizian universe mirrors that universe from a different point of view, and thus mirrors a different aspect or perspective of that universe" (PP 201). In Mead's social psychology this Leibnizian/Whiteheadian perspectivism provides a cosmological basis for C. H. Cooley's famous notion of the social self as a "looking-glass self" which functions as a mirror reflecting its primary social group. Mead's developmental psychology of the social self is based on the notion of perspectivism or perspective-taking, the ability of entering into the perspective of others in the community so as to take on the common perspective of the generalized other: "This principle is that the individual enters into the perspectives of others, in so far as he is able to take their attitudes, or occupy their points of view" (PP 165).

Mead's perspectivist model underscores not only the "social" character of self as an individual microcosm of the social macrocosm (PP 201), but also the *temporal* character of self as a creative advance into novelty (PP 172). Like Whitehead's process cosmology Mead rejects the idealist notion of an "absolute perspective" in that it undermines the reality of finite events in the temporal process of creative advance (PP 161). In the process cosmology of Mead and Whitehead there is an emphasis on the *emergent* character of spatio-temporal perspectives in the creative advance of nature. For this reason, Mead singles out as major points of orientation for contemporary philosophy the two correlate notions of "emergence" and "perspective" (PA 640). Each objective perspective in nature arises during the course of emergent evolution as the spontaneous, creative, and novel response of a unique organism to its deterministic social environment. Mead summarizes his Whiteheadian concept of nature as a temporal process of creative advance into novelty based on a process theory of emergent perspectives when he writes: "What I am suggesting is that this process, in which . . . new common perspectives arise, is an instance of the organization of perspectives in nature, of the creative advance of nature" (PP 172).

It has now been seen that Nishida in modern Japanese philosophy as well as Whitehead and Mead in American process thought have each developed a Leibnizian perspectivist cosmology wherein the social self reflects its world as an individual microcosm of the social macrocosm. Moreover, all three have revised the perspectivism of Leibiniz with a theory of *discontinuous* temporal perspectives in order to allow for self-creativity. As shown above, Nishida's idea of discontinuous perspectives is underscored by his recurrent notion of temporal selfhood as a "continuity of discontinuity" (*hirenzoku no renzoku*) (NKZ VII, 268), which itself functions similarly to the process notion of temporal selfhood as discontinuous continuity formulated by both Whitehead (SMW 135; PR 35) and Mead (SW 345–54). In contrast to Leibniz's more deterministic notion of a "metaphysical point," Nishida describes his perspectival self as a "creative point" (NKZ XI, 135), whereas Mead, following Whitehead, speaks of the *emergence* of discontinuous temporal perspectives in the "creative advance of nature" (PP 172).

However, elsewhere I have developed a thoroughgoing criticism of Kegon Buddhism, including those schools based on the Kegon infrastructure like Zen and the modern philosophy of Nishida Kitarō, from the standpoint of Whiteheadian process metaphysics (see Odin 1982). I argue that Whiteheadian process thought, like Kegon Buddhism and the modern Japanese philosophy of Nishida, has a theory of perspectives wherein each event mirrors its universe from its own perspectival locus in nature as a microcosm of the macrocosm. To this extent it can be said that a Whiteheadian event functions like a jewel in Indra's net which mirrors its world from a perspective. Both Whiteheadian process cosmology and Zen/Kegon Buddhism articulate what visionary physicist David Bohm describes in *Wholeness and the Implicate Order* (1980) as the holographic structure of reality, an ever-flowing "holomovement" or "holo-flux" in which the undivided whole of the implicate order is enfolded in each nonlocal hologram. However, while Kegon Buddhism holds that each perspectival event holographically mirrors past, present, and future alike so as land in causal determinism, for Whitehead, each perspectival event mirrors only its past in order to allow for a fully open-ended universe wherein nature is conceived as a temporal process of creative advance into novelty. The difference is that while both Whitehead and the Zen/Kegon infrastructure of Nishida's philosophy describes the world in terms of becoming, process, or universal flux, unlike the former, Nishida does not articulate a theory of emergent evolution which recognizes the *irreversibility* of temporal flux, the *asymmetry* of temporal process, and the *cumulative* nature of temporal becoming. In contrast, Whitehead adheres to the asymmetrical, cumulative, and irreversible structure of temporal process as creative advance so as to fully preserve the *arrow of time.*

Generally speaking, Nishida's Buddhist cosmology of absolute Nothingness follows the direction of Kegon, whereas Mead follows the direction of Whitehead and American process cosmology. Although Nishida revises Leibniz's perspectivist idea of a monad or metaphysical point with his own idea of a "creative point" (*sōzōten*), at the same time he emphasizes that each creative point extends into the infinite future and the infinite past as a self-determination of the absolute present (NKZ XI, 135). For Mead and Whitehead in the West, as for Nishida in the East, the self functions as the source of creative synthesis which unifies the many into the one. But while for Mead and Whitehead the present self unifies only its predecessors, for Nishida each present self unifies its contemporaries and successors as well as its predecessors. That is to say, while Nishida, like Mead and Whitehead, describes the self as a creative advance from many into one, for Nishida the "many" refers to *all* events of the past, present and future as unified in the bottomless depths of an eternal now, in contrast to the Whitehead-Mead position, whereby the "many" refers to the pluralistic field of *antecedent* events alone. In the asymmeterical theory of Whitehead and Mead, the creative advance from many into one whereby each event actualizes itself in the present signifies an emergent creative synthesis of antecendent multiplicity into a novel unity so that the sum total of events increases with each passing moment. Takeuchi Yoshinori, a leading scholar of the Kyoto school, has clarified this fundamental contrast between the perspectivism of Nishida's philosophy and Western process cosmology as follows:

> Bergson and more recently an American philosopher, Professor Charles Hartshorne, think that all events of the past are restored in a metaphysical remembrance. It seems that Nishida thought through the problem above more radically: not only events of the past, but also those of the future, are all present in the eternal now. (1982, 193)

To conclude, it has been shown that both Nishida and Mead have articulated an explicit theory of the twofold social self based on a dialectic of

I-Other relationships, what Nishida calls his dialectic of I and Thou, and what Mead calls his dialectic of I and Me. Also, both Nishida and Mead ground their social-self theories and I-Other dialectics upon a cosmology of perspectives whereby the self is likened to a Leibnizian monad which mirrors its world as an individual microcosm of the social macrocosm. Furthermore, both revise their Leibnizian perspectivist cosmologies with a doctrine of creativity so that each perspectival self represents a creative synthesis of the many into the one. However, insofar as Nishida argues that each perspectival self mirrors all events of the past, present, and future, he develops a *symmetrical* theory of social relations, so that his theory bears a closer structural proximity to Leibniz' doctrine of monads in the West or Kegon Buddhism in the East. In contrast, the evolutionary process cosmology of Mead and Whitehead develops an *asymmetrical* theory of social relations in which each perspectival self mirrors only events of the past, thereby to allow for both self-creativity in the present as well as the emergence of genuine novelty in the future. Or in terms of their respective I-Other dialectics of the social self, for Nishida the I-Thou relation is symmetrical while for Mead the I-Me relation is asymmetrical in character. According to this asymmetical, irreversible, and cumulative time structure underlying Mead's bipolar model of the social self as an I-Me dialectic, the emerging perspectival self arises from its deterministic social environment inherited from the *past* at the Me pole, but then responds to it with spontaneity, creativity, and freedom in the *present* as an individual organism at the I pole. In contrast to Mead's theory of *emergent perspectives*, Nishida may be said to have developed a theory of *total perspectives* like both Leibniz in the West and Kegon Buddhism in the East. To the extent that Nishida retains the symmetrical time framework of the Zen/Kegon infrastructure wherein each event constitutes a total perspective mirroring past, present, and future at once, it falls into a position of social determinism, and thus does not allow for the same kind of individual freedom, creativity, and novelty established through the asymmetrical time framework of Whitehead and Mead. In the evolutionary process cosmology of Whitehead and Mead, then, it is this notion of *emergent* temporal perspectives based on a *asymmetrical* theory of becoming in the *arrow of time* which overcomes the problem of social determinism and constitutes the autonomous nature of selfhood as a creative advance into novelty.

# ～11～

## Selfhood in the Social Psychology of Mead and Doi

G. H. Mead's doctrine of the social self has been presented here as a unifying model which integrates philosophy and the social sciences into a single framework governed by the experimental method which at the same time is grounded in an organismic process metaphysics of creative advance. The main task of the present work has been the expansion of Mead's intersubjective communication model of the social self into an East-West contextualist model of personhood by means of which to illuminate the East Asian concept of self in general and the Japanese concept of self in particular. Whereas previously I have considered the social-self theory worked out by Mead and other American pragmatists in relation to representative figures of modern Japanese philosophy like Nishida Kitarō and Watsuji Tetsurō, in this section I focus specifically upon Mead's *social psychology* from the standpoint of recent developments in modern Japanese psychiatry, psychotherapy, and psychology. Here I take up Mead's social psychology in relation to the *amae* (dependency) psychology of the eminent Japanese psychiatrist Doi Takeo. In this context I show the correspondence between the twofold structure of Doi's group-centered model of Japanese selfhood as a dialectic between *honne* (private feeling) and *tatemae* (public institutions) and Mead's bipolar model of the social self as a dialectic between I and Me. Furthermore, I clarify the extent to which Mead's symbolic interactionist framework of social psychology has in fact directly influenced Doi's *amae* psychology including his developmental model of Japanese socialization and his twofold social conception of Japanese selfhood.

### The Social Psychology of Mead and Doi's Amae Psychology

It has been seen that one of Mead's greatest contributions to the social sciences has been his articulation of a comprehensive *social psychology* based upon his communication theory of the bipolar social self as an individual-society interaction. To reiterate the words of Charles Morris in his introduction to Mead's work, *Mind, Self, and Society:* "Philosophically, Mead was a pragmatist; scientifically, he was a social psychologist" (MSS ix). In contrast to Freud's ego-directed individualistic psychology based on narcissistic id-instincts of sex and aggression, Mead pioneered the development of an other-directed social psychology which provides an empirically based genetic account of the social formation of mind and self through communicative interaction between the individual and society. It is worth recalling the words of the eminent sociologist Peter Berger, who evaluates the significance of Mead's symbolic interactionist framework of social psychology as follows:

> [I]t is through the work of George Herbert Mead and the Meadian tradition of the 'symbolic-interactionist' school that a theoretically viable social psychology has been founded. . . . in this achievement lies the most important theoretical contribution to the social sciences in America. (1970, 373)

When viewed from a cross-cultural perspective Mead's social psychology has also provided us with the most comprehensive theoretical framework by means of which to interpret the structure and dynamics of the Japanese self. At the outset of *Mind, Self, and Society* (1934) Mead defines "social psychology" as an investigation into "the effect which the social group has in the determination of the experience and conduct of the individual members" (MSS 1). According to the social psychology of Mead, then, the self cannot be understood as an isolated Cartesian subject having independent existence but must always be relationally defined in terms of its reference to a social group. For Mead there is no self which exists apart from or prior to membership in a social group in that the self is ontologically constituted by its social relations to others. It is precisely this group reference aspect of Mead's social psychology which makes it especially relevant to the "groupism" characterizing Japanese selfhood. The significance of Mead's social psychology for illuminating the traditional Japanese group-centered model of self has been mentioned by several scholars, notably Robert J. Smith, who remarks: "In the mid-1930's George Herbert Mead . . . attempted to develop a social psychology that fits almost perfectly what we are told is the peculiarly Japanese case" (1985, 39). Elsewhere, Smith criticizes those scholars who have endeavored to interpret the Japanese self using the "individual psychology of Freud" instead of "the social psychology of figures like George Herbert Mead and Henry Stack Sullivan [sic]" (1983, 74). He adds that if scholars had employed the symbolic interactionist framework of social psychology developed by Mead instead of Freud's individualistic psychology, "we should long since have had an eminently plausible picture of the Japanese conception of the self" (1983, 74).

If the symbolic interactionist framework of Mead has established the most theoretically viable social psychology in America as claimed by Berger (1970, 373), it can likewise be said that one of the greatest contributions to social psychology in Japan is the *amae* psychology of Doi Takeo. In *Amae no kōzō* (*The Structure of Amae*, 1971), translated into English as *The Anatomy of Dependence* (1973), Doi argues that the social nature of Japanese selfhood can best be explained through the principle of *amae*, defined in psychiatric terms as "the need of an individual to be loved and cherished or the prerogative to presume and depend upon the benevolence of another." As discussed earlier, Doi (1971, 89) indicates that his *amae* principle can itself be traced back to *The Structure of Iki* (*Iki no kōzō*, 1930) by the Japanese philosopher Kuki Shūzō, who analyzes linguistically related words like *amae*, *amaeru*, and *amami* as components of the Edo period aesthetic ideal of *iki* or "chic," defined as representing a polar contrast between *amami* (sweetness) or the positive value which establishes intimate social and intersexual contact with others, and *shibumi* (astringency) or the negative value of "elegant restraint" which functions to establish a psychological distance from others. It is this same principle of *amae* which Doi transforms into his key psychological principle, now understood as a nonlibidinous drive to seek human affiliation with others. The social psychology of Doi thus posits *amae* (indulgent dependency) as an intrapsychic "drive," "motive," "wish," "need," "trait," "disposition," or "instinct" which is more primary than the narcissistic sexual and aggressive instincts postulated by the individualistic psychology of Freud.

Doi agrees with the view of many other scholars that the American self represents a form of "individualism" (*kojinshugi*) and that the Japanese self is to be characterized by "groupism" (*shūdanshugi*) (1985, 53). However, Doi's contribution here is to have explained the phenomenon of Japanese groupism in terms of his psychological notion of *amae*, the "drive to dependence." In Doi's words, "*amae* is the psychology underlying Japanese groupism" (1985, 55). Hence, according to Doi, "Japanese group-consciousness" (*nihon no shūdan-ishiki*) is to be explained as a psychological function of *amae*, the primary need to depend on others. In this way Doi's social psychology based on the underlying principle of *amae* or "dependency drive" has come to establish a theoretical framework by means of which to explicate the Japanese sense of self as a nexus of dependency relationships.

## The Bipolar Model of Selfhood in Doi and Mead

Since the publication of *The Structure of Amae* (*Amae no kōzō*, 1971), much has been written about Doi's concept of *amae* in both Japanese and English. However, what has gone all but completely unmentioned is the significant extent to which Doi's *amae* psychology has itself been influenced by the social psychology of William James, Charles Horton Cooley, and especially George Herbert Mead in classical American pragmatism. Even Frank A. Johnson's impressive and detailed study of Doi's *amae* psychology called *Dependency and Japanese Socialization* (1993) fails to make any reference to the social psychology of Mead. Yet Doi's theory of Japanese selfhood as well as his theory of Japanese socialization is best understood in terms of Mead's symbolic interactionist framework of the social self. In Doi's analysis of Japanese selfhood he argues that the person in relationship to others has a twofold structure; that of *tatemae* (= social institutions) and *honne* (= individual reactions). He then asserts that the dual *honne-tatemae* structure of Japanese selfhood corresponds to the I-Me dialectic of the social self described by G. H. Mead. Furthermore, Doi explains the "socialization" (*shakaika*) of the individual in Japanese culture by a developmental process whereby *honne* or the private side of the twofold self internalizes the public institutions of *tatemae*, just as for Mead one achieves personhood as a bipolar social self with reflexive self-consciousness through a socialization process whereby the I or individual pole takes on the roles, perspectives and attitudes of the Me or institutional pole, otherwise called the "generalized other." He also describes the breakdown and fragmentation of Japanese self-identity through a split between *tatemae* and *honne* in terms of the multiple self theories of James and Mead. Doi's *amae* psychology thus represents an East-West synthesis of the Japanese contextualist theory of selfhood as an opposition of *honne* and *tatemae* and G. H. Mead's concept of the social self as a dialectic of I and Me.

It should be recalled how in his work called *Omote to Ura* (Front and Back, 1985), translated into English as *The Anatomy of Self: The Individual Versus Society* (1986), Doi goes on to articulate the "double-sidedness" (*nimensei*) or "twofold" (*futae, nijū*) structure of the Japanese self in terms of such distinctions as *omote-ura* (front/back), *soto/uchi* (outside/inside), and *tatemae-honne* (public institution/private reaction). The twofold Japanese self is divided into "front" (*omote*) and "back" (*ura*) or "outside" (*soto*) and "inside" (*uchi*) according to the restraint verses the expression of *amae*, the infantile dependency wish. According to this twofold model of Japanese selfhood, while it is appropriate to presume upon the love of others or to freely express the infantile dependency needs of *amae* on the "inside" (*uchi*) with family and friends, it is necessary to conform to the ritual conventions of society on the "outside" (*soto*).

Doi next proceeds to clarify the *omote-ura* or "outside-inside" contrast of the twofold Japanese self in terms of the distinction of *tatemae-honne* (1985, 25–42). He says that in Japanese *tatemae* is often used with the implication that it is only an "external facade" while *honne* represents one's true "inner feelings" (1985, 25). However, as Doi analyzes these terms, *tatemae* designates the ritualized conventions of one's social group established by consensus, while *honne* represents the individual's personal responses operating within the framework of these conventions (1985, 27). This is later clarified in terms of the contrast between "institutions" (*seido*) and the "individual" (*kojin*). He points out that the English word "institution" comes from Latin, where it was derived from the verb *instituere*, meaning "to stand [something] up," which is the same etymological meaning as *tatemae* in Japanese (1985, 44). According to Doi, *tatemae* in fact signifies the aspect of "social institutions" which are incorporated into the self in its public aspect. He summarizes his understanding of *tatemae* and *honne* when he writes: "Above, we considered the concepts of institutions and the individual by asserting that they were analogous to *tatemae* and *honne*" (1985, 52). Hence, for Doi the aforementioned "double-sidedness" of the person as *ningen* consists of the fact that it is constituted by a twofold interaction between *tatemae* and *honne*, wherein *tatemae* corresponds to the "social institutions" on the public or *omote* side, and *honne* corresponds to the "individual responses" on the private or *ura* side of the Japanese self in its relations to others in society.

Doi next proceeds to articulate the twofold *tatemae-honne* structure of the Japanese context-dependent self in terms of the social psychology of William James, Charles Horton Cooley, and George Herbert Mead in American pragmatism. In order to further clarify how the *tatemae* aspect of the self can be understood to denote social institutions established by group consensus, Doi quotes from the writings of C. H. Cooley, who together with G. H. Mead, advanced a symbolic interactionist notion of the "social self." Moreover, while summarizing his interpretation of the *tatemae-honne* structure of twofold Japanese selfhood he directly cites from Mead's work *Mind, Self, and Society*:

> Finally, I would like to say a word about how *tatemae* and *honne* are formed. It is established in the home environment during childhood, and afterwards, through human relations developed through school education and social education. If we view it in this way, *tatemae* and *honne* overlap with psychological and sociological concepts of socialization

and self-consciousness. *Tatemae* is precisely a product of socialization and *honne* is the expression of self-consciousness. Furthermore, socialization and self-consciousness are intimately related, and can be seen as two sides of the same coin. For instance, G. H. Mead writes: "To be self-conscious is essentially to become an object to one's self in virtue of one's social relations to other individuals" [Mead: MSS 172]. The "I" reacts to the self which arises through the taking of the attitudes of others. Through taking these attitudes we have introduced the "me" and we react to it as an "I." [Mead: MSS 74] (Doi: 1985, 45)

As Doi indicates in the above passage, when the *tatemae-honne* distinction is understood through the social psychology of G. H. Mead, *tatemae* represents the process of "socialization" (*shakaika*) whereby the self internalizes the attitudes of its social group by taking on the roles of others, while *honne* represents the individual self-consciousness (*jiga-ishiki*) which reacts to it. Moreover, by his references to Mead's thought Doi wishes to underscore that the individual self-consciousness of *honne* arises only by becoming an object to itself through this socialization process of taking the attitude of others, or as it were, by internalizing the social institutions of *tatemae*. Following Cooley and Mead in American pragmatism, Doi regards the distinction between *honne* and *tatemae* corresponding to "individual" and "society" as representing two sides of the same coin. However, at this point Doi now endeavors to explicitly articulate the twofold *honne-tatemae* structure of Japanese selfhood in terms of Mead's bipolar model of the social self as an I-Me dialectic. In an important passage, Doi states:

> Mead's concept of "Me" corresponds to *tatemae,* and his "to become an object to one's self" is related to the formation of *tatemae.* Again, his "I" corresponds to *honne.* (1985, 42)

According to Doi's *amae* psychology, then, when the double-sided structure of Japanese selfhood as a *tatemae-honne* relationship is understood in terms of Mead's bipolar "social self" theory and correlate I-Me dialectic, *honne* comes to represent the *I* or individual pole, and *tatemae* denotes the *Me* or institutional pole. That is to say, *tatemae* is that public aspect of the social self which Mead calls the Me or the internalized social group formed by taking on the attitudes, roles, and perspectives of the generalized other, while *honne* is that private aspect which reacts to it as an individual I. Moreover, Doi explains Japanese socialization in terms of Mead's developmental process of becoming a social self with reflexive self-consciousness by taking on the role of the other and then by seeing oneself as an object from the standpoint of that other.

For the *amae* psychology of Doi, as for the social psychology of Mead, "self-identity" is constituted only through relationships with others. Doi (1985, 85) asserts that the Japanese translation of "identity" (*dōitsusei*) has two meanings: to identify with someone or something (*dōitsuka*), and to identify something as such (*dōtei*). While the former refers to the binding of oneself to another person or thing, the latter refers to identifying a thing as that thing. He thus asserts: "In accordance with this, if we say it simply, identity is to be aware of oneself as oneself. But its meaning as a technical concept lies in the suggestion that this consciousness of self is constituted by its connections with others" (1985, 85). In Doi's *amae* psychology, then, self-identity is intersubjectively constituted through social interaction between *honne* and *tatemae*, the private aspect of the individual and the public aspect of social institutions. Similarly, in the social psychology of Mead, self-identity is intersubjectively constituted through communicative interaction between the *I* or individual pole and the *Me* or institutional pole. Hence, in this way both Doi and Mead have arrived at the insight that one becomes a person with self-identity and reflexive self-consciousness only through communication with others in society.

Doi attempts to further clarify the manner in which *honne* and *tatemae* are both necessary components of Japanese selfhood through his psychological interpretation of various creative works of fiction in the tradition of modern Japanese literature, including famous novels by representative Meiji period authors like Natsume Sōseki (1867–1916) and Mori Ōgai (1862–1922). Here Doi can be said to follow the example of Watsuji Tetsurō, who received inspiration for his *ningen* concept of Japanese selfhood as *hito to hito to no aida* or the "betweenness of persons" from Sōseki's novels and literary essays based upon his Buddhist idea of *sokuten kyoshi* (= *ten ni nottotte watakushi o saru*) "departing from the self and following the way of heaven." In this way Doi, like Watsuji, attempts to ground his theoretical notion of Japanese selfhood deep within the aesthetic, literary, and cultural dimensions of traditional Japanese society itself. Doi (1985, 62) analyzes the Meiji period comic novel *Botchan* (Little Master) by Natsume Sōseki, whose protagonist named Botchan provides an excellent case study of an individual who has not learned how to use the social institutions of *tatemae* and attempts to go through life with only with the impulsive behavior of *honne*. Botchan lacks the basic skills of competent social navigation known in Japanese as *kejime* (discrimination), which as Takie S. Lebra has pointed out is "the Japanese person's keen awareness of the discrepancy between *honne* and *tatemae*" (1976, 136). As a result of this

lack of *kejime* or "discrimination," Botchan gives free expression to the infantile dependency wishes of *amae* and the personal feelings of *honne* without
conforming to the ritualized constraints ordinarily imposed on an individual
by the social institutions of *tatemae*. Doi also discusses another Meiji period
Japanese literary work, *Abe Ichizoku* (The Abe Family) by Mori Ōgai, whose
main characters illustrate the attempt to live solely by the public institutions
of *tatemae* without the personal feelings of *honne*. Through his psychological
analysis of Sōseki's *Botchan* and Mori Ōgai's *Abe Ichizoku*, Doi thus endeavors
to show that neither *tatemae* nor *honne* are effective as a single guiding principle for human conduct (1985, 73). Both *honne* and *tatemae*, both individual
reactions and social institutions, are necessary elements of Japanese selfhood
in its wholeness. From the standpoint of Mead's social psychology, Sōseki's
character Botchan represents the imbalance arising when an individual acts
by the unrestrained impulses of his *I* at the instinctive pole of the twofold
bio-social self without having fully internalized the social roles, attitudes,
and perspectives of the *Me* or "generalized other." On the other hand the
characters of Ōgai's novel represent the development of oversocialized selves
whose conduct is regulated by the internalized public institutions of the generalized other at the Me pole without the spontaneous responses originating
at the I pole. Mead (MSS 198) thus emphasizes that both the I and the Me are
essential to the bipolar social self in its full expression.

Doi then shows how the dual consciousness of *tatemae* and *honne* breaks
down in the pathology of the Japanese psyche. He asserts that "the privileging of *honne* and the devaluation of *tatemae* have become the dominant trends
in contemporary Japanese society" (1985, 93). Moreover, he describes how
this devaluation of *tatemae* in contemporary Japanese society has occurred
to the point that ancient social institutions previously held in esteem are
now objects of skepticism. The collapse of the institution of the family is one
of the most destructive aspects of this disregard for *tatemae* in contemporary
Japanese society. Doi (1985, 88) writes: "To begin with, the family can be
thought of as the first knot which binds together *tatemae* and *honne*. Consequently, it is the break up of the family that most dramatically indicates a
split between them" (1985, 88). According to Doi, when *tatemae* and *honne*
fall apart into sharp conflict, they are no longer able to coexist, so that the
self-identity of the Japanese psyche splits asunder into a double or multiple
existence devoid of unity. To clarify this idea of psychic conflict between
*tatemae* and *honne* from which emerges a divided, fragmented self, he then
makes direct reference to William James's arguments for the multiple existence of the social self. In this context, Doi (1985, 97–98) cites the following
passage from James's *Principles of Psychology*:

Properly speaking, a man has as many social selves as there are individuals who recognize him and carry an image of him in their mind . . . he has as many different social selves as there are distinct groups of persons whose opinion he cares. He generally shows a different side of himself to each of these different groups.

For Doi, James describes a discordant splitting in which a person's various social selves are mutually divided and in conflict. Doi (1985, 98–99) goes on to again cite Mead in order to clarify the multiple existences of the social self. When the conflict between *omote* and *ura*, *soto* and *uchi*, or *tatemae* and *honne* become deep, the self-identity of the Japanese psyche is shattered into fragments.

## Conclusion

It has now been shown how both G. H. Mead in America and Doi Takeo in Japan have abandoned the individualism of Freudian psychology based on a narcissistic concept of self and worked out a social psychology grounded in a social concept of self. Furthermore, both have articulated a twofold concept of selfhood whereby the person constitutes himself as a unity through communicative interaction between two poles, what Mead calls the *I* or individual pole and the *Me* or institutional pole, and what Doi refers to as *honne* or the "private reaction" of an individual and *tatemae* or the "public institutions" of society. Again, both have provided a genetic account of the social nature, origin, and formation of the self through a developmental process of socialization. Both develop an account of the socialization process according to which an individual becomes a person as a twofold social self with reflexive self-consciousness only by becoming an object to itself, which for Mead occurs when the I takes on the social roles of the Me so as to see itself from the standpoint of the generalized other, and which for Doi arises when the *honne* aspect of self incorporates the social institutions of the *tatemae* aspect. Mead thus argues that both the I and the Me are essential to the bipolar social self in its full expression, just as Doi holds that both *tatemae* and *honne* are necessary components of the Japanese self.

As for some of the discrepancies between their two frameworks it should first of all be pointed out that there is an important difference in their approach to the fundamental problem of freedom versus determinism. Both Doi and Mead have framed a twofold model of selfhood expressed through a dialectic of individuality and sociality, or what Doi calls his dialectic of *honne* and *tatemae* and what Mead refers to as his dialectic of I and Me. For Doi *tatemae* represents the aspect of social determinism while *honne* represents the aspect of personal freedom. Similarly, in Mead's bipolar model of self the Me pole signifies the aspect of social determinism while the I pole accounts for personal freedom. However, Doi explains the distinction of *honne* and *tatemae* in terms of the expression versus constraint of *amae*, the infantile dependency wish. As Doi argues in chapters 8 and 9 of *The Structure of Amae* (*Amae no kōzō*, 1971, 94–108), *jiyū* or "freedom" in Japanese society means *amaeru jiyū*, "freedom to depend upon others." Mead, on the other hand, defines personal freedom in more positive terms as the emergent creativity, spontaneity, and originality of the I or individual pole in its adjustive response to the social determination by the Me or institutional pole. There is also a fundamental difference which arises in their two systems regarding the nature of human drives. In Doi's social psychology the principle of *amae* (indulgent dependency) is an intrapsychic "drive" or "instinct" which is more primary than the narcissistic sexual and aggressive instincts of Freud's psychology. Likewise, Mead describes human conduct as being rooted in "social instinct" (SW 98). But the social psychology of Mead rejects the notion that there is any fixed content, essence, or nature defining human selfhood and only affirms the general character of self as an ever-changing social process which develops through role-taking. For this reason Mead generally substitutes the notion of intrapsychic "drives" or "instincts" with the more flexible and open concept of *impulses* which undergo extensive modifications in the process of emergent evolution (MSS 337). Finally, it has been shown how both Mead in the West and Doi in the East have worked out a thoroughgoing social psychology based on an analysis of the twofold structure of human selfhood as an individual-society interaction. But while Doi's *amae* psychology represents a *nihonjinron* theory which seeks to identify the essence of Japanese uniqueness, Mead provides a universal account of human self and society in general. Thus, while Doi's *amae* psychology attempts to explain the social character of Japanese selfhood and the groupism of Japanese society, Mead instead argues that *every* self in *every* society is by necessity a social self although it reflects the particular social group from which it emerges.

# ~:12:~

## The Social Self as a Body-Mind Interaction

From the tradition of European modernism we have inherited a concept of self based upon the dualism of body and mind. Although the separation of a material body from the ether of mind, soul, or spirit has characterized much of Western philosophy since Plato, it was fully reified by Descartes and his seventeenth-century contemporaries. Cartesianism, like Platonism, not only posits a dualistic ontology; it also accords an *ontological priority* of the spiritual over the material so as to privilege the mind over the body, the mental over the physical, the psychic over the somatic, and the subjective over the objective. This Cartesian bifurcation of mind and body has established the agenda for modern Western philosophy ever since, including those who accept the distinction, those attempting to surmount it, and those adopting one side while rejecting or subordinating the other.

However, in the twentieth century we have seen bold efforts on the part of several Western thinkers to revolt against the Cartesian dualism of body and mind. To begin with, the paradigm figure in Western psychology is the psychiatrist Wilhelm Reich, who argued that all mental contents are mirrored in the physical body as expressed through his principle of *psychosomatic identity*. Because of what he terms the "functional identity of body and mind," there is an exact correspondence between the defensive system of repressed emotions and psychic conflicts in the unconscious mind (character armor), and its reflection in the chronic pattern of muscular tensions, inhibited impulses, and depressed respiration of the physical body (body armor). Reichian body-oriented psychotherapy aims at self-actualization by releasing all physical and mental blocks to the bioenergetic flow of cosmic Orgone-energy from center to periphery in the achievement of full orgastic potency. Reich's key principle of "psychosomatic identity" is of great value for understanding the Japanese Buddhist concept of self as a bodymind unity.

The classic treatment of the body in twentieth-century Continental philosophy is no doubt *Phenomenology of Perception* by Maurice Merleau-Ponty. In this work Merleau-Ponty critically undermines the Cartesian idea of self as a disembodied subject through an extraordinary phenomenological account of the embodied self based on a description of the intertwining of subjectivity and objectivity in the flesh of the "lived body" at the prereflective level of primordial perception. Merleau-Ponty's descriptive profile reveals how in contrast to the object body which is "in" space, the lived body "inhabits" or pervades space—it embodies its surrounding spatial environment so as to physically incarnate the whole figure/ground *gestalt* contexture of the perceptual field as a "corporeal situation" or "global sensorium" of intersensory synaesthesia.

Moreover, the twentieth-century tradition of classical American philosophy running through Peirce, James, Dewey, Whitehead, and Mead represents a sustained effort to overturn Cartesian dualism. In American philosophy this revolt against Cartesian mind-body dualism is especially brought into focus by G. H. Mead's empirical account of the social self as an I-Me dialectic grounded in a behavioristic psychology of embodied gestures. For Mead the social self is not just an I or disembodied Cartesian subject but a dialectic of I and Me representing the unity of subject and object, mind and body, mental and physical, or psychic and somatic. Mead's concept of the embodied social self as a dialectic between the I or individual pole and the Me or institutional pole describes not only the relation of mind to the physical body of the five senses but also to the larger *body of culture* with its corpus of embodied norms, laws, rites, customs, and institutions. In terms of his methodological approach, Mead rejects introspectionism and adopts a holistic, nonreductive, and social form of behavioristic psychology which studies human consciousness, mind, and self as externally manifested through the embodied *gestures* of observable human conduct.

In contrast to Platonic and Cartesian philosophy in the West and Samkya Yoga philosophy in the East, for which body and mind are by definition ontologically distinct, the nondual worldview of Japanese Buddhism argues for the oneness of body and mind. Although twentieth-century Western thinkers like Mead and Merleau-Ponty have attempted to develop a nondual model of selfhood which overturns the Cartesian subjectivism, Japanese Buddhism has from the very start assumed that the true self is a unified bodymind experience as codified by the Zen Buddhist doctrinal formula: *shinjin ichinyo*— "oneness of bodymind." Moreover, this nondual Zen Buddhist model of the self as body-mind unity has been appropriated in the frameworks of representative modern Japanese philosophers like Nishida Kitarō and Watsuji Tetsurō. However, in contemporary Japanese philosophy the "body" has especially been thematized by Yuasa Yasuo. In *The Body* (1987) and other works, Yuasa analyzes the Japanese concept of self as a bodymind unity in both traditional and modern Japanese Buddhist thought while at the same time working out his own model of embodied selfhood through a synthesis of Japanese and Western perspectives on the body.

Whereas previously I have shown how representative thinkers in modern Japanese philosophy and G. H. Mead in classical American philosophy have converged upon an intersubjective model of the social self as a self-other interaction, I now attempt to further clarify how they have converged upon a psychosomatic model of the *embodied self* as a body-mind interaction. The parallels between Mead and modern Japanese philosophers can be seen through the proximity of both to Merleau-Ponty's phenomenology of the lived body. Just as the Yuasa Yasuo (1987) has established the parallels between Merleau-Ponty and modern Japanese philosophy, so coauthors S. B. Rosenthal and P. L. Bourgeois (1991) have established the parallels between Merleau-Ponty and G. H. Mead. It is thus shown that like Merleau-Ponty's phenomenology of the lived body, both Mead and modern Japanese Buddhist philosophers have developed a intersubjective concept of embodied selfhood as a unified bodymind experience.

## The Social Self as a Bodymind Unity in the Behaviorism of G. H. Mead

Mead's communication model of the social self is at once anti-Cartesian in that it understands the person as an integral unity of body and mind. In *Movements of Thought in the Nineteenth Century* (1936), Mead characterizes Descartes's version of mind-body dualism as follows: "For Descartes, mind and body were distinct substances neither of which depended upon the other for its being" (MTNC, 307). However, in contrast to the dualistic framework of Cartesian subjectivism, Mead conceives of the social self as a unified bodymind experience. The central importance of bodymind unity for Mead's theory of the social self is clarified in his 1927 Lectures on Social Psychology, now available in a volume called *The Individual and the Social Self: Unpublished Works of George Herbert Mead* (1982). In this essay Mead argues for the inseparability of self and body: "We are thus tied to the body insofar as we have a self" (ISS 148). Elsewhere he asserts that "Our bodies are parts of our environment" (MSS 171). For Mead the self is always connected to its surrounding environment through a physical body. He maintains that such disciplines as social psychology in the human sciences and evolutionary theory in the natural sciences function to undermine Cartesian mind-body dualism and instead reveals the continuity between the mind, body, and surrounding physical environment of nature: "For Descartes there was a physical and a psychical realm, but . . . Mind and body are not to be separated on the basis of our present physical science" (ISS 167). From the modern scientific evolutionary perspective there is an unbroken continuity between the mind and body in that both emerge from out of, and are thus continuous with, the surrounding physical environment of nature. According to Mead, "There is an organic union between mind and body, they could not exist without each other, but we can think of them separately" (ISS 173). Hence, while body and mind can be distinguished through analysis, they are not separable within the organic unity of the social self. Elsewhere in the text he states: "The self involves a unity; it is there in the social process. . . . It is the center about which the individual is organized, and the body is an integral part of the self" (ISS 148). He further argues, "The self . . . is a social entity that must be related to the entire body, and only insofar as the self is related to the body is it related to the environment" (ISS 148). Mead thus holds that because the self is a social self which is always tied to a body and the body is a part of the environment, it is through the medium of the body that the self is anchored in its surrounding environment.

Mead's revolt against Cartesian dualism in all of its forms can be summed up through his *bipolar* concept of the social self as an I-Me dialectic. It has already been seen that while for Descartes the self is an I or atomic individual, for Mead the self is a bipolar social self arising through a "conversation of 'I' and 'Me'," thus representing the two interactive poles of *individuality* and *sociality*. In this context Mead employs his I-Me dialectic of intersubjectivity to clarify how the social self is constituted through an individual-society interaction. However, his I-Me dialectic functions in other contexts to explain how the self is an *embodied self* constituted through a body-mind interaction. For Mead the self is not just an I or disembodied Cartesian subject but a "dialectic of 'I' and 'Me'," thereby representing the dialectical unity of subject and object, mind and body, mental and physical, or psychic and somatic. At the cosmological level Mead's concept of the social self as a dialectic between two poles of I and Me can be compared to A. N. Whitehead's process theory of selfhood as a serially ordered society of creative, novel, and aesthetic events, wherein each event is *bipolar* with both a "physical pole" and a "mental pole." In *Process and Reality* (1929) Whitehead states: "Each actuality is essentially bipolar, physical and mental, and the physical inheritance is essentially accompanied by a conceptual reaction" (PR 108). According to Whitehead an event or occasion of experience arises through its multiplicity of causal relations (physical prehensions or feelings) inherited from the past at the "physical pole" and then reacts with creativity in the present at the "mental pole." Likewise, for Mead the self is a series of psychosomatic events which arise through social relations inherited from the past as a Me corresponding to the *physical pole* followed by a spontaneous response in the present as an "I" corresponding to the *mental pole*. Hence, in the organismic process cosmology of both Mead and Whitehead, the self arises by embodying its social situation in the past at the Me or physical pole and then by introducing novelty in the present at the I or mental pole.

Mead's effort to overturn the Cartesian dualism of body and mind is to be found not only in terms of his theoretical framework but also in terms of his method: namely, his "social behaviorism" based on a Wundtian psychology of *gestures*. At the outset of *Mind, Self, and Society* Mead identifies his basic method as that of behavioristic psychology, or social behaviorism (MSS 1), which he then defines as follows: "Behaviorism . . . is simply an approach to the study of the experience of the individual from the point of view of his conduct . . . as it is observable by others" (MSS 2). He rejects introspectionism and adopts behavioristic psychology as an observational method which provides an empirical basis for the study of human consciousness, mind and self through their manifestations in overt human behavior, conduct, actions, and practices. However, Mead asserts that unlike the behaviorism of John Watson, which is reductionistic and individualistic, his own method is a holistic, nonreductive, and social behaviorism in that it recognizes the parts of the act that do not come to external observation (images, feelings, sensations), and it emphasizes the act of an individual in a social situation (MSS 6).

The key to Mead's social behaviorism is his theory of the "gesture" which he incorporates from the psychology of Wundt (MSS 42). Based upon his nondualistic concept of the social self as an inseparable unity of mind and body, Mead's behavioristic psychology is an empirical method which studies the human mind as externally objectified through the embodied gestures of observable human conduct. He defines the "gesture" as the initial phase of a social act of communication functioning as a *stimulus* which calls out for a *response* in the final phase of the act (MSS 43). He further clarifies that while the "gesture" is the *stimulus*, the *response* is the "meaning" of that gesture: "The gesture stands for a certain resultant of the social act . . . so that the meaning is given or stated in terms of response" (MSS 76). Mead's pragmatic theory of meaning is a refinement of Dewey's psychology as developed in "The Reflex Arc Concept in Psychology" (1896), which replaces the dualistic S-R (stimulus-response) model of the reflex arc with the notion of a "circuit of coordination," whereupon it is only in terms of the whole "circuit" that the initial phase becomes the stimulus and the final phase becomes the response. Mead refines Dewey's concept of a "circuit of coordination" and make it the basis for his own analysis of the "social act" as the fundamental unit of communicative interaction which stretches across the dualism of stimulus (gesture) and response (meaning). For Mead all social acts of communication are to be understood in behavioristic terms as a "conversation of gestures" (MSS 47). Even *thinking* is defined in behaviorist terms as a social process of communication which arises by internalizing the external "conversation of gestures" (MSS 47). But while animal communication is restricted to a conversation of nonsignificant gestures, human communication involves a conversation of *significant gestures* at the symbolic level of interaction. A gesture functions as a significant symbol or significant gesture when it calls out to oneself the same response that it calls out to another, thereby to have a shared or common meaning (MSS 47). Although any kind of gesture can function as a significant gesture, such as the conversation of bodily gestures employed in the sign language of the American Indians and the deaf, Mead holds that the development of a social self with reflexive self-awareness is above all fostered through speech acts of communicative interaction by means of a conversation of "vocal gestures" which call out the same meaning for both the speaker and the listener (SW 387).

It can now be seen how the social behaviorism of Mead functions to completely overturn the dualistic framework of Cartesian subjectivism. First of all, his behavioristic psychology undermines the individualistic method of Cartesian subjectivism in that interior mental states are not directly examined through introspection, but through their external manifestation in the embodied gestures of overt human conduct, wherein each gesture is *publicly observable* to others. Hence, in opposition to the introspective method of Cartesian subjectivism with its appeal to private verification by a solitary thinker, social behaviorism follows the scientific experimental method of pragmatism which requires *public verification* by an intersubjective community of inquirers. Secondly, insofar as behavioristic psychology examines the human mind through its *embodiment* in a "language of gestures," including bodily, vocal, and linguistic gestures, it completely undermines the Cartesian dualism of body and mind. In that Mead's behavioristic psychology establishes a direct correlation between inner mental states and outer physical gestures, it presupposes a *functional relation of body and mind*. For as the psychiatrist Wilhelm Reich has argued, the correspondence which can be observed between mental and physical states requires an explanatory principle of *psychosomatic identity*. The upshot of Mead's behavioristic psychology of gestures is that the Cartesian dualism of body and mind is now wholly abandoned for a nondual concept of embodied selfhood as a unified bodymind experience.

The significance of Mead's behavioristic method for philosophy and the social sciences is highlighted by Jürgen Habermas in *The Theory of Communicative Action*. He points out that at the turn of the century Cartesian subjectivism was undermined by analytic philosophy of language and behavioristic psychology, both of which were strongly indebted to C. S. Peirce, who defined meaning in terms of shared, observable practices. Habermas (1989, 3) further asserts that both the linguistic and behavioristic aspects of Peirce's method were first integrated in the symbolic interactionist framework of social behaviorism formulated by G. H. Mead. Both the philosophy of language and behaviorism implicit in Peirce's theory of meaning are at once combined through Mead's behavioristic understanding of linguistic communication as a "conversation of gestures" (MSS 47). It should be recalled how Peirce assaulted Cartesian subjectivism through his semiotic concept of human selfhood as a web of linguistic "signs." To repeat the words of Peirce: "the word or sign which man uses is the man himself. For, as the fact that every thought is a sign, taken in conjunction with the fact that life is a train of thought, proves that man is a sign. . . . Thus my language is the sum total of myself; for the man is the thought" (1955, 249; also, CP, 5.314). Building upon Peirce's theory of signs, Royce developed a semiotic view of self in a community of interpretation in terms of a metaphysics of absolute idealism whereupon the self and all reality is understood to be pure mind or thought. Mead learned of Peirce's theory of signs from his teacher Royce, and went on to articulate the intersubjective constitution of human mind and self in society through social acts of linguistic communication, but as defined in *behavioristic* terms as a "conversation of gestures" wherein the observable "gesture" is the stimulus, and the observable response is the "meaning" evoked by the gesture. Whereas for Royce the meaning of a sign is always another sign so that all relations are between minds, for Mead the meaning of a sign is not another sign but an observable embodied *response*. Hence, for Mead the linguistic meanings of signs or significant symbols are not only "mental," as for Royce, but also *physical* as embodied in a gestural language. Mead's paradigm shift beyond Cartesian subjectivism to an intersubjective communication model of the social self thus represents a fully *embodied* mode of human existence as a "conversation of gestures."

As various authors have noted, there are many points in common between G. H. Mead's description of the social self as a bodymind unity which physically embodies the social situation from which it has been constituted, and Maurice Merleau-Ponty's intersubjective account of the self as anchored in the environment through a lived body as a global sensorium which incarnates or embodies the spatial locus of its whole perceptual field as a corporeal situation. The parallels between these two thinkers have been especially clarified in a work entitled *Mead and Merleau-Ponty* (1991) by S. B. Rosenthal and P. L. Bourgeois. At the methodological level both Mead and Merleau-Ponty employ a behavioristic psychology based on the analysis of psychic contents through an observation of human conduct which presupposes an underlying functional relation between body and mind. Furthermore, both Mead and Merleau-Ponty are described as overcoming introspective accounts of self through a holistic, nonreductive form of behavioristic psychology which focuses upon how consciousness, mind, and self are externally manifested through the embodied *gestures* of observable human behavior (1991, 11). Just as Mead's concept of the social act is based on Dewey's notion of a "circuit of coordination" between stimulus (gesture) and response (meaning), so Merleau-Ponty rejects the "constancy hypothesis" according to which a one-to-one correspondence obtains between stimulus and response in favor of an *intentional arc* or "circuit of existence" (1991, 148). Like the "circuit of coordination" in Mead's social act of communication, Merleau-Ponty's "circuit of existence" represents the organic interaction or intertwining of subjectivity and objectivity within a social situation. Rosenthal and Bourgeois also emphasize the social, communicative, and intersubjective character of selfhood as a bodymind unity in both Mead and Merleau-Ponty. Speaking of the social concept of self in both thinkers, they write: "The respective views of the self found in the positions of Mead and Merleau-Ponty include a common focus on the nature of the self as social or intersubjective and the importance of a type of role taking in the development of the self which involves the mutual interrelation of the emergence of self-awareness and the awareness of the other" (1991, 86). In this context the authors go on to underscore the central role of the *lived body* in the decentered self theory and intersubjective self-other dialectic of both Mead and Merleau-Ponty. They state that for Mead, "The 'I' and the 'me' are functional relations, not metaphysical distinctions, because they represent two ways in which the lived body, the decentered subject, functions" (1991, 106). Similarly, Merleau-Ponty has developed a concept of "social subjectivity which, as non ego-logical, is decentered in the interacting and intertwining of self and others achieved through the central role of the lived body" (1991, 98). They conclude that both thinkers develop a nondualistic concept of self as a unity of body and mind as well as an intersubjective notion of self as a unity of self and other: "Thus, it is clear that Merleau-Ponty, like Mead, has overcome solipsism, has rejected dualism involving body and mind, and in the process, has developed a view of the essentially intersubjective or social nature of the self" (1991, 96).

## The Self as a Bodymind Unity in Japanese Buddhism

The psychosomatic concept of self as a unified bodymind experience has long been a recurrent theme in traditional Japanese Buddhist philosophy. Different sects of Japanese Buddhism have encapsulated the principle of psychosomatic unity by means of various doctrinal formulas such as *sokushin jobutsu* or "enlightenment in this very body" in the Shingon Mikkyō (Esoteric) Buddhism of Kūkai (774–835), *shinjin ichinyo* or "oneness of body-mind" in the Rinzai Zen of Eisai (1141–1215), *shinjin gakudō* or "studying the Way with body-mind" in the Sōtō Zen of Dōgen, and *shikishin funi* or "nonduality of body-mind" in the Nichiren Buddhism of Nichiren (1222–82). From the standpoint of the unity of the "three truths" in the Tendai Buddhist philosophy of Saichō (766–822), the body signifies *ketai* or material truth and the mind represents *kūtai* or spiritual truth, both of which are seen to be nondual aspects of *chūtai*, the truth of the middle way. A fundamental assumption of Japanese Buddhism is that the realization of self as a oneness of body-mind is not merely given but is itself an achievement that requires "cultivation" (*shūgyō*). At the level of self-cultivation, the *kōan* meditation of Eisai's Rinzai Zen, the *shikantaza* or "sitting-only" exercise of Dōgen's Sōtō Zen, the *sanmitsu* or "three secrets" exercise of *mudra, mantra,* and *mandala* in Kūkai's Mikkyō, the *shikan* or "tranquility and insight" practice of Saichō's Tendai, and the chanting of *daimoku* ("*Namu myōhō renge kyō*") in Nichiren Buddhism, are all directed toward the realization of the true self as a nondual bodymind experience. Moreover, the oneness of bodymind has been a recurrent theme in the Zen Buddhist influenced aestheticism of Geidō—the Way of the artist, for instance, the tea ceremony, inkwash painting, and Nō drama, as well as Bushidō—the Way of the Samurai warrior, including maritial arts like Judō, Karate, Kendō, and Aikidō. Based upon the notion of self as a bodymind unity the Japanese Buddhist tradition assumes that one can transform the mind by disciplining the body and vice versa. Thus, the Japanese concept of embodied selfhood can be said to presuppose the Reichian principle of *psychosomatic identity*, otherwise expressed as the "functional relation of body and mind."

*The Bodymind Experience in Japanese Buddhism* (1985) by David Edward Shaner uses the phenomenological method established by Edmund Husserl in order to explicate the Japanese Buddhist concept of self as a primoridal unity of bodymind in both the Zen teachings of Dōgen and the Shingon Mikkyō philosophy of Kūkai. Shaner argues that both the Zen meditation of Dōgen and the Tantric mandala-visualization of Kūkai result in the achievement of a unified bodymind experience, or what he otherwise calls "first-order bodymind awareness" characterized by the spatial embodiment of "an expanded periphery and horizon *in toto*" (1985, 48). He asserts that while in ordinary perception various "thetic positings" (mental discriminations) constitute experience so that a specifiable noetic vector intends a privileged noematic focus, the Tantric practice of mandala contemplation and the Zen practice of seated meditation both function to neutralize all mental positings, thereby leading to the first-order bodymind experience of an expanded periphery and total horizon of boundless empty space. However, while Shaner's work lucidly explains in Husserlian phenomenological terms how Japanese Buddhism is oriented toward a realization of the true self as a unified bodymind experience of an expanded horizon of space, he does not go on to articulate the notion of *social space*, nor does he describe *the social nature of Japanese selfhood* through its embodiment of a spatial locus. By contrast the modern Japanese philosopher Watsuji Tetsurō develops a phenomenological description of Japanese selfhood not only in terms of its individual existence in time but also in terms of its social existence in a "climate" (*fūdo*) of space. Watsuji's phenomenology of embodied spatial existence thus functions to disclose the social, relational, and contextual nature of Japanese selfhood as intersubjectively constituted through a dialectic of self-other relationships.

The concept of self as a bodymind unity in traditional Japanese Buddhism as well as in the modern Japanese philosophy of Watsuji Tetsurō and Nishida Kitarō has been especially clarified by Yuasa Yasuo in his important work, *The Body: Toward and Eastern Mind-Body Theory* (1987). While Shaner employs Husserl's phenomenology to explicate the focus/horizon structure of embodied spatial existence in Japanese Buddhism, Yuasa instead makes recourse to Merleau-Ponty's phenomenology of perception. The advantage of this latter approach is that Merleau-Ponty explicitly thematizes the notion of the *lived body* in relation to "lived space." Furthermore, Merleau-Ponty discusses the intersubjective constitution of embodied selfhood in lived space. In this context Yuasa (1987, 174) clarifies Merleau-Ponty's phenomenological description of how the human subject is physically incarnated in the network of interconnections, and how for Merleau-Ponty space-consciousness comes to bear a more fundamental importance than the subject's time-consciousness as for Heidegger. Yuasa (1987, 169) further clarifies how Meleau-Ponty rejects the Cartesian dualism between mind and body by positing a third term that underlies them both; namely, the "habitual body" (*le corps habituel*) which underlies the "actual body" (*le corps actuel*) and is the fundamental layer making the body a lived body, or as it were, the bodily scheme (*le scheme corporeal*) (1987, 169). From the standpoint of East-West comparative philosophy Yuasa (1987, 167–79) then argues that like Merleau-Ponty, both traditional Japanese Buddhism as well as the modern Japanese philosophy of Nishida Kitarō and Watsuji Tetsurō articulate a notion of the "somatic self" which completely overcomes Cartesian mind-body dualism. Moreover, Yuasa (1987, 38) points out that similar to Watsuji's *ningen* theory of Japanese personhood as embodying a *fūdo* or spatial "climate" of society and nature, Nishida develops a somatic idea of selfhood as embodying a *basho* or spatial "locus" (place, matrix, field). It can thus be said that just as for Merleau-Ponty the self embodies its entire spatial environment as a corporeal situation, so for Nishida the self embodies a *basho* or spatial "locus," and for Watsuji the person as *ningen* embodies a *fūdo* or spatial "climate."

Yuasa goes on to quote Nishida's definition of the body: "A body is that which is seen as well as that which sees [NKZ, vol. 8, 326]" (Yuasa: 1987, 50). Again, he directly cites Nishida as follows: "There is no ego without a body. . . . Even our own bodies are seen from the outside. Yet our body is that which sees as well as that which is seen. There is no seeing without a body [NKZ, vol. 8, 328]" (Yuasa: 1987, 51). Yuasa clarifies that a body, as that which sees, indicates how the embodied self exists in the world as a "subject," while its being that which is seen indicates how it exists as an "object "(1987, 51). He adds that as a subject which sees as well as an object which is seen, the embodied self is ambiguous in its being. In this context Yuasa points out the similarity between the concept of the lived body in both Nishida and Merleau-Ponty as that which both sees and is seen: "Merleau-Ponty also defined the body as both 'the seeing' (*le voyant*) and 'the visible' (*le visible*)" (1987, 51). For both Nishida and Merleau-Ponty, then, insofar as the body is both that which sees and that which is seen, the embodied self has the reflexive character of being both subject and object at the same time. Yuasa explains that similar to Merleau-Ponty's description of embodied selfhood through an analysis of human behavior, Nishida formulates a theory of "acting intuition" (*koi chokkan*), wherein the acting self in the *basho* or space of the lifeworld is grasped as a dialectical unity of action and intuition (1987, 65). Hence, similar to Merleau-Ponty's analysis of the embodied self as a "circuit of existence" wherein subjectivity and objectivity are intertwined, Yuasa describes Nishida's theory of acting intuition as a dialectic wherein "the self and the world are linked together in terms of the centripetal-centrifugal circuit of intuiting and acting" (1987, 55).

## The Self as a Bodymind Unity in Mead and Japanese Buddhist Philosophy

Now I would like to briefly consider how the psychosomatic theory of selfhood as a bodymind unity developed in both traditional Japanese Buddhism as well as the modern Japanese philosophy of Watsuji, Nishida, and Yuasa can be elucidated in terms of Mead's nondualistic theory of the embodied social self as a dialectic of I and Me. It has been seen that for Mead the human self is not a merely an I or disembodied Cartesian subject but a conversation of I and Me, thereby expressing the dialectical unity of subject and object, mind and body, psychic and somatic, or physical and mental. Hence, both Mead and Japanese Buddhism are at once anti-Cartesian in that they reject dualism for a concept of embodied selfhood as a unity of body and mind. Similar to Japanese Buddhism the Chicago school pragmatism of Mead holds that the self is always connected to a body and the body is a part of the environment so that only through the body is the self related to its surrounding physical environment of society and nature. The Japanese concept of embodied selfhood as a unified bodymind experience of an expanded periphery and horizon *in toto* is articulated throughout the tradition of classical American philosophy in terms of the "focus/field" or "foreground/background" structure of immediate experience wherein each individual organism in the foreground focus is surrounded by a social environment in the background field. Mead's nondualistic model of the social, temporal, and multiple self as a unity of body and mind provides an empirically based social scientific Western framework by means of which to articulate the traditional Zen Buddhist concept of selfhood as *shinjin ichinyo* or "oneness of body-mind." Also, Mead's communicative interaction model of the social self expressed in behavioristic terms as a conversation of significant gestures, including the full range of bodily, vocal, and linguistic gestures, provides a framework by means of which to elucidate the Japanese Mikkyō (Tantric) Buddhist concept of realizing the true self as a bodymind unity by means of the "three secrets" (*sanmitsu*) practice of transforming body, speech, and mind through *mudra* (bodily gestures), *mantra* (vocal incantations), and *mandala* (mental images).

A most important parallel is to be seen in their essential agreement that the self as as unified bodymind experience is something to be achieved. As clarified especially by the research of Yuasa Yasuo, the Japanese Buddhist traditions "generally treat mind-body unity as an *achievement*, rather than an essential relation" (Yuasa: 1987, 1). In Japanese Buddhist thought, he argues, the integration of mind and body is only partial in the everyday self so that full integration is the result of prolonged self-cultivation (1987, 9). For Yuasa the Japanese Buddhist tradition is directed toward the realization of an "achieved body-mind unity" (1987, 3). Likewise, it has been seen how for Mead the self is not initially there at birth, but is something which requires development through intersubjective praxis (MSS 135). According to Mead the individual becomes a social self as a bodymind unity through a dialectical process wherein the self must constantly reconcile the I and the Me, thereby integrating the individual and social, subjective and objective, and physical and mental aspects. Thus, like both traditional and modern Japanese Buddhism, the philosophy of Mead emphasizes that the social self as a unity of body and mind is not simply given as an essential relationship; it is something which must be *realized* through a process of development.

Parallels between Mead and modern Japanese philosophy on the self as a bodymind unity can be articulated through the similarities of both to Merleau-Ponty's account of the lived body. Just as Yuasa (1987) sees a close affinity between the bodymind theory of selfhood developed by Japanese philosophy in the East and Maurice Merleau-Ponty in the West, so Rosenthal and Bourgeois (1991) see an intimate connection between the unified bodymind theory of selfhood established by Mead and Merleau-Ponty. Yuasa (1987, 38) shows how in modern Japanese philosophy Nishida's spatial notion of *basho* or "locus" (place, field, matrix) and Watsuji's idea of *fūdo* or "climate" both denote an embodied social space of the lifeworld in which the person arises through a mutual encounter between self and other. Similarly, in the West both Mead and Merleau-Ponty abandon the Cartesian ontology of subjects and objects for an ontology of "situations," whereupon the social self physically embodies its value-laden figure/ground gestalt situation functioning as the spatial locus for self-other relations. Just as Mead adopts Dewey's notion of a "circuit of coordination" between stimulus and response as the basis for his notion of the social act as organic interaction between self and other, and Merleau-Ponty analyzes the embodied self as a "circuit of existence" wherein subjectivity and objectivity are intertwined, so Yuasa has described Nishida's theory of acting intuition as a dialectic wherein the self and the world are linked through a "circuit of intuiting and acting" (1987, 55). Again, just as Yuasa (1987, 51) has demonstrated how Nishida and Merleau-Ponty similarly define the lived body in reflexive terms as both *that which sees* (the subject) and *that which is seen* (the object), it has likewise been discussed how for Mead the embodied social self has a reflexive character as a dialectical unity of the I and Me representing the two interacting poles of subjectivity and objectivity. As Mead explicitly asserts: "This characteristic is represented in the word 'self,' which is a reflexive, and indicates that which can be both subject and object" (MSS 137). Mead thus argues that the individual I becomes an embodied social self with reflexive self-consciousness by taking on the attitudes of the "Me" or generalized other and then by seeing itself as an object from the standpoint of that other, thereby to function as both subject (*that which sees*) and object (*that which is seen*) at the same time. In this way modern Japanese philosophers like Nishida, Watsuji, and Yuasa in the East along with philosophers like Merleau-Ponty and Mead in the West have together converged upon a nondualistic model of embodied selfhood as a unified bodymind experience.

## The Cultural Body of the Social Self in Mead and Asian Thought

Like the Zen/Confucian *ningen* concept of contextual persons in Japanese philosophy, Mead's bipolar model of a social self as a dialectical interaction between the I or physiological pole and the Me or institutional pole represents the notion of an embodied subject which includes not only the unity of the mind and its physical body, but also the wider "body" of culture and society. It has been seen that a primary concept in the Confucian tradition of China, Korea, and Japan is the principle of *li* or "ritual propriety" signifying the established norms which govern human relationships, thereby constituting both person and community in East Asian culture. For Confucianism, ritual acts of *li* establish the *tao* or Way for all norm-governed aesthetic, moral, and religious existence in human society. As pointed out by Hall and Ames (1987, 87–88), in the Confucian tradition of China there is a direct connection between ritual action and the body of cultural tradition as revealed through the cognate relationship between the two Chinese characters, "ritual action" (*li*) and "body" (*ti*). Both of these characters share the *li* phonetic, "ritual vase" (*li*), which associates ritual with the sacred and sacrificial. Like a "body" of literature or a "corpus" of music, the Confucian rituals of *li* are embodied social institutions which continue through time as a repository of the religious, ethical, and aesthetic insights of those who have gone before in the ancient traditions of East Asia. The Japanese *ningen/kanjin* model of contextual persons governed by symbolic interaction rituals in social groups patterned after the family system is itself wholly permeated by this Confucian principle of *li* (J. *rei*) or "ritual propriety." Insofar as relationships between the contextual persons, social selves, or ritual men of Japanese group-centered society are governed by the Confucian principle of *li* they incorporate the "cultural body" of ancient tradition with its inherited fund of institutions, rituals, laws, norms, and customs. This concept of a wider body of cultural institutions is implicit in the Japanese word *dantai* or "group," which assumes special importance in that Japanese selfhood is usually classified as a form of groupism (*dantai-shugi*). Like the Japanese word *taiken* or "experience," the word *dantai* contains the character pronounced *tai*, "body." However, while *taiken* indicates that "experience" is always "bodily experience" rooted in one's physical body, *dantai* (= group + body) literally designates one's "group-body," or as it were, the larger *corpus* of society, tradition, and culture with its embodied institutions, customs, laws, and rituals.

A similar principle to the Confucian idea of *li* is to be found in the ancient Indian Vedic principle of *Rta*, embodied Norm. The Vedic concept of *Rta* or "embodied Norm" functions similarly to the Confucian idea of *li* in that it provides the basis for all norm-governed rational thought, ethical conduct, and aesthetic experience. This understanding of *Rta* as an embodied Norm or cultural body establishing the Way for moral action in society has been especially clarified by Antonio T. de Nicholas in his work *Meditations through the Rg Veda* (1976, 155–77). De Nicholas states that "*Rta* is perhap the most significant contribution both to practical reason and to social acting which Indian Tradition has to offer" (1976, 160). According to De Nicolas, *Rta* provided Rg Vedic man the basic normative principles which governed moral and social life in that it is the store of all that has been rightly formed as the common body of culture. De Nicholas variously characterizes the Vedic principle of *Rta* or "embodied Norm" as signifying "activity which has become embodied in a universal Norm" (1976, 158), the "practical body of acting for a community" (1976, 158), a "common body of Law, a Norm" (1976, 161), the "body of the Norm" (1976, 163), the "moving body of the social group" (1976, 163), the "embodied community" (1976, 163), and so forth. Defined as an embodied norm the Vedic principle of *Rta* now comes to be understood as the accumulation of practices, customs, rituals, and institutions governing moral action within the common body of a social community. De Nicholas thus asserts that the ancient Vedic principle of *Rta* underscores the long neglected "social-embodied dimension of Indian philosophy" (1976, 163).

Like the Confucian principle of *li* in East Asia and the Vedic principle of *Rta* in India, Mead's principle of sociality functions to clarify how the individual subject incorporates the wider "body" of cultural memories represented by the institutions of society. Mead clarifies the double structure of the bio-social self as having "two poles" (MSS 229), namely, what he calls the "individual or physiological pole," and the "institutional pole" (MSS 230). Thus in terms of his I-Me dialectic of the bio-social self, while the *I* signifies the individual aspect of the physiological pole, the *Me* or generalized other designates the social-embodied aspect of the institutional pole. By defining the Me as the "institutional pole," Mead has made fully explicit the process whereby the self becomes a social self through internalizing the embodied institutions of society. His definition of the Me as the institutional pole clarifies that the social self represents not only "man in society" but also *society in man*. The bio-social self constitutes itself as a unity by first taking on the common body of social institutions, customs, rites, norms, and traditions inherited from the *past* at the "institutional pole" represented by the Me or generalized other and then responds with individual creativity, spontaneity, and originality in the *present* at the physiological pole represented by the I. Mead's basic definition of the social self as a "conversation between I and Me" is restated in behavioristic terms as a "conversation of *gestures*," wherein embodied selfhood is achieved to the degree which the individual calls out that institutionalized group of responses in himself (MSS 265). Mead specifically asserts that the social self can be understood to *embody* the institutionalized system of reactions, responses, and attitudes of the Me or generalized other. "The social self," writes Mead, can be said to "embody those reactions which can be common to him in a great community" (MSS 324). Mead's concept of the *generalized other* as a cultural body of rules guiding norm-governed conduct is expressed by J. M. Charon as follows: "Mead used the word 'generalized other' to describe the shared culture of the group. . . . 'generalized other' places the emphasis on culture as a *shared body of rules*" (1989, 165). Hence, like the Confucian tradition of East Asia and the Vedic tradition of India, Mead clarifies how at the institutional pole of the Me or generalized other, the self embodies the social institutions, customs, laws, habits, practices, norms and rituals of its society, thereby taking on the "corpus" of its tradition or "body" of its culture. Furthermore, like the Confucian idea of *li* and the Vedic idea of *Rta*, the Me or generalized other at the institutional pole of the bio-social self functions to provide those embodied universal norms governing social relationships in society. Like the Confucian idea of *li* and the Vedic idea of *Rta*, the Me or generalized other at the "institutional pole" is the embodied community, the embodied tradition, the embodied law, and the embodied norm which is necessary for all norm-governed rational thought, moral conduct, and aesthetic experience. Mead's concept of the Me or generalized other as the embodiment of social institutions can in part be seen as a secularized reformulation of Royce's salvific and religious idea of community. In his Christian soteriological theory, Royce views salvation as a social process of achieving self-realization through membership in the beloved community of the church, understood in St. Paul's terms as representing the "body of Christ." In Mead's naturalistic reworking of this concept, self-realization occurs through membership in the common body of a secular liberal democratic community by means of norm-governed social acts of communicative interaction through a conversation of embodied gestures. It can thus be said that for Mead in American pragmatism, as for the Confucian dimensions of Japanese thought and culture, the idea of becoming a person carries with it the goal of achieving a social self as an integrated bodymind experience, thereby to form a *single body* with the embodied norms, rites, and institutions of society. However, Mead has best of all articulated the dialectic wherein the self arises by incorporating embodied institutions of society inherited from the past as a socialized Me, and then *reconstructing* those institutions through creative activity in the present as an autonomous I.

# ~:13:~

## The Social Self as a Human–Nature Interaction

The concept of a *social self* as developed both in the traditions of American pragmatism and modern Japanese philosophy is here set forth as a unifying principle for an East-West model of ecology, including a philosophy of nature as well as an environmental ethics and a conservation aesthetics. Whereas previously I have underscored the sociological dimensions of the social self as an individual-society relation, in this section of the present work I focus especially upon the *ecological* dimensions of the social self as an *organism-environment interaction*. An ecological concept of the social self which establishes a *continuity* between the individual and its total surroundings of society and nature has been developed by John Dewey, Alfred North Whitehead, and George Herbert Mead in American pragmatism as well as representative thinkers like Nishida Kitarō and Watsuji Tetsurō in modern Japanese philosophy. It is thus my contention that in the twentieth century, both in the East and the West, there has been a shift beyond the narrow egocentric perspective of individualism to an *eco-centric* model of the social self as an organism-environment interaction which can provide the theoretical basis for a comprehensive system of environmental ethics.

## The Environmental Ethics of Aldo Leopold

In the West the main inspiration for the field of environmental ethics is a volume by Aldo Leopold entitled *A Sand County Almanac* (1949), especially the capstone essay of this work called "The Land Ethic." It is here where he makes a threefold division of ethics: "The first ethics dealt with the relation between individuals. . . . Later accretions dealt with the relation between the individual and society" (1966, 238). He then goes on to enlarge the discipline of ethics to include a third factor: man's relation to the land, or as it were, the land ethic:

There is as yet no ethic dealing with man's relation to land and to the animals and plants which grow upon it . . . The land-relation is still strictly economic, entailing privileges but not obligations. The extension of ethics to this third element in the human environment is, if I read the evidence correctly, an evolutionary possibility and an ecological necessity. (1966, 238–39)

Leopold defines ethics in terms of his key notion of "community." However, whereas previously, ethics has confined itself to the relationship between individuals and the human community, Leopold suggests that the field be expanded to include a land ethic or an environmental ethic which includes the relation of the individual to the "biotic community" of soil, plants, and animals. In Leopold's words:

All ethics so far evolved rest upon a single premise: that the individual is a member of a community of interdependent parts. . . . The land ethic simply enlarges the boundaries of the community to include soils, waters, plants, and animals, or collectively: the land. (1966, 239)

Leopold goes on to argue that "a land ethic changes the role of *Homo sapiens* from conqueror of the land-community to plain member and citizen of it" (1966, 240). Furthermore, his land ethic redefines conservation from maximizing the utility of natural resources to "a state of harmony between men and the land" (1966, 243). For Leopold, the principles of a land ethic not only impose obligations in the legalistic sense, but entail the evolution of what he terms an "ecological conscience" (1966, 243), understood as an "extension of the social conscience from people to the land" (1966, 246). According to Leopold, then, a land ethic reflects the existence of an ecological conscience, and this in turn reflects an inner conviction of individual responsibility for the health of the land (1966, 258).

Leopold grounds his "land ethic" on what he calls his "land aesthetic." As he writes in the original 1947 Foreword to his work: "These essays deal with the ethics and esthetics of land." He thus concludes *A Sand County Almanac* with a chapter entitled "Conservation Aesthetic." Leopold argues that it is the beauty or aesthetic value of nature which places a requirement upon us to extend ethics to include the symbiotic relation between man and land, to extend the social conscience from the human community to the biotic community, and thereby to establish an ecological harmony between people and their natural environment of soil, plants, and animals. According to Leopold, the norm for governing behavior in relation to land-use is whether or not our conduct is aesthetically right as well as ethically: "A thing is right when it tends to preserve the integrity, the stability, and beauty of the biotic community" (1966, 262). Hence our moral love and respect for nature is based on an aesthetic appreciation of the beauty of the land. In this way, the environmental ethic of Aldo Leopold is grounded in the value theory of a conservation aesthetic.

It should be further clarified how the ecological worldview of Leopold presupposes a metaphysics, not of separate substances with simple location, but of interrelational fields where the parts are dependent on the whole and vice versa, thereby constituting a synergistic ecosystem of organisms interacting with their environment. In his article "The Metaphysical Implications of Ecology," J. Baird Callicott describes the "field theory of living nature adumbrated by Leopold" (1989, 57). Following the insights of Leopold, Callicott argues the "object-ontology is inappropriate to an ecological description of the natural environment," and adds, "Living natural objects should be regarded as ontologically subordinate to 'events' . . . or 'field patterns'" (1989, 58). According to Callicott, for the ecology and environmental ethics of Leopold, as for the New Physics, organisms in nature are a "local perturbation, in an energy flux or 'field'," so that "subatomic microcosm" is analogous to "ecosystemic macrocosm," "moments in [a] network," or "knots in [a] web of life" (1989, 59). Hence, the ecological worldview of Aldo Leopold, including both the land ethic and land aesthetic, is to be conceived as involving a paradigm shift from atomism based on the premise of substance with independent existence to a field theory of reality based upon the notion of interconnected events.

## The Self as a Human–Nature Relation in American Pragmatism

The tradition of American philosophy has developed not only a "social" concept of the self as an individual-society relation, but also an *ecological* notion of the self as an organism-environment interaction. As such, the social self is understood as not only a unity of man and society; it is also a unity of man and nature. From the standpoint of a phenomenology of perception, the tradition of American philosophy articulates a "focus/field" or "foreground/background" model of immediate experience which is unified by a pervasive aesthetic quality with intrinsic value. According to this "foreground/background" model of selfhood, the self is always a social self in that the individual organism in the foreground is dependent for its existence upon the wider social and natural environment in the background. In American philosophy a concept of the twofold social self as a holistic foreground/background situation emerging through an organism-environment interaction unified by pervasive aesthetic quality is developed in such classic works as *Experience and Nature* (1929) by John Dewey, *Process and Reality* (1929) by Alfred North Whitehead, and *Mind, Self, and Society* (1934) by George Herbert Mead. This definition of the social self as arising through a valuative transaction between the organism and the environment functions to overcome what has been termed by A. N. Whitehead the fallacy of the bifurcation of nature and its correlate error, the fallacy of simple location, in that it establishes an unbroken *continuity* between the individual and its total surroundings of society and nature. For this reason the concept of the social self has significant implications for the extension of moral philosophy into an "environmental ethics"—what Aldo Leopold refers to in *A Sand County Almanac* (1949) as a "land ethic."

## John Dewey

It has been seen that John Dewey defines human selfhood as a function of *social interactions* between an individual and its total surroundings. To repeat his definition of selfhood from the chapter on "Nature, Mind and the Subject" in *Experience and Nature*: "Personality, selfhood, subjectivity are eventual functions that emerge with complexly organized interactions, organic and social" (EN 209). As a function of social interactions the self cannot be localized either in the subject or in the object but is instead coextensive with the whole field of social relationships from which it emerged so as to be continuous with its total environment of society and nature. Indeed, the central theme of Dewey's *Experience and Nature* (1925) is that since human experience arises as an organism-environment interaction, there is a *continuity* between the inner world of experience and the outer world of nature. At the outset of this work, he thus states: "The chief obstacle to a more effective criticism of current values lies in the traditional separation of nature and experience, which is the purpose of this volume to replace by the idea of continuity" (EN, xvi). Similar to Peirce's doctrine of Firstness or qualitative immediacy, the "pure experience" of James, and the "immediate experience" of Whitehead and Mead, Dewey articulates a nondualistic theory of immediate experience which is characterized by a whole in which there is continuity between foreground and background, subject and object, organism and environment, experience and nature, the act of experience and the material of experience. In Dewey's words: "[Experience] is 'double-barrelled' in that it recognizes in its primary integrity no division between act and material, subject and object, but contains them both in an unanalyzed totality" (EN 8). According to Dewey, it is in the prereflective, unanalyzed totality of immediate experience arising prior to the division of subject and object wherein there exists an unbroken continuity between man and nature: "[N]ature and experience are not enemies or alien. Experience is not a veil that shuts man off from nature; it is a means of penetrating continually further into the heart of nature . . . a growing progressive self-disclosure of nature itself" (EN x). There is no gap between the subjective world of human experience and the objective world of nature because experience penetrates down into the very depths of nature itself: "[E]xperience is *of* as well as *in* nature. It is not experience which is experienced, but nature . . . Experience thus reaches down into nature; it has depth" (EN 4a).

By overcoming the conventional dualism of experience and nature or subject and object, he at the same time endeavors to surmount the correlate dualism of facts and values. For Dewey, "values" are the immediately felt aesthetic qualities which are intrinsic to events in nature: "Values are naturalistically interpreted as intrinsic qualities of events in their consummatory reference" (EN xvi). However, because of the continuity between experience and nature, the immediately felt value qualities of events cannot be localized either in the organism or in the environment: "The qualities never were 'in' the organism; they were *qualities of interactions* in which both extra-organic things and organisms partake . . . they are as much qualities of the things engaged as of the organism" (EN 259; emphasis added). His polemic here is that since human experience arises through a "valuative transaction" between an organism and its natural environment, there is a continuity between the subjective qualities of experience and the objective qualities of nature. For Dewey the basic unit of existence is not "substance," but what he calls a foreground/background *situation*, otherwise termed an "event," "affair," "field," "context," or "transaction," all of which emerge as a function of social relationships and interactions. Dualisms like foreground-background, subject-object, organism-environment, mind-body, or experience-nature are *functional distinctions* within these units, derived by abstraction, and must not be taken as concrete or ultimate in any way. By this view, the immediately felt qualities of events are not to be simply located either in the organism or in the environment, either in experience or nature, but are instead located throughout the whole organism-environment situation as their pervasive aesthetic quality. As Dewey argues in *Art as Experience*, just as there is no dualism between experience and nature, there is also no dualism between experience and art in that each experience is a function of social interactions bound together with pervasive aesthetic quality. To establish a continuity between experience and nature means that the aesthetic qualities of experience *are* the aesthetic qualities of nature. Dewey's nondualistic conception of the social self as transactional situation in which there is a *continuity of experience and nature* unified by pervasive aesthetic quality thus suggests a new model of personhood that can function as the theoretical basis for an ecological theory including both a land ethics and a land aesthetics.


## Alfred North Whitehead

Like John Dewey, A. N. Whitehead defines immediate experience in holistic terms as an organism-environment interaction so as to establish the continuity between self and nature. In his *Concept of Nature* (1920), Whitehead criticizes the "bifurcation of Nature into two systems of reality" (CN 152) underlying the dualistic worldview of scientific materialism, which divides reality into an interior subjective world of "secondary" qualities (flavor, scent, color, sound, etc.), and an exterior objective world of "primary" qualities (extension, motion, configuration). As a consequence of the fallacy of the bifurcation of nature, and its correlate error, the fallacy of simple location (SMW 58), the dualistic worldview of scientific materialism is forced to rip out the vivid, immediately felt pervasive qualities suffusing all events in the undivided aesthetic continuum of nature, and to "simply locate" them in the private mental substance of an isolated Cartesian subject, such that the objective world of nature is now reduced to a meaningless nihilistic flux of material particles, thus being wholly divested of the beauty which funds it with intrinsic value. Hence, for Whitehead it is the fallacy of "simple location" underlying Western substance metaphysics which has resulted in the false bifurcation of self and nature.

According to Whitehead, the dualistic and nihilistic worldview of scientific materialism is based upon the fallacy of misplaced concreteness (SMW 58), the error of mistaking vacuous, simply located, enduring material substances for the concrete actualities from which they were abstracted; namely, the aesthetic, novel, and self-creative events or occasions of experience unified by pervasive qualities. Just as for Dewey, the "fallacy of selective emphasis" is defined as being *the* philosophical fallacy (EN 27–29), for Whitehead the fallacies of simple location, vacuous actuality, and the bifurcation of nature are all aspects of this fundamental error, the fallacy of misplaced concreteness. Against the dualistic worldview of scientific materialism, Whitehead articulates an organismic concept of nature as an undivided aesthetic continuum wherein the human self and all events are "occasions of experience" which arise through an interpenetration of the many and the one so as to both contain and pervade the whole continuum of nature as a microcosm of the macrocosm. Whitehead describes the aesthetic continuum of nature in pluralistic terms as an irreducible multiplicity of transitory events or epochal occasions which arise and perish whole through their causal interconnections to every other event, thereby forming a relational web in which the parts and the whole are mutually dependent within a symbiotic ecosystem. In order to overcome the nihilistic depiction of nature as a meaningless flux of particles in the worldview of scientific materialism, Whitehead develops a profoundly aesthetic concept of nature as a creative advance into novelty wherein each event attains some measure of beauty. He thus states, "the teleology of the Universe is directed to the production of Beauty" (AI 265). In his chapter entitled "The Romantic Reaction" from *Science and the Modern World*, he cites the empirical testimony provided by English romantic nature poetry as an argument on behalf of a philosophy of organism, which rejects the separation of facts from values in modern scientific materialism, and instead holds that beauty or aesthetic value is intrinsic to all events by virtue of the haunting presence of the whole of nature within each of its parts: "Both Shelly and Wordsworth emphatically bear witness that nature cannot be divorced from aesthetic values; and that these values arise from the cumulation, in some sense, of the brooding presence of the whole on to its various parts" (SMW 88). In his chapter on "Organisms and the Environment" from *Process and Reality*, as in his discussion of beauty in *Adventures of Ideas*, Whitehead develops a foreground/background model of immediate experience wherein each occasion of experience is characterized by an individual organism in the foreground arising through its interactions with the entire social and physical environment in the background; the *patterned contrast* between foreground focus and background field elicits maximum depth of intensity of feeling in an occasion of experience. Hence the interdependence of organism and environment or part and whole as characterized by the foreground-background pattern of immediate experience constitutes the primordial structure of beauty or depth. Whitehead repudiates the "fallacy of vacuous actuality" (PR 159), the concept of nature as comprised by lifeless substances devoid of intrinsic worth, and instead elaborates a panpsychic vision of living nature consisting of aesthetic events or occasions of experience which aim toward the realization of intrinsic values. Whitehead explicitly describes the primacy of aesthetic experience in the process metaphysics underlying his value-centric concept of nature when he asserts: "The metaphysical doctrine, here

expounded, finds the foundations of the world in the aesthetic experience . . .
All order is therefore aesthetic order, and the moral order is merely certain
aspects of aesthetic order" (RM 101). For Whitehead, then, our moral love
and respect for nature is based upon an aesthetic appreciation for the beauty
or aesthetic value of nature. In such a manner Whitehead's philosophy of
organism establishes a systematic theoretical framework in which to ground
the metaphysics of relational events implicit in the ecological worldview of
Aldo Leopold, including both his land ethic and land aesthetic.

For Whitehead, as for Aldo Leopold, ethics is grounded upon the notion that the individual is a member of a community of interdependent parts.
Also, like Leopold he *enlarges* the notion of "community or "society" so that
it includes the surrounding environment of living nature. Throughout his
chapter on "Organisms and the Environment" in *Process and Reality*, as elsewhere, Whitehead argues the social nature of reality consists in the fact that
each organism is dependent for its existence upon its relationships to a wider
background of environmental conditions. By extending the category of "the
social" beyond human society to the larger community of nature, he thus
formulates the metaphysical groundwork for an environmental ethics.
Whitehead extends the notion of "society" to encompass all of nature and
the universe when he writes: "[T]he Universe achieves its value by reason of
its co-ordination into societies of societies, and into societies of societies of
societies" (AI 264). For Whitehead, the human self is a "society" of actual
occasions, or as it were, a serially ordered "society of societies" occurring
within the larger society of nature, comprehended as a "society of societies
of societies." Elsewhere he develops his concept of nature as a "community"
of epochal occasions, each of which arises through its social relationships to
all the others: "Then the actual world is a community of epochal occasions . . .
The epochal occasions are the primary units of the actual community, and
the community is composed of the units. But each unit has in its nature a
reference to every other member of the community, so that each unit is a
microcosm representing in itself the entire all-inclusive universe" (RM 89). In
*Process and Reality* Whitehead argues that ethical theory presupposes the concept of man as a "social animal" (PR 204). However, he then goes on to enlarge the category "the social" into a generalized metaphysical category, so
that not only the human self, but *all* events are social in the community of
nature in that their existence depends upon an organization of societies of
occasions in the surrounding environment. In Whitehead's words, "the philosophy of organism appears as an enlargement of the premise in ethical
discussions: that *man is a social animal*. Analogously, *every actual occasion is
social*, so that when we have presumed the existence of any persistent type of

actual occasions, we have thereby made presumptions as to types of *societies comprised in its environment*" (PR 204; emphasis added). Hence, the most significant aspect of Whitehead's philosophy of organism for the construction of an environmental ethics is that it underscores the *social* character of the self and all occasions of experience in the biotic community of living nature, thus allowing for the extension of morality into an ethics which deals with human conduct in relation to the land.

George Herbert Mead

For G. H. Mead, as for Dewey and Whitehead, the individual emerges through a process of interaction between the organism and the environment. The individual self, mind and consciousness arise from communication between organisms as well as between organisms and their environment, thus mutually influencing each other's development. Mead's analysis clearly shows the strong imprint of nineteenth-century social Darwinism with its emphasis on the mutual adjustment of organisms and their environment in the evolutionary process. Mead's understanding of the self and nature as an evolving system of organisms interacting with their environment has also been deeply influenced by the tradition of American process philosophy, as demonstrated by the fact that he often cites with approval Dewey's *Experience and Nature* (see Mead PP 18), as well as the earlier works by Whitehead, including *The Principles of Natural Knowledge, The Concept of Nature*, and *Science in the Modern World* (see Mead, PP 10 fn.). Hence, similar to the process theories of Whitehead and Dewey, Mead develops a concept of selfhood as a function of social interactions between the individual and its surroundings which attempts to overcome the dualism between mind and nature. At the same time, there are important innovations in Mead's approach in that he synthesizes Darwinian evolutionism with the process thought of Dewey, Whitehead, and others within the context of his own social-self theory and I-Me dialectic based upon an underlying "principle of sociality." The social-self paradigm of Mead represents a nondual framework which shows how the individual, society, and nature all interact in various ways, each determining the other, so as to provide a unifying model in which ecology can be integrated with philosophy and the social sciences.

Mead's organismic concept of self and nature as a creative advance into novelty is especially influenced by Whitehead's philosophy of nature as an organization of perspectives. In Mead's words: "What I wish to pick out of Professor Whitehead's philosophy of nature is this conception of nature as an organization of perspectives, which are there in nature" (PP 163). As he further emphasizes, "Whitehead's principle of organization of perspectives is . . . the abandonment of simple location as the principle of physical existence" (PP 164). Whitehead's concept of nature as an organization of perspectives represents the abandonment of notion of independent substance with "simple location" for a notion of relational events whose location is coextensive with the entire field of social relationships from which they emerge. According to this Leibnizian perspectivist cosmology worked out by Whitehead and Mead, the human self and every other organism is a living mirror which reflects its total environment from a unique perspective so as to both contain and pervade the whole continuum of nature as an individual microcosm of the social macrocosm. In his essay "The Process of Mind in Nature" contained in *The Philosophy of the Act,* Mead closely follows Whitehead's effort to undermine the dualistic worldview of scientific materialism based on simple location and the bifurcation of nature. Mead describes the bifurcation of nature into two systems of reality and the simple location of aesthetic qualities in the private mind of a solitary Cartesian subject when he writes: "Color, sound, temperature as felt, odor, taste, as well as all the affective characters of things could not reside in nature in its reality. The simplest treatment of such characters was to place them in mind, as the effects on mind of the action of a nature which was nothing but matter in motion" (PA 358). However, like Whitehead, he rejects the fallacies of bifurcation and simple location so as to overcome the dualism between mind and nature: "If we abandon with Whitehead the bifurcation of nature, the colors, sounds, tastes, odors, and temperatures are there in nature quite as genuinely as spatiotemporal extension" (PA 337). Hence, for Mead, as for Dewey and Whitehead, there is a continuity between the subjective world of human experience and the objective world of living nature so that the immediately felt aesthetic qualities of experience *are* the aesthetic qualities of nature.

Throughout his various works Mead repeatedly argues that the locus of self, mind, and consciousness as well as that of experience and perception is not in an individual but in a social situation or perspective which arises through an interaction between organism and environment. The individual self, like mind and consciousness, cannot be localized within the boundaries of a private subject but is a field which is *coextensive* with the entire matrix of social relationships and interactions by which it is constituted (MSS 223 fn.). In a discussion on consciousness he writes: "Consciousness as such refers to both the organism and its environment and cannot be *located simply* in either" (MSS 332; emphasis added). Again, he states: "The suggestion I have made is that consciousness, as such, does not represent a separate substance . . . but rather that the term 'consciousness' represents a certain sort of an environment in its relation to sensitive organisms" (MSS 329). Similarly, he argues that the mind cannot be simply located in an isolated subject but instead takes place in a field of social conduct between an organism and its environment: "Mind . . . lies in a field of conduct between a specific individual and the environment. . . . Mind is then a field that is not confined to the individual, much less is located in a brain" (SW 247). He elsewhere describes human perception as an interaction of organism and environment, stating: "Perception is a relation between a highly developed physiological organism and an object, or an environment in which selection emphasizes certain elements" (PA 8). Thus, insofar as self, mind, consciousness, experience, and perception are all defined as an organism-environment relation, they are continuous with their total surroundings of society and nature.

Mead emphasizes that the organism is not simply determined by its social relationships to the environment, but that the "determining relationship is bilateral" (MSS 215). In other words, there is a "mutual determination of the individual and his environment" (SW 86). Again, he states: "That reaction is not simply a determination of the organism by the environment, since the organism determines the environment as fully as the environment determines the organism" (MSS 129). He clarifies the manner in which the organism and environment are mutually determining when he states: "In general, we consider the determination of the organism by the environment as *causal*, while we consider the determination of the environment by the organism as *selective*" (PA 412). This "mutual determination" of organism and environment is explained in terms of his *bipolar* model of the social self as an I-Me dialectic, whereby the self arises by internalizing its whole environment as a Me, and then reacts to it as an emergent organism with creativity, spontaneity, and novelty as an individual I. The bipolar theory of selfhood worked out by Mead is thus not a one-sided doctrine of social determinism since the organism and environment influence each other in a reciprocal way. Mead underscores the fact that it is precisely because the organism determines its environment as much as the environment determines the organism which places a moral responsibility upon an individual in relation to its surroundings:

> *The organism, then, is in a sense responsible for its environment.* Since organism and environment determine each other and are mutually dependent for their existence, it follows that the life-process, to be adequately understood, must be considered in terms of their interrelations. (MSS 130; emphasis added)

In his essay "The Philosophical Basis of Ethics" (1908), Mead expresses a similar point, arguing that it is the "mutual determination" of organism and environment in each social situation which imposes a moral obligation on the organism with regard to its environment:

> But if we admit that the evolutionary process consists in a mutual determination of the individual and his environment—not the determination of the individual by his environment, moral necessity in conduct is found in the very evolutionary situation. (SW 86)

In the same text Mead goes on argue that the evolution of moral conduct is rooted in the mutual determination of organism and environment characterizing the structure of "immediate experience." He writes that "environment as well as individual appears in immediate experience; the one coterminous with the other, and moral endeavor appears in the mutual determination of one by the other" (SW 88).

For Mead ethics is grounded in a social concept of selfhood wherein the person is constituted by his relationships to others in a community. Furthermore, he enlarges the notion of "community" beyond the sphere of human society so as to also include the wider society of living nature. One of the innovations of Mead's social-self paradigm is that he generalizes his "principle of sociality" (PP 65) into a universalized metaphysical category so that not only the human self but all events in the community of nature and the cosmos are ultimately social in character. In his introduction to Mead's *Philosophy of the Present*, A. E. Murphy correctly asserts: "The most original feature of these lectures is the daring extension of 'the social' into what is at least a philosophy of nature, and, if the name did not offend a pragmatist, might also be called a metaphysic" (Mead 1932, xv–xvi). Mead's generalization of the principle of sociality into a metaphysical category is expressed when he writes: "I wish to emphasize the fact that the appearance of mind is only the culmination of that *sociality* which is found throughout the universe" (PP 86; emphasis added). It is precisely this extension of "the social" beyond the human community to include the biotic community of nature which establishes the theoretical basis for an environmental ethics in the framework of G. H. Mead.

As pointed out by J. D. Baldwin, in that Mead's social-self paradigm clarifies how the individual, society, and nature all interact through mutual determination of organism and environment, it establishes a theoretical basis for integrating ecology with sociology and other disciplines in a unified social science model:

> Although Mead did not develop the ecological facets of his theory as well as he developed other parts, he did provide the basic theoretical structure that shows how people, society and the environment interact—each influencing the other . . . Mead's theoretical system that integrates physiology, behavior, society, and ecology in one unified model offers a useful tool for interweaving ecological variables into sociological theories. (1986, 135)

In this way Mead's unified social-self paradigm and I-Me dialectic with its underlying principle of sociality may be said to provide the basis for a comprehensive ecological theory, including the extension of morality into an environmental ethics.

## The Self as a Human-Nature Relation in Japanese Philosophy

### Traditional Japanese Buddhism

As I have elsewhere discussed at length (1992), Japanese Buddhism articulates an ecological concept of personhood a fusion of man and nature based on an underlying metaphysic of relational fields which provides us with an important resource for the construction of an East-West model of environmental ethics. There is a profound ecological worldview implicit not only in the indigenous Japanese nature religion of Shintoism, but also throughout the Kegon, Tendai, Shingon, Zen, Pure Land, and Nichiren schools of Japanese Buddhism as well as in modern Japanese Buddhist philosophy represented by such thinkers as Nishida Kitarō and Watsuji Tetsurō. The Japanese Buddhist concept of nature is at once deeply aesthetic and religious in character. For traditional Japanese Buddhism the spiritual reverence for nature as well as the moral love and respect for nature is itself partly inspired by a poetic appreciation for the beauty of nature with its immediately felt pervasive aesthetic qualities like *aware* (tragic beauty), *yūgen* (profound mystery), *wabi* (rustic poverty), and *sabi* (solitariness). Also, Japanese Buddhism expounds a religious and soteric concept of nature wherein the natural environment becomes the ultimate locus of salvation for all sentient beings. In his article "Probing the Japanese Experience of Nature," Omine Akira traces the soteric concept of nature in the Japanese literary tradition beginning with the earliest eighth-century anthology called the *Man'yō-shū* (Collection of Myriad Leaves), running through Saigyō (1118–1190), Ippen (1239–1289), and

Bashō (1644–1694) as set in the context of the Japanese Buddhist worldview formulated by Zen master Dōgen as well as the founder of Jōdo Shinshū or True Pure Land Buddhism, Shinran (1173–1263). In this context he cites directly from Dōgen's "Sutra of Mountains and Waters" (*Sansui-kyō*), the 29th chapter of *Shōbōgenzō*: "Mountains and rivers right now are the emerging presence of the ancient Buddhas" (Omine 1987, 19). As Dōgen propounds in the *Genjōkōan* chapter of *Shōbōgenzō*, to study Zen is to study the self, and to study the self is to empty or negate the self, thus to be enlightened by all *dharmas* in the living scripture of nature, with its mountains and rivers all "presencing just as they are" (*genjōkōan-su*) in their primordial suchness so as to disclose the Buddha-nature inherent in all things, understood in Dōgen's philosophy of *uji* or "being-time" as as *mujō-busshō*, "impermanence-Buddha-nature." Omine makes further reference to Shinran's Pure Land theory of salvation by the grace of "Other-power" (*tariki*), reformulated in his later writings through his famous doctrine of *jinen honi*, "naturalness." To be saved by Buddha, to be born into the Pure Land of Bliss, is simply a function of *jinen* (*shizen*), "nature," defined by Shinran as "from the very beginning made to become so" (Omine 1987,28). Omine concludes with his assessment that Shinran's Pure Land Buddhist notion of *jinen honi* or "naturalness" reflects an ancient Japanese concept of living nature as the ground and source of human salvation.

This traditional religio-aesthetic concept of nature in Japan is itself grounded in a Mahāyāna Buddhist metaphysic of *śūnyatā* (J. *kū*) or "emptiness," wherein the mountains and rivers of nature, just as they are here and now in the concrete immediacy of the present moment, are the revelation of impermanence-Buddha-nature in the dynamic and nonsubstantial flux of being-time. According to the Japanese Buddhist doctrine of *śūnyatā*, there is nothing which is "more real" beyond the interdependence of everything in nature. The Buddhist metaphysic of *śūnyatā* with its explicit identification of *samsara* and *nirvana* therefore results in the complete dialectical interfusion of transcendence and immanence, absolute and relative, or the sacred and the profane. In this way Japanese Buddhism overturns all models of transcendence and dualism such as to effect a radical shift from "other-worldiness" to "this-worldliness." For Japanese Buddhism, ultimate reality is not to be found in a transcendent or supernatural beyond, but in fields of interrelationships which confer to each event a boundless depth of aesthetic, moral, and religious value. It is in this philosophical context that nature becomes the "locus of salvation" in traditional Japanese Buddhism as reflected by poet seers following the religio-aesthetic path of Geidō, the Way of the artist.

At the heart of the ecological worldview to be found in traditional Japanese thought lies its nondualistic concept of personhood as a human-nature relationship. Kimura Bin has clarified the traditional Japanese concept of personhood as a unity of "self" (*mizu-kara*) and "nature" (*onozu-kara*) in his essay "The Japanese Concept of Nature" (1969), as well as in chapter 18 entitled *Mizukara and Onozukara* (Self and Nature) from his book called *Betweenness* (*Aida*, 1988). The common Japanese term for "nature" is *shi-zen* (also pronounced *ji-nen*), which originally derived from the Chinese word *tsu-jan*, literally denoting "spontaneity" or "what is so of itself." An alternate word for nature which is indigenous to Japan is *onozukara*, written with the first of the two characters for *shi-zen*. However, as Kimura further points out, the Japanese word *onozukara*, meaning "nature," also stands for another original Japanese term, *mizukara*, meaning "self." That is to say, in the Japanese language, both the words for "self" (*mizukara*) and "nature" (*onozukara*) can be expressed by the same character. Kimura explains the implications of this as follows:

> As of itself *Onozukara* expresses an objective state . . . *Mizukara* as self expresses, on the other hand, a subjective state. . . . That the Japanese believe they can express these seemingly autonomous terms by means of a single character points towards a deeper insight by which they apprehend *Onozukara* and *Mizukara*, nature and self, as originating from the same common ground. (1969, 154–5)

For Kimura, in that both the "self" and "nature" can be expressed by the same character in Japanese, it reveals that the person is an inseparable unity of *mizukara/onozukara* or "self/nature." In the traditional Japanese notion of personhood, then, both *mizukara* and *onozukara* or "self" and "nature" are grounded in a transpersonal locus of reality as the subjective and objective aspects of a single continuum of pure experience.

This nondualistic concept of personhood as an indivisible unity of self (*mizukara*) and nature (*onozukara*) has been expressed through a variety of doctrinal formulas in traditional Japanese Buddhism. Nichiren Buddhism, the only indigenous form of Japanese Buddhism and by far the largest Buddhist sect in present day Japan, is characterized by its emphasis on the *social* dimensions of Buddhism. More than any other traditional Japanese Buddhist thinker, Nichiren (1222–82) emphasizes the need to establish the proper social environment for the correct study and practice of Buddhism. However, Nichiren was equally concerned with the relation of the individual to both the social and the natural environment. Nichiren articulates an explicit notion of personhood as a unity of self and nature through his principle of *eshō funi,* the "oneness of life and its environment." In *Fundamentals of Buddhism,* Yasuji Kirimura summarizes Nichiren's principle of *eshō funi* as follows:

> The relationship between human life and its environment is explained in terms of *eshō funi.* *Eshō* is the combination of the first syllables of *ehō* and *shōhō.* *Shōhō* means the living subject, or something which performs activities associated with life, while *ehō* is the object, that which supports *shōhō.* *Shōhō* denotes a living being and *ehō* its environment on which it is dependent for its life-activities and survival . . . *eshō funi* means that life and its environment are two independent phenomena but one in their fundamental essence. Man and his environment are inseparable. (1977, 69)

Because of the principle of *eshō funi* an internal change in the subjective realm of human life produces a corresponding effect in the objective realm of the environment and vice versa. In Nichiren Buddhism, the practical means for spritual transformation of both human life and its surrounding environment is chanting the mantric formula derived from the *daimoku* or sacred title of the *Lotus Sutra:* "*Myōhō Renge Kyō.*" By chanting the mantra of "*Namu myōhō renge kyō*" while facing the *gohonzon* or object of worship upon which the mantra is inscribed, the practice of Nichiren Buddhism aims to awaken the nondual wisdom expressed by such Tendai principles as *eshō funi,* the "one-ness of life and its environment," *shikishin funi,* "the oneness of body and mind," *nimpō ikka,* "the oneness of the person and the Law [of *Namu myōhō renge kyō*]," and ultimately, the master principle of *ichinen sanzen,* "three thou-sand worlds in a single life-moment." Hence, while there are many dimensions to Nichiren Buddhist theory and practice, the principle of *eshō funi* or "oneness of life and its environment" articulates a profoundly ecological notion of personhood as a unity of the self and nature which at once consti-tutes the doctrinal basis for an environmental ethics.

The Japanese ecological concept of personhood as a unity of self and nature also finds powerful expression in the teachings of traditional Zen Bud-dhism as influenced by the Kegon (Ch. *Hua-yen*; Skt. *Avatamsaka*) philosophy of interpenetration between subject and object. The ecological worldview implicit in the Kegon Buddhist philosophy is expressed by the metaphor of Indra's net, which visualizes nature as a vast web of social interrelationships wherein the parts and the whole are mutually dependent. The Kegon philos-ophy has in turn deeply influenced various Buddhist modes of thought in

Japan including both traditional Zen Buddhism as well as the modern Japanese philosophy of Nishida Kitarō and the Kyoto school. In the final chapter
of his book *Zen and Japanese Culture* entitled "Love of Nature," D. T. Suzuki
underscores the Kegon infrastructure underlying the traditional aesthetic
concept of nature in Japanese Zen Buddhism. Thus, Suzuki writes: "The balancing of unity and multiplicity or, better, *the merging of self with others* in the
philosophy of Avatamsaka (Kegon) is absolutely necessary to the [Zen] aesthetic understanding of Nature" (1959, 354). According to the Kegon philosophy
Zen Buddhism, nature is an undivided aesthetic continuum characterized by
the unobstructed interfusion of subject and object, self and other, or unity
and multiplicity. It is the mutual penetration of subject and object which
establishes an unbroken continuity between man and nature. In Suzuki's
words:

> Zen proposes to respect Nature, to love Nature, to live its own life; *Zen*
> *recognized that our Nature is one with objective Nature* . . . in the sense that
> *Nature lives in us and we in Nature.* For this reason, Zen asceticism
> advocates simplicity, frugality, straightforwardness, virility, making no
> attempt to utilize Nature for selfish purposes. (1959, 351–352)

This Zen/Kegon concept of the person as an interpenetration of self and
nature thus provides us with an ecological worldview in which a land ethic is
grounded in a land aesthetic.

## Nishida Kitarō

In twentieth-century Japanese philosophy Nishida Kitarō has reformulated
the traditional Zen concept of personhood as a unity of man and nature in
terms of his notion of the "social self" (*shakaiteki jiko*) as a contradictory self-
identity of "I and Thou" (*ware to nanji*) in the *basho* or locus of absolute Nothingness. As he states in *Fundamental Problems of Philosophy* (*Tetsugaku no kompon
mondai*, 1934): "The I is an I by facing a Thou, and the individual is an individual by facing other individuals. The self must be social" (NKZ, VII, 382).
Moreover, he understand the social self as a dialectic of intersubjective I-Thou
relations whereby there is a "mutual determination" (*sōgo gentei*) between
the individual (*kobutsu*) and the environment (*kankyō*). In the following passage Nishida describes the "mutual determination" of I and Thou in terms of
his concept of the "individual-as-environment" (*kobutsuteki gentei soku kankyōteki gentei*):

The I becomes an I only through recognition of a Thou, just as a Thou becomes a Thou only through recognition by an I. There is no merely solitary personal self. This is the meaning of the determination of the individual-as environment and of the environment-as-individual. (NKZ VII, 169)

Nishida emphasizes that the social self as a mutual determination of individual organism and social environment is constituted by a dialectic of I-Thou relationships not only between man and society but also between man and his natural surroundings. He writes: "That which stands over against the I must always be a Thou . . . everything which stands opposed to the self—even the mountains, rivers, trees and stones—is a Thou. In such a sense, the concrete world becomes a metaphysical society" (NKZ VII, 59). For Nishida, then, in the I-Thou dialectic by virtue of which the person is constituted as a social self, the Thou which faces the I is not only human society, but also the larger metaphysical society of nature with the mountains, rivers, trees, and stones of the land.

## Watsuji Tetsurō.

It has already been seen that for Watsuji Tetsurō the basis of ethics is to be found in his twofold *ningen* concept of Japanese personhood as an individual-society relation. Thus, in his *Ethics* (*Rinrigaku*, 1937), Watsuji states: "The primary meaning of the effort to define ethics (*rinri*) as a study of the 'person' (*ningen*) is that it escapes the error of the modern world which understands ethics as only a problem of individual consciousness (*kojinshiki no mondai*)" (1937, 1). For Watsuji the starting point for an ethical system is the *ningen* concept of personhood defined in terms of the *aidagara* or "betweenness" of individuals, as codified in terms of his standard doctrinal formula, *hito to hito to no aidagara*, the "betweenness of person and person." Insofar as the second character of *ningen*, alternatively pronounced *aida* or "betweenness," is also referred to as *ma* in the canon of traditional Japanese aesthetics, the person as *ningen* implies not only a moral, but also an aesthetic mode of existence. However, Watsuji's concept of the person as *ningen* is not limited only to human-society relations but involves human-nature relations as well. In his work entitled *Climate, an Anthropological Investigation* (*Fūdo ningengakuteki kosatsu*, 1935) Watsuji develops as his main philosophical theme the embodied spatiality of human existence in various social environments, so that the individual both influences and is influenced by the family, the community, the nation, and the natural environment of a *fūdo* or "climate." Hence, Watsuji clearly formulates an ethics in which the individual must be conceived as being situated in a spatial field of betweenness not only to human society, but also to a surrounding "climate" (*fūdo*) of living nature as the ultimate extension of embodied subjective space in which man dwells. Watsuji's ethical philosophy is therefore one of the most suggestive Asian resources for environmental ethics as outlined by Aldo Leopold, in which morality is enlarged so as to include the encompassing human-nature relation between man and the land.

This ethical concept of personhood as a unity of man and nature articulated by Watsuji's "climate" theory social space has been clearly explained by the modern Japanese philosopher Yuasa Yasuo: "Watsuji wrote a book called *Climates* in which he said that to live in nature as the space of the life-world—in other words, to live in a 'climate'—is the most fundamental mode of being human. . . . In short, to exist in a climate, to exist in the concrete aspect of space, is to exist in living Nature" (1987, 38–39). For Yuasa, Watsuji's theory of "climates" is further related to a theory of the body where the person as *ningen* physically embodies its entire spatial locus of society and nature. Moreover, Yuasa connects Watsuji's idea concerning the embodied spatial mode of human existence in the *aidagara* or "betweenness" of things to the technical term of *basho* indicating a field, locus or matrix of lived space, introduced into modern Japanese philosophy by Nishida Kitarō: "But what does it mean to exist in betweenness (*aidagara*) ? . . . our betweenness implies that we exist in a definite, spatial *basho*" (1987, 38). According to Yuasa's synthesis of Watsuji and Nishida, then, that the person as *ningen* exists in the "betweenness" (*aidagara*) of events means the self always embodies the concrete spatial *basho* of a surrounding *fūdo* or "climate" of living nature.

In *The Betweenness of Person and Person* (Hito to hito to no aida, 1972), especially in chapter 3 called *Fūdo to ningensei* (Climate and Human Nature, pp. 81–128), the psychiatrist Kimura Bin further develops Watsuji's theory of "climates" (*fūdo*) wherein the person as *ningen* exists not only in the *aidagara* or "betweenness" of the individual and human society, but also in the "betweenness" of the individual and the encompassing spatial locus of nature. Like Watsuji, Kimura holds that the human self is always conditioned by a *fūdo* or spatial "climate." The surrounding cultural and natural climate of a *fūdo* determines the structure of human nature and relationships between persons. Like Yuasa Yasuo, Kimura (1972, 65) also integrates Watsuji's theory of *fūdo* or "climates" with key notions from the philosophy of Nishida Kitarō, especially the latter's idea of "pure experience" (*junsui keiken*) and the doctrine of *basho* or spatial "locus" (field, place, matrix). In this context he argues that *aida* or "betweenness" functions as a transpersonal *basho* or spatial locus in which the self arises through its social relationships with its total surroundings (1972, 65). Moreover, he says that in the dualistic mode of reflective consciousness, subject and object are separate. However, what Nishida terms "pure experience" is the nondualistic and prereflective state which arises prior to subject-object dualism since it is anterior to all cognition and judgment. Kimura asserts that we encounter nature the same as we encounter other human individuals. Hence, in the nondual and prereflective mode of "pure experience" there is as yet no bifurcation between subject and object, seer and seen, or self and nature. Kimura writes:

> We are used to seeing nature as an object. But this relation between two opposite things, subjectivity and objectivity, comes from reflected consciousness. In *pure experience* without any reflection, there is no opposite relationship between subjectivity and objectivity. Then the self, which is the act of seeing, and nature, which is the seen, are still completely inseparable with each other. (1972, 85)

Kimura goes on to emphasize the relationship between the notion of "climate" and the concept of the "body" in the prereflective state of pure experience, stating that when people are born with a physical body, the body is already a part of a *fūdo* or climate. Hence, Kimura states that the climate of nature is also the human body (1972, 123). In pure experience there is no body-mind dualism so that the human self physically *embodies* the transpersonal spatial locus of its entire surrounding "climate" including both the locus of society and and the more encompassing locus of living nature. For Kimura, then, Watsuji's *ningen* theory of personhood as existing in the concrete space of a "climate" of living nature is itself a modern reformulation of the traditional Japanese understanding of man as a unity of "self" (*mizukara*) and "nature" (*onozukara*), comprehended as the subjective and objective aspects of a transpersonal locus of reality at the level of pure experience.

## An East-West Model of the Social Self as a Basis for Environmental Ethics

It has already been seen that there are many significant points of contact between the "social self" models of personhood developed in both American pragmatism and modern Japanese philosophy. But here I will focus on the ecological implications of this parallel. Just as Watsuji Tetsurō has developed a Zen/Confucian model of the person as *ningen* wherein the self is both an individual and a part of society, so G. H. Mead develops the notion of a social self as having two component systems, the I or individual pole and the Me or social pole. Similar to Watsuji's concept of *aidagara*, wherein the individual is located in the "betweenness" of the individual and society, Mead's "principle of sociality" (PP 47) states that the individual is located "betwixt and between" the old system representing the Me or deterministic social environment of the past, and the new system representing the I or spontaneous organism emerging in the present. For Mead the social self exists betwixt and between the individual organism and its total social environment including both the human community and the biotic community of living nature. Similarly, for Watsuji, the social self as *ningen* is located in the betweenness of an individual organism and the natural environment of a *fūdo* or "climate." At the level of value theory, Watsuji *ningen* theory of self underscores the aesthetic dimensions of Japanese personhood as a betweenness of the individual and its surrounding climate of society and nature, just as Dewey, Whitehead, and Mead in American philosophy have all described the social self as an organism/environment situation unified by a pervasive aesthetic quality which constitutes its wholeness and funds it with intrinsic value. Hence, the social-self theories of both Watsuji and Mead both functions to expand the discipline of ethics to include not only a social ethics of the human-society relation but also an environmental ethics of the human-nature relation. Moreover, both thinkers show how an environmental ethics in turn depends upon a conservation aesthetics.

The parallels between the social-self theories of G. H. Mead and Nishida Kitarō are no less significant for ecology. Just as for Mead the social self arises through a dialectic of I and Me, for Nishida the social self (*shakaiteki jiko*) arises through the dialectic of I and Thou (*ware to nanji*). Moreover, both define the social self in ecological terms by defining it as an organism-environment relation. Just as for Mead the I-Me dialectic of the social self is constituted by a process of interaction between an individual organism and its total environment, Nishida defines the I-Thou dialectic of the social self in terms of his notion of "determination of the individual-as-environment" (*kobutsuteki gentei soku kankyōteki gentei*) and the "determination of environment-as-individual" (*kankyōteki gentei soku kobutsuteki gentei*). Also, both thinkers restate their ecological concept of the social self as an organism-environment relation in phenomenological terms as the foreground/background structure of immediate experience whereby the individual organism located in the foreground focus is surrounded by the social environment in the background field. Moreover, both Mead and Nishida avoid falling into a mechanistic doctrine of social determinism by underscoring the "mutual determination" of organism and environment. Just as for Mead there is a mutual determination between the individual I and the social Me, for Nishida there is a mutual determination (*sōgo gentei*) between the I and the Thou.

## Conclusion

In this essay I first described the inspiration for environmental ethics in the writings of Aldo Leopold. It was Leopold who put forth the bold idea that ethics must be enlarged beyond the social relations between individuals or between the individual and society so as to include the wider sphere of relations between the individual and nature—what he refers to as the "land ethic." It was shown how Leopold's land ethic and land aesthetic presupposes the abandonment of a metaphysics of substance with simple location for that of a metaphysics of relational fields establishing a symbiotic ecosystem wherein the parts depend on the whole and vice versa. It was then argued that the organismic process philosophy of Dewey, Whitehead, and Mead, which describes nature as an aesthetic continuum of interconnected events based on a field paradigm of reality is the most adequate metaphysical framework in which to ground the ecological worldview of Aldo Leopold. Within the context of this organismic process metaphysics the American philosophers, like Aldo Leopold, generalize the category of "the social" to include the environment as the basis of a land ethic. Moreover, it was pointed out that in American pragmatism, as well as Aldo Leopold, the "land ethic" is grounded in a *land aesthetic* in that our moral love and respect for nature is related to a deeply poetic appreciation of the beauty of nature.

From here there was an effort to construct a parallel between the social-self theories in both American pragmatism and modern Japanese philosophy. The basic argument here is that the ecological worldviews of twentieth-century American philosophy as well as both traditional and modern Japanese thought is unified in terms of their respective notions of a "social self" as a human-nature interaction. To recapitulate some of these basic insights into the self: Dewey, Whitehead and Mead in American philosophy all define the self in holistic terms as arising through a valuative transaction between an individual organism and its entire social environment so as to overcome the fallacy of simple location and establish the unbroken *continuity* between man and nature. Again, they reformulate the social self as an organism-environment interaction or human-nature relation in phenomenological terms whereby the individual organism in the foreground focus of attention is encircled by a field of social relationships in the spatial background. On the side of Asian thought, Kimura Bin clarifies the traditional Japanese notion of personhood as a unity of "self" (*mizukara*) and "nature" (*onozukara*), understood as the subjective and objective aspects of the same transpersonal locus of reality at the level of pure experience. Nichiren Buddhism expresses this traditional Japanese concept of personhood as a human-nature relation in terms of its principle of *eshō funi*, the "oneness of life and its environment." Similarly, Zen Buddhism argues for the unity of man and nature based on the Kegon philosophy of unobstructed interfusion between subject and object or self and other. This traditional Japanese model of personhood as a human-nature relation is then reformulated by leading thinkers in the tradition of modern Japanese philosophy like Nishida Kitarō and Watsuji Tetsurō as well as the synthesis of both these thinkers in the writings of Yuasa Yasuo and Kimura Bin. In this context a parallel was constructed between Mead's key notion of a social self as a dialectic of I and Me with Watsuji's *ningen* concept of personhood, *aidagara* theory of self-other relations, and doctrine of *fūdo* or "climates," followed by a consideration of Nishida's idea of a social self as a dialectic of I and Thou. Mead, Whitehead, and Dewey in the West, like Nishida and Watsuji in the East, formulate a social concept of the person as arising through the interaction of an individual with its total surroundings including both society and nature. It was thus argued that similar to Mead and others in American process philosophy, representative Japanese philosophers like Nishida and Watsuji have elaborated a model of the social self as a symbiotic human-nature relationship which can function as an integrative principle for environmental ethics. The upshot of this entire discussion is that all of the thinkers under consideration here have enlarged the ethical concept of man as a social being so as to extend morality into a land ethic which considers the wider relation of the self to its natural environment. Like the environmental ethics of Aldo Leopold, the ecological model of the social self as an organism-environment interaction developed both in the East and the West expands the boundaries of "society" beyond the human community to that of the biotic community of soil, water, plants, and animals of the land, so that man's relation to nature entails not only rights and privileges, but also moral obligations, duties, and commitments.

Following the assertion of Jürgen Habermas (1987) it has been argued throughout the present work that the social science framework of G. H. Mead represents a radical paradigm shift beyond subject-centered consciousness wherein selfhood is located in a private ego, to an intersubjectivist communication model of the *social self* located in the betweenness of I and Me. Building up on the theme of Habermas, I would argue that in the twentieth century, both in the East and the West, there has been a major shift beyond the narrow egocentric standpoint of individualism to the *eco-centric* perspective of the social self as an organism-environment interaction or human-nature relationship which can function as a unifying model in which to integrate ecology with philosophy and the social sciences. Dewey, Whitehead, and Mead in America, along with Nishida, Watsuji, Kimura, and others in Japan, have together converged upon a model of the social self as a unity of man, society, and nature. The concept of a "social self" as an organism-environment interaction can thus be regarded as a unifying principle for an East-West ecological model which includes a comprehensive philosophy of nature as well as an environmental ethics and a conservation aesthetics.

# ⌒14⌒
## The Social Turn in Philosophical Anthropology

Philosophical anthropology may be defined in the most general sense as that discipline which undertakes the study of "self," "person," or "human nature." The discipline of philosophical anthropology began in the modern period as a German historical movement including such figures as Kant, Fichte, Hegel, Feuerbach, Marx, Nietzsche, Scheler, Husserl, Heidegger, Cassirer, and Buber. It was Kant who set the agenda for the German movement by positing *Anthropologie* as that fundamental philosophical science which endeavors to answer the most basic of all questions: "What is man?" Yet in its general meaning as the study of self the discipline of philosophical anthropology can be traced back to its origins in ancient Greek thought. The basic task of philosophical anthropology is at once expressed in the dictum said to have been inscribed upon the ancient Greek oracle at Delphi: *gnothi sauton*—"Know thyself." The Greek injunction to "Know thyself" first appears in a dialogue entitled *Alcibiades I*, attributed to Plato. When the young Alcibiades wishes to begin his public life (123d), Socrates intervenes and, with reference to the Delphic inscription, seeks to lead Alcibiades to a knowledge of himself (124a–124b), for, by knowing oneself, the political leader knows the proper affairs of other selves, and thereby the affairs of state (133d–134a). Plato's dialogue *The Republic*, with its tripartite analysis of the *psyche* or "soul" of man (the appetitive, spirited, and rational natures), the moral virtues corresponding to each (temperance, courage, and wisdom), their correlation to divisions in the political state (the merchant, warrior, and ruling classes), and the normative principle of justice as a "harmony" of all three elements, may be regarded as the first great systematic treatise on philosophical anthropology. Ever since the *Alcibiades I* and other Platonic dialogues, the Delphic principle of self-knowledge has been at the very center of ethical thought in the West. Hence, the discipline of philosophical anthropology is here to be defined as that *investigation of self*, which began with the ancient Delphic injunction to "Know thyself," and has continued up until the present, from the modern German movement of *Anthropologie* wherein selfhood becomes the exclusive object of philosophy and anthropology the universal science, to the postmodern tradition of French deconstructionism which announces the "disappearance of man" and the "dissolution of self"—the total liquidation of the human subject!

In his masterful overview of the history of philosophical anthropology entitled *Between Man and Man,* Martin Buber (1878–1965) traces the development of the concept of self through its various phases of individualism and collectivism, finally describing what he regards to be the epoch-making "turn" initiated by Feuerbach from a monological view of self as an isolated I or Cartesian subject to a fully *dialogical* concept of self as an I-Thou relationship. Here I employ Buber's account of this turning point or Copernican revolution in the history of philosophical anthropology to further clarify what Jürgen Habermas (1989) refers to as the "paradigm shift" in G. H. Mead from Cartesian subjectivism to an intersubjective communication model of the social self as an I-Me relationship. Buber's account is further used to edify what Hans Joas (1993, 24) has called the "social turn" initiated by Mead in classical American pragmatism. As noted by H. Richard Niebuhr (1963) and other scholars there is a profound similarity between Martin Buber's twofold concept of self as a dialogue between I and Thou and Mead's bipolar concept of the social self as a conversation between I and Me. However, I point out that the similarity of their two frameworks can in part be traced to a common source of influence, in that Mead, like Buber, studied for several years in Germany under Wilhelm Dilthey—the founder of the study of the history of philosophical anthropology. It is shown how after studying philosophical anthropology in Germany under Dilthey, Buber and Mead went on to formulate a dialogical concept of self as an I-Other relation so as to establish a *via media* between individualism and collectivism. I further develop Mead's framework in conjunction with Ernst Cassirer's work on philosophical anthropology entitled *An Essay on Man* (1944), arguing that Mead's definition of personhood as a "social self" arising through *symbolic interaction* functions to unify Aristotle's notion of a "social animal" and Cassirer's notion of a "symbolic animal." Mead's symbolic interactionism is then juxtaposed with John Macmurray's influential work *Persons in Relation* (1961), whereupon I show that both thinkers have developed a linguistic communication model of the self as a relation between I and Other, what Mead calls the relation of I and Me, and what Macmurray calls the relation of I and You. Macmurray's vision of the self as an *I-You relationship* arising through communication in a community of persons in relation is seen to have many parallels with both Mead's communication model of the social self as an *I-Me relationship* and Buber's dialogical concept of man as an *I-Thou relationship.*

Although twentieth-century Japanese philosophy has been deeply influenced by the anthropological orientation of traditional Zen Buddhism as *koji kyūmei* or "investigation of self," it has also been directly influenced by the German tradition of *Anthropologie* from Kant to Heidegger. In this context I show how like Buber and Mead in the West, modern Japanese thinkers such as Watsuji Tetsurō and Nishida Kitarō have developed a philosophical anthropology based on a social concept of self as an I-Other relation. After undergoing his radical "turn" (*tenkō*) from romantic individualism to a socioethical standpoint, Watsuji Tetsurō articulates a fully social, relational, and contextual concept of Japanese selfhood. Similar to Buber's bipolar concept of self as existing in the "between" (*das Zwischen*) of I and Thou, Watsuji develops an "anthropology" or "study of the person" (*ningengaku*) as the groundwork for a system of ethics focusing upon his twofold Zen/Confucian *ningen* concept of personhood located in the "between" (*aidagara*) of self and society. Moreover, both simultaneously with and independently of Buber, Nishida Kitarō worked out a philosophical anthropology based on a social concept of self as an I-Thou relationship in three spheres; the self in relation to society, the self in relation to nature, and the self in relation to God as the eternal Thou and absolute Other. Here I demonstrate that Buber (1965, 147–48) and Nishida (NKZ VII, 175) in fact both derive their dialogical concepts of selfhood as an I-Thou relationship from Ludwig Feuerbach's *Principles of the Philosophy of the Future*, first published in 1843. Both Nishida in the East and Buber in the West identify Feuerbach's shift from a monological to a dialogical concept of self as an I-Thou relationship as the turning point in the history of philosophical anthropology. Like Buber, both Watsuji and Nishida level strong criticism against the German tradition of philosophical anthropology, claiming that thinkers such as Heidegger failed to establish a truly social concept of man as an I-Other relationship. Similarly, it is shown how recent German scholars influenced by American pragmatism such as E. Tugendhat, H. Joas, and J. Habermas argue that while a breakthrough to an intersubjective or social concept of self was not achieved in the German tradition of philosophical anthropology leading up to and including Heidegger's concept of *Dasein* as "being-with" (*Mitsein*), it is at last achieved in G. H. Mead's communication theory of the social self as an I-Me dialectic. In his account of the history of philosophical anthropology, the German scholar Hans Joas therefore describes G. H. Mead as "the most important theorist of intersubjectivity between Feuerbach and Habermas" (1985, 2). By adopting a transcultural approach to the history of philosophical anthropology it will thus be shown how in the twentieth century, both in the East and the West, there has been a social turn to a new concept of the person as a bipolar social self which arises through a dialectical interplay between individuation and sociation.

## Martin Buber on the History of Philosophical Anthropology

Martin Buber describes the turn from a monological concept of self as an I to a fully dialogical concept of self as an I-Thou relationship in his essays on the history of philosophical anthropology collected under the title *Between Man and Man* (1965), especially his 1938 essay called "What is Man?" (*Was ist der Mensch?*). Buber's historical approach is especially influenced by his teacher Wilhelm Dilthey, whom he credits as being the founder of the study of the history of philosophical anthropology (1965, 126). Although Buber's historical overview provides a brief account of earlier periods it focuses upon the modern European and especially German tradition of *Anthropologie* from Kant to Heidegger. Buber (1965, 119) asserts that the real agenda for modern philosophical anthropology was established by Kant, who asks in the *Handbook* to his lectures on logic: (1) What can I know? (2) What ought I to do? (3) What may I hope? and (4) What is man? These questions are in turn answered by (1) metaphysics/epistemology, (2) ethics, (3) religion, and (4) anthropology. Kant is next cited as stating: "Fundamentally all this could be reckoned as anthropology, since the first three questions are related to the last" (Buber: 1965, 119). For Kant, then, human existence is determined to be the central topic for philosophy such that "anthropology" now becomes the universal science as a study of the self. Yet Buber maintains that Kant fails to answer the question which he put to anthropology—What is man? (1965,119).

According to Buber's account, philosophical anthropology after Kant has been characterized throughout its history by the false alternatives of individualism and collectivism, thus leading to the development of an individualistic anthropology on the one side and a collectivist sociology on the other: "As life erroneously supposes that it has to choose between individualism and collectivism, so thought erroneously supposes that it has to choose between an individualistic anthropology and a collectivist sociology" (1965, 202). Hence, while some thinkers like Kierkegaard, Nietzsche, and Heidegger fall into individualism, others like Hegel and Marx fall into the opposite extreme of collectivism.

For Buber the "Copernican revolution" (1965, 148) or turning point in the history of philosophical anthropology occurs in the work of Ludwig Feuerbach. Feuerbach rejected the theological approach and instead carried out an anthropologicial reduction whereby the human self now becomes the exclusive topic for philosophical inquiry. Buber quotes from Feuerbach's *Principles of the Philosophy of the Future* (*Philosophie der Zukunft*, 1843), wherein the latter states: "The new philosophy makes man . . . the exclusive, universal . . . object of philosophy, and thus makes anthropology . . . the universal science" (cited by Buber 1965, 147). He asserts that it was Feuerbach who first established the fundamental distinction between "monological" versus "dialogical" approaches to the self. Whereas previous concepts of self have been essentially monological in character, the philosophy of the future must have as its new starting point a fully dialectical concept of self as arising through a dialogue between the I and the Thou. In this context, he cites Feuerbach as saying, "True dialectic is not a monologue of the solitary thinker with himself, it is a dialogue between *I* and *Thou*" (Buber 1965, 127). Buber thus clarifies that when Feuerbach establishes "man" (*Mensch*) as the basic subject for philosophical anthropology, he does not refer to man as an individual, but "the connexion of *I* and *Thou*" (1965, 147). He cites Feuerbach as saying: "Man's being is contained only in community, in the unity of man with man—a unity which rests, however, only on the reality of the difference between I and Thou" (cited by Buber 1965, 147–48). As Buber then goes on to point out, in Feuerbach there is a coupling of the human *thou* and the divine *Thou*, as shown by his assertion: "man with man—the unity of I and Thou is God" (1965, 210).

However, this epoch-making discovery of the self as an I-Thou relation was neither developed further by Feuerbach nor by his successors in the German tradition of philosophical anthropology. Buber points out that although Nietzsche was inspired by Feuerbach's anthropological reduction so as to render human existence the center of his thought, he still failed to grasp the latter's social concept of personhood as an I-Thou relation and instead develops a theory of heroic individualism based on his notion of the superman: "Nietzsche depends much more solidly on Feuerbach's anthropological reduction than is usually admitted. He falls short of Feuerbach in that he loses sight of the autonomous sphere of the relation between *I* and *Thou*" (1965, 148). On the other side of this false dualism is that of a collectivist sociology as represented by Marxism. In his *Sixth Thesis on Feuerbach*, Marx provides his famous definition of man as "the ensemble of social relations." Marx follows the anthropological reduction of Feuerbach which abandons the theological approach and establishes human selfhood as the exclusive topic of philosophical discourse. Also, he adopts Feuerbach's notion that human selfhood is not contained within itself but only in community. However, he does not appropriate Feuerbach's notion that the self in community is grounded in an irreducible difference between I and Thou. Thus, Buber argues that despite the great influence which Feuerbach exerted on Marx, the latter fails to grasp the essence of Feuerbach's definition of self as an I-Thou relation, and therefore goes on to develop a one-sided collectivist notion of self whereby social relationships always supercede the individual: "Marx did not take up into his concept of society the element of the real relation between the really different *I* and *Thou,* and for that very reason opposed an unreal individualism with a collectivism which was just as unreal" (1965, 148). In criticism of Marx's sociological reduction to an abstract collectivism, he adds: "But if individualism understands only a part of man, collectivism understands only as a part: neither advances to the wholeness of man, to man as a whole. Individualism sees man only in relation to himself, but collectivism does not see *man* at all, it sees only 'society'" (1965, 200). For Buber it is Feuerbach's turn from a monological concept of self as an I to a dialogical concept of self as an I-Thou relation which at last opens the way to establishing a *via media* between individualism and collectivism. But while Feuerbach exercised a profound influence upon many subsequent thinkers in the German tradition of *Anthropologie,* they nonetheless all failed to grasp his dialogical concept of self as an I-Thou unity. Hence, while some thinkers influenced by Feuerbach, like Nietzsche, fall into an individualistic anthropology, others, like Marx, fall into a collectivist sociology.

The rediscovery of Feurbach's concept of self as an I-Thou relation is not to be found until the publication of Martin Buber's own landmark work called *I and Thou (Ich und Du,* 1923). In this prophetically inspired work Buber develops his social concept of the person as a dialogical encounter between the two poles of *I* and *Thou.* This dialogical relation between I and Thou is said by Buber to constitute the "twofold" (1958, 3) or "bipolar" (1958, 81) structure of the person conceived as a whole. The I-Thou (*Ich-Du*) relation is in turn distinguished from that of I-It (*Ich-Es*). Whereas I-Thou designates an interpersonal relation between two subjects, I-It denotes a mere connection with experienced objects, resulting in an isolated and alienated individual devoid of any relation with a genuine Other. Moreover, this twofold dialogical relation between I and Thou occurs in three spheres: man with nature, man with man, and man with God (1958, 6; also 101). While the I-Thou relationship with nature is only at the threshold of speech, and the I-Thou relation with God transpires in deepest silence, the I-Thou relation with others in the human community takes the form of an interpersonal dialogue using language, signs, and speech (1958, 101). For Buber, one is only a true person or self as an *I* responding to a *Thou* in all three spheres of relationship—with society, nature, and God.

Buber goes on to argue that the dialogical medium of language establishes a sphere of communication between I and Thou, a sphere which is common to them both but which reaches out beyond the special sphere of each; namely, what he terms the "between" (*das Zwischen*), or the "sphere of 'between'" In Buber's own words:

> I call this sphere . . . the sphere of "between" . . . The view which establishes the concept of "between" is to be acquired by no longer localizing the relation between human beings, as is customary, either within individual souls or in a general world which embraces and determines them, but in actual fact *between* them. (1965, 203)

Buber's discussion of the "sphere of 'between'" in *Between Man and Man* is in fact reintroducing the concept of the *between* already articulated in previous works including *I and Thou* and *Paths in Utopia*. In his earlier book *I and Thou* Buber had already asserted that the divine presence of "Spirit" does not reside within a self-enclosed individual but only in the *betweenness* of I-Thou relations. In Buber's words: "Spirit is not in the I, but between *I* and *Thou*" (1958, 39). The final paragraph of Buber's *I and Thou* is itself concluded with yet another discussion of the "sphere of 'between'," where it is now revealed to be the locus for the divine theophany: "And the theophany becomes ever nearer, increasingly near to the sphere that lies *between* beings, to the Kingdom that is hidden in our midst, there between us" (1958, 119–20). Hence, the Kingdom of God, like the Holy Spirit, does not exist within the depths of our soul nor outside in a transcendent beyond but only in that intermediary realm comprehended now as the "sphere of 'between'," the *betweenness* of persons in relation.

According to Buber, then, the linguistically mediated social world of human interrelationships always consists of three factors: the *I*, the *Thou*, and the *between*. Buber's category of "between" can be said to represent the culmination of his I-Thou paradigm of a social, relational, and dialogical self. The basic social fact of human existence is neither the I nor the Thou but a third aspect, the *betweenness* of I and Thou. In one of his most memorable statements, Buber thus asserts: "On the far side of the subjective, on this side of the objective, on the narrow ridge where I and Thou meet, there is the realm of 'between'" (1965, 204). He further propounds that this sphere of betweenness is not only existential but also *ontological* in character: "'Between' is not an auxiliary construction, but the real *place* and bearer of what happens between men" (1965, 203; emphasis added). The "between" is now described as the ontological *place* of I-Thou relationships, or the "place" in which both self and others arise through a dialogical encounter. Buber ends his overview of the history of philosophical anthropology by proclaiming that with the advent of the twentieth century there has occurred a turn from the monological view of self as an I to a fully dialogical view of self as the *between* of I and Thou. For Buber this dialogical concept of self as the *between* of I and Thou points the way to a new philosophical anthropology which avoids the reduction to either an individualistic anthropology or a collectivist sociology. "This reality, whose disclosure has begun in our time, shows the way, leading beyond individualism and collectivism, for the life decision of future generations" (1965, 205). It is this turn to a new dialogical concept of self as an I-Thou relation grounded in the ontological reality of *between* which at last provides the basis for a *via media* between abstract individualism and abstract collectivism.

Although Buber speaks from within the prophetic Biblical tradition of Judaism and Hasidic mysticism he also explores the grounds for interreligious dialogue and East-West encounter theology. In *I and Thou*, Buber discusses what he regards to be the difference between the spiritual traditions of Judaism and Buddhism. According to Buber, while Jewish spirituality is based on interhuman I-Thou relationships in the sphere of *between*, the Buddha's teaching is based on an introspective mysticism or absorptionism which points away from human relations altogether. In criticism of the Buddhist faith, he thus writes: "All doctrine of absorption is based on the colossal illusion of the human spirit that is bent back on itself, that exists in man. Actually spirit exists with man as starting point—between man and that which is not man" (1958, 93). Buber goes on to say that the Buddhist teaching of immersion within the self denotes the illusion of man turned back on himself which leads to the renunciation of the basic meaning of the spirit as relation (1958, 93). As he states here and elsewhere in his treatise, spirit does not exist within an isolated subject but only in the *betweenness* of I-Thou relations. Buddhologists might argue that Buber is wholly mistaken in his understanding of Buddhism as representing a kind of introspectionism, mysticism, or absorptionism, and that Buddhist philosophy is *par excellence* that view which defines the self not as substance but in terms of social relations. However, at the same time it shows that traditional Buddhism has long needed to clarify if not actually reform its concept of the "social" as an ultimate category of existence. It is for this reason that I have endeavored to bring to light the "social turn" of modern Japanese Buddhism wherein thinkers like Watsuji Tetsurō and Nishida Kitarō have developed philosophical anthropologies based on an intersubjective model of self which is at once reminiscent of Buber's own dialogical concept of self as the *between* of I and Thou.

## The Philosophical Anthropology of Mead and Buber

In the tradition of classical American pragmatism a landmark contribution to philosophical anthropology is also to be found in the writings of George Herbert Mead. More than any other thinker in the tradition of classical American pragmatism Mead explicitly thematizes and problematizes the concept of selfhood. The entire philosophy of Mead can be regarded as an effort to answer the basic question of philosophical anthropology: "What is the self?" And his answer is precisely this: that the self is a "social self" arising through communicative interaction between the individual and society. The pervasive motif in all of Mead's writings is the nature, origin, and development of self. Mead's framework thus assumes the general character of a philosophical anthropology as a sustained inquiry into the human self.

As has been clarified especially in the work of H. Richard Niebuhr (1963), and his student Paul Pfuetze (1973), there is a profound similarity between Martin Buber's twofold dialogical self as a betweenness of I and Thou and G. H. Mead's bipolar social self as a betweenness of I and Me. It has already been noted that this resemblance between the thought of Buber and Mead can to some extent be explained by the fact that both studied in Germany under the direction of Wilhelm Dilthey, the founder of the history of philosophical anthropology as a distinctive field of inquiry. After his graduate studies at Harvard University Mead spent three years abroad in Germany (1889–1891), during which time his research advisor was none other than Wilhelm Dilthey—the founder of the study of the history of philosophical anthropology. As documented by G. A. Cook (1993, 24), during Mead's study at Berlin he took two courses from Dilthey. It is partly through Mead's study of philosophical anthropology under Dilthey which led to his preoccupation with theories of the self in general and the social dimensions of the self in particular. Hence, both Mead and Buber acquired from Dilthey their primary orientation toward philosophical anthropology, which takes as its basic subject matter the problem of the human self. But in contrast to Buber, who develops philosophical anthropology in the direction of theology and existentialism as the basis for a religious concept of selfhood, Mead instead takes it in the secular direction of pragmatism, humanism, and naturalism as the basis for a social scientific research program. Nonetheless, both thinkers attempt to work out an intersubjective or social concept of self as as an I-Other relation which overcomes the limitations of both individualism and collectivism in the history of philosophical anthropology.

Whereas Buber has clarified the intersubjective constitution of self through a "dialogue" between I and Thou, Mead has similarly demonstrated the social nature, origin, and development of the self through a "conversation" between I and Me. Like Buber's dialogical notion of self as an I-Thou relation, Mead's concept of a bipolar social self as an I-Me dialectic represents the effort to overcome the reduction to either an individualist anthropology or a collectivist sociology. In accord with the linguistic turn both Mead and Buber analyze the self as emerging through an intersubjective process of communication using linguistic signs and symbols. Furthermore, both Mead and Buber describe the linguistic process of symbolic communication in terms of a dialogical principle of "betweenness." For Mead, as for Buber, human existence lies in the *between* of I-Other relationships. An especially suggestive parallel emerges when considering Buber's category of the "between" (*das Zwischen*), in connection with Mead's "principle of sociality," defined in *The Philosophy of the Present* as the "betwixt and between" (1932, 47) of the old system represented by the Me pole or deterministic social environment inherited from the past, and the new system represented by the I pole or emergent individual organism which responds to it with creative spontaneity in the present. It should be recalled that Mead has been deeply influenced on this point by his teacher Josiah Royce, who employs "the *between*" as a technical category to express the intermediary relation between Ego and Alter constituting the "greater social self" as described throughout his work *The World and the Individual*. Mead repeatedly argues that the self, like mind and consciousness, is not to be conceived as an independent substance with simple location, but as a field of relations which exists between an organism and its environment. The movement of symbolic interactionism in American sociology inspired by the thought of G. H. Mead is so named precisely because it finds the locus of personhood neither in the individual nor in society but in the dynamic process of *communicative interaction* which occurs "between" the two poles of I and Me constitutive of the social self. As J. M. Charon writes: "Instead of focusing on the individual . . . or on how the social structure or social situation causes individual behavior, symbolic interactionism focuses on the *nature of interaction*, the dynamic social activities taking place *between* persons" (1989, 22). It can thus be said that for both Mead and Buber, the human self cannot be simply located either in the individual or in society but is instead located within a continuum extending between the two poles of I and Other, what Mead calls the I and the Me, or what Buber calls the I and the Thou. By underscoring the ontological reality of "betweenness" they shift the focus away from both the individual and society to a third factor — the process of linguistically mediated dialogue, conversation, or communication which occurs *between* persons in relation.

The first to systematically combine the frameworks of Mead and Buber was H. Richard Niebuhr (1963), who synthesized Mead's social self and I-Me dialectic with Buber's dialogic self and I-Thou relation as the basis for a new Christian ethics of responsibility. Niebuhr's appropriation of the social self developed by Mead and other American social psychologists like Charles Horton Cooley and Harry Stack Sullivan is especially found in chapter two of his work entitled *The Responsible Self* (1963), wherein he asserts:

> [M]any lines of inquiry have converged on the recognition that the self is fundamentally social, in this sense that it is a being which not only knows itself in relation to other selves but exists as self only in that relation. . . . In America the work of Charles Horton Cooley, of George Herbert Mead, of Harry Stack Sullivan, and many others has led to the understanding that the self is a being which comes to knowledge of itself in the presence of other selves and its very nature is that of a being which lives in response to other selves. (1963, 71)

In this context, Niebuhr develops Mead's idea of the social self as coming to reflexive self consciousness by becoming an object to itself through *dialogue* with others (1963, 71–72). Niebuhr then goes on to reformulate the "social self" in moral terms as what he calls the *responsible self*, a self that lives in response-relations to others, which in turn becomes an *accountable self*. He writes: "The self before nature remains a social self, responding to other selves in all responses to nature. It is also an accountable self . . . Responsiveness now becomes responsibility in the sense of accountability when response is made not to one being alone but to that being as related with the self to a third reality" (1963, 81–82). Niebuhr distinguishes three elements characterizing the social nature of the responsible self, which as he admits, is deeply influenced by Josiah Royce's (Peircean) semiotic concept of the triadic stucture of all dialectical interaction within the community of interpretation (1963, 83). The first element is that of *response*, that all moral action of a social self is a response to action upon us (1963, 61). The second element in the action of a self is not called moral action unless it is response to *interpreted* action upon us (1963, 62). A third element is *accountability*, understood as a part of the future-oriented response pattern of our self-conduct. Our actions are responsible not only insofar as they are reactions to interpreted actions upon us but also insofar as they are made in anticipation of answers to our answers (1963, 63). This third element in responsibility, the anticipation of reaction to our reaction, in turn results in *social solidarity* (1963, 65). These three elements altogether constitute the *dialogical* nature of responsible action made by a social self in the community of interpretation:

> An agent's action is like a statement in a dialogue. Such a statement not only seeks to meet, as it were, to fit into the previous statement to which it is an answer, but is made in anticipation of reply. It looks forward as well as backward. . . . It is made as part of a total conversation that leads foreward and is to have meaning as a whole. (1963, 64)

Hence, Niebuhr's responsible self based on the triadic nature of dialogue is itself heavily influenced by the holistic model of semiotic communication developed by Peirce and Royce, wherein the present self is always interpreting the past self to the future self in a community of interpretation. Moreover, Neibuhr's analysis further reflects the holistic model of semiotic communication developed by G. H. Mead, whereby it is the anticipation of the response of the other that gives one's own gesture (stimulus) its meaning within the organic unity of a social act.

Niebuhr then argues that the Meadian idea of a social or responsible self is a new symbolic form through which to understand Jesus Christ as well as a new root metaphor for comprehending the dialogical nature of Christian ethics (1963, 154–59). Furthermore, this new root metaphor of social responsibility and accountability can be understood through the symbol of *homo dialogicus*, the "dialogical animal," the paradigm of which is the person and teaching of Jesus Christ (1963, 159–60). It can thus be said that in the theological anthropology of Niebuhr, the person of Jesus Christ becomes the ultimate exemplar of Mead's notion of the social self constituted by a dialectic of I and Me.

Niebuhr sees the deep affinity of G. H. Mead's notion of the social self as a dialogical conversation between the I and the Me with Martin Buber's idea of self as an intersubjective dialogue between the I and the Thou (1963, 72). He argues that both the prophetic Biblical tradition of Buber and the social psychology of Mead show how human personhood emerges in dialogue with the generalized other. He thus attempts to combine these two traditions in his own Christian ethics based on the notion of a "responsible self," comprehended as the spontaneous response to the other with whom all individuals are bound within a community of mutual accountability. Niebuhr writes:

> The social psychology of G. H. Mead and his successors was developed in the context of evolutionary, biocentric, and behavioristic thinking,

but a group of men with very different general orientations has led to similar results. Among them Martin Buber is best known. In his existentialist reflections he has come upon the primordial character of "I-Thou" and "I-It" as prior to any atomic I or atomic object. (1963, 72)

In this way, the responsible self of Niebuhr's Christian ethics of accountability takes the form of a synthesis of Josiah Royce's (Peircean) semiotic notion of the church as a community of interpretation with G. H. Mead's idea of a social self as a dialectic between I and Me as well as Martin Buber's dialogical concept of self as a relation between I and Thou. He thus states that the social self is an I-Thou or I-You self, responding to a Thou that is always a member of an interacting community (1963, 78).

Under the influence of his teacher H. Richard Niebuhr's lecture series delivered at Yale University in 1940, P. E. Pfuetze (1954, 1973) has written a systematic comparative study of Mead and Buber which takes as its central theme the notion of the "social self" as analyzed from both a philosophical and religious point of view. In his work entitled *Self, Society, Existence*, Pfuetze uses the term *social self* to establish the similarity between Mead's I-Me relation and Buber's I-Thou dialogue. As points of comparison he emphasizes that both Mead and Buber underscore relationships between persons and the social nature of reality. Reality itself has a social structure and is constituted by interrelationships. The predominant motif in their writing is that all life is a complex of relationships, and that on the human level it is only within a social matrix that the "self" arises. For Mead and Buber, the self is not a birthright but something to be realized, and there are graduated levels of self-realization up to the achievement of personhood. It is only through social relationships between persons involving dialogue or symbolic communication with others that human selfhood is realized. The use of speech, language and signs in symbolic communication and dialogue is the basic mechanism constitutive of selfhood. In the context of establishing these parallels between Mead and Buber, Pfuetze emphasizes that both thinkers have developed the notion of a social self as a middle position between individualism and collectivism, or as it were, between atomistic subjectivism and organic monism. He writes: "Mead and Buber . . . reject the extremes of both individualism and collectivism . . . and seek instead a middle axiom in the social self in which self and society are correlative terms" (1973, 333). He further points out that for both thinkers the locus of reality is the *betweenness* of person and person in society, that is, the betweenness of *I* and *Me* for Mead and the betweenness of *I* and *Thou* for Buber. In Pfuetze's words: "Both Mead and Buber are saying . . . that the essential and constitutive character of human life and selfhood is something that takes place *between* one person and another in a society of persons" (1973, 6).

## Mead and John Macmurray on the Self as an I-Other Relationship

In his influential book entitled *Persons in Relation* (1961, 1983), John Macmurray sets forth his inspired vision of the self as an I-You relation constituted by linguistic communication with others in a community of persons in relation. Macmurray's concept of the self as a relation of I and You shares much in common with both Mead's communication theory of the social self as a relation of I and Me as well as Buber's dialogical self as a relation of I and Thou. From the outset of his text Macmurray articulates the self in *bipolar* terms, stating that the person is not a solitary I, but an "'I-You' relationship" (1983, 40). According to Macmurray, "Persons . . . are constituted by their mutual relation to one another. 'I' exists only as one element in the complex 'You and I'." (1983, 24). Again: "Formally stated, 'I' am one term in the relation 'You and I' which constitutes both the 'I' and the 'You'" (1983, 28). And as he elsewhere asserts: "The unit of the personal is not the 'I', but the 'You and I'" (1983, 61). The I and the You are in and of themselves to be regarded as abstractions from the "original 'You and I' situation" (1983, 70). For Macmurray, then, the I and the You are not separate atomic entities which later form a relationship; but rather, the "'You and I' relation" is itself the basic ontological unit from which both the I and the You are constituted by the mutuality of their relation (1983, 91). Finally, Macmurray's concept of self as an I-You relation is developed in terms of his doctrine of "community" as a fellowship of persons in relations.

In his introduction to *Persons in Relation*, F. G. Kirkpatrick underscores the resemblance between Macmurray's concept of personhood and the organismic model of self articulated in A. N. Whitehead's process metaphysics, the latter which he says "introduced into much of contemporary philosophy a . . . feeling for *community*, the union of the many into one" (Macmurray: 1983, xiv). While there is no doubt a most significant parallel between Macmurray's concept of self in a community of persons in relation and Whitehead's organismic process model of self in the metaphysical community of many into one, there is an even greater parallel to be found in the process philosophy of G. H. Mead. Macmurray's concept of the self as an *I-You relationship* is at once reminiscent of Mead's bipolar notion of the social self as an *I-Me relationship*. For both thinkers the self is not an isolated I or Cartesian subject but a unity of "I and Other," what Mead calls the unity of "I and Me" and what Macmurray calls the unity of "I and You." Mead asserts that, "The self is both the 'I' and the 'me'; the 'me' setting the situation to which the 'I' responds" (MSS 277). Similarly, Macmurray states: "The unit of the personal is not the 'I', but the 'You and I'" (1983, 61). Mead defines the self in *reflexive* terms, stating that "The self has the characteristic that it is an object to itself" (MSS 136). Hence, for Mead the individual becomes a social self with reflexive self-consciousness and personal identity only insofar as it functions as both an "I" or subject and a "Me" or object at the same time. Macmurray likewise asserts: "A personal being is at once subject and object . . . As subject he is 'I', as object he is 'You', is always 'the Other'" (1983, 27) Just as for Mead the social self arises through interaction between I and Me within the ontological context of a "situation" (MSS 228), so Macmurray speaks of the "original 'You and I' situation" (1983, 70). For both thinkers, then, the *I-Other relation* is a situational transaction functioning as the basic ontological unit from which both "I" and "Other" are constituted through mutual encounter.

Mead and Macmurray both go on to develop their respective notions of selfhood as an I-Other relationship in conjunction with a doctrine of *community*. The theme of self-realization through community is a recurrent motif in classical American philosophy, including Peirce's intersubjective community of scientific inquirers, Royce's religious community of loyalty, Dewey's secular liberal democratic community, and Whitehead's metaphysical community based on harmonic interpenetration between the many and the one. In the philosophy of Mead the notion of "community" is designated by his most famous concept: the generalized other. According to Mead the self is constituted as a unity through its internalization of the generalized other representing the attitudes of its entire community: "The organized community or social group which gives to the individual his unity of self may be called 'the generalized other.' The attitude of the generalized other is the attitude of the whole community" (MSS 154). Likewise, Macmurray asserts that "the Self exists only in dynamic relation with the Other" (1983, 17). He further specifies that the "reference to the Other is therefore to a community" (1983, 78). And elsewhere: "The Other acquires the character of a community of which I am a member" (1983, 77). Hence, both thinkers hold that the self is always to defined through its relations to "the Other" understood as a collective representation of the entire community to which it belongs. In this way both have overcome the conventional dichotomy of self versus society through a more holistic model of human selfhood as an individual-community relationship.

From what has been said above it can now be asserted that both Mead and Macmurray have abandoned the notion of a separate self as an isolated I or Cartesian subject for a *communicative self* as the unity of I and Other. Both explicitly define their concepts of self in terms of communication, just as both argue that the individual becomes a person or social self only through communication with the others in a community. Mead writes: "[T]he individual reaches his self only through communication with others" (MSS 233). Similarly, Macmurray asserts: "To be a person is to be in communication with the Other" (1983, 77). Hence, the ultimate goal of life for both thinkers is to achieve self-realization through communication with others in a community, which for Mead is to become a social self as an I-Me relationship, and which for Macmurray is to become a "person" as an I-You relationship. In this way both G. H. Mead and John Macmurray have converged upon a communication model of human selfhood defined as arising through linguistically mediated communication between the I and the Other, or what Mead calls the I and the Me, and what Macmurray calls the I and the You.

## The Self as an I-Other Relation in Macmurray, Buber, and Mead

In his overview of the history of philosophical anthropology entitled *Between Man and Man*, Martin Buber underscores the turn initiated by Ludwig Feuerbach in 1843 from a monological concept of self as an individual I to a dialogical concept of self as a "connexion of *I* and *Thou*" (1965,147), or a "dialogue between *I* and *Thou*" (1965, 127). Under the influence of Feuerbach, Buber sets forth his own concept of self as an I-Thou relation in his celebrated work *I and Thou* (*Ich und Du*, 1923). In *Mind, Self, and Society* (1934), G. H. Mead likewise asserts that, "The self is both the 'I' and the 'me'" (MSS 277). Although he makes no reference to either Mead or Buber, John Macmurray's concept of self as an *I-You relation* at once bears a striking resemblance to both Mead's communication model of the social self as an *I-Me relation* and Buber's dialogical self as an *I-Thou relation*. In *Persons in Relation* Macmurray therefore states: "Persons . . . are constituted by their mutual relation to one another. 'I' exists only as one element in the complex 'You and I'" (1983, 24). Generally speaking, all three argue that the self is not an isolated I or Cartesian subject but a relation of "I and Other"—what Macmurray calls the relation of "I and You," what Mead calls the relation of "I and Me," and what Buber calls the relation of "I and Thou." For all three, the I and Other are not separate atomic entities that are subsequently related, but rather the I-Other relation is itself the primary ontological unit from which both the I and Other are constituted through their mutuality of relation. Hence, all three have crystallized the *bipolar* or twofold structure of the human self as an I-Other relation which underscores both the individuality of the self as an I and the sociality of the self through relationship to an Other. Moreover, all three have developed a communication model of personhood whereby the individual becomes a self only through a linguistic process of communication, conversation, and dialogue between the I and the Other. The upshot in all three frameworks is that the human self is not a solitary ego but an individual-community relationship which arises through communication with others in the intersubjective medium of language. It can thus be said that in the twentieth-century tradition of Western philosophy, Mead, Macmurray, and Buber are three paradigmatic figures representing the turn from a monological notion of self as an I to a dialogical vision of self as a relation of I and Other. Yet the advantage of Mead's formulation of the self-society interaction as a dialectic of I and Me is that while underscoring the irreducible otherness of the Other, it also clarifies that others are not simply external to oneself, but are constitutive of one's own selfhood as the Me. The *Me* component of Mead's I-Me dialectic thus describes not only the "self-in-society," but also *society-in-the-self*.

It is especially with regard to their treatment of God that we find the single major discrepancy between the frameworks of Mead, Buber, and Macmurray. Buber speaks of the I-Thou relation in three spheres insofar as the self is related not only to other selves but also to nature and to God (1958, 6; also, 101). Likewise, Macmurray describes the person as an I-You relationship involving not only other persons, but also nature (1983, 165), and God (1983, 164). Macmurray explicates the I-You relation to God in his role as the universal Other, stating: "the idea of a universal personal Other is the idea of God" (1983, 164). However, while Buber speaks of God as the absolute Other and eternal Thou, and Macmurray refers to God as the universal personal Other, the Generalized Other of Mead remains a wholly secular concept with no reference to the concept of God. Thus, while Buber and Macmurray both move in the direction of a theological anthropology, Mead carries out an anthropological reduction which rejects the theological approach and establishes the human self as the object for philosophical reflection. In his comparative study of Buber and Mead, Pfuetze (1973) criticizes Mead's secular doctrine of human intersubjectivity with its connections to the natural sciences from the standpoint of Buber's theological anthropology and existentialist personalism. He asserts that for Mead, social relations are always horizontal and there is no place for a vertical man-God relation (1973, 250). In contrast, for Buber the horizontally structured interhuman relation of *I* and *thou* is grounded in the vertically structured human-divine relation of *I* and *Thou*. Pfuetze ends his work by trying to bring Mead's secular notion of human intersubjectivity closer to Buber's theological anthropology in which the self is related not only to society and nature but also to God. He thus comes to agree with the Chicago school pragmatist Edward Scribner Ames, who criticized Mead for his unwillingness to recognize the religious implications of the generalized other (see Pfuetze 1973, 86). For Pfuetze, as for E. S. Ames, Mead's idea of the generalized other must finally be expanded beyond its secular meaning to its ultimate religious significance as the transcendent being of God, the absolute Other and the eternal Thou. Nonetheless, it cannot be questioned that for Mead himself the generalized other has no connotations of a metaphysical ultimate or religious absolute, but remains a wholly regulative and functional concept: namely, the generalization of the process of role-taking within a social group. In Mead's secular framework the generalized other does not represent God but the *universalized human community* by means of which the individual is constituted as a social self. As the universalized human community the generalized other also functions as the impartial jury which legislates for all norm-governed rational thought and moral conduct. Hence, Mead's concept of the generalized other is to be understood as a naturalistic reformulation of Josiah Royce's notion of God as the beloved community, just as his genetic account of how the greater social self is constituted as a unity by taking on the roles of the generalized other is a secularization of Royce's Christian religious theme of self-realization through the community. While Buber and Macmurray recognize the I-Other relationship as constitutive of the human self in its wholeness, the Other is first of all God, a being who is believed to have a transcendent existence apart from man. But for Mead the "generalized other" emerges from out of the social process of communicative interaction itself and has no existence apart from or prior to this social process. Mead's communication model of the social self is therefore completely nondualistic in that it accounts for the social origin and formation of self through its incorporation of the generalized other without any reference whatsoever to a transcendent or supernatural principle.

### Mead and Cassirer on the Symbolic Nature of Human Selfhood

From what has been stated above it can now be seen how the frameworks of such thinkers like Mead, Buber, and Macmurray represent a *social turn* from the monological concept of self as an atomic I or Cartesian subject to a dialogical concept of self as an I-Other relation, respectively codified as the I-Me relation for Mead, the I-Thou relation for Buber, and the I-You relation for Macmurray. Among these three it is especially Mead who posits the "social" as an ultimate category of human existence. However, the adequacy of defining the essence of self as "social" has been questioned by one of the great works of philosophical anthropology in the twentieth century, *An Essay on Man* (1944) by Ernst Cassirer. In the final chapter of this work Cassirer specifically criticizes the limitations of Aristotle's definition of man as a "social animal," arguing that it provides no basis for distinguishing man from other animals, all of which to some extent have a social characteristic. He writes:

> Aristotle's definition of man as a "social animal" is not sufficiently comprehensive. It gives us a generic concept but not the specific difference. Sociability as such is not an exclusive characteristic of man, nor is it the privilege of man alone. In the so-called animal states among bees and ants, we find a . . . suprisingly complicated social organization. (1944, 223)

Cassirer's polemic here is that since both man and animals have a social nature, since bees and ants as well as humans are highly socialized, the generic notion of "sociability" cannot function as the *differentia* which separates man from other living creatures.

After criticizing previous concepts of human nature formulated in the history of philosophical anthropology, including Aristotle's notion of man as a "social animal," Cassirer then provides his own well-known definition of man as an *animal symbolicum*:

> Reason is a very inadequate term with which to comprehend the forms of man's cultural life in all their richness and variety. But all these forms are symbolic forms. Hence, instead of defining man as an *animal rationale*, we should define him as an *animal symbolicum*. (1944, 26)

In opposition to the narrower concept of man as a "rational animal" (*animal rationale*), man is now conceived as a "symbolic animal" (*animal symbolicum*) who lives in a culture built up of "symbolic forms." Cassirer takes up a neo-Kantian position wherein human experience is constituted not simply by "rational forms" of the understanding as for Kant, but also by *symbolic forms* from the deeper levels of mythic, poetic, and imaginative consciousness. In her work *Philosophy in a New Key* (1942), Suzanne Langer further develops Cassirer's philosophical anthropology based on the notion of "symbolic forms." She argues that new disciplines which have emerged only in the twentieth century ranging from symbolic logic to depth psychology have converged upon the insight that human experience is essentially "symbolic" in character. Adopting Cassirer's definition of self as an *animal symbolicum*, Langer goes on to assert that human existence is to be distinguished from animal existence through the *symbolic transformation of experience*. Hence, for Langer, as for Cassirer, the distinctive trait of human experience is that it is translated into symbols, including not only the "discursive symbols" of science, logic, and mathematics, but also the "nondiscursive symbols" of art, religion, and mythology.

The problem which arises for our consideration here is whether Cassirer's criticism of Aristotle's concept of the social animal is also applicable to the G. H. Mead's concept of the social self. It must further be asked if Cassirer's rejection of "sociability" as the defining characteristic of human exitence at the same time undermines the Meadian principle of sociality. Another question to be addressed is whether Cassirer's definition of man as a "symbolic animal" is itself a more adequate criterion for distinguishing human and nonhuman animals than Mead's generic definition of a social self. It has already been seen how Mead's notion of the social self was influenced *via* the latter writings of Josiah Royce by Peirce's concept of personhood as arising through communication in an intersubjective community. According to Justus Buchler, Peirce's communication theory of self represents a modern reformulation of Aristotle's concept of man as a social animal. However, Buchler further clarifies that for Peirce the self is a social animal precisely because it emerges through a semiotic process of symbolic communication using linguistic signs and symbols. To repeat the words of Buchler:

> Peirce maintains that in so far as thought is cognitive it must be linguistic or *symbolical* in character—that is, it must presuppose communication. *Communication takes place by means of signs,* and Peirce's theory, in its investigation of the nature and conditions of the sign-relation, endows with a new and vital significance the old truth that man is a *social animal*. (Peirce 1955, xi–xii; italics added)

Cassirer's insightful criticism of Aristotle's concept of man as a social animal therefore does not hold for Peirce, in that for the latter, the "social" nature of self is developed in terms of the *symbolic* nature of human communication.

A. N. Whitehead is another leading figure in the tradition of classical American philosophy who explicitly affirms the notion of the human self as a social animal (PR 204). Furthermore, like Peirce and other American thinkers,

Whitehead underscores the *symbolic* nature of the self as a social animal. In his chapter entitled "Symbolic Reference" from *Process and Reality* (1929), and in his book *Symbolism* (1927), Whitehead argues that there are three levels of perception: (1) causal efficacy, (2) presentational immediacy, and (3) symbolic reference. While all living organisms experience the social environment through nonsensuous perception in the primordial mode of causal efficacy, and more highly evolved animals experience through sense perception in the mode of presentational immediacy, human experience is characterized by perception in the mode of symbolic reference, wherein the clear and distinct sense data of presentational immediacy function as symbols referring to the dim feelings of causal relationship at the level of causal efficacy. Hence, insofar as Whitehead's generic definition of the human self as a "social animal" is distinguished from nonhuman animals by virtue of its capacity for perception in the mode of symbolic reference, it is not open to the charges which Cassirer levels against Aristotle's theory.

The semiotic communication model of personhood developed in the tradition of American philosophy running through Peirce, James, Royce, Dewey, Cooley, Whitehead, and others reaches it clearest and most systematic expression in Mead's concept of the "social self" as a communication process of symbolic interaction using significant symbols. Mead, like Cassirer, fully recognizes that not only human but also nonhuman animals are "social" in character. In fact, Mead generalizes his "principle of sociality" into a universal metaphysical category which is applicable not only to both human and nonhuman animals but to *all* events in the creative advance of nature: "I wish to emphasize the fact that the appearance of [human] mind is only the culmination of that *sociality* which is found throughout the universe, its culmination lying in the fact that the organism, by occupying the attitudes of others, can occupy its own attitude in the role of the other" (PP 86; italics added). Mead, like Cassirer, makes reference to the high level of social organization found in the beehive and the ant's nest (MSS 232), as well as schools of fishes, packs of wolves, flocks of birds, herds of cattle, and other animal groups (MSS 238). Thus far Mead's concept of a social self in not yet adequate in that it only provides a generic concept but not the specific difference between human and nonhuman animals. However, Mead goes on to further specify that while both human and nonhuman animals possess the character of "sociality," the human is social in a unique and special manner which differentiates it from all other living creatures. As Mead asserts: "The human being is social in a *distinguishing* fashion" (MSS 241; italics added).

How is the sociality of humans to be distinguished from that of other animals? First of all, similar to Cassirer's philosophical anthropology wherein man is defined as an *animal symbolicum,* and Whitehead's concept of human experience as characterized through perception in the mode of *symbolic reference,* Mead's concept of the social self is further defined through the notion of *symbolic interaction,* or *symbolic communication.* The "symbolic interactionist" movement of sociology in America which was originally inspired by G. H. Mead and then further developed by Herbert Blumer, Erving Goffman and others takes the communication process of "symbolic interaction" using *significant symbols* to be the distinguishing characteristic of human nature as a social self. As clarified by Herbert Blumer in *Symbolic Interactionism* (1969), Mead identifies two levels of communicative interaction in human society, "the conversation of gestures," or nonsymbolic communication, and "the use of significant symbols," or symbolic communication (1986, 8). While animals communicate through the conversation of gestures at the nonsymbolic level, only humans communicate with significant gestures having shared meanings at the symbolic level so as to develop a social self with reflexive self-consciousness. Consequently, while for Mead all animals are social, human beings are "social" in a *distinguishing fashion* through symbolic communication.

Let us now review this developmental process of becoming a social self through a communication process of symbolic interaction as described by Mead. At the outset of his chapter on "The Self" from *Mind, Self, and Society,* Mead defines the self in reflexive terms as the development of self-consciousness by becoming its own object: "The self has the characteristic that it is an object to itself" (MSS 136). He then asks: "How can an individual get outside himself (experientially) in such a way as to become an object to himself? This is the essential psychological problem of selfhood or of self-consciousness" (MSS 138). His answer to this question is that "he becomes an object to himself only by taking the attitudes of other individuals toward himself within a social environment" (MSS 138). Furthermore, the individual can go outside itself and view himself as an object only by taking the role of the other through symbolic communication using "significant symbols" (MSS 138–39). The "significant symbol" functions to call out the same response in the speaker as the listener so as to have a common, shared, or universal meaning. For this reason the "significant symbol" is the primary mechanism for *role-taking* whereby the individual can go outside himself through taking the role of the other and see himself as an object from the standpoint of that other.

While communication between animals is limited to a "conversation of gestures," humans instead communicate through symbolic interaction using "significant gestures" or "significant symbols":

The importance of what we term "communication" lies in the fact that it provides a form of behavior in which the organism or the individual may become an object to himself. It is that sort of communication which we have been discussing—not communication in the sense of the cluck of the hen to the chickens, or the bark of a wolf to the pack, or the lowing of cow, but communication in the sense of *significant symbols,* communication which is directed not only to others but also to the individual himself. (MSS 138–139; italics added)

Mead again makes this fundamental distinction between human versus non-human communication when he writes:

> The socialized human animal takes the attitude of the other toward himself . . . The socialized non-human animal, on the other hand, does not take the attitude of the other toward himself . . . Hence, it is only in human society . . . that mind arises or can arise; and thus also human beings are evidently the only biological organisms which are or can be self-conscious or possessed of selves. (MSS 235n.)

To summarize the basic elements of Mead's argument: the self is to be defined "reflexively" as a process of developing *self-consciousness* by becoming an object to itself; the self goes outside itself and becomes its own object only by the mechanism of *role-taking* or taking the attitudes of the generalized other and then by seeing itself as an object from the standpoint of that other; the self takes the role of the generalized other only through "symbolic interaction," or by symbolic communication using *significant symbols*; the function of significant symbols is to call out the same response in the speaker as in the listener to whom they are addressed so as to have a shared or common meaning. He then asserts that while both man and the animals are able to communicate, only man communicates through significant symbols, and consequently, only man can go outside himself by taking on the social roles of others and see himself as an object from the standpoint of others. He then argues that since man alone has the capacity for role-taking through communication with significant symbols, only man can develop into a "social self" with personal identity and reflexive self-consciousness (MTNC 398).

It can now be seen precisely how Mead's symbolic interactionist theory of self establishes a clear *differentia* between the "social self" of human animals and the more generic sociality of nonhuman animals. While all animals are characterized by the generic principle of "sociality," the human is social in a distinguishing fashion, insofar as only the human self arises through *symbolic interaction*. Although other animals besides the human are capable of "communication," unlike the nonsymbolic communication between animals through a "conversation of gestures," the human self alone interacts through symbolic communication using "significant symbols" or "significant gestures." Moreover, while ants, bees, and other animals besides humans exhibit a degree of "socialization," the socialized nonhuman animal does not take the attitude of the other toward himself, whereas the socialized human animal does take the attitude of the other toward himself through communication with significant symbols. Finally, since a "self" is acquired only by becoming an object to oneself, and since only the human takes the attitude of the other toward himself through symbolic communication with significant symbols, only the human develops a social self with reflexive self-consciousness and personal identity. For Mead, then, it is only insofar as the human communicates with *symbols* that it can become a social self. Insofar as Mead specifies that the "social" character of human selfhood is itself a function of symbolic interaction, he undercuts Cassirer's arguments against Aristotle's definition of man as a social animal. Mead's concept of man as a social self arising through symbolic interaction provides both the *generic* concept of human existence as a social animal as well as the specific *difference* as a symbolic animal. Thus, Mead's definition of man as a "social self" arising through *symbolic interaction* in one stroke elegantly combines Aristotle's definition of man as a "social animal" and Cassirer's definition of man as a "symbolic animal."

## Philosophical Anthropology in Modern Japanese Thought

If philosophical anthropology in the West traces back to the ancient Delphic injunction *gnothi sauton* or "Know thyself" as recorded in the Platonic dialogue *Alcibiades I* (124a–124b), the anthropological orientation of modern Japanese philosophy has its origins in traditional Zen Buddhism understood as *koji-kyūmei*, "investigation of self." It has already been seen how in his essay "The Standpoint of Zen" (1984, 1), Nishitani Keiji from the Kyoto school of modern Japanese philosophy traces this characterization of Zen Buddhism as *koji-kyūmei*, or "investigation of self" to Zen master Daitō Kokushi (1281–1338), founder of Daitokuji in Kyoto. Nishitani thus asserts: "Zen is that standpoint which exhaustively investigates the self itself" (1984, 1). The distinguished modern Japanese philosopher Abe Masao further elucidates the characterization of Zen Buddhism as an inquiry into self versus the theistic orientation of Christianity as an inquiry into God: "The basic question of Christianity is What is God? . . . By contrast, the basic question of Zen is

What is the self? . . . This is why the primary concern of Zen traditionally has been *koji-kyūmei*, 'investigation of self'" (see Ives 1992, viii). In the West it was L. Feuerbach who first explictly rejected the theological approach to man and instead carried out an anthropological reduction whereby the "human self" becomes the sole object of philosophical inquiry (see Buber 1965, 147). However, as the above statement by Abe makes clear, such an anthropological reduction was carried out from the very beginning in traditional Japanese Zen Buddhism conceived as *koji-kyūmei*, "investigation of self."

In twentieth-century Japanese philosophy thinkers related to the Kyoto school like Watsuji Tetsurō and Nishida Kitarō have been influenced not only by the anthropological direction of traditional Zen Buddhism as *koji kyūmei* or "investigation of self," but also the German tradition of *Anthropologie* from Kant to Heidegger. Furthermore, representative modern Japanese philosophers like Nishida Kitarō and Watsuji Tetsurō have rejected all subjectivist concepts of human existence in favor of a social or intersubjectivist model of self as a twofold individual-society interaction. The anthropological direction of Watsuji Tetsurō's framework is clearly indicated by the very title of the first chapter of his *Ethics* (*Rinrigaku*, 1937), called "The Significance of Ethics as Anthropology," or as it might also been translated, "The Significance of Ethics as the Study of the Person" (*Ningen gaku to shite no rinrigaku no igi*). Similarly, the full title of Watsuji's book on "climate" (*fūdo*) theory reads: *Climate: An Anthropological Investigation* (*Fūdo ningengakuteki kōsatsu*, 1935). Watsuji, like Buber and Mead, studied for a period in Germany and was deeply influenced the writings of Wilhelm Dilthey. Hence, like Buber and Mead, Watsuji focuses upon the central problem of philosophical anthropology: that of defining the nature of the human self. Moreover, Watsuji provides an historical account of the European and especially German tradition of philosophical anthropology running through such figures as Kierkegaard, Nietzsche, Dilthey, Scheler, Husserl, and Heidegger, arguing that all are still bound by the limits of individualism. From this standpoint Watsuji asserts that the standpoint of "individualism" (*kojinshugi*) must now be overcome with a double concept of Japanese personhood based on a dialectic of "self-other" (*ji-ta*) relations.

Influenced by Heidegger's etymological analysis of words to bring into the open their implicit meaning, Watsuji endeavors to disclose the social character of Japanese self and society by an examination of the Japanese language. For Watsuji, among the languages of the world it is especially the Japanese term *ningen* or "person" which reflects the double-sided character of the self as an individual-society interaction. Watsuji (1937, 9) holds that the Japanese *ningen* model of personhood has a "twofold character" (*nijū seikaku*) as a self-other dialectic. As has already been seen, Watsuji unfolds the etymological meaning of the two Sino-Japanese characters for the word *ningen* or person as disclosing the double structure of the self as both an "individual" (*hito, kojin*) and a part of "society" (*shakai, yo no naka, seken*). In his *Ethics*, Watsuji asserts: "Thus, I must also clarify the idea of 'person' (*ningen*), which I have used vaguely up to now. This is especially needed in order to distinguish it from the 'Philosophical Anthropology' which has become popular in recent times" (1937, 7). For Watsuji, the notion of a Cartesian subject in the sense of a solitary individual or isolated ego-self is always an abstraction from this twofold dialectical structure of personhood as *ningen* in its concrete wholeness. Contrasting the individualistic notions of man expressed in Western languages to the Japanese word for the person, he thus states: "[S]uch words like *anthropos, homo, man,* and *Mensch* signify [only] the individual man . . . A man must be able to exist both as an individual and as a social being. The word which best expresses this twofold character (*nijū seikaku*) is the term *ningen*" (1937, 9). As emphasized by Kumon Shumpei (1979, 1982), Watsuji's "contextual" (*kanjin*) model of Japanese personhood as *ningen* wherein the self is always understood in relation to its surrounding "context" (*aidagara*) represents a middle position between individualist and collectivist accounts of the self.

Like Mead, Buber, and others who have taken the social turn in the Western tradition of philosophical anthropology, Watsuji has formulated a social or intersubjective concept of personhood based upon a dialogical principle of *betweenness*. In the philosophical anthropology of Watsuji the person as *ningen* is understood through the fundamental notion of *aidagara*, "betweenness," or as it were, *hito to hito to no aidagara*, the "betweenness of person and person." Let us recall the following passage from Watsuji's *Ethics*: "The locus of ethical problems is not in the consciousness of the isolated individual but in the betweenness of person and person (*hito to hito to no aidagara*). Therefore ethics is a study of the person (*ningen*)" (1937, 2–3). In Kimura Bin's work *The Betweenness of Man and Man* (*Hito to hito to no aida,* 1972), the very title of which at once reminds us of Martin Buber's text on philosophical anthropology entitled *Between Man and Man* (1965), he elaborates Watsuji's *ningen* model of self based on the dialogical notion of *aida* (= *aidagara*), "betweenness." He reformulates Watsuji's notion of *aida* in terms of Nishida's idea of a transpersonal *basho* or spatial locus wherein both self and non-self arise through mutual encounter. In this context Kimura also discusses Buber's notion of personhood a betweenness of I and Thou. He emphasizes that Japanese psychiatry and psychology in the twentieth century have been profoundly influenced by Martin Buber's fundamental categories of *I* and *Thou*, which Kimura himself denotes by means of the Japanese equivalent, *ware to nanji* (1972, 140). In his more recent work entitled *Betweenness* (*Aida*, 1988), Kimura further discusses Buber's notion of selfhood as the "between" of I-Thou relations in connection with the Japanese dialogical principle of betweenness:

> Dialogue philosophers like Martin Buber, are the first people who considered relations between I and Thou, the *aida* or between of self and others, not as an interchange of communication after their first meeting, but as a field of the possibility of such communication . . . Buber paid attention to the field of betweenness (*aida*) as a place of encounter wherein I and Thou come into existence mutually, and regarded this field as primary in that it is the origin of human reality. Naturally his thought is important for us. But his religious thought, and in particular his model of encounter with God as an eternal Thou . . . is beyond our consideration in this book. (1988, 116)

For Kimura the most significant point of contact between the philosophical anthropology of Buber and the Japanese *ningen* concept of personhood as developed by Zen Buddhism as well as the modern Japanese philosophy of Nishida and Watsuji is that for both the self is understood to be a function of the dialogical principle of *aida*, "betweenness." The *aida* or "between" of I and Thou is the ultimate ontological field of social relationships in which both the I and the Thou are both constituted through mutual encounter. However, while Kimura acknowledges that Buber was among the first to elucidate the dialogical principle of betweenness (*aida*) as the basic category of human selfhood, at the same time he is critical of the latter's illicit theological extension of this principle beyond the interhuman sphere of social relationships. Kimura goes on to contrast the "vertical" relation of transcendence in Buber's notion of the man-God encounter to that of the "horizontal" relation in the interhuman encounter described by the Japanese dialogical principle of *aida*. Relating the principle of *aida* to both Zen Buddhism and the philosophy of Nishida Kitarō, Kimura writes:

> It is certain that the field of *aida* has a kind of religious meaning as a place of encounter with human others instead of God. If we ignore the reality of *aida* when we discuss the relation of human existence to morality, it would be just an academic discussion. But we would like to ask how *aida* could be a place of encounter with God, and what the structure of this encounter would be. In Zen Buddhism it is said:

"Meeting Buddha, kill him. Meeting ancestors, kill them." On the other hand, it is said: "To know the self is to forget the self. To forget the self is to be enlightened by the world" [Dōgen]. Nishida says: "Things come and enlighten me." Please remember our insistence that "The self is nothing but the principle of relation to the world in the between (*aida*) of ourselves and the world." . . . If the self is a principle of betweenness (*aida*) itself, it is to be found not only in special religious experiences, but also in everyday life. (1988, 116–18)

As indicated above, the modern Japanese philosopher Nishida Kitarō has also developed a philosophical anthropology based on an intersubjective concept of the social self as an I-Thou relation. It should be remembered that in his maiden work *A Study of Good* (*Zen no kenkyū*, 1911), while under the influence of James's process philosophy based on the method of radical empiricism, Nishida articulates a relational and temporal view of the self understood as a series of momentary events of "pure experience" (*junsui keiken*) devoid of any subject-object dualism which arise and perish in the stream of consciousness. In chapter 26 of *A Study of Good* Nishida then goes on to sketch out a theory of the "social self" (*shakaiteki jiko*) as a middle position between the extremes of "individualism" (*kojinshugi*) and "collectivism" (*kyōdōshugi*). In his ideology critique of *nihonjinron* (the study of Japanese identity) entitled *The Myth of Japanese Uniqueness* (1986, 220–23), Peter N. Dale argues that Nishida Kitarō's Zen Buddhist idea of selfhood as "pure experience" (*junsui keiken*), understood as the "oneness of subject and object" (*shukaku gōitsu*), like Watsuji Tetsurō's *ningen* concept of self and *aidagara* principle of relationships, signifies a psychological theory of infantile regression to the pre-ego state as well as a political totalitarianism which erroneously conflates the existential "I-Thou" distinction into a disindividualized collectivity whereby the individual collapses into the whole and the self is fused with the other. Dale thus writes: "In constructing a mythology of culture which denies the existential distinction between 'I' and 'Thou', and in supplanting that original and ineluctable estrangement between self and other with a cosy affirmation of the identity of subject and object as an ethnic ontology . . . neither the individual nor the group may obtain a pregnantly dialectical relationship of enhancing exchange" (1986, 222). However, Dale's ideology critique is flawed in that it concentrates exclusively upon the "pure experience" phase of Nishida's earlier work. In the later period of his philosophical career Nishida's concept of the social self is dialectically reformulated in terms of an I-Thou relation of intersubjectivity.

According to Nishida, his articulation of the I-Thou relation, first developed at length in a chapter entitled "I and Thou" (*ware to nanji*) from *Self-Conscious Determination of Nothingness* (*Mu no jikakuteki gentei*, 1932), represents a critical turn in the development of his speculative thought (NKZ VI, 341 fn). The I-Thou relation of intersubjectivity thereafter becomes a fundamental motif in Nishida's philosophy of absolute Nothingness. And as has been seen, the I-Thou relationship constituting the Zen self in the locus of absolute Nothingness has also been developed in various ways by members of the Kyoto school of modern Japanese philosophy inspired by the writings of Nishida Kitarō, including Nishitani Keiji (1969), Ueda Shizuteru (1982), and Abe Masao (1985). This I-Thou dialectic constitutive of the social self is concisely expressed in *Fundamental Problems of Philosophy* (*Tetsugaku no kompon mondai*, 1934), when Nishida writes: "The I is an I by facing a Thou, and the individual is an individual by facing other individuals. The self must be social" (NKZ VII, 382). In terms of Nishida's Zen logic of paradox, the social self is now to be understood as a contradictory self-identity of I and Thou in the locus of absolute Nothingness. The I is the individual aspect of the self in its *discontinuity*, while the Thou is the social aspect of the self in its *continuity*, thereby constituting the unity of the self as a "continuity of discontinuity" (*hirenzoku no renzoku*). The Thou (*nanji*) which stands over against the I (*ware*) represents an absolute Other in relation to the self. The irreducible creativity and uniqueness of the I or individual aspect together with the absolute otherness of the Thou or social aspect are in this way both preserved in Nishida's dialectical concept of personhood as a contradictory self-identity of self and not-self. In his book called *Betweenness* (*Aida*, 1988), Kimura Bin describes the I-Thou relational structure of selfhood in Nishida's philosophy as follows:

> It is Nishida Kitarō who emphasized the absoluteness of "Thou" as the Other. Nishida says that "Thou should be independent from me, and something outside of me." But the "absolute Other" is not different from me. "When self sees self as the self, self sees the absolute other as the self, and the absolute other means the self itself." The process is to see the self in the absolute Other, and the restriction of the Other is the restriction of the self. (1988, 137)

Like Buber, Nishida rejects the notion of a solitary I and develops an intersubjective theory of self as an I-Thou relation. Moreover, like Buber he applies the I-Thou relation beyond the human community to both nature and God. Nishida asserts that the I-Thou dialectic is not just a relation between individuals within the human community, since everything which opposes the I, even the mountains, rivers, trees, and stones in the metaphysical society of nature, has the meaning of a Thou (NKZ VII, 59). Elsewhere he further extends the I-Thou dialectic to God, whereupon he distinguishes the divine *Thou* used to address God, and the interhuman *thou* used when we call our neighbor a *thou* (NKZ VII, 210). Consequently, for Nishida, as for Buber, the I becomes an I not only by facing an Other at the horizontal level of inter-human relationships, but also by facing a transcendent God as the absolute Other and eternal Thou at the vertical level of divine-human relationships. Yet Nishida emphasizes that the dialectic of I and Thou makes God wholly immanent to the self, thus constituting what he calls an "immanent tran-scendence" (*naizaiteki chōetsu*). For Nishida, both God and the human self are emptied through *kenōsis* into a paradoxical self-identity of I and Thou in the *basho* or locus of absolute Nothingness, so that transcendence moves not in the direction of an other-worldly beyond, but in the direction of bottom-less depths in the absolute present.

The double I-Thou structure of the social self in the spatial *basho* or locus of absolute Nothingness is further articulated in terms of the category of the "between" (*aidagara*) by Nishida's eminent disciple Ueda Shizuteru, a leading representative of the Kyoto school of modern Japanese philosophy. Nishida (NKZ VII, 59) himself uses the Japanese word *aida* or "between" to express the relation of I and Thou. However, Ueda highlights the use of "between" (*aidagara*) as a technical category in such a way that the I-Thou dialectic of the social self formulated by Nishida Kitarō is synthesized with the *ningen* model of personhood based on the notion of *aidagara* or "between" in the philosophical anthropology of Watsuji Tetsurō. A conceptual bridge is thus formed between Watsuji's idea of *ningen* understood as *hito to hito to no aidagara* or the "betweenness of person and person," and Nishida's idea of the "social self" (*shakaiteki jiko*) as the betweenness of I and Thou. In par-ticular, Ueda (1982) uses the *Ten Oxherding Pictures* to illustrate the Kyoto school logic of *śūnyatā* as a threefold emptying process whereby the substantial ego-self at the eternalistic standpoint of Being (*u*), which dies or is negated in a void at the nihilistic standpoint of relative Nothingness (*sōtaiteki mu*) is then resurrected as the fully enlightened "selfless self" of Zen Buddhism located in the *between* of I and Thou at the middle way standpoint of absolute Nothing-ness (*zettaiteki mu*). To repeat Ueda's words, "the self, cut open by absolute nothingness and laid bare, unfolds as this 'between' . . . I am 'I and thou,' 'I and thou' is I. The self is seen as a double self in virtue of selflessness" (1982, 20–21). Hence, for Nishida and Ueda of the Kyoto school, as for Buber in the

West, the person is to be conceived as a twofold social self which is located in the between of I and Thou.

There is yet another connection to be found between Buber's ontological notion of *das Zwischen* or "between" and Nishida's ontological concept of *basho*, "place." Buber sets forth his dialogical notion of "between" as an actual *place* with ontological status when he writes: "'Between' is not an auxiliary construction, but the real place and bearer of what happens between men" (1965, 203). Similarly, in his work *Climate* (*Fūdo*, 1935) Watsuji Tetsurō develops the principle of "between" (*aidagara*) in terms of his ontological notion of "climate" (*fūdo*), the spatial locus for self-other relations. Furthermore, it should be recalled that Watsuji's dialogical principle of *aida* or "betweenness" is explicitly identified with Nishida's ontological concept of *basho* or "place" by Kimura Bin (1972, 65) as well as Yuasa Yasuo (1972, 65). To repeat the words of Kimura Bin:

> The "betweenness of person and person" (*hito to hito to no aida*) and "betweenness" (*aida*) do not signify merely a relationship between two individuals. The "betweenness of person and person" is the "place" (*basho*) functioning as the source from out of which both I and others arise. (1972, 65)

Hence, just as Buber's concept of "between" has ontological reality as the "place" for I-Thou relationships, both Kimura and Yuasa identify Watsuji's principle of "betweenness" (*aida*) with Nishida's ontological concept of *basho* or "place" as the spatial locus where both I and Thou arise through mutual encounter.

It should be further emphasized that Nishida's intersubjective concept of self as an I-Thou relation was developed independently from the thought of Buber in the West. The evidence shows that both Nishida and Buber initially derived their own notions of the self as a unity of I and Thou from Ludwig Feuerbach's *Principles of the Philosophy of the Future* (*Grundsatze der Philosophie der Zukunft*, 1843). In *Between Man and Man*, Buber attributes the discovery of the I-Thou relation to Feuerbach, a discovery which he regards as the critical turning point or Copernican revolution in the history of philosophical anthropology (1965, 210). Although Nishida's pioneering essay entitled "I and Thou" (*ware to nanji*) appeared in 1932, in fact, he began to thematize the I-Thou relation of intersubjectivity as early as *Art and Morality* (*Geijutsu to dōtoku*), published in 1923, the same year which marked the publication of Buber's work entitled *I and Thou* (*Ich und Du*, 1923). While Nishida at no time cites the work of Buber as the source of inspiration for his I-Thou concept of a social self, he does make explicit reference to Feuerbach. In *Fundamental Problems of Philosophy,* Nishida writes: "As Feuerbach has said, in opposition to previous philosophy which has taken its starting point from only the I, philosophy should take as its starting point the I-Thou relationship" (NKZ VII, 175). Yet Nishida then goes on to criticize Feuerbach in a manner which again approximates the views of Buber, stating that the free and personal acting self in the social-historical world has no meaning seen from the materialistic standpoint which takes matter to be the basis of the I-Thou relationship, as is the case in Feuerbach's atheistic philosophy. He adds that the I-Thou relation can only be understood as a "determination of *basho*" (locus, place, field), namely, what he otherwise calls *mu no basho,* the locus of Nothingness (NKZ VII, 175). It can thus be said that Martin Buber in the West and Nishida Kitarō in the East both simultaneously and independently came to recognize the epoch-making significance of Feuerbach's turn to a dialogical concept of self as a unity of I and Thou, and thereafter proceeded to thematize the I-Thou relation of intersubjectivity within the specific contexts of their own philosophical frameworks.

## Philosophical Anthropology in Mead and Japanese Thought

It can now be seen how in the history of philosophical anthropology, both in the East the West, there has occurred a *social turn* from a subjectivist model of self as an I to an intersubjectivist model of self as an I-Other relation. The social turn to a bipolar concept of self as an I-Me relation which has been formulated by G. H. Mead in American pragmatism can be used to clarify all the various Eastern and Western frameworks under consideration here, including not only Buber's concept of self as an I-Thou relation and Macmurray's concept of the person as an I-You relation in the West, but also Watsuji's *ningen* concept of the person as an I-Other relation and Nishida's concept of the self as an I-Thou relation in modern Japanese thought. The bipolar structure of this I-Other relation has been further specified by such thinkers in terms of a dialogical principle of betweenness. On the side of Western philosophy a significant parallel to Mead's principle of sociality, according to which the the social self exists "betwixt and between" the I and the Me, is to be found in Buber's category of the "between." Whereas for Buber the self arises through dialogue between I and Thou, for Mead the self emerges by means of a process of communicative interaction between I and Me. Hence, in their analysis of personhood both thinkers focus neither on the individual nor on society but instead focus on the interactive process of dialogue, conversation, and communication which occurs *between* persons in relation.

On the side of modern Japanese philosophy, Watsuji Tetsurō's key notion of *aidagara* meaning " between" or " betweenness" is no doubt the most remarkable parallel to Mead's principle of sociality as the "betwixt and between," and Buber's category of *das Zwischen*, the "between." Buber's concept of a dialogical self articulated in terms of such notions as "I and Thou," "man with man," and the "between" in his work on philosophical anthropology entitled *Between Man and Man*, is in many fundamental respects analogous to Watsuji's *ningen* concept of personhood which he codifies by the doctrinal formula *hito to hito to no aidagara*, the "betweenness of person and person." This parallel between the philosophical anthropology of Watsuji and that of Buber has been further clarified by Kimura Bin, who in his book entitled *Betweenness* (*Aida*, 1988) describes how Buber and Japanese thought both define the social character of selfhood in terms of a dialogical principle of "betweenness" (*aida*). Kimura clarifies how *aida* or betweenness functions as the transpersonal locus of relationships in which both self and not-self emerge through interaction. Finally, in the thought of Nishida Kitarō and the Kyoto school the fully enlightened selfless self or emptied self of Zen Buddhism is analyzed precisely as a social self located in the *betweenness* of I-Thou relations of intersubjectivity in the spatial *basho* or locus of absolute Nothingness. Ueda Shizuteru illustrates this Zen process of becoming a person through the pictorial images of the *Ten Oxherd Pictures*, wherein the substantial ego at the level of being is emptied into a nihilistic void at the level of relative Nothingness, finally being resurrected as a compassionate Bodhisattva at the level of absolute Nothingess, depicted by the tenth and final diagram of the series as a twofold social self located in the *between* of I and Thou. It can therefore be said that Mead's *principle of sociality* defined as the "betwixt and between" of I and Me, Buber's principle of *das Zwischen* defined as the between of I and Thou and the Japanese principle of *aida* defined as the between of self and other, all represent a dialogical principle of "betweenness" in interpersonal relationships functioning as the basis for a social theory of self. Each of these thinkers develop the "between" as an ontological category functioning to signify the social field of relationships in which both self and others arise through mutual encounter. Hence, from the standpoint of the history of philosophical anthropology, G. H. Mead in American pragmatism and Martin Buber in European existentialism as well as Watsuji Tetsurō, Kimura Bin, Nishida Kitarō, Ueda Shizuteru and others in the tradition of modern Japanese philosophy, have together converged upon an intersubjective communication model of the social self based on a dialectic of I-Other relations and a dialogical principle of betweenness.

According to Buber (1958, 6), the Thou which stands in relation to the I applies not only to the human community but to other living creatures in the community of nature. Similarly, Nishida asserts that the I-Thou dialectic is not just a relation between individuals within the human community, since everything which opposes the I, even the mountains, rivers, trees, and stones in the metaphysical society of nature, has the meaning of a Thou (NKZ VII, 59). To this extent, the positions of Nishida and Buber are close to G. H. Mead's idea of the social self as an interaction between an individual organism with its whole environment of society and nature, as well as to Watsuji's concept of *ningen* as a relationship between an individual with its embodied spatial "climate" (*fūdo*) of society and nature. Or in terms of the thought of Kimura Bin, the Japanese notion of personhood as the betweenness of I and Thou signifies a concept of human existence as the unity of *mizukara* (self) and *onozukara* (nature). Hence, each of these thinkers enlarges the sphere of I-Other relationships so that the social self is constituted not only by its I-Other relations with the sphere of human society, but also by its I-Thou relations with the wider sphere of living nature. They thus develop not only a sociological concept of self as an individual-society relation providing the basis for an interhuman ethics, but also an ecological concept of self as a human-nature relation with significant implications for environmental ethics.

However, there is a significant discrepancy between these various thinkers concerning their respective concepts of God. For Buber the I-Thou relation exists in three spheres, including man and man, man with nature, and man with God. (1958, 6; also, 101). Similarly, Nishida applies his I-Thou dialectic not only to inter-human relationships (NKZ VII, 382), but also to the human-nature relationship (NKZ VII, 59), as well as the human-divine relationship wherein God becomes the eternal Thou or absolute Other (NKZ VII, 210). As opposed to the more humanistic approaches to intersubjectivity based on an I-Other dialectic developed by secular thinkers like Feuerbach and Mead in the West or Watsuji and Kimura in Japan, Nishida instead develops a theological orientation to I-Other relationships closer to that of Buber and Macmurray. It has been seen how twentieth-century Western philosophers of intersubjectivity like Martin Buber, John Macmurray, and G. H. Mead all formulate a dialogical concept of self as a relation of I and Other, what Buber calls the relation of I and Thou, what Macmurray calls the relation of I and You, and what Mead calls the relation of I and Me. However, Buber and Macmurray both develop an I-Other dialectic in the direction of a theological anthropology whereby God becomes the absolute, eternal, and universal Other. For Nishida, the true self is a social self arising through a dialectical interaction between *ware to nanji,* which can be translated either as "I and Thou" following Buber, or as "I and You" following Macmurray. Similar to the theological anthropology of Buber and Macmurray, Nishida extends the I-Other relation into a third sphere: that of the relation between the self and God. Consequently, for Nishida, as for Buber and Macmurray, the I becomes an I not only by facing an Other at the horizontal level of inter-human relationships, but also by facing an immanently transcendent God as the absolute Other and eternal Thou at the vertical level of divine-human relationships. In contrast, Mead formulates a secular, humanistic, and naturalistic concept of self as an I-Other dialectic whereby the generalized other has no implication whatsoever of a metaphysical ultimate or religious absolute, but instead represents the universalized human community. Mead's concept of the generalized other, which is essential for all norm-governed rational thought and moral conduct, arises from within the social process of communicative interaction itself, and has no existence apart from or prior to the social process. Thus, each of the Eastern and Western frameworks considered here establishes a dialogical notion of self as an I-Other dialectic of intersubjectivity; but while Nishida, Buber and Macmurray develop a theological anthropology in which God signifies the absolute Other, both Watsuji and Mead carry out the anthropological reduction initiated by Feuerbach, which rejects the theological approach and posits the human self as the fundamental topic for philosophical reflection.

Finally, while all of the Eastern and Western frameworks considered here establish a breakthrough into a social or intersubjective model of self as an I-Other relation, only the Whiteheadian process framework of G. H. Mead clarifies the *asymmetrical* nature of these relations so as to allow for both individuality and sociality, creativity and contextuality, indeterminacy and determinacy. Although the I-Me relation of Mead in many ways resembles the I-Thou relation of Buber and the I-You relation of Macmurray in the West as well as the I-Thou relation of Nishida and the I-Other relation of Watsuji in the East, only the asymmetrical framework of Mead specifies how the self is intersubjectively constituted by its social environment inherited from the *past* at the Me pole and then responds with creativity in the *present* at the I pole. For Mead it is precisely this asymmetry of the I-Me relation which explains how the self is determined by its social relations from the past as a Me yet is at the same time a creative autonomous agent in the locus of the present as an I, thereby to resolve the problem of freedom and determinism. Moreover, for Mead it is only this asymmetrical structure of the I-Me relationship constitutive of selfhood which preserves the irreversible structure of time's arrow as a creative advance to novelty in the flux of emergent evolution.

## The Critique of Heidegger

The *social turn* to an intersubjective model of self initiated by thinkers like Mead and Buber in the West along with Nishida and Watsuji in Japan signifies a radical overcoming of the German tradition of philosophical anthropology. Buber traces the history of philosophical anthropology through its various stages of individualism and collectivism with the aim of demonstrating the turn from a monological to a dialogical concept of self as an I-Thou relation. From this standpoint he argues that the existentialist tradition of Nietzsche, Kierkegaard, and Heidegger is deeply flawed insofar as it is commited to an individualistic anthropology. Even Heidegger's concept of *Dasein* as "being-with" (*Mitsein*) fails to grasp the social character of selfhood, the centrality of communication, the primacy of the "between" as an ultimate ontological category, and the bipolar structure of human existence as an I-Thou relation of intersubjectivity.

According to Buber, despite Heidegger's analysis of *Dasein* as "being-with" (*Mitsein*) articulated in section 26 of *Being and Time,* nonetheless, he essentially develops an an individualistic concept of man in which authentic human existence is discovered in the aloneness and solitude of *Dasein* as a "being-in-time" and a "being-toward-death." As Buber asserts: "Thus it looks as though Heidegger fully knew and acknowledged that a relation to others is essential. But this is not actually the case" (1965, 169). For Buber, although Heidegger's anthropology makes the pretension of being dialogical, it is in fact wholly *monological* in character: "Heidegger's 'existence' is monological. And monologue may certainly disguise itself ingeniously for a while as dialogue" (1965, 168). He argues that for Heidegger authentic selfhood is achieved not through communication with others in society but only by living in communication with oneself through self-being (1965, 168). Heidegger describes the human community of others in negative terms as the anonymous "one" (*das Man*), which like Kierkegaard's notion of the "crowd" and Nietzsche's concept of the "herd" is not an essential relation constitutive of one's existence, but is in fact an obstacle to achieving authentic selfhood (1965, 173). Although Heidegger's notion of "being-with" involves a resolution to co-existence, it does not yet arrive at an understanding of human selfhood as being intersubjectively constituted by its relationships to others: "We have seen that Heidegger does not look on the highest level as an isolation, but as resolution to co-existence with others. We have also seen, however, that this resolution only confirms solicitude on a higher plane, but knows nothing of any essential relation with others or any real I-Thou with them which could breach the barriers of the self" (1965, 174). For Buber, then, Heidegger entirely fails to grasp the significance of Feuerbach's turn from a monological to a dialogical concept of self as an I-Thou relation and instead falls into a radical individualism: "Existence is completed in self-being; there is no ontic way beyond this for Heidegger. What Feuerbach pointed out, that the individual does not have the essence of man in himself, that man's essence is contained in the unity of man with man, has entirely failed to enter Heidegger's philosophy" (1965, 171). Hence, despite Heidegger's emphasis on the "openness" of *Dasein*, he in fact does not develop a theory of an open self in relation with others, but instead articulates an individualistic notion of selfhood as enclosed in self-being: "Heidegger's 'openness' of the existence to itself thus in truth involves its being finally closed" (1965, 173). Buber argues that Heidegger mistakenly privileges the individuality over the sociality of *Dasein* based on an underlying phenomenological description which privileges the temporal over the spatial aspect of human existence. His polemic here is that Heidegger's individualistic notion of authentic selfhood in its aloneness and solitude is an abstraction from the concrete wholeness of man resulting from his absolutization of the temporal aspect of *Dasein*. In Buber's words: "Heidegger isolates the wholeness of life the realm in which man is related to himself, since he absolutizes the temporally conditioned situation of the radically solitary man" (1965, 168).

In his hermeneutic phenomenology of selfhood developed in *Oneself as Another*, Paul Ricoeur (1992, 328) makes a similar point, arguing that Heidegger's overemphasis on temporality leads to an inadequent description of spatiality, which subsequently results in his failure to articulate an intersubjective concept of self as ontologically constituted by the Other. Although Ricoeur (1992, 188) does not cite Buber, he relies heavily upon Emmanuel Lévinas's dialogical concept of selfhood as an I-Thou relationship, which is in turn directly influenced by Buber. Ricoeur states his own primary thesis as follows: "*Oneself as Another* suggests from the outset that the selfhood of oneself implies otherness to such an intimate degree that one cannot be thought of without the other" (1992, 3). Hence, like Lévinas and Buber, Ricouer aims to establish an intersubjective notion of self as a relation of self and Other. Furthermore, Ricouer works out a *narrative* concept of self influenced by Alasdair MacIntyre's *After Virtue* (1981), wherein self-identity is not constituted by sameness or unbroken continuity, but through a "narrative unity of life" (1992, 178). This concept of narrative unity is further meant to clarify W. Dilthey's hermeneutic concept of an autobiographical "life history," or what the latter calls "the connectedness of life" (*Zusammenhang des Lebens*) (1992, 141). In the context of formulating his narrative concept of self-identity, Ricouer, like Buber, criticizes Heidegger's inadequate phenomenology of spatial relationships in the ontological constitution of *Dasein*. First he points out that paragraph 24 of Heidegger's *Being and Time* is specifically devoted to the spatiality of *Dasein* as determined by the structure of solicitude or care (*Sorge*). However, "the spatial dimension of being-in-the-world appears to involve mainly the inauthentic forms of care" (1992, 328). Ricoeur clarifies that by the inauthentic form of care he means that "it is the backdrop of the spatiality of available and manipulable things that *Dasein's* spatiality is made" (1992, 328). He adds: "We may then wonder if it is not the unfolding of the problematic of temporality, triumphant in the second section of *Being and Time*, that prevented an authentic phenomenology of spatiality . . . as though the authentic features of spatiality were finally to be derived from those of temporality" (1992, 328). For Ricoeur, Heidegger's ideas of care, being-with, and being-in-the-world represent an artifical otherness that is added on to selfhood from the outside, as though to prevent its solipsistic drift, in contrast to a dialectical notion of personhood as a relation to the Other wherein the self is ontologically constituted by otherness in a spatial field of relationships from the very beginning (1992, 317).

Leading contemporary German philosophers who have come under the influence of American pragmatism such as Jürgen Habermas, Ernst Tugendhat, and Hans Joas, have likewise underscored the "social turn" represented by the paradigm shift in G. H. Mead. Furthermore, Joas, Tugendhat and Habermas all have described the significant advance represented by Mead's communication model of the social self and I-Me dialectic over that of Heidegger's concept of self as *Dasein* and other alternatives within the German tradition of philosophical anthropology. In *The Philosophical Discourse of Modernity* (1987), Habermas shows through detailed textual analysis how a shift from the paradigm of subject-centered consciousness to an intersubjectivist paradigm of communicative action was *a path opened but not followed* by Heidegger and others in the German tradition of philosophical anthropology (1987, xvi). Habermas marks the places where Hegel, Marx and Heidegger stood before alternative paths which they did not choose (1987, 295). Although Heidegger suggests the way out of the paradigm of subject-centered reason as a knowledge of objects to an intersubjectivist paradigm to communicative reason based on mutual understanding through dialogue, he nonetheless always falls back into a notion of the self-assertive and self-sufficient subjectivity of *Dasein* (1987, 151). Moreover, Habermas is extremely critical of Heidegger's enthusiastic support of Hitler and Nazism as well as how fascist ideology played into the very development of Heidegger's concept of *Dasein* (1987, 156–58). He maintains that while thinkers like Hegel, Marx, and Heidegger did not achieve this paradigm-change from subject-centered reason to communicative reason (1987, 296), it was fully realized in the American pragmatism of C. S. Peirce and G. H. Mead (1987; 137, 138, 148, 325). Habermas claims that Heidegger's notion of the mineness of *Dasein* is still tinged with the solipsism of Husserlian phenomenology, who posits as originary the subjectivity of sense-giving acts rooted in the Transcendental Ego, as opposed to the linguistically created intersubjectivity of mutual understanding through communication. He adds: "Heidegger does not take the path to a response in terms of a theory of communication . . . The idea that subjects are individuated and socialized in the same stroke cannot be accommodated in the latter framework" (1987, 149). By contrast, he sums up the achievement of Mead's communicative interaction model of the social self as follows: "If, with George Herbert Mead, we understand the process of socialization itself as one of individuation, the sought-for mediation between individual and society is less 'puzzling'" (1987, 334). For Habermas, then, while Heidegger's concept of *Dasein* is still rooted in the old subjectivist paradigm in which individuation precedes sociation, Mead was the first to clearly articulate the paradigm shift to an intersubjectivist communication model of the social self as a dialectical interplay between individuation and sociation.

In his essay "Mead: Symbolic Interaction and the Self," Ernst Tugendhat argues that aside from Heidegger, George Herbert Mead is the only philosopher who has attempted to free the relation of oneself to oneself from the conception of a reflexive relation (1991, 169). According to Mead, the relation of oneself to oneself must be understood as a form of *conversation* or "talking to oneself," and this in turn is to be understood as the internalization of communicative talking to others, so that the relation of oneself to oneself is in its essence both linguistically and socially conditioned by others in society. In comparison with Mead's notion of the social self, Tugendhat finds the social aspects of Heidegger's notion of man as "being-with" (*Mitsein*) to be inadequately developed. Tugendhat asserts that "it is true for [Heidegger] that human existence is essentially being-with (*Mitsein*), a being with and for (or against) others (BT Sec. 26). But this aspect remained peculiarly faint and undeveloped in his work" (1991, 192). He adds that "Mead's view corrects Heidegger's conception not only with regard to its social deficiency but also with regard to its rational deficiency" (1991, 200).

Complementing the views of Habermas and Tugendhat is that of Hans Joas, who calls Mead "the most important theorist of intersubjectivity between Feuerbach and Habermas" (1985, 2). It is especially Joas (1993, 34) who has clarified the "social turn" of classical American pragmatism initiated by G. H. Mead and the Meadian tradition of symbolic interactionism. In this context he describes "the steps that Mead took toward a 'social' or 'intersubjective' turn of the fundamental pragmatist model of action" (1993, 250). Evaluating Mead's significance for the history of philosophical anthropology, Joas states: "I myself see in Mead's work a possiblity of escaping aporiae which occured in the development of German philosophy from Dilthey and Husserl to Heidegger and Philosophical Anthropology, and which are important for the grounding of the social sciences" (1985, 41). Joas maintains that the German tradition of philosophical anthropology failed to achieve an adequate doctrine of human sociality based on a thoroughgoing principle of intersubjectivity. He admits that Heidegger's philosophical anthropology introduces an element of intersubjectivity in the form of "being-with" (*Mitsein*), praxis in the form of "care" (*Sorge*), and the structure of the relation between the self and society in the form of "being-in-the-world" (*In-der-Welt-Sein*) (1985, 43). Yet Heidegger's idea of *Mitsein* still falls short of an intersubjectivist model of personhood wherein the self is essentially and ontologically constituted by its social relationships with others. Joas maintains that it is through the reference to death that Heidegger seeks to show the individual's ultimate and radical isolation. Within the framework of Heidegger's thought, the willingness to accept this isolation is the equivalent to the formation of the self. He thus states that in Heidegger's anthropological concept of man as *Dasein*, "intersubjectivity must make a forced appearance in the exposition because it was not, as in Mead's work, made implicit in the concept of subjectivity from the outset" (1985, 197). Moreover, the German tradition of philosophical anthropology leading up to Heidegger is beset with problems of relativism and the commitment to transcendentalism. For Joas, it is in the social science framework of Mead that we first see the articulation of a non-relativist and nontranscendentalist theory of the social self based on a principle of sociality and an adequate notion of intersubjectivity:

> What was thereby not achieved in the German tradition [of Philosophical Anthropology] is a theory of the fundamental structure of human sociality that is based in a thoroughgoing way on intersubjectivity and is not apriorist and transcendentalist, that is non-relativist, and draws upon and is consistent with the findings of natural and social science. To such a theory, I believe, Mead made a significant contribution. (1985, 44)

Hence, while Heidegger's anthropological concept of self as "being-with" (*Mitsein*) remains highly suggestive, it cannot be said to have achieved a fully social, intersubjective, and dialogical theory of selfhood whereby the person emerges through communication with others in society. For German thinkers like Habermas, Turgendhat and Joas, this breakthrough to a fully intersubjective communication model of personhood is finally attained within the Western tradition of philosophical anthropology through G. H. Mead's conception of the bipolar social self as a dialectic of I and Me.

In twentieth-century Japanese thought the social turn in philosophical anthropology is to be found in the framework of Watsuji Tetsurō. Although in his youth Watsuji was initially attracted to the romantic individualism of existentialist philosophy, after the "turn" (tenkō) announced in the preface to his *Revival of Idols* (1918) he attempted to work out a social concept of personhood under the influence of various Asian sources, including his teacher Nitobe Inazō's Bushidō ethic of self-renunciation and group loyalty, Natsume Sōseki's idea of *sokuten kyoshi* or "departing from the self and following heaven," along with ideals of self-negation, derived from Confucian and Buddhist modes of thought. In his later work he thus goes on to overcome the problem of "individualism" (*kojinshugi*) through the Japanese notion of personhood as *ningen*, understood as expressing the double nature of self as an individual-society relation. Similar to Buber and Ricouer, and other Western thinkers cited above, the Japanese thinker Watsuji Tetsurō has articulated a philosophical anthropology based on an intersubjective concept of self as ontologically constituted by its relation to the Other. Like Buber and Ricouer, Watsuji critically undermines the individualism underlying the German tradition of philosophical anthropology leading up to Heidegger's concept of self as *Dasein*. It is especially illuminating that like Buber (1965, 168) and Ricouer (1992, 328), Watsuji also traces Heidegger's privileging of the individual over the social aspects of self based on a phenomenology of human existence which accords priority to the temporal over the spatial dimensions of self. Watsuji argues that Heidegger's notion of *Dasein* is basically individualistic in that it focuses on the *temporal* structure of authentic human existence in its solitude, while neglecting the social aspects of personhood associated with the *spatial* aspect of existence. For this reason, Heidegger arrives at an individualistic understanding of authentic human existence as a "being-in-time" and "being-toward-death," such that he fails to articulate the social dimensions of the self as a being-in-space. Just as Watsuji etymologically analyzes the two Sino-Japanese characters of *ningen* or "person" as expressing the double structure of selfhood as both "individual" and "social" (1937, 12), so he unfolds the meaning of the Japanese word *sonzai* or "existence" as a compound whose two characters designate both "time" (= *son*) and "space" (= *zai*) (1937, 20–22). He contrasts this spatio-temporal character of "existence" (*sonzai*) and "human existence" (*ningen sonzai*) underlying the Japanese *ningen* model of self with Heidegger's analysis of the temporal structure of *Sein* (being, existence) in *Being and Time*. Hence, while Heidegger focuses primarily on the individualistic nature of *Dasein* as a being-in-time, Watsuji instead understands the person (*ningen*) as an individual-society relation whose existence (*sonzai*) is both temporal and spatial in character. This point is made with special clarity in the preface to Watsuji's book entitled *Climate: An Anthropological Investigation* (*Fūdo ningengakuteki kōsatsu*, 1935), wherein he directly criticizes Heidegger's overemphasis on the temporal structure of *Dasein*, arguing that the twofold structure of *ningen* as both individual and social must be understood not only in relation to time, but also in relation to its encompassing "climate" (*fūdo*) of space:

> It was in the early summer of 1927 when I was reading Heidegger's *Zein und Seit* in Berlin that I first came to reflect on the problem of climate. I found myself intrigued by the attempt to treat the structure of man's existence in terms of time but I found it hard to see why, when time had thus been made to play a part in the structure of subjective existence, at the same juncture space also was not postulated as part of the basic structure of existence . . . I perceived that herein lay the limitations of Heidegger's work . . . because his *Dasein* was the *Dasein* of the individual only. He treated human existence as being the existence of a man. From the standpoint of the dual structure—both individual and social—of human existence, he did not advance beyond an abstraction of a single aspect. (1961, v–vi)

In his *Ethics* (*Rinrigaku*, 1937, 14–16) Watsuji further develops his critique of Heidegger's notion of *Dasein* as representing a one-sidedly temporal and individualistic mode of human existence. He points out that Heidegger reformulates Husserl's phenomenological concept of "intentionality" in terms of human existence as "being-in-the world" (*yo no naka ni aru koto*) (1937, 14–15). Yet, similar to Ricouer, Watsuji argues that Heidegger understands man's being-in-the-world not so much in terms of relationship with others in human society, but as a relationship with tools. That is to say, the *aidagara* or "betweenness" of persons is hidden in the shadow of the relationships between man and his tools or equipment, such that the aspect of human social relationships is given a subordinate role to a relationship with things. He then points out that Heidegger's student Karl Lowith (in his *Das Individuum in der Rolle des Mitmenschen*, 1928) has attempted to develop the notion of being-in-the-world into an explicit concept of man as defined through relationships with others in society. While Heidegger's work represents fundamental

*Ontologie,* Lowith instead moves to *Anthropologie.* According to Watsuji, Lowith's philosophical anthropology does not focus on the individual, but instead underscores the "betweenness of self and other" (*jita no aidagara*) (1937, 15). Moreover, Lowith's anthropological concept of human existence as mutual relatedness itself establishes the basis for ethics, now understood as a study of the betweenness of person and person (1937, 16).

Similar to both Watsuji in Japan and Buber in the Europe, Nishida Kitarō criticizes the various individualistic accounts of selfhood formulated within the German tradition of philosophical anthropology, ranging from the heroic individualism of Nietzsche's superman, to the subjectivist notion of a transcendental ego developed in various forms by Kant's transcendental idealism, Husserl's phenomenology, and Heidegger's existentialism, finally arriving at the turn toward a fully intersubjectivist paradigm of the social self as a unity of I and Thou. Furthermore, like Watsuji (1961, 5–6) in Japan as well as Buber (1965, 171) and Ricouer (1992, 238) in the West, Nishida (NKZ VII, 179–80) undermines the individualism of Heidegger's notion of self, arguing the structure of *Dasein* as "being-in-the-world" is still essentially subjectivistic in character and thus fails to arrive at the social nature of selfhood as an I-Thou relation of intersubjectivity. Nishida writes:

> Even Heidegger's philosophy of existence, which was influenced by Dilthey, does not account for the world determined by human action, but rather a world of the understanding. . . . It is neither the world which determines the individual, nor the world which includes the relation of I and Thou. (NKZ VII, 179–80)

Finally, it should be noted that in the *Heart of Buddhism,* Takeuchi Yoshinori (1983, 122) of the Kyoto school likewise criticizes Heideger's idea of authentic human existence as a radically temporal "being-toward-death" and even as *Mitsein* or "being-with," arguing that such notions have only a private meaning which ignores the positive role of intersubjective I-Thou relationships in the existentialism of Buber.

For reasons stated above I have underscored the inherent limitation of efforts to interpret the Zen Buddhist concept of selfhood in terms of either Nietzsche's idea of the superman or Heidegger's notion of man as *Dasein.* Within the tradition of modern Japanese philosophy both Nishitani Keiji and Abe Masao of the Kyoto school have emphasized the close proximity of German existentialism to the Zen Buddhist philosophy of Japan. Nietzsche's superman who overcomes nihilism through affirmation of nature as the innocence of becoming, and Heidegger's authentic self whose ecstatic existence in time is understood as being held out suspended in nothing, are thus said to designate two Western philosophical currents which approach the Zen Buddhist standpoint of a true self of absolute Nothingness. And indeed there are many significant points of contact between the thought of Japanese Zen Buddhism and that of both Nietzsche and Heidegger. However, to the extent that the existentialism of Nietzsche and Heidegger signifies a philosophy of radical individualism, it is unable to articulate the profoundly social concept of personhood at the heart of both Confucian and Zen Buddhist modes of thought, or their synthesis in the work of such modern Japanese philosophers as Watsuji and Nishida.

The possibilities for comparison between Buddhism and Heidegger's concept of self as *Dasein* is brought into sharper focus in a work by Stephen Batchelor called *Alone With Others* (1983). In this work Batchelor endeavors to interpret the two poles constitutive of Buddhahood in terms of Heidegger's existentialist categories of "being-alone" and "being-with." After elucidating Heidegger's description of the ontological structures of authentic human existence as *being-alone* and *being-with,* he then proceeds to apply these categories to the notion of Buddhahood as follows: "Buddhahood, as the optimum mode of being, is the end point in which the two essential, interwoven strands of our being—being-alone and being-with—are purposefully fulfilled. It is the mode wherein both meaningful being-for-oneself and meaningful being-for-others are realized" (1983, 88). Yet as has been persuasively demonstrated by many leading scholars in their accounts of the the the history of philosophical anthropology, including Martin Buber (1965, 163–75), Paul Ricouer (1992, 328), Jürgen Habermas (1987, 151), Ernst Tugendhat (1991, 169–200), and Hans Joas (1985, 41–44), in the West, as well as Watsuji Tetsurō (1961, v–vi), Nishida Kitarō (NKZ VII, 179–80), and Takeuchi Yoshinori (1983, 122) in Japan, Heidegger's notion of *Mitsein* or "being-with" is inadequately developed and fails to articulate a truly social, relational, and dialogical concept of personhood as an I-Thou relation of intersubjectivity.

In his comparative study of Zen Buddhism and American philosophy, Van Meter Ames at once clarifies how the bipolar I-Me structure of the social self as formulated by Mead articulates the two poles of "aloneness" and "sociality" constituting the Bodhisattva ideal of Zen Buddhism when he writes: "There is the *social* and the *alone* come together in the social self, its civilized 'me' guiding the aboriginal 'I'" (1962, 278; italics added). Whereas the solitude, aloneness, and private aspect of self is represented by what Mead calls the I, the social, relational, and public aspect of self is designated by the Me. This relationships between the two poles of human existence, the *social* and the *alone*, are also to be found in Whitehead's process model of selfhood.

Throughout *Religion in the Making,* Whitehead analyses religious experience in terms of such categories as the social, society, and community. Like Royce and Mead, Whitehead describes how religion involves the realization of one's greateter social self through membership in a community. However, more than either Royce or Mead, Whitehead gives equal importance to the roles of both *community* and *solitude* in religion. He writes, "Religion is what the individual does with his own solitariness" (RM 16). Further describing the existential dimension of solitude or aloneness he states that religion involves a confrontation with "the awful ultimate fact, which is the human being, consciously alone with itself, for its own sake" (RM 16). Whitehead states that the "great religious conceptions which haunt the imaginations of civilized mankind are scenes of solitariness," and as examples he cites "Mohamet brooding in the desert, the meditations of the Buddha, the solitary Man on the Cross" (RM 19, 20). Yet at the same time, the great religious personages of world history like Buddha and Christ culminate their existence not in a state of aloneness but in a *return from solitariness to society.* He writes:

> Expression . . . is the return from solitariness to society. There is no such thing as absolute solitariness. Each entity requires its enviroment. Thus man cannot seclude himself from society . . . what is known in secret must be enjoyed in common, and must be verified in common. (RM 137–38)

Hence, in this way both G. H. Mead and A. N. Whitehead in American philosophy have worked out a concept of human selfhood as being constituted by two poles, the *social* and the *alone,* or what Mead calls the "Me pole" and the "I pole," and what Whitehead calls the "physical pole" and the "mental pole." Moreover, corresponding to this bipolar concept of human existence is an explanation of the dual structure of religious experience as combining both solitariness and the sense of community.

It can now be seen that Mead's bipolar concept of self as a dialectic of I and Me differs in significant respects from Heidegger's notion of man as "being-alone" and "being-with." First of all, in contrast with Heidegger's individual aspect of *Dasein* as "being-alone," the I pole in Mead's I-Me dialectic of self accounts for not only the existential aspect of aloneness, solitude, or privacy in human existence, but also for the positive elements of emergence, creativity, spontaneity, originality, and autonomy. Consequently, while Heidegger underscores the unbroken continuity of *Dasein* as a being-in-time and a being-toward-death, for Mead the creative, spontaneous, and novel act of *emergence* represented by the I constitutes the self in time as a continuity of discontinuity, so that with each arising and perishing event the old self is replaced with a partly new self. Secondly, in contrast to Heidegger's social aspect of *Dasein* as "being-with" (*Mitsein*) which presupposes that the self has an existence apart from its social relations, the Me pole of Mead's I-Me dialectic clarifies how the self is socially constructed by its relationships to others in a community and has no existence apart from or prior to these relationships. For Mead the self is social not only in that is "co-exists" with others in society, but in the much deeper sense whereby the self is essentially and ontologically constituted by its social relationships to others. Whereas for Heidegger's notion of *Dasein* the concept of "being-with" has been added on to selfhood from the outside to prevent its solipsistic drift, for Mead the Me or internalized social pole of the generalized other is constitutive of selfhood from the very beginning. For Heidegger the self is something which first exists and then enters into relations with others; whereas for Mead the others are not simply external to the self but are constitutive of one's own selfhood. The radical difference between their two positions is that whereas Heidegger's concept of *Dasein* as "being-with" assumes that individuation *precedes* sociation, Mead's concept of the self as an I-Me dialectic clarifies how individuation and sociation are *simultaneous* processes. While Heidegger describes the human community of others in negative terms as the anonymous "one" (*das Man*) which is not an essential relation constitutive of human existence but instead an obstacle to realizing authentic selfhood, for Mead the self can achieve self-realization only through its social relations to others in the community. In short, Heidegger's concept of authentic selfhood lacks a strong theory of "otherness" and in the end falls into moral nihilism, egocentrism, and chauvinism. The point to be underscored here is that Heidegger's concept of man is a form of radical individualism which cannot be simply corrected by adding hyphens or little prepositional hooks so that *Dasein* is "with" and "for" other things and people who are "at hand"; whereas Mead's framework represents a complete breakthrough to an intersubjective model of the self according to which the human mind and self are socially constructed by relations to others in society through social acts of linguistically mediated communicative interaction.

Insofar as the Zen model of selfhood in modern Japanese philosophy represents an intersubjective concept of the social self as an individual-society relation it cannot be adequately expressed in terms of Heidegger's individualistic concept of man as *Dasein*. Although Watsuji Tetsurō studied under Heidegger and was deeply influenced by Heidegger, his Zen/Confucian *ningen* model of self is developed in the context of critically undermining Heidegger's individualistic account of *Dasein* as a being-in-time. Watsuji's Zen/Confucian idea of the Japanese self as *ningen* constituted through the dependent co-arising of individual and society is therefore much closer to Mead's inter-subjective account of the social self as constituted by the dialectical interplay between individuation and sociation. Furthermore, not only is Heidegger's attempt to establish a social theory of *Dasein* as being-with completely inadequate as a framework by means of which to interpret Nishida Kitarō's Zen idea of the social self as an I-Thou dialectic; his temporal concept of *Dasein* as a being-in-time is also inadequate because he emphasizes the sheer "continuity" (*Kontinuität*) of time, while for Nishida the self in time is constituted as a "continuity of discontinuity" (*hirenzoku no renzoku*). In contrast, G. H. Mead's concept of the social self as an I-Me dialectic is the single most adequate framework by means of which to elucidate Nishida's Zen model of the social self as an I-Thou dialectic. Moreover, Nishida's Zen model of the temporal self as a "continuity of discontinuity" is best understood through Mead's process theory of the social self whereby the "Me" or social pole represents the *continuous* aspect of causal conditioning from the past, and the "I" or individual pole represents the *discontinuous* aspect of creativity, spontaneity, and emergent novelty in the locus of the present. Likewise, in Nishida's concept of the social and temporal self as an I-Thou relation, the I is the individual aspect of self in its discontinuity, while the Thou is the social aspect of self in its continuity, thereby constituting the unity of the self as a contradictory self-identity of continuity and discontinuity. Finally, it has also been seen how both Mead and Nishida ground their notions of the social self within the framework of a Leibnizian cosmology of perspectives so that the self is a mirror which reflects the social-historical world from its own perspective as a microcosm of the macrocosm.

Let us further consider the extent to which Heidegger and Mead have articulated the notion of an "open self" and the relation of both to the Zen concept of self. Heidegger's language is often very suggestive of Zen Buddhism, insofar as for both Heidegger and Zen the self is envisioned through poetic images as a "nothingness" or "openness" in which the play of nonsubstantial phenomena occurs. Similar to Nishida's *basho* or "place," Heidegger's *Dasein* is a place of nothingness or openness functioning as the horizon of dis-closure wherein the self and all phenomena come to presence in their suchness, unhiddenness, and nonconcealment. But as argued by Martin Buber (1965, 171–173), despite Heidegger's emphasis on the the "openness" of *Dasein*, he in fact does not develop a theory of an open self in relation with others but instead articulates an individualistic notion of man as closed in its own self-being. On the other hand, scholars of American pragmatism like Andrew J. Reck, Charles W. Morris, and David L. Miller have all characterized Mead's idea of a social self arising through an interaction of I and Me as an *open self*. As stated by Reck: "Ideally both 'I' and 'me' are functions of a single self. Such a self is, in Charles Morris' phrase, an 'open self'" (Mead SW xxxii). Similarly, Miller (1973, 168–69) argues that Mead's idea of the social self as an I-Me dialectic in fact represents a genuine breakthrough to an "open self," just as his political vision of a liberal democracy of free and equal persons represents a breakthrough to an "open society." The "openness" represented by Mead's concept of the social self is the openness of unblocked communicative interaction with significant others in an ideal communication community. Mead's concept of the social self represents an open system which is constantly interacting with its surrounding environment of society and nature. Hence, like the self envisaged by Zen, the ideal social self of Mead is truly an "open self" by virtue of its open communication with others in a community.

In the present work I have attempted to clarify the twofold, bipolar or double-sided nature of the social self as an I-Other relationship through its various formulations in Asian philosophy, including among its paradigmatic expressions the Confucian ideal of the authoritative self as a dialectic between *yi* (creative response) and *li* (ritual propriety), the neo-Confucian ideal of the "scholar official" who exists in the continuum between a private pole and a public pole so as to establish the continuity of thought and action, the Maoist-Marxist/Confucian ideal of bio-social man with two essences—the biological and the social, the traditional Zen ideal of Buddhahood with its two poles of spontaneity and sociality, Watsuji Tetsurō's syncretic Zen/Confucian ideal of Japanese selfhood as *ningen* as the *aidagara* or "betweenness" of the individual and society in *kū* or emptiness, Nishida Kitarō's ideal social self as a dialectic of I and Thou in the locus of absolute Nothingness, Ueda Shizuteru's Zen Buddhist ideal of the true self as a compassionate Bodhisattva in the *between* of I and Thou, and Doi Takeo's *amae* or "dependency" model of Japanese selfhood with its two directional coordinates of "inner" (*uchi, ura, honne, ninjō*) and "outer" (*soto, omote, tatemae, giri*). From the perspective of East-West comparative philosophy I have further argued that this Asian concept of man as a twofold individual-society relation cannot be adequately conceptualized through the German tradition of philosophical anthropology leading up to Heidegger's individualistic notion of human existence as *Dasein*, but instead requires a fully intersubjective model of self as an I-Other relationship, including such paradigmatic expressions as Martin Buber's notion of man as an I-Thou relationship, John Macmurray's concept of the person as an I-You relationship, and especially George Herbert Mead's idea of the social self as an I-Me relationship. It has been my position that above all others the most adequate standpoint by means of which to illuminate the East Asian concept of self in general and the Japanese notion of self in particular is to be found in the tradition of classical American pragmatism and process cosmology leading up to G. H. Mead's concept of the social self as a dialectical interplay between the two poles of I and Me or individuation and sociation. Mead's nondualistic framework of the human self as a dialectic of I and Me represents a breakthough to an intersubjective model of the social self as an individual-society interaction as well as a psychosomatic model of the self as body-mind interaction and an ecological model of self as a human-nature interaction. Finally, Mead's framework crystallizes the axiological basis of classical American pragmatism to the extent that his I-Me dialectic of the social self designates a value-centric model of the person as aesthetic and creative action. I would therefore suggest that Mead's communicative interaction model of the bipolar social self as an I-Me dialectic can function as a unifying theory for an East-West transcultural model of philosophical anthropology in which various insights into the social construction of mind and self in society can all be integrated within a single coherent framework.

## Summary and Conclusion

In his overview of the history of philosophical anthropology Martin Buber has underscored the epoch-making significance of Ludwig Feuerbach's turn in 1843 from a *monological* concept of man as an I to a *dialogical* concept of man as a unity of I and Thou. It was then Buber himself who thematized this dialogical concept of self as an I-Thou relationship in his celebrated work called *I and Thou* (*Ich und Du*, 1923). For Jürgen Habermas, however, the first to provide an account of the social nature, origin, and formation of self in the context of an empirically based social scientific research program grounded in the experimental laboratory method was George Herbert Mead in American pragmatism. Thus, in volume II of *The Theory of Communicative Action* (1989), Habermas describes the "paradigm shift" in Mead beyond the Cartesian philosophy of subject-centered consciousness to an intersubjective communication model of the social self arising through symbolically mediated communicative interaction between I and Me. Habermas emphasizes that against the tradition of Cartesian subjectivism for which individuation precedes sociation, Mead's concept of self as an I-Me dialectic was the first to clarify how individuation and sociation proceed together. Again, in *Moral Consciousness and Communicative Action* (1990) Habermas further describes Mead's paradigm shift to a communicative discourse ethics through a social reformulation of Kant's universalist moral theory, whereupon the categorical imperative is no longer a "monological" procedure conducted by a solitary individual, but a *dialogical* procedure for securing universally valid ethical norms carried out by a community of social selves through open communication, mutual participation, and intersubjectively mounted public discourse. The German scholar Hans Joas therefore refers to Mead as "the most important theorist of intersubjectivity between Feuerbach and Habermas" (1985, 2). For Joas (1993, 24), Mead's symbolic interactionist concept of self represents a "social turn" in classical American pragmatism. While the breakthrough to an intersubjective or social concept of self was not fully achieved in the German tradition of philosophical anthropology leading up to Heidegger's individualistic notion of human existence as *Dasein,* it was at last realized through Buber's concept of man as a dialogue between I and Thou and through Mead's concept of the social self as a conversation between I and Me. Although Feuerbach exerted a profound influence upon the German tradition of philosophical anthropology, some thinkers fall into an individualistic anthropology while others fall into a collectivist sociology. In contrast both Buber's concept of man as an I-Thou relation and Mead's concept of the social self as an I-Me relation function to establish a *via media* between the extremes of individualism and collectivism. Furthermore, John Macmurray's inspired vision of the self as an *I-You relationship* constituted through linguistic communication in a community of persons has been seen to have much in common with both Mead's communication model of the "social self" as an *I-Me relationship* and Buber's dialogical concept of man as an *I-Thou relationship.* It has been demonstrated how leading Western philosophers of intersubjectivity like Mead, Macmurray, and Buber have all rejected the individualistic notion of self as an isolated I or Cartesian subject and instead set forth an explicit bipolar concept of self as a relation between I and Other—what Mead calls the relation between "I and Me," what Macmurray calls the relation between "I and You," and what Buber calls the relation between "I and Thou." For this reason Mead, Macmurray, and Buber have been described as three paradigmatic figures in twentieth-century Western thought representing the social turn from a monological to a dialogical notion of man as a relation between I and Other.

However, I have endeavored to view this turning point in the history of philosophical anthropology from the broader perspective of East-West comparative thought so as to include those intersubjective models of selfhood as an I-Other relationship which have been formulated in twentieth-century Japanese Buddhist philosophy. It has been seen that while the anthropological orientation of modern Japanese philosophy has been deeply influenced by the German movement of *Anthropologie*, it can be traced back to the traditional concept of Zen Buddhism as *koji-kyūmei*, "investigation of self." In *Revival of Idols* (WTZ 17, 15–16), Watsuji describes his "turn" (*tenkō*) from romantic individualism to a socio-ethical concept of self. Watsuji thereupon comes to reject the Western tradition of "individualism" (*kojinshugi*) and develops his own anthropology or study of the person (*ningen-gaku*) based on a Zen/Confucian model of Japanese selfhood as *ningen* which exists as the *aidagara* or "between" of the individual and society in *kū* or emptiness defined as dependent coorigination. Also, both simultaneously with and independently of Martin Buber in the West, Nishida Kitarō recognized the epoch-making significance of Feuerbach's turn to a concept of self as a unity of I and Thou, and then proceeded to thematize the I-Thou (*ware to nanji*) relationship constituting the social self in the context of his own Zen Buddhist philosophy of absolute Nothingness. Following Nishida, Ueda Shizuteru of the Kyoto school has gone on to clarify how the *Ten Oxherding Pictures* illustrating the Zen process of becoming a person culminates with the realization of the true self as a compassionate Bodhisattva located in the *between* of I and Thou at the standpoint of Nothingness. Ueda's interpretation of the *Ten Oxherding Pictures* from the standpoint of Nishida's philosophy of Nothingness thereby makes fully explicit that the goal of Zen is not simply an inner state of tranquility but the social reconstruction of self. This turning point described in the philosophical anthropologies of Watsuji and Nishida in modern Japanese thought has thereby converged with the social turn of classical American pragmatism initiated by G. H. Mead. It has therefore been suggested that Mead's turn to a communication model of the social self as an I-Me relation shares much in common with not only Buber's dialogical self as an I-Thou relation and Macmurray's personal self as an I-You relation in the West, but also Watsuji's Zen/Confucian *ningen* concept of self as an I-Other relation and Nishida's Zen notion of the social self as an I-Thou relation in Japan. Yet it has further been emphasized that only the Whiteheadian process framework of Mead clarifies the *asymmetrical* structure of the social, temporal, and multiple self as an I-Me relation whereby the self arises from its social situation inherited from the *past* as an objective Me and then responds with creativity in the *present* as a subjective I. For Mead it is only this asymmetrical time-structure of the social self as an I-Me relation which can establish a true *via media* between individualism and collectivism, freedom and determinism, or liberalism and communitarianism.

In the final analysis all of the Eastern and Western frameworks considered here establish a philosophical anthropology directed toward the ultimate goal of becoming fully human as a person or social self through communication with others in a norm-governed community. Furthermore, all of these frameworks have shifted from a monological concept of self as a solitary I to a fully dialogical concept of self located in the *between* of "I and Thou." Again, all of these frameworks have shifted from a subjectivist model of self wherein individuation precedes sociation to an intersubjectivist model of self as an interplay of individuation and sociation. It can thus be said that in the twentieth century, both in the East and in the West, there has been a *social turn* in the history of philosophical anthropology; namely, a paradigm shift to a new ideal of personhood as a bipolar social self arising through communicative interaction between the individual and society.

# Notes

1. The concept of a turn, or turning point, has come to be used in order to clarify the paradigm shifts characterizing recent trends in philosophy. The "linguistic turn" of twentieth-century philosophy was popularized through Richard Rorty's anthology *The Linguistic Turn* (Chicago: The University of Chicago Press, 1967). In *Consequences of Pragmatism* (Minneapolis: University of Minnesota Press, 1982, xviii) Rorty associates this linguistic turn with the "pragmatization" of twentieth-century philosophy, or as it were, the pragmatic turn. Elsewhere in this text Rorty (1982, 204) speaks of the "interpretive turn" marking a shift from epistemology to hermeneutics. According to Rorty (1979, 139), the pragmatism or antifoundationalism of the linguistic turn is to be contrasted with the quest for absolute foundations underlying Descartes's "epistemological turn." For Rorty, pragmatism denotes "anti-essentialism" and "anti-foundationalism" to the point of deconstructionism and relativism. This trend has been aptly characterized as the "deconstructive turn" through Christopher Norris's anthology by the same title (see Norris's *The Deconstructive Turn* [New York: Methuen Publishers, 1983]). However, the pragmatism of G. H. Mead has instead been characterized in more positive and constructive terms by Hans Joas as the "social turn" (see Joas's *Pragmatism and Social Theory* [Chicago: The University of Chicago Press, 1993], 24). In the present work I extend this characterization to both Western and Eastern modes of thought, arguing that in the twentieth century there has been a Social Turn from a monological concept of self as an "I" to a dialogical concept of self as an "I-Other relation" both in classical American pragmatism and the Zen Buddhism of modern Japanese philosophy.

2. Steve Odin, "The Social Self in Japanese Philosophy and American Pragmatism: A Comparative Study of Watsuji Tetsurō and George Herbert Mead," in *Philosophy East & West* (42, no. 3, July 1992).

3. In *Process Metaphysics and Hua-Yen Buddhism* (1982) I argue that both A. N. Whitehead and Hua-Yen (J. Kegon) Buddhism have formulated a perspectivist cosmology wherein each occasion is a mirror reflecting the whole universe from its own perspective in the aesthetic continuum of nature as a microcosm of the macrocosm. However, whereas Hua-yen posits a symmetrical theory of social relations in which each occasion is a total perspective reflecting past,

present, and future at once, Whitehead instead develops an asymmetrical concept of social relations preserving the irreversibility of time's arrow so that each occasion is an emergent perspective which reflects only the past in the creative advance toward novelty. Whereas Nishida Kitarō's philosophy is based on the Kegon infrastructure so that each occasion is like a jewel in Indra's net or a Leibnizian monad which reflects past, present, and future at once in an eternal now, G. H. Mead's perspectivist concept of the social self instead follows the asymmetrical framework of Whitehead's process cosmology so that the self is a perspectival mirror which reflects the past at the Me or social pole and responds with creative novelty in the present at the I or individual pole.

4. I have critically analysed the parallel between Christian *kenōsis* and Buddhist *śūnyatā* as developed the the Kyoto school of modern Japanese philosophy in the following articles: "Kenōsis as the Foundation for Buddhist-Christian Dialogue: The Kenotic Buddhology of Nishida and the Kyoto School in relation to the Kenotic Christology of Thomas J. J. Altizer" in *The Eastern Buddhist* (Spring 1987); "A Critique of the *Kenōsis/Śūnyatā* Motif in Nishida and the Kyoto School" in *Buddhist-Christian Studies* (Vol. 9, 1989); and "Abe Masao and the Kyoto School on Christian *Kenōsis* and Buddhist *Śūnyatā*" in *Japanese Religions* (Vol. 15 / No. 3, January 1989). In the present work I am underscoring the social dimensions of this interfaith dialogue whereby both the self-emptying love of Jesus in Christianity and the self-negating compassion of a Bodhisattva in Buddhism are to be understood not only in mystical terms as emptying the mind into an imageless void, but in intersubjective terms as representing the ethical ideal of a social self which pours itself out for the sake of others.

5. In his book *George Herbert Mead: The Making of a Social Pragmatist* (1993), Gary A. Cook brings to light previously unknown aspects of Mead's life based on a careful study of Mead's personal letters. As documented by Cook (1993, 17–18), during Mead's year at Harvard University (1887–88), at which time he was living in the home of William James as a tutor of his children, he became romantically involved with Margaret Gibbens—the sister of Mrs. James! It was apparently due to Mead's great embarrassment over this complicated romantic interlude with Mrs. James's sister which led to his decision not to return to Harvard in the fall of 1888, but instead to enroll at the university of Leipzig in Germany, where he studied under Wundt, and then at Berlin, where he studied under Dilthey. Mead eventually married Helen Castle, the sister of his close friend Henry Castle.

6. As documented by Gary A. Cook (1993, 138), on September 14, 1926, both G. H. Mead and A. N. Whitehead delivered papers at a session of the Sixth International Congress of Philosophy meeting at Harvard University. Later that day Mead reported in a letter that his paper, which dealt in part with the work of Whitehead, had gone very well and that he then had a brief conversation with

Whitehead himself. Cook (1993, 138–60) goes on to discuss the profound influence of Whitehead's cosmology on the social pragmatism of G. H. Mead.

7. In *The Theory of Communicative Action* (1989, 1–112), Jürgen Habermas employs the phrase "paradigm shift" to dramatize the turn toward intersubjectivity in the social pragmatism of George Herbert Mead. However, as the term is used in the present work it does not refer to Thomas Kuhn's notion of a paradigm shift as a gestalt switch representing a discontinuous rupture or break with previous models. While Mead argues for the concept of "emergence" or "discontinuity" in his evolutionary process cosmology of creative advance to novelty, at the same time he adopts a rationalist notion of theory change as occuring in a gradual, continuous process of problem-solving through the experimental laboratory method. Siding with Kuhn over against Mead, Kathy Ferguson writes: "Mead's description of the progress of science as a methodical, incremental, cumulative process of gradual change does not square with historical accounts of major innovations. In *The Structure of Scientific Revolutions* [1962], Thomas Kuhn points out that changes in the theoretical perspective by which research is ordered generally come through a relatively sudden and unstructured experience that resembles a gestalt switch. This description had little in common with Mead's idea of a gradual and orderly process of problem-solving" (K. Ferguson, *Self, Society, and Womankind,* 1980, 53). G. H. Mead's view is more in accord with the historically grounded position of Larry Laudan (1984), who opposes the discontinuous model of Kuhn with the "reticulated" or continuous model wherein theory changes occur in a gradual, incremental, step-by-step process of problem-solving. See especially Laudan's forcefully argued critique of Kuhn developed in *Science and Values* (Berkeley: University of California Press, 1984).

8. Jürgen Habermas (1989) argues that Mead's ontogenetic account of the social construction of human mind and self in society through communicative interaction is complemented by Durkheim's phylogenetic account of how ethical norms evolved through the secularization of sacred rites in the ancient world. In this work I have focused upon Mead's ontogenetic analysis of the social construction of selfhood as an intercultural framework by which to interpret the Japanese notion of self. However, Durkheim's explanation of the social origins of the sacred in collective consciousness and the evolutionary transformation of rites from the sacred to the secular provide a valuable comparative framework for interpreting the phylo-genesis of Confucian rites of *li* or "ritual action" in East Asian culture.

# Glossary of Sino-Japanese Terms

*aida* (betweenness)
間

*amae* (drive to dependence)
甘え

*basho* (place, locus, field)
場所

*engi* (dependent coorigination,
interrelational existence)
縁起

*fūdo* (climate)
風土

*geidō* (way of the artist)
芸道

*hirenzoku no renzoku* (continuity of
discontinuity)
非連続の連続

*hito to hito to no aida* (betweenness
of person and person)
人と人との間

*ie* (family, household)
家

*iki* (chic)
粋

*jihi* (compassion)
慈悲

*jinkaku* (personality)
人格

*junsui keiken* (pure experience)
純粋経験

*kanjin* (contextual person)
間人

*kojinshugi* (individualism)
個人主義

*kokka* (nation)
国家

*kokutai* (national polity)
国体

*ku* (emptiness)
空

*kyōdōshugi* (cooperationism,
collectivism)
共同主義

*kyōryaku* (continuous passage)
経歴

*kyomu* (nihility)
虚無

*li* (ritual action)
禮

*ma* (space and/or time in-between)
間

*mizukara/onozukara* (self/nature)
自ら/自から

*mu* (nothingness)
無

459

*muga*   (no-self, non-ego)
無我

*mujō*   (impermanence)
無常

*naizaiteki chōetsu*   (immanent transcendence)
內在的超越

*nihonjinron*   (study of Japanese identity)
日本人論

*ningen*   (person)
人間

*nikon*   (right now)
而今

Nishida Kitarō   (1870–1945)
西田幾多郎

*omote/ura*   (front/back)
表/裏

*onore o munashiku suru koto*   (to empty oneself, to make oneself nothing)
己を空しくすること

*riji muge*   (interpenetration of particular and universal)
理事無礙

*rinrigaku*   (ethics)
倫理学

*shakaiteki jiko*   (social self)
社会的自己

*sonzai*   (existence)
存在

*soto/uchi*   (outside/inside)
外/內

*soku/hi*   (is/is not)
即/非

*sōtaiteki mu*   (relative nothingness)
相対的無

*sōzōten*   (creative point)
創造点

*tatemae/honne*   (social institutions/personal feelings)
建前/本音

*ta to ichi to no mujunteki jiko dōitsu*   (self-identity of the one and the many)
多と一との絶対矛盾的自己同一

*tsukurareta mono kara tsukuru mono e*   (from the creating to the created)
作られたものから作るものへ

*uji*   (being-time)
有時

*ware to nanji*   (I and Thou)
我と汝

Watsuji Tetsurō (1889–1960)
和辻哲郎

*zettaiteki hiteisei*   (absolute negativity)
絶対的否定性

*zettai mu*   (absolute nothingness)
絶対無

# References

[Abbreviations used in text are placed in brackets following the title ]

## Selected Bibliography of Japanese Language Works

Dōgen Kigen
1969–70    *Dōgen zenji zenshū*. Edited by Okubo Doshu. 2 vols. Tokyo: Chikūma
           Shobo.

Doi Takeo
    1971    *Amae no kōzō*. Tokyo: Kobundo.
    1985    *Omote to ura*. Tokyo: Kobundo.

Hamaguchi Eshun
    1977    *'Nihonrashisa' no saihakken*. Tokyo: Nihon Keizai Shinbunsha.
    1982    *Kanjinshugi no shakai nikon*. Tokyo: Toyo kezai.

Kimura Bin
    1972    *Hito to hito to no aida*. Tokyo: Kobundo.
    1988    *Aida*. Tokyo: Kobundo.

Kosaka Kunitsugu
    1991    *Nishida tetsugaku no kenkyū*. Kyoto: Mineruva Shobo.

Kuki Shūzō
    1930    *Iki no kōzō*. Tokyo: Iwanami Shoten.

Kumon Shumpei
    1979    *Bunmei to shite no ie shakai*. Tokyo: Chuo Koronsha.

Mutō Kazuo
    1974    *Shūkyōtetsugaku no atarashii kanōsei*. Tokyo: Sobunsha.

Nishida Kitarō
    1965    *Nishida Kitarō zenshū* [NKZ], 19 vols. 2nd edition. Tokyo: Iwanami Shoten.
    1984    *Zen no kenkyū*. Tokyo: Iwanami Shoten.

Nishitani Keiji
    1961    *Shūkyō to wa nani ka*. Tokyo: Sobunsha.

Tanabe Hajime
  1963    *Tanabe Hajime zenshū* [THZ], Vol. 10. Tokyo: Chikūma shobo.

Watsuji Tetsurō
  1937    *Rinrigaku.* Tokyo: Iwanami Shoten.
  1962    *Watsuji Tetsurō zenshū* [WTZ]. Tokyo: Iwanami Shoten.

## Selected Bibliography of English Language Works

Abe, Masao
  1985    *Zen and Western Thought.* Edited by W. R. LaFleur. Honolulu: University
          of Hawaii Press.
  1991    "Kenotic God and Dynamic Shunyata." In *The Emptying God*, edited by
          John B. Cobb Jr. and Christopher Ives (Maryknoll, New York: Orbis
          Books).

Aboulafia, Mitchell
  1986    *The Mediating Self: Mead, Sartre and Self-Determination.* New Haven and
          London: Yale University Press.
  1991    *Philosophy, Social Theory, and the Thought of George Herbert Mead.* Edited
          by M. Aboulafia. Albany: State University of New York Press.

Adachi, Yasushi
  1969    "Aspects of Pragmatism in Japan." M.A. Thesis, University of Texas.

Adler, Alfred
  1927,1941  *Understanding Human Nature.* Tower Book Edition. Cleveland, Ohio: The
          World Publishing Company.

Ames, Roger T.
  1980    "Bushidō: Mode or Ethic?" *Traditions* 10. (Vol. III, No.2).

Ames, Van Meter
  1962    *Zen and American Thought.* Honolulu: University of Hawaii Press.

Arisaka, Y., and A. Feenberg
  1990    "Experiential Ontology: The Origins of the Nishida Philosophy in the
          Doctrine of Pure Experience." *International Philosophical Quarterly* 30,
          no. 2 (June 1990).

Baldwin, John D.
  1986    *George Herbert Mead: A Unifying Theory for Sociology.* Newbury Park: Sage
          Publications.

Barthes, Roland
  1982    *Empire of Signs.* Translated by R. Howard. New York: Hill and Wang.

# References

Batchelor, Stephen
    1983    *Alone With Others.* New York: Grove Press.

Bellah, Robert N.
    1965    "Japan's Cultural Identity: Some Reflections on the Work of Watsuji Tetsurō." *The Journal of Asian Studies* 24, no. 4: 573–94.

Benedict, Ruth
    1967    *The Chrysanthemum and the Sword: Patterns of Japanese Culture.* New York: New American Library.

Benhabib, Seyla
    1986    *Critique, Norm and Utopia.* New York: Columbia University Press.

Berger, Peter L.
    1963    *Introduction to Sociology.* New York: Doubleday, Anchor Books.
    1966    *The Social Construction of Reality: A Treatise in the Sociology of Knowledge.* New York: Anchor Books/Doubleday.
    1970    "Identity as a Problem in the Sociology of Knowledge." In J. E. Curtis and J. W. Petras (eds.) *The Sociology of Knowledge.* New York: Praeger Publishers.

Bernstein, Richard J.
    1988    *Beyond Objectivism and Relativism.* Philadelphia: University of Pennsylvania Press.

Blumer, Herbert
    1986    *Symbolic Interactionism.* Berkeley: University of California Press.

Bourgeois, Patrick L., and Sandra B. Rosenthal
    1991    *Mead and Merleau-Ponty.* Albany: SUNY Press.

Buber, Martin
    1958    *I and Thou.* Translated by Ronald Gregor Smith. New York: Collier Books/Macmillan Publishing Company.
    1965    *Between Man and Man.* Translated by R. G. Smith. London: Kegan, Paul, Trench, Trubner & Co.

Buchanan, Allen E.
1988–89    "Assessing the Communitarian Critique of Liberalism." *Ethics* 99.

Buchler, Justus
1951, 1979    *Toward a General Theory of Human Judgment.* Second revised edition. New York: Dover Publications.
1955, 1985    *Nature and Judgment.* New York: University Press of America.
1966, 1990    *Metaphysics of Natural Complexes.* Second expanded edition. Edited by Kathleen Wallace and Armen Marsoobian, with Robert S. Corrington. Albany. SUNY Press.

Callicott, Baird J.
   1989   "The Metaphysical Implications of Ecology." In *Nature in Asian Traditions of Thought: Essays in Environmental Philosophy*. Edited by J. Baird Callicott and Roger T. Ames (Albany: SUNY Press).

Charon, J. M.
   1989   *Symbolic Interactionism*. Englewood Cliffs, New Jersey: Prentice Hall.

Collcutt, Martin C.
   1983   "Bushidō." *Kodansha Encyclopedia of Japan*. Tokyo: Kodansha. Vol.1.

Cohen, Marshall J.
   1982   *Charles Horton Cooley and the Social Self in American Thought*. New York & London: Garland Publishing, Inc.

Colapietro, Vincent M.
   1989   *Peirce's Approach to the Self: A Semiotic Perspective on Human Subjectivity*. Albany: SUNY Press.

Cook, Gary A.
   1993   *George Herbert Mead: The Making of a Social Pragmatist*. Urbana and Chicago: University of Illinois Press.

Cooley, Charles Horton.
   1902 [1964]   *Human Nature & the Social Order*. Foreward by George Herbert Mead. New York: Schocken Books.

Culler, Jonathan
   1981   *The Pursuit of Signs: Semiotics, Literature, Deconstruction*. Ithaca, New York: Cornell University Press.

Dale, Peter N.
   1986   *The Myth of Japanese Uniqueness*. New York: St. Martin's Press.

De Nicolas, Antonio T.
   1978   *Meditations through the Rg Veda*. Boulder & London: Shambala.

Dewey, John
   1908   *Ethics*. J. Dewey and J. H. Tufts. New York: Henry Holt & Company.
   1931   "George Herbert Mead." *The Journal of Philosophy*, 48: 310–11.
   1939   "Experience, Knowledge and Value: A Rejoinder." In Paul Arthur Schilpp (ed.), *The Philosophy of John Dewey* (Evanston and Chicago: Northwestern University Press; New York: Tudor Publishing Company, 1951).
   1958   *Experience and Nature* [EN]. New York: Dover Publications.
   1971–72   *The Early Works of John Dewey*. Edited by Jo Ann Boydston. 6 vols. Carbondale: University of Southern Illinois Press.
   1980   *Art as Experience*. New York: Perigee Books / G. P. Putnam's Sons.

Dilworth, David A.

1974    "Watsuji Tetsurō (1889–1960): Cultural Phenomenologist and Ethician."
        *Philosophy East and West* 24, no. 1.

Doi, Takeo

1973    *The Anatomy of Dependence.* Translated by J. Bester. Tokyo: Kondansha
        International.

1986    *The Anatomy of Self: The Individual Versus Society.* Translated by Mark A.
        Harbison. Tokyo: Kodansha International.

Dore, R. P.

1967    *City Life in Japan.* Berkeley: University of California Press.

Ferguson, Kathy E.

1980    *Self, Society, and Womankind.* Westport, Connecticut: Greenwood Press.

Feuerbach, Ludwig

1966    *Principles of the Philosophy of the Future.* Translated by M. H. Vogel. New
        York: The Bobbs-Merrill Company.

Fingarette, Herbert

1972    *Confucius: The Secular as Sacred.* New York: Harper Torchbooks.

Furukawa, Tesshi

1967    "The Individual in Japanese Ethics." In Charles A. Moore, ed, *The Japa-
        nese Mind* (Honolulu: The University Press of Hawaii).

Giddens, Anthony

1979    *Central Problems in Social Theory.* Berkeley and Los Angeles: University of
        California Press.

1984    *The Constitution of Society: Outline of the Theory of Structuration.* Berkeley
        and Los Angeles: University of California Press.

Goffman, Erving

1959    *The Presentation of Self in Everyday Life.* New York: Anchor Books.

1951    *Asylums* New York: Anchor Books.

1967    *Interaction Ritual.* New York: Anchor Books.

Gutmann, Amy

1985    "Communitarian Critics of Liberalism." *Philosophy & Public Affairs* 14,
        no. 3 (Summer 1985).

Habermas, Jürgen

1968    *Knowledge and Human Interests.* Translated by Jeremy J. Shapiro. Boston:
        Beacon Press.

1979    *Communication and the Evolution of Society.* Translated by T. McCarthy.
        Boston. Beacon Press.

1984	*The Theory of Communicative Action* (vol. I). Translated by T. McCarthy. Boston. Beacon Press.

1987	*The Philosophical Discourse of Modernity.* Translated by F. G. Lawrence. Cambridge, Massachusetts: MIT Press.

1989	*The Theory of Communicative Action* (vol. II). Translated by T. McCarthy. Boston: Beacon Press.

1990	*Moral Consciousness and Communicative Action.* Translated by C. Lenhardt and S. W. Nicholsen. Cambridge, Massachusetts: MIT Press.

1992	*Postmetaphysical Thinking.* Translated by W. M. Hohengarten. Cambridge, Massachusetts: MIT Press.

Hall, David, and Roger Ames

1987	*Thinking Through Confucius.* Albany: SUNY Press.

Hamaguchi, Eshun

1985	"A Contextual Model of the Japanese: Toward a Methodological Innovation in Japan Studies." *Journal of Japanese Studies* 11, no. 2 (Summer): 289–321.

Hanson, Karen

1986	*The Self Imagined: Philosophical Reflections on the Social Character of Psyche.* New York and London: Routledge & Kegan Paul.

Hartshorne, Charles

1942	"Review of World Hypotheses." *Ethics,* 53: 73–74.

1972	*Whitehead's Philosophy.* Lincoln: University of Nebraska Press.

1984	*Creativity in American Philosophy.* Albany: SUNY Press.

1987	"Bergson's Aesthetic Creationism Compared to Whitehead's." In *Bergson & Modern Thought.* New York: Harwood Academic Publishers.

Hegel, G. W. F.

1977	*Phenomenology of Spirit.* Translated by A. V. Miller. Oxford: Oxford University Press.

Hewitt, John P.

1976	*Self & Society: A Symbolic Interactionist Social Psychology.* Fifth edition. Boston: Allyn and Bacon Publishers.

Inada, Kenneth K.

1984	"The American Involvement With Śūnyatā: Prospects." In *Buddhism and American Thinkers,* edited by Kenneth K. Inada and Nolan P. Jacobson. Albany: SUNY Press.

Izutsu, Toshihiko

1982	*Toward a Philosophy of Zen Buddhism.* Boulder: Prajñā Press.

James, William
  1983      *The Principles of Psychology.* Cambridge, Massachusetts and London,
            England: Harvard University Press.

Joas, Hans
  1985      *G. H. Mead: A Contemporary Re-examination of his Thought.* Translated by
            R. Meyer. Cambridge, Massachusetts: The MIT Press.
  1987      "Symbolic Interactionism." In *Social Theory Today,* edited by A. Giddens
            and J. Turner (Stanford, California: Stanford University Press).
  1993      *Pragmatism and Social Theory.* Chicago and London. The University of
            Chicago Press.

Johnson, Frank A.
  1993      *Dependency and Japanese Socialization: Psychoanalytic and Anthropological
            Investigations into Amae.* New York and London: New York University Press.

Kalupahana, David J.
  1987      *The Principles of Buddhist Psychology.* Albany: SUNY Press.

Kant, Immanuel
  1987      *Fundamental Principles of the Metaphysic of Morals.* Translated by T. K.
            Abbot. Buffalo, New York: Prometheus Books.

Kasulis, Thomas P.
1981,1985   *Zen Action / Zen Person.* Honolulu: University of Hawaii Press.

Keller, Catherine
  1986      *From A Broken Web: Separation, Sexism, and Self.* Boston: Beacon Press.
  1991      "On Feminist Theology and Dynamic Self-Emptying." In *The Emptying
            God,* edited by John B. Cobb Jr. and Christopher Ives (Maryknoll, New
            York: Orbis Books).

Kerouac, Jack
  1986      *The Dharma Bums.* New York: Penguin Books.

Kimura, Bin
  1989      "The Japanese Concept of Nature." In *Nature in Asian Traditions of
            Thought: Essays in Environmental Philosophy,* edited by J. Baird Callicott
            and Roger T. Ames. Albany: SUNY Press.

Kirimura, Yasuji
  1977      *Fundamentals of Buddhism.* Tokyo: Nichiren Shoshu International.

Kodera, James T.
  1987      "The Romantic Humanism of Watsuji Tetsurō." *Dialogue & Alliance.* 1
            no. 3: 4–11.

Kondo, Dorinne K.

    1990    *Crafting Selves: Power, Gender, and Discourses of Identity in a Japanese Workplace*. Chicago: The University of Chicago Press.

Kumon, Shumpei

    1982    "Some Principles Governing the Thought and Behavior of Japanists (Contextualists)." *The Journal of Japanese Studies* 8, no. 1.

Kurtz, Lester R.

    1984    *Evaluating Chicago Sociology*. Chicago: University of Chicago Press.

Kurokawa, Kisho

    1982    "Rikyu Gray: An Open-ended Aesthetic." *Chanoyu Quarterly: Tea and the Arts of Japan*, 36: 33–52.

Kuwayama, Takami

    1992    "The Reference Other Orientation." In Nancy J. Rosenberger, ed., *Japanese Sense of Self* (Cambridge: The Cambridge University Press).

LaFleur, William

    1978    "Buddhist Emptiness in the Ethics and Aesthetics of Watsuji Tetsurō." *Religious Studies* 14: 237–50.

Leopold, Aldo

    1966    *A Sand County Almanac*. New York: Ballantine Books.

Lebra, Takie.

1974,1986    *Japanese Culture and Behavior*. Edited by Takie and William Lebra. Honolulu: University of Hawaii Press.

    1992    "Self in Japanese Culture." In Nancy J. Rosenberger, ed., *Japanese Sense of Self* (Cambridge: Cambridge University Press).

MacIntyre, Alasdair

    1981    *After Virtue: A Study in Moral Theory*. London: Duckworth Press.

Macmurray, John

    1983    *Persons in Relation*. New Jersey and London: Humanities Press.

Magliola, Robert

    1984    *Derrida on the Mend*. West Lafayette, Indiana: Purdue University Press.

Mead, George H.

    1932    *The Philosophy of the Present* [PP]. Edited by A. E. Murphy with a Preface by John Dewey. Chicago: University of Chicago Press.

1934, 1962    *Mind, Self & Society* [MSS]. Edited by C. W. Morris. Chicago: University of Chicago Press.

    1936    *Movements of Thought in the Nineteenth Century* [MTNC]. Edited with an Introduction by Charles W. Morris. Chicago: University of Chicago Press.

1938    *The Philosophy of the Act* [PA]. Edited by C. D. Morris, in collaboration with J. M. Brewster, A. M. Dunham, and D. L. Miller. Chicago: University of Chicago Press.

1956    *George Herbert Mead on Social Psychology.* Edited with an Introduction by Anselm Strauss. Chicago: The University of Chicago Press.

1964    *George Herbert Mead: Selected Writings* [SW]. Edited by A. J. Reck. Chicago and London: The University of Chicago Press.

1982    *The Individual and the Social Self: Unpublished Work of George Herbert Mead* [ISS]. Edited with an Introduction by David L. Miller. Chicago and London: The University fo Chicago Press.

Meltzer, Bernard N.
1972    *The Social Psychology of George Herbert Mead.* Kalamazoo: Center for Sociological Research.

Meltzer, B., J. Petras, and L. Reynolds
1975    *Symbolic Interactionism: Genesis, Varieties and Criticism.* Boston: Routledge & Kegan Paul.

Merton, Thomas
1968    *Zen and the Birds of Appetite.* New York: New Directions.

Miller, David L.
1973    *George Herbert Mead: Self, Language and the World.* Chicago and London: University of Chicago Press.

1975    "Josiah Royce and George H. Mead on the Nature of the Self." In *Transactions of the Charles S. Peirce Society* 11, no. 2 (Spring), 67–89.

Miyanaga, Kuniko
1991    *The Creative Edge: Emerging Individualism in Japan.* New Brunswick and London: Transaction Publishers.

Munro, Donald J.
1977    *The Concept of Man in Contemporary China.* Ann Arbor, Michigan: University of Michigan Press.

Nagami, Isamu
1981    "The Ontological Foundation in Tetsurō Watsuji's Philosophy: *Kū* and Human Existence." *Philosophy East and West* 31, no. 3: 279–96.

Nakamura, Hajime
1964, 1981    *Ways of Thinking of Eastern Peoples.* Honolulu: University of Hawaii Press.
1984    "Interrelational Existence." In *Buddhism and American Thinkers,* eds. K. K. Inada and N. P. Jacobson (Albany: SUNY Press).

Nakane, Chie
1970    *Japanese Society.* Berkeley and Los Angeles: University of California Press.

Neville, Robert Cummings
    1987    *The Puritan Smile: A Look Toward Moral Reflection.* Albany: SUNY Press.

Niebuhr, Richard
    1963    *The Responsible Self: An Essay in Christian Moral Philosophy.* New York: Harper & Row.

Nishida, Kitarō
    1960    *A Study of Good.* Translated by V. H. Viglielmo. Tokyo: Japanese Government Printing Bureau.
    1970    *Fundamental Problems of Philosophy.* Translated by David A. Dilworth. Tokyo: Sophia University / A *Monumenta Nipponica* Monograph.
    1987    "An Explanation of Beauty." Translated with Introduction and Notes by Steve Odin. *Monumenta Niponica* 42, no. 2 (Summer).
    1990    *An Inquiry into the Good.* Translated by Masao Abe and Christopher Ives. New Haven: Yale University Press.

Nishitani, Keiji
    1982    *Religion and Nothingness.* Translated by Jan Van Bragt. Berkeley: University of California Press.

Nitobe, Inazō
    1969    *Bushidō—The Soul of Japan.* Tokyo: Charles E. Tuttle Company.

Nolte, Sharon H.
    1987    *Liberalism in Modern Japan.* Berkeley: University of California Press.

Odin, Steve
    1982    *Process Metaphysics & Hua-yen Buddhism.* Albany: SUNY Press.
    1990    "Derrida & the Decentered Universe of Zen Buddhism." In *Journal of Chinese Philosophy* 17. (To be reprinted in *Japan in Traditional and Postmodern Perspectives,* eds. Steven Heine and Charles W. Fu. [Albany: SUNY Press. Forthcoming]).
    1992    "The Japanese Concept of Nature in Relation to the Environmental Ethics & Conservation Aesthetics of Aldo Leopold." *Journal of Environmental Ethics* (Spring).
    1992    "The Social Self in Japanese Philosophy & American Pragmatism: A Comparative Study of Watsuji Tetsurō & George Herbert Mead." *Philosophy East & West* (Spring).

Oh, Sadaharu
    1984    *Sadaharu Oh.* New York: Times Books / Random House.

Omine, Akira
    1987    "Probing the Japanese Expereince of Nature." Translated by Dennis Hirota in *Chanoyu Quarterly: Tea and the Arts of Japan* 51.

Peirce, Charles, Sanders
    1931    *Collected Papers of Charles Sanders Peirce* [CP]. Volumes 1 and 2. Edited by Charles Harshorne and Paul Weiss. Cambridge, Massachusetts: The Belknap Press of Harvard University Press.
    1933    *Collected Papaers of Charles Sanders Peirce*. Volumes 3 and 4. Edited by C. Hartshorne and P. Weiss. Cambridge, Massachusetts: The Belknap Press of Harvard University Press.
    1934–35    *Collected Papers of Charles Sanders Peirce*. Volumes 5 and 6. Edited by C. Hartshorne and P. Weiss. Cambridge, Massachusetts: The Belknap Press of Harvard Unversity Press.
    1955    *Philosophical Writings of Peirce*. Selected and Edited with an Introduction by Justus Buchler. New York: Dover Publications. (First published in 1940 under the title *The Philosophy of Peirce: Selected Writings* by Routledge & Kegan Paul Ltd.)

Pepper, Stephen C.
    1942    *World Hypotheses*. Berkeley and Los Angeles: University of California Press.
    1961    "Whitehead's 'Actual Occasion'." *Tulane Studies in Philosophy* 10., 71–88.
    1969    "On Donald Keene's 'Japanese Aesthetics'." *Philosophy East & West* 19, no. 3 (July).

Pilgrim, Richard B.
    1986    "Ma: A Cultural Paradigm." *Chanoyu Quarterly: Tea and the Arts of Japan*, 46.

Piovesana, Gino K.
    1969    *Contemporary Japanese Philosophical Thought*. New York: St. John's University Press.

Pfuetze, Paul E.
    1961    *Self, Society, Existence: Human Nature and Dialogue in the Thought of George Herbert Mead and Martin Buber*. New York: Harper & Row, Torchbooks. (Originally published as *The Social Self*. New York: Bookman Associates, 1954).

Plath, David
    1990, 1992    *Long Engagements: Maturity in Modern Japan*. Stanford, California: Stanford University Press.

Preston, David L.
    1988    *The Social Organization of Zen Practice*. Cambridge: Cambridge University Press.

Ricoeur, Paul
    1992    *Oneself As Another*. Translated by K. Blamey. Chicago and London: University or Chicago Press.

472 References

Robinson, John

1963     *Honest to God.* Philadelphia: The Westminster Press.

Rosenberger, Nancy R.

1992     *Japanese Sense of Self.* Cambridge: Cambridge University Press.

Royce, Josiah

1885     *The Religious Aspect of Philosophy.* Boston: Houghton Mifflin.
1908     *The Philosophy of Loyalty.* New York: Macmillan.
1913     *The Problem of Christianity,* 2 vols. New York: Macmillan.
1959     *The World and the Individual,* 2 vols. New York: Dover.

Sandel, Michael

1982     *Liberalism and the Limits of Justice.* Cambridge: Cambridge University Press.

Shaner, David E.

1985     *The Bodymind Experience in Japanese Buddhism.* Albany: SUNY Press.

Singer, Beth J.

1983     *Ordinal Naturalism: An Introduction to the Philosophy of Justus Buchler.* Lewisburg: Bucknell University Press.

Smith, Robert J.

1983     *Japanese Society: Tradition, Self and the Social Order.* Cambridge: Cambridge University Press.
1985     "A Pattern of Japanese Society: *Ie* Society or Acknowledgment of Interdependence?" *The Journal of Japanese Studies* (Symposium on *Ie* Society) 11, no. 1: 29–45.

Stcherbatsky, F. Th.

1927     *The Conception of Buddhist Nirvana.* Leningrad: Public Office of the Academy of Sciences of the USSR.

Sullivan, Harry Stack

1945     *Conceptions of Modern Psychiatry.* New York: Norton.
1970     "Self as Concept and Illusion." In *Social Psychology through Symbolic Interaction*, ed. G. Stone and H. Farberman (Waltham, Mass.: Xerox College Publication).

Suzuki, D. T.

1959     *Zen and Japanese Culture.* Princeton, New Jersey: Princeton University Press.

Takeuchi, Yoshinori

1982     "The Philosophy of Nishida." In *The Buddha Eye: An Anthology of the Kyoto School.* New York: Crossroads.
1983     *The Heart of Buddhism.* Translated by J. Heisig. New York: Crossroads.

Tanabe, Hajime
1986    *Philosophy as Metanoetics.* Translated by Takeuchi Yoshinori with Valdo Viglielmo and James Heisig. Berkeley: University of California Press.

Tatsuo, Arima
1969    *The Failure of Freedom: A Portrait of Modern Japanese Intellectuals.* Cambridge, Massachusetts: Harvard University Press.

Taylor, Charles
1979    *Hegel and Modern Society.* Cambridge: Cambridge University Press.
1989    *Sources of the Self.* Cambridge Massachusetts: Harvard University Press.

Tremmel, W. C.
1957    "The Social Concepts of George Herbert Mead." *Emporia State Research Studies* 5, no. 4: 6–11.

Tugendhat, Ernst
1991    "Mead: Symbolic Interaction and the Self." In *Philosophy, Social Theory, and the Thought of George Herbert Mead*, edited by M. Aboulafia (Albany: SUNY Press).

Ueda Shizuteru
1982    "Emptiness and Fullness: *śūnyatā* in Mahayana Buddhism." *The Eastern Buddhist*15, no. 1: 9–37.
1982    "'Nothingness' in Meister Eckhart and Zen Buddhism." In *The Buddha Eye: An Anthology of the Kyoto School*, edited by Frederick Franck (New York: Crossroads).

Von Bertalanffy, Ludwig
1981    *A Systems View of Man.* Edited by Paul A. LaViolette. Boulder, Colorado: Westview Press.

Waldenfels, Hans
1980    *Absolute Nothingness: Foundations for a Buddhist-Christian Dialogue.* Translated by J. W. Heisig. New York: Paulist Press.

Watsuji Tetsurō
1961    *A Climate: A Philosophical Study.* Translated by Geoffrey Bownas. Tokyo: Unesco.
1971    "Japanese Literary Arts and Buddhist Philosophy." Translated by Hirano Umeyo, *The Eastern Buddhist* 4, no. 1 (May): 88–115.

Whitehead, Alfred North
1954    *Religion in the Making* [RM]. New York: New American Library.
1959    *Symbolism: Its Meaning and Effect* [S]. Capricorn.
1967    *Science and the Modern World* [SMW]. New York: The Free Press.

1978    *Process and Reality* [PR]. Corrected edition, ed. David Ray Griffin and Donald W. Sherburne. New York: Free Press.

Yuasa Yasuo

1987    *The Body: Toward an Eastern Mind-Body Theory.* Translated by Nagatomo Shigenori and T. P. Kasulis. Albany: SUNY Press.

Yusa, Michiko

1987    "The Religious Worldview of Nishida Kitarō." *The Eastern Buddhist* (Autumn).

# Note on Centers

This series is published under the auspices of the Center for a Postmodern World and the Center for Process Studies.

*The Center for a Postmodern World* is an independent nonprofit organization in Santa Barbara, California, founded by David Ray Griffin. It promotes the awareness and exploration of the postmodern worldview and encourages reflection about a postmodern world, from postmodern art, spirituality, and education to a postmodern world order, with all this implies for economics, ecology, and security. One of its major projects is to produce a collaborative study that marshals the numerous facts supportive of a postmodern worldview and provides a portrayal of a postmodern world order toward which we can realistically move. It is located at 6891 Del Playa, Isla Vista, California 93117.

*The Center for Process Studies* is a research organization affiliated with the School of Theology at Claremont and Claremont University Center and Graduate School. It was founded by John B. Cobb, Jr., Director, and David Ray Griffin, Executive Director; Mary Elizabeth Moore and Marjorie Suchocki are also Co-Directors. It encourages research and reflection upon the process philosophy of Alfred North Whitehead, Charles Hartshorne, and related thinkers, and upon the application and testing of this viewpoint in all areas of thought and practice. This center sponsors conferences, welcomes visiting scholars to use its library, and publishes a scholarly journal, *Process Studies*, and a quarterly *Newsletter*. It is located at 1325 North College, Claremont, California 91711.

Both centers gratefully accept (tax-deductible) contributions to support their work.

# Index of Authors